WISDOM AND INNOCENCE

The Chestershaw through the eyes of Max Beerbohm

Wisdom and Innocence

A Life of G. K. Chesterton

Joseph Pearce

IGNATIUS PRESS SAN FRANCISCO

For Sarah

Copyright © Joseph Pearce, 1996, 2004

First published in Great Britain 1996
Hodder & Stoughton, London

The right of Joseph Pearce to be identified as the Author of
the Work has been asserted by him in accordance with the
Copyright, Designs and Patents Act 1988.

ISBN 0–89870–700–5
Library of Congress catalog number 2004115168

Typeset by Hewer Text Composition Services, Edinburgh
Printed and bound in the United States of America
by Thomson-Shore, Inc., Dexter, Michigan ∞

CONTENTS

v

PREFACE

On 28 May 1995 the lead article in the *Sunday Telegraph*'s 'Review' section was headlined 'A Saint Among Journalists?' The article was prompted by a letter from Argentina signed by politicians, diplomats and an archbishop and addressed to Cardinal Hume of Westminster. The letter called for the 'initiation of the formal procedures towards the eventual canonisation of Gilbert Keith Chesterton'.

Regardless of whether Chesteron warrants canonisation, the arrival of such a letter served as a timely reminder of his continuing influence throughout the world. Indeed, sixty years after his death, there appears to be a considerable revival of interest in both his life and work. There are flourishing Chesterton Societies in Canada, Japan, Australia, France, Poland, Norway and Britain – and there are various separate societies scattered throughout the United States. The *Chesterton Review*, a scholarly quarterly, is published from Canada, and the Ignatius Press of San Francisco is currently issuing Chesterton's Collected Works.

The fact is that Gilbert Keith Chesterton appears to many as one of the giants of twentieth-century literature. His wit was a match for that of Bernard Shaw, H. G. Wells and a host of others. To Oscar Wilde's statement that we cannot appreciate sunsets because we cannot pay for them Chesterton's riposte was that Oscar Wilde could pay for sunsets by not being Oscar Wilde.[1] Similarly, he was asked, following a speech in America on the 'Coming Peril', whether he considered Bernard Shaw a coming peril. 'Heavens, no,' he replied. 'He is a disappearing pleasure.'[2] Shaw, in turn, referred to Chesterton as a 'colossal genius'.[3]

Yet it was in the depths of his philosophy and not in the speed of his wit that his genius resided. Chesterton was, in the literal sense of the words, a radical thinker. He went back to the very roots of the issue in order to understand it: 'The modern man is more like a traveller who has forgotten the name of his destination, and has to go back whence he came, even to find out where he is going.'[4] This ability was described by Monsignor Ronald Knox:

> It was a favourite principle of Chesterton that it is possible to see a thing again and again until it has become utterly staled to you by familiarity, and then suddenly to see it for the first time ... it was possible to have a vision of the truth in the same way – to see a thing as it really is for the first time, because all your nine hundred and ninety-nine previous glimpses of it had given you a merely conventional picture of it, and missed its essential truth.[5]

It is apparent from this exposition of Chesterton's thought that his main complaint against Oscar Wilde was not that he could not appreciate the sunset but that he could not even see it. Aware of this blindness in others, he continually expressed his gratitude for the sight he'd been given:

> Give me miraculous eyes to see my eyes,
> Those rolling mirrors made alive in me,
> Terrible crystal, more incredible
> Than all the things they see.[6]

With those rolling mirrors of terrible crystal Chesterton cut through the commonplace and discovered common sense: 'I am the man who with the utmost daring discovered what had been discovered before.'[7] Thus the miraculous perceived the miracle.

Monsignor Knox, in the panegyric he preached at Chesterton's requiem mass in Westminster Cathedral, said that 'he will almost certainly be remembered as a prophet in an age of false prophets'.[8] Malcolm Muggeridge, writing fifty years later, agreed:

> He felt a deep, instinctive distaste for the way the twentieth century was going which enabled him, in his early years of pessimism, to be an impressive prophet. 'The earnest Freethinkers,' he wrote in 1905, 'need not worry themselves so much about the persecutions of the past. Before the Liberal idea is dead or triumphant, we shall see wars and persecutions the like of which the world has never seen.' Stalin, then a young man of twenty-six, and Hitler, ten years younger, were, along with others, to make good his words to a fabulous degree.

It is surprising, in a way, that, when Chesterton has so often been proved right in his judgments, he should still be less seriously regarded than contemporaries like Wells and the Webbs who were almost invariably wrong.[9]

Chesterton's powers of prophecy were evident at the lecture he gave on 'Culture and the Coming Peril' in Toronto in 1930. The Coming Peril, he explained, was not Bolshevism because Bolshevism had now been tried and 'the best way to destroy a Utopia is to establish it. The net result of Bolshevism is that the modern world will not imitate it.' Nor was the Coming Peril another world war, although the next war 'would happen when Germany tried to monkey about with the frontiers of Poland'. The Coming Peril was 'the intellectual, educational, psychological, artistic overproduction which, equally with economic overproduction, threatened the wellbeing of contemporary civilisation. People were inundated, blinded, deafened, and mentally paralysed by a flood of vulgar and tasteless externals, leaving them no time for leisure, thought, or creation from within themselves.'[10]

The astounding perception of this speech, delivered three years before the Nazis came to power, nine years before the outbreak of war and many years before the final downfall of communism, illustrates Chesterton's grasp of reality. It is in this light that one should read Richard Ingrams's introduction to the 1992 reissue of Chesterton's *Autobiography*:

> The new reader of Chesterton will be surprised by two things. One is how contemporary a figure he is . . . in the *Autobiography* as in his other books we find that the issues that obsessed Chesterton and his generation are very topical – Imperialism, pacifism, Darwinism, religious orthodoxy – how he would have relished the Bishop of Durham – and especially Distributism, the political creed which he and Belloc embraced and which finds an echo in our modern concern with self-sufficiency and Dr Schumacher's creed of 'Small is Beautiful' . . .
>
> The second thing which I realise myself every time I return, as I regularly do, to his writing is how persuasively reassuring he is to those of us brought up as Christians who doubt and dither about our beliefs.[11]

It is interesting that Ingrams should make the connection between Chesterton's contemporary relevance and his Christian faith, a connection emphasised by Chesterton himself in his *Autobiography*: 'The first thing to note, as typical of the modern tone, is a certain effect of toleration which actually results in timidity. Religious liberty might be supposed to mean that everybody is free to discuss religion. In practice it means that hardly anybody is allowed to mention it.'[12]

Such timidity is not possible in any study of Chesterton because his faith is absolutely central to his life and to an understanding of his character. His motto could almost be *credo, ergo sum*. Hilaire Belloc, his friend and comrade-in-arms, understood this when he wrote, 'Chesterton's connection with the faith is much the most important aspect of his literary life and deserves more detailed treatment than any other part of his activity.'[13]

Etienne Gilson, the French historian and renowned Thomist scholar, once said that 'with Chesterton, more than literature is at stake . . . we value him most of all as a theologian'.[14] This valuation was exemplified by Gilson's praise for Chesterton's biography of St Thomas Aquinas: 'I consider it as being without possible comparison the best book ever written on St Thomas. Nothing short of genius can account for such an achievement.'[15]

Yet, although philosophy may seldom be seen as fun, it was, to Chesterton, not only fun but funny. He once claimed that 'the secret of life lies in laughter and humility'[16] and Christopher Hollis argued that 'it was Chesterton's first achievement that he turned the joke against the sceptic. Just as General Booth refused to let the devil have all the best tunes, so Chesterton refused to let him have all the best jokes, and claimed that those who had the faith should also be allowed to have the fun.'[17]

In this rare combination of fun and philosophy, and in the linking of logic with laughter, lies the secret of Chesterton's charm and the secret of his success as a defender of Christianity. It is a combination which has unlocked the agnosticism and atheism of many. C. S. Lewis, Evelyn Waugh and Graham Greene all admit the profound influence of Chesterton on their respective conversions. Another who professed a debt to Chesterton was Dorothy L. Sayers. 'He was,' she wrote in 1952, 'a Christian liberator. Like a beneficent bomb, he blew out of the Church a quantity of stained glass of a very poor period, and let in gusts of fresh air, in which the dead leaves of doctrine danced with all the energy and indecorum of our Lady's Tumbler.'[18] One suspects that the list of the famous who found faith, at least in part, through contact with Chesterton is only the tip of a much larger spiritual iceberg. For every C. S. Lewis or Sir Alec Guinness how many unknown conversions have there been?

When confronted with such examples of the contemporary relevance of Chesterton one is reminded of the extract from 'The Queer Feet', published in *The Innocence of Father Brown*, when the priest remarks, 'He has made me a fisher of men.' The story continues:

> 'Did you catch this man?' asked the colonel, frowning.
>
> Father Brown looked him full in his frowning face. 'Yes,' he said, 'I caught him, with an unseen hook and an invisible line which is long enough to let him wander to the ends of the world, and still to bring him back with a twitch upon the thread.'[19]

This passage, which was an inspiration to Evelyn Waugh who called the second book of *Brideshead Revisited* 'A Twitch Upon The Thread', was not the only example of Chesterton casting the Church as the fisher of men:

> The moment men cease to pull against the Catholic Church they feel a tug toward it. The moment they cease to shout it down they begin to listen to it with pleasure. The moment they try to be fair to it they begin to be fond of it. But when that affection has passed a certain point it begins to take on the tragic and menacing grandeur of a great love affair.[20]

Here, in barely a paragraph, Chesterton has presented his life's journey in microcosm: the initial pull against the Church, the subsequent tug he felt towards it, his desire to be fair leading to a fondness and thence, in time, to a great love affair with it. Certainly there were other love affairs in his life, most notably and obviously with his wife, Frances, but also with his brother, Cecil, and his great friends Belloc and Shaw. Yet these were only subplots, subsisting within the great love affair with Christ.

Chesterton put the matter poetically: 'If seeds in the black earth can turn into such beautiful roses what might not the heart of man become in its long journey towards the stars?'[21]

ACKNOWLEDGMENTS

First and foremost I must acknowledge a debt of gratitude to Aidan Mackey at the Chesterton Study Centre in Bedford. Without his patient and invaluable assistance it would have been impossible to source so much previously unpublished material. He is to be thanked also for supplying the many hitherto unpublished photographs which illustrate this volume. In fact, the photofiles at the Study Centre were so rich with previously unseen material that even now I am haunted by the sins of omission forced upon me in making the final selection. As well as being the fortunate recipient of Aidan's knowledge and experience, I was also the grateful recipient of his hospitality. After being a regular guest at Bedford over the past four years, I am of the opinion that he and Dorene offer the most comfortable surroundings for research imaginable, complete with bed and breakfast!

I am grateful to Sarah Hollingsworth for reading the initial draft of each chapter, and I am especially grateful for her judgment and criticism. Although this was ruthless on occasions, I am certain that the subsequent revisions have improved the text considerably.

Father Laurie Locke offered constant help and encouragement as well as free access to his extensive library – itself a Chesterton Study Centre in microcosm.

Alfred Simmonds deserves special mention for his unceasing support in ways too numerous to mention.

The following people have also helped in a variety of ways: Kevin Allard, David Barnard, Dennis Barrow, Mike and Elizabeth Butler, Richard Callan, Robert Gilbey, Alison Gillings, John Kingsmill, Robert Sneesby, Alan and Frances Staton, Adrian Stimpson and Alan Young.

Special thanks should be given to Father Joseph Fessio, S J, of the

Ignatius Press in San Francisco for granting me permission to quote extensively from the works of Chesterton. It should also be noted that several of the poems cited in the notes as being unpublished have since been collected as part of the Ignatius Press's printing of Chesterton's *Collected Works*. Thanks are also due to Father Ian Boyd, editor of the *Chesterton Review*, for permission to quote from several issues of that excellent publication.

I should like to thank the following for granting me permission to quote from previously published works. A. P. Watt Ltd, on behalf of the Turstees of the Maurice Baring Will Trust, for the five-line extract from 'Vita Nuova' from Baring's *Collected Poems*; Douglas Hyde for the extract from *I Believed*; Walter Hooper for the short quotation from his and the late Roger Lancelyn Green's biography of C. S. Lewis; George Sassoon for Siegfried Sassoon's *Fight to a Finish*; Oxford University Press for the short quotation from C. S. Lewis's *The Allegory of Love*; Burns & Oates Ltd for the various quotes from Ferdinand Valentine's biography of Father Vincent McNabb; Plexus Publishing for the extract from Donald Spoto's biography of Alfred Hitchcock; Macmillan Publishers Ltd for the quotation from George Sayer's biography of C. S. Lewis; Sheed & Ward for the various quotations from Maisie Ward's *Gilbert Keith Chesterton, Insurrection v. Resurrection* and *Return to Chesterton*, and for the extracts from F. J. Sheed's *The Church and I* and Belloc's essay *On the Place of Gilbert Keith Chesterton in English Letters*; Random House UK Ltd for permission to quote from several books, including Michael Holroyd's biography of Shaw, Arthur Ransome's *Autobiography*, Hilaire Belloc's *Complete Verse* and Father John O'Connor's *Father Brown on Chesterton*, originally published by Frederick Muller; Harper Collins for the short quotes from *Blessings in Disguise* by Sir Alec Guinness and *Surprised by Joy* by C. S. Lewis; Element Books Ltd of Shaftesbury, Dorset, for the three short quotes from *Alan Watts: Modern Mystic*; and Chapman & Hall Ltd for the quotes from Mrs Cecil Chesterton's book, *The Chestertons*.

Last, but emphatically not least, I am grateful to Elspeth Taylor and James Catford for putting their faith in my efforts.

Father of the Man

The Child is father of the Man;
And I could wish my days to be
Bound each to each by natural piety.
WILLIAM WORDSWORTH, 'My Heart Leaps Up'

A CRITICISM OFTEN LEVELLED against G. K. Chesterton is that he never grew up. He was hopelessly romantic and helplessly naïve. At first glance his own opinions may give the impression that such a view is correct. A few months before his death he wrote candidly of his childhood: 'I have never lost the sense that this was my real life; the real beginning of what should have been a more real life; a lost experience in the land of the living.'[1]

It would be very easy to see such sentiments as naïve but to do so is to fall into the trap of naïvety oneself or at least to make the mistake of being naïve about Chesterton. Indeed, although Chesterton confessed to being a romantic, he always insisted that romance was closer to reality than cynicism. Hence he was hopefully romantic and never hopelessly so. As he would have taken great joy in proclaiming, it is the cynic and not the romantic who is without hope. For Chesterton, the romance of reality was hidden in the innocence of childhood:

I was subconsciously certain then, as I am consciously certain now, that there was the white and solid road and the worthy beginning of the life of man; and that it is man who afterwards darkens it with dreams or goes astray from it in self-deception. It is only the grown man who lives a life of make-believe and pretending; and it is he who has his head in a cloud.[2]

I

By way of disarming and dispelling the allegations of naïvety, Chesterton presented a curriculum vitae, appropriately enough in his *Autobiography*, demonstrating that he was a 'man of the world':

> Without giving myself any airs of the adventurer or the globetrotter, I may say I have seen something of the world; I have travelled in interesting places and talked to interesting men; I have been in political quarrels often turning into faction fights; I have talked to statesmen in the hour of destiny of States ... There are many journalists who have seen more of such things than I; but I have been a journalist and I have seen such things.[3]

With these words he sought to nail the lie of his naïvety. Yet he still delivered the punchline that all these episodes in his life 'will be unmeaning if nobody understands that they still mean less to me than Punch and Judy on Campden Hill'.[4]

The profound importance of puppet-show memories is evident in Chesterton's description of the 'very first thing I can ever remember seeing with my own eyes'. He recalled a young man walking across a bridge with 'a curly moustache and an attitude of confidence verging on swagger'. He was wearing a gold crown and carried a disproportionately large key. Even more dramatically, the bridge traversed 'a highly perilous mountain chasm':

> To those who may object that such a scene is rare in the home life of house-agents living immediately to the north of Kensington High Street, in the later seventies of the last century, I shall be compelled to admit, not that the scene was unreal, but that I saw it through ... the proscenium of a toy theatre constructed by my father; and that (if I am really to be pestered about such irrelevant details) the young man in the crown was about six inches high and proved on investigation to be made of cardboard. But it is strictly true to say that I saw him before I can remember seeing anybody else; and that, so far as my memory is concerned, this was the sight on which my eyes first opened in this world.[5]

As an adult in the final years of his life Chesterton readily admitted the importance of these embryonic childhood memories but he foresaw that some psychologists might try to read more into it. To the 'laborious reader of little books on child-psychology', who might come to the conclusion that his romanticism was due to such childhood memories, he gave the following reply:

> Yes, fool, yes. Undoubtedly your explanation is, in that sense, the true one. But what you are saying, in your witty way, is simply that I associate these things with happiness because I was so happy. It does not even begin to consider the question of why I was so happy. Why should looking through a square hole, at yellow pasteboard, lift anybody into the seventh heaven of happiness at any time of life? Why should it specially do so at that time of life? That is the psychological fact that you have to explain; and I have never seen any sort of rational explanation.[6]

Elsewhere Chesterton goes on to attempt an explanation of why there has been no explanation:

> Boyhood is a most complex and incomprehensible thing. Even when one has been through it, one does not understand what it was. A man can never quite understand a boy, even when he has been the boy. There grows all over what was once the child a sort of prickly protection like hair; a callousness, a carelessness, a curious combination of random and quite objectless energy with a readiness to accept conventions.[7]

Here in true Chestertonian fashion was encapsulated the paradox of childhood; it is a mystery we know exists but can't explain. The child is father of the man. He is paradoxically older than the man. His existence is older, his memories are older. The child has been with the adult all his life. He was even with the adult before the adult was born. Yet the adult neither knows nor understands the child.

So much for the child as father of the man. What of the father of the child?

Edward Chesterton's influence on his son's early development was considerable, a fact exemplified by the part he played as creator of the toy theatre which formed the first universe Gilbert discovered. One of six sons, and known affectionately by the family as 'Mister' or 'Mr Ed', Edward Chesterton was put jointly in charge of the family estate-agent business with his brother Sydney. His heart, however, was not in commerce but in art and literature. Edward Chesterton was a frustrated artist. He dabbled at drawing and was the author of several books for children, at least one of which, *The Wonderful Story*

3

of Dunder Van Haedon, he illustrated.[8] In his *Autobiography* Chesterton
wrote of 'a certain book with pictures of old Dutch houses' which
furnished his imagination as a child: 'The book was one my father
had written and illustrated himself, merely for home consumption.'[9]
Gilbert also recalled that his father's talents extended far beyond the
writing and illustrating of books: 'His den or study was piled high
with the stratified layers of about ten or twelve creative amusements;
water-colour painting and modelling and photography and stained
glass and fretwork and magic lanterns and medieval illumination.'[10]
In an early letter to his schoolfriend E.C. Bentley, Chesterton recounts
a childhood experience of one of these hobbies: 'I went to a party at
my uncle's where my father, known in those regions as Uncle Ned,
showed a magic lantern display, most of the slides I had seen before
with the exception of one beautiful series, copied and coloured by
my cousin, illustrating the tragical story of Hookybeak the Raven.'[11]

Bentley, writing many years later, paid tribute to the healthy
influence Edward Chesterton exerted on his son, stating that he had
never met 'with greater kindliness – to say nothing of other sterling
qualities – than that of his father, the businessman whose feeling
for literature and all beautiful things worked so much upon his sons
in childhood'.[12] This influence was freely admitted by Gilbert who
remembered that his father 'knew all his English literature backwards'
with the result that 'I knew a great deal of it by heart, long before
I could really get it into my head. I knew pages of Shakespeare's
blank verse without a notion of the meaning of most of it; which is
perhaps the right way to begin to appreciate verse.'[13]

Perhaps the most endearing description of Edward Chesterton
is recounted in Gilbert's *Autobiography*, in which a charming, if
mischievous, side of his character is depicted:

> My father . . . had all the Pickwickian evenness of temper and pleasure
> in the humours of travel. He was rather quiet than otherwise, but his
> quietude covered a great fertility of notions; and he certainly liked
> taking the rise out of people. I remember, to give one example of
> a hundred such inventions, how he gravely instructed some grave
> ladies in the names of flowers; dwelling especially on the rustic names
> given in certain localities . . . after affecting to provide them with the
> full scientific name . . . They followed him without revulsion when
> he said lightly: 'Merely a sprig of wild bigamy.' It was only when he
> added that there was a local variety known as Bishop's Bigamy, that
> the full depravity of his character began to dawn on their minds.[14]

4

Unfortunately, Chesterton's *Autobiography* is notably devoid of similar anecdotes about his mother, Marie Louise Grosjean. According to family legend his mother's people 'were descended from a French private soldier of the Revolutionary Wars, who had been a prisoner in England and remained there'.[15] In this instance, however, the romantic notion appears to bear little relation to reality. It seems likely that the family had in fact come to England from the French-speaking region of Switzerland two generations earlier and were of wealthy background. Marie Louise's father had been a Temperance Movement pioneer and a Wesleyan lay preacher. Her mother's family, surnamed Keith, were from Aberdeen. Bearing in mind Chesterton's outspoken opposition to the Temperance Movement and to Prohibition in the United States, coupled with his public crusades against Protestant theology, it is safe to assume that Gilbert inherited relatively little from his maternal grandfather. None the less he liked to feel that from his maternal grandmother he had derived 'a certain vividness in any infusion of Scots blood or patriotism . . . a sort of Scottish romance in my childhood'.[16]

If the family legend about the arrival of his mother's family bears little relation to reality, the real-life adventures of a certain member of his father's family more than re-establish the romantic credentials. Captain George Laval Chesterton was a veteran of the Napoleonic Wars, a soldier of fortune, a prison governor and reformer and a friend of Charles Dickens. He fought in the Peninsular War and then joined the British Army and its loyalist and Indian allies in the war of 1812 against the Americans. He wrote several autobiographical books in which he recorded the harsh realities of army life during the age of Waterloo, recalling hardened soldiers being 'made ill by the sight of a private receiving five hundred strokes of the lash'.[17] After his experiences in Europe and North America, Captain Chesterton offered his services as a mercenary fighting with the British Legion expedition to Venezuela. Both there and in Spain he fought, was imprisoned and several times faced death from fever and from execution by his captors.

His soldiering days over, Captain Chesterton returned to England where he was offered the governorship of Cold Bath Fields Prison. It was here that he became friendly with Charles Dickens and the prison reformer Elizabeth Fry. He became an outspoken campaigner for prison reform, writing a book entitled *Revelations of Prison Life*. Perhaps he was still recoiling from the memories of the floggings he witnessed in the British army when he wrote disdainfully about the whipping of a thief at the tail of a cart: 'My first reflection, after this exhibition, was that I and the police had been degraded, and the public outraged by so savage a spectacle, and I heartily rejoiced when the custom fell into desuetude, or became prohibited . . .'[18]

The adventures of other members of the Chesterton clan could be told, such as those of an Arthur Chesterton who went to sea in 1829 and wrote home in 1830 about his experiences in Jamaica. However, the main concern is that Edward Chesterton eventually met, fell in love with and married Marie Louise Grosjean. Gilbert was destined to be their second child.

As to the specific details of Chesterton's birth, they can scarcely be put more poignantly or imaginatively than in the opening lines of his *Autobiography*:

> Bowing down in blind credulity, as is my custom, before mere authority and the tradition of the elders, superstitiously swallowing a story I could not test at the time by experiment or private judgment, I am firmly of opinion that I was born on the 29th of May, 1874, on Campden Hill, Kensington; and baptised according to the formularies of the Church of England in the little church of St. George opposite the large Waterworks Tower that dominated that ridge.[19]

In fact, his parents were themselves bowing down in blind credulity before mere authority and the tradition of the elders when they decided to get Gilbert baptised in an Anglican church. Certainly they felt no affiliation to the creed of the Church into which their son was baptised. They were 'freethinkers' in the best Victorian tradition, paying lip-service to a Unitarian form of worship and thus rejecting 'the formularies of the Church of England'. One can only assume, therefore, that the parents consented to their son's baptism from a position more of social standing than spiritual standpoint. The 'mere authority' was not that of the Church but of convention. None the less, the Reverend Alexander Law Watherston performed the ceremony on 1 July at St George's church, Campden Hill, during which Gilbert received the surname of his godfather, Tom Gilbert, and the family name Keith.[20]

Gilbert had an older sister named Beatrice who was five years his senior. Beatrice was the 'idol of the household' and she seems to have accepted the new baby's arrival lovingly. They became the best of playmates, receiving the nicknames 'Birdie' and 'Diddie', presumably Gilbert's own earliest efforts at speech.[21] The nicknames were short-lived. Tragedy struck the family when Beatrice died, aged eight.

It is hard to gauge how his sister's death affected him, and his own words shed little light on the subject:

> I had a little sister who died when I was a child. I have little to go on; for she was the only subject about which my father did not talk ... I do not remember her dying; but I remember her falling off a rocking-horse ... the greater catastrophe must somehow have become confused and identified with the smaller one. I always felt it as a tragic memory, as if she had been thrown by a real horse and killed. Something must have painted and repainted the picture in my mind; until I suddenly became conscious about the age of eighteen that it had become the picture of Amy Robsart lying at the foot of the stairs, flung down by Varney and another villain. This is the real difficulty about remembering anything; that we have remembered too much – for we have remembered too often.[22]

There are few clues to be gleaned from this candid confession, illustrating yet again the ever-elusive but all-pervasive power of childhood. It is clear that he regrets never being able to talk the matter through with his father but, beyond that, it is clear that nothing else is clear. The trouble with thinking about something often, Chesterton explained, is that 'it becomes more and more our own memory of the thing rather than the thing remembered'.[23] This quote immediately precedes the discussion of his sister and is an admission that he thought of her death often over the following years of childhood and adolescence. How it affected the subsequent course of his life is open to conjecture, but perhaps it was as important to Chesterton as the death of another Beatrice proved to be to the life of a greater poet.

Apart from the tragic death of his sister, Gilbert's childhood appears almost idyllic, so much so that he felt compelled to apologise for it in his *Autobiography*. The apology, however, was made with tongue firmly embedded in cheek and one suspects that he had the child psychologist in mind when he wrote it:

> ... such were the people among whom I was born. I am sorry if the landscape or the people appear disappointingly respectable and even

7

reasonable, and deficient in all those unpleasant qualities that make
a biography really popular . . . I regret that . . . I cannot do my duty
as a true modern, by cursing everybody who made me whatever I
am . . . I am compelled to confess that I look back to the landscape
of my first days with a pleasure that should doubtless be reserved
for the Utopias of the Futurist.[24]

The landscape of Chesterton's first days was brightened considerably in November 1879 by the arrival of a second son, Cecil Edward,
in the family. Gilbert was reported to have greeted the news that he
had a brother by saying that 'now I shall always have an audience'.[25]
If this is so, the young Gilbert was about to get more than he bargained
for. As soon as Cecil learned to talk he learned to argue. Gilbert's
audience was a heckler:

> it was a case of there being simultaneously two orators and no
> audience. We argued throughout our boyhood and youth until we
> became the pest of our whole social circle. We shouted at each other
> across the table, on the subject of Parnell or Puritanism or Charles
> the First's head, until our nearest and dearest fled at our approach,
> and we had a desert around us.[26]

The most important thing to remember about this juvenile jousting
was the good-natured way in which it was conducted. As Gilbert
explained: 'I am glad to think that through all those years we
never stopped arguing; and we never once quarrelled.'[27] Modern
idiom has blurred and cheapened the words 'quarrel' and 'argue',
treating them synonymously. Chesterton is an incarnation of the
difference between the two, since his whole life was an argument
but he rarely, if ever, quarrelled. He put the matter whimsically
when he said that 'the principal objection to a quarrel is that it
interrupts an argument'.[28]

Neither should the fact that the brothers argued be taken as an
indication that they weren't close. Gilbert idolised his younger brother
and was very protective towards him. Whenever Cecil is mentioned in
any of Gilbert's writings it is invariably in terms of adoration. He quite
literally will hear nothing said against him, frequently eulogising him
to excess.

Shortly after Cecil's birth, the family moved to Warwick Gardens
in another part of Kensington. Ada Chesterton, Cecil's wife, later

described the family home. Its exterior was adorned with flowers in dark-green window boxes. The interior remained substantially unchanged year after year; the walls of the dining-room continually renewing their original shade of bronze green, while the mantelboard was perennially wine-coloured. The tiles of the hearth, Edward Chesterton's own design, grew more and more mellow as the years passed. Books lined as much of the wall space as was feasible and the shelves reached from floor to ceiling. The furniture, described as 'graceful' by Ada Chesterton, included a slim mahogany dining-table, a small sideboard, generously stocked with bottles, and deep chairs. On the wall facing the fireplace was a portrait of Gilbert, aged six, by the Italian artist Bacceni. Through the vista of a rose-coloured drawing-room could be seen a 'long and lovely garden, burgeoning with jasmine and syringa, blue and yellow iris, climbing roses and rock plants'. The garden was surrounded by high walls, with tall trees standing sentinel at the far end. It was here that Edward Chesterton, on special occasions, 'would hang up fairy lamps in absurd and ravishing loops among the flowers and trees'.[29]

The concluding lines of Ada Chesterton's description of family life at Warwick Gardens serve as a further illustration of the influence of Gilbert's father. As well as introducing his sons to toy theatres, magic lanterns and fairy lamps, he introduced them to fairy stories. One such story was George MacDonald's *The Princess and the Goblin*, a book which Gilbert's father gave him as a gift. It had a profound effect. Gilbert later stated that it had made 'a difference to my whole existence, which helped me to see things in a certain way from the start'. It was a tale of goblins lurking in hidden corners of the house and fairy allies hiding in others. It was a tale of good and evil. Here, in a nutshell, is the secret of Chesterton's spiritual growth. Fairy stories had introduced him to morality and he came to believe that only in morality was reality. Perhaps it was fortuitous that Chesterton had been introduced to the concept of morality through the reading of fairy stories because in the agnostic air of Victorian England it was conspicuous by its absence. Echoing the words of Nietzsche, many Victorians considered themselves 'beyond good and evil'. They were too modern to be moral.

> The general background of all my boyhood was agnostic [wrote Chesterton]. I remember when my friend Lucian Oldershaw ... said to me suddenly, looking back on the tired lessons in the Greek

Testament at St. Paul's School, 'Of course, you and I were taught our religion by agnostics;' and I, suddenly seeing the faces of all my schoolmasters, except one or two eccentric clergymen, knew that he was right. [30]

Elsewhere he wrote: 'The truth is that for most men about this time Imperialism, or at least patriotism, was a substitute for religion. Men believed in the British Empire precisely because they had nothing else to believe in.' [31] And again: 'what I wish to attest, merely as a witness to the fact, is that the background of all the world was not merely atheism, but atheist orthodoxy, and even atheist respectability. That was quite as common in Belgravia as in Bohemia. That was above all normal in Suburbia . . .' [32]

This background of agnosticism and atheism coloured everything with doubt, or at least it seemed that way to Gilbert's parents, and although they persisted in taking their children to church, their choice of religious affiliation was itself coloured with doubt. They attended Bedford Chapel, where a Unitarian minister named Stopford Brooke preached. He had caused some controversy in 1880 by leaving the Anglican Church, where he had been a royal chaplain, because of his lack of belief in miracles.

At about the same time Stopford Brooke was leaving the Anglican Church, the young Gilbert, then only six years old, experienced his first encounter with Catholicism. He remembered walking with his father along Kensington High Street and coming across a crowd of people. Although he had seen crowds before, this particular crowd behaved rather oddly:

> In a flash a sort of ripple ran along the line and all these eccentrics went down on their knees on the public pavement . . . Then I realised that a sort of little dark cab or carriage had drawn up . . . and out of it came a ghost clad in flames . . . lifting long frail fingers over the crowd in blessing. And then I looked at his face and was startled with a contrast; for his face was dead pale like ivory and very wrinkled and old . . . having in every line the ruin of great beauty. [33]

The scarlet ghost was Cardinal Manning, a prince of the Church enshrined as an ageing Prince Charming in the memory of an ageing Chesterton writing more than fifty years after the event. The vividness of the memory indicates two things very clearly. First, that the vision of the cardinal retained a potency which may have affected Chesterton subconsciously in later years; and second, that Chesterton's romantic retelling of the tale only months before his death illustrates his retention of childlike qualities.

Another prominent Catholic introduced to Chesterton in these formative years was to have an even greater influence on his destiny. St Francis of Assisi was the hero of a story read to him by his parents when he was still a small boy and it was to prove the beginning of a lifelong relationship. From the moment the wide-eyed Gilbert first heard the story of St Francis he knew he had found a friend.

A further factor in Chesterton's early formation was the experience of Dickensian Christmases. He remembered the Christmases of his childhood vividly. As a result, he 'believed in the spirit of Christmas before I believed in Christ . . . and from my earliest years I had an affection for the Blessed Virgin and the Holy Family, for Bethlehem and the story of Nazareth'.[34] This infant piety was expressed in a couple of drawings by the young Gilbert, preserved for posterity by his ever-doting father who had collected and dated the child's scribblings. Both drawings date from 1882 when Gilbert was seven or eight years old. The first is a vigorous drawing of Christ crucified surrounded by large ministering angels.[35] The second is perhaps even more noteworthy in the light of his later conversion. It shows a smiling monk holding a crucifix aloft being pursued by angry, sword-wielding men; in the background a man kneels before another crucifix.[36] The truly remarkable aspect of the drawing is the young Chesterton's perception, considering the general background of agnosticism. In Victorian England it was not usual for Christians other than Catholics to portray Christ on the Cross so the inclusion of a crucifix as opposed to a naked cross is surprising. Somewhere, even at this early age, Chesterton had seen, and was influenced by, the images of Catholic Christianity.

Inevitably and more predictably he was also influenced by the prevailing Victorian view of history, a view echoed and espoused by his father. This view made the Catholic Church very much the villain, while its heroes were Henry the Eighth, Elizabeth, Oliver Cromwell and William of Orange, all of whom were praised for striking a blow against the Church. It is scarcely surprising, therefore, that the young Chesterton was the author of a couple of anti-Catholic poems. The first and earlier of the two is an ironic parody of Aytoun's *Lays of the Scottish Cavaliers*:

Drive the trembling Papists backwards
Drive away the Tory's hord
Let them tell thier hous of villains
They have felt the Campbell's sword.[37]

The poem is undated, but the poor spelling indicates its early origin. Elsewhere the same poem rejoices:

That same morn we drove right backwards
All the servants of the Pope.

The second poem is somewhat later, probably around 1886 when Gilbert was eleven or twelve. Entitled 'The Hero', it climaxed as follows:

He had chased all Holland's navy
Back into the Zuyder Zee
As he smote the Papish tyrant
On the Spaniard's native sea.[38]

The underlying trend in both these early efforts at poetry, aside from the anti-Catholicism, is a swashbuckling love for heroics. It is the hero-worship of childhood.

With these poems the sun set on Chesterton's childhood and the moon rose on the darker world of adolescence and early manhood. At the age of twelve he entered St Paul's School. In the new world in which he found himself the innocence of childhood was threatened. For every glimmer of light there was a lurking shadow. Contrary opinions and contradictions fought for supremacy. Yet the influence of these formative pre-school years would always be important to his later life. Whenever the vaunt of woe appeared triumphant and the darkness of despair descended, a gleam of childlight would disperse the shadows. Years later, when the battle was won and the man emerged victorious, he owed a debt of gratitude to the child.

« 2 »

Soul in a Ferment

The imagination of a boy is healthy, and the mature imagination of a man is healthy; but there is a space of life between, in which the soul is in a ferment, the character undecided, the way of life uncertain, the ambition thick-sighted: thence proceeds mawkishness, and all the thousand bitters which those men I speak of must necessarily taste in going over the following pages.

KEATS, from the Preface to *Endymion*

GILBERT'S FORMAL EDUCATION BEGAN in 1881 when his parents sent him to Colet Court preparatory school. An early school exercise book, dating from the following year, indicates that the eight-year-old Chesterton was making good progress in both English and arithmetic. His efforts at taking dictation are of particular interest, with his form mistress, Miss Seamark, underlining the misspelt words and instructing Gilbert to write them out correctly at the bottom of the page: 'Great was the surprise of Montcalm when he was told, one morning at day *brake*, that an English *armany* was drawn up on the heights of Abraham, the plain overlooking Quebec on the south west.'[1]

At the end of 1886 Gilbert's time at Colet Court came to an end. In January 1887, at the age of twelve, he entered St Paul's School, situated directly opposite Colet Court on the Hammersmith Road.

St Paul's was a public school with impeccable credentials. It boasted a fine history of celebrities among its scholars, including Milton and Marlborough, Pepys and Judge Jeffreys, but in later life Chesterton made no secret of the fact that he didn't care for institutionalised learning, describing education as 'being instructed by somebody I did not know about something I did not want to know'.[2]

Not surprisingly, considering this negative attitude, he failed to make any impression academically during his first years at St Paul's. Neither was he worried by the fact, explaining that 'personally, I was perfectly happy at the bottom of the class'.[3] He also expressed the belief that 'the chief impression I produced, on most of the masters and many of the boys, was a pretty well-founded conviction that I was asleep'.[4] This belief was borne out by Lawrence Solomon, the boy who sat next to him in class, who remembered him as sleepy and indifferent in manner but able to master anything when he took the trouble – as he seldom did. Certainly, his teachers were unimpressed by his lack of academic effort, as these extracts from his half-yearly reports indicate:

December 1887 Too much for me: means well by me, I believe, but has an inconceivable knack of forgetting at the shortest notice, is consequently always in trouble, though some of his work is well done, when he does remember to do it. He ought to be in a studio not at school. Never troublesome, but for his lack of memory and absence of mind.

July 1888 Wildly inaccurate about everything; never thinks for two consecutive moments to judge by his work . . .

December 1890 Takes an interest in his English work, but otherwise has not done well.

July 1892 Not on the same plane with the rest: composition quite futile, but will translate well and appreciate what he reads. Not a quick brain, but possessed by a slowly moving tortuous imagination.[5]

Masters and pupils also remembered his absent-minded eccentricities: 'I can see him now, very tall and lanky, striding untidily along Kensington High Street, smiling and sometimes scowling as he talked to himself, apparently oblivious of everything he passed.' Others recall him striding along 'apparently muttering poetry, breaking into inane laughter'.[6]

Much of this apparent eccentricity and insularity was the result of short-sightedness. Gilbert was not perceived as myopic and was consequently misunderstood. The brooding expression, the distant look in the eyes, the scowling can all be traced to his poor sight. So, perhaps, can his reticence.

Inevitably the eccentricity and absent-mindedness led to his being teased at school and he became the butt of practical jokes. Lucian Oldershaw, a schoolfriend who later became his brother-in-law, remembered how the young Chesterton's pockets had been filled with snow in the playground and how he had returned to the classroom unaware of the prank played on him. As he sat at his desk the snow began to melt, leaving a pool of water at his feet.[7]

Chesterton, it seems, was seen as a donkey by his fellow pupils and as an intellectual ass by his tutors. The most extreme case of the attitude of the latter was displayed by one master who exclaimed: 'You know, Chesterton, if we could open your head, we should not find any brain but only a lump of white fat!'[8] In fairness, however, the assessment of his abilities was not made any easier by his own dogged determination not to stand out in the classroom:

> I can remember running to school in sheer excitement repeating militant lines of *Marmion* with passionate emphasis and exultation; and then going into class and repeating the same lines in the lifeless manner of a hurdy gurdy, hoping that there was nothing whatever in my intonation to indicate that I distinguished between the sense of one word and another.[9]

The attitude reminds one instantly of two lines from Chesterton's poem 'The Donkey': 'Starve, scourge, deride me: I am dumb,/I keep my secret still.'

The insularity and reticence were cured, or at least alleviated, by the acquisition of friends. One boy in particular was to become his best friend at St Paul's and was to remain one of Gilbert's closest companions for the rest of his life. The boy was Edmund Clerihew Bentley. He was two years Gilbert's junior but the age difference proved no barrier to their friendship. Neither did other differences. For example, Bentley's athleticism stood in stark contrast to Chesterton's clumsiness. Commenting on his friend's physical prowess, Gilbert recalled that it was 'a poetic pleasure to see him walk, a little pompously, down the street and suddenly scale a lamppost like a monkey . . . and then drop down and resume his walk with an unchanged expression of earnestness and serenity'.[10] Chesterton, on the other hand, was always an object of fun in the gymnasium, with the other boys forming parties to observe his bizarre efforts on the trapeze or parallel bars. On one occasion an exercise on the rings required hands and feet to be inserted and the body turned. Gilbert, hands in rings, could not get his feet up. The instructor seized his feet and pushed them in, whereupon Gilbert let go with his hands, leaving the instructor staggering under the full weight of his limp body.

However, beneath the superficial differences the two boys discovered a unity of spirit. They shared a love of literature and a similar sense of humour which came together in their first joint literary endeavour. It was an adventure story, in which they wrote alternate chapters, about two of their favourite masters at school carrying around a third who turned out to be a robot.

In later years Bentley also became a writer of renown, and it is a mark of the depth of their friendship that he dedicated his bestselling detective story, *Trent's Last Case*, to Gilbert:

> ... I have been thinking again today of those astonishing times when neither of us ever looked at a newspaper; when we were purely happy in the boundless consumption of paper, pencils, tea, and our elders' patience; when we embraced the most severe literature and ourselves produced such light reading as was necessary ... in short, when we were extremely young.[11]

He was, in fact, returning the compliment, since Gilbert had already dedicated his third novel, *The Man Who was Thursday*, to Bentley:

> A cloud was on the mind of men, and wailing went the weather,
> Yea, a sick cloud upon the soul when we were boys together ...
> This is the tale of those old fears, even of those emptied hells,
> And none but you shall understand the true thing that it tells –
> The doubts that drove us through the night as we two talked amain
> And day had broken on the streets e'er it broke on the brain.[12]

Whereas Bentley's dedication concentrates on the untroubled innocence of boyhood, Chesterton's touches on the doubts and fears of adolescence. None the less, the days at St Paul's were essentially happy ones. The more serious doubts and anxieties would not arise until later, and Bentley's memories of their schooldays concentrate on Chesterton's cheerfulness:

> G. K. C., when I knew him first, was an unusually tall, lanky boy with a serious, even brooding, expression that gave way very easily to one of laughing happiness. He was by nature the happiest boy

and man I have ever known; even in the adolescent phase of morbid misery that so many of us go through, and that he has described so thoroughly, laughter was never far away, in my recollection . . .

So far as it is possible for an awakened mind to go through the world as we know it in a temper of prevailing cheerfulness, Gilbert Chesterton, I think, achieved it. He had an ideally happy home; he was devoted to his friends, and they to him; he had not an enemy; he had at least a double dose of the faculty of enjoying things, from a nineteenth-century sausage-and-mash to a fifteenth-century Madonna and Child. Even as a boy, he knew the peculiar delight of creative work, both with pencil and with pen; even as a boy, his sense of humour was as enormously developed as were his sense of beauty and his sense of reverence – things which, I can assure my conscientiously low-minded and hard-boiled friends, do somehow make for happiness . . .[13]

Although Bentley was the first, and foremost, of Chesterton's friends he was but one of a growing circle. Two extracts from the notebook Gilbert kept at this time indicate that he had at last found the audience he had hoped for at the birth of his brother:

A List

I know a friend, very strong and good. He is the best friend in
    the world.
I know another friend, subtle and sensitive. He is certainly the best
    friend on earth.
I know another friend, very quiet and shrewd, there is no friend so
    good as he.
I know another friend, who is enigmatical and reluctant, he is the
    best of all.
I know yet another: who is polished and eager, he is far better than
    the rest.
I know another, who is young and very quick, he is the most beloved
    of all friends.
I know a lot more and they are all like that.

                                   Amen.[14]

In the other extract these anonymous friends are identified:

The Cosmic Factories

What are little boys made of?
Bentley is made of hard wood with a knot in it, a complete set of
      Browning and a strong spring;
Oldershaw of a box of Lucifer matches and a stylographic pen;
Lawrence of a barrister's wig: files of *Punch* and salt,
Maurice of watch-wheels, three riders and a clean collar.
Vernede is made of moonlight and tobacco,
Bertram is mostly a handsome black walking-stick.
Waldo is a nice cabbage, with a vanishing odour of cigarettes,
Salter is made of sand and fire and an university extension ticket.
But the strongest element in all cannot be expressed; I think it is a
      sort of star.[15]

Together this motley crew comprised the Junior Debating Club
(JDC), the founding of which was the inspiration of Lucian Oldershaw,
described by Chesterton as 'the third member of our original trio' (i.e.,
Chesterton, Bentley and Oldershaw). The son of an actor, Oldershaw
had travelled about the country, had been to other schools and, in
consequence, had an air of confidence and experience unknown to
his contemporaries. 'Above all,' wrote Chesterton, 'there possessed
him, almost feverishly, a vast, amazing and devastating idea, the idea
of *doing* something . . . in the manner of grown-up people, who were
the only people who could be conceived as doing things.'[16]

The first meeting of the Junior Debating Club was held at
Oldershaw's house, in Talgarth Road, on 1 July 1890. Oldershaw
also took the minutes which recorded the club's purpose: 'to get a few
friends together to amuse one another with a literary or something
approaching a literary subject'.[17] Gilbert was the elected chairman
and Oldershaw the secretary. Ten other boys made up the original
club members and subscribed to the rules, namely that they must agree
with the club's motto, 'Hence loathed Melancholy', and undertake to
pay the fine of sixpence should they fail to read a literary paper to the
assembled members when required to do so. The members also agreed
to pay a fine of sixpence if absent from two consecutive meetings
without a valid and convincing excuse. Meetings would take place
in the members' houses after school and sometimes on Saturdays.

Apart from Chesterton, Oldershaw and Bentley the members
of the original Junior Debating Club were an intriguing group.
Robert Vernede, a poet of some promise, was killed in the First
World War. Lawrence Solomon became Senior Tutor at University

College, London. His brother Maurice became a leading director of the General Electric Company. Edward Fordham, a writer of satiric poetry, became a successful barrister. Another member, F. R. Salter, became Gilbert's solicitor and was to write a history of St Paul's School.

The JDC was an instant success. The minutes of a meeting held several months after its inauguration testify that Chesterton, as chairman, 'said a few words stating his pride at the success of the Club, and his belief in the good effect such a literary institution might have as a protest against the lower and unworthy phases of school life. His view having been vehemently corroborated, the meeting broke up.'[18] In one fairly typical month papers were read on 'Three Comedies of Shakespeare', 'Pope' and 'Herodotus'. At a meeting when no paper was produced there was a discussion on capital punishment. In another month there were papers on 'The Brontës', 'Macaulay as an Essayist' and 'Tennyson'.

Before long the club had developed sundry offshoots over and above the weekly literary debates. It spawned in due course a library, a chess club, a naturalists' society and a sketching club. Yet the effervescent Oldershaw was not content. He published a magazine, the *Debater*, in which members could disseminate their views and literary contributions.

Eighteen issues of the *Debater* were to be published, written in laborious longhand by the club's members and then transported to the typewriting studio of Miss Davidson at 13 Charleville Road in West Kensington. The circulation was between sixty and a hundred copies, sold at sixpence each. Issue one contained Chesterton's first appearance in print, an article entitled 'Dragons', and later his first poems were published.

As the debate on capital punishment at an early JDC meeting demonstrates, the club did not restrict itself to literary themes. Indeed, as the boys got older they began, inevitably, to develop political views. In most cases these were in sympathy with the Marxian socialism which was in vogue intellectually during the 1890s. Two motions offered for debate at a meeting of the club in 1892 illustrate the adoption of the socialist creed by Gilbert and most of his friends: 'That this house is of opinion that a competitive state of society is at present detrimental to the real progress of humanity' and 'That this house favours the assumption by the state of all means of production and distribution, to be managed in the common interest and for the common profit'.[19] This new-found socialism was evident in 'The Song of Labour', a poem that Chesterton sent to the *Speaker*, a radical magazine:

> God has struck all into chaos, princes and priests down-hurled,
> But he leaves the place of the toiler, the old estate of the world.
> When the old Priest fades to a phantom, when the old King nods
>   on his throne,
> The old, old hand of labour is mighty and holdeth its own.[20]

With the passage of time it was not the priest but the politician who faded to a phantom in Chesterton's estimation. Yet even at this time his attitude to religion was ambiguous and ambivalent. He was certainly not as negative towards the priest as the poem suggested. Indeed, many of the other poems he wrote at this time were avowedly Christian. 'Adveniat Regnum Tuum', published in the *Debater* in 1891, has a theme similar to that of 'The Song of Labour' but a very different moral:

> Not that the widespread wings of wrong brood o'er a moaning
> earth,
> Not from the clinging curse of gold, the random lot of birth;
> Not from the misery of the weak, the madness of the strong,
> Goes upward from our lips the cry, 'How long, oh Lord, how
>   long!' . . .
> Though death shall close upon us all before that hour we see,
> The goal of ages yet is there – the good time yet to be:
> Therefore, tonight, from varied lips, in every house and home,
> Goes up to God the common prayer, 'Father, Thy Kingdom Come.'[21]

The camaraderie inherent in the JDC did more than offer Chesterton the audience he desired. It also afforded him the opportunity to be part of an audience, part of a group with a common set of interests. Amidst the friendships, and the sense of belonging they cemented, Gilbert began to flourish. Even his tutors began to take notice of the talent he displayed. Frederick Walker, the High Master at St Paul's, told him that he had some literary merit and capability as long as he could 'solidify' his potential.[22] Within the pages of the *Debater* the potential solidified exceedingly. In 1892 the inexperienced Gilbert, still only eighteen, got to grips with Shelley:

He was not a bad man; he was not a good man; he was not an ordinary man; he was a sincere philanthropist and Republican; yet he was often as lonely and ill-tempered as a misanthrope; he had far purer feelings towards women than either Burns or Byron, yet he was a far worse husband than they: he was one of those men whose faults and failures seem due, not to the presence of tempting passions or threatening disasters, so much as to a mysterious inner weakness, a certain helplessness in the hands of circumstances.[23]

Although the conclusion may have been more fatalistic than Chesterton would have professed later in life, the analysis of Shelley's character is remarkable for one so young. Even more remarkable was the insight exhibited in an early paper on Queen Mary and Queen Elizabeth:

It must indeed have been a terrible scene, the execution of that unhappy Queen . . . But the continually lamented death of Mary of Scotland seems to me happy compared with the end of her greater and sterner rival. As I think on the two, the vision of the black scaffold, the grim headsman, the serene captive, and the weeping populace fades from me and is replaced by a sadder vision: the vision of the dimly-lighted state-bedroom of Whitehall. Elizabeth, haggard and wild-eyed, has flung herself prone upon the floor and refuses to take meat or drink, but lies there, surrounded by ceremonious courtiers, but seeing with that terrible insight that was her curse, that she was alone, that their homage was a mockery, that they were waiting eagerly for her death to crown their intrigues with her successor, that there was not in the whole world a single being who cared for her: seeing all this, and bearing it with the iron fortitude of her race, but underneath that invincible silence the deep woman's nature crying out with a bitter cry that she is loved no longer: thus gnawed by the fangs of a dead vanity, haunted by the pale ghost of Essex, and helpless and bitter of heart, the greatest of Englishwomen passed silently away. Of a truth, there are prisons more gloomy than Fotheringay and deaths more cruel than the axe. Is there no pity due to those who undergo these?[24]

On reading these lines one is struck not only by the deep and profound insight displayed but by the development of a distinctive prose style. One is witnessing a writer in the making.

In the summer term of 1892 Chesterton reached the pinnacle

of his literary achievement at school when he entered a poetry competition. His entry, a poem on St Francis Xavier, was awarded the Milton Prize. The choice of subject serves as further illustration of his embryonic spirituality:

> He died: and she, the Church that bade him go,
> Yon dim Enchantress with her mystic claim,
> Has ringed his forehead with her aureole-glow,
> And monkish myths, and all the whispered fame
> Of miracle, has clung about his name . . .[25]

The quality of this poem was enough to convince Frederick Walker, the High Master, that Gilbert had 'solidified' his potential. He told Chesterton's mother, when she visited him in 1894, that her son was 'six foot of genius. Cherish him, Mrs Chesterton, cherish him.'[26]

As a reward for winning the Milton Prize, Gilbert's father took him to France for a holiday. It was his first journey abroad. They took the train to Rouen and thence to Arromanche. Gilbert recounted these first impressions of foreign life in a letter to Bentley: 'A foreign town is a very funny sight with solemn old *abbés* in their broad brims and black robes and sashes and fiery bronzed little French soldiers staring right and left under their red caps, dotted everywhere among the blue blouses of the labourers and the white caps of the women.'[27] Before returning to England, father and son visited Paris and enjoyed a guided tour of Notre Dame cathedral.

Perhaps the tour made a lasting impression because religious themes proliferate in the poetry Gilbert wrote in the following year. 'Ave Maria', a poem which appeared in the *Debater* in 1893, begins:

> Hail Mary, thou blessed among women, generations shall rise up
> to greet,
> After ages of wrangles and dogma, I come with a prayer to thy feet.[28]

Yet Chesterton, for all his romantic Marianism, was not a Christian of any conviction. He directed another poetic prayer to the Unknown God or, to employ the imagery he chose, the Unknown Goddess:

> O strange old shadow among us, O sweet-voiced mystery,
> Now in the hour of question I lift my voice unto thee.
> Stricken, unstable the creeds and old things fall and are not.

The temples shake and groan and whisper we know not what.
The shapes and the forms of worship wherein the divine was seen
Are scattered and cast away on the fields of the things that have been.
A terrible stir of change and waking through all the land,
Till we know not what things to believe of what knowledge be near
    at hand.
Therefore I turn to thee, the nameless infinite,
Mother of all the creeds that dawn and dwell and are gone,
Voice in the heart of man, imperative, changeless, blind,
The call to the building of faith through the ages of all mankind.[29]

A call to the building of faith . . . But faith in what? A strange old shadow? The nameless infinite?

In the November issue of the *Debater* Chesterton wrote a poem about St Francis of Assisi. Buried in the poem is a question of his own that begs an answer: 'Is it God's bright house we dwell in, or a vault of dark confusion?'[30]

On 16 December 1892 the Junior Debating Club reached a crisis point. A meeting was held at which its very future was called into question, 'as members were already beginning to leave St Paul's, and in a year or so more would be scattered over different parts of the world'.[31]

It was a sad day for Gilbert. The JDC had constituted the centre of his schoolboy universe and he argued that it should continue. It was a vain hope that it could ever do so in anything but name. Time had rolled relentlessly on. Gilbert had left St Paul's six months earlier and most of his friends were about to follow suit, destined for Oxford or Cambridge. For Chesterton, who remained in London to study art, his friends would soon seem a world away. In February 1893 the final issue of the *Debater* was published: 'Regretful though we may be at losing our Magazine, we may still claim that enthusiasm which prompted us to start it, and a belief that the idea which it was intended to embody, has been helped rather than hindered by its championship.'[32]

With the ending of the *Debater* much more ceased to exist than the magazine. It was the end of the camaraderie and *joie de vivre* to which it gave expression. Chesterton, more sensitive than most, felt the loss intensely. He had lost his audience but, much worse, he had lost his friends and comrades. Those he loved had left for pastures new. About this time he wrote a short verse called 'Love'. It was a cry from the heart:

Do I say no-one has loved as I love?
I believe thousands have loved as I love
And if thousands have loved a thousand times more than I love
Why so much the better.[33]

For the first time since the death of his sister, Gilbert had loved and lost. It had a profound and, in the short term at least, a negative effect. As well as heralding a return to the old reticence and brooding, the loss of innocence which accompanies the onset of adulthood had added a new and more ominous dimension to his feelings. He now suffered from a deep and recurring depression, nurtured by doubt and morbidity. 'I deal here,' wrote Chesterton in his *Autobiography*, 'with the darkest and most difficult part of my task; the period of youth which is full of doubts and morbidities and temptations; and which, though in my case mainly subjective, has left in my mind for ever a certitude upon the objective solidity of Sin.'[34] In *Orthodoxy*, a book he wrote in 1908, he confessed that 'I was a pagan at the age of twelve, and a complete agnostic by the age of sixteen.'[35] In 1893, at the age of nineteen, he had regressed further:

I am not proud of believing in the Devil. To put it more correctly, I am not proud of knowing the Devil. I made his acquaintance by my own fault; and followed it up along lines which, had they been followed further, might have led to devil-worship or the devil knows what.[36]

In truth, Chesterton did not 'know' the devil at the age of nineteen, any more than he was a pagan at twelve or an agnostic at sixteen. He had not formulated a final view in any of these areas at these ages. He was still searching, groping, exploring. He was asking the questions but, as yet, had not received the answers. Catholicism, Protestantism, paganism, agnosticism, socialism and spiritualism were all influences to varying degrees at varying times. During these formative years he caught these influences for short periods much as a man catches influenza. None of them was a permanent state but temporary aberrations battling for supremacy. He didn't accept them as facts but fed on them as fads.

The fad to which Chesterton was referring when he spoke of knowing the devil was spiritualism: 'What I may call my period of madness coincided with a period of drifting and doing nothing; in which I could not settle down to any regular work. I dabbled in a number of things . . . among these dabblings in this dubious time, I dabbled in Spiritualism.'[37] Cecil was his partner in these dabblings, and together they experimented with the planchette, or what the Americans call the ouija board. Although their experiments were carried out in a mischievous and playful spirit, Gilbert

> saw quite enough of the thing to be able to testify, with complete certainty, that something happens which is not in the ordinary sense natural, or produced by the normal and conscious human will. Whether it is produced by some subconscious but still human force, or by some powers, good, bad or indifferent, which are external to humanity, I would not myself attempt to decide. The only thing I will say with complete confidence, about that mystic and invisible power, is that it tells lies. The lies may be larks or they may be lures to the imperilled soul or they may be a thousand other things; but whatever they are, they are not truths about the other world; or for that matter about this world.[38]

Many years later Chesterton discussed this early fascination with spiritualism with his friend Father John O'Connor. Father O'Connor had mentioned in casual conversation that the Sacred Congregation of Rites had just condemned the use of the planchette after forty years of carefully weighing the evidence. Chesterton told the priest of his youthful experiences but explained that he had stopped using the planchette after headaches ensued: 'But after the headaches came a horrid feeling as if one were trying to get over a very bad spree, with what I can best describe as a bad smell in the mind.'[39] Father O'Connor diagnosed the feelings as 'the beginning of despair'. In his *Autobiography* Gilbert appeared to give some credence to his friend's diagnosis:

> I have sometimes fancied since that this practice, of the true psychology of which we really know so little, may possibly have contributed towards the disturbed or even diseased state of brooding and idling through which I passed at that time. I would not dogmatise either way; it is possible that it had nothing to do with it . . . I would leave planchette with a playful farewell, giving her the benefit of the doubt; I would allow that she may have been a joke or a fancy or a fairy or anything else; with the proviso that I would not touch her again with a bargepole.[40]

On 6 October 1893 Gilbert began to study at University College, London. His course was Fine Art and included English, French and

Latin. His professor of Latin was Alfred Edward Housman, later to achieve fame as the author of *A Shropshire Lad*. Chesterton, however, did not benefit greatly from Housman's lectures and after one year of his Latin course was asked, and agreed, to give up the subject. As ever, he was finding it hard to fit into an institutionalised system of study.

Many years later he returned to University College to deliver the seventh of a series of centenary addresses. At the commencement of his speech he recalled his days as a student:

> It was at the Slade School that I discovered that I should never be an artist; it was at the lectures of Professor A. E. Housman that I discovered that I should never be a scholar; and it was at the lectures of Professor W. P. Ker that I discovered that I should never be a literary man. The warning, alas! fell on heedless ears, and I still attempted the practice of writing, which, let me tell you in the name of the whole Slade School, is very much easier than the practice of drawing and painting.[41]

Chesterton the misfit and outcast was missing the relative security of the Junior Debating Club more than ever. At the beginning of his second year at University College Bentley wrote from Merton College, Oxford:

> You will be charmed to hear that the Human Club exists . . . It was decided that it would be well to discuss things, and read papers, until it got homogeneous enough to come together for the fun of the thing alone, like the J.D.C. . . . By the way, will you write to Vernede and tell him there is a God? He's getting frightfully dogmatic in his Agnosticism and wants somebody to unreason with him on the point.[42]

To Chesterton, alone in London, news of a born-again JDC being launched in Oxford by his friends Bentley, Oldershaw and Vernede must have accentuated his feelings of isolation. His comrades had quite literally bypassed him and were continuing an idyllic life without him. Musing on their absence, he wrote a poem entitled 'An Idyll':

> Tea is made; the red fogs shut round the house but the gas burns.
> I wish I had at this moment round the table
> A company of fine people.

Two of them are at Oxford and one in Scotland and two at
  other places.
But I wish they would all walk in now, for the tea is made.[43]

Neither was it the best time for Bentley to suggest that Chesterton
write to Vernede 'and tell him there is a God'. Chesterton, by 1894,
had ceased to be convinced that there was a God:

> At a very early age I had thought my way back to thought itself.
> It is a very dreadful thing to do; for it may lead to thinking that
> there is nothing but thought. At this time I did not very clearly
> distinguish between dreaming and waking; not only as a mood, but
> as a metaphysical doubt, I felt as if everything might be a dream
> . . . I was simply carrying the scepticism of my time as far as it
> would go. And I soon found it would go a great deal further than
> most of the sceptics went. While dull atheists came and explained
> to me that there was nothing but matter, I listened with a sort of
> calm horror of detachment, suspecting that there was nothing but
> mind . . .
>
> And as with mental, so with moral extremes. There is something
> truly menacing in the thought of how quickly I could imagine the
> maddest, when I had never committed the mildest crime. Something
> may have been due to the atmosphere of the Decadents, and their
> perpetual hints of the luxurious horrors of paganism; but I am not
> disposed to dwell much on that defence; I suspect I manufactured
> most of my morbidities for myself. But anyhow, it is true that there
> was a time when I had reached that condition of moral anarchy
> within, in which a man says, in the words of Wilde, that 'Atys with
> the blood-stained knife were better than the thing I am.' I have never
> indeed felt the faintest temptation to the particular madness of Wilde;
> but I could at this time imagine the worst and wildest disproportions
> and distortions of more normal passion . . . As Bunyan, in his morbid
> period, described himself as prompted to utter blasphemies, I had an
> overpowering impulse to record or draw horrible ideas and images;
> plunging deeper and deeper as in a blind spiritual suicide.[44]

Although Chesterton played down the importance of the 'atmosphere of the Decadents', the fact remains that the Slade School of
Art, where he studied at this time, was firmly under their influence.
Indeed, Chesterton gives a potent account of one such 'Decadent',
a fellow student he'd befriended:

... It was strange, perhaps, that I liked his dirty, drunken society; it was stranger still, perhaps, that he liked my society. For hours of the day he would talk with me about Milton or Gothic architecture; for hours of the night he would go where I have no wish to follow him, even in speculation. He was a man with a long, ironical face, and close red hair; he was by class a gentleman ... And I shall never forget the half-hour in which he and I argued about real things for the first and last time ... He had a horrible fairness of the intellect that made me despair of his soul. A common, harmless atheist would have denied that religion produced humility or humility a simple joy; but he admitted both. He only said, 'But shall I not find in evil a life of its own? Granted that for every woman I ruin one of those red sparks will go out; will not the expanding pleasure of ruin ...'

'Do you see that fire?' I asked. 'If we had a real fighting democracy, someone would burn you in it; like the devil-worshipper that you are.'

'Perhaps,' he said, in his tired, fair way. 'Only what you call evil I call good.'

He went down the great steps alone, and I felt as if I wanted the steps swept and cleaned. I followed later, and as I went to find my hat in the low, dark passage where it hung, I suddenly heard his voice again, but the words were inaudible. I stopped, startled; but then I heard the voice of one of the vilest of his associates saying, 'Nobody can possibly know.' And then I heard those two or three words which I remember in every syllable and cannot forget. I heard the Diabolist say, 'I tell you I have done everything else. If I do that I shan't know the difference between right and wrong.' I rushed out without daring to pause; and as I passed the fire I did not know whether it was hell or the furious love of God.

I have since heard that he died; it may be said, I think, that he committed suicide; though he did it with tools of pleasure, not with tools of pain. God help him, I know the road he went; but I have never known or even dared to think what was that place at which he stopped and refrained.[45]

It is clear that Chesterton's acquaintance with this student, and doubtless others like him, had a lasting and beneficial effect. Filled with horror and revulsion, he rebelled against everything they epitomised:

When I had been for some time in these, the darkest depths of the contemporary pessimism, I had a strong inward impulse to revolt; to dislodge this incubus or throw off this nightmare. But as I was still thinking the thing out by myself, with little help from philosophy and no real help from religion, I invented a rudimentary and makeshift mystical theory of my own. It was substantially this: that even mere existence, reduced to its most primary limits, was extraordinary enough to be exciting. Anything was magnificent as compared with nothing. Even if the very daylight were a dream, it was a day-dream; it was not a nightmare.[46]

There can be little doubt that Gilbert was helped in this formulation by the happy memories of childhood, which were anything but a nightmare. Reality, as enshrined in the memory, contradicted the illusion of pessimism. It is also clear that Chesterton owed his positive outlook to the influence of Dickens, Robert Louis Stevenson and Walt Whitman. His favourite writers had always been those great romantics who had vanquished the Giant Despair.

Examples of his new 'makeshift mystical theory' are exhibited in the poetry he wrote at the time:

> I thank thee, O Lord, for the stones in the street
> I thank thee for the hay-carts yonder and for the houses built and
> half-built
> That fly past me as I stride.
> But most of all for the great wind in my nostrils
> As if thine own nostrils were close.[47]

The religious nature of Chesterton's positive philosophy is evident in this poem. Another, written about the same time, is more specifically Christian:

> There was a man who dwelt in the east centuries ago,
> And now I cannot look at a sheep or a sparrow,
> A lily or a cornfield, a raven or a sunset,
> A vineyard or a mountain, without thinking of him;
> If this be not to be divine, what is it?[48]

Writing many years later, Chesterton remembered this battle of the mind from which he emerged triumphant:

> if He did not come to do battle . . . even in the darkness of the brain of man, I know not why He came. Certainly it was not only to talk about flowers or to talk about Socialism. The more truly we can see life as a fairy-tale, the more clearly the tale resolves itself into war with the dragon who is wasting fairyland.[49]

Even in the darkest hour of Chesterton's morbidity he never lost sight of the memory and imagery of childhood. It was the light at the beginning of the tunnel into which he had wandered and, looking back, he could always see it behind him. It was also the light at the end of the tunnel because in remembering the happiness of childhood he forgot the despair. He remembered reality and was thankful for it: 'I hung on to the remains of religion by one thin thread of thanks.'[50]

« 3 »

The Chesterblogg

That dear, dreamy old bachelor notion – that notion that the unity of marriage, the being one flesh, has something to do with being perfectly happy, or being perfectly good, or even with being perfectly and continuously affectionate! I tell you, an ordinary honest man is a part of his wife even when he wishes he wasn't. I tell you, an ordinary good woman is part of her husband even when she wishes him at the bottom of the sea. I tell you that, whether the two people are for the moment friendly or angry, happy or unhappy, the Thing marches on, the great four-footed Thing, the quadruped of the home. They are a nation, a society, a machine. I tell you they are one flesh, even when they are not one spirit.[1]

WHEN CHESTERTON WROTE THESE lines, in 1905, he had been married for four years. Yet in 1894 he had still not met Frances Blogg, the other half of the quadruped, a woman who would affect the course of his life more profoundly than anyone. The story of their first meeting, courtship and marriage are all monumental milestones on Chesterton's road through life. First, however, one must become acquainted with the young Gilbert, recently emerged from the doldrums of despair, who was growing ripe for romance.

During a visit to Florence in 1894 he escaped the scepticism of the 'moderns' at the Slade School and found solace in the city's masterpieces. A letter home to Bentley bubbles with enthusiasm. He has seen in the space of twenty-four hours 'the frescoes of Santa Croce, the illuminations of St. Marco; the white marbles of the tower of Giotto; the very Madonnas of Raphael, the very David of Michael Angelo'. In Santa Maria Novella, he saw some of the most interesting pieces of mediaeval painting I have ever seen, interesting not so much from an artistic as from a moral and historical point of view. Particularly noticeable was the great fresco expressive of the grandest mediaeval conception of the Communion of Saints, a figure of Christ surmounting a crowd of all ages and stations, among whom were not only Dante, Petrarca, Giotto, etc., etc., but Plato, Cicero, and best of all, Arius.[2]

If this letter, written from the Hotel New York in Florence, illustrated Chesterton's appreciation of Catholic art and doctrine, a letter to Bentley from the Grand Hotel de Milan displayed a more worldly romanticism:

I write you a third letter before coming back, while Venice and Verona are fresh in my mind. Of the former I can really only discourse *viva voce*. Imagine a city, whose very slums are full of palaces, whose every other house wall has a battered fresco, or a gothic bas-relief; imagine a sky fretted with every kind of pinnacle from the great dome of the Salute to the gothic spires of the Ducal Palace and the downright arabesque orientalism of the minarets of St. Mark's; and then imagine the whole flooded with a sea that seems only intended to reflect sunsets, and you still have no idea of the place I stopped in for more than 48 hours.

In Verona the balconies made a lasting impression, 'with young ladies hanging over them; really quite a preponderating feature. Whether this was done in obedience to local associations and in expectation of a Romeo, I can't say.'[3]

In May 1895 Chesterton celebrated his twenty-first birthday. He was tall, standing a little over six feet two inches, and his slender frame belied the obesity of later years. His mother wrote a note to him in Oxford where he was staying and enclosed a birthday gift of some money to cover expenses or to buy some books: 'My heart is full of thanks to God for the day that you were born and for the day on which you attain your manhood . . . I wish you a long happy and useful life. May God grant it. Nothing I can say or give would express my love and pleasure in having such a son.'[4]

In a letter to Bentley, commemorating his coming of age, he wrote:

Being twenty-one years old is really rather good fun. It is one of those occasions when you remember the existence of all sorts of miscellaneous people. A cousin of mine, Alice Chesterton, daughter of my Uncle Arthur, writes me a delightfully cordial letter from Berlin, where she is a governess; and better still, my mother has received a most amusing letter from an old nurse of mine, an exceptionally nice and intelligent nurse, who writes on hearing that it is my twenty-first birthday . . . Yes, it is not bad, being twenty-one, in a world so full of kind people . . .[5]

The Chesterton who wrote this letter was not only at peace with the world around him, he was in love with it. Indeed, his love affair with life is celebrated in the same letter:

I have just been out and got soaking and dripping wet; one of my favourite dissipations. I never enjoy weather so much as when it is driving, drenching, rattling, washing rain. As Mr Meredith says in the book you gave me, 'Rain, O the glad refresher of the grain, and welcome water-spouts of blessed rain.' . . . Seldom have I enjoyed a walk so much. My sister water was all there and most affectionate. Everything I passed was lovely, a little boy pickabacking another little boy home, two little girls taking shelter with a gigantic umbrella, the gutters boiling like rivers and the hedges glittering with rain. And when I came to our corner the shower was over, and there was a great watery sunset right over No. 80, what Mr Ruskin calls an 'opening into eternity'. Eternity is pink and gold . . . Yes, I like rain. It means something, I am not sure what; something freshening, cleaning, washing out, taking in hand, not caring-a-damn-what-you-think, doing-its-duty, robust, noisy, moral, wet. It is the Baptism of the Church of the Future.[6]

Gilbert captured this spirit in a short story published in the second volume of the *Quarto*, the Slade School magazine. It was entitled 'A Crazy Tale' and tells the story of a boy considered mad by his neighbours because he is astonished by the common things of life they take for granted. Standing in a field the boy perceives that 'every inch of the green place was a living thing . . . Treading fearfully amid the growing fingers of the earth, I raised my eyes, and the next moment shut, as at a blow. High in the empty air blazed and streamed a great fire, which burnt and blinded me every time I raised my eyes to it.'[7] In this story the spectre of scepticism is finally exorcised and an earlier innocence regained. Chesterton the Child is saying thank you for the restoration of sight after a period of blindness: 'I am the first that ever saw a dandelion as it is . . . I tell you religion is in its infancy . . . some day a creature [will] be produced . . . with an intellect capable of performing a new function never before conceived truly; thanking God for his creation.'[8]

The poetry Chesterton wrote at this time also reflected his new-found gratitude. Yet it was tempered by a lingering mistrust of the Church and, in particular, a prejudiced view of the priesthood. Thus 'Easter Sunday', written in 1895, seems to imply that the Resurrection of Christ would be an insurrection against the Church:

> The wheels that rack, the lips that rave
> Stern is God's guard about the grave.
>
> Peace – for the priests in gold array –
> Peace – for today is Easter Day.
>
> The bannered pomp: the pontiffs wise
> (Great God – methinks he might arise)
>
> Might break for once from death's eclipse
> To smite these liars on the lips.[9]

Similarly, 'The Song of the Children', written a couple of years later, contains barbed references to the priesthood:

> Had he stayed here for ever,
> Their world would be wise as ours –
> And the king be cutting capers,
> And the priest be picking flowers.
>
> But the dark day came: they gathered:
> On their faces we could see
> They had taken and slain our brother,
> And hanged him on a tree.[10]

In the face of Chesterton's anti-clericalism there still remained his love for the Blessed Virgin. 'An Old Riddle', written about the time of his twenty-first birthday, is a meditation on the mysteries of the Annunciation:

> But a maid's choice is as God's choice
> And who shall challenge it.[11]

'A Christmas Carol', an unfinished poem written a year or so later, continues in the same vein:

> At Bethlehem, that city blest
> Did Our Lady take her rest
> Mary, fair and undefiled
> There conceived and bore a Child
> > Mater sanctissima
> > Ora pro nobis

> And Saint Joseph, when he saw
> Christ asleep upon the straw,
> In great love he worshipped there
> Mary and the Child she bare
> > Ave plena gratia
> > Ave Rosa Mundi[12]

Chesterton left the Slade School of Art at the end of the summer term, 1895, without a degree. In the opinion of his friend E. C. Bentley he had learned nothing while he was there. None the less, his failure had at least convinced him that his vocation was not art but writing, a view given added weight by the publication of 'Easter Sunday' in the *Clarion* on 20 April 1895. 'Now that I have tried other kinds of hurry and bustle, I solemnly pledge myself to the opinion that there is no work so tiring as writing, that is, not for fun, but for publication.'[13] In a letter to Bentley he discussed the rigours of his new way of life:

Other work has a reputation, a machinery, a reflex action about it somewhere, but to be on the stretch inventing things, making them out of nothing, making them as good as you can for a matter of four hours leaves me more inclined to lie down and read Dickens than I ever feel after nine hours' ramp at Redway's [a small publishing house specialising in the ocult].The worst of it is that you always think the thing so bad, too, when you're in that state. I can't imagine anything more idiotic than what I've just finished.[14]

One suspects the real key to the tiring nature of Chesterton's writing was not the four hours of creation itself but the 'nine hours' ramp at Redway's' which preceded it. He was forced to do all his writing in the evenings because of his first full-time job as a reader at Redway's. He was horrified by some of the manuscripts he read while he worked there, rejecting lurid offerings and returning them to addresses which he imagined 'must be private asylums'.[15] He spent only a few months at Redway's before gaining employment at the larger and more prosperous publishing house of T. Fisher Unwin. He remained at Fisher Unwin until 1901, when his growing reputation as a writer finally offered him the prospect of a full-time living. In the intervening six years he would be forced to constrain his literary creativeness to the evenings after work. As well as burning the midnight oil to build his own literary career, Chesterton was probably responsible for launching Somerset Maugham's career. Maugham's first novel, *Liza of Lambeth*, was published by Fisher Unwin in 1897 and it is likely that Chesterton was the reader who recommended it.

By 1896 he had settled into this solid and solitary routine of a hard day's reading followed by a hard night's writing. However, not all the writing was intended for publication, and the notebook he kept at the time included jottings intended for his eyes only. Among these were a couple of short poems giving voice to his innermost feelings:

Suddenly in the Midst

Suddenly in the midst of friends,
Of brothers known to me more and more,
And their secrets, histories, tastes, hero-worships,
Schemes, love-affairs, known to me
    Suddenly I felt lonely.
Felt like a child in a field with no more games to play
Because I have not a lady
    to whom to send my thought at that hour
    that she might crown my peace.

Madonna Mia

About Her whom I have not yet met
I wonder what she is doing
Now, at this sunset hour,
Working perhaps, or playing, worrying or laughing,
Is she making tea, or singing a song, or writing,
    or praying, or reading?
Is she thoughtful, as I am thoughtful?
    Is she looking now out of the window
    As I am looking out of the window?[16]

It was this love-sick Chesterton, ripe, perhaps over-ripe, for romance, who spent a week at Margate in the summer of 1896, followed by a short trip to France. Considering his frame of mind, or heart, it is not surprising that he looked longingly at the young female friends who accompanied the Chestertons to France. He wrote to Bentley from the Hotel St Pierre at Ault: 'Judging by the first day at Ault, I shall be getting horribly fond of those Cowton girls here before the fortnight is out ... As soon as we got near the place we found them in white dresses and red berets, dotting the town like scarlet poppies.'[17] When he wasn't pining after the English girls in their white dresses and red berets he was admiring the French girls 'with black pigtails in red ribbons'. Unfortunately for the frustrated Englishman the *mesdemoiselles* 'run after and take care of the little French boys in cropped hair and oblique eyebrows whether I had ever been born or no'.[18]

Gilbert would not play the lovelorn spectator for long. A few months later he would meet the woman he was destined to marry. The woman in question was Frances Blogg, daughter of a diamond merchant who had died when she was young. The family was of French descent, the name de Blogue being anglicised to Blogg. Although the Bloggs had been a family of considerable wealth, they had fallen into a degree of poverty that necessitated the three daughters earning a living. Lucian Oldershaw, Gilbert's friend from Junior Debating Club days, was courting, and was later to marry, Ethel Blogg, Frances's younger sister.

During the autumn of 1896 Chesterton accompanied Oldershaw to the Blogg family home in Bedford Park, where he met Frances for the first time. He fell in love at first sight: 'She wore a green velvet dress barred with grey fur, which I should have called artistic, but that she hated all the talk about art; and she had an attractive face, which I should have called elvish, but that she hated all the talk about elves.'[19] Alone in his room, late at night, Gilbert scribbled his devotion to Frances Blogg:

To My Lady
God made you very carefully,
He set a star apart for it,
He stained it green and gold with fields
And aureoled it with sunshine;

He peopled it with kings, peoples, republics,
And so made you, very carefully.
All nature is God's book, filled with his rough sketches
for you.[20]

In his notebook he began *An Encyclopaedia of Bloggs*. Blanche
(Mrs Blogg), Gertrude and their brother Knollys were nothing
but names written at the head of a virgin page. Ethel is described
as 'a quite demoralisingly kind girl. When Christ was made
everybody's brother, Miss Ethel Blogg was made everybody's sister.'
Frances was

> a harmony in green and brown. There is some gold somewhere in
> it, but cannot be located on examination. Probably the golden crown.
> Harp not yet arrived. Physically there is not quite enough of her to
> carry all that temperament: she looks slight, fiery and wasted, with
> a face which would be a Burne-Jones if it were not brave: it has the
> asceticism of cheerfulness, not the easier asceticism of melancholy.
> Devouring appetite for sensations; very fond of the Bible; very fond
> of dancing. When she is enjoying herself thoroughly, one has a sense
> that it would be well for her to go to sleep for a hundred years. It
> would be jolly fun for some prince too.[21]

Gilbert's love for Frances was reciprocated. His wish had come
true. He was to be her prince. A letter to a friend, Mildred Wain,
indicates that he was a regular visitor *chez* Blogg:

> In your last letter you enquired whether I saw anything of the Bloggs
> now. If you went and put that question to them there would be a
> scene. Mrs Blogg would probably fall among the fire-irons, Knollys
> would foam in convulsions on the carpet, Ethel would scream and
> take refuge on the mantelpiece and Gertrude faint and break off her
> engagement. Frances would – but no intelligent person can affect an
> interest in what she does.[22]

Although this letter was written light-heartedly Chesterton was very
concerned to gain the approval of Frances's family and, particularly,
that of her mother. With this in mind he made regular gifts to Mrs
Blogg, including a copy of Matthew Arnold's *Culture and Anarchy*, with
the inscription 'Mrs Blogg – Charity covereth a multitude of virtues.
G. K. C. June 10th, 1897'. Another gift to her, Arnold's *St Paul and
Protestantism*, contains the added lines:

Nor without honour my days ran
Nor yet without a boast shall end
For I was Shakespeare's countryman,
And were you not my friend?[23]

The reason for Gilbert's desire to ingratiate himself with Mrs Blogg is patently obvious. He hoped to marry her daughter. Gilbert joined the ranks of the betrothed in the summer of 1898, proposing to Frances on a small bridge in the middle of St James's Park. That evening he wrote his new fiancée a long letter:

> You will, I am sure, forgive one so recently appointed to the post of Emperor of Creation, for having had a great deal to do tonight before he had time to do the only thing worth doing . . .
>
> Little as you may suppose it at the first glance, I have discovered that my existence until today has been, in truth, passed in the most intense gloom . . . Intrinsically speaking it has been very jolly. But I never knew what being happy meant before tonight. Happiness is not at all smug: it is not peaceful or contented, as I have always been till today. Happiness brings not peace but a sword: it shakes you like a rattling dice; it breaks your speech and darkens your sight. Happiness is stronger than oneself and sets its palpable foot upon one's neck.
>
> . . . I think it is no exaggeration to say that I never saw you in my life without thinking that I under-rated you the time before. But today was something more than usual: you went up seven heavens at a run.
>
> . . . I am overwhelmed with an enormous sense of my own worthlessness – which is very nice and makes me dance and sing – neither with great technical charm. I shall of course see you tomorrow. Should you then be inclined to spurn me, pray do so. I can't think why you don't, but I suppose you know your own business best . . .
>
> God bless you, my dear girl.[24]

Any comment on such a letter would be superfluous. Suffice it to say that it was fortunate Frances 'went up seven heavens at a run' because Gilbert was now residing in the seventh heaven, from where he wrote to her again:

> Dear Love,
> Mr Swinburne, in a devout moment, calls his Maker a 'mystery many-faced.' I suppose we each see one face only. For me, when

the clouds break and float from the face of the throne and the last and best is made clear, I shall see, high above all the angels that face of yours as it was, lit up by the sunset . . .

At least I can imagine nothing better . . . There is, I am convinced, a kind of outward bodily beauty which one must be good in order to have . . . I know that there was a Cleopatra of Egypt, who, in your temporary but unavoidable absence, attracted the male sex to a large extent. But these people do not possess beauty in your sense, I am sure: what they had was animal regularity. There is one kind of beauty which begins inside and works out: first it makes spring in the heart and then the whole blossoms like a tree, on every twig and spray. The soul is like a flame and it makes the whole body transparent. Any actress with a pot of rouge and a stick of grease-paint could make herself like Helen of Troy. But no one *could* look like you, without having a benediction in her heart . . .[25]

Both he and Frances had certainly experienced a benediction of the heart, and the spiritual purity of their relationship is manifest in Gilbert's letter. Yet there was scarcely parity between the spiritual purity and the material possessions Gilbert had to offer. In 1898 he was a struggling writer working as a publisher's reader to make ends meet. He was not, in the financial sense, much of a catch. None the less, Gilbert treated his financial circumstances lightly, making a joke of his penury. He wrote to her, explaining that he had been 'endeavouring to reckon up the estate I have to offer you'. The letter comprised a list of his possessions, including a straw hat, a walking stick, a copy of Walt Whitman's poems, a pocket knife, a box of matches, a tennis racket and 'about three pounds in gold and silver'. The twelfth, and final, item on the list was 'A Heart – mislaid somewhere. And that is about all the property of which an inventory can be made at present. After all, my tastes are stoically simple. What more does man require? . . .'[26]

Perhaps the first real test of the strength of their relationship came when a personal tragedy struck the Blogg family. In the first week of July 1899 Gertrude was knocked off her bicycle by an omnibus and fatally injured. She died a few days later. Frances was inconsolable. For several months Gilbert did his best to comfort her:

I do not know what Gertrude's death was – I know that it was beautiful, for I saw it. We do not feel that it is so beautiful now – why? Because we do not *see* it now. What we see now is her absence:

but her Death is not her absence, but her Presence somewhere else. That is what we *knew* was beautiful, as long as we could see it. Do not be frightened, dearest, by the slow inevitable laws of human nature, we shall climb back into the mountain of vision . . .[27]

When Frances recovered from the depression brought on by her sister's death, she pinned a prayer into one of Gilbert's notebooks: 'If in aught I can minister to her peace, be pleased of thy Love to let this be . . .'[28]

Gilbert and Frances were married at Kensington Parish Church on 28 June 1901 by the Reverend Conrad Noel. Their honeymoon was spent on the Norfolk Broads. A poem entitled 'Creation Day', dated July 1901, was written either during or immediately after the honeymoon:

> Between the perfect marriage day
> > And that fierce future proud, and furled,
> I only stole six days – six days
> > Enough for God to make the world.
>
> For us is a creation made
> > New moon by night, new sun by day,
> That ancient elm that holds the heavens
> > Sprang to its stature yesterday –
>
> Dearest and first of all things free,
> > Alone as bride and queen and friend,
> Brute facts may come and bitter truths,
> > But here all doubts shall have an end.
>
> Never again with cloudy talk
> > Shall life be tricked or faith undone,
> The world is many and is mad,
> > But we are sane and we are one.[29]

'We are sane and we are one . . .' This was an accurate reflection of Chesterton's view of marriage, yet if he and Frances were one, he had a lot to take on board. Most notably, he had to take on board the fact that Frances was a practising Anglo-Catholic. Indeed, her religious observance was one of the things he had found attractive about her when they first met:

... she actually practised a religion. This was something utterly unaccountable both to me and to the whole fussy culture in which we lived. Any number of people proclaimed religions, chiefly oriental religions, analysed or argued about them; but that anybody could regard religion as a practical thing like gardening was something quite new to me and, to her neighbours, new and incomprehensible. She had been, by an accident, brought up in the school of an Anglo-Catholic convent; and, to all that agnostic or mystic world, practising a religion was much more puzzling than professing it.'[30]

One result of his relationship with a practising Christian was an increasing sympathy for institutional religion. Following his meeting with Frances there were no more anti-ecclesiastical poems and no more attacks on the priesthood. From this embryonic acceptance his faith grew stronger. By 1911, ten years after their marriage, he could dedicate *The Ballad of the White Horse* to Frances in gratitude for the faith she'd given him:

> Therefore I bring these rhymes to you,
> Who brought the cross to me.[31]

Thus far the relationship between Frances and Gilbert has been recounted in the words of the husband. Frances remains a silent partner, and one is almost tempted to say, in classic Victorian tradition, that she was seen and not heard. Yet if this was so, it was because she wanted it that way. She was always an intensely private individual and was virtually written out of her husband's *Autobiography* at her own request. 'The truth is,' she told an American reporter years later, during one of Gilbert's lecture tours, 'that I care more for my dog, donkey and garden in the little English village where we live than for all the publicity in the world.' She continued: 'Thank Heaven my husband is thoroughly normal and unaffected; he doesn't care for popularity any more than I do, and we are just terribly homesick for our home in England.' Then, in a witticism more reminiscent of her husband, she added: 'While my husband is going on a lecture tour, I am organising a campaign for the emancipation of the wives of famous men.'[32]

This rare display of wit is an indication of the intellect she possessed. Her few extant literary endeavours also serve as illustrations of her hidden talents. Frances had written poetry all her life, collecting her own compositions in a notebook dating back to 1893, three years before she met Gilbert. Her first published poem appeared in the *Westminster Gazette* in 1909 and her well-known carol, 'How Far is It to Bethlehem?', written in 1917, won a prize in 1922 and is today included in the *Oxford Book of Carols*.

The essential point is that Frances remained in the background because she *chose* to. She wasn't forced to through inability or lack of confidence. And Gilbert, better than anyone, understood his wife's abilities and the hidden intricacies of her personality. This should be borne in mind when allegations are levelled at him that he didn't understand women. This particular misconception is best laid to rest by a woman who was closer to Chesterton than anyone other than Frances herself. The woman in question was Dorothy Collins, who started as his secretary and became, effectively, his adopted daughter:

> He had a mystical regard for women. I have even seen him rise from his chair when a young girl came into the room. He always remembered what he had seen and those with whom he had talked, not so much by their faces as by their minds – for that is how he saw people.
>
> His wife Frances, who was a very great friend of mine, gave him the security he needed. She was a profound character with depths of understanding and sympathy, and he was entirely dependent on her for his happiness.[33]

Chesterton's 'mystical regard for women' is the root of the misunderstanding about his attitude to the female half of the species. To him the female was quite simply the fairer sex. One could almost envisage his believing that God created man only as an excuse to create woman. As he maintained in an article entitled 'The Heroines of Shakespeare', the Elizabethans believed that 'man was natural, but woman was supernatural'. Shakespeare epitomised this view:

> Shakespeare had conceived, with extraordinary force, humour and sympathy, a man to express the ideal of technical justice, formal morality, and the claim of a man to his rights: the man was Shylock. Over against him he set a figure representing the larger conception of generosity and persuasion, the justice that is fused of a score of genial passions, the compromise that is born of a hundred worthy enthusiasms. Portia had to represent the ideal of magnanimity in

law, morality, religion, art and politics. And Shakespeare made this figure a good woman because, to the mind of his day, to make it a good woman was to ring it with a halo and arm it with a sword.[34]

For Chesterton this idea of sublime femininity had become incarnate in Frances. He told a friend, Freda Riviere, that he particularly liked an unusually placed window at their home: 'I like that window. When the light catches her hair, it gives Frances a halo and makes her look something like what she really is.'[35]

Neither would Chesterton deny that he was totally dependent on his wife. Indeed, he admitted as much in his *Autobiography*. Referring to the familiar image he sported at the height of his fame, he wrote that the reader

> must not be misled at this stage by that Falstaffian figure in a brigand's hat and cloak, which has appeared in many caricatures. That figure was a later work of art; though the artist was not merely the caricaturist; but a lady artist touched on as lightly as possible in this very Victorian narrative. That caricature merely commemorates what the female genius could do with the most unpromising materials.[36]

These lines were written only months before his death but the affirmation that he was shaped by his wife, in externals at least, goes back much further. In 1907, nearly thirty years earlier, he made the same observation in an interview with a journalist from the *Daily News*. Before Chesterton arrived, the interviewer talked with Frances:

> 'The best thing your husband ever wrote,' so I began, 'was that "if a thing is worth doing at all –"'
>
> 'It is worth doing badly,' replied Mrs Chesterton. 'I know it well, because I have opened debates on the point and got everyone to agree. Look at children playing with paints,' she continued, 'and you will realise the truth of the paradox. Music and dancing and singing have all been banished from our lives because we are all afraid to do things badly.'
>
> ... 'I do not apologise,' said Mr Chesterton, as, with a gesture of importance, he drew aside a curtain and stood suddenly revealed in the lamplight – 'I do not apologise for my personal appearance because, in my opinion, which may, of course, be quite ridiculous, a married man's personal appearance is simply the artistic creation of his wife's fancy. She makes him look precisely what she wants.'

At this point, somewhat perturbed by the sweeping generalisation of her husband's remark, Frances protested hastily that this was true only 'within limits'.

> 'My dear,' proceeded Mr Chesterton, undeterred, 'you unfortunately have had to mould a mass of mud; other wives have the advantage of carving marble. The mud remains mud and the marble remains marble, but, mud or marble, the wife is the artist. You are the deity who says to these preposterous locks of hair, "Thus far shalt thou grow and no further."[37]

When the flippancy of the language is stripped aside, the profundity of the statement is striking. He is saying that, within the sacramental union of marriage, woman creates man in her image. Whether one agrees with him or not, his view is scarcely chauvinistic. Even if he is misguided, he is not a misogynist. On the contrary, his error lies, if anything, in idolising and idealising women.

One wonders, however, if it is possible to idealise one's spouse too much. Speaking of her husband, Frances once told Father Ignatius Rice, 'I am in a perpetual state of wonder at him.'[38] Speaking of his wife, Gilbert wrote candidly that he had fallen in love with her at first sight. She had looked straight at him during the course of a conversation and he said to himself: 'If I had anything to do with this girl I should go on my knees to her: if I spoke with her she would never deceive me: if I depended on her she would never deny me: if I loved her she would never play with me: if I trusted her she would never go back on me: if I remembered her she would never forget me.'[39]

Whether it be called intellect, intuition or anything else, his first impressions were completely correct. Yet love at first sight was not enough for Chesterton unless it could be coupled with love at last sight: love at first sight till death us do part. Thus, even in the early days of his courtship with the young woman he loved, he had a vision of an old woman he loved. It would be a further forty years before she even existed but he loved her already:

> A wan new garment of young green,
> > Touched, as you turned your soft brown hair;
> And in me surged the strangest prayer
> > Ever in lover's heart hath been.

That I who saw your youth's bright page,
    A rainbow change from robe to robe,
    Might see you on this earthly globe,
Crowned with the silver crown of age.

Your dear hair powdered in strange guise,
    Your dear face touched with colours pale,
    And gazing through the mask and veil
The mirth of your immortal eyes.[40]

Clearly Gilbert idolised this one particular woman, but it is equally clear that he idolised women in general. Thus, in true paradoxical fashion, he opposed the suffragette movement because he believed that women would debase themselves if they became 'equal' to men. It is an unfashionable opinion in the last decade of the twentieth century but fashions change. It is possible that the fashion, and not Chesterton, is wrong.

There is an old maxim that behind every great man there is a great woman. One can imagine Chesterton saying, for maximum comic and controversial effect, that behind every great man there is a greater woman. Certainly he was fascinated by the wives of great men, and he longed to hear the view of William Cobbett's wife who, he wrote, 'remains in the background of his life in a sort of powerful silence'.[41] Chesterton was too modest to imagine himself a great man but he understood the importance of marriage in the lives of men, great or otherwise. He would have seen a parallel between Mrs Chesterton and Mrs Cobbett.

Above all, there can be no true understanding of the man who was G. K. Chesterton without understanding that he was only one half of a quadruped. The other half walked with him in everything he did. Gilbert and Frances were in a mystical but very real sense One. She exerted on him an influence which was unseen but far greater than that exerted by anyone else in his life. She was the powerful silence in which he found peace.

« 4 »

The Chesterbelloc

> Wells has written . . . about Chesterton and Belloc without stopping
> to consider what Chesterton and Belloc is. This sounds like bad
> grammar; but I know what I am about. Chesterton and Belloc is
> a conspiracy, and a most dangerous one at that. Not a viciously
> intended one: quite the contrary. It is a game of make-believe of
> the sort which all imaginative grown-up children love to play . . .
>   Now at first sight it would seem that it does not lie with me to rebuke
> this sort of make-believe. The celebrated G. B. S. is about as real as a
> pantomime ostrich. But it is less alluring than the Chesterton-Belloc
> chimera, because as they have four legs to move the thing with,
> whereas I have only two, they can produce the quadrupedal illusion,
> which is the popular feature of your pantomime beast.[1]

THESE LINES, PUBLISHED IN the *New Age* in 1908, are part of Bernard
Shaw's reply to an article by H. G. Wells. The subject of both articles
was the relationship between Chesterton and Hilaire Belloc. Shaw's
reply was entitled 'The Chesterbelloc: A Lampoon', and its purpose
was to suggest that Chesterton and Belloc were seen so synonymously
that they formed 'a very amusing pantomime elephant'.

Not everyone was amused by Shaw's lampoon. Maurice Baring
wrote to Chesterton from Moscow: 'I hated GBS's article on you
and Hilaire. I thought it rude, beastly and untrue.'[2] None the
less, Shaw's satire struck home and the Chesterbelloc was born.
Henceforth many would see Belloc and Chesterton merely as
mouthpieces of the Chesterbelloc, a monster larger than both
of them.

There are conflicting reports of how the two friends first met. It
seems clear, however, that they were introduced by either Bentley
or Oldershaw. The former had first met Belloc in January 1895

when he had come up to Balliol College, Oxford, to try to win the Brackenbury history scholarship for the glory of St Paul's. Bentley had found himself sitting opposite Belloc, 'who fell upon each paper and tore it limb from limb with ... startling rapidity'.[3] He was not surprised when Belloc won the scholarship.

In June 1895 Belloc won first-class honours in history but failed to gain a fellowship at All Souls College. (He always believed he was passed over because of his Catholic faith.) Yet he stayed on at Oxford for several years, writing and tutoring, and during this time he developed a lasting friendship with both Bentley and Oldershaw. Eventually, in 1906, Bentley signed Belloc's citizenship papers so that he could run for Parliament, a formality made necessary by the latter's Anglo-French ancestry.

Belloc was born in the village of La Celle St Cloud, near Paris, in 1870. He was the son of a French barrister, Louis Belloc, and his English wife. His father died when he was two years old and the family moved to England, where he was educated under Cardinal Newman at the Oratory School, Birmingham. He returned to France to do his military service and then went up to Balliol. He travelled widely across the United States, marrying Elodie Hogan, an Irish-American, in California in 1896. In November the same year *The Bad Child's Book of Beasts* was published, a collection of nonsense verse for children written by Belloc and illustrated by Basil Blackwood. The first edition was sold out within four days. Other books followed and at the time of the first meeting with Chesterton he was already an established writer. Gilbert, on the other hand, had had only the odd article or poem published and was yet to see his first book in print.

The scene was thus set for the fated first meeting, the importance of which can be gauged by Oldershaw's view of the event: 'I lost Gilbert first when I introduced him to Belloc, next when he married Frances, and finally when he joined the Catholic Church ... I rejoiced, though perhaps with a maternal sadness, at all these fulfilments.'[4]

An element of mystery surrounds the first meeting. Although it is probable that Lucian Oldershaw made the first formal introduction, it is likely that Belloc and Chesterton were aware of each other prior to this. Indeed, Belloc's first reported words upon being introduced were, 'Chesterton, you write very well.'[5] Chesterton, on the other hand, wrote a letter to Frances, in April 1900, in which he glows with admiration for Belloc:

... a moment after there was a movement and we were conscious of a young man rising and saying three words quietly: yet we felt somehow it was a cavalry charge.

> The furious Frenchman comes with his clarions and his drums
> His tactics of Sadowa and his maxims of Jean-Paul,
> He is bursting on our flanks,
> Grasp your pikes and close your ranks
> For Belloc never comes but to conquer or to fall.

You hate political speeches: therefore you would not have hated Belloc's. The moment he began to speak one felt lifted out of the stuffy fumes of forty-times repeated arguments into really thoughtful and noble and original reflections on history and character. When I tell you that he talked about 1. the English aristocracy; 2. the effects of agricultural depression on their morality; 3. his dog; 4. the Battle of Sadowa; 5. the Puritan Revolution in England; 6. the luxury of the Roman Antonines; 7. a particular friend of his who had by an infamous job received a political post he was utterly unfit for; 8. the comic papers of Australia; 9. the mortal sins in the Roman Catholic Church – you may have some conception of the amount of his space that was left for the motion before the house. It lasted for half-an-hour and I thought it was five minutes.[6]

Many authorities believe Oldershaw's introduction was several months later than the date of this letter. If this is so, Gilbert was clearly already enamoured with, and in awe of, Hilaire Belloc at the time of their first meeting. However, the undertones of familiarity evident in the letter suggest that the introduction may have been earlier, perhaps very early in 1900. Chesterton's most famous account of the meeting is in his *Autobiography*. He had arranged to meet Oldershaw in a little French restaurant in Soho, the Mont Blanc in Gerrard Street, one of the 'delightful little dens off Leicester Square, where in those days a man could get a half-bottle of perfectly good red wine for sixpence'.[7] Oldershaw entered,

followed by a sturdy man with a stiff straw hat of the period tilted over his eyes, which emphasised the peculiar length and strength of his chin. He had a high-shouldered way of wearing a coat so that it looked like a heavy overcoat, and instantly reminded me of the pictures of Napoleon; and, for some vague reason, especially of the pictures of Napoleon on horseback. But his eyes, not without anxiety, had that curious distant keenness that is seen in the eyes of sailors; and there was something about his walk that has even been compared to a sailor's roll . . . He sat down heavily on one of the benches and began to talk at once about some controversy or other . . .

As Belloc went on talking, he every now and then volleyed out very provocative parentheses on the subject of religion . . . All this amused me very much, but I was already conscious of a curious undercurrent of sympathy with him, which many of those who were equally amused did not feel. And when, on that night and many subsequent nights, we came to talk about the war, I found that the subconscious sympathy had something of a real significance . . . It was from that dingy little Soho café, as from a cave of witchcraft, that there emerged the quadruped, the twiformed monster Mr Shaw has nicknamed the Chesterbelloc.[8]

A lesser-known account is given by Chesterton in an introduction he wrote to a book entitled *Hilaire Belloc: The Man and His Work*:

When I first met Belloc he remarked to the friend who introduced us that he was in low spirits. His low spirits were and are much more uproarious and enlivening than anybody else's high spirits. He talked into the night, and left behind in it a glowing track of good things . . .

. . . What he brought into our dream was his Roman appetite for reality and for reason in action, and when he came to the door there entered with him the smell of danger.[9]

Reason in action and the smell of danger. In these words Chesterton has unwittingly unlocked one of the secrets of the Chesterbelloc. Whatever else attracted him to Belloc, the real attraction for Gilbert was the fact that his new friend was a man of action. As he admired Frances not only for professing a faith but for practising it, so he admired Belloc not only for believing in romantic adventures but for living them out. Chesterton dreamed of the adventure, Belloc was the adventurer. Chesterton imagined the excitement of the high seas, Belloc was an accomplished sailor. Chesterton imagined the bravery of battle, Belloc had been a soldier in the French army. Chesterton imagined the exhilaration of exploring wild frontiers, Belloc had walked and hiked across the United States from the east to the west coast, discovering the 'Wild West' in the 1890s. Last but not least, Chesterton was grappling with religious truths in the abstract while Belloc lived religious truth ritually. Quite literally, Belloc gave body to the ideas in Chesterton's head. He gave them substance.

The influence Belloc exerted on Chesterton would appear to be considerable, yet Gilbert was not merely a passive disciple. The two halves of the Chesterbelloc have much in common but they also differ in crucial respects. In order to understand the relationship between them it is necessary to dissect Shaw's creation and to reveal that many aspects of Shaw's 'pantomime elephant' are not as he would have us believe.

It is symbolically apt that the first encounter with Belloc occurred in the opening months of a new century. The year 1900 marked the beginning of Chesterton's published work and consequently the beginning of his public life. Belloc, the author of a biography of Danton the previous year, had a selection of satirical essays entitled *Lambkin's Remains* published in 1900. Chesterton's first two books, *Greybeards At Play* and *The Wild Knight and Other Poems*, both published in this year, were collections of his poetry.

Gilbert was never very pleased with *Greybeards At Play*. None of the light nonsense verse from the book was included in his *Collected Poems* and he fails to acknowledge its publication in his *Autobiography*. Instead he referred to *The Wild Knight* as his 'introduction to literature'.

A copy of *The Wild Knight* was sent to Rudyard Kipling by Brimley Johnson. The link between these two was Gertrude Blogg who, prior to her death, had been Johnson's fiancée and Kipling's secretary. Seen in this light, Kipling's reply is of particular interest:

> Many thanks for *The Wild Knight*. Of course I knew some of the poems before, notably 'The Donkey' which stuck in the mind at the time I read it.
>
> I agree with you that there is any amount of promise in the work – and I think marriage will teach him a good deal too. It will be curious to see how he'll develop in a few years. We all begin with arranging and elaborating all the Heavens and Hells and stars and tragedies we can lay our poetic hands on – Later we see folk – just common people under the heavens – Meantime I wish him all the happiness that there can be and for yourself such comfort as men say time brings after loss. It's apt to be a weary while coming but one goes the right way to get it if one interests oneself in the happiness of other folk. Even though the sight of this happiness is like a knife turning in a wound.

PS. Merely as a matter of loathsome detail, Chesterton has a bad attack of 'aureoles'. They are spotted all over the book. I think everyone is bound in each book to employ unconsciously some pet word but that was Rossetti's.

Likewise I notice 'wan waste' and many 'wans' and things that 'catch and cling'. He is too good not to be jolted out of that. What do you say to a severe course of Walt Whitman – or will marriage make him see people?[10]

As 1900 drew to a close, Gilbert gave Frances a copy of the new book as a Christmas present, writing a poem on the flyleaf. On Christmas Eve he accompanied Hilaire and Elodie Belloc to midnight mass. It was almost certainly his first attendance at a Catholic mass and his presence proves the closeness of his friendship with Belloc, which would continue to flourish, as would the relationship between their respective wives. A letter Elodie wrote to Frances from the Hotel de la Chaine d'Or, Les Andelys, offers an insight into this relationship:

My sister has come to me from the Equator and I have brought her to France. I was a broken reed and Dr Penny said I must go away, so I left Courthill under the regime of Hilairius Primus and came here a fortnight ago. We stayed a joyous week in Paris and we have been here a week. I have still a few days of paradise left me. We saw the Review at Longchamps on July 14 – Eleanor's birthday. How I wish that you and Gilbert had seen it . . .

When are we, my beloved friend, to have a week together in Paris? In the Name of God let us have it before we are much older or the grand crash comes. I can see the Frogs dilating with joy as we four or five would go by them. Let us complete these plans for some day before we die. It has been a miracle to me, to see Paris and the French as I have seen them during this fortnight.[11]

And in the spring of 1904, when Chesterton dedicated his first novel to her husband, Elodie wrote to Gilbert in gratitude:

I am lost in my efforts to choose which thing I must most thank you for – the book, the inscription or the glorious dedication! My loyalty to you and my memories . . . drive me towards the book; my egotism and my violence and my security in the soundness of my views in all things drive me towards the inscription in which

you have so sweetly and so kindly included me; my passionate love
of Liberty and my mild Irish belief in the final victory of all the good
over the miserable muddy muggy streams of evil that drip under
our unhappy noses (here and in Holy France) and the love for my
beloved Man and the joy that I always have when he is recognised
drive me to the dedication. I beg you and Frances to come and tell
me which is the thing of all these three that should make me most
happy.[12]

One is struck by the forthright, almost brash, personality which
comes across in Elodie's correspondence. She appears as extroverted
and opinionated as her husband and, at first sight, she certainly seems
to have little in common with the quiet and emotionally restrained
Frances.

By the beginning of 1901 Chesterton's writing began to attract
widespread attention. As well as the two collections of verse he
was gaining a reputation as a journalist. He contributed regular
articles to the *Speaker* and the *Daily News*. The extent of his growing
fame can be gauged from a comment in a letter to Frances, dated
8 February 1901:

Another rather funny thing is the way in which my name is being
spread about. Belloc declares that every one says to him 'Who
discovered Chesterton?' and that he always replies, 'The genius
Oldershaw.' . . .
Belloc, by the way, has revealed another side of his extraordinary
mind. He seems to have taken our marriage much to heart, for he
talks to me, no longer about French Jacobins and Mediaeval Saints,
but entirely about the cheapest flats and furniture, on which, as on
the others, he is a mine of information, assuring me paternally that
'it's the carpet that does you.' I should think this fatherly tone would
amuse you.[13]

Following their marriage, Gilbert and Frances moved into a
house in Edwardes Square, Kensington. As this was lent to
them on a temporary basis by one of Frances's friends, they
soon moved to Overstrand Mansions in Battersea. Commenting
in his 'fatherly tone' on their new home, Belloc penned a poem
which the Chestertons pinned to the wall of their dining-room.
It began:

Frances and Gilbert have a little flat
At eighty pounds a year and cheap at that . . .[14]

The move to Battersea made the Chestertons and Bellocs virtually
neighbours. Hilaire and Elodie had moved to 104 Cheyne Walk
on the Chelsea Embankment during the previous year. The house
stood a few yards beyond Battersea Bridge, on the opposite side of
the Thames from Battersea. A sketch map drawn by Chesterton,
probably in 1902, shows the site of both homes depicted by crude
figures marked 'GKC' and 'Belloc'. About half way between the
two Chesterton has marked the site of a public house with the
words 'beer excellent' beneath.[15] It is a safe assumption that this
particular hostelry had been selected as a mutually convenient
meeting place.

In the years that followed there developed a *joie de vivre* in their
relationship which became almost legendary, so much so that
H. G. Wells, many years later, complained of the air of Catholic
conviviality which surrounded them. 'Chesterton and Belloc,' he
said, 'have surrounded Catholicism with a kind of boozy halo.'[16]
Another example of this joy of life is given by Edward Marsh, who
remembers a visit to the theatre to see Pelissier's Follies. Marsh was
seated between Chesterton and Belloc as Pelissier, a great mountain
of a man, was pushed across the stage in a pram to the song of 'Baby
Mine'. Elsewhere during the performance Pelissier's ad libs and gags
reduced his supporting band of Follies to such helpless laughter that
no one could go on. Chesterton and Belloc laughed so much

> that when the curtain came down they couldn't stop and went on
> all through the *entr'acte*, so that the people in front stood up and
> turned round to see what the matter was while I sat shrinking and
> shrivelling like Alice between the Red Queen and the White, or a
> mouse new-born of two mountains, both in a state of eruption, and
> feeling, as the saying is, my position acutely.[17]

For a few weeks, late in the summer of 1903, Hilaire and Elodie
rented a house at Slindon, a picturesque village in Sussex. Frances
and Gilbert came to visit and an interesting reminiscence is given
by Eleanor Jebb, the Bellocs' second eldest child: 'Gilbert and H. B.
seemed to talk the whole time. We children could not understand one
word of the torrent. H. B. was lying on the lawn with head pillowed

on his arm. Talk, talk, talk! We heard it through the bushes, where we were up to mischief as usual.'[18] Two years after this visit the Bellocs left London for good and returned to Slindon, where they leased Courthill Farm, standing on the northern slope of the hill behind the village. A year later they moved to King's Land in the village of Shipley, seven miles south of Horsham. It was far from the main road and had an acre of walled garden. The house had once been a shop, and its oldest parts dated from the fourteenth century. The newest part had been added in 1890, but its eleven gables were so similar in aspect that it was not easy to discern the old from the new. It was held together by dark oak beams. This was to be home to Hilaire and Elodie for the rest of their lives.

Soon after moving to King's Land, Belloc wrote the following letter to Chesterton:

It will annoy you a good deal to hear that I am in town tomorrow Wednesday evening and that I shall appear at your Apartment at 10.45 or 10.30 at earliest. P.M.! You are only just returned. You are hardly settled down. It is an intolerable nuisance. You heartily wish I had not mentioned it.

Well, you see that [arrow pointing to 'Telegrams, Coolham, Sussex'], if you wire there before One you can put me off, but if you do I shall melt your keys, both the exterior one which forms the body or form of the matter and the interior one which is the mystical content thereof.

Also if you put me off I shall not have you down here ever to see the Oak Room, the Tapestry Room, the Green Room, etc.[19]

A superficial perusal of this letter may give the impression of brusqueness but it is, of course, a light-hearted, good-humoured letter from one friend to another. The apparent brusqueness is only banter between confidants who have long since forsaken the formalities of less intimate relationships. In any case, one may assume that Chesterton extended his hospitality at such short notice, or that Belloc relented on his threats, because Frances and Gilbert were soon regular guests in Sussex. One such visit to King's Land is recounted by Chesterton in his *Autobiography*:

Among the memories that are blown back to me, as by a wind over the Downs, is that of the winter day when Belloc dragged us through

Sussex to find the source of the Arun. The company included his wife and mine; none of us had been long married, and perhaps we knew less than we do now of the diversity of human temperaments, not to say temperatures. He and I were fond of cold weather; my wife and his wife, who was a very charming Californian, were not. We did find the place where the Arun rose in the hills; and it was indeed, of all the sights I have seen, one of the most beautiful . . . For it rose in a (partly frozen) pool in a small grove of slender trees, silver with the frost, that looked somehow like the pale and delicate pillars of a temple. But I think the ladies, though both of them sensitive to scenery, looked on that cold paradise with something of a cold eye. When this began to be discovered, Belloc instantly proposed the remedy of hot rum, in large tumblers at an adjoining inn; and we were puzzled by the fact that the remedy was regarded with almost as much distaste as the disease . . .

We then returned to Belloc's house; where he rather neutralised the effects of the restoring warmth, by continually flinging open the door and rushing out to a telescope in the garden (it was already a frosty starlight) and loudly hallooing to the ladies to come and see God making energy. His wife declined, in terms of not a little humour . . .

Needless to say, however, his hospitality terminated with a magnificent feast of wine, and all ended in a glow of gaiety; but there lingers a sort of legend of that day in winter, when some of us were so much more interested in the barometer than the telescope.[20]

Chesterton recounts 'another rather ridiculous private incident' in his *Autobiography* which 'involved the meeting of Belloc and a very famous and distinguished author'.[21] The author in question was Henry James and the meeting occurred during 1908 in Rye, where Frances and Gilbert had rented a house for a short holiday. James lived next door and when he heard of their arrival he paid a visit, accompanied by his brother William. Henry and William James were both in their mid-sixties and both enjoyed international reputations, the former for novels such as *The Bostonians*, *The Wings of a Dove* and *The Ambassadors* and the latter for his pioneering work in psychology and pragmatic philosophy. Chesterton described Henry James as 'a very stately and courteous old gentleman' in a 'formal frock-coat', and he likened the visit to 'a very stately call of state'. It was in this air of puritanical decorum that the meeting was conducted. The two authors discussed the plays of Shaw and then 'proceeded to consider gravely the work of Hugh Walpole, with many delicate degrees of appreciation and doubt'. All of a sudden the decorum was shattered by a noise resembling that of 'an impatient fog-horn'. It was Belloc bellowing for beer and bacon. His arrival was something of a surprise because Chesterton believed his friend to be in France. Indeed, he had been in France, 'walking with a friend of his in the Foreign Office, a co-religionist of one of the old Catholic families'. However, 'by some miscalculation they had found themselves in the middle of their travels entirely without money':

> Their clothes collapsed and they managed to get into some workmen's slops. They had no razors and could not afford a shave. They must have saved their last penny to re-cross the sea ... They arrived, roaring for food and drink and derisively accusing each other of having secretly washed, in violation of an implied contract between tramps. In this fashion they burst in upon the balanced tea-cup and tentative sentence of Mr Henry James.
>
> Henry James had a name for being subtle; but I think that situation was too subtle for him. I doubt to this day whether he, of all men, did not miss the irony of the best comedy in which he ever played a part. He left America because he loved Europe, and all that was meant by England or France; the gentry, the gallantry, the tradition of lineage and locality, the life that had been lived beneath old portraits in oak-panelled rooms. And there, on the other side of the tea-table, was Europe, was the old thing that made France and England, the posterity of the English squires and the French soldiers; ragged, unshaven, shouting for beer, shameless above all shades of poverty and wealth; sprawling, indifferent, secure. And what looked across at it was still the Puritan refinement of Boston; and the space it looked across was wider than the Atlantic.[22]

Although Chesterton tells the tale humorously it is hardly surprising that James, a very Victorian old gentleman, was not amused. In fact, the whole episode displays an obvious and stark difference between Belloc and Chesterton which far outweighs any difference between Belloc and James. Belloc's bellowing arrival contrasts with Chesterton's efforts, 'a little nervously', to entertain his guests. Chesterton is the gentleman and perfect host, Belloc the noisy gatecrasher.

How typical is this isolated incident as an indication of the difference between the two friends?

Chesterton loved Belloc as a kindred spirit but also as a man of action and bravado. To Chesterton his friend's adventurism and carefree attitude made him something of a lovable rogue. Yet Belloc's carefree approach to life often made him careless in his relationships with others. He lacked decorum and tact, a fact which made him many enemies.

F. J. Sheed, the publisher and writer, compared this flaw in Belloc's character with Chesterton's more charitable approach:

> Each had his own way of being himself, which means that they had their different ways of forcing men to listen. I shall tell a story of each, well known to men of my generation, not perhaps to our juniors.
>
> 1. Belloc was kneeling at Mass in Westminster Cathedral. A sacristan whispered to him, 'Excuse me, sir, we stand here.'
> *Belloc*: 'Go to hell.'
> *Sacristan*: 'I'm sorry, sir, I didn't know you were a Catholic.'
> 2. Chesterton was a vast man physically – over twenty stone, say three hundred pounds. During the war a patriotic lady accused him of cowardice.
> *Patriotic lady*: 'Why aren't you out at the Front?'
> *Chesterton*: 'Madame, if you will go round to the side, you'll see that I am.'
> The stories are typical – Belloc rude to the polite stranger, Chesterton polite to the rude stranger . . .[23]

Sheed sums up the difference succinctly: 'Belloc went about as if he owned the earth, Chesterton as if he didn't care who owned it.'[24]

Neither is Sheed's observation unique. Frank Swinnerton, a contemporary of both Chesterton and Belloc, made this comparison: 'One reason for the love of Chesterton was that while he fought he sang lays of chivalry and in spite of all his seriousness warred against wickedness rather than a fleshly opponent, while Belloc sang only after the battle and warred against men as well as ideas.'[25] And Christopher Hollis wrote that Chesterton's first achievement was to turn the joke against the sceptic:

> Just as General Booth refused to let the devil have all the best tunes, so Chesterton refused to let him have all the best jokes, and claimed that those who had the faith should also be allowed to have the fun . . . Belloc made jokes which were as excellent as those of Chesterton.

But Belloc's jokes were all too often bitter and satiric. Their aim was to make the object of them ridiculous. He struck to wound. There was, as Chesterton himself said of him to Douglas Woodruff, a sundering quality in his controversies. Chesterton's jokes were warm jokes – the jokes of a kindly man.[26]

A similar conclusion was reached many years earlier by H. G. Wells. In an article published at the beginning of 1908 Wells described his wish to be 'a painted Pagan God' living upon a ceiling:

> The company about me on the clouds varies greatly with the mood of the vision, but always it is in some, if not always a very obvious way, beautiful. One frequent presence is G. K. Chesterton, a joyous whirl of brushwork, appropriately garmented and crowned. When he is there, I remark, the whole ceiling is by a sort of radiation convivial. We drink limitless old October from handsome flagons, and we argue mightily about Pride (his weak point) and the nature of Deity . . . Chesterton often – but never by any chance Belloc. Belloc I admire beyond measure, but there is a sort of partisan viciousness about Belloc that bars him from my celestial dreams. He never figures, no, not even in the remotest corner, on my ceiling.[27]

One suspects that Belloc wouldn't be seen dead on Wells's celestial ceiling even if invited. His response, a perfect example of the 'partisan viciousness' of which Wells speaks, could be expressed in his poem 'The Sailor's Carol'. It ends with the following sentiments of seasonal cheer:

> May all good fellows that here agree
> Drink Audit Ale in heaven with me,
> And may all my enemies go to hell!
> Noel! Noel! Noel! Noel!
> May all my enemies go to hell!
> Noel! Noel![28]

It would seem that Wells doesn't figure in the remotest corner of Belloc's celestial ceiling either.

Although it would be wrong to ignore the joke in such poems, and clearly Belloc intends them to raise a smile, they do reveal an acerbity in his character. Indeed, Belloc accepted acerbity almost as a virtue and criticised its absence in Chesterton's writing:

You do not rise from the reading of one of Chesterton's appreciations with that feeling of being armed which you obtain from the great satirists and particularly from the masters of irony.

He wounded none, but thus also he failed to provide weapons wherewith one may wound and kill folly. Now without wounding and killing, there is no battle; and thus, in this life, no victory; but also no peril to the soul through hatred.

Of the personal advantage to himself of so great and all-pervading a charity, too much cannot be said; but I believe it to be a drag upon his chances of endurance upon paper – for what that may be worth – and it is worth nothing compared with eternal things.[29]

There is an absence of logic in one key aspect of Belloc's analysis. It does not follow that one must wound people in order to provide weapons to wound and kill folly. It was a central tenet of Chesterton's outlook that one could kill folly without killing a person or his personal reputation. Chesterton, like Belloc, saw himself as being fearlessly at war with the fallacies of the age. He once said that 'you can't be moderate with a battle axe'. Yet his battle axe smashed ideas, never people. It cracked skulduggery, never skulls. It wasn't moderate but neither did it murder.

Another episode in the life of the Chesterbelloc throws even more light on the nature of the beast. One night in London, Chesterton, Belloc and J. B. Morton, a friend who would later become Belloc's biographer, were sharing a taxi. Chesterton signalled for the driver to go in the direction of his home.

'Where are you going?' asked Belloc.

'Home,' Chesterton replied.

'Right,' said Belloc, 'I will drop you. But first I have one or two places to call at.'

He mentioned the places, and one of them was in Hampstead. Chesterton said it would be simpler for him to get another cab and go home.

'No, no,' said Belloc, 'I will drop you.'

Chesterton laughed and told Morton that this was Belloc's idea of 'strategy'.

The strategy worked and Chesterton was dragged round London before being allowed to return home.[30]

Once again, a superficial reading of the event will render a wrong interpretation. Belloc appears to be a bully determined to get his own way. However, as with his letter demanding to stay the night, he adopted the attitude of brusqueness in the secure knowledge of the depth of their relationship. He knew that Chesterton would not be offended. On the contrary, he knew his friend would be amused at the absurdity of a journey which bore a remarkable resemblance to 'the night we went to Birmingham by way of Beachy Head'.

Morton, the third passenger in the cab, understood the situation when he commented that 'the rich absurdity of the arrangement' appealed to Chesterton's sense of humour.[31] None the less, some commentators have taken this and other incidents at face value. In consequence, they have drawn rash, and wrong, conclusions. Sheed, for instance, forgetting the profound insight of his earlier observation that 'Belloc went about as if he owned the earth, Chesterton as if he didn't care who owned it', went on to make the following assertion: 'Belloc had so much to do with the making of Chesterton, and Chesterton not much with the making of Belloc.'[32] The earlier statement gets to the root of their relationship, the latter is a shallow travesty of it. Unfortunately, many writers have slavishly accepted the latter view.

One writer who would not have accepted this view is Hilaire Belloc himself. He considered Chesterton 'a thinker so profound and so direct that he had no equal'.[33] And there are many other instances of Belloc's humility in the face of his friend's abilities. Father O'Connor recalled walking in Leeds with Belloc and listening to him reciting French verse. By way of a riposte Father O'Connor recited the following:

> Sleeps Hector on Scamander side
> And Harold by the Sussex sea,
> And Egypt's awful eyes undried
> Above the bones of Antony.

Belloc grasped his arm excitedly: 'Whose is that? Who wrote that?'

'Why, who could, except Gilbert?' replied the priest.

'Ah! the Master!' said Belloc.[34]

On another occasion he remarked that Chesterton's poem 'Lepanto' was the 'summit of high rhetorical verse in all our generation'. He was strangely moved when he heard that Chesterton admired one of his poems and once exclaimed that 'Chesterton expresses everything so much better than I do.'[35] Having bowed to Chesterton as a thinker beyond equal, and a poetic master, Belloc bows to his style as a writer: 'No one whatsoever that I can recall in

the whole course of English letters had his amazing – I would almost
say superhuman – capacity for parallelism.'[36]

Belloc was, of course, no mere sycophant given to an endless
torrent of panegyrics. On the contrary, he could be Chesterton's
sternest critic. For example, when Lady Juliet Duff took him to see
Magic, Chesterton's first play, he thought it got worse as it went on
and that many of the speeches had nothing to do with the stage
at all.[37] However, his high regard for Chesterton's literary talent
and his admiration of his power as a thinker suggest that he was
influenced by his friend far more than Sheed suggests.

Perhaps the most amusing tribute Belloc paid to Chesterton was
the following untitled ballade:

> I like to read myself to sleep in Bed,
> A thing that every honest man has done
> At one time or another, it is said,
> But not as something in the usual run;
> Now I from ten years old to forty-one
> Have never missed a night: and what I need
> To buck me up is Gilbert Chesterton,
> (The only man I regularly read).
>
> The Illustrated London News is wed
> To letterpress as stodgy as a bun,
> The Daily News might just as well be dead,
> The Idler has a tawdry kind of fun,
> The Speaker is a sort of Sally Lunn,
> The World is like a small unpleasant weed;
> I take them all because of Chesterton,
> (The only man I regularly read).
>
> The memories of the Duke of Beachy Head,
> The memoirs of Lord Hildebrand (his son)
> Are things I could have written on my head,
> So are the memories of the Comte de Mun,
> And as for novels written by the ton,
> I'd burn the bloody lot! I know the Breed!
> And get me back to be with Chesterton
> (The only man I regularly read).
>
> *Envoi*
> Prince, have you read a book called 'Thoughts upon

The Ethos of the Athanasian Creed'?
No matter – it is not by Chesterton
(The only man I regularly read).[38]

There was also one very practical way in which Belloc owed a debt of gratitude to Chesterton. Over the years Chesterton illustrated many of Belloc's novels which, since Chesterton was the more popular writer, helped to enhance and rekindle his failing literary reputation. Belloc claimed that Chesterton's illustrating of his initial rough ideas gave them form.

Once a proper sense of proportion has been returned to the relative importance of each half of the Chesterbelloc, perhaps the next question begging an answer is whether the influence they exerted on each other was benignant. Certainly Shaw thought not:

> But a pantomime animal with two men in it is a mistake when the two are not very carefully paired ... Chesterton and Belloc are so unlike that they get frightfully into one another's way. Their vocation as philosophers requires the most complete detachment: their business as the legs of the Chesterbelloc demands the most complete synchronism.[39]

A similar view is expressed by C. S. Lewis, who considered that Belloc was 'always, on the intellectual side, a disastrous influence on Chesterton'.[40]

The fact is that Belloc and Chesterton exerted on each other an influence that affected their intellectual outlooks. Chesterton gave Belloc a sharpness of philosophical insight he would otherwise not have possessed; Belloc gave Chesterton a broad perspective of European history which enabled him to see England within a wider context. Belloc possessed a deeper understanding of economics and Chesterton accepted Belloc's distributist ideas. He wrote of distributism that Belloc was 'the founder and father of this mission; we were the converts but you were the missionary'.[41] Whether this intellectual influence was disastrous, as C. S. Lewis maintains, depends on one's own subjective views on philosophy, or history, or economics.

None the less, to get to the real heart of the Chesterbelloc requires delving below the intellectual level. At the heart of both men was their Christian faith. It was the pearl of great price which neither would sacrifice for anything the world had to offer. Yet Belloc's grip on the pearl was not as strong as Chesterton's. 'By my nature,' he once confided to a friend, 'I am all sceptical and sensual – so much so as hardly to understand how others believe unseen things.'[42] Temperamentally tempted by doubt, Belloc held on to his faith by a constant act of the will. As Christopher Hollis pointed out: 'He was quite open to the sceptical fear that nothing was true at all.'[43]

By contrast, Chesterton's faith grew ever stronger the longer Belloc knew him. If Gilbert, in the early days of their friendship, had admired Belloc for being the adventurer when he had only dreamed of the adventure, Belloc came to see Chesterton as the fortitude of faith in a world of falsehood. When Belloc found it difficult to believe the unseen things, Chesterton was the thing he could see. In times of darkness, Chesterton was a beacon. Seen in this light, Belloc's relationship to Chesterton appears totally afresh. Far from Belloc having much to do with the making of Chesterton, Chesterton had much to do with the sustaining of Belloc.

One is drawn to a parallel between the Chesterbelloc and the Chesterblogg. Frances was Gilbert's powerful silence; Chesterton, in turn, was a powerful silence in which Belloc found peace. Meanwhile, Chesterton, listening to Belloc's bombastic tirades, found peace but seldom quiet.

« 5 »

Enter G. K. C.

On 22 January 1901 Queen Victoria died at Osborne House. She had been on the throne for more than sixty years and during her reign Britain's economic, military and political power had triumphed worldwide. Her death marked the end of an era. It was also to mark the beginning of the end of Britain's unrivalled status. With the passing of the Queen the sun began to set on the British Empire. Whether or not Chesterton detected these ominous portents he was, like the vast majority of his fellow countrymen, deeply moved by her death. Somers Cocks, a friend of Belloc, reported that Gilbert cried when he heard the news, and a letter to Frances poignantly conveys his last respects:

> Today the Queen was buried. I did not see the procession . . . I like a crowd when I am triumphant or excited: for a crowd is the only thing that can *cheer*, as much as a cock is the only thing that can crow . . . But I think that reverence is better expressed by one man than a million. There is something unnatural and impossible, even grotesque, in the idea of a vast crowd of human beings all assuming an air of delicacy. All the same, my dear, this is a great and serious hour and it is felt so completely by all England that I cannot deny the enduring wish I have, quite apart from certain more private sentiments, that the noblest Englishwoman I have ever known was here with me to renew, as I do, private vows of a very real character to do my best for this country of mine which I love with a love passing the love of Jingoes. It is sometimes easy to give one's country blood and easier to give her money. Sometimes the hardest thing of all is to give her truth.[1]

Chesterton carried a deep respect for Queen Victoria throughout his whole life. Evidence of this occurred more than thirty years later when Thomas Derrick contributed a cartoon to *G. K.'s Weekly* on the subject of a proposed *entente* between Britain and Nazi Germany. The cartoon depicted a bashful John Bull offering a bouquet of flowers to a smiling Gretchen dressed in a frock dotted with swastikas. Above them Queen Victoria, floating on a cloud, gave her blessing. At either side of her were two passages from her letters, each in the warmest praise of Germany, describing it as the home of peace and extolling the virtues of 'a strong Prussia'. Derrick was convinced that Chesterton would be amused at the irony of the whole thing but he refused to print it. It was the only drawing Derrick ever submitted that Chesterton rejected.[2]

If the beginning of 1901, and the death of the Queen, heralded the setting of the sun on the Empire it coincided with the rising of the sun over Chesterton's literary career. His first two published books of poetry had achieved an element of critical acclaim, the articles in the *Speaker* were attracting attention and he had become a regular columnist for the *Daily News*. This early period in his journalistic career was remembered by Frank Swinnerton: 'At the *Daily News* office, Gardiner, who loved him, told me he would sit with a book before him, reading a few words here and there, ruffling his thick locks, and scribbling away at speed. The result of the haphazard dipping so impressed readers that they set up a buzz of excitement about him.'[3] On 8 February Chesterton wrote to Frances about this newfound success at the *Daily News*:

> The *Daily News* have sent me a huge mass of books to review, which block up the front hall. A study of Swinburne – a book on Kipling – the last Richard Le Gallienne – all very interesting. See if I don't do some whacking article, all about the stars and the moon and the creation of Adam and that sort of thing. I really think I could work a revolution in daily-paper writing by the introduction of poetical prose.[4]

Chesterton's thoughts very quickly became reality because his peculiar brand of poetical prose mixed with journalism formed a volatile cocktail. Hammond, the editor of the *Speaker*, showed him letters 'from Cambridge dons and such people demanding the identity of G. K. C. in a quite violent tone. They excuse themselves by offensive phrases in which the word "brilliant" occur . . .'[5]

Chesterton's success at the *Speaker* can be gauged by the fact that a series of articles he wrote for the paper were, by popular demand, published together as a book. *The Defendant* received much more attention than either of the collections of poetry, and most of it was highly complimentary. The *Whitehall Review* described it as 'one of the most delightful companions possible for a man to have with him, and if it does not run through two or three editions rapidly then there is no virtue of honour left in these decadent days'.[6] Sir Arthur Quiller-Couch wrote in the *Bookman* of Chesterton's 'courageous innocence' and commented that 'the most ordinary occurrences in the world are marvellous in his eyes, and his optimism proceeds from a blessed contentment with a planet which provides so many daily miracles.'[7]

Appropriately enough, this 'blessed contentment' with the planet was exemplified in the essay 'A Defence of Planets' in which Chesterton praises the poetry of science:

> ... for some mysterious reason this habit of realising poetically the facts of science has ceased abruptly with scientific progress, and all the confounding portents preached by Galileo and Newton have fallen on deaf ears. They painted a picture of the universe compared with which the Apocalypse with its falling stars was a mere idyll. They declared that we are all careering through space, clinging to a cannon-ball, and the poets ignore the matter as if it were a remark about the weather. They say that an invisible force holds us in our armchairs while the earth hurtles like a boomerang; and men still go back to dusty records to prove the mercy of God.[8]

This ability in Chesterton to see everything poetically, however apparently mundane, was the secret of the book's success. A further example was 'A Defence of Skeletons':

> The importance of the human skeleton is very great, and the horror with which it is commonly regarded is somewhat mysterious ... One would think it would be most unwise in a man to be afraid of a skeleton, since Nature has set curious and quite insuperable obstacles to his running away from it.
>
> One ground exists for this terror: a strange idea has infected humanity that the skeleton is typical of death. A man might as well say that a factory chimney was typical of bankruptcy. The factory may be left naked after ruin, the skeleton may be left naked after bodily dissolution; but both of them have had a lively and workmanlike life of their own, all the pulleys creaking, all the wheels turning, in the

House of Livelihood as in the House of Life. There is no reason why this creature (new, as I fancy, to art), the living skeleton, should not become the essential symbol of life.[9]

Another key to the charm which captivated his readership was Chesterton's ability to put his finger on profound truth while keeping his tongue firmly in his cheek. For example, the serious aspects of his defence of skeletons didn't prevent the article's punchline: 'And, however much my face clouds with sombre vanity, or vulgar vengeance, or contemptible contempt, the bones of my skull beneath it are laughing for ever.'[10]

In the final analysis, *The Defendant* received favourable reviews rather than hostile criticism because its subject matter was safe and uncontroversial. Among the other things defended in the book were china shepherdesses, heraldry and detective stories, none of which was likely to elicit the ire of his public. The essays raised eyebrows, they raised laughs, but they raised few objections.

If Chesterton's writing at this time was relatively uncontroversial, the company he kept was not. First, of course, there was his blossoming friendship with Belloc, who was religiously and politically militant and who relished the thrill of intellectual combat. Another religious and political militant he became acquainted with during 1901 was the Rev. Conrad Noel, the Anglo-Catholic priest who presided at his wedding. Noel was something of an eccentric. The son of a poet and the grandson of a peer, he had, according to Chesterton, 'all the incalculable elements of the eccentric aristocrat'.[11] In Conrad Noel's case the eccentricity boiled over into controversy. He was a leading member of the Christian Social Union (CSU), an organisation which combined traditional theology with revolutionary politics. Theologically the CSU was Anglo-Catholic. Politically it was radical socialist. Many years later, Conrad Noel was to achieve notoriety by flying the red flag from his parish church at Thaxted in Essex.

As with Gilbert's first meeting with Belloc, confusion surrounds the details of how Chesterton and Noel first met. Chesterton 'cannot remember exactly' but he believes their first meeting was during a debate on Nietzsche at which one of the participants had praised the German philosopher for his opposition to 'false Christianity'. Chesterton was struck by the logic of a curate 'with dark curly hair and a striking face, who got up and pointed out that Nietzsche would be even more opposed to True Christianity than to False Christianity'.[12]

Conrad Noel's account of the first meeting is somewhat more precise:

> We met G. K. C. for the first time at the Stapleys in Bloomsbury
> Square, at a series of meetings of the Christo-Theosophic Society
> . . . We had been much impressed by the weekly contribution of
> an unknown writer to the *Speaker* and the *Nation* – brilliant work,
> and my wife and I, independently, came to the conclusion when
> we heard this young man speak that it must be he. The style was
> unmistakable.
>
> I thought of writing to him to congratulate him on his speech,
> but before I could do so, I got a letter from him, saying that he was
> coming to hear me in the same series in a week or so; it was thus we
> first became acquainted, and the acquaintance ripened into a warm
> friendship with us both. He and his brother Cecil were in and out of our
> flat in Paddington Green, where I was assistant curate. He was genial,
> bubbling over with jokes, at which he roared with laughter.[13]

The influence Noel exerted on Gilbert and his brother Cecil
can best be gauged by Chesterton's own words: 'When Noel first
appeared on the horizon of my brother and myself, my brother was
frankly anti-religious and I had no religion except the very haziest
religiosity.'[14] However, 'the Anglo-Catholic party in the Anglican
Church . . . really had a great deal to do with the beginning of
the process by which Bohemian journalists, like my brother and
myself, were drawn towards the serious consideration of the theory
of a Church. I was considerably influenced by Conrad Noel; and
my brother, I think, even more so.'[15]

Meanwhile, Chesterton's journalistic career continued apace. In
October 1902 his second book of essays, *Twelve Types*, was published.
Like *The Defendant*, this book was a collection of articles which had
originally appeared in the *Daily News* and the *Speaker*. Now, however,
he was growing in confidence and the subject matter reflected this.
Instead of writing about relative trivia he turned his attention to
twelve famous people. He was beginning to tread on dangerous
ground and objections as well as eyebrows were being raised. One
reviewer in the *Academy and Literature* was alarmed at his confident
dissecting of the various 'types' discussed in the book:

> For sheer cleverness there is probably no one at the present moment
> to compare with Mr Chesterton. His gift of brilliant improvisation is

amazing. But we must confess to being a little appalled by his new book: it is so confident, so assertive, its rhetoric is so breathless. The spectacle of a young man putting Savonarola and Scott, St Francis and Tolstoy each in his place with the assurance and familiarity that Mr Chesterton exerts strikes us as a little uncanny.[16]

The other eight 'types' included in the book were Charlotte Brontë, William Morris, Byron, Pope, Rostand, Charles II, Stevenson and Carlyle. Of Byron he deduced 'with the certainty of logic that he is very young and very happy'.[17] This, of course, flagrantly contradicted the established view that Byron was the arch-pessimist. Yet, Chesterton argued, anyone who voluntarily chose to walk alone in winter near the crashing waves of the sea was an optimist at heart. Similarly the beauty of Byron's poetic style betrays his deeper feelings. While the words are woeful the metre dances 'a bounding *pas de quatre*':

> Oh, there's not a joy the world can give like that it takes away
> When the glow of early youth declines in beauty's dull decay.[18]

Chesterton conceded that Byron may have considered himself a pessimist but he 'is one of a class who may be called the unconscious optimists, who are very often indeed, the most uncompromising conscious pessimists'.[19] It was the crux of Chesterton's argument that a man must be optimistic in order to see a sunset, even if the sunset causes sadness. A true pessimist wouldn't even notice the sunset. Since Chesterton seemed to be saying that he knew Byron better than Byron knew himself, however, it is no wonder that some critics were 'a little appalled' by his latest book.

None the less, *Twelve Types* was a success, serving to enhance his reputation still further. A classic example of the incisive insight which pervaded the short character studies in the book was his description of the Italian religious reformer Savonarola: 'Men like Savonarola are the witnesses to the tremendous psychological fact at the back of all our brains, but for which no name has ever been found, that ease is the worst enemy of happiness, and civilisation potentially the end of man.'[20]

Commenting on this view, a reviewer in the *New Age* said Chesterton saw Savonarola as much more than a great religious reformer. He was also a great social deliverer intent on saving his generation from the hedonistic coma of the Italian Renaissance which was 'drugging the spirits of men with the lotus-brew of a degenerate luxury'.[21]

Chesterton was clearly captivated by the character of Savonarola and at one stage considered writing a full-length biography. It was advertised once or twice as 'in the course of preparation' but, sadly, never materialised. One is also drawn irresistibly to the conclusion that Chesterton saw parallels between Savonarola, the religious and political revolutionary who shook fifteenth-century Florence, and Conrad Noel, a latter-day Savonarola who sought to shake twentieth-century London. The fact that the first meeting with Noel coincided with the writing of *Twelve Types* seems to reinforce such a conclusion.

At about this time, autumn 1902, Chesterton became embroiled in his first public religious controversy. It was conducted through the correspondence columns of the *Daily News* and was ostensibly concerned with Balfour's Education Bill, which was then before Parliament. In particular, Gilbert objected to the stand taken by Dr John Clifford, a Baptist minister of militant Protestant views who was at the forefront of the Nonconformist opposition to the Bill. Dr Clifford's main objection was that the Bill might further the cause of Catholicism. 'Popery in politics we will not have,' he declared; 'the capture of the machinery and resources of the whole State for sectarian ends we cannot endure.'

Chesterton entered the debate in the third week in September under the heading 'Dr Clifford and the "No Popery" Cry'. Although he was also against the Bill, on the grounds that 'it violates an elementary liberal principle in not equalising contribution and control', he objected to Dr Clifford's anti-Catholicism. 'Let us attack the Education Bill as Liberals,' he exhorted, 'without binding the living body of Liberalism to the slimy corpse of the Protestant Truth Society.'

Although, in September 1902, Chesterton denied being anything as doctrinaire as an Anglo-Catholic, let alone anything as unthinkable as a Roman Catholic, the correspondence illustrated a growing awareness of the issues at stake:

> The principle that the English Church Union is Popish, or the principle that it ought to be Protestant, are not only disputed, but are, *pace* Dr Clifford, highly disputable propositions. They are historical propositions about which we most of us know little or nothing. To decide whether the English Church is Catholic, as

Bishop Gore says, or Protestant, as Prebendary Webb-Peploe says, we ought to be familiar with Bulls and judgments, with Councils of the Fourth Century, with Statutes of the Sixteenth Century, with the controversies about the Sarum Rite and the Statute of Praemunire. Most of us, as a matter of fact, have not read even the introduction to the Prayer Book. It is one of the hardest things in human history to say exactly what happened in England at the Reformation.

Regardless of whether Chesterton professed any specific creed at this time, the hidden hands of Noel, the Anglo-Catholic, and Belloc, the Roman Catholic, are clearly detectable as influences.

Similarly, Chesterton understood enough of the difference between Catholicism and Protestantism to conclude that the Liberal 'compromise' of simple Bible teaching for all the state schools could not be expected to satisfy Catholics. He wrote in the *Daily News*:

> The Bible compromise is certainly in favour of the Protestant view of the Bible. The thing, properly stated, is as plain as the nose on your face. Protestant Christianity believes that there is a Divine record in a book; that everyone ought to have free access to that book; that everyone who gets hold of it can save his soul by it, whether he finds it in a library or picks it off a dustcart. Catholic Christianity believes that there is a Divine army or league upon earth called the Church; that all men should be induced to join it; that any man who joins it can save his soul by it without ever opening any of the old books of the Church at all. The Bible is only one of the institutions of Catholicism, like its rites or its priesthood; it thinks the Bible only efficient when taken as part of the Church . . . This being so, a child could see that if you have the Bible taught alone, anyhow, by anybody, you do definitely decide in favour of the first view of the Bible and against the second.[22]

In spite of these reservations about aspects of Liberal policy Chesterton was still an active supporter of the party. It would be several years before he grew sceptical about the effectiveness of parliamentary politics and during the election of 1902 he canvassed actively for the Liberal cause. Charles Masterman recounted how Chesterton canvassed a street with him. Both started at the same end on opposite sides of the road. Masterman completed his side and came back on the other to find Gilbert still earnestly arguing at the first house.[23] This singular, though scarcely effective, method of canvassing was something of a Chesterton speciality. During the previous election in 1900 he and Lucian Oldershaw had rushed down to Frome in Somerset to offer their support to the Liberal candidate. They were to produce a special edition of the *Beacon*, a magazine of strongly radical character, and to make themselves generally useful in the campaign. Chesterton wandered about the constituency, often unaccompanied, and wherever he could get an audience he would harangue it on the iniquities of the Government. In the evenings he visited a pub which was the unofficial headquarters of his Tory opponents and would engage all and sundry in debate. So popular did these evenings become that the Tory organisers complained bitterly that their canvassers forsook their job of house-to-house visiting to discuss politics in the pub with Chesterton. The special edition of the *Beacon*, filled with excellent propaganda but continually delayed by new suggestions and revisions, was published the day after the poll.[24]

As well as being courted by canvassers in public houses Gilbert was being canvassed by courtiers in public life. In May 1902, for instance, the celebrated writer and caricaturist, Max Beerbohm, wrote the following:

I have seldom wished to meet anyone in particular: but you I should very much like to meet.

I need not explain who I am, for the name at the end of this note is one which you have more than once admitted, rather sternly, into your writings.

By way of personal and private introduction, I may say that my mother was a friend of your grandmother, Mrs Grosjean, and also of your mother.

As I have said, I should like to meet you. On the other hand, it is quite possible that *you* have no reciprocal anxiety to meet *me*. In this case, nothing could be easier than for you to say that you are very busy, or unwell, or going out of town, and so are not able – much as you would have liked – to lunch with me here either next Wednesday or next Saturday at 1.30.

I am, whether you come or not, yours admiringly

MAX BEERBOHM

P.S. I am quite different from my writings (and so, I daresay, are you from yours). So that we should not necessarily fail to hit it off.

I, in the flesh, am modest, full of common sense, very genial, and rather dull.

What you are remains to be seen – or not to be seen by me, according to your decision.

Any answer to this note had better be directed to

48 Upper Berkeley Street, W.

for the porter of this club is very dilatory.[25]

It can be assumed that Chesterton answered in the affirmative because he and Beerbohm became good friends. In fact, as the tone of Beerbohm's letter demonstrates, Chesterton was becoming something of a sought-after celebrity. He was now rubbing shoulders with the rich and famous and counted among his acquaintances not only members of the literati but also leading political statesmen. In 1902 he was a guest at a social evening presided over by a Conservative Cabinet Minister, George Wyndham. Among the other guests was a young man, six months younger than Gilbert, who had been elected recently as the Conservative Member of Parliament for Oldham. The man was Winston Churchill. Chesterton's memory of the evening was recounted in his *Autobiography*:

> George Wyndham had all sorts of odd and original notions; and one of his eccentricities was to set a subject for conversation and ask for opinions all round, as if it were an examination or a game. One day I remember he sternly announced 'Japan,' and asked me to start with a few words. I said: 'I distrust Japan because it is imitating us at our worst. If it had imitated the Middle Ages or the French Revolution, I could understand; but it is imitating factories and materialism . . .'[26]

Churchill, on the other hand, said that what amused him was that 'as long as Japan was beautiful and polite, people treated it as barbarous; and now it has become ugly and vulgar, it was treated with respect . . .'[27]

Although Gilbert was now accorded celebrity status, he and Frances remained far from wealthy. Mrs Saxon Mills, one of their earliest neighbours and closest friends in Battersea, remembered the hardships vividly: 'We were very poor in those days. When we were short, they used to feed us. When they were short, we used to feed them.' Commenting on Mrs Saxon Mills's husband, Chesterton remarked that 'the difference between Saxon Mills and me is that he is frightfully unpractical and thinks he isn't. I am frightfully unpractical and know I am.'[28]

Another neighbour who became a great friend was Rann Kennedy. He had a large library and Chesterton would leave the flat after a visit with his pockets crammed with books. These would be returned later by Frances with a note apologising for 'my thief of a husband'.[29]

In the same year, 1902, Chesterton reviewed Belloc's latest book, *The Path to Rome*. It was, he wrote, 'the product of the actual and genuine buoyancy and thoughtlessness of a rich intellect'.[30] *The Path to Rome* proved a great success when it was published in April, eventually selling 112,000 copies. However, although Belloc and Chesterton both had grounds for optimism as their reputations grew apace, Chesterton's popularity was already outpacing Belloc's. A writer in the *Sunday School Chronicle* proclaimed that 'if there is a more popular journalist just now than Mr G. K. Chesterton, I should like to know him.' Another religious journal, the *Christian World*, noted that 'Mr Chesterton, to use his own words, has as his principal amusement "kicking up a row".'[31]

In 1903 he began 'kicking up a row' with Robert Blatchford, editor of the *Clarion*. Blatchford was a radical socialist who had published a determinist credo entitled *God and My Neighbour*. Confident of the strength of his own position, Blatchford had invited a free and open exchange of views on its central tenets in the pages of the *Clarion*. Chesterton responded instantly to the challenge:

> The first of all the difficulties that I have in controverting Mr Blatchford is simply this, that I shall be very largely going over his own ground. My favourite textbook of theology is *God and My Neighbour*, but I cannot repeat it in detail. If I give each of my reasons for being a Christian, a vast number of them would be Mr Blatchford's reasons for not being one . . .
>
> The Blatchfordian position really amounts to this – that because a certain thing has impressed millions of different people as likely or necessary, therefore it cannot be true . . .
>
> . . . the Secularist . . . tries to prove that there is no such thing as supernatural experience by pointing at the people who have given up everything for it. He tries to prove that there is no such thing by proving that there are people who live on nothing else.[32]

Thus the Chesterton attack continued. To the secularist charge that Christianity had produced tumult and cruelty, he replied that high ideals often led to abuses, citing the French Revolution as an example:

The mere flinging of the polished pebble of Republican Idealism into the artificial lake of eighteenth century Europe produced a splash that seemed to splash the heavens, and a storm that drowned ten thousand men. What would happen if a star from heaven really fell into the slimy and bloody pool of a hopeless and decaying humanity? Men swept a city with the guillotine, a continent with a sabre, because Liberty, Equality, and Fraternity were too precious to be lost. How if Christianity was yet more maddening because yet more precious?[33]

Chesterton's last riposte to the Blatchfordian position was on the subject of biblical tradition:

The Secularist constantly points out that the Hebrew and Christian religions began as local things; that their god was a tribal god; that they gave him material form, and attached him to particular places . . .

If there be such a being as God, and He can speak to a child, and if God spoke to a child in the garden, the child would, of course, say that God lived in the garden. I should not think it any less likely to be true for that. If the child said: 'God is everywhere; an impalpable essence pervading and supporting all constituents of the Cosmos alike' – if, I say, the infant addressed me in the above terms, I should think he was much more likely to have been with the governess than with God.

So if Moses had said God was an Infinite Energy, I should be certain he had seen nothing extraordinary. As he said He was a Burning Bush, I think it very likely that he did see something extraordinary. For whatever be the Divine Secret, and whether or no it has (as all people have believed) sometimes broken bounds and surged into our world, at least it lies on the side furthest away from pedants and their definitions, and nearest to the silver souls of quiet people, to the beauty of bushes, and the love of one's native place.

Thus, then, in our last instance (out of hundreds that might be taken), we conclude in the same way. When the learned sceptic says: 'The visions of the Old Testament were local, and rustic, and grotesque,' we shall answer: 'Of course. They were genuine.'[34]

With this article, and others written during the same debate, Chesterton made a dramatic debut as a Christian apologist. Henceforth religious controversy would form an integral part of his published output. Indeed, the debate with Blatchford marks a watershed in Chesterton's life, heralding the nailing of his Christian colours to the mast. Before the debate he had been perceived by many as, if not a secularist, then at least nothing more than a lukewarm fellow-traveller with the Anglican Church. This is illustrated by the fact that Blatchford, in the early days of their debate, asked Chesterton whether he was a Christian. Chesterton replied to this, and the three other questions Blatchford put to him, in his column in the *Daily News*. It amounted to a public profession of faith:

1. *Are you a Christian?* Certainly.
2. *What do you mean by the word Christianity?* A belief that a certain human being whom we call Christ stood to a certain superhuman being whom we call God in a certain unique transcendental relationship which we call sonship.
3. *What do you believe?* A considerable number of things. That Mr Blatchford is an honest man, for instance. And (but less firmly) that there is a place called Japan. If he means what do I believe in religious matters, I believe the above statement (answer 2) and a large number of other mystical dogmas, ranging from the mystical dogma that man is the image of God to the mystical dogma that all men are equal and that babies should not be strangled.
4. *Why do you believe it?* Because I perceive life to be logical and workable with these beliefs and illogical and unworkable without them.[35]

Throughout the course of the controversy Chesterton managed to retain his sense of humour. For example, one can imagine him chuckling aloud as he replied to Blatchford's claim that no English judge would accept the evidence for the Resurrection. Christians, he said, have not 'such an extravagant reverence for English judges as is felt by Mr Blatchford himself. The experiences of the Founder of Christianity have perhaps left us in a vague doubt of the infallibility of Courts of law.'[36]

In its closing stages the debate centred on the question of free will. Blatchford, a dogmatic determinist, denied the existence of abstract will, insisting that man was a slave to the forces of heredity and environment. Chesterton disagreed: 'There is an error of logic in your whole article, so obvious that it can be dealt with in a few lines. You indicate that I typify revenge and you forgiveness. Is it possible you do not see that forgiveness, like every other virtue, stands and falls with free will? A man who forgives is noble, but only because he could reproach if he liked.'[37]

One aspect of Blatchford's determinism was his belief that bad environment inevitably produced bad men. Chesterton, in an article entitled 'The Eternal Heroism of the Slums', deplored 'this association of vice with poverty, the vilest and the oldest and the dirtiest of all the stories that insolence has ever flung against the poor'.[38] In the same article he continued his defence of free will:

> More numerous than can be counted, in all the wars and persecutions of the world, men have looked out of their little grated windows and said, 'At least my thoughts are free.' 'No, no,' says the face of Mr Blatchford, suddenly appearing at the window, 'your thoughts are the inevitable result of heredity and environment. Your thoughts are as material as your dungeons. Your thoughts are as mechanical as the guillotine.' So pants this strange comforter, from cell to cell.
>
> I suppose Mr Blatchford would say that in his Utopia nobody would be in prison. What do I care whether I am in prison or no, if I have to drag chains everywhere. A man in his Utopia may have, for all I know, free food, free meadows, his own estate, his own palace. What does it matter? He may not have his own soul.[39]

Chesterton developed this theme in a private letter to Blatchford:

> selfishness is *not* a disease, an abnormal accident . . . Selfishness is a permanent and natural danger which arises from the existence of a self . . . While you are turning over the musty folios of early Victorian materialism, newer things are happening: a fresh and fierce philosophy of oligarchy and the wise few is spreading from Germany all over the world. We have a logical answer to that philosophy. You have none. We have a basic defence of democracy. You have none. Our answer is 'There are no wise few; for in all men rages the folly of the Fall. Take your strongest, happiest, handsomest, best born, best bred, best instructed men on earth and give them special power for half an hour and because they are men they will begin to [perform] badly . . .'[40]

It is important to note that these words were written early in 1904, ten years before the outbreak of the First World War and thirty years before the emergence of the Third Reich. Even as a young man in his twenties Chesterton knew enough of human nature to be wary of the politics of pride. He foresaw the dangers of dictatorship before the emergence of the dictators and perceived that the philosophical denial of free will could evolve into the political denial of freedom. On the other hand, people like Blatchford, blinded by the naïvety of their Utopian dreams, stared wide-eyed into a future mythical Golden Age.

The religious controversy with Robert Blatchford dragged on for much of 1903, and not everyone was amused by the affair. Even some of Chesterton's admirers found the debate tedious. A correspondent to the *Daily News* in January 1904 wrote the following 'lines written on reading Mr G. K. Chesterton's forty-seventh reply to a secularist opponent':

> What ails our wondrous G. K. C.
> > Who late, on youth's glad wings,
> Flew fairylike, and gossip'd free
> > Of translunary things?

> That thus, in dull didactic mood,
> > He quits the realm of dream,
> And like some pulpit-preacher rude,
> > Drones on one dreary theme?

> Stern Blatchford, *thou* hast dashed the glee
> > Of our Omniscient Babe;
> Thy name alone now murmurs he,
> > Or that of dark McCabe.

> All vain his cloudy fancies swell,
> > His paradox all vain,
> Obsessed by that malignant spell
> > Of Blatchford on the brain.[41]

One can't help but sympathise with the writer of this poem. Chesterton had put aside the flippant and disarmingly innocent trivia of his early essays. Instead he sought and courted controversy. The Omniscient Babe was awake and his great desire was to wake his fellow men. Not surprisingly, those who were happier asleep, or if not happier at least more comfortable, resented his interference. For Chesterton, however, there was no turning back. Exactly a month before the plaintive poem was sent to the *Daily News* he had pre-empted it in an article in the same paper:

> You cannot evade the issue of God: whether you talk about pigs or the binomial theory, you are still talking about Him . . . If Christianity

should happen to be true – that is to say, if its God is the real God of the universe – then defending it may mean talking about anything and everything. Things can be irrelevant to the proposition that Christianity is false, but nothing can be irrelevant to the proposition that Christianity is true. Zulus, gardening, butchers' shops, lunatic asylums, housemaids and the French Revolution – all these things not only may have something to do with the Christian God, but must have something to do with Him if He lives and reigns.[42]

At the end of 1901 the figure of G. K. C. had taken Fleet Street by storm, defending penny dreadfuls, nonsense, farce, skeletons and detective stories. Two years later he was defending God. The new approach was not welcomed by those who believed that religion should be seen and not heard, but by others he was regarded as a champion of common sense in an increasingly mad world. To the cynical wit, seated on the sidelines, Chesterton's earlier defence of nonsense and farce had reached its logical conclusion in his defence of God. Whatever one's opinion, Chesterton, by the end of 1903, had become a household name.

« 6 »

Robert Browning and Father Brown

In 1903, in the midst of the long religious controversy with Robert Blatchford, Chesterton was asked to write a biography of Robert Browning. It was the most prestigious assignment of his literary career thus far. Chesterton remembered it as 'a crown of what I can only call respectability'.[1] The crown had been presented to him by the publishers Macmillan, who had asked him to write the study of Browning as part of the 'English Men of Letters' series. He was in illustrious company because others who had contributed to the series included Anthony Trollope, who had written the book on Thackeray, and Viscount Morley, who had written the study of Edmund Burke. These, and others who had written for the same series such as Henry James and Thomas Huxley, were the doyens of the literary establishment. Chesterton, on the other hand, was a novice of only twenty-eight when he was approached to write the study of Browning and as yet he had not written a single full-length book, his previous published works being either collections of essays or verse. It is no wonder that he described it as 'a very flattering invitation'.[2]

He set to work researching the book in the British Museum Reading Room and in due course the completed manuscript was presented to the publishers. They were not impressed. Stephen Gwynn, a junior editor at Macmillan who had promoted the idea of Chesterton writing the Browning biography, had to face the consequences:

Old Mr Craik, the Senior Partner, sent for me and I found him in white fury, with Chesterton's proofs corrected in pencil; or rather not corrected; there were still thirteen errors uncorrected on one page; mostly in quotations from Browning. A selection from a Scottish ballad had been quoted from memory and three of the four lines were wrong. I wrote to Chesterton saying that the firm thought the book was going to 'disgrace' them. His reply was like the trumpeting of a crushed elephant. But the book was a huge success.[3]

A huge success? It was certainly a popular success, becoming a bestseller, but it received a mixed reception from the critics. He was vilified by some and vindicated by others. Writing in his diary twenty-one years later, a young C. S. Lewis, who was only five when the book was first published, joined the ranks of those who lambasted him: 'I walked into town and went to the library in College. I looked into G. K. Chesterton's *Browning* – a thoroughly bad book, full of silly generalisations.'[4] This is a scathing criticism, especially as it comes from an intellect as sharp as Lewis's and even more so considering that Lewis, on the whole, was a great admirer of Chesterton's work. None the less the force of the criticism is tempered by the fact that Lewis was himself only an undergraduate of twenty-five when he made the comments, and it would be rash to insist that they are the views of the mature thinker of later years.

Perhaps the most interesting judge of the Browning biography, if not the most objective, is Chesterton himself. In his *Autobiography* he made the following confession:

> I will not say that I wrote a book on Browning; but I wrote a book on love, liberty, poetry, my own views on God and religion (highly undeveloped), and various theories of my own about optimism and pessimism and the hope of the world; a book in which the name of Browning was introduced from time to time, I might almost say with considerable art, or at any rate with some decent appearance of regularity. There were very few biographical facts in the book, and those were nearly all wrong. But there is something buried somewhere in the book; though I think it is rather my own boyhood than Browning's biography.[5]

Elsewhere he makes an apology for the lack of chronological detail in his own *Autobiography*: 'I have written several books that were supposed to be . . . lives of really great and remarkable men, meanly refusing them the most elementary details of chronology; and it would be a more than mortal meanness that I should now have the arrogance to be accurate about my own life, when I have failed to be thus accurate about theirs. Who am I that I should be dated more carefully than

Dickens or Chaucer? What blasphemy if I reserved for myself what I had failed to render to St Thomas and St Francis of Assisi. It seems to be a clear case, in which common Christian humility commands me to continue in a course of crime.'[6]

Although these views are coloured by conscious self-abasement, the fact remains that he pleads guilty to the charge of inaccuracy. There is only one line of defence. It is scrawled in one of Gilbert's notebooks, probably dating around 1910: 'Not Facts first Truth first.'[7] According to Chesterton's criteria a book should be judged by the truth it imparts more than by the facts it contains. If this is so, one must ask whether his *Browning* enlightens one about the person of Browning and the poetry of Browning. If it does it is a success; if it doesn't, it isn't. Either way, the portrait of Browning is unmistakably painted by the brush of Chesterton. Thus, for instance, he discusses at some length whether it was morally permissible to publish the most private correspondence between Browning and Elizabeth Barrett. He concludes that 'our wisdom, whether expressed in private or public, belongs to the world, but our folly belongs to those we love'.[8] In a similar vein he comments on Wordsworth's reaction to the news that Browning and Barrett had eloped to Italy:

> Wordsworth when he heard afterwards of their eventual elopement said with that slight touch of bitterness he always used in speaking of Browning, 'So Robert Browning and Miss Barrett have gone off together. I hope they understand each other – nobody else would.' It would be difficult to pay a higher compliment to a marriage.[9]

Immediately prior to the elopement Elizabeth Barrett did something which Chesterton believed truly heroic:

> The sullen system of medical seclusion to which she had long been subjected has already been described. The most urgent and hygienic changes were opposed by many on the ground that it was not safe for her to leave her sofa and her sombre room. On the day on which it was necessary for her finally to accept or reject Browning's proposal, she called her sister to her, and to the amazement and mystification of that lady asked for a carriage. In this she drove into Regent's Park, alighted, walked on to the grass, and stood leaning against a tree for some moments, looking round her at the leaves and the sky. She then entered the carriage again, drove home, and agreed to the elopement. This was possibly the best poem that she ever produced.[10]

The same poetry pervaded the tragedy of Elizabeth Barrett's death:

> One event alone could really end the endless life of the Italian Arcadia. That event happened on June 29, 1861. Robert Browning's wife died ... She died alone in the room with Browning, and of what passed then, though much has been said, little should be. He, closing the door of that room behind him, closed a door in himself, and none ever saw Browning upon earth again but only a splendid surface.[11]

Predictably, Chesterton used Browning's poetry as an excuse to attack modern notions of which he disapproved, for instance the belief that novelty was necessarily a virtue:

> Poetry deals with primal and conventional things – the hunger for bread, the love of woman, the love of children, the desire for immortal life. If men really had new sentiments, poetry could not deal with them. If, let us say, a man did not feel a bitter craving to eat bread; but did, by way of substitute, feel a fresh, original craving to eat brass fenders or mahogany tables, poetry could not express him. If a man, instead of falling in love with a woman, fell in love with a fossil or a sea anemone, poetry could not express him. Poetry can only express what is original in one sense – the sense in which we speak of original sin. It is original, not in the paltry sense of being new, but in the deeper sense of being old; it is original in the sense that it deals with origins.[12]

Perhaps the most profound point on the importance of poetry appears in the chapter entitled 'The Philosophy of Browning':

> The practical value of poetry is that it is realistic upon a point upon which nothing else can be realistic, the point of the actual desires of man. Ethics is the science of actions, but poetry is the science of motives ... in poetry, as in music, a note is struck which expresses beyond the power of rational statement a condition of mind, and all actions arise from a condition of mind.[13]

Lest we should forget, amid these detours, that the book is about Browning, Chesterton reintroduces him:

> Now the supreme value of Browning as an optimist lies in this that we have been examining, that beyond all his conclusions, and deeper

than all his arguments, he was passionately interested in and in love with existence ... He is a great poet of human joy for precisely the reason of which Mr Santayana complains: that his happiness is primal, and beyond the reach of philosophy. He is something far more convincing, far more comforting, far more religiously significant than an optimist: he is a happy man.[14]

Immediately preceding this passage Chesterton wrote that 'poetry can tell us whether the happiness is the happiness that sends a man to a restaurant, or the richer and fuller happiness that sends him to church.'[15] In 1903 he attended restaurants far more frequently than he attended church, but the happiness he ascribed to Browning he possessed himself. Furthermore, he was grateful for it and wrote as much in an article in the *Daily News* of 20 June 1903 entitled 'The Philosophy of Gratitude'.

In September 1903 *Varied Types* was published. It was essentially a reprint of *Twelve Types* except that a further eight character studies were tacked on to the original twelve. These included Alfred the Great, Ruskin, Queen Victoria, Tennyson and Elizabeth Barrett Browning.

Chesterton's second full-length biography was a portrait of the painter George Frederick Watts. As with his biography of Browning, however, *Watts* is memorable as much for the thoughts of the author as for the life of the subject: 'It is not so much the fact that there is no such thing as allegorical art, but rather the fact that there is no art that is not allegorical.'[16] The book is also dotted with thought-provoking aphorisms, such as Chesterton's assertion that 'purity is the only atmosphere for passion'.[17]

G. F. Watts died in the year Chesterton's biography was published, but not before he had read the book. On 5 April 1904 Frances recorded in her diary that Mrs G. F. Watts had written Gilbert 'a charming note' saying that her husband is 'really pleased with the little book'.[18]

As well as writing about the giants of the Victorian age which had recently passed away, Gilbert was meeting and debating with the giants of the Edwardian age which had replaced it. Frances's diary for 1904 illustrates her husband's absorption into the Edwardian literary scene:

Gilbert and I meet all sorts of queer, well-known, attractive, unattractive people and I expect this book will be mostly about them ...

Feb 17th. We went together to Mr and Mrs Sidney Colvin's . . .
It was rather jolly but too many clever people there to be really
nice. The clever people were Mr Joseph Conrad, Mr Henry James,
Mr Laurence Binyon, Mr Maurice Hewlett, and a great many
more . . .

Feb 23rd. Gilbert went as Mr Lane's guest to a dinner of the
'Odd Volumes' at the Imperial Restaurant. The other guest was
Baden Powell. He and Gilbert made speeches . . .[19]

A picture of life in literary London at this time is painted by a
twenty-year-old Arthur Ransome. His own literary career had yet
to materialise but would come to fruition many years later with
children's books such as *Swallows and Amazons*. On his way home
during 1904 he used to take a detour through a quiet street behind
Westminster Abbey to see if his cousin Laurence Binyon's light was
burning, and to 'exult in the thought of the poems that might result
from such midnight labour'. Sometimes he would glimpse Chesterton
'rolling up Fleet Street laughing to himself and bumping into other
pedestrians without noticing'.[20]

In fact, Ransome had recently befriended Gilbert, probably having
been introduced to him by Cecil who was a close friend. In his
Autobiography Ransome described Cecil as being a 'regular visitor' to
his home, where he listened passively while his guest talked politics.
Ransome also provided an interesting insight into domestic life at
Warwick Gardens at this time:

> Cecil Chesterton was then still living with his father and mother in
> Warwick Gardens. I remember coming in there with him unexpectedly
> and finding them at some meal in their dining-room, each behind a
> rampart of books, with food grown cold beside them. He told me
> that all their meals were like that, and that often, engrossed in their
> reading, they would forget to eat at all until startled by the arrival
> of their next meal with the other still waiting on the table. When
> he and his brother were both at home, there was usually argument
> instead of reading, with much the same result. I never knew so
> united a family with such a passion for debate. Gilbert Chesterton
> had lately married and was living in a flat across the river, by Battersea
> Park, and here I met E. Nesbit and her husband, the rather florid
> Hubert Bland, with his monocle dangling from a broad silk ribbon,
> a confident, blustering creature for whose works both Chestertons
> had an exaggerated respect and I had none, though I had a great
> deal for the works of his wife.[21]

Meanwhile, Frank Swinnerton remembered Chesterton debating with Ramsay MacDonald during these early years:

> Used to chivalrous combat with Shaw, Chesterton used the same methods when he was persuaded to debate with Ramsay MacDonald. MacDonald, handsome, rasping, aggressive, scorned them. He harangued. He punched the whole time, seeking victory, hitting his left hand with his right, a conscious orator. I think he was pretty good; for he was not then the ass he became when Prime Minister; but he had a shallow mind.[22]

Another debate was recorded in Frances's diary on 22 March: 'Meeting of Christo Theosophical Society at which G. lectured on "How Theosophy appears to a Christian". He was very good. Herbert Burrows vigorously attacked him in debate afterwards.'[23]

In the same day's entry in her diary Frances noted that *The Napoleon of Notting Hill* was published. This was Gilbert's first novel and, according to his own estimation, it was his first important book. The story behind the writing of it illustrates the tenuous financial position he and Frances were in during 1904:

> I was 'broke' – only ten shillings in my pocket. Leaving my worried wife, I went down Fleet Street, got a shave, and then ordered for myself, at the Cheshire Cheese, an enormous luncheon of my favourite dishes and a bottle of wine. It took my all, but I could then go to my publishers fortified. I told them I wanted to write a book and outlined the story of *Napoleon of Notting Hill*. But I must have twenty pounds, I said, before I begin . . . They gave it.[24]

Remembering this incident, Frances told Maisie Ward how she had sat at home thinking hard thoughts of Gilbert's disappearance with their last remaining coin when he returned dramatically and poured twenty golden sovereigns into her lap.

The book itself is an enigma defying easy categorisation. Its theme is hinted at by one of the novel's characters, the President of Nicaragua, a mysterious figure who makes one fleeting appearance before disappearing from the plot without trace: 'And with a pleasant smile he finished his coffee and rose, bowing profoundly, passed out into the fog, which had again grown dense and sombre. Three days afterwards they heard that he had died quietly in lodgings in Soho.'[25] Before taking his bow, however, he has neatly set the scene for what is to follow: '"Nicaragua has been conquered like Athens. Nicaragua has been annexed like Jerusalem," cried the old man, with amazing fire. "The Yankee and the German and the brute powers of modernity have trampled it with the hoofs of oxen. But Nicaragua is not dead. Nicaragua is an idea."'[26] In a spirited defence of the cultural integrity of small nations, the exiled President attacks the forces of imperialism:

> That is what I complain of your cosmopolitanism. When you say you want all peoples to unite, you really mean that you want all peoples to unite to learn the tricks of your people. If the Bedouin Arab does not know how to read, some English missionary or schoolmaster must be sent to teach him to read, but no one ever says, 'This schoolmaster does not know how to ride on a camel; let us pay a Bedouin to teach him.' You say your civilisation will include all talents. Will it? Do you really mean to say that at the moment when the Esquimaux has learnt to vote for a County Council, you will have learnt to spear a walrus?[27]

The scene thus set by a peripheral character, the two central figures in the story take over: Auberon Quin and Adam Wayne. Quin, the cynical joker who has become the King of England, is determined to laugh at mankind's expense: ' "At any rate, I have said my last serious word today, and my last serious word I trust for the remainder of my life in this Paradise of Fools. The remainder of my conversation with you today, which I trust will be long and stimulating, I propose to conduct in a new language of my own by means of rapid and symbolic movements of the left leg." ' The King then begins 'to pirouette slowly round the room with a preoccupied expression'.[28]

In this spirit of tomfoolery, Auberon Quin conceives his greatest joke yet: 'A revival of the arrogance of the old mediaeval cities applied to our glorious suburbs. Clapham with a city guard. Wimbledon with a city wall. Surbiton tolling a bell to raise its citizens. West Hampstead going into battle with its own banner.'[29]

The joke becomes the law of the land in the form of the Great Proclamation of the Charter of the Free Cities. Great fun is had by all, or at least great fun is had by the King at the expense of all, until someone fails to get the joke. Adam Wayne, determined to defend

Pump Street from developers, declares war in the name of Notting Hill. The rest is histrionics.

Many critics have attempted to get to grips with the deeper meaning of Chesterton's first foray into full-length fiction. E. C. Bentley, reviewing the book for the *Bystander*, described it as the story of 'the triumph of a spiritual idea over the multitude of common-minded men, a possibility of which Mr Chesterton is, to his great honour, one of the resolute maintainers'.[30]

Ronald Knox was only sixteen, 'a schoolboy just beginning to think', when *The Napoleon of Notting Hill* was published. It influenced him profoundly and many years later he was still puzzling over its underlying message:

> The book concludes . . . by opening up a wider problem; which was right? Quin, who invented Notting Hill for a joke, or Wayne, who did not see that it was a joke and turned it into a reality? Which is right – the cynic who sees everything as amusing, or the fanatic who has no sense of humour at all? The answer to that is, that the two men are in reality only two lobes of one brain; it is only when the world goes wrong that the pure precipitation of cynic or of fanatic is formed; the normal man, living in normal surroundings, is a blend of both. Laughter and love are everywhere; in healthy people there is no war between them.[31]

Perhaps a more obvious interpretation was made by Michael Collins, the Irish politician and Sinn Féin leader who was largely responsible for negotiating the treaty with Britain in 1921. Collins was only fourteen when *The Napoleon of Notting Hill* was published and, although it is not clear at what age he actually first read the book, it influenced his political outlook in its formative stages. Collins described it as his favourite book and there can be no doubt that he derived inspiration for his Irish nationalism from the words of Chesterton's fictitious President of Nicaragua and also, possibly, from Adam Wayne's local patriotism which proclaimed that a place, however small, 'which is large enough for the rich to covet . . . is large enough for the poor to defend'.[32] It is said that Lloyd George, hearing of Michael Collins's literary taste, presented a copy of *The Napoleon of Notting Hill* to every member of his Cabinet prior to their meeting with the Irish delegation during negotiations for the Irish Treaty so that they might the better understand the Irish leader's mind.[33]

Another admirer of *The Napoleon of Notting Hill* is Terry Pratchett, the modern author of popular comic fantasy. In the September 1991 issue of the magazine *Interzone* he is quoted as saying that Chesterton 'in small doses taken regularly [is] good for the soul'. He also had the following to say about two of Chesterton's novels:

> It's worth pointing out that in *The Man Who was Thursday* and *The Napoleon of Notting Hill* he gave us two of the most emotionally charged plots in the twentieth century: one being that both sides are actually the same side; it doesn't matter which side we're talking about, both sides are the same. This has been the motor of half the spy novels of this century. The other plot can't be summarised so succinctly, but the basic plot of *The Napoleon of Notting Hill* is that someone takes seriously an idea that wasn't intended to be taken seriously and gives it some kind of nobility by so doing.[34]

Pratchett paid Chesterton a further tribute when he and his co-author Neil Gaiman dedicated their novel *Good Omens* 'to the memory of G. K. Chesterton, a man who knew what was going on'.[35] In the same book the character Crowley describes Chesterton as 'the only poet in the twentieth century to even come close to the Truth'.[36]

Frances's next entry in the diary after her announcement of the publication of *The Napoleon of Notting Hill* is dated 31 March: 'Ilkley. The country is wonderful and there is room to breathe.'[37]

The entry was written in the peace and relative seclusion of the Yorkshire moors where Frances and Gilbert were enjoying a holiday. It was while they were there that they met a man who was to become a close friend of both of them. The man was Father John O'Connor, an Irish priest who was curate at St Anne's Church in Keighley. Maisie Ward described the friendship which developed between Gilbert and Father O'Connor as 'perhaps the closest of Gilbert's life'.[38]

There are, as ever, conflicting reports of how the two friends were originally introduced. Certainly Father O'Connor had been an admirer of Chesterton long before they met. Over a year earlier, in February 1903, he had written to Gilbert telling him that he was a 'Catholic priest, and though I may not find you quite orthodox in details, I first wish to thank you very heartily, or shall I say, to thank God for having gifted you with the spirituality which alone makes literature immortal, as I think'.[39]

As to the first meeting itself, Father O'Connor and Chesterton give similar but differing accounts. Father O'Connor wrote that they met

> at Keighley in the spring of 1904, at the house of Mr Herbert Hugill, who was a much older Chesterton fan than I was . . . There we agreed to walk over the moor to Ilkley, where Chesterton was spending a short holiday, and I was his willing guide. The actual conditions for both of us were as near the ideal as makes no difference: he was on holiday, having delivered his lecture to the Keighley intelligentsia, and I was in possession of the heart's desire, which was to talk with him.[40]

Meanwhile, Chesterton's memory of the occasion is somewhat more detailed:

> I had gone to give a lecture at Keighley on the high moors of the West Riding, and stayed the night with a leading citizen of that little industrial town; who had assembled a group of local friends such as could be conceived, I suppose, as likely to be patient with lecturers; including the curate of the Roman Catholic Church; a small man with a smooth face and a demure but elvish expression. I was struck by the tact and humour with which he mingled with his very Yorkshire and very Protestant company; and I soon found out that they had, in their bluff way, already learned to appreciate him as something of a character . . . I liked him very much; but if you had told me that ten years afterwards I should be a Mormon Missionary in the Cannibal Islands, I should not have been more surprised than at the suggestion that, fully fifteen years afterwards, I should be making to him my General Confession and being received into the Church that he served.
>
> Next morning he and I walked over Keighley Gate, the great wall of the moors that separates Keighley from Wharfedale, for I was visiting friends in Ilkley; and after a few hours' talk on the moors, it was a new friend whom I introduced to my old friends at my journey's end. He stayed to lunch, he stayed to tea; he stayed to dinner; I am not sure that, under their pressing hospitality, he did not stay the night; and he stayed there many nights and days on later occasions; and it was there that we most often met.[41]

The old friend with whom the Chestertons were staying in Ilkley was Francis Steinthal, a Jew of Frankfurt descent with whom they lodged on many occasions in subsequent years. It was *chez* Steinthal on 5 April that Frances recorded her first impressions of Father O'Connor in her diary:

> Father O'Connor came over. He is delightful. So boyish. So wise. So young. So old. There is a sort of charm about him difficult to define. He uses his hands to help out his meaning very effectively and yet never suggests affectation or theatricality. It is wonderful that he should lead that quiet life of a parish priest in Keighley when he appears so dazzling.[42]

Frances was clearly as charmed by the Irish priest as was her husband. Indeed, if anything, Frances became a closer friend of Father O'Connor's than did Gilbert. Throughout the years she and Father O'Connor kept up a steady correspondence, always friendly and intimate, and when Father O'Connor wrote his book on Gilbert he dedicated it to Frances. The book, entitled *Father Brown on Chesterton*, was published in 1937, a year after Gilbert's death. Ten years earlier, Chesterton's book *The Secret of Father Brown* had been dedicated 'to Father John O'Connor of St Cuthbert's, Bradford, Whose Truth is Stranger than Fiction, With a Gratitude Greater than the World'.[43]

Gilbert's gratitude was due primarily to Father O'Connor's role in assisting him to the Catholic faith, but he was also indebted to his friend in another important respect, namely that the Irish priest was the original model and inspiration for Father Brown, Chesterton's fictional priest detective. Yet Chesterton's inspiration came primarily not from his friend's physical appearance but from his worldly wisdom masquerading as innocence. The story is that Father O'Connor had startled Gilbert by revealing his knowledge of the more lurid side of human nature, a knowledge gained as a direct result of his priestly life. The paradox of innocent wisdom was a fertile source for Chesterton's imagination and it was heightened still further by an episode at the house at which they arrived immediately after the startling conversation. Two Cambridge undergraduates, who were guests at the house, spoke disparagingly about the clergy being 'all shut up in a sort of cloister' and not knowing 'anything about the real evil in the world'. To Chesterton, who was 'still almost shivering with the appallingly practical facts' of which the priest had warned him, the comments sounded with 'such a colossal and crushing irony' that he 'nearly burst into a loud harsh laugh in the drawing-room'. At that moment it dawned on him that, compared with Father O'Connor, the two Cambridge gentlemen 'knew about as much of real evil as two babies in the same perambulator'.[44]

Then came the moment of inspiration:

> . . . there sprang up in my mind the vague idea of making some artistic use of this comic yet tragic cross-purposes; and constructing a comedy in which a priest should appear to know nothing and in fact know more about crime than the criminals. I afterwards summed up the special idea in the story called 'The Blue Cross', otherwise very slight and improbable, and continued it through the interminable series of tales with which I have afflicted the world. In short, I permitted myself the grave liberty of taking my friend and knocking him about; beating his hat and umbrella shapeless, untidying his clothes, punching his intelligent countenance into a condition of pudding-faced fatuity, and generally disguising Father O'Connor as Father Brown.[45]

Chesterton goes on to explain the disguise as 'a deliberate piece of fiction, meant to bring out or accentuate the contrast that was the point of the comedy'.[46] No doubt this is true, but another reason for the Irishman's transfiguration was Chesterton's desire for his hero to be English. As long as he was English it was not particularly important which part of England he came from, as is testified to by the fact that Father Brown is described as a Suffolk dumpling in Gilbert's *Autobiography* but was introduced to literature in 'The Blue Cross' as having 'a face as round and dull as a Norfolk dumpling'.[47]

Gilbert's dedication to Father O'Connor had exclaimed that the Irishman's 'Truth is Stranger than Fiction'. Yet Chesterton had turned that truth into a stranger fiction. He had met an Irish priest and had transformed him into an English hero.

« 7 »

Heretics and Orthodoxy

DURING 1904 CHESTERTON'S POPULARITY scaled new heights on both sides of the Atlantic. Shan F. Bullock, writing in the *Chicago Evening Post* on 9 April, feared that the young Gilbert was becoming a victim of his own success:

> I see that Chesterton has just issued a volume on the art of G. F. Watts. His novel was published yesterday. Soon his monograph of Kingsley should be ready. I believe he has a book on some modern aspects of religious belief in the press. He is part-editor of the illustrated booklets on great authors issued by the *Bookman*. He is contributing prefaces and introductions to odd volumes in several series of reprints. He is a constant contributor to the *Daily News* and the *Speaker;* he is conducting a public controversy with Blatchford of the *Clarion* on atheism and free-thinking; he is constantly lecturing and debating and dining out; it is almost impossible to open a paper that does not contain either an article or review or poem or drawing of his, and his name is better known now to compositors than Bernard Shaw.
>
> Now, both physically and mentally Chesterton is a Hercules, and from what I hear of his methods of work he is capable of a great output without much physical strain; nevertheless, it is clear, I think, to anyone that at his present rate of production he must either wear or tear . . . Not often is a man like Chesterton born. He should have his full chance. And that can only come by study and meditation, and by slow, steady accumulation of knowledge and wisdom.[1]

The American journalist who wrote these lines shared the concern of many that Chesterton was wasting his talents by spreading himself too thinly. Father O'Connor was one of those who advised him to 'cease to spread and dissipate his gifts on daily papers, and begin to print on handmade paper with gilt edges. In other words, to go in for Literature.'[2] In response, Frances told Father O'Connor that her husband would not change because he was 'bent on being a jolly journalist, to paint the town red . . . All he wants is buckets and buckets of red paint.'[3]

Perhaps the real reason for his prolific output was given unwittingly by Chesterton himself in an introduction he wrote to the Everyman Library edition of *Barnaby Rudge*. Although he was writing of Dickens it is clear that the description was equally applicable to his own situation:

> The calls upon him at this time were insistent and overwhelming; this necessarily happens at a certain stage of a successful writer's career. He was just successful enough to invite offers and not successful enough to reject them . . . there was almost too much work for his imagination, and yet not quite enough work for his housekeeping . . . And it is a curious tribute to the quite curious greatness of Dickens that in this period of youthful strain we do not feel the strain but feel only the youth. His own amazing wish to write equalled or outstripped even his readers' amazing wish to read. Working too hard did not cure him of his abstract love of work. Unreasonable publishers asked him to write ten novels at once; but he wanted to write twenty novels at once.[4]

Chesterton's own love of work may have led him to accept too many literary and journalistic commitments but he still found time to collaborate with Belloc on the latter's first novel. *Emmanuel Burden* was published by Methuen in September 1904, complete with thirty-four illustrations by Chesterton. It was the first of several such collaborations. Dorothy Collins, Gilbert's secretary for six of the eleven 'Chesterbellocs', remembered how they took shape:

> Belloc needed Chesterton, and would come like a whirlwind with the plot of one of his satirical novels, saying that he could not possibly write the story until Gilbert had drawn the pictures. They would go into the study after lunch and for the length of a hilarious afternoon they would be closeted together. At tea-time they would emerge, Belloc triumphant with twenty-five illustrations for his book. The characters had come to life through the medium of the drawings.[5]

One by-product of Chesterton's growing popularity was his continued incorporation into the London literary scene. The entries in Frances's diary in 1904 are dotted with references to society dinners:

May 8th The Literary Fund Dinner. About the greatest treat I have had in my life. J. M. Barrie presided. He was so splendid and so complimentary . . . It is wonderful the way in which they all accept Gilbert, and one well-known man told me he was the biggest man present . . .

May 12th Went to see Max Beerbohm's caricature of Gilbert at the Carfax Gallery . . .

June 9th A political 'at home' at Mrs Sidney Webb's – Saw Winston Churchill and Lloyd George . . .[6]

The jaunty innocence of these accounts of evenings with the rich and famous contrasts starkly with the sinister nature of Chesterton's encounter with the infamous Aleister Crowley three months later. On 24 September Chesterton reviewed Crowley's poem *The Sword of Song*: 'Mr Crowley begins his poem, I believe, with an earnest intention to explain the beauty of the Buddhist philosophy; he knows a great deal about it; he believes in it. But as he went on writing one thing became stronger and stronger in his soul – the living hatred of Christianity . . .'[7] In the wake of the review, Crowley wrote to Chesterton seeking an open debate on the issues raised:

Dear Sir,
I was very disappointed, after risking a whole halfpenny on the *Daily News* of Saturday, to find that your promised article on Buddhism had suffered from the Gladstonian 'Ireland blocks the way'. If I am right in surmising that the 'certain reasons' of which you speak refer to the exigencies of journalism, not those of controversy, and that therefore the digression is likely to be permanent, perhaps it would be a pleasant suggestion to you that the affair should be transferred to some other journal.
    I am anxious to meet you in fair fight . . .[8]

In spite of Crowley's promptings Chesterton refused resolutely to be drawn into open debate. Since Gilbert was usually more than eager to accept the challenge of those wishing to meet him 'in fair fight' his reticence is both surprising and out of character. Indeed, his refusal to debate allowed Crowley to publish a pamphlet in which he gloated that 'on the appearance of his article . . . I signified my intention to reply. It aborted his attack on me, and he has not since been heard of.

> In the midst of the words he was trying to say,
> In the midst of his laughter and glee,
> He has softly and suddenly vanished away –'[9]

It is likely that Chesterton saw in Crowley a vision of the diabolist acquaintance of his student days at the Slade who 'had a horrible fairness of the intellect that made me despair of his soul'; who sought to 'find in evil a life of its own'; who sought to corrupt women for no other reason than 'the expanding pleasure of ruin'.[10] Certainly Crowley's own life appeared to parallel that of Chesterton's student acquaintance. He was a year younger than Chesterton and had become interested in the occult while an undergraduate at Cambridge. He was expelled from the Order of the Golden Dawn for extreme practices and founded his own occultist order, the Silver Star. He settled with a group of disciples in Sicily but was expelled from Italy after rumours of drugs, orgies and magical ceremonies involving the sacrifice of babies. In 1921 a series of newspaper reports gained him the notoriety he craved. He liked to be known as 'the great beast' and 'the wickedest man alive' – and certainly many who associated with him died tragically, including his wife and child.

Crowley could indeed gloat that Chesterton had retreated from his challenge, yet Chesterton would sooner be defeated than defiled. Once before he had 'softly and suddenly vanished away' when retreating from the other diabolist. On that occasion he had 'rushed out without daring to pause; and as I passed the fire I did not know whether it was hell or the furious love of God'.[11]

In spite of the unpleasantness of his brief relationship with Crowley, 1904 was the most successful year so far in Gilbert's young and blossoming literary career. In the following year he continued to be the 'jolly journalist', contributing regularly to a variety of journals, and he continued to lecture up and down the country. Two of the most memorable lectures were given at St Paul's Church in Covent Garden on 16 and 30 March as part of a series sponsored by the London Branch of the Christian Social Union.

The year 1905 saw the publication of two more books. The first was a light-hearted collection of short stories under the title of *The*

Club of Queer Trades. The club in question was defined as 'an eccentric and Bohemian Club, of which the absolute condition of membership lies in this, that the candidate must have invented the method by which he earns his living'.[12] Having invented such a club, the author uses it as an excuse to invent the sort of eccentrics who would join it. The result is flippant and whimsical. Although *The Club of Queer Trades* is not one of the most memorable of Chesterton's books, one particular extract is of interest because it reiterates Chesterton's assertion that truth transcends fact: '"Facts," murmured Basil, like one mentioning some strange, far-off animals, "how facts obscure the truth . . . Facts point in all directions, it seems to me, like the thousands of twigs on a tree. It's only the life of the tree that has unity and goes up – only the green blood that springs, like a fountain, at the stars."'[13]

The Club of Queer Trades was eclipsed both in merit and in impact by the book which followed it. *Heretics* was published on 6 June to immediate acclaim and immediate condemnation. The book, by its very nature, was bound to offend even though its author attacked only the philosophy of the people he wrote about, never the people themselves:

> I for one have come to believe in going back to fundamentals. Such is the general idea of this book. I wish to deal with my most distinguished contemporaries, not personally or in a merely literary manner, but in relation to the real body of doctrine which they teach. I am not concerned with Mr Rudyard Kipling as a vivid artist or a vigorous personality; I am concerned with him as a Heretic – that is to say, a man whose view of things has the hardihood to differ from mine. I am not concerned with Mr Bernard Shaw as one of the most brilliant and one of the most honest men alive; I am concerned with him as a Heretic – that is to say, a man whose philosophy is quite solid, quite coherent, and quite wrong. I revert to the doctrinal methods of the thirteenth century, inspired by the general hope of getting something done.[14]

Neither did the book restrict itself to Kipling and Shaw. Many other giants of literature and philosophy were branded heretics by the precocious newcomer:

> The thing which is resented, and, as I think, rightly resented, in that great modern literature of which Ibsen is typical, is that while the eye that can perceive what are the wrong things increases in an uncanny and devouring clarity, the eye which sees what things are

right is growing mistier and mistier every moment, till it goes almost blind with doubt. If we compare, let us say, the morality of the *Divine Comedy* with the morality of Ibsen's *Ghosts*, we shall see all that modern ethics have really done. No one, I imagine, will accuse the author of the *Inferno* of an early Victorian prudishness or a Podsnapian optimism. But Dante describes three moral instruments – Heaven, Purgatory, and Hell, the vision of perfection, the vision of improvement, and the vision of failure. Ibsen has only one – Hell.[15]

Chesterton also declared war on the philosophy of Nietzsche: 'Nietzsche's Superman is cold and friendless . . . A great man is not a man so strong that he feels less than other men; he is a man so strong that he feels more. And when Nietzsche says, "A new commandment I give to you, be hard," he is really saying, "A new commandment I give to you, be dead." Sensibility is the definition of life.'[16]

In attacking the principle of H. G. Wells's novel *The Food of the Gods*, published the previous year, he inadvertently sets against it the underlying principle of his own novel, *The Napoleon of Notting Hill*: '*The Food of the Gods* is the tale of Jack the Giant-Killer told from the point of view of the giant. This has not, I think, been done before in literature; but I have little doubt that the psychological substance of it existed in fact . . . The modern world, like Mr Wells, is on the side of the giants . . .'[17] In Chesterton's eyes Jack represented the small nation fighting for its independence against the giants of Empire, or the small businessman fighting for his existence against the giants of multinationalism. If Jack stood in the way of 'progress', 'progress' and not Jack should go. He adopted a similar stance against the ethical standpoint of Bernard Shaw:

After belabouring a great many people for a great many years for being unprogressive, Mr Shaw has discovered, with characteristic sense, that it is very doubtful whether any existing human being with two legs can be progressive at all. Having come to doubt whether humanity can be combined with progress, most people, easily pleased, would have elected to abandon progress and remain with humanity. Mr Shaw, not being easily pleased, decides to throw over humanity with all its limitations and go in for progress for its own sake.[18]

However, if Chesterton was sceptical about the naïvety of believing in progress for its own sake, he was even more sceptical about scepticism:

The vice of the modern notion of mental progress is that it is always something concerned with the breaking of bonds, the effacing of boundaries, the casting away of dogmas. But if there be such a thing as mental growth, it must mean the growth into more and more definite convictions, into more and more dogmas. The human brain is a machine for coming to conclusions; if it cannot come to conclusions it is rusty. When we hear of a man too clever to believe, we are hearing of something having almost the character of a contradiction in terms. It is like hearing of a nail that was too good to hold down a carpet; or a bolt that was too strong to keep a door shut.[19]

He proceeds with characteristic humour, observing that when a man

drops one doctrine after another in a refined scepticism, when he declines to tie himself to a system, when he says that he has outgrown definitions, when he says that he disbelieves in finality, when, in his own imagination, he sits as God, holding no form of creed but contemplating all, then he is by that very process sinking slowly backwards into the vagueness of the vagrant animals and the unconsciousness of the grass. Trees have no dogmas. Turnips are singularly broad-minded.[20]

Chesterton was none the less aware that dogmatism had become synonymous with bigotry to the modern mind. This was yet another example of the modern mind being mistaken:

A common hesitation in our day touching the use of extreme convictions is a sort of notion that extreme convictions, specially upon cosmic matters, have been responsible in the past for the thing which is called bigotry. But a very small amount of direct experience will dissipate this view. In real life the people who are most bigoted are the people who have no convictions at all. The economists of the Manchester school who disagree with Socialism take Socialism seriously. It is the young man in Bond Street, who does not know what socialism means, much less whether he agrees with it, who is quite certain that these socialist fellows are making a fuss about nothing. The man who understands the Calvinist philosophy enough to agree with it must understand the Catholic philosophy in order to disagree with it. It is the vague modern who is not at all certain what is right who is most certain that Dante was wrong. The serious opponent of the Latin Church in history, even in the act of showing that it produced great infamies, must know that it produced great saints. It is the hard-headed stockbroker, who knows no history and believes no religion, who is, nevertheless, perfectly convinced that all these priests are knaves ... Bigotry may be roughly defined as the anger of men who have no opinions. It is the resistance offered to definite ideas by that vague bulk of people whose ideas are indefinite to excess. Bigotry may be called the appalling frenzy of the indifferent.[21]

Amidst the debunking of the 'heresies' of Shaw and others, *Heretics* contains a few swipes at aspects of modern life such as 'motor-car civilisation' which was 'outstripping time, consuming space, seeing all and seeing nothing'.[22] Against this, Chesterton was one of the first exponents of the 'green' alternative:

The truth is that exploration and enlargement make the world smaller ... It is inspiriting without doubt to whizz in a motor-car round the earth, to feel Arabia as a whirl of sand or China as a flash of rice-fields. But Arabia is not a whirl of sand and China is not a flash of rice-fields. They are ancient civilisations with strange virtues buried like treasures. To conquer these places is to lose them. The man standing in his own kitchen-garden, with fairyland opening at his gate, is the man with large ideas. His mind creates distance; the motor-car stupidly destroys it.[23]

On the whole, though, *Heretics* turned a stern and critical eye on many giants of the literary world. One writer, however, was conspicuous by the absence of criticism levelled against him. For Dickens there was nothing but praise:

... the living and invigorating ideal of England must be looked for in the masses; it must be looked for where Dickens found it – Dickens, among whose glories it was to be a humorist, to be a sentimentalist, to be an optimist, to be a poor man, to be an Englishman, but the greatest of whose glories was that he saw all mankind in its amazing and tropical luxuriance, and did not even notice the aristocracy; Dickens, the greatest of whose glories was that he could not describe a gentleman.[24]

This evident admiration for the genius of Dickens found fruition the following year in a full-length biography. *Charles Dickens* was received with enthusiasm by critics and public alike. The French novelist and biographer André Maurois considered it one of the best biographies ever written; while T. S. Eliot found the book a delight to read and thought that there was no better critic of Dickens than Chesterton. Bernard Shaw wrote to Chesterton on 6 September, a week after the book was published: 'As I am a supersaturated Dickensite, I pounced on your book and read it, as Wegg read Gibbon and other authors, right through.'[25]

Chesterton began his study of Dickens with an appeal to his readers:

> I put this appeal before any other observations on Dickens. First let us sympathise, if only for an instant, with the hopes of the Dickens period, with the cheerful trouble of change . . . For you, perhaps, a drearier philosophy has covered and eclipsed the earth . . . If, then, you are a pessimist, in reading this story, forgo for a little the pleasures of pessimism. Dream for one mad moment that the grass is green.[26]

On 8 September James Douglas, writing in the *Throne*, stressed that Chesterton's sympathy for Dickens was grounded in his similarity to Dickens: 'He is, like Dickens, an imaginative caricaturist, an artist in grotesque humour, an apostle of exaggeration. "Exaggeration," says Mr Chesterton roundly, "is the definition of art." It is certainly the definition of Dickensian art and Chestertonian art.'[27] Whether one approved or otherwise, it was certainly true that the subject of Dickens afforded Chesterton the opportunity to flaunt his own imagination:

> Dickens was a mythologist rather than a novelist . . . He did not always manage to make his characters men, but he always managed, at the least, to make them gods . . . It was not the aim of Dickens to show the effect of time and circumstance upon a character; it was not even his aim to show the effect of a character on time and circumstance . . . It was his aim to show character hung in a kind of happy void, in a world apart from time . . .[28]

Similarly, with the art of exaggeration of which he stood accused, Chesterton described Dickens as more than merely 'the last of the mythologists, and perhaps the greatest'. He was also the last of the democrats and perhaps the greatest: 'Dickens stands first as a defiant monument of what happens when a great literary genius has a literary taste akin to that of the community . . . Dickens and his school had a hilarious faith in democracy and thought of the service of it as a sacred priesthood.'[29]

Developing the theme of Dickens's popularity, Chesterton emphasised that Dickens 'wanted what the people wanted' because he was at one with the common mind:

> But with this mere phrase, the common mind, we collide with a current error. Commonness and the common mind are now generally spoken of as meaning in some manner inferiority and the inferior mind; the mind of the mere mob. But the common mind means the mind of all the artists and heroes; or else it would not be common. Plato had the common mind; Dante had the common mind; or that mind was not common. Commonness means the quality common to the saint and the sinner, to the philosopher and the fool; and it was this that Dickens grasped and developed. In everybody there is a certain thing that loves babies, that fears death, that likes sunlight: that thing enjoys Dickens . . . And when I say that everybody understands Dickens I do not mean that he is suited to the untaught intelligence. I mean that he is so plain that even scholars can understand him.[30]

Only five days before the publication of *Charles Dickens*, the Chestertons' marriage was shaken by a family tragedy. On 25 August Frances's brother, Knollys, was washed up, dead, on a beach in Sussex. He had committed suicide. Ever since the tragic death of his sister Gertrude he had suffered from recurring bouts of depression. None the less, his death came as a shock because he had shown signs of improvement in recent months and had apparently gained solace from his recent conversion to the Catholic faith.

Frances hastened to Newhaven to identify her brother's body and arrange the funeral. She was plunged into grief and sought to share it with Father O'Connor: 'I have to write in a great trouble. My dear brother was found drowned at Seaford a few days ago. It was a terrible shock to us all – we were so happy about him . . . He seemed to have quite recovered from his terrible illness but he sought his own death.'[31]

Gilbert did his awkward best to comfort his wife during the difficult weeks following the tragedy. She slipped into a deep depression and he watched helplessly from the sidelines as she sought solace in the cult of spiritualism. Endeavouring desperately to contact her dead brother and sister, she called on the help of a medium. Gilbert disapproved intensely. His earlier experiences with the planchette had convinced him of the sinister nature of spiritualism and, no doubt, the recent liaison with Aleister Crowley had reinforced this. His disapproval is evident in 'The Crystal'. It is one of his best poems, yet remained unpublished because of the deeply personal nature of the subject.

The Crystal

I saw it; how she lay as one in dreams,
    And round that holy hair, round and beyond
My Frances, my inviolable, screamed
    The scandal of the dead men's demi-monde.

Close to that face, a window into heaven,
    Close to the hair's brown surf of broken waves
I saw the idiot face of the ghosts
    That are the fungus, not the flower, of graves.

You whom the pinewoods robed in sun and shade
    You who were sceptred with thistle's bloom,
God's thunder! What have you to do with these
    The lying crystal and the darkened room?

Leave the weird queens that find the sun too strong,
    To mope and cower beneath Druidic trees,
The still, sweet gardens of the dastard's dream.
    God's thunder! What have you to do with these?

Low fields and shining lie in crystal land
    Peace and strange pleasure: wonder-lands untrod,
But not plain words, nor love of open things,
    Truth, nor strong laughter, nor the fear of God.

I will not look: I am a child of earth,
    I see the sun and wood, the sea, and grass.
I only saw one spirit. She is there
    Staring for spirits in a lump of glass.[32]

Amid the domestic worries which followed the suicide of Frances's brother, Gilbert found comfort in his work. In February 1907 J. M. Dent & Son issued *The Old Curiosity Shop*, with an introduction by Chesterton, in the Everyman Library. In September of the same year ten more Dickens titles were published, all with introductions by Chesterton. By 1911 Chesterton had written introductions to Dickens's complete works in the series. Frank Swinnerton, who was employed with Dent's until May 1907, remembered an encounter with Chesterton in the early days of his involvement with the Dickens reprints:

> ... after the office was closed, he drove up one evening in a hansom cab, bearing a bundle of manuscript which contained his introduction to either *David Copperfield* or *Martin Chuzzlewit* (I was not allowed to handle it) for Everyman ... while, because I could not pay cash for it, he refused to leave his manuscript ... his manner was the reverse of harsh. It was that of one who thought he and I were engaged in an unfortunate but risible non-transaction, and was both friendly and amusing. I suspect that having worked in two publishing offices and for a number of unremunerative papers he had developed a preference for ready-money transactions ...[33]

Although Chesterton, like Dickens, was a great believer in democracy, there was at this time a metamorphosis in his political outlook which was influenced in no small part by Belloc. In essence it was a growing disillusionment with those who governed at Westminster, a belief that parliamentary democracy was undemocratic and representative government unrepresentative: 'The speaking in the House of Commons is not only worse than speaking was. It is worse than speaking is, in all or almost all other places: in small debating clubs or casual dinners. England shows us the blind leading the people who can see.'[34] This theme was echoed in one of his best-known poems, 'The Secret People', which was published during the summer of 1907 in the first number of the *Neolith*:

> We hear men speaking for us of new laws strong and sweet,
> Yet is there no man speaketh as we speak in the street.
> It may be we shall rise the last as Frenchmen rose the first,
> Our wrath come after Russia's wrath and our wrath be the worst.
> It may be we are meant to mark with our riot and our rest
> God's scorn for all men governing. It may be beer is best.
> But we are the people of England; and we have not spoken yet.
> Smile at us, pay us, pass us. But do not quite forget.

Another interesting feature of 'The Secret People' was its acceptance of the Catholic view of English history, as championed by Belloc:

And the eyes of the King's Servants turned terribly every way,
And the gold of the King's Servants rose higher every day.
They burnt the homes of the shaven men that had been quaint
        and kind,
Till there was no bed in a monk's house, nor food that man could find.
The inns of God where no man paid, that were the wall of the weak,
The King's Servants ate them all. And still we did not speak.
And the face of the King's Servants grew greater than the King:
He tricked them, and they trapped him, and stood round him
        in a ring.
The new grave lords closed round him, that had eaten the
        abbey's fruits,
And the men of the new religion, with their bibles in their boots,
We saw their shoulders moving, to menace or discuss,
And some were pure and some were vile; but none took heed of us.
We saw the King as they killed him, and his face was proud and pale;
And a few men talked of freedom, while England talked of ale.

The extent to which Chesterton accepted the Catholic position in 1907 can be gauged by two letters he wrote to the *Nation* in December of that year:

> Sir, – I trust you will take it as the candid phrase of a friend if I tell you that the strange irritation which always attracts you to the discussion of Catholic philosophy will strike us rather as a tribute to its strength than as any evidence of its decline ... Of all the converging objections to Catholicism which once rent Europe to its roots, you have only managed to retain one objection: the objection to a collective authority in religion. But the more pathetically you cling to this one last Protestant doctrine, the more we shall be reminded that you have openly abandoned all the others.[35]

The editor of the *Nation* responded by asking whether Chesterton was a Roman Catholic, to which Chesterton replied the following week, 'I am not. I shall not be until you have convinced me that the Church of England is really the muddle-headed provincial heresy that you make it out.'[36]

Yet he must have fuelled rumours of his Roman sympathies still further the following month when he wrote in defence of the Sacrament of Penance in the *Daily News* on 18 January. In answer to a critic's claim that confession of sins was morbid, Chesterton responded that 'the morbid thing is not to confess them. The morbid thing is to conceal your sins and let them eat your heart out, which is the happy state of most people in highly civilised communities.'[37]

Chesterton's first published book in 1908 was his second novel, *The Man Who was Thursday*. It is arguably the best and is certainly the most perplexing of his works of fiction. On a superficial level the plot is literally a plot, in the sense of the Gunpowder Plot. It revolves around a group of anarchists apparently intent on destruction. When asked if their intention is to abolish government one of the anarchists proclaims that this is not enough; their aim is

> To abolish God! . . . We do not only want to upset a few despotisms and police regulations; that sort of anarchism does exist, but it is a mere branch of the Nonconformists. We dig deeper and we blow you higher. We wish to deny all these arbitrary distinctions of vice and virtue, honour and treachery, upon which mere rebels base themselves. The silly sentimentalists of the French Revolution talked of the Rights of Man! We hate Rights as we hate Wrongs. We have abolished Right and Wrong.[38]

This is not mere amorality or immorality; it is anti-morality. It is the shadow of Aleister Crowley and the dream of the diabolist. In the diabolist's dreams he has gone beyond good and evil . . . and discovered something worse. It is no wonder that Chesterton subtitled the book 'A Nightmare'. And as a dreamer has difficulty unravelling the meaning of his dreams – if, indeed, his dreams have any meaning at all – Chesterton has difficulty unravelling the meaning of his nightmare. Asked in an interview to explain the enigmatic nature of Sunday, the novel's most mysterious character, he said that 'you can take him to stand for Nature as distinguished from God'. Yet in the very same interview he stated that 'you tear off the mask of Nature and you find God'.[39] It all appears to be contradiction and conundrum; even the author, who set the riddle, is seemingly unable to give the answer. This being so, it is perhaps apposite that Chesterton admitted, albeit whimsically, that in the case of *The Man Who was Thursday*, he needed a psychiatrist.[40]

Years later C. S. Lewis drew a surprising parallel between *The Man Who was Thursday* and the works of the Czech writer Franz Kafka:

> Is the difference simply that one is 'dated' and the other contemporary? Or is it rather that while both give a powerful picture of the loneliness and bewilderment which each one of us encounters in his (apparently)

single-handed struggle with the universe, Chesterton, attributing to the universe a more complicated disguise, and admitting the exhilaration as well as the terror of the struggle, has got in rather more; is more balanced: in that sense, more classical, more permanent?[41]

In the light of Lewis's comments it is interesting to note that Kafka was familiar with *The Man Who was Thursday*. Discussing both *Orthodoxy* and *The Man Who was Thursday*, Kafka remarked that Chesterton 'is so gay, that one might almost believe he had found God . . . in such a godless time one must be gay. It is a duty.'[42]

Chesterton's second book of that year was published by Methuen on 10 September 1908. It was a collection of articles originally written for the *Illustrated London News* and entitled *All Things Considered*. The author's own view of the collection was given on the first page: 'I cannot understand the people who take literature seriously; but I can love them, and I do. Out of my love I warn them to keep clear of this book. It is a collection of crude and shapeless papers . . . their vices are too vital to be improved with a blue pencil, or with anything I can think of, except dynamite.'[43] In spite of the author's derision of his own work, *All Things Considered* is an example, or rather an exhibition, of Chesterton's journalism at its very best. If he was content, as his wife claimed, to be simply the 'jolly journalist', *All Things Considered* displays the journalist at his jolliest. Take, for instance, the essay 'On Running After One's Hat': There is an idea that it is humiliating to run after one's hat; and when people say it is humiliating they mean that it is comic. It certainly is comic; but man is a very comic creature . . . A man running after a hat is not half so ridiculous as a man running after a wife.'[44]

However, for all the entertainment intermingled with pearls of wisdom to be obtained from the collection of essays, it was over-shadowed by its successor. *Orthodoxy* was published only two weeks after *All Things Considered* on 25 September. Chesterton explained his reasons for writing it in his *Autobiography*:

> I had published some studies of contemporary writers . . . I gave the book the title of *Heretics*. It was reviewed by Mr G. S. Street, the very delightful essayist, who casually used the expression that he was not going to bother about his theology until I had really stated mine. With all the solemnity of youth, I accepted this as a challenge; and wrote an outline of my own reasons for believing that the Christian theory, as summarised in the Apostles' Creed, would be found to be a better criticism of life than any of those that I had criticised. I called it *Orthodoxy* . . .[45]

Maisie Ward considered *Orthodoxy* so important that 'more must be said of it than his other published works'.[46] Her father, Wilfrid Ward, considered it a major milestone in the development of Christian thought and proclaimed as much in an enthusiastic article in the *Dublin Review*. Chesterton's paradoxical style was, Ward wrote, 'the administration of intellectual stimulants, or the application to a tired and bored world of a tremendous shower-bath in order to brace it and renew its normal activities'. In fact, Wilfrid Ward's enthusiasm for Chesterton's *Orthodoxy* knew no bounds: 'I class his thought – though not his manner – with that of such men as Burke, Butler and Coleridge . . .

'The spectacle of this intensely active and earnest modern intellect . . . reminds us how much that is indispensable in the inheritance of Christendom our own age has ceased adequately to realise and is in danger of lightly abandoning.'[47]

Certainly *Orthodoxy* is one of Chesterton's best books, and it illustrates a greater consistency of thought than any of his earlier writing. It contains, moreover, a development of many ideas he had championed earlier, such as the philosophy of gratitude: 'The test of all happiness is gratitude; and I felt grateful though I hardly knew to whom . . . We thank people for birthday presents of cigars and slippers. Can I thank no one for the birthday present of birth?'[48] It also contained incisive insights into the objectivity of Christianity: 'Christianity came into the world firstly in order to assert with violence that a man had not only to look inwards, but to look outwards, to behold with astonishment and enthusiasm a divine company and a divine captain.'[49] Most controversially, however, *Orthodoxy* championed both dogma and doctrine: 'The spike of dogma fitted exactly into the hole in the world – it had evidently been meant to go there – and then the strange thing began to happen. When once these two parts of the two machines had come together . . . all the other parts were repeating that rectitude, as clock after clock strikes noon. Instinct after instinct was answered by doctrine after doctrine.'[50] A similar metaphor was used when Chesterton described the Creed as the key to understanding both Christianity and the cosmos: 'When once one believes in a creed, one is proud of its complexity, as scientists are proud of the complexity of science. A stick might fit a hole or a stone a hollow by accident. But a key and a lock are both complex. And if a key fits a lock, you know it is the right key.'[51]

It is clear from these extracts that the popularity and success of *Orthodoxy* had almost as much to do with the potency of Chesterton's prose as with the cogency of his arguments. For example, one can scarcely fail to be caught up in the excitement of the imagery of the Church as a heavenly chariot 'thundering through the ages, the dull heresies sprawling and prostrate, the wild truth reeling but erect'.[52]

It was an imagery which excited the young Dorothy L. Sayers, rekindling her faith at a time when it was threatened by the doubts of adolescence. She had read *Orthodoxy* as a schoolgirl disillusioned with the low-church Puritanism to which she was accustomed. She told a friend in later years that if she hadn't been inspired by the 'invigorating vision' of *Orthodoxy*, she might in her schooldays have given up Christianity altogether.[53] In 1952 she wrote of her debt to Chesterton: 'To the young people of my generation. G. K. C. was a kind of Christian liberator. Like a beneficent bomb, he blew out of the Church a quantity of stained glass of a very poor period, and let in gusts of fresh air in which the dead leaves of doctrine danced with all the energy and indecorum of Our Lady's Tumbler.'[54]

Another writer who was affected profoundly by *Orthodoxy* was Theodore Maynard: 'There was, however, one book which deeply impressed me . . . This was Chesterton's *Orthodoxy*. It still seems to me a most extraordinary work and it sank deeply into my mind . . . Chesterton did not himself enter the Church until thirteen years later . . . long before that he had made a Catholic of me.'[55]

The publication of *Orthodoxy* led many to change the way they viewed the young, precocious writer. He was now provocative and controversial in a way which was a threat to the agnostic *status quo*. Chesterton was acutely aware of this change of attitude:

> Very nearly everybody, in the ordinary literary and journalistic world, began by taking it for granted that my faith in the Christian creed was a pose or a paradox. The more cynical supposed that it was only a stunt. The more generous and loyal warmly maintained that it was only a joke. It was not until long afterwards that the full horror of the truth burst upon them; the disgraceful truth that I really thought the thing was true. And I have found, as I say, that this represents a real transition or border-line in the life of the apologists. Critics were almost entirely complimentary to what they were pleased to call my brilliant paradoxes; *until* they discovered that I really meant

what I said. Since then they have been more combative; and I do not blame them.[56]

Orthodoxy brought to a conclusion the transition which began with the publication of *Heretics* three years earlier. The jolly journalist had become the Christian controversialist. The Omniscient Babe had become the Babe-in-Arms.

« 8 »

Uncle Chestnut

IN THE SUMMER OF 1909 Gilbert and Frances moved from Battersea to the small town of Beaconsfield, twenty-five miles west of London.[1] Here they would spend the rest of their lives. Their first home was a small house known as Overroads, but some years later they bought the land adjacent to it, upon which they built Top Meadow, a larger house which would be their permanent home thereafter.

It appears that the decision to move was made principally at Frances's behest. She was in poor health and desperate to escape the hustle and bustle of London. Her state of mind and body at the time of the move is apparent from a letter Gilbert wrote to Father O'Connor on 3 July:

> I would not write this to anyone else, but you combine so unusually in your own single personality the characters of 1. priest, 2. human being, 3. man of the world, 4. man of the other world, 5. man of science, 6. old friend, 7. new friend, not to mention Irishman and picture dealer, that I don't mind suggesting the truth to you. Frances has just come out of what looked bad enough to be an illness, and is just going to plunge into one of her recurrent problems of pain and depressions. The two may be a bit too much for her and I want to be with her every night for a few days – there's an Irish Bull for you!
>
> One of the mysteries of Marriage (which must be a Sacrament and an extraordinary one too) is that a man evidently useless like me can yet become at certain instants indispensable. And the further oddity (which I invite you to explain on mystical grounds) is that he never feels so small as when he knows that he is necessary.[2]

Frances's bouts of depression were nothing new, as she had suffered prolonged periods of anxiety following the tragic deaths of her sister and brother. None the less the cause of the black moods in 1909 was not so obvious. Certainly she was in a great deal of physical pain, due to the curvature of the spine from which she had long suffered, and perhaps her anxiety to leave London had also contributed to a general feeling of dejection. There was, however, one other possible explanation. Frances and Gilbert had always cherished the prospect of starting a family, but their efforts hadn't borne fruit. Eventually it was decided that Frances should have an operation to enable her to have children. The operation was unsuccessful, and the couple were burdened with the sobering fact that they would never have a family of their own. The period of convalescence following the operation was recalled by Frances's doctor:

> I received a telephone call from the matron of the nursing home in which Mrs Chesterton was staying, suggesting that I should come round and remonstrate with Mr Chesterton. On my arrival I found him sitting on the stairs, where he had been for two hours, greatly incommoding passers up and down and deaf to all requests to move. It appeared that he had written a sonnet to his wife on her recovery from the operation and was bringing it to give her. He was not however satisfied with the last line, but was determined to perfect it before entering her room to take tea with her.[3]

This amusing anecdote aside, the failure of the operation was a great blow and Frances found it difficult to come to terms with the awful reality. For instance, when a friend, Mrs Saxon Mills, told her she was expecting her second baby, Frances confessed that it was some days before she could make up her mind to see her again. Similarly, when her sister visited Frances with her first child she admitted that she could hardly bear it. Many years later she would confess her deepest regret to one of her husband's secretaries: 'I wanted to have seven beautiful children.'[4]

By the time she and Gilbert finally left London Frances was learning to accept that her dreams of children would not come true. Instead she sought solace, and found security, in the creation of a home in Beaconsfield, building a nest even if there were to be no nestlings. From this sound base any remnants of bitterness evaporated and soon other people's children were enlivening the home. In fact, Gilbert and Frances positively welcomed youngsters into their new home, preferring the company of the children to that of their parents. For example, all adults were excluded from the

Christmas parties held by the Chestertons at Overroads and, in the absence of nurses or parents, the children would hang on Gilbert's neck in anarchic affection. Meanwhile, in an effort to restore some method to the madness, he and Frances devised endless games for them. A favourite party pastime was the toy theatre Gilbert created by cutting out and painting figures and scenery. He devised many plots for the plays, two of the most popular being 'St George and the Dragon' and 'The Seven Champions of Christendom', and he frankly admitted that he got as much pleasure from playing with the theatre as did the children. This is borne out by the reminiscences of Eleanor Jebb, Belloc's daughter, who remembered Gilbert 'making his puppets come to life for us in the nursery, sitting perilously on a chair far too small for his vast form and rumbling out romances and feuds, at which he laughed almost more than we did'.[5] Eleanor Jebb also nurtured fond childhood memories of Frances, who 'had a deep tenderness of heart for children and a great understanding of them. She gave me the first carnation I had ever seen – it was in her buttonhole – and I carry the undimmed magic of its scent and beauty to this day. It had to be left for the night when I was put to bed – but I only parted from it having seen it safely in a cup of water and put in the doll's house.'[6]

Chesterton's relationship with children throughout his life was summed up by Ronald Knox:

> To be sure there was always a childlike element in his character. I like the story of a small guest at a children's party in Beaconsfield, who was asked when he got home whether Mr Chesterton had been very clever. 'I don't know about clever,' was the reply, 'but you should see him catch buns in his mouf.' He did not, like many grown-ups who are reputedly 'fond of children', exploit the simplicity of childhood for his own amusement. He entered, with tremendous gravity, into the tremendous gravity of the child.'[7]

This childlike element in his character was evident during an episode in Beaconsfield involving the doctor's son. The little boy was observed by Chesterton running along the top of a wall, his nurse threatening punishment if he didn't get down that minute. Chesterton looked at the boy and told him that 'this wall is meant for little boys to run along'.[8] Similarly, there is a story of Chesterton with a slipper in hand demanding of Frances that the children be allowed to stay up late, slapping the slipper on the table, much to the children's delight, and saying, 'You see, I am putting my foot down.'[9] There are numerous other anecdotes. Peter Oldershaw, the son of Frances's sister and Gilbert's schoolfriend, called Chesterton 'the Big Uncle' who roared and padded about like a lion. When Peter was sick 'the Big Uncle' sent postcards with a special poem and a serialised weekly story about a boy who pulled a rope and found a bear tied to the end of it. All of the children remembered that their 'uncle' never acted as if they were smaller or less important than he.

Perhaps the best picture of life in Beaconsfield at this time is given in an article Chesterton wrote for the *Daily News* in 1910:

A monstrously lazy man lives in South Bucks partly by writing a column in the Saturday *Daily News*. At the time he usually writes it (which is always at the last moment) his house is unexpectedly invaded by infants of all shapes and sizes. His secretary is called away; and he has to cope with the invading pygmies. Playing with children is a glorious thing; but the journalist in question has never understood why it is considered a soothing or idyllic one. It reminds him, not of watering little budding flowers, but of wrestling for hours with gigantic angels and devils.

Moral problems of the most monstrous complexity besiege him incessantly. He has to decide before the awful eyes of innocence, whether, when a sister has knocked down a brother's bricks, in revenge for the brother having taken two sweets out of his turn, it is endurable that the brother should retaliate by scribbling on the sister's picture book, and whether such conduct does not justify the sister in blowing out the brother's unlawfully lighted match. Just as he is solving this problem upon principles of the highest morality, it occurs to him suddenly that he has not written his Saturday article; and that there is only about an hour to do it in. He wildly calls to somebody (probably the gardener) to telephone to somewhere for a messenger; he barricades himself in another room and tears his hair, wondering what on earth he shall write about . . .

He sits down desperately; the messenger rings at the bell; the children drum on the door; the servants run up from time to time to say the messenger is getting bored; and the pencil staggers along, making the world a present of fifteen hundred unimportant words. Then the journalist sends off his copy and turns his attention to the enigma of whether a brother should commandeer a sister's necklace because the sister pinched him at Littlehampton. That is how an article is really written.[10]

As well as offering a candid view through the keyhole at Overroads, the article displays Chesterton's love affair with children. It was a love affair that lasted the whole of his life, always one between equals. An affirmation of this equality was inscribed in a picture book he gave to a young child:

> This is the sort of book we like
> (For you and I are very small),
> With pictures stuck in anyhow,
> And hardly any words at all.
>
> You will not understand a word
> Of all the words, including mine;
> Never you trouble; you can see,
> And all directness is divine –
>
> Stand up and keep your childishness:
> Read all the pedants' screeds and strictures;
> But don't believe in anything
> That can't be told in coloured pictures.[11]

Nicolas Bentley recalled that he enjoyed Chesterton's company when he was a small boy because Gilbert treated him

> as though the difference in our ages was the only difference between us. It was not, as is sometimes cosily and fallaciously supposed, that he became like a small boy, but that he made small boys feel that they had become men. I could not have understood very much of 'Lepanto' when he recited it to me one afternoon in the garden (I must have been about eight or nine at the time), but the fact that mine was the ear he had chosen, as much as the flashing and reverberating words of 'Lepanto' itself, impressed and excited me . . .
> He was never in the least didactic, never patronising, and consequently one never felt, as small boys can so easily be made to feel, guilty of being a fool or ashamed of one's ignorance.'[12]

Small girls were equally privileged. Grace, the daughter of Mrs Saxon Mills, remembered how Chesterton used to sit her on his knee and recite poetry: 'When I was alone with him I felt I was an important person worth talking to.'[13]

Dorothy Fagan, being slightly older than most of the other children who stayed with the Chestertons in Beaconsfield, was often put in charge of the younger visitors: 'My memory of G. K. C. is not as a great man – I was not in a position to judge him as that – but as one of the kindest humans it was my fortune to meet.'[14] She remembered many specific examples of his kindness, such as the day her cat had to be destroyed. On that occasion, blinded by tears, she suddenly realised with dismay that she had inadvertently got into a railway carriage which Gilbert and Frances had to themselves. Gilbert seemed very busy with masses of papers and she felt embarrassed and apologetic. But they both welcomed her, and Gilbert, 'stuffing the papers underneath him', began to talk about cats through the ages 'right down from the Egyptian dynasties. I didn't have to say a word, and it was so interesting I soon stopped crying.'[15]

Another young female visitor, Patricia Burke, remembered how Chesterton helped her overcome the fear of thunderstorms. He took 'immense pains' to reassure her that she was safe and told her to make the sign of the Cross when a clap or a flash startled her.[16] (Since Gilbert was not a Catholic at this time it is perhaps surprising that he should give such advice. Yet the extent of his latent Catholicism was exhibited by the fact that he drew pictures of the patron saints of many of the children on their respective birthdays. Drawings of St Michael, St Joan, St Cecilia, St Clare and St Patrick were presented to their namesakes as birthday gifts.)

All the children who stayed at Beaconsfield retained vivid memories of the two dogs, Winkle and his successor Quoodle, whom Gilbert would surreptitiously feed during meals until Frances called a halt. This was the cue for Gilbert to fix his eyes on Quoodle, who in turn would fix his mournful Scottie eyes on him. At this point Gilbert recited the words:

> No more, no more, no more!
> Such language holds the solemn sea,
> The sands upon the shore shall bloom
> The thunder-blasted tree
> Or the stricken eagle soar
> – No more, old man, no more.

At the last 'no more' Quoodle would bow his head and slink under the table.[17]

If Chesterton's chastisement of his pets was so light-hearted and mild, it is scarcely surprising that the children were never seriously scolded. There was, however, a notable exception. On one occasion a small visitor to Beaconsfield spoke rudely to the maid and Chesterton told her to apologise. The child retorted: 'What does it matter? She's only a servant.' Gilbert responded in rare wrath and sent the girl up to her bedroom. It was, according to Frances, the only time Gilbert ever punished a child.[18]

While it pained Chesterton to reprimand his young friends, it gave him pleasure to see them grow and develop. In particular, he took a great interest in their education. Felicity Walpole remembered his invaluable role as an educator who helped open her mind to history and great literature: 'I asked him what "panache" meant, and he told me the whole story of Cyrano with immense chunks of quotation.' Another time they spoke of the medieval theory of love and he introduced her to the *Morte d'Arthur* by reciting the death of Lancelot. He also introduced her to Chaucer by presenting her with a copy of his own biography of him. It contained a characteristic inscription:

CHAUCER
as clumsily, ramblingly and irrelevantly rendered in this
patchy and partly unreadable book, is introduced to
FELICITY
who could doubtless express the same views with very much
greater
FELICITY.[19]

On another occasion Felicity asked Chesterton a question about a medieval picture of St Augustine on the seashore. He told her the story of the great philosopher strolling on the beach meditating on the mystery of the Holy Trinity. Suddenly the saint saw a small boy scooping water from the sea and pouring it into a hole. Upon asking the child to explain what he was doing, St Augustine received the reply that he was putting the sea into the hole in the sand. The saint smiled at the sight of the vast sea and the small hole and the child said to him: 'As easy to put the sea into a hole as the mystery of the infinite God into a human mind.'

The children to whom the Chestertons formed the closest attachment, perhaps, were five sisters – Clare, Dorothy, Cecilia, Joan and Barbara Nicholl. Maisie Ward referred to the Nicholl family as Chesterton's 'last family' because he didn't meet them until 1927. From then until his death a decade later they were an integral part of his life.

The story of the first meeting with the Nicholl sisters is especially interesting. During a holiday in the West Country Frances and Gilbert intended to stay in Lyme Regis for two nights before moving on. In the event they stayed for two weeks and returned again the two following summers. The chain of events which led to their change of plan began when they spied two little girls gazing into a toyshop window, their noses glued to the glass. The Chestertons overheard them ardently discussing which toys they wanted and whether they had enough money to make a purchase. Alas, the money was short and dejectedly they turned away.

'Could we offer them half-a-crown to make it up?' Gilbert suggested.

'They look such well-brought-up little girls, their mother might not like it.'

Meanwhile the children had spotted the Chestertons and rushed home excitedly to their older sister.

'Clare, we've seen the man you like so much. You taught us about him in literature.'

Clare had been an admirer of Chesterton for a long time. Years before, as a young child, she had read *The Blue Cross* and had said to herself: 'One day I must know this Mr Chesterton. He is the friend I have always been looking for.' Indeed, only moments before her sisters had rushed in excitedly she had been reading him again and had closed the book on the sentence 'When the chord of monotony is stretched at its tightest, it breaks with the sound of a song.'

Scarcely able to believe what her sisters were saying, and wondering whether dreams really do come true, she grabbed Barbara's hand and informed her mother that they were going to ask Mr Chesterton to tea.

They entered the lounge of the Three Cups hotel where the younger sisters thought he was staying and, sure enough, they saw him sitting there, but their courage failed and they returned home empty-handed. Clare then wrote a note asking Chesterton if he knew he was the reincarnation of Shakespeare, assuring him that the family were neither tourists nor autograph-hunters – and would he *please* come to tea? Returning to the hotel, they sent up the note and waited in the hall for an answer.

They remembered Gilbert's grey-trousered legs appearing first on the stairs, looking like the front-quarters of a particularly large and friendly elephant. In no time he was shaking hands with them: 'Am I really the ghost of Shakespeare? And may we come to tea?'[20]

This was the beginning of a flourishing friendship and soon it was the turn of the Chestertons to invite the Nicholls to tea. On that occasion Gilbert solemnly presented a poem to Barbara and Dorothy to thank them for coming:

> Saint Nicholas Patron of Nicholls
> And also of Children and Thieves
> (For he burgles our houses at Christmas
> As every good Christian believes).
>
> But he comes not to take but to give,
> And his Nicholls are even as he:
> For they bring us the Wine of their Youth in exchange
> For a chemical puddle called Tea.[21]

Dorothy Nicholl remembered an occasion when Chesterton called while she was the only person at home. Being a shy girl she could not bring herself to answer the bell:

> I saw him coming to the door and I heard the bell ring several times. In a panic of shyness I hid behind the curtain. Then I watched him go down the path and out at the gate. Suddenly I felt horribly sad and ashamed. I ran up the road after him, and when I caught up with him I told him that I had been there all the time and how sorry I was and I asked him to come back and have tea and macaroons with me. He was so sweet to me and I never forgot how he looked. He put his hand on my shoulder with his big characteristic gesture and said, 'That *would* be jolly,' as if it was the one thing he really felt like doing! I never felt shy of him again.'[22]

Visits to Lyme Regis eventually became unnecessary because the Nicholl family moved to Beaconsfield – and not only to Beaconsfield but to Christmas Cottage in the very same road as Top Meadow. After this the intercourse became almost daily. One sister or another would call at Top Meadow and Gilbert and Frances would sometimes eat Sunday supper at Christmas Cottage. And presently another generation of Nicholls was added when the girls' only brother, who was older than any of his sisters, brought home Bernard, their first nephew. Little Bernard didn't live at Christmas Cottage but on his visits he would inform his grandmother, 'I'll be off to Top Meadow now, Granny, to see my Uncle Chestnut.'[23]

Gilbert missed the sisters whenever they were away from home. In particular, he missed them one Christmas when the Nicholl family went to spend the festivities with relatives in Bournemouth. Upon their return they were greeted with 'A Curse in Free Verse', which begins:

> I CURSE PARADOX –
> I curse the contradictory inconsistencies of the Modern Mind:
> I curse and curse and curse . . .

and ends, after a list of those inconsistencies:

> But what are all these aversions . . .?
> Compared with the blighting blistering horror and hatred
> With which I regard
> THOSE WHO CALL THEIR HOUSE CHRISTMAS COTTAGE
> AND THEN GO AWAY FROM IT AT CHRISTMAS?[24]

These lines were obviously written in jest, and the mock malice is only an instrument of mirth. Yet if Chesterton was incapable of real malice, he was, on occasion, capable of anger. According to Clare Nicholl, 'unkindness or uncharitable gossip were the things that made him angry, as well as speciousness or cheap "cleverness".' Nor, she continued,

> did personal affection for the sinner in question prevent him showing his anger – on the contrary, the closer the affection the more severe the rebuke. He very rarely found fault openly, but the offender would know by his silence and sudden lack of response that she had transgressed. One's thoughtless words would sound against the silence of G. K. C. like counterfeit coin against a touchstone. It was infallible as a test of integrity. Even unconscious lapses of taste were illumined by that silence. One would think, 'Now why on earth should he object to that . . .' and, thinking it over afterwards, one would realise that the rash remark had been prompted by exhibitionism, vanity or malice, though one had not realised it at the moment of speaking.'[25]

It is clear from this reminiscence that the relationship by this stage was no longer one of adult and child but of older adult and younger adult. The Nicholl sisters were growing into women before Gilbert's eyes and he recorded the fact poetically:

> Rejoice all nations under the sun;
> Their bishops dance, their aged statesmen run,
> Paint the world red and think it frightful fun
> That Barbara, Barbara is Twenty-One.
> > But the Crier is crying
> > In Lyme of the King
> > Lost, Stolen or Strayed
> > Is the Marvellous Thing.
> I will ring for the sea-gulls
> That dance in the spray
> But the girls that go dancing
> > Go dancing away,
> The girls that go dancing,
> > Go dancing
> > go dancing,
> The girls that go dancing
> > Go dancing away.[26]

Of course, the 'Marvellous Thing' which has been lost or stolen is childhood, and there is certainly a hint of regret and an element of lament in the poem. Yet there is also real rejoicing at his young friend's coming of age. In this attitude to the evolution from childhood to adulthood via adolescence a notable difference existed between Frances and Gilbert. Frances loved the joy and innocence of childhood but found the trials and tribulations of adolescence a problem. Felicity Walpole made the following observation about Frances: 'She loved us dearly when we were small. And she loved us again if we got married and had babies of our own. But she didn't understand the time when young people get rebellious. It frightened her.'[27] Gilbert, on the other hand, was far more sympathetic to his young friends as they groped their way towards adulthood. The difference between Gilbert and Frances was typified by their respective attitudes to a young cousin who had managed to get hold of a dilapidated car and was always having difficulties with it. As far as Frances was concerned he shouldn't have been allowed to drive until he had learned to mend a puncture, to which Gilbert responded that one might as well say that no one should ride a horse unless he is a vet.[28]

If anything, Chesterton seemed to understand his friends better when they were adolescents than when they were children. After all, his own soul had been in ferment when he was their age. Joan Nicholl remembered that Gilbert was the only one who understood Clare because 'she is less obvious and easy to understand than the rest of us'.[29] This observation was confirmed by Clare herself: 'Our friendship with G.K. was the daily bread of life: he made one feel at home in the world and he himself was like a huge comfortable house with great windows opening on to vistas and letting in the daylight ... For us he belongs (it is impossible to think of him in the past tense) not to the limelight, but to the firelight.'[30] Barbara Nicholl echoed the sentiments of her sister: 'I shall never be grateful enough for knowing him. It is not only what he did and meant at the time, but what he meant later, remembering it in a more grown-up way.' She recalled how he had helped her during a period of loneliness and moral difficulty:

> One of the things I loved and honoured most in him and one of the things which made me feel 'exalted' and 'humbled' together, as in the *Magnificat*, was his *deep* chivalry and honour of women. And one felt and knew that it was based on no whimsy and namby-pamby ideas of colourless innocence and lack of temptation, but on the contrary on a very profound and understanding experience. I remember being terribly worried soon after I came to France by the reasoning of many of the young men I met, who were perfectly sincere themselves and who argued that love was good and beautiful in itself – so why be so selfish? Why think so much of oneself as though one was too precious to touch? Why not be entirely generous? etc. etc. With lots of this, part of me agreed, and in any case I found my arguments sounding very narrow, dry and difficult. One day when I was alone with Unclet at Top Meadow I managed, in a very incoherent way, to come out with some of this. He was moved, like he always was, over a genuine trouble, and I remember at the moment he wasn't *very* much more coherent than I. He patted my hand and rumbled, 'My dear, don't let them bother you.' But the next day a poem arrived, putting, as I think he did in verse, even more than in prose, everything in a nutshell; and giving that wonderful feeling of blessedness.[31]

Other young friends were suffering from similar spiritual growing pains. Rhoda Bastable, for instance, expressed to him her fear that she was a hypocrite. He wrote:

My Dear Rhoda,

Hypocrites do not call themselves hypocrites. The very fact that you use such a word about yourself proves that you do not deserve it . . .

Simply do not think at all about the misunderstandings of people, who think you a saint or a hypocrite. Think about your old friends – who know you are neither. Friends are facts; and the good things you have done to them are facts . . . So cheer up till we all meet; for I will say only one more thing now. You speak of Faith: that also is a fact and, believe me, it refers to facts. I can think at least as well as most who will tell you to the contrary: and I doubt if there is a doubt anywhere I have not entertained, examined and dismissed. I believe in God the Father Almighty, Maker of Heaven and Earth and in the other extraordinary things in the same statement. I believe them more, the more I see of human experience. And when I say, 'God bless you, my dear girl,' I have no more doubt of Him than of you.[32]

This resolute defence of the Faith in the face of adolescent doubt was echoed in another incident. When one of the Nicholl sisters expressed the fear that the Faith may be nothing but a fable his response was instant: 'You may be perfectly sure that if anything can get *me* out of bed five minutes before I need to get up, there is certainly something in it.'[33]

However, he was equally able to urge caution as to offer comfort. For instance, one of his most interesting and perceptive letters was written to a girl intending to try her vocation in a convent:

If you are really For It (I use, not without justice, the jovial phrase commonly used about people going to be jailed or flogged or hanged) – if you are For It, it is the grandest and most glorious and deific thing that any human being can be For. It is far beyond my imagination. But never, for one instant, among all my sins, have I doubted that it was *above* my imagination. I have no more doubt that a man like Father McNabb is walking on a crystal floor over my head than I have that Quoodle has a larger equipment of legs than I have: and (with all respect to his many virtues) a rather simpler intellectual plan of life. If that is your Way Out, then everybody must stand out of your Way, as out of the way of a Celestial Fire-Engine. If one of my friends is caught up to Heaven in a fiery chariot – you will not think me capable of being a stout and stolid speed-Cop or Traffic Policeman to hold her up for enquiries. No: that is unanswerable. If that is so, nobody has a right to say anything except – 'God will love you even more than we do.'

But – there is still one little worrying thought left in the dregs of what I call my mind. You will be generous enough to forgive if the hesitation sounds personal. [My friend] I have often hailed as she rushed by: but I have met her rushing *from* places as well as to places. If you must rush, this is a place you must rush to and cannot rush from. I don't mean any material nonsense of the Walled-Up Nun – I mean that you yourself could not go from something greater to anything less great. Now you do have black fits, don't you? Reactions – scruples and the rest. What I want you to be quite clear about (I expect you are and grovel again) is that if you have one of those black reactions *after* this, it may do you what Professor Bobsky would call psychological harm, and those who talk English would call spiritual harm. It doesn't matter if you get tired of the Middlesex Mummies Exploration Fund and rush to the East Ealing Ethical Dance Movement – because we all live in that world and laugh at it and earn our living in it. But if you have a reaction from this greater thing – you will feel quite differently. You may be in danger of religious melancholia: for you will say 'I have had the Best and it did not help.' Anyhow you may be hurt . . . and I hate your being hurt.

Reassure me on this one point and I am absolutely with you – if I am worthy to say so. Let me know (by a Wink or any recognised ritual) that you see what I mean, and have allowed for it, and I am at once a Trappist. Not your nearest and dearest – let alone a dubious acquaintance – have a right to speak. It is only in God that we all love each other.[34]

It is easy to perceive the ways in which young people benefited from Chesterton's wisdom; in return he clearly enjoyed 'the wine of their youth' and derived enormous pleasure from their friendship.

Bernard Nicholl was ten years old when he was told of Chesterton's death. Upon hearing the news he was silent for a moment, then he said: 'I will always be lonely for him. Do you know, I think my Uncle Chestnut was not quite so fat as he pretended to be.'[35] To Clare Nicholl, Bernard's aunt, who was a young woman when her 'Unclet' died, we have seen that Gilbert was 'like a huge comfortable house with great windows opening on to vistas and letting in the daylight'. One suspects that Chesterton would prefer these two tributes as a memorial to his name to any of the obituaries written by 'adults'. One also suspects that he was happier being Uncle Chestnut than he was being anything else.

The Chestershaw

If THE MOVE TO Beaconsfield in the summer of 1909 marked an important personal milestone for Chesterton, a major publishing milestone was reached at the same time. During the third week of August his biography of Bernard Shaw was published, a book which was more a critical appraisal of Shaw's work than a chronological account of his life. Its publication gave Chesterton an opportunity to state his case against Shaw and, paradoxically, served as his greatest tribute to the man who had been his main adversary in the preceding five years. The key to the paradox is found in Chesterton's *Autobiography* when he differentiates between intellectual enmity and personal friendship:

> My principal experience, from first to last, has been in argument with him. And it is worth remarking that I have learned to have a warmer admiration and affection out of all that argument than most people get out of agreement. Bernard Shaw, unlike some whom I have had to consider here, is seen at his best when he is antagonistic, I might say that he is seen at his best when he is wrong. I might also add that he generally is wrong. Or rather, everything is wrong about him except himself.[1]

The same point was put poignantly in a magazine article in 1912: 'I believe I have two true affections – one for truth, and the other for Mr Shaw. I follow truth with reluctance.'[2]

In spite of the hyperbolical nature of this statement there was always an affectionate warmth in their relationship which defied the intellectual antagonism. They were friends as well as enemies and each gained immensely from both the friendship and the enmity. Maisie Ward writes:

I don't think the country has appreciated sufficiently how much G. K. C. and G. B. S. contrived to make one another. Their natural opposition helped largely to make their separate reputations and their perpetual watchfulness helped to define the limits of each. Until G. K. C. turned up G. B. S. had the world of controversy to himself. But as soon as G. K. stepped into the ring he had to watch his step in a new way and make the most of his ring-craft. G. K. could always get through the old man's guard; and that made it especially exciting when they met either on the platform or in the pages of *G. K.'s Weekly* or the *New Witness*.[3]

She quotes a journalist from the *New York Times* stating that 'the main meaning of Chesterton's life, aside from the religious meaning, is to be found in the running debate . . . with George Bernard Shaw'.[4]

It is appropriate that Mrs Ward employs the imagery of the boxing or wrestling ring in her description of Shaw's relationship with Chesterton since the two, locked in perpetual combat, often merge in the mind's eye into a unified, if struggling, whole. The fact that many people perceived Chesterton and Shaw synonymously, even though their views differed profoundly, was not lost on Chesterton. Many years later he wrote with wry amusement of their relationship:

Wherever I wandered in the United States people leapt out upon me from holes and hedges with the question pointed like a pistol, with all the promptitude of a gun in the hand of a gunman: 'How is Bernard Shaw?' It is not surprising that they should be interested in Bernard Shaw; so are we all, however much we disagree with him . . . what is extraordinary is that they should be so intensely interested in me in connection with Bernard Shaw. They seem to suppose that I am his brother or his keeper; though I admit that, if we travelled together, there might be a dispute among the schools as to which was the keeper and which the lunatic . . . By this time I am driven to go about declaring that I am Bernard Shaw; the difference is a mere matter of two disguises: of alternative cushions and a beard.[5]

There can be little doubt that Chesterton had Shaw's article on the Chesterbelloc in mind when he wrote this. His claim that he and Shaw were really one and the same person bears a striking similarity to Shaw's earlier claim that Chesterton and Belloc made up two halves of the same pantomime elephant. However, Shaw's invention of the Chesterbelloc was based on the striking similarity of the two halves, Chesterton and Belloc being united in their attitude to most of the intellectual issues of the day. Shaw and Chesterton, on the other hand, had nothing in common. Shaw was a vegetarian; Chesterton championed the carnivore. Shaw was a teetotaller; Chesterton relished wine and beer. Shaw believed that man had created God; Chesterton that God had created man. Shaw was a socialist who believed in abolishing private property in favour of common ownership; Chesterton was a distributist who believed in abolishing common ownership in favour of genuine private property. Yet, in spite of this, people persisted in seeing them as one. In May 1909, three months before the publication of Chesterton's book on Shaw, Max Beerbohm, a friend of both men, drew a caricature of the two in profile facing each other, one fat, the other thin, entitled 'Leaders of Thought'. Indeed, if the mythical Chestershaw can be imagined at all, it would bear a remarkable resemblance to the Pushmi-Pullyu in *The Story of Doctor Dolittle* by Hugh Lofting. This creature, described as 'the rarest animal of all', had one body but two heads pointing in opposite directions, a unique feature which prompted an obvious question: '"Lord save us!" cried the duck. "How does it make up its mind?"' The Chestershaw, unable to make up its collective mind, was able to make up both its individual minds through the process of arguing with itself.

The roots of their relationship stretched back to the turn of the century. Obviously, Chesterton was aware of Shaw long before Shaw became aware of him, since the Irishman enjoyed a considerable reputation as both playwright and critic years before Chesterton's literary career had even begun. However, Shaw was impressed with an article on Sir Walter Scott written by Chesterton on 10 August 1901, which convinced him that a new talent in the field of literary criticism had emerged:

> I cannot remember when I first met Chesterton. I was so much struck by a review of Scott's *Ivanhoe* which he wrote for the *Daily News* in the course of his earliest notable job as feuilletonist to that paper that I wrote to him asking who he was and where he came from, as he was evidently a new star in literature. He was either too shy or too lazy to answer. The next thing I remember is his lunching with us on quite intimate terms, accompanied by Belloc.[6]

In failing to reply to this letter Chesterton inadvertently delayed the commencement of their friendship – perhaps by as much as five years.

It is impossible to date the intimate luncheon referred to by Shaw, and it is not even clear whether this was the first meeting. Lucian Oldershaw, Gilbert's brother-in-law, claimed that he was the first to introduce Chesterton to Shaw at the studio of Rodin in Paris in 1906. The French sculptor was in the process of creating a bust of the Irish playwright; according to Oldershaw, he introduced Gilbert to Shaw during one of the sittings, at which Shaw had been explaining the nature of the Salvation Army to the puzzled sculptor, presumably in relation to his play *Major Barbara*, which had premièred the previous year. According to Rodin's secretary, the Frenchman was less than impressed by his subject's rhetoric, complaining that Shaw's grasp of the French language was poor and that his manner of expression was too imposing. Oldershaw also complained of Shaw's imperious nature on that occasion, stating that he 'talked Chesterton down'.[7]

It is open to debate whether Rodin's studio was the venue for the fated first meeting. It is possible that the intimate luncheon referred to by Shaw predates the meeting in Paris, calling Oldershaw's claim into question, as it seems odd that Shaw should fail to remember the Paris meeting. Alternatively, it is possible that Shaw was barely aware of Chesterton's presence during the sittings because Rodin's studio had taken on the nature of a theatre, with all manner of people dropping in to watch the proceedings. According to Michael Holroyd, Shaw's biographer, an audience assembled every day and 'sat in mesmerised silence as Shaw ("*ce modèle extraordinaire*") collected and concentrated himself and Rodin filled the place with "his raging activity, his gigantic movements", and volleys of unintelligible sound'.[8]

Although an air of mystery continues to shroud the occasion of their first meeting, Chesterton was at loggerheads with Shaw long before they met in the flesh. As early as 1900 he disagreed with him over the controversy surrounding Britain's involvement in the Boer War:

> I began arguing with Mr Bernard Shaw in print almost as early as I began doing anything. It was about my pro-Boer sympathies in the South African War. Those who do not understand what the Fabian political philosophy was may not realise that the leading Fabians were nearly all Imperialists. Mr and Mrs Sidney Webb were in that matter strong Imperialists; Hubert Bland was a still stronger Imperialist; my brother was as strong an Imperialist as Hubert Bland. And even Bernard Shaw, though retaining a certain liberty to chaff everybody, was quite definitely an Imperialist, as compared with myself and my friends the pro-Boers.[9]

In fact, Shaw had broken with the radical Liberals who opposed the Boer War because of what he called 'the inefficiency of leaving stray little States lying about in the way of great powers'.[10]

The difference of opinion with Shaw and the other Fabians over the Boer War bore fruit four years later as the inspiration for *The Napoleon of Notting Hill*:

> All at once I realized how completely lost this bit of Notting Hill was in the modern world. It was asked to be interested in the endowment of a public library in Kamschatka by an American millionaire, or a war between an oil trust and another oil trust in Papua, or the splendid merger of all the grocery interests in Europe and America or the struggles between the brewers and the Prohibitionists to give us worse beer or less beer.
>
> In all these world-shaking events this little bit of Notting Hill was of no account. And that seemed idiotic. For to this bit of Notting Hill the bit was of supreme importance.
>
> In the same instance I saw that my Progressive friends were more bent than any on destroying Notting Hill. Shaw and Wells and the rest of them were interested only in world-shaking and world-making events. When they said, 'Every day in every way better and better,' they meant every day bigger and bigger – in every way . . .
>
> In that half-second of time, gazing with rapt admiration at the row of little shops, nobly flanked by a small pub and a small church, I discovered that not only was I against the plutocrats, I was against the idealists. In the comparatively crystalline air of that romantic village I heard the clear call of a trumpet. And, once for all, I drew my sword – purchased in the old curiosity shop – in defence of Notting Hill.[11]

Neither was it solely in the fields of economics and politics that Chesterton differed with Shaw. On the contrary, Chesterton's first published broadsides levelled at Shaw, published in the *Daily News* in April 1905, were on the subject of Shakespeare. Shaw had criticised Shakespeare, implying that he was overrated, and Chesterton had rallied to the Bard's defence:

> The fault of Mr Shaw as a philosopher or a critic of life . . . is altogether on the side of being too grave, too stern, too fanatical, too unbending and austere. Mr Bernard Shaw is too serious to enjoy Shakespeare. Mr Bernard Shaw is too serious properly to enjoy life. Both these things are illogical where he is logical, chaotic where he

is orderly, mystical where he is clear. In all the great Elizabethan writers there is present a certain thing which Mr Shaw, with all his astounding abilities, does not really understand – exuberance, an outrageous excess of words, a violent physical pleasure in mere vocabulary, an animal spirit in intellectual things.[12]

The accusation that Shaw was 'too serious' would be a recurring theme in Chesterton's future writing and a central tenet in his case against Shaw in the full-length study of 1909. However, these early differences were nothing compared to the explosion of interest created by the controversy between Chesterton, Shaw, Wells and Belloc in 1908. In this year the differences burst like fireworks in front of an admiring and amused public.

The controversy was conducted in the pages of the *New Age*, a radical journal edited by Alfred Orage. The curtain-raiser was provided by Belloc, who wrote an article entitled 'Thoughts about Modern Thought', which was followed by Chesterton's 'Why I am not a Socialist' in the edition of 4 January. A week later Wells responded with an article, 'About Chesterton and Belloc', to which Chesterton replied with an essay entitled 'On Wells and a Glass of Beer'. A further contribution by Belloc was followed on 15 February by Shaw's first foray into the fray. His article, 'The Chesterbelloc: a Lampoon', is seen by posterity as the most memorable of the articles in the series, and it is certainly an example of Shaw at his wittiest and best. His creation of the Chesterbelloc formed an image of Belloc and Chesterton in the mind of the public which neither was ever able to shake off, if indeed they ever desired to do so. Shaw concluded his article with an invitation to Chesterton to reply:

> And now, what has the Chesterbelloc (or either of its two pairs of legs) to say in its defence? But it is from the hind legs that I particularly want to hear: because South Salford will very soon cure Hilaire Forelegs of his fancy for the ideals of the Catholic peasant proprietor. He is up against his problems in Parliament: it is in Battersea Park that a great force is in danger of being wasted.[13]

Chesterton's reply to Shaw, 'The Last of the Rationalists', appeared two weeks later, on 29 February:

> I have just seen Bernard Shaw's very jolly article and I hope you will allow me to reply. I have reluctantly come to the conclusion that

Belloc and I must be horribly fascinating men. We never suspected it ourselves; but I have been forced to the belief by the discussion in the *New Age*. We offered certain objections to Socialism. We were honoured by being answered, not only by the two most brilliant Socialists alive, but by the two most brilliant writers alive, who both happen to be Socialists. Bernard Shaw and H. G. Wells undertook to reply to us about Socialism. They both forgot to say anything whatever about Socialism, but they insisted on talking (with the utmost humour and luxuriance) about us. The fact can be tested by anyone who cares to look up the file of this paper and compare the articles. My article may have been vague and mystical, but it was about Socialism; Wells's article was about me. Belloc's article may have been harsh or academic, but it was about Socialism; Shaw's article was about Belloc.[14]

Following this somewhat defensive introduction, Chesterton moved on to the attack. On this occasion the subject was not socialism but the doctrine of Miracles which Shaw had attacked in his previous article:

The plain fact is that Shaw does not know what the Catholic doctrine of Miracles is; but he has (to his eternal glory) almost discovered it for himself. He has toiled and panted in the train of the Catholic doctrine of Miracles; and whenever he picked up a piece of it, he was hugely and legitimately proud. The Catholic doctrine of Miracles is this. That the highest power in the universe is not (as the Materialists say) Law: the highest power in the universe is Will, the will of God which is Good Will. Akin to this, though much weaker, is the will of man. There is also in the universe another element of routine and law; but Will, being the higher, can overpower law, the lower . . . Now for the last five years Shaw has been preaching this doctrine of the transforming power of will. But it will give him a great shock when he discovers that it is only the Christian doctrine of Miracles: then, very likely, he will drop it like a hot potato.[15]

The controversy continued in the pages of the *New Age* throughout the year. The following month, for instance, Hilaire Belloc penned 'A Question' to which Wells provided 'An Answer'. Neither was the debate confined to the *New Age* but spilled over on to platforms at sundry public meetings. One such debate was held at the Surrey Masonic Hall in Camberwell on 18 November. On that occasion Chesterton and Belloc argued against socialism while Shaw and Cecil Chesterton argued for it.

By this time Chesterton and Shaw had become great friends as well as intellectual enemies, so much so that Chesterton could describe Shaw in 1908 as having 'a heroically large and generous heart; but not a heart in the right place'.[16] An illuminating insight into their relationship was given by Lance Sieveking, one of Chesterton's many godchildren, who had nicknamed his godfather 'Mr Tame Lion':

I was present in my godfather's house when those four giants – Wells, Shaw, Belloc and Chesterton – were shouting, interrupting each other, arguing and laughing . . .

Once, I remember, they argued about the desirability or reverse of personal immortality. Chesterton remarked: 'H. G. suffers from the disadvantage that if he's right he'll never know. He'll only know if he's wrong.' Wells gave an exasperated exclamation, whereupon Belloc said: 'There is something sublimely futile about discussing the desirability or undesirability of the inevitable.' At which Shaw accused Belloc of habitually begging the question and then he trounced Chesterton for consistent evasion of all points at issue in any argument on any subject and then, without letting the other three get a word in, he proceeded to hold forth on immortality, personal, impersonal, metaphorical, mythological and so on and so on and so on. At last, after twenty minutes, he paused and Mr Tame Lion observed to the ceiling: 'That, I suppose, is what is known as putting the whole thing in a nutshell.'[17]

The intellectual combat of 1908 set the scene for Chesterton's *George Bernard Shaw*. Indeed, the high public profile of both the author and the subject of the study, combined with their much publicised differences of opinion, served to whet the appetite of a readership anxious to digest the latest instalment in the continuing war of words. They were not to be disappointed.

Typically, Chesterton began his study epigrammatically, claiming that 'Shaw is like the Venus of Milo; all that there is of him is admirable.'[18] Yet the compliment, though meant charitably, was deliberately barbed and carried the subtle implication that Shaw's sins were those of omission. The rest of the book incisively dissects Shaw to discover what is missing. Thus Chesterton discusses Shaw's Irishness and discovers that he is not as Irish as he seems:

Bernard Shaw is not merely an Irishman; he is not even a typical one. He is a certain separated and peculiar kind of Irishman, which

133

is not easy to describe. Some Nationalist Irishmen have referred to him contemptuously as a 'West Briton'. But this is really unfair; for whatever Mr Shaw's mental faults may be, the easy adoption of an unmeaning phrase like 'Briton' is certainly not one of them. It would be much nearer the truth to put the thing in the bold and bald terms of the old Irish song, and to call him 'The anti-Irish Irishman' . . . This fairly educated and fairly wealthy Protestant wedge which is driven into the country at Dublin and elsewhere is a thing not easy superficially to summarise in any terms. It cannot be described merely as a minority; for a minority means the part of a nation which is conquered. But this thing means something that conquers, and is not entirely part of a nation . . . There is only one word for the minority in Ireland, and that is the word that public phraseology has found; I mean the word 'Garrison'. The Irish are essentially right when they talk as if all Protestant Unionists lived inside 'The Castle'. They have all the virtues and limitations of a literal garrison in a fort. That is, they are valiant, consistent, reliable in an obvious public sense; but their curse is that they can only tread the flagstones of the courtyard or the cold rock of the ramparts; they have never so much as set their foot upon their native soil.[19]

The same point is reiterated later:

All the influences surrounding Bernard Shaw in boyhood were not only Puritan, but such that no non-Puritan force could possibly pierce or counteract. He belonged to that Irish group which, according to Catholicism, has hardened its heart, which, according to Protestantism, has hardened its head, but which, as I fancy, has chiefly hardened its hide, lost its sensibility to the contact of the things around it. In reading about his youth, one forgets that it was passed in the island which is still one flame before the altar of St Peter and St Patrick. The whole thing might be happening in Wimbledon . . . That is the philosophical atmosphere; those are the religious postulates. It could never cross the mind of a man of the Garrison that before becoming an atheist he might stroll into one of the churches of his own country, and learn something of the philosophy that had satisfied Dante and Bossuet, Pascal and Descartes.[20]

Since Chesterton, as ever, failed to allow facts to fog the truth, it is necessary to fill in some of the details of Shaw's ancestry in order to buttress Chesterton's arguments. The family had originally come from Scotland, then moved to England. In 1689 Captain William Shaw sailed from Hampshire to Ireland to fight at the Battle of the Boyne. His reward for rescuing his wounded commander was a large grant of land in Kilkenny. There, as landed gentry, the Shaws lived out lives of exceptional ease, marrying into the families of those who had come to Ireland as part of the Danish, Norman and Cromwellian invasions, all of whom, being of respectable Garrison stock, took their morality, politics and religion from Dublin Castle.

It is worth noting also that Chesterton's views are reflected by Michael Holroyd, Shaw's biographer:

> The Shaws made no secret of being aristocrats. They knew nothing of the middle class. Their aristocracy was a fact of natural history and the unpromiscuous social order of Ireland. No Shaw could form a social acquaintance with a Roman Catholic or tradesman. They lifted up their powerful Wellingtonian noses and spoke of themselves, however querulously, in a collective spirit (as people mentioning the Bourbons or Habsburgs) using the third person: 'the Shaws'.[21]

Chesterton goes further still, drawing psychological conclusions that push his argument to the limit:

> He who has no real country can have no real home. The average autochthonous Irishman is close to patriotism because he is close to the earth; he is close to domesticity because he is close to the earth; he is close to doctrinal theology and elaborate ritual because he is close to the earth. In short, he is close to the heavens because he is close to the earth. But we must not expect any of these elemental and collective virtues in the man of the Garrison. He cannot be expected to exhibit the virtues of a people, but only (as Ibsen would say) of an enemy of the people.[22]

The psychological interrogation intensified as Chesterton probed the reason for Shaw's abhorrence of alcohol. After commenting that Shaw's father was in theory a teetotaller but in practice often a furtive drinker, Chesterton launches into an attack on the puritanical attitude to drink:

> The dipsomaniac and the abstainer are not only both mistaken, but they both make the same mistake. They both regard wine as

a drug and not as a drink . . . it is the whole point of the matter that Bernard Shaw comes of a Puritan middle-class family of the most solid respectability; and the only admission of error arises from the fact that one member of that Puritan family took a particularly Puritan view of strong drink. That is, he regarded it generally as a poison and sometimes as a medicine, if only a mental medicine. But a poison and a medicine are very closely akin, as the nearest chemist knows; and they are chiefly akin in this; that no one will drink either of them for fun. Moreover, a medicine and a poison are also alike in this; that no one will by preference drink either of them in public.[23]

Again, Chesterton's insight into the nature of Shaw's aversion to alcohol can be buttressed by facts which his study overlooked. For example, Shaw's father was by no means the only guilt-ridden alcoholic in the family. Two of his uncles were also alcoholics. His uncle Fred's drinking bouts were so excessive that he suffered from delirium tremens, whereas his uncle Barney was frequently drunk by dawn and lived a largely fuddled life until he was past fifty. 'They avoided observation whilst drinking,' Shaw noted, '. . . [but] their excesses rendered them wretched . . . They all, when well-advanced in life, gave up drinking at once and for ever.'[24] In the light of this experience Shaw wrote, 'I know as much about drink as anybody outside a hospital of inebriates.'[25] It is interesting in the light of Chesterton's comments that Shaw associates drink with a hospital but, confronted with the drinking habits of his family, it is perhaps not surprising.

One particularly tragic incident in his childhood highlights the destructive effects of alcoholism. Observing for the first time that his father's behaviour was somewhat out of the ordinary, the young Shaw whispered his awful discovery into his mother's ear: 'Mama, I think Papa's drunk.' This was too much for his mother, who retorted with disgust: 'When is he ever anything else?' The rash response of his mother had a devastating effect: 'The wrench from my childish faith in my father as perfect and omniscient to the discovery that he was a hypocrite and a dipsomaniac was so sudden and violent that it must have left its mark on me.' Recalling this incident many years later he wrote, 'I have never believed in anything since: then the scoffer began.' Although he subsequently claimed that this had been a 'rhetorical exaggeration', there may have been more truth in it than he cared, or dared, to admit.[26] Either way, he confessed to one of his cousins that 'the least suggestion of drink, however jocular, is deadly to a Shaw. Drink is the biggest skeleton in the family cupboard.'[27]

Following the revelation that his father was 'a hypocrite and a dipsomaniac', Shaw made the sobering discovery that he also lacked a mother's love. He tried to gain his mother's attention and affection but found he could do nothing to interest her. He grew miserable by neglect, confessing that 'she was simply not a wife or mother at all' and, utterly disillusioned, admitted, 'I shall carry traces of that disillusion to the grave.'[28]

One can't help but compare Shaw's wretched childhood with the relative bliss of Chesterton's early years, and conjecture the extent to which their childhoods affected their adult personalities. Perhaps their later attitude to children offers a clue. Compare Chesterton's love for children to Shaw's belief that love was wasted on them because nobody was capable of love until he had earned it.[29] If the latter view seems somewhat hard-hearted, Shaw would no doubt consider it a compliment. He confessed in 1939 that 'fortunately I have a heart of stone: else my relations would have broken it long ago'.[30]

It was inevitable that Chesterton would delve into the realms of child psychology in his efforts to understand Shaw and explain him to his readers. He had always been convinced that the formative years were truly formative, even though they were subject to the freedom of the will to reform them in later years. Yet his study of Shaw was not intended solely, or even primarily, as a biography, but as an assessment of his life and work. In this respect he was surprisingly positive in his approach. For example, he was quick to praise Shaw's artistic and intellectual originality: he 'thoroughly thrashed all competitors in the difficult art of being at once modern and intelligent ... No one ever approximately equalled Bernard Shaw in the power of finding really fresh and personal arguments for these recent schemes and creeds. No one ever came within a mile of him in the knack of actually producing a new argument for a new philosophy.'[31]

Yet originality was not, for Chesterton, a virtue in itself. On the contrary, one of man's first acts of originality, in Chesterton's view, had been the Original Sin. Originality could be destructive:

It would be untrue to say that he was a cynic; he was never a cynic, for that implies a certain corrupt fatigue about human affairs, whereas he was vibrating with virtue and energy. Nor would it be fair to call him even a sceptic, for that implies a dogma of hopelessness and definite belief in unbelief. But it would be strictly just to describe him at this time, at any rate, as a merely destructive person. He was one whose main business was, in his own view, the pricking of illusions, the stripping away of disguises, and even the destruction of ideals. He was a sort of anti-confectioner whose whole business it was to take the gilt off the gingerbread.[32]

It is clear, none the less, that Chesterton preferred the destructiveness of Shaw to the decadence of Wilde or Whistler:

Now when people heard that Bernard Shaw was witty, as he most certainly was, when they heard his *mots* repeated like those of Whistler or Wilde . . . they expected another of these silent sarcastic dandies who went about with one epigram, patient and poisonous, like a bee with his one sting. And when they saw and heard the new humorist they found no fixed sneer, no frockcoat, no green carnation, no silent Savoy Restaurant good manners, no fear of looking a fool, no particular notion of looking a gentleman. They found a talkative Irishman with a kind voice and a brown coat; open gestures and an evident desire to make people really agree with him. He had his own kind of affections no doubt, and his own kind of tricks of debate; but he broke, and, thank God, for ever, the spell of the little man with the single eyeglass who had frozen both faith and fun at so many tea-tables. Shaw's human voice and hearty manner were so obviously more the things of a great man than the hard, gem-like brilliancy of Wilde or the careful ill-temper of Whistler. He brought in a breezier sort of insolence; the single eyeglass fled before the single eye.[33]

Yet the single eye could be singularly blind to the truth and, according to Chesterton, Shaw's criticism of Shakespeare was an example of this:

His misunderstanding of Shakespeare arose largely from the fact that he is a Puritan, while Shakespeare was spiritually a Catholic. The former is always screwing himself up to see the truth; the latter is often content that truth is there. The Puritan is only strong enough to stiffen; the Catholic is strong enough to relax. Shaw, I think, has entirely misunderstood the pessimistic passages of Shakespeare. They are flying moods which a man with a fixed faith can afford to entertain. That all is vanity, that life is dust and love is ashes, these are frivolities, these are jokes that a Catholic can afford to utter. He knows well enough that there is a life that is not dust and a love that is not ashes. But just as he may let himself go more than the Puritan in the matter of enjoyment, so he may let himself go more than the Puritan in the matter of melancholy. The sad exuberances of Hamlet are merely like the glad exuberances of Falstaff. This is not conjecture; it is the text of Shakespeare. In the very act of uttering his pessimism, Hamlet admits that it is a mood and not the truth.[34]

Perhaps, in describing Shakespeare as spiritually a Catholic, Chesterton had fallen into Falstaffian exuberance himself. In fairness, he did offer a tentative apology for calling Shakespeare a Catholic with a big C but maintained he was a catholic with a small one. Either way, the point that Shaw's psychological Puritanism rendered him unable to see the frivolities and humour in the text of Shakespeare was a valid one. Once again Chesterton had returned to his old allegation that Shaw was too serious by half.

Romance was another victim of this Puritanism.

Shaw is wrong about nearly all the things one learns early in life and while one is still simple. Most human beings start with certain facts of psychology to which the rest of life must be somewhat related. For instance, every man falls in love; and no man falls into free love. When he falls into that he calls it lust, and is always ashamed of it even when he boasts of it. That there is a connection between a love and a vow nearly every human being knows before he is eighteen. That there is a solid and instinctive connection between the idea of sexual ecstasy and the idea of some sort of suicidal constancy, this I say is simply the first fact in one's own psychology; boys and girls know it almost before they know their own language. How far it can be trusted, how it can best be dealt with, all that is another matter. But lovers lust after constancy more than after happiness; if you are in any sense prepared to give them what they ask, then what they ask, beyond all question, is an oath of final fidelity.[35]

Chesterton concluded that this flaw in Shaw's psychology was also a fatal flaw in his art: 'For dramatic purposes, G .B. S., even if he despises romance, ought to comprehend it. But then, if once he comprehended romance, he would not despise it.'[36] A practical example of the anti-romantic flaw is given in the discussion of Shaw's play, *Man and Superman*:

In this play . . . woman is made the pursuer and man the pursued. It cannot be denied, I think, that in this matter Shaw is handicapped by his habitual hardness of touch, by his lack of sympathy with the romance of which he writes . . . The result is that while he makes Anne, the woman who marries his hero, a really powerful and convincing woman, he can only do it by making her a highly objectionable woman . . . In short, Bernard Shaw is still haunted with his old impotence of the unromantic writer; he cannot imagine the main motives of human life from the inside. We are convinced successfully that Anne wishes to marry Tanner, but in the very process we lose all power of conceiving why Tanner should ever consent to marry Anne.[37]

The last section of the study deals with Shaw the philosopher:

I must frankly say that Bernard Shaw always seems to me to use the word God not only without any idea of what it means, but without one moment's thought about what it could possibly mean. He said to some atheist, 'Never believe in a God that you cannot improve on.' The atheist (being a sound theologian) naturally replied that one should not believe in a God whom one could improve on; as that would show that he was not God. In the same style in *Major Barbara* the heroine ends by suggesting that she will serve God without personal hope, so that she may owe nothing to God and He owe everything to her. It does not seem to strike her that if God owes everything to her He is not God. These things affect me merely as tedious perversions of a phrase. It is as if you said, 'I will never have a father unless I have begotten him.'[38]

Yet, after the last note of criticism is struck, Chesterton ends as he began – on a positive note:

quite apart from all particular theories, the world owes thanks to Bernard Shaw for having combined being intelligent with being intelligible. He has popularised philosophy, or rather he has re-popularised it, for philosophy is always popular, except in peculiar corrupt and oligarchic ages like our own. We have passed the age of the demagogue, the man who has little to say and says it loud. We have come to the age of the mystagogue or don, the man who has nothing to say, but says it softly and impressively in an indistinct whisper . . .

Against all this mystification both of silence and verbosity Shaw has been a splendid and smashing protest. He has stood up for the fact that philosophy is not the concern of those who pass through Divinity and Greats, but of those who pass through birth and death. Nearly all the most awful and abstruse statements can be put in words of one syllable, from 'A child is born' to 'A soul is damned.' If the ordinary man may not discuss existence, why should he be asked to conduct it? . . .

This plain, pugnacious style of Shaw has greatly clarified all controversies. He has slain the polysyllable, that huge and slimy centipede which has sprawled over all the valleys of England like the 'loathly worm' who was slain by the ancient knight. He does not think that difficult questions will be made simpler by using difficult words about them.[39]

Following the publication of *George Bernard Shaw* the principal question was not so much whether Shaw had slain the polysyllable but whether Chesterton had slain Shaw. The critics, in their role as a self-appointed jury, returned their verdicts. Charles Marriot in the *Manchester Guardian* believed that

Mr Chesterton is the right man, or at least a good man, to size up Mr Shaw. Mr Shaw's is one of the cyclonic kind of talents that charge through their time as an express train tears through small stations, and if your mind be only a piece of straw or an empty paper bag, or is not pulled in some other direction by something else, it leaves all and follows the express until the express drops it a little further on. Mr Chesterton's is a substantial mind, rammed pretty full of hard sense, very slightly disguised by a kind of defiant and skittish bluntness . . . Besides, Mr Chesterton is moored. He is a sworn romantic; he is devout; when he is near it is not safe for thin lucidities and facile false finalities to be about . . . And yet Mr Chesterton's comment is not an attack. He is as generous as anyone now writing, and he feels the comradeship of the generous with all who, whatever their cause, have scorned mean compromises and accommodations and have not fawned on whoever seemed to have success to give.[40]

A review in *Outlook* on 28 August found the book equally praiseworthy:

The opening of this book treats with remarkable brilliancy of the spiritual origins of Bernard Shaw. These three chapters are, in our judgment, the best in a book containing very little that is not good.

Even when the author is betrayed by some lapse of memory into a mistake of fact as to a date, or as to a point of a play which he has not seen recently, he is full of matter; but this treatment of the influences that made Shaw, under the headings of 'The Irishman', 'The Puritan', and 'The Progressive', is perhaps the most mature and clear-sighted piece of psychological discussion that Mr Chesterton has written yet.[41]

Ironically, the most amusing review was by the reviewer who was least amused. Vivian Carter, writing in the September 1909 issue of the *Bystander*, was not impressed by the book but sensed a comic conspiracy behind it:

> The issue of a book, entitled *George Bernard Shaw*, by G. K. Chesterton, is heralded by the Shaw–Chesterton fraternity as only another link in a long chain of imposition. For months they have wondered how Mr Shaw would deal with the threatened exposure of his dual identity, for by now it is, they say, surely general knowledge that Shaw and Chesterton are one and the same person. Shaw, it is said, tired of Socialism, weary of wearing Jaegers, and broken down by teetotalism and vegetarianism, sought, some years ago, an escape from them. His adoption, however, of these attitudes had a decided commercial value, which he did not think it advisable to prejudice by wholesale surrender. Therefore he, in order to taste the forbidden joys of Individualistic philosophy, meat food and strong drink, created 'Chesterton'. This mammoth myth, he decided, should enjoy all the forms of fame which Shaw had to deny himself. Outwardly, he should be Shaw's antithesis. He should be beardless, large in girth, smiling of countenance, and he should be licensed to sell paradoxes only in essay and novel form, all stage and platform rights being reserved for Shaw.[42]

However, joking aside, Carter was not impressed:

> Seeing that it is a life of George Bernard Shaw, you will ask yourself whether it is a good or a bad biography. And you will probably agree with me that it is a bad one. For it approaches the subject with the fatal purpose of seeking to explain it. Mr Chesterton, the last of all men to be suspected of such an intention, has attempted to analyse Mr Shaw. He makes him out to be the creature of environment. He traces one of Mr Shaw's characteristics after another to the fact that he is, respectively, an Irishman, a protestant, a Puritan, a rebel, a mathematician, a musician, and goodness knows what else.[43]

Overall, the critics gave a majority verdict in Chesterton's favour. Shaw, however, had words to say in his own defence – quite a few words. Prior to the book's publication Shaw had stated that it 'will not contain any facts; but it will be exceedingly interesting'.[44] Following its publication, Shaw found himself in the rare position of being able to review a biography of himself: Shaw on Chesterton on Shaw! This he did in the 25 August issue of the *Nation*: 'This book is what everybody expected it to be: the best work of literary art I have yet provoked. It is a fascinating portrait study; and I am proud to have been the painter's model.' None the less, although he evidently admired the skill of the artist he didn't like the portrait:

> Generally speaking, Mr Chesterton's portrait of me has the limitations of a portrait, which is, perhaps, fortunate in some respects for the original. As a picture, in the least personal and most phenomenal sense, it is very fine indeed. As an account of my doctrine, it is either frankly deficient and uproariously careless or else recalcitrantly and . . . madly wrong.

He also made a fighting defence of teetotalism:

> Teetotalism is, to Chesterton, a strange and unnatural asceticism forced on men by an inhuman perversion of religion. Beer drinking is to him, when his imagination runs away with him on paper, nothing short of the communion. He sees in every public-house a temple of the true catholic faith . . . Have I survived the cry of Art for Art's Sake, and War for War's Sake, for which Mr Chesterton rebukes Whistler and Mr Rudyard Kipling, to fall a victim to this maddest of all cries: the cry of Beer for Beer's Sake?[45]

Several hundred words later, and not before he had fulminated on subjects such as fairy tales, Calvinism and Christmas, Shaw wrote, 'I must stop arbitrarily or my review will be longer than the book!' Even then it was another couple of hundred words before he did stop arbitrarily. Clearly Chesterton's study had not slain Shaw, who was as ready to fight as ever. In the years ahead he and Chesterton would keep up a running intellectual battle without ever losing the deep affection each felt for the other.

An insight into their relationship from Shaw's viewpoint is provided by a discarded segment of his play *Back to Methuselah* in which Chesterton is caricatured in the character of Immenso

Champernoon, 'A man of colossal mould, with the head of a cherub on the body of a Falstaff . . . friendly, a little shy, and jokes frequently enough to be almost either still enjoying the last or already anticipating the next'.[46] Through the medium of Mrs Etteen, an archetypal Shavian heroine, Shaw voices his impatience and annoyance at this flippancy in Chesterton's character: 'You flirt with religions, with traditions, with politics, with everything that is most sacred and important. You flirt with the Church, with the Middle Ages, with the marriage question, with the Jewish question, even with the hideous cult of gluttony and drunkenness . . . you are not a bit in earnest . . .'[47] It seems that Shaw is countering Chesterton's accusation that he is too serious by complaining that Chesterton is not serious enough. Yet Shaw's Preface to this segment of the play displays his evident fondness for Chesterton:

> My thumbnail sketch, inadequate and libellous as it is, may give a hint or two to some future great biographer as to what the original of Immenso Champernoon was like in the first half of his career when, in defiance of the very order of nature, he began without a figure as a convivial immensity with vine leaves in his hair, deriding his own aspect, and in middle life slimmed into a Catholic saint, thereby justifying my reminder to those who took him too lightly of old, that Thomas Aquinas began as a comically fat man and ended as The Divine Doctor.[48]

It is in this genuine 'love for thine enemy' that the beauty of their relationship resides, but, regardless of any lack of affectation or animosity, they were still enemies, intellectually at least, and it is pertinent to consider whether there was a victor in the seemingly endless public sparring.

Christopher Hollis appeared in no doubt that Chesterton gained the upper hand: 'Shaw, though his position was ultimately irrational, used reason most brilliantly as an incidental weapon,' while Chesterton, 'though deeply rational in his conclusions, was pictorial and romantic in his manner'. Yet 'on the plane of thought it was certainly Chesterton who was by far the deeper thinker – a man of 'colossal genius' as Shaw confided with characteristic generosity to T. E. Lawrence.'[49]

Hollis's conclusions are, of course, subjective and open to debate, but, if nothing else, Shaw's credulity must cast a shadow of doubt over his position. For instance, he wrote to Chesterton during the time of Prohibition in the United States that 'the success of Prohibition is so overwhelming that it is bound to become a commonplace of civilisation'.[50]

Similarly, his belief in a socialist Utopia was scorned by Malcolm Muggeridge, who witnessed the 'collectivisation famine' in Kiev 'while Bernard Shaw and newspaper correspondents were telling the world of the bursting granaries and apple-cheeked dairymaids in the Ukraine'.[51] Compare this inability to see the truth even after the event with Chesterton's prophetic prediction before the event: 'The best way to destroy a Utopia is to establish it. The net result of Bolshevism is that the modern world will not imitate it.'[52]

Again, witness Shaw's naïve view of the police state with Chesterton's stark realism. Shaw considered that Chesterton's aversion to socialism was due, in part, to his dislike of wholesome discipline: 'A Socialist state might make the lazy man work, the fat man diet or take exercise. It might limit the number of glasses of beer allowed to an individual. It would, in fact, police him.' Chesterton responded to this by drawing a picture entitled 'When The Revolution Happens' which depicted Shaw tied to a lamp-post, surrounded by armed and angry revolutionaries and refusing to drink from a flagon offered to him. The caption underneath read: 'Mr Bernard Shaw refuses to drink the blood of aristocrats on grounds of vegetarianism and kindness to the lower animals. He is murdered.'[53] One senses Chesterton's acute awareness of Shaw's credulity when, during a debate in Toronto on the subject of 'Culture and the Coming Peril', Chesterton was asked whether George Bernard Shaw was a coming peril. 'Heavens, no,' was the instant reply. 'He is a disappearing pleasure.'[54]

In spite of the witticism, Shaw was always a reappearing pleasure in Chesterton's life, and in deference to the triumph of friendship over adversity which their relationship represented Chesterton paid his friend the following tribute:

> There is one fundamental truth in which I have never for a moment disagreed with him. Whatever else he is, he has never been a pessimist; or in spiritual matters a defeatist. He is at least on the side of Life, and in that sense of Birth. When the Sons of God shout for joy, merely because the creation is in being, Mr Shaw's splendid Wagnerian shout or bellow will be mingled with my less musical but equally mystical song of praise.[55]

« IO »

Innocence and Wisdom

As WELL AS SETTLING down in a new home in Beaconsfield and settling
old intellectual scores with Shaw, Chesterton's life in 1909 revolved
around being both a public speaker and a journalist. In the former
capacity he spoke in the lounge of *The Times* Book Club on 'The
Romances of the Future' on 17 December. Following his speech he
found himself surrounded by admiring women.

'I tried hard to understand your *Orthodoxy*,' said one.

'You seem to know everything,' said another.

'I know nothing, Madam,' Chesterton replied. 'I am a journalist.'[1]

In spite of such characteristic self-effacement, Chesterton had
acquired celebrity status. On 12 November, a month before his
address to these female admirers, Constance Smedley wrote the
following description of him in *T. P.'s Weekly*:

> Fleet Street crowds have been used to the ways of great men since
> Dr Johnson and Dean Swift trod the paving stones. Chesterton is
> enveloped in an abstraction so mighty that it neutralises the attention
> of the passer-by. His huge figure, enveloped in its cloak and shaded by
> a slouch hat, rolls through the streets unheeding his fellow beings. His
> eyes stare before him in a troubled dream; his lips move, muttering,
> composing, arguing. He is an imposing figure; of immense proportions,
> almost balloon-like with a fine impetuous head which rises over the
> surrounding crowds; his hair is properly shaggy, his countenance
> open and frank, wearing indeed a curious childlike unconsciousness
> in spite of the thought intensity that clouds his brow.[2]

The result of this 'thought intensity' was exhibited in a multitude
of journals, not least of which was the *Daily News*, to which he still
contributed a regular column. A collection of Chesterton's *Daily*

News essays appeared together in September 1909 under the title *Tremendous Trifles*. He described the essays as 'fleeting sketches' but they also provided glimpses of the childlike qualities in Chesterton's character that so beguiled his readership: 'Personally, of course, I believe in Santa Claus; but it is the season of forgiveness, and I will forgive others for not doing so.'[3] In another of the essays he describes an imaginary meeting with Santa Claus in which Santa bemoans the fact that the modern world misunderstands him:

> 'How can one be too good, or too jolly? I don't understand. But I understand one thing well enough. These modern people are living and I am dead.'
> 'You may be dead,' I replied. 'You ought to know. But as for what they are doing – do not call it living.'[4]

The underlying innocence in this and the other essays is seen as laudable by some and laughable by others, but to Chesterton innocence is the beginning of wisdom. In a similar vein he argued that great religious architecture was not only artistic but miraculous. Alluding to the words of Christ that the very stones would cry out if the crowds were silent, he wrote:

> With these words He called up all the Wealth of artistic creation that has been founded on this creed. With those words He founded Gothic architecture. For in a town like this [Bruges], which seems to have grown Gothic as a wood grows leaves, anywhere and anyhow, any odd brick or moulding may be carved off into a shouting face. The front of vast buildings is thronged with open mouths, angels praising God, or devils defying Him. Rock itself is racked and twisted, until it seems to scream. The miracle is accomplished; the very stones cry out.[5]

This was one of several essays in *Tremendous Trifles* that were inspired by the writer's recent excursions to France, Germany and Belgium. He was impressed by Bruges but not by Brussels: 'Except for some fine works of art, which seem to be there by accident, the City of Brussels is like a bad Paris, a Paris with everything noble cut out, and everything nasty left in.'[6]

Amid these travels, and the tremendous trifles he wrote for the *Daily News*, Chesterton was, of course, embroiled in serious controversy. His public battles with Shaw may have taken centre-stage but he was also involved in a less publicised but equally significant controversy in the pages of the *Church Socialist Quarterly*. This magazine was superficially in sympathy with the Anglican high-church position but its editorial line was theologically Modernist and economically Marxist. It was the journal of the Church Socialist League, founded in 1906 by radical Anglo-Catholics who regarded the Christian Social Union as insufficiently radical and the Guild of St Matthew as excessively Anglo-Catholic. The controversy began in the January 1909 edition of the magazine with an article by Chesterton entitled 'Of Sentimentalism and the Head and Heart'. Its theme was the difference between Traditionalism and Modernism, the former of which he labelled the philosophy of the Tree and the latter the philosophy of the Cloud:

> I mean that a tree goes on growing, and therefore goes on changing; but always in the fringes surrounding something unchangeable. The innermost rings of the tree are still the same as when it was a sapling; they have ceased to be seen, but they have not ceased to be central. When the tree grows a branch at the top, it does not break away from the roots at the bottom; on the contrary, it needs to hold more strongly by its roots the higher it rises with its branches. That is the true image of the vigorous and healthy progress of a man, a city, or a whole species. But when the evolutionists I speak of talk to us about change, they do not mean that. They do not mean something that produces external changes from a permanent and organic centre, like a tree; they mean something that changes completely and entirely in every part, at every minute, like a cloud . . .
>
> Now, if this merely cloudy and boneless development be adopted as a philosophy, then there can be no place for the past and no possibility of a complete culture. Anything may be here today and gone tomorrow; even tomorrow. But I do not accept that everlasting evolution, which merely means everlasting chaos. As I only accept the organic and orderly development of a thing according to its own design and nature, there is for me such a thing as a human culture that is reasonably complete. Only the modern, advanced, progressive, scientific culture is unreasonably incomplete.[7]

Chesterton's article brought a scathing response from Robert Dell, a Roman Catholic Modernist. He wrote that the 'awakening of the social conscience' and 'the spread of the sentiment of compassion' were not the achievement of the Church, as Chesterton had claimed, but of the French Revolution. Dell's article proceeded to ridicule the social teaching of the modern popes, describing the Catholic Church as 'the chief reactionary force in every country in Europe'. He then launched a bitter attack on Pope Pius X, whose encyclical *Pascendi*, published two years earlier, had condemned Modernism. He concluded the article by advocating the total destruction of 'the papal Church'.[8]

In answer to Dell, Chesterton wrote 'The Staleness of Modernism', which was published in the July issue of the *Quarterly*:

> Why is it that Mr Dell cannot become a new-fashioned Catholic without immediately becoming an old-fashioned Protestant? Why cannot he argue with the Pope without playing to the No-Popery gallery?
>
> ... For instance, he says that a man becoming a Catholic 'leaves his responsibility on the threshold', and is converted to be saved 'the trouble of thinking'. Why, quite so, and the 'Mass is a Mummery', and the Pope is the Beast in Revelation, and Papists can swear anything for the good of the Church, and Home Rule is Rome Rule ... Unless Modernism has some strange and softening influence on the brain, Mr Dell *must* know better. He must know whether men like Newman and Brunetière left off thinking when they joined the Roman Church. Moreover, because he is a man of lucid and active mind, he must know that the whole phrase about being saved the trouble of thinking is a boyish fallacy. Euclid does not save geometricians the trouble of thinking when he insists on absolute definitions and unalterable axioms. On the contrary, he gives them the great trouble of thinking logically. The dogma of the Church limits thought about as much as the dogma of the solar system limits physical science. It is not an arrest of thought, but a fertile basis and constant provocation of thought.[9]

Chesterton concluded his article by implying that Dell had unwittingly brought him closer to the Roman Catholic Church by his attacks upon it:

> That we shall be right in the long run if we feel the roots of mercy inside Catholicism, and wrong in the long run if we look for them outside, all history and reason convinces ... About the seat of the Catholic authority I do not disguise from any one that I am still in some doubt; and I agree much more with the high Anglicans than the Roman Modernists. Nevertheless, I never felt so near to Mr Dell's communion as after I had read his attack on it. And since,

despite Mr Dell's perverse ways, one cannot doubt his fidelity to his Church, it will certainly be a great pleasure to him to think that he has, even unconsciously, brought any lamb so near his fold.[10]

Once again, as with so many other controversies in which he'd become engaged, Chesterton was led closer to orthodoxy by the 'heretics'. However, he was never destined to be a lamb in the same flock as Robert Dell – or at least they would never be in the same flock at the same time. Dell left the Roman Catholic Church before Chesterton joined it, becoming a revolutionary socialist and committed agnostic.

In the midst of the controversy with Dell, one of Gilbert's closest friends, Maurice Baring, had overcome the doubts Chesterton still felt about 'the seat of the Catholic authority'. At Brompton Oratory, on the eve of Candlemas, Baring was received into the Roman Catholic Church by Father Sebastian Bowden. Many years later he wrote of his conversion as 'the only action in my life which I am quite certain I have never regretted'.[11]

In the same month that his reply to Robert Dell was appearing in the *Church Socialist Quarterly*, Chesterton had been invited to reply to an article in the *Hibbert Journal* which had denied the divinity of Christ. The writer of the original article had been fundamentally wrong, he claimed, in assuming that

when we look, so to speak, through the four windows of the Evangelists at this mysterious figure, we can see there a recognisable Jew of the first century, with the traceable limitations of such a man. Now this is exactly what we do not see. If we must put the thing profanely and without sympathy, what we see is this: an extraordinary being who would certainly have seemed as mad in one century as another, who makes a vague and vast claim to divinity . . . For some of his utterances men might fairly call him a maniac; for others, men long centuries afterwards might justly call him a prophet. But what nobody can possibly call him is a Galilean of the time of Tiberius . . . That is not how he appeared to his own nation, who lynched him, still shuddering at his earth-shaking blasphemies . . .

If I take it for granted (as most modern people do) that Jesus of Nazareth was one of the ordinary teachers of men, then I find Him splendid and suggestive indeed, but full of riddles and outrageous demands, by no means so workable and everyday an adviser as many heathens and many Jesuits. But if I put myself hypothetically into the other attitude, the case becomes curiously arresting and even thrilling. If I say 'Suppose the Divine did really walk and talk upon the earth, what should we be likely to think of it?' – then the foundations of my mind are moved. So far as I can form any conjecture, I think we should see in such a being exactly the perplexities that we see in the central figure of the Gospels ... I think he would seem to us to contradict himself; because, looking down on life like a map, he would see a connection between things which to us are disconnected. I think, however, that he would always ring true to our own sense of right, but ring (so to speak) too loud and too clear. He would be too good but never too bad for us: 'Be ye perfect.' I think there would be, in the nature of things, some tragic collision between him and the humanity he had created, culminating in something that would be at once a crime and an expiation ... I think, in short, that he would give us a sensation that he was turning all our standards upside down, and yet also a sensation that he had undeniably put them the right way up.[12]

It is scarcely surprising that Chesterton, always ready to plunge headlong into debate, was gaining a reputation for being dogmatic and opinionated. The essayist E. V. Lucas expressed this view light-heartedly in a mock epitaph:

> Poor G. K. C., his day is past –
> Now God will know the truth at last.[13]

Yet Lucas, in spite of the whimsical jesting, was aware of the humility behind Chesterton's opinions. Indeed, the mock epitaph was written in reply to a letter of Chesterton's in which Gilbert expressed the view that future biographers, 'if they find any trace of me at all', will find it 'difficult to understand the cause even of such publicity' as he obtained in his own day.[14]

A further example of Chesterton's humility is given by Father O'Connor. In the early months of 1910 Father O'Connor bought a copy of Chesterton's new novel, *The Ball and the Cross*, in Kensington High Street before proceeding to Beaconsfield to visit his friend. Having been asked to inscribe the copy, Gilbert disappeared for a while and returned it with the following inscription:

> This is a book I do not like,
> Take it away to Heckmondwike,
> A lurid exile, lost and sad

To punish it for being bad.
You need not take it from the shelf
(I tried to read it once myself:
The speeches jerk, the chapters sprawl,
The story makes no sense at all)
Hide it your Yorkshire moors among
Where no man speaks the English tongue.[15]

In spite of Chesterton's self-criticism, *The Ball and the Cross*, published on 24 February, received critical acclaim. An unsigned review in the *Pall Mall Gazette* was typical of the response:

> The theme in Mr Chesterton's new novel is largely the same that he treated in *Orthodoxy*; there he contrasted the cross with its symbolism of four arms stretching away infinitely and the circle with its narrow completeness, and here he develops the contrast . . . the story has far less fireworks and far more good solid work than any of Mr Chesterton's essays in fiction . . . there is far less sidetracking than is usual with Mr Chesterton . . . the story is concerned with the effort of the two honest men to fight a duel on the most vital problem in the world, the truth of Christianity.[16]

If the unknown author of this review seemed impressed with *The Ball and the Cross*, a better-known author, writing many years later, was equally impressed by the novel. In the mid-1970s Cardinal Luciani, the patriarch of Venice, wrote a series of articles in the form of letters, each addressed to real or fictional characters from the past. These characters were known collectively as the *Illustrissimi* (the Most Illustrious) and they included, among others, Charles Dickens, Mark Twain, St Bernard of Clairvaux, Goethe, King David, St François de Sales, Sir Walter Scott, Hippocrates, St Theresa of Lisieux, St Bonaventure, Christopher Marlowe, St Luke, Petrarch, St Teresa of Avila – and Jesus. One of these 'letters' was addressed to Chesterton:

> Dear Chesterton,
> On Italian television during the past few weeks we have been seeing Father Brown, your surprising detective-priest – a character who is typically yours. A pity we haven't also had Professor Lucifer and the monk Michael. I'd very much have liked to see them as you described them in *The Ball and the Cross*, sitting beside each other on the flying ship . . .

The monk's conclusion, which is yours, dear Chesterton, is quite right. Take God away and what is left, what do men become? What sort of a world are we reduced to living in? 'Why, the world of progress!' I hear someone say. 'The world of affluence!' Yes, but this famous progress isn't all it was once cracked up to be. It contains other things in itself: missiles, bacteriological and atomic weapons, the present process of pollution – all things that, unless they are dealt with in time, threaten to plunge the whole human race into catastrophe ... Progress that involves men who don't recognise a single Father in God becomes a constant danger: without a parallel moral progress, which is continuous and internal, it develops what is lowest and cruellest in man, making him a machine possessed by machines, a number manipulated by numbers ...

Dear Chesterton, you and I go down on our knees before a God who is more present than ever. Only he can give a satisfactory answer to the questions which, for everyone, are the most important of all: Who am I? Where did I come from? Where am I going?[17]

A few years after this 'letter' was written Albino Luciani, who wasn't even born when *The Ball and the Cross* was first published, became Pope John Paul I. In view of Chesterton's self-effacement, and his apparent belief that future biographers would scarcely remember his name, this is surely a case of the humble being exalted.

About the time *The Ball and the Cross* was published Chesterton was asked by an Anglican society to lecture in Coventry. When he asked what they wanted him to lecture on he was told he could choose his subject: 'Anything from an elephant to an umbrella.' 'Very well,' he said, 'I will lecture on an umbrella.' He proceeded to demonstrate that the umbrella was an example of increasing artificiality. Hair is worn to protect the head, a hat is worn to protect the hair and an umbrella is used to protect the hat.

After the lecture two Catholic priests saw him at the railway bookstall in Coventry station and asked him whether it was true that he was thinking of joining the Church. 'It's a matter that is giving me a great deal of agony of mind,' he replied, 'and I'd be very grateful if you would pray for me.'[18] The rumours of Chesterton's imminent conversion to Catholicism were more widespread than ever at this time. In Canada, for instance, the *Toronto Catholic Register* described Chesterton as 'the eminent English publicist and the most noteworthy convert to the faith in recent years'.[19] In fact, it would be over a decade before he did finally convert.

On 7 May 1910 the *Daily News* published an article by Chesterton in which he wrote that he would 'very much like to write one last, roaring, raging book telling all the rationalists not to be so utterly irrational'. The book would be 'a string of violent vetoes, like the Ten Commandments'. The remainder of the article sets out these vetoes:

> Don't use a noun and then an adjective that crosses out the noun. An adjective qualifies, it cannot contradict. Don't say 'Give me a patriotism that is free from boundaries.' It is like saying 'Give me a pork pie with no pork in it.' Don't say 'I look forward to that larger religion that shall have no special dogmas.' It is like saying 'I look forward to that larger quadruped who shall have no feet.' A quadruped means something with four feet; and a religion means something that commits a man to some doctrine about the universe. Don't let the meek substantive be absolutely murdered by the joyful, exuberant adjective . . .
>
> Don't say 'There is no true creed; for each creed believes itself right and the other wrong.' Probably one of the creeds is right and the others are wrong. Diversity does show that most of the views must be wrong. It does not by the faintest logic show that they all must be wrong . . . I believe (merely upon authority) that the world is round. That there may be tribes who believe it to be triangular or oblong does not alter the fact that it is certainly some shape, and therefore not any other shape. Therefore I repeat, with the wail of imprecation, don't say that the variety of creeds prevents you from accepting any creed. It is an unintelligent remark.[20]

The article concluded abruptly; it was 'getting much too long. I apologise. I beg your pardon. I thought I was writing a book.'[21]

In fact, the article could have served as an introduction to his next book, *What's Wrong with the World*, published on 28 June. It was dedicated to Charles Masterman, MP:

> My Dear Charles,
>
> I originally called this book *What is Wrong*, and it would have satisfied your sardonic temper to note the number of social misunderstandings that arose from the use of the title. Many a mild lady visitor opened her eyes when I remarked casually, 'I have been doing *What is Wrong* all this morning.' And one minister of religion moved quite sharply in his chair when I told him (as he understood it) that I had to run upstairs and do what is wrong, but should be down again in

a minute. Exactly of what occult vice they silently accused me I cannot conjecture, but I know of what I accuse myself; and that is, of having written a very shapeless and inadequate book, and one quite unworthy to be dedicated to you. As far as literature goes, this book is what is wrong, and no mistake.[22]

The change of title from *What is Wrong* to *What's Wrong with the World* was the decision of the publishers, who were no doubt convinced that the more dogmatic and affirmative title would be beneficial to sales. They appeared to be vindicated in this conviction because six editions were necessary within the first two months of publication. However, the decision was somewhat unfair on the author, since the more forthright title gave the impression of arrogance and self-righteousness. Although such an impression should have been dispelled by the humility of the dedication, many reviewers were suspicious. For example, the *Evening Standard* commented: 'We haven't the faintest notion what's wrong with the world, and after reading Mr Chesterton's book – nearly 300 pages – we regretfully come to the conclusion that he doesn't either.'[23]

The book itself was indeed 'shapeless' in many respects, and 'inadequate' as a genuinely comprehensive outline of what was wrong with the world. Max Beerbohm was singularly unimpressed, describing it as 'very cheap and sloppy, though with gleams – gleams of gas-lamps in Fleet Street, mud and slush'.[24] None the less it contained some pearls of Chestertonian wisdom:

If I am to discuss what is wrong, one of the first things that are wrong is this: the deep and silent modern assumption that past things have become impossible. There is one metaphor of which the moderns are very fond; they are always saying, 'You can't put the clock back.' The simple and obvious answer is 'You can.' A clock, being a piece of human construction, can be restored by the human finger to any figure or hour. In the same way society, being a piece of human construction, can be reconstructed upon any plan that has ever existed.

There is another proverb, 'As you have made your bed, so you must lie in it'; which again is simply a lie. If I have made my bed uncomfortable, please God I will make it again.[25]

One of the central tenets of *What's Wrong with the World* was his belief in widely distributed property as an alternative to the concentration of ownership in the hands of either the capitalist combines or the socialist state:

> I am well aware that the word 'property' has been defiled in our time by the corruption of the great capitalists. One would think, to hear people talk, that the Rothschilds and the Rockefellers were on the side of property. But obviously they are the enemies of property; because they are the enemies of their own limitations. They do not want their own land, but other people's ... A man with the true poetry of possession wishes to see the wall where his garden meets Smith's garden; the hedge where his farm touches Brown's. He cannot see the shape of his own land unless he sees the edges of his neighbour's. It is the negation of property that the Duke of Sutherland should have all the farms in one estate; just as it would be the negation of marriage if he had all our wives in one harem.[26]

Chesterton ended the book with a final note on the idea of widely distributed private property:

> I have not dealt with any details touching distributed ownership, or its possibility in England, for the reason stated in the text. This book deals with what is wrong, wrong in our root of argument and effort. This wrong is, I say, that we will go forward because we dare not go back. Thus the Socialist says that property is already concentrated in Trusts and Stores: the only hope is to concentrate it further in the State. I say the only hope is to unconcentrate it; that is, to repent and return; the only step forward is the step backward.[27]

However, perhaps the most controversial aspect of *What's Wrong with the World*, at least from the perspective of the late twentieth century, is the author's outspoken views on feminism. Probably the best-known of Chesterton's utterances on the subject is his witticism that women asserted that they would not be dictated to but then became stenographers. On a less flippant level he believed that the question was not whether women were good enough for votes, but whether votes were good enough for women: 'Most of the Feminists would probably agree with me that womanhood is under shameful tyranny in the shops and mills. But I want to destroy the tyranny. They want to destroy the womanhood. That is the only difference.'[28] As ever, Chesterton was enshrining women in an idealised femininity. In all his works of fiction the female characters were spotless heroines, devoid of the ugly masks of masculinity, and in this work of sociological non-fiction he asked 'whether we can recover the clear vision of woman as a tower with many windows, the fixed eternal feminine . . . whether we can preserve the tradition of a central thing which is even more human than democracy and even more practical than politics; whether, in a word, it is possible to re-establish the family, freed from the filthy cynicism and cruelty of the commercial epoch . . .'[29]

Chesterton saw something sublimely symbolic in the actions of suffragettes chaining themselves to railings. They were unwittingly chaining themselves to the 'filthy cynicism' which he so despised in modern capitalism. He believed in a matriarchy where the woman was at the centre of the family and the family was at the centre of society and, in rebelling against this, women, he thought, would lose far more than they could possibly gain. Chesterton's views were based on a profound respect for womanhood, a respect which was arguably exaggerated beyond the call of reason. He saw the 'eternal feminine' as the keystone upon which any healthy society rested. Perhaps he painted women whiter than white – and certainly whiter than many women wished to be painted.

One woman who was impressed by Chesterton's writing at this time was the young Dorothy L. Sayers. She had read *What's Wrong with the World* as a student at Oxford and had found parts of it 'very pleasing'.[30] She had also seen both Chesterton and Shaw give lectures at Oxford, being impressed with Chesterton, who was 'much sounder' than she had expected, but not with Shaw who was 'not particularly original'.[31]

If Chesterton's writing of *What's Wrong with the World* had unwittingly influenced the future career of Dorothy L. Sayers, an article he wrote in the *Illustrated London News* in October 1910 was due to have an even wider influence. He observed that the emerging Indian nationalism 'seems to be not very Indian and not very national'. The crux of his argument was that the Nationalists in India had merely accepted European ideas and sought European forms of government instead of recognising the

distinction between a people asking for its own ancient life and a people asking for things that have been wholly invented by somebody else . . . The right of a people to express itself, to be itself in arts and action, seems to me a genuine right. If there is such a thing in

India, it has a right to be Indian. But Herbert Spencer is not Indian; 'Sociology' is not Indian; all this pedantic clatter about culture and science is not Indian. I often wish it were not English either. But this is our first abstract difficulty, that we cannot feel certain that the Indian Nationalist is national.'[32]

The article had a profound influence on Mahatma Gandhi, who was then a struggling student living in London. He immediately translated it into Gujurati, and its penetrating analysis formed the basis of the future Indian leader's campaigns.

During November 1910 two more books were published. *Alarms and Discursions* was a further collection of essays from his weekly journalism, and *William Blake* was a book in the Popular Library of Art series, a companion to his earlier study of G. F. Watts. Reviewing the latter book, a writer in the *Nation* complained: 'Although Mr Chesterton's "Blake" appears in a series of books about art he has not troubled much to give any special consideration of Blake as a draughtsman, painter, or engraver. The immensely important question, for instance, of Blake's power of design, its amazing successes and its unaccountable failures, is entirely ignored.'[33] The criticism was entirely justified because Chesterton was much more concerned with Blake's heart and mind, 'his mental and spiritual endowment', than with any detailed consideration of his practical output.

Alarms and Discursions had its high points, one of which was an essay entitled 'The Wheel':

> wheels are the mark of a man quite as much as wings are the mark of an angel. Wheels are the things that are as old as mankind and yet are peculiar to man; they are prehistoric but not pre-human.
>
> . . . Many modern philosophers . . . are ready to find links between man and beast, and to show that man has been in all things the blind slave of his mother earth. Some . . . are even eager to show it; especially if it can be twisted to the discredit of religion. But even the most eager scientists have often admitted in my hearing that they would be surprised if some kind of cow approached them moving solemnly on four wheels. Wings, fins, flappers, claws, hoofs, webs, trotters, with all these the fantastic families of the earth come against us and close around us, fluttering and flapping and rustling and galloping and lumbering and thundering; but there is no sound of wheels.
>
> . . . The wheel is an animal that is always standing on its head

... Or if the phrase be felt as more exact, it is an animal that is always turning head over heels and progressing by this principle ... A wheel is the sublime paradox; one part of it is always going forward and the other part always going back ...

Why should people be so scornful of us who stand on our heads? Bowing down one's head in the dust is a very good thing, the humble beginning of all happiness. Then (leaving our heads in the humble and reverent position) we kick up our heels behind in the air. That is the true origin of standing on one's head; and the ultimate defence of paradox. The wheel humbles itself to be exalted; only it does it a little quicker than I do.[34]

On the evening of 4 November Chesterton, accompanied by Frances, visited the Roman Catholic college of St Edmund's at Ware. He lectured on chivalry and the occasion was considered important enough for Monsignor Barnes, the Catholic chaplain at Cambridge, to bring over a party of undergraduates. Chesterton was in fine form, contrasting the civilising influence of the Roman Empire with the modern barbarism of worshipping a mythical superman.

In January 1911 a collection of Chestertonian aphorisms and short extracts from previous books was published as *A Chesterton Calendar*. This novel idea, in which there was a different quote from Chesterton for every day of the year, was a great success, prompting the publication of a second collection in 1916. Another volume of essays published early in 1911 was his *Appreciations and Criticisms of the Works of Charles Dickens*, containing Chesterton's introductions to Dickens's works in the Everyman Library series.

However, a collection of short stories, published in July by Cassell, was destined to dwarf all his previous books in terms of popularity. The twelve stories in *The Innocence of Father Brown* had originally appeared separately during the previous ten months in either the *Storyteller* or Cassell's own magazine. Their appearance in a single volume was considered a mistake by a reviewer in *Country Life*: 'The stories of Father Brown should have been left to their proper place scattered in the pages of a magazine, where their effect, not being cumulative, would have been greater.'[35] This was a sentiment with which the public emphatically did not agree. The character of Father Brown, the priest-detective modelled loosely on Chesterton's friend Father O'Connor, won the hearts of a whole new generation of readers. He was destined also to reach the hearts of many future generations, something which would not have been possible had the stories remained scattered and ultimately lost to posterity in the pages of sundry magazines.

Evidence of the enduring popularity of Father Brown is manifold, from his emergence as a film star in the hands of Sir Alec Guinness to his transformation into a television celebrity by Kenneth More in the mid-seventies. Guinness confessed a debt of gratitude to the priest-detective in his autobiography:

> My friendship with Cyril Tomkinson had reduced my anti-clericism considerably but not my anti-Romanism. Then came the film of *Father Brown* . . . and on location in Burgundy I had a small experience the memory of which always gives me pleasure . . .
>
> . . . By the time dusk fell I was bored and, dressed in my priestly black, I climbed the gritty winding road to the village . . . I hadn't gone far when I heard scampering footsteps and a piping voice calling, 'Mon père!' My hand was seized by a boy of seven or eight, who clutched it tightly, swung it and kept up a non-stop prattle. He was full of excitement, hops, skips and jumps, but never let go of me. I didn't dare speak in case my excruciating French should scare him. Although I was a total stranger he obviously took me for a priest and so to be trusted. Suddenly with a 'Bonsoir, mon père', and a hurried sideways sort of bow, he disappeared through a hole in a hedge. He had had a happy, reassuring walk home, and I was left with an odd calm sense of elation. Continuing my walk I reflected that a Church which could inspire such confidence in a child, making its priests, even when unknown, so easily approachable, could not be as scheming and creepy as so often made out. I began to shake off my long-taught, long-absorbed prejudices.[36]

Another doyen of the cinema was also greatly influenced by Chesterton in general and Father Brown in particular. Alfred Hitchcock's taste in literature as a teenager during the First World War was 'the detective fiction of the Catholic novelist G. K. Chesterton, whose sleuth Father Brown was delighting thousands of readers'. Hitchcock's biographer laid great stress on the formative nature of Chesterton's writing on the young filmmaker:

> Much admired and celebrated by the Catholic clergy, and read by Catholic schoolboys, Chesterton's popular essays . . . entertained the adolescent Hitchcock, and provided him with ideas for the formation of his own style and vision when he was an apprentice filmmaker. It was Chesterton who defended popular literature, Chesterton who pointed

out the archetypal, fairy-tale structure of police stories, and Chesterton who defended the exploration of criminal behaviour . . .

Chesterton and Hitchcock shared not only Catholicism but also a sense of irony. And what Chesterton wrote of the popular literature, Hitchcock took to heart, for it provided, if ever he needed, the justification for his apparently slight moral tales about all the garden varieties of villainy.[37]

In the very first Father Brown story Chesterton had introduced his new character as 'a very short Roman Catholic priest going up from a small Essex village'. He had 'a face as round and dull as a Norfolk dumpling' and his eyes were 'as empty as the North Sea'. The priest was observed by a sophisticated and sceptical French detective who had no love for priests but could pity them and this one, he thought, 'might have provoked pity in anybody'. Father Brown 'had a large, shabby umbrella, which constantly fell on the floor. He did not seem to know which was the right end of his return ticket. He explained with a moon-calf simplicity to everybody in the carriage that he had to be careful, because he had something made of real silver "with blue stones" in one of his brown-paper parcels. His quaint blending of Essex flatness with saintly simplicity continuously amused the Frenchman.'[38]

Certainly this saintly simplicity also amused the public at large who followed the priest's adventures avidly. Yet, although there is little doubt that many found *The Innocence of Father Brown* charming, it was the potent combination of this innocence with a profound wisdom that was the key to his popularity. Chesterton always asserted that wisdom and innocence were intertwined and he embodied both qualities in his clerical detective. Through the medium of Father Brown, he illustrated how cynicism pollutes and destroys wisdom as much as it pollutes and destroys innocence. One cannot see objectively through cynical eyes because the vision is obscured by dark, sceptical clouds. Consequently, only the eyes of innocence see clearly. Indeed, it was no mere coincidence that the second volume of Father Brown stories, published in 1914, was entitled *The Wisdom of Father Brown*. Another volume, published in 1927, was entitled *The Secret of Father Brown*. Chesterton knew the secret all along. The synthesis of innocence and wisdom was the secret of Father Brown.

II

A Man Alive

Perhaps you do not know where Ethandune is. Nor do I; nor does anybody. That is where the somewhat sombre fun begins. I cannot even tell you for certain whether it is the name of a forest or a town or a hill. I can only say that in any case it is of the kind that floats and is unfixed ... Over a vast dim region of England this dark name of Ethandune floats like an eagle doubtful where to swoop and strike, and, indeed, there were birds of prey enough over Ethandune, wherever it was. But now Ethandune itself has grown as dark and drifting as the black drifts of the birds.[1]

THESE LINES APPEARED IN an essay in *Alarms and Discursions,* published in November 1910. Another essay in the same book recounted the day Chesterton had hired a car 'because I wanted to visit in very rapid succession the battle-places and hiding-places of Alfred the Great'.[2] The link between the two essays was Chesterton's research for an epic poem which would be published the following August under the title of *The Ballad of the White Horse.* Yet the poetic imagery was already evident in these earlier essays in which the author was clearly besotted by the ballad he was in the process of writing:

But the other day under a wild sunset and moonrise I passed the place which is best reputed as Ethandune, a high, grim upland, partly bare and partly shaggy ... The darkness, the red wreck of sunset, the yellow and lurid moon, the long fantastic shadows, actually created that sense of monstrous incident which is the dramatic side of landscape. The bare grey slopes seemed to rush downhill like routed hosts; the dark clouds drove across like riven banners; and the moon was like a golden dragon, like the Golden Dragon of Wessex.'[3]

These were the words of a man possessed. Chesterton, so often content to be merely a 'jolly journalist', was so drunk with a vision of Ethandune and Alfred the Great that the writing of his ballad became an obsession, a crusade. He believed that Ethandune was the place 'where you and I were saved from being savages for ever'.[4] Already as mysterious as Camelot, it deserved to be as mighty. Thus *The Ballad of the White Horse* sought to put Ethandune on the map – even if no one knew exactly where on the map it was supposed to be.

According to Father O'Connor, Chesterton's initial inspiration came in a dream when a whole stanza emerged in his subconscious:

> People, if you have any prayers,
> Say prayers for me:
> And lay me under a Christian stone
> In that lost land I thought my own,
> To wait till the holy horn is blown,
> And all poor men are free.[5]

He could scarcely have been blessed with a more important or more productive dream because *The Ballad of the White Horse* became one of his most acclaimed works.

George Wyndham echoed the sentiments of many when he wrote to Chesterton soon after it was published:

I must thank you for the *White Horse*. I cannot go on reading it to myself (4 times) and reading it aloud at the top of my voice (5 times) and refrain any longer from thanking you. It is your due to be told that many eyes shine with delight at its strength, and that knots climb up the throats of men and women at its beauty. It is wisdom we shall patiently learn. 'At last,' and 'Thank God,' are what people say when they read it or hear it read. I thank you in addition to thanking God and my stars for having given what I most needed in largest measure. I am not selfish over it. I do not hoard it for my own satisfaction. On the contrary I read it aloud to all my friends and have a huge joy in watching it working in them. This I can easily do over the top of the book, as I know most of the plums by heart. Like all great gifts, it goes round, it can be shared. It is not like a diamond or a sonnet in a language which few people know. To read the *White Horse* aloud is like bathing in the sea or riding over the downs in a company that becomes good company because of the exhilaration.[6]

On 17 June 1912 Chesterton received an equally enthusiastic letter from John Galsworthy: 'A really splendid stir and thrum in it, and that passage beginning: *"Brothers at arms," said Alfred* rouses me to high enthusiasm.'[7]

Many years later this splendid stir and thrum was to have a marked effect on Douglas Hyde during a train journey through south London:

> Through my mind, in rhythm with the wheels, ran a verse from Chesterton's *Ballad of the White Horse* I had re-read not long before:
>
> > Therefore I bring these rhymes to you,
> > Who brought the cross to me,
> > Since on you flaming without flaw,
> > I saw the sign that Guthrum saw
> > When he let break the ships of awe,
> > And laid peace on the sea.
>
> Could there be so many Catholic churches? I asked myself, as cross followed cross. Why had I not seen them before? Through Herne Hill, Tulse Hill, smug, suburban Streatham, the crosses came and went. And still the wheels hammered out Chesterton's lines:
>
> > Out of the mouth of the Mother of God
> > Like a little word come I;
> > For I go gathering Christian men
> > From sunken paving and ford and fen,
> > To die in a battle, God knows when,
> > By God, but I know why.[8]

Hyde was, at this time, a leading member of the Communist Party and news editor of its paper, the *Daily Worker*. Soon after, he resigned from its ranks and became a Catholic.

More than twenty years after its publication the historian Christopher Dawson wrote to Chesterton, expressing his debt to the *Ballad*:

> I have ventured to send you a copy of my new book, *The Making of Europe*, in the hope it may be of interest to you. Years ago, when I

was an undergraduate, your *Ballad of the White Horse* first brought the breath of life to this period for me when I was fed up with Stubbs and Oman and the rest of them . . . I have tried to write a history that does not leave out everything that matters, in the academic fashion, and that gives a proper place to spiritual factors.[9]

Another undergraduate who was influenced by the *Ballad* was George Sayer, who remembered a conversation with C. S. Lewis, later his English tutor at Oxford:

'Tell me, Sayer, why do you want to read English?' he asked.
   'I suppose it's mainly because I enjoy reading, especially poetry.'
   'Well, that's a good answer. What poetry do you like?'
   'Oh, lots. Wordsworth, Shelley, Keats, and, of course, Shakespeare.'
   'Have you read any long poems, such as *The Prelude*?'
   'No, I haven't read that,' I said. (In fact, I did not know who had written it.) 'But I've read some of *The Revolt of Islam* and the whole of *The Ballad of the White Horse*.'
   'Good. What can you quote from that?'
   I quoted the one verse that had stuck in my memory:

> The great Gaels of Ireland
> Are the men that God made mad.

I got no further on my own, for with gusto and a glowing face he declaimed the next lines with me:

> For all their wars are merry,
> And all their songs are sad.

'Marvellous stuff, isn't it? Don't you like the way Chesterton takes hold of you in that poem, shakes you, and makes you want to cry? I think I like best of all the last part. What's it called? "Ethandune". Here and there it achieves the heroic, the rarest quality in modern literature.' His face glowed with delight as he declaimed:

> 'The high tide!' King Alfred cries,
> 'The high tide and the turn!
> As a tide turns on the tall grey seas,
> See how they waver in the trees,
> How stray their spears, how knock their knees,
> How wild their watchfires burn!'[10]

A further giant of English literature who was impressed by *The Ballad of the White Horse* was Graham Greene. In an interview published in the *Observer* on 12 March 1978 he called Chesterton 'another underestimated poet'. To illustrate the point he cited the *Ballad*: 'Put *The Ballad of the White Horse* against *The Waste Land*. If I had to lose one of them, I'm not sure that . . . well, anyhow, let's just say I re-read *The Ballad* more often!'[11]

One notable dissenting voice amid the chorus of praise was that of J. R. R. Tolkien. Although he had been much impressed by the poem when he had first read it as a young man, he came to have many reservations about it in later life. In a letter to his son during the Second World War, he wrote:

> P . . . has been wading through *The Ballad of the White Horse* for the last many nights; and my efforts to explain the obscurer parts to her convince me that it is not as good as I thought. The ending is absurd. The brilliant smash and glitter of the words and phrases (when they come off, and are not mere loud colours) cannot disguise the fact that G. K. C. knew nothing whatever about the 'North', heathen or Christian.[12]

However, although the critics would remain divided as to the *Ballad*'s literary merits, one suspects that Chesterton gained more joy from the way the poem was received by the public at large than he ever derived from the praise of his literary peers. During the First World War many of the soldiers in the trenches carried it for comfort and inspiration and a sailor's widow wrote to Gilbert soon after her husband's death: 'I want to tell you that a copy of the *Ballad of the White Horse* went down into the Humber with the R.38. My husband loved it as his own soul – never went anywhere without it.'[13]

During the Second World War *The Times*, under the heading '*Sursum Corda*', carried a brief statement of the defeat in Crete, followed by the words of the Blessed Virgin to King Alfred:

> I tell you naught for your comfort,
> Yea, naught for your desire,
> Save that the sky grows darker yet
> And the sea rises higher.
>
> Night shall be thrice night over you,
> And heaven an iron cope.

Do you have joy without a cause,
Yea, faith without a hope?

Following its publication many wrote to *The Times* seeking the source of the quotation. The evocation of a thin yet unbreakable thread of faith in the face of adversity summed up the hopes and fears of England at the time. Months later, when Winston Churchill spoke of 'the end of the beginning', *The Times* returned to the *Ballad*, giving the opening lines of Alfred's speech at Ethandune:

'The high tide!' King Alfred cried.
'The high tide and the turn!'

Perhaps, to recall another of Churchill's wartime speeches, this was Chesterton's Finest Hour. To be called upon as a spokesman for England at the time of her greatest need would have meant more to him than the praise of any Oxbridge don.

In 1911, however, both wars were in the future. For the present Chesterton was still conducting his own private war with Shaw. On 29 May Shaw had addressed a debating society calling itself the Heretics at the Victoria Assembly Rooms in Cambridge. His subject was 'The Religion of the Future'. He was as controversial as ever, incurring the wrath of the press for his assertion that Christ was a failure. the *Academy* protested against 'the dissemination of poisonous theories amongst young persons', describing Shaw's lecture as 'vile and blasphemous'.[14] The *Fortnightly Review* called it 'an unwarrantable assault upon some of the loftiest and noblest spirits of our times and something of an insult to the most sacred of our dead'.[15]

When Chesterton was invited by the Heretics to reply to Shaw, he began by defending his friend from these attacks, stating that the *Academy* report had been 'not merely written by an idiot but by an idiot who had no belief in Christianity'.[16] Chesterton's reply to Shaw took place in front of a packed audience of nearly a thousand at the Guildhall in Cambridge on 17 November. Shaw's address had been entitled 'The Religion of the Future'; Chesterton's riposte was entitled 'The Future of Religion'.

As was often the case when he was giving lectures, he arrived late and began his address by apologising. On this occasion he explained that his late arrival was due to the fact that he had come in a cab and had constantly urged the driver to go more slowly so that he might see the beauties of the city and also begin to make up what he was going to say. He continued by explaining that the Heretics had sent him a pamphlet giving the substance of Shaw's earlier lecture. It is likely that Chesterton didn't bother to prepare his lecture until he was in the Cambridge cab because his notes were scribbled hurriedly on the text of the pamphlet he'd been sent. On the cover he'd sketched a scanty plan of the main points he wished to discuss: 1. Blasphemy; 2. Nonsense; 3. Machinery; 4. Idolatry; 5. Liberty. Inside the pamphlet he'd scrawled comments in the margins, some of which found their way into his speech. On the inside cover he'd written: 'It has taken about 1800 years to build up my religion. It will not take 18 minutes to destroy Mr Shaw's.'[17]

In the earlier address Shaw had defined his religion in the following terms:

> We are all experiments in the direction of making God. What God is doing is making Himself, getting from being a mere powerless will or force. This force has implanted into our minds the ideal of God. We are not very successful attempts at God so far, but I believe that if we can drive into the heads of men the full consciousness of moral responsibility that comes to men with the knowledge that there never will be a God unless we make one – that we are instruments through which that ideal is trying to make itself a reality – we can work towards that ideal until men become supermen, and then super-supermen, and then a world of organisms who had achieved and realised God.

In the margin alongside this passage in the pamphlet Chesterton had written 'Outside Reason'. In his own speech he elaborated:

> If he [Shaw] said: 'Here are five poor children. They haven't got a mother; let them all come together and manufacture a mother,' we would agree that there was a certain slip in the logic of the observation. That is what, literally, Mr Shaw had said in his address. He said, 'We must come together and make a religion,' and then he said, 'A God doesn't exist yet, but we must help to make him exist,' or words to that effect.[18]

In spite of his hasty preparation, Chesterton's talk was received warmly. Yet the real highlight of the evening was the questioning by the audience when he had finished. To an enquirer who asked for his views on Hell he responded that, although he could not speak from personal experience, he regarded it as a thing to be avoided. When asked how he thought Christianity should be practised he replied that he was more than ever inclined to think that the claims of the Greek and Anglican Churches were less near the truth than the Roman Catholic Church. A member of the audience asked him to reconcile his belief in reason with a belief in miracles. Chesterton replied, 'I have always believed in miracles, even before I believed in Christianity. I have never been able to see why spirit should not alter matter, and I have never been able to see the philosophic objection to miracles.'[19] Another questioner asked for his opinion on the expulsion of Father Tyrrell from the Roman Catholic Church. He replied that personally he was a member of the National Liberal Club, but if he continued to make speeches which were inconsistent with Liberal principles he could have no objection in the abstract if he were requested to resign his membership. He added: 'I can assure you, and I would prove it to you if I had time, that the Popes have done a hundred times more for Liberty than any of the Protestant Churches ever have.'[20]

Reporting on the evening's events, the *Cambridge Review* stated, 'Mr Chesterton's address lasted an hour, and was followed by a long and animated discussion, during which Mr Chesterton was seen to great advantage; his resource and humour in debate would be hard to equal.'[21] But perhaps the greatest praise for Chesterton's achievement was published in the *Gownsman* on 25 November:

A surprisingly successful and lengthy debate followed this vigorously reverent Apologetic. Seldom can a discussion in the Guildhall have continued unabated for over an hour. Whether replying to worshippers of Osiris, to grandsons of Bradlaugh, to Physicists, to Medicine Men, or to Mr Lowes Dickinson . . . Mr Chesterton's acumen was expugnable. From whatever side he was attacked, it was impossible to get round him, impossible to impinge on the *esprit de corps* of this phalanx of orthodoxy.

It was a rare pleasure to observe the agility with which he pounced upon the gist or motive of a question, his scrupulous fairness, his exacerbating aplomb. Deplore as we may the dissipation of endowments of such breadth and profundity in acceptance of the Miraculous, and the palliation of Papal Oppression, we must be grateful indeed to a speaker who can occasionally introduce Humour into the Divine. Perhaps the sinister influence of Mr Belloc is to

blame for the present mission of Mr Chesterton out of his element
– to bolster up a sinking ship.[22]

The introduction of Belloc's name as an influence, real or imagined,
on Chesterton's embryonic Catholicism was predictable. It was
universally known that they were inseparable friends, and Belloc's
public defence of the Catholic faith was always robust and candid.
Yet it should be remembered that Shaw was also on friendly terms
with Belloc, and on 27 October, just three weeks before Chesterton's
appearance at the Guildhall in Cambridge, Shaw wrote to Chesterton
concerning plans for a three-star show – a public debate between
the two of them with Belloc as the chairman. After stating that
he was 'prepared to accept any conditions', Shaw argued that too
many conditions would stifle Belloc's ability, as chairman, to enter
the fray:

> The disadvantages for us are that we both want Belloc to let himself
> go . . . We shall all three talk all over the shop . . . and Belloc will not
> trouble himself about the rules of public meeting and debate, even if
> there were any reason to suppose that he is acquainted with them
> . . . I therefore conclude that we had better make it to some extent
> a clowns' cricket match . . . In a really hostile debate it is better to
> be as strict as possible; but as this is going to be a performance in
> which three Macs who are on the friendliest terms in private will
> belabour each other recklessly . . . we need not be particular . . .
> My love to Mrs Chesterton . . . To hell with the Pope![23]

Others recalled Belloc's ability to bend the rules of debate in the
way Shaw described in his letter. Thomas Derrick remembered an
occasion when Gilbert was lecturing, Shaw and Cecil Chesterton
were in the audience and Belloc was in the chair:

> When G. K. started to wander, H. B. in an apparently absent-minded
> way would write hints on scraps of paper, and put them across the
> top of the water-tumbler that stood on the table at G. K.'s side.
> As he spoke, G. K. took up a succession of these notes. Shaw . . .
> replied. After he had spoken, I remember that H.B. could stand the
> constraint of the chair no longer. He beckoned to Cecil to act as
> proxy, and rose to reply to Shaw. In conclusion, he summed up on
> his fingers what Shaw's points had been, and as he did so, Shaw
> nodded in assent that his case had been fairly condensed. Then

Belloc threw out his arms in a kind of despair and shouted: 'If that's what you think, then all I can say is, you *haven't travelled*, and you *don't know men*.' Then he sat down.

On the same occasion, there was a very fluent working-man Socialist at the back of the hall, who rose in opposition after G. K. had finished. 'As for Mr Chesterton's jokes,' he said, 'WE' (meaning the Socialists) 'had one present' (meaning Shaw) 'who could beat Mr Chesterton hollow at it.' ('Hear, hear!' from G. K.) 'I'll tell you wot the matter is with Mr Chesterton,' he went on. 'Mr Chesterton is *Middle Class*.' Chesterton at once responded to this. He dropped his pencil, and tried to tuck his notes under one arm while clapping his hands and repeating: 'Hear, hear!'[24]

Neither was this anonymous proletarian alone in his belief that Shaw was superior to Chesterton in debate. Frank Swinnerton was evidently of the same opinion:

> The first time I ever saw Shaw was at a lecture delivered by G. K. Chesterton (from notes hastily made while the chairman 'introduced' him) before the Humanitarian Society. Chesterton suggested cheerfully that Humanitarianism, like Charity, should begin, but did not begin, with one's next-door neighbour; and he embroidered this sound proposition with his own fancies until the meeting seethed with misunderstanding. I, a boy, sniggered with delight at the ferocious exclamations uttered all about me by the humane. Just as hysteria threatened to ruin the meeting, a tall, bony, energetic man with a brogue and a brain sprang to his feet near the low platform. With his hands upon his hips, his head back, his words full of subtle aitches and lovely variations of emphasis, he put everybody right. The lecturer was eclipsed; the audience was appeased; everybody clapped and glowed; my friends said, 'Well, that was Shaw.' We streamed out of the hall filled with elation.[25]

Yet not everyone was convinced of Shaw's superiority. As we have seen, Dorothy L. Sayers was singularly unimpressed by Shaw and thought Chesterton a far better lecturer. Meanwhile, another Dorothy, not destined to become as well known as Sayers, came to the same conclusion. Dorothy Salmon was a Fabian socialist committed to the views of Shaw when she attended a lecture, given by Chesterton, which ended in an acrimonious attack by Shaw on Chesterton's faith. The majority of the audience, being Fabians themselves, were with Shaw, but Chesterton chuckled with delight and held his ground happily. After the meeting Dorothy was very silent. Then she exclaimed in a surprised tone that Chesterton was right. The revelation changed her life. She died many years later as Mother Mary Raphael, Abbess of the Poor Clare community in Workington.[26]

Whether Chesterton was Shaw's equal in open debate is itself, it seems, open to debate. However, there is no doubting his ability to deal with Shaw's lesser disciples. One such disciple was Holbrook Jackson, joint editor of the *New Age*, editor of *T. P.'s Weekly* and biographer of both Shaw and William Morris.

Chesterton and Jackson were acquaintances, if not close friends, having met originally at the Yorkshire home of the Steinthals, where Chesterton had first met Father O'Connor several years earlier. The acquaintance continued in print when Chesterton reviewed Jackson's *Great English Novelists* in the *Daily News*. On that occasion he had written, 'I should like to write an article upon almost every one of Mr Jackson's paragraphs.'[27] In 1911 Jackson published *Platitudes in the Making*, a slim volume which he presented to Chesterton with the inscription 'To G. K. Chesterton with esteem'. This time Chesterton almost fulfilled his wish to write an article upon all of Jackson's paragraphs by countering each of Jackson's 'platitudes' with an anecdote, or antidote, of his own. Each reply was scribbled between the lines of the text. Although Chesterton's comments remained unpublished, only being discovered many years later when his personal copy of *Platitudes in the Making* turned up in a second-hand bookshop in San Francisco, they display his intellect and wit at its sharpest:

JACKSON: Be contented, when you have got all you want.
CHESTERTON: Till then, be happy.
JACKSON: Don't think – do.
CHESTERTON: Do think! Do!
JACKSON: A lie is that which you do not believe.
CHESTERTON: This is a lie: so perhaps you don't believe it.
JACKSON: As soon as an idea is accepted it is time to reject it.
CHESTERTON: No: it is time to build another idea on it. You are always rejecting: and you build nothing.
JACKSON: Truth and falsehood in the abstract do not exist.
CHESTERTON: Then nothing else does.
JACKSON: Truth is one's own conception of things.
CHESTERTON: The Big Blunder. All thought is an attempt to discover if one's own conception is true or not.

JACKSON: No two men have exactly the same religion: a church, like
society, is a compromise.

CHESTERTON: The same religion has the two men. The sun shines on
the Evil and the Good. But the sun does not compromise.

JACKSON: Only the rich preach content to the poor.

CHESTERTON: When they are not preaching Socialism.

JACKSON: In a beautiful city an art gallery would be superfluous. In
an ugly one it is a narcotic.

CHESTERTON: In a real one it is an art gallery.

JACKSON: Negations without affirmations are worthless.

CHESTERTON: And impossible.

JACKSON: Theology and religion are not the same thing. When
the churches are controlled by the theologians religious people
stay away.

CHESTERTON: Theology is simply that part of religion that requires
brains.

JACKSON: Desire to please God is never disinterested.

CHESTERTON: Well, I should hope not!

JACKSON: We are more inclined to regret our virtues than our vices;
but only the very honest will admit this.

CHESTERTON: I don't regret any virtues except those I have lost.

JACKSON: Every custom was once an eccentricity; every idea was once
an absurdity.

CHESTERTON: No, no, no. Some ideas were always absurdities. This
is one of them.

JACKSON: No opinion matters finally: except your own.

CHESTERTON: Said the man who thought he was a rabbit.

JACKSON: The future will look upon man as we look upon the
ichthyosaurus – as an extinct monster.

CHESTERTON: The 'future' won't look upon anything. No eyes. [28]

Although this was Chesterton exercising his mind purely for his own
amusement, he continued in the closing months of 1911 to exercise
his mind for the amusement of others. In particular, the last weeks
of the year found him working on his latest novel, *Manalive*, which
was published the following February. Not generally considered one
of his best works of fiction, perhaps it is sadly underrated. It contains
the charm, mystery and adventure of *The Man Who was Thursday* or
The Ball and the Cross, but it also has a depth beyond either of these,
most notably in its characterisation of women. In the earlier novels
female characters play a peripheral role, whereas in *Manalive* they
are central to the plot. Moreover they have a depth and mystery

of their own which is lacking, or at least only hinted at, in the earlier books.

The mystique of Mary Gray, the novel's heroine, is illustrated in an extract where her friends try to deter her from marrying Innocent Smith, the novel's misunderstood hero:

'Mary, Mary,' cried Rosamund, almost breaking down, 'I'm so sorry about it, but the thing can't be at all. We – we have found out all about Mr Smith.'

'All?' repeated Mary, with a low and curious intonation; 'why, that must be awfully exciting.'

Another character, Dr Pym, then explains exactly what they have found out:

'To begin with,' he said, 'this man Smith is constantly attempting murder. The warden of Brakespeare College – '

'I know,' said Mary, with a vague but radiant smile; 'Innocent told me.'

'I can't say what he told you,' replied Pym quickly, 'but I'm very much afraid it wasn't true. The plain truth is that the man's stained with every known human crime. I assure you I have all the documents. I have evidence of his committing burglary, signed by a most eminent English curate. I have – '

'Oh, but there were two curates,' cried Mary, with a certain gentle eagerness; 'that was what made it so much funnier.'

. . . 'But don't you understand, Mary,' cried Rosamund in despair; 'don't you know that awful things have happened even before our very eyes? I should have thought you would have heard the revolver shots upstairs.'

'Yes, I heard the shots,' said Mary almost brightly; 'but I was busy packing just then. And Innocent had told me he was going to shoot at Dr Warner; so it wasn't worth while to come down.'

'Oh, I don't understand what you mean,' cried Rosamund Hunt, stamping, 'but you must and shall understand what I mean. I don't care how cruelly I put it, if only I can save you. I mean that your Innocent Smith is the most awfully wicked man in the world. He has sent bullets at lots of other men and gone off in cabs with lots of other women. And he seems to have killed the women too, for nobody can find them.'

'He is really rather naughty sometimes,' said Mary Gray, laughing softly as she buttoned her old gray gloves.[29]

The plot thickens and one is left puzzled not only by the curious, possibly homicidal, nature of Innocent Smith but also by the oblivious, apparently masochistic, nature of Mary Gray. Chesterton strings the mystery along. The novel's more mundane characters are intrigued by the presence of someone hidden in a tree:

'Who is there?' shouted Arthur. 'Who are you? Are you Innocent?'

'Not quite,' answered an obscure voice among the leaves. 'I cheated you once about a penknife.'

The wind in the garden had gathered strength, and was throwing the tree backwards and forwards with the man in the thick of it . . .

'But are you Smith?' asked Inglewood, as in an agony.

'Very nearly,' said the voice out of the tossing tree.

'But you must have some real names,' shrieked Inglewood in despair. 'You must call yourself something.'

'Call myself something,' thundered the obscure, shaking the tree so that all its ten thousand leaves seemed to be talking at once. 'I call myself Roland Oliver Isaiah Charlemagne Arthur Hildebrand Homer Danton Michaelangelo Shakespeare Brakespeare – '

'But, manalive!' began Inglewood in exasperation.

'That's right! That's right!' came with a roar out of the rocking tree; 'that's my real name.'[30]

It is two hundred pages later that the mystery of Innocent Smith finally begins to unfold:

There is but one answer, and I am sorry if you don't like it. If Innocent is happy, it is because he *is* innocent. If he can defy the conventions, it is just because he can keep the commandments. It is just because he does not want to kill but to excite to life that a pistol is still as exciting to him as it is to a schoolboy . . . It is just because he does not want to commit adultery that he achieves the romance of sex; it is just because he loves one wife that he has a hundred honeymoons. If he had really murdered a man, if he had really deserted a woman, he would not be able to feel that a pistol or a love-letter was like a song – at least, not a comic song.[31]

This is a return to familiar territory. The intrinsic wisdom of innocence and its unobtainability by the naïvely cynical is the novel's whole *raison d'être*. Innocent Smith is misunderstood because his innocence is inaccessible to those around him. He is so innocent that they think he must be guilty and so honest that he must be lying.

Yet there is a postscript which belongs to Mary Gray: '"Oh, what's the good of talking about men?" cried Mary impatiently; "why, one might as well be a lady novelist or some horrid thing. There aren't any men. There are no such people. There's a man; and whoever he is he's quite different."' After this appeal for an end to stereotypes, she does moderate her earlier statement slightly: 'there's only two things generally true of them. At certain curious times they're just fit to take care of us, and they're never fit to take care of themselves.'[32]

Whether this statement is true of men and women in general, it is certainly true of one man and one woman in particular, namely Gilbert and Frances. Above all, *Manalive* was a parable of the Chesterblogg. Innocent Smith was Gilbert, trying always to stir the world from its cynical slumber, while Mary Gray was Frances, the silence on which he depended utterly, the power behind the throne.

With the completion of *Manalive*, 1911 drew to a close. It had been a singularly successful year. During the previous twelve months the first Father Brown book had been published, *The Ballad of the White Horse* had established Gilbert as a poet of distinction and his reputation as a journalist and public debater had been firmly established. It was perhaps appropriate then that he should end the year with a novel which was a veritable song of contentment, a hymn of optimism about the triumph of innocence over adversity. It would also represent the calm before a coming storm. The following few years would bring a series of trials which would shake him from the comfort of complacency – or the complacency of comfort. From now on his innocence, though always emerging victorious, would be tempered by pain and bitter experience.

« 12 »

Brothers in Arms

IN OCTOBER 1912 a further collection of Chesterton's *Daily News* articles was published. Entitled *A Miscellany of Men*, it contained essays written for the paper between 1909 and 1912. One of the articles, 'The Romantic in the Rain', displayed the author at his most charming:

> All around me as I write is a noise of Nature drinking: and Nature makes a noise when she is drinking, being by no means refined. If I count it Christian mercy to give a cup of cold water to a sufferer, shall I complain of these multitudinous cups of cold water handed round to all living things; a cup of water for every shrub; a cup of water for every weed? I would be ashamed to grumble at it.[1]

Far from grumbling at it, he seemed determined to receive his share of this communion which feeds every plant:

> I could never reconcile myself to carrying an umbrella; it is a pompous Eastern Business, carried over the heads of despots in the dry, hot lands. Shut up, an umbrella is an unmanageable walking-stick; open, it is an inadequate tent. For my part, I have no taste for pretending to be a walking pavilion . . .[2]

In keeping with the ebullience of the previous year, Chesterton, the man alive, concludes with a song of praise to the rain:

> For indeed this is one of the real beauties of rainy weather, that while the amount of original and direct light is commonly lessened, the number of things that reflect light is unquestionably increased. There is less sunshine; but there are more shiny things; such beautifully

shiny things as pools and puddles and mackintoshes. It is like moving in a world of mirrors.[3]

In another memorable essay, 'The Architect of Spears', published originally on 13 May 1911, Chesterton brings Gothic architecture to life:

> The truth about Gothic is, first, that it is alive, and second, that it is on the march. It is the Church Militant; it is the only fighting architecture. All its spires are spears at rest; and all its stones are stones asleep in a catapult. In that instant of illusion, I could hear the arches clash like swords as they crossed each other. The mighty and numberless columns seemed to go swinging by like the huge feet of imperial elephants. The graven foliage wreathed and blew like banners going into battle; the silence was deafening with all the mingled noises of a military march; the great bell shook down, as the organ shook up its thunder. The thirsty-throated gargoyles shouted like trumpets from all the roofs and pinnacles as they passed; and from the lectern in the core of the cathedral the eagle of the awful evangelist clashed his wings of brass.[4]

Although these essays are perhaps the best of those collected in *A Miscellany of Men*, they are by no means typical. In most of Chesterton's journalism at this time, the poetic beauty of the prose had given way to the prosaic demands of the author's politics. Romance was replaced by rhetoric and even the Church Militant had given way to the Chesterton Militant. An essay entitled 'The Free Man' was representative of the new abrasive style:

> The mere love of liberty has never been at a lower ebb in England than it has been for the last twenty years. Never before has it been so easy to slip small Bills through Parliament for the purpose of locking people up. Never was it so easy to silence awkward questions, or to protect high-placed officials. . .
>
> Political liberty . . . means the power of saying the sort of things that a decent but discontented citizen wants to say. He does not want to spit on the Bible, or to run about without clothes, or to read the worst pages of Zola from the pulpit of St Paul's . . . But the normal man, the decent discontented citizen, does want to protest against unfair law courts. He does want to expose brutalities of the police. He does want to make game of a vulgar pawnbroker who is made a Peer. He does want publicly to warn people against unscrupulous

capitalists and suspicious finance. If he is run in for doing this (as he will be) he does want to proclaim the character or known prejudices of the magistrate who tries him. If he is sent to prison (as he will be) he does want to have a clear and civilised sentence, telling him when he will come out. And these are literally and exactly the things that he now cannot get. That is the almost cloying humour of the present situation. I can say abnormal things in modern magazines. It is the normal things that I am not allowed to say. I can write in some solemn quarterly an elaborate article explaining that God is the devil; I can write in some cultured weekly an aesthetic fancy describing how I should like to eat boiled baby. The thing I must not write is rational criticism of the men and institutions of my country.

The present condition of England is briefly this: That no Englishman can say in public a twentieth part of what he says in private. One cannot say, for instance, that – But I am afraid I must leave out that instance, because one cannot say it. I cannot prove my case – because it is so true.[5]

This dissident polemic was echoed in another essay in the same collection: 'All government is representative government until it begins to decay. Unfortunately (as is also evident) all government begins to decay the instant it begins to govern.'[6]

Chesterton's increased militancy was due primarily to the influence of both his brother Cecil and his friend Belloc. These two had launched the first number of the *Eye Witness*, a hard-hitting radical weekly, during the summer of 1911. A year later, in June 1912, the magazine was renamed the *New Witness* and Cecil became editor. In October 1912, the month that *A Miscellany of Men* was published, Belloc had published *The Servile State*, a definitive critique of modern industrial society and its evils. Previously Belloc and Cecil Chesterton had collaborated on a book entitled *The Party System*, which they had written 'to support the tendency now everywhere apparent and finding expression, a tendency to expose and ridicule as it deserves, to destroy and to supplant the system under which Parliament, the governing institution of this country, has been rendered null'.[7]

The extent to which Chesterton was influenced by the campaigning of his brother and Belloc can be gauged by, for instance, the essay from *A Miscellany of Men* entitled 'The Voter and the Two Voices', which accords with the central tenet of *The Party System*:

The real evil of our Party System is commonly stated wrong. It was stated wrong by Lord Rosebery, when he said that it prevented the best men from devoting themselves to politics, and that it encouraged a fanatical conflict. I doubt whether the best men ever would devote themselves to politics. The best men devote themselves to pigs and babies and things like that. And as for the fanatical conflict in party politics, I wish there was more of it. The real danger of the two parties with their two policies is that they unduly limit the outlook of the ordinary citizen. They make him barren instead of creative, because he is never allowed to do anything except prefer one existing policy to another. We have not got real Democracy when the decision depends upon the people. We shall have real Democracy when the problem depends upon the people. The ordinary man will decide not only how he will vote, but what he is going to vote about.[8]

These are clearly the words of disillusionment. Chesterton, ever the romantic in terms of philosophy, theology and the practical realities of life, was on the verge of cynicism as far as Britain's two-party system was concerned. He concluded the same article with a scenario which could have proved the inspiration for a typically Chestertonian novel but instead would come to fruition many years later in the nightmare visions of Huxley and Orwell:

The democracy has a right to answer questions, but it has no right to ask them. It is still the political aristocracy that asks the questions. And we shall not be unreasonably cynical if we suppose that the political aristocracy will always be rather careful what questions it asks. And if the dangerous comfort and self-flattery of modern England continues much longer there will be less democratic value in an English election than in a Roman saturnalia of slaves. For the powerful class will choose two courses of action, both of them safe for itself, and then give the democracy the gratification of taking one course or the other. The lord will take two things so much alike that he would not mind choosing them blindfold – and then for a great jest he will allow the slaves to choose.[9]

As well as being deeply influenced himself by the agitational propaganda of Cecil and Belloc, Chesterton came to meet others who had been similarly influenced. Father Vincent McNabb was drawn to their battle-cry in 1911 and made his first contribution to the *Eye Witness* in August of that year. A Dominican who was the parish priest of Holy Cross, Leicester, Father McNabb infused the social and ethical principles of the Catholic Church into the radicalism of the *Eye Witness*. He had derived his own views from the encyclical of Pope Leo XIII, *Rerum Novarum*, which had been published twenty years earlier. Known popularly as the Workers' Charter, this encyclical had condemned the rule of a 'few very rich men' who were laying upon 'the teeming masses of the labouring poor a yoke little better than slavery itself'. Father McNabb, however, took the Pope's teaching to a fundamentalist extreme, proclaiming that all industrialism was morally evil. Although Chesterton was always more pragmatic in his approach to industrialism, he and Father McNabb became close friends. In fact, part of the attraction of this Dominican monk in Chesterton's eyes was the way he practised what he preached. A devout advocate of the simple life, Father McNabb walked everywhere whenever possible, spurning modern forms of transport. He wore homespun robes and even refused to use a typewriter on the grounds that it was machinery.

Over the years their friendship matured but Chesterton remained in awe of the monk's spirituality. As we have seen, he wrote on one occasion, 'Father McNabb is walking on a crystal floor over my head.'[10] On the occasion of Father McNabb's golden jubilee celebrations at the London Priory, after the monk had spoken for over half an hour about the way that God had blessed his priestly life, Chesterton rose and told the audience that 'when Father Vincent was speaking to us I felt as if I was in the presence of God'.[11] These comments, taken cynically or superficially, may seem inapt, even crass, yet the sincerity of his words were borne out by Dorothy Collins, Chesterton's secretary, who picked him up from the Priory at the conclusion of the celebration: 'I called for Gilbert in the car and he had *thoroughly* enjoyed himself; and he spoke of Father Vincent as being "spiritually the greatest man in England at the present time".'[12] And in an introduction to Father McNabb's *Francis Thompson and Other Essays* Chesterton wrote the following tribute:

> I am nervous about writing here what I really think of Father Vincent McNabb, but I will say briefly and firmly that he is one of the few great men I have met in my life: that he is great in many ways – mentally and morally and mystically and practically and that next to nobody nowadays has ever heard of him. But there is a further development which has already made a considerable difference, and

that also is an interesting criticism of our time and of the type of effort needed to affect it, for at least nobody who ever met or saw or heard of Father McNabb has ever forgotten him.[13]

The influence of Father McNabb on Chesterton is evident, yet his own on Father McNabb was not inconsiderable. Ferdinand Valentine, one of Father McNabb's students when he was Prior of Hawkesyard, remembered Chesterton's influence on his tutor with an element of frustration: 'We couldn't help noticing that he tended to ruin his own graceful and accomplished style of speaking and writing, by imitating the paradoxes of Chesterton, which on the publication of *Orthodoxy* in 1909 were very much in vogue.'[14]

Another priest who was exerting a benign influence on Chesterton in 1912 was his old friend Father O'Connor. Already the inspiration for Father Brown, Father O'Connor also appears to have been instrumental in developing Chesterton's idea for his epic poem 'Lepanto'. In the late spring of 1912 both Chesterton and Father O'Connor took part in a meeting of the Ladies' Debating Society at Leeds. Chesterton gave the main address, after which Father O'Connor spoke a few words in his support:

> At the end of this discriminating support, I, with a kind of remorse, rallied to him with the age-long resistance of the Popes to the Grand Turk . . .
>
> I told of Lepanto, how Philip the Second of Spain had been assembling his Armada to invade England, and could only spare two ships to face the hundred galleys of the Porte; and how Don John of Austria, the only commander under whom Genoa would agree with Venice, burst the battle-line on a sinking ship, after fighting through all the hours of daylight. And the story of the Pope's prayer all that day, and his vision of the crisis of the action at three in the afternoon, with his vision of the victory about the time of the Angelus. Thus, I take it, came Chesterton to write the incomparable Ballad of *Lepanto* . . .
>
> On the way home I got fierce about what trash it made of English history, and what rubbish we talked and sang of Nelson and Trafalgar. What was at stake at Trafalgar? Only the Industrial Revolution and the Financial Supremacy of the City of London, with child-labour and Gin Palaces, only one small department of the gilded manure-heap called Modern Progress.
>
> He interrupted me – we were alone in the train going back to Ilkley – by telling me he had made up his mind to be received into the Church and was only waiting for Frances to come with him,

as she had led him into the Anglican Church out of Unitarianism.
'Because I think I have known intimately by now all the best kinds
of Anglicanism, and I find them only a pale imitation.' I was thrilled,
naturally, but not surprised.[15]

The ballad of 'Lepanto' reinforced Chesterton's reputation as a
poet, building on the respect which *The Ballad of the White Horse* had
earned him. As ever, one of his staunchest supporters and admirers
was Hilaire Belloc. In his essay *On the Place of Gilbert Keith Chesterton
in English Letters*, Belloc wrote: 'the whole of that poem *Lepanto* is
not only the summit of Chesterton's achievement in verse but the
summit of high rhetorical verse in all our generation. I have said
this so often that I am almost tired of saying it again, but I must
continue to say it. People who cannot see the value of *Lepanto* are
half dead. Let them so remain.'[16]

Belloc's championing of 'Lepanto' was remembered by the poet
Alfred Noyes:

> I had a great admiration for some of Chesterton's poems, particularly
> his *Lepanto*. Belloc asked me if I did not think it one of the finest
> of contemporary poems, and before I could express my cordial
> agreement, he added, 'Oh, but of course you wouldn't. All poets
> are jealous.' My only possible reply was, 'In that case I'm not a
> poet,' after which he became quite charming and conciliatory, and
> later added to the treasures of my library by sending me a pleasantly
> inscribed copy of that brilliant tour-de-force *Belinda*.[17]

Amid all the praise of his literary peers perhaps the tribute which
pleased Chesterton more than any other was a short note from John
Buchan, dated 21 June 1915: 'The other day in the trenches we
shouted your *Lepanto*.'[18]

Meanwhile, in Beaconsfield horizons were expanding. By the
summer of 1912 Frances and Gilbert had purchased the meadow
facing Overroads, where they built a brick-and-timber studio to
accommodate the large number of guests and young friends they regularly entertained. Father O'Connor, whose name appeared frequently
in the Overroads visitors' book, remembered that Chesterton's toy
theatre and puppet shows were popular 'with children of any age' and
that charades was another favourite pastime. He recalls playing the
part of Canon Crosskeys, in a charade in which Lily Yeats, the poet's
sister, also took part, one evening that was to end unhappily:

'The evening waxed late, and I offered my arm to Gilbert going over to the house, but he refused it with a finality foreign to our friendship. So I went on ahead. As I entered the house ten yards in front, he fell over a tree-pot at the corner, and broke his arm at 11.45 p.m. Six weeks in bed was the result.'[19]

As well as entertaining at home, the Chestertons had woven themselves into the social fabric of Beaconsfield. Chesterton designed a poster advertising a Dickens evening on Saturday, 17 February 1912, at the New Hall, Beaconsfield, 'by kind permission of Lord Burnham'.[20] This was a social event close to Chesterton's heart, since his love for Dickens had already found expression in two books, the biography of 1906 and his *Appreciations and Criticisms of the Works of Charles Dickens* published the previous year.

In 1913 *The Victorian Age in Literature* was to give him the opportunity to sing the praises of his favourite author yet again:

> Dickens was a mob – and a mob in revolt; he fought by the light of nature; he had not a theory, but a thirst. If anyone chooses to offer the cheap sarcasm that his thirst was largely a thirst for milk-punch, I am content to reply with complete gravity and entire contempt that in a sense this is perfectly true. His thirst was for things as humble, as human, as laughable as that daily bread for which we cry to God.[21]

The Victorian Age in Literature is, however, more memorable for the author's outspoken views on other aspects of nineteenth-century literature. Indeed, his views were sufficiently controversial in some respects to warrant a disclaimer from the publishers at the start of the book: 'The editors wish to explain that this book is not put forward as an authoritative history of Victorian literature. It is a free and personal statement of views and impressions about the significance of Victorian literature made by Mr Chesterton at the Editors' express invitation.'

Chesterton began his study by putting the Victorian era into its historical context:

> The previous literary life of this country had left vigorous many old forces in the Victorian time, as in our time. Roman Britain and Mediaeval England are still not only alive but lively; for real development is not leaving things behind, as on a road, but drawing life from them, as from a root ... The ancient English literature was

like all the several literatures of Christendom, alike in its likeness, alike in its very unlikeness. Like all European cultures, it was European; like all European cultures, it was something more than European. A most marked and unmanageable national temperament is plain in Chaucer and the ballads of Robin Hood; in spite of deep and sometimes disastrous changes of national policy, that note is still unmistakable in Shakespeare, in Johnson and his friends, in Cobbett, in Dickens. It is vain to dream of defining such vivid things; a national soul is as indefinable as a smell, and as unmistakable.[22]

Perhaps the most incisive – and the most inciting – of Chesterton's views were those concerning the women novelists of the Victorian era:

This is the first fact about the novel, that it is the introduction of a new and rather curious kind of art; and it has been found to be peculiarly feminine . . . It is a hearty and exhaustive overhauling of that part of human existence which has always been the woman's province, or rather kingdom; the play of personalities in private . . . What the novel deals with is what women have to deal with; the differentiations, the twists and turns of this eternal river. The key of this new form of art, which we call fiction, is sympathy. And sympathy does not mean so much feeling with all who feel, but rather suffering with all who suffer.[23]

After discussing the female novelists in general Chesterton dissected several of them individually. The works of George Eliot and Jane Austen were reviewed, then the Brontës came under scrutiny:

Undoubtedly the Brontës exposed themselves to some misunderstanding by . . . perpetually making the masculine creature much more masculine than he wants to be. Thackeray (a man of strong though sleepy virility) asked in his exquisite plaintive way: 'Why do our lady novelists make the men bully the women?' It is, I think, unquestionably true that the Brontës treated the male as an almost anarchic thing coming in from outside nature . . . The reply may be made that the women in men's novels are equally fallacious. The reply is probably just.[24]

To illustrate the point more specifically, Emily Brontë's creation is considered: 'Her imagination was sometimes superhuman – always inhuman. *Wuthering Heights* might have been written by an eagle. She is the strongest instance of these strong imaginations that made the other sex a monster: for Heathcliffe fails as a man as catastrophically as he succeeds as a demon.'[25]

The Victorian Age in Literature emphasised Chesterton's talent as an original and provocative literary critic. Yet in February 1913, when the book was published, he was too preoccupied as a critic of English society to devote much time to being a critic of English literature. His increasingly outspoken views were becoming too controversial for the columns of the *Daily News*, and its editor A. G. Gardiner wrote to inform him that his services as a weekly columnist were no longer required. His last article appeared on 1 February, ending twelve years of association with the paper.

There is no doubt that Gardiner, who was on very friendly terms with Chesterton, was being forced to comply with the will of George Cadbury, the paper's owner. Cadbury was being attacked continually in the pages of the *New Witness*, and an issue in January had contained several derogatory references to his 'Cocoa Press'. It was known that Cecil was the author of these; Gilbert could have claimed that he wasn't his brother's keeper. Gilbert, however, had no intention of making such a defence, since he now perceived himself and Cecil as brothers in arms against a corrupt plutocracy. The final straw, as far as Cadbury was concerned, and the final nail in Gilbert's coffin as a *Daily News* columnist, was the publication of his poem 'A Song of Strange Drinks' in the *New Witness* on 23 January. After praising wine and water and tolerating tea, which 'although an Oriental, is a gentleman at least', the third stanza proclaimed:

> Cocoa is a cad and coward,
> Cocoa is a vulgar beast,
> Cocoa is a crawling, cringing,
> Lying, loathsome swine and clown,
> And may very well be grateful
> To the fool that takes him down.

Gardiner, explaining that he hated all separations, expressed the belief and the hope that the columns of the *Daily News* would still be open to Chesterton in the near future. He was wrong. It would be fifteen years before the *Daily News* published anything else by him. Chesterton, for his part, seemed relatively undeterred by the dismissal and immediately began negotiations with the socialist paper, the *Daily Herald*. His first article for the *Herald* was published on 12 April.

If anything, Gilbert's running battle with, and subsequent dismissal from, the *Daily News* was only a minor sideshow compared with his brother's involvement in what became known as the Marconi Scandal. Cecil, through the pages of the *New Witness*, had exposed insider trading in the sale of Marconi shares. Briefly, the scandal arose when the managing director of the Marconi Company, Godfrey Isaacs, used inside knowledge to trade in his company's shares. The affair took on a potentially explosive nature because of the involvement of senior government officials. The financial beneficiaries included Rufus Isaacs, the Attorney General, who was Godfrey Isaacs's brother, Lloyd George, the Chancellor of the Exchequer, and the Master of Elibank, the Government Chief Whip.

Eventually a Select Committee of the House of Commons was appointed in an attempt to get at the truth of the affair. Cecil, who was summoned to appear before the Committee on 2 January 1913, was convinced that it would never have been appointed if he hadn't raised 'a pretty considerable agitation'. Although the *New Witness*, under his editorship, had been at the forefront of those demanding an inquiry, it would be wrong to imply that it was the only journal seeking action. The *National Review* and the *Morning Post*, as well as the financial press, were also prominent in their condemnation of the ministers' actions.

Meanwhile, Godfrey Isaacs, no doubt working on the principle that the best means of defence was attack, had sued Cecil for criminal libel. The preliminary hearing at Bow Street police court was held on 28 February. Gilbert, in the company of Belloc, attended the hearing, at which the defendant was committed for trial. Belloc reported to Maurice Baring that Cecil's speech had made a powerful impression. In response to the claim by Isaacs's counsel that the *New Witness* was a 'gutter rag', Cecil listed the literati who had contributed to it. 'When any man acquainted with letters were to make out a list of, say, the twenty best-known literary men in England today, I will undertake to find twelve of them among the contributors to my paper.'[26] He went on to mention Quiller-Couch, Wells, Shaw and Belloc by name. Tactfully, perhaps, he omitted to mention his own brother, but he might well have added Arthur Ransome, Maurice Baring, E. Nesbit and Desmond MacCarthy.

In the interval between Cecil's appearance at Bow Street and the commencement of the full trial at the Central Criminal Court on 27 May, Gilbert himself became embroiled in the issue. Ever protective of his younger brother, he was increasingly bitter towards those he perceived to be his persecutors. On 3 April he wrote a scathing attack on Sir Rufus Isaacs in the *New Witness*:

> If ever a human being on this earth most distinctly did not tell people 'what was in his mind' even when he professed to doing it, he is Sir Rufus Isaacs. What was in his mind was the recent memory of shovelling Marconis in and out as a croupier does coins; what was on his lips was a distinct denial proper to an intellectual man who had hardly heard of such things.

In the following week's edition of the *New Witness* he renewed his attack with even more venom:

> The politics of Sir Rufus Isaacs are as wearisome to the flesh as his religion would be a revelation to the soul. It must also be remembered that in the days when theological tests united and divided men clearly, it was much easier to look at an alien thing with the clean curiosity of the artist. Anti-Semitism is a sour fruit – but it is the fruit of Crypto-Semitism.

Cecil's trial lasted ten days, and Gilbert, accompanied by Frances, attended each day's proceedings. On the ninth day he was called and questioned on oath about his brother's character, as were Maurice Baring and Conrad Noel. When asked how long he had known 'the accused gentleman', Chesterton replied, 'Since he was born, I think'; and when asked what he had to say about him, he answered, 'I can only say I rather envy him the dignity of his present position.' Finally, after being brought to the point, he added, 'His character is good in my opinion and most other people's opinion.'[27]

However, the matter principally under consideration at the trial was whether the character of Godfrey Isaacs was good. The case, as the judge emphasised, had nothing to do with the question of whether there had been unethical trading in Marconi shares but 'whether the individual Godfrey Isaacs, in his career as a company-promoter previous to the Marconi Case, had been unfairly described by the individual Cecil Chesterton'.[28] The jury found Cecil guilty as charged and the judge, before passing sentence, questioned whether Cecil had thought deeply enough about the effects of his actions:

When I consider the cruelty of some of these charges, the effect I daresay not considered but obvious to anybody who did consider them, it might have rendered Godfrey Charles Isaacs a beggar and driven him from his employment as well as driven him from all fame and respect and good name, and when I remember the sending of those placards along the front of his place of business in the Strand, it is extremely difficult to restrain oneself from sending you to prison.[29]

None the less, the judge did restrain himself from passsing the three-year prison sentence Cecil was expected to receive if found guilty. Instead he was only fined £100. This was taken as being indicative of a moral victory, and there was much cheering from Cecil's supporters in the public gallery when the sentence was announced. However, those of a more cynical or conspiratorial disposition could not help but notice that the judge, Mr Justice Phillimore, was a cousin of John Phillimore, a great friend of both Chesterton and Belloc, who held the Chair of Classics at Glasgow University and whose review of *The Oxford Book of Latin Verse* was published in the *New Witness* the very week that Cecil was sentenced.

There was another twist in the tale. Cecil, in the middle of the trial, had sought out the same Father Bowden at the Brompton Oratory who had converted Maurice Baring four years earlier. On 7 June he was received into the Catholic Church at Corpus Christi, Maiden Lane. But the final *coup de grâce* belonged to Godfrey Isaacs, who was received into the Catholic Church himself some years later. Truth, it seems, is infinitely stranger than fiction. Gilbert recorded his views about Isaacs's conversion in his *Autobiography*:

And there is to be added to this a curious and ironic conclusion to the matter; for many years after my brother received the Last Sacraments and died in a hospital in France, his old enemy, Godfrey Isaacs, died very shortly after being converted to the same universal Catholic Church. No one would have rejoiced more than my brother; or with less bitterness or with more simplicity. It is the only reconciliation; and it can reconcile anybody. *Requiescant in pace.*[30]

At the height of Cecil's trial Gilbert was himself threatened with a libel action by Sir William Lever. The action was brought because Chesterton had referred to Port Sunlight, the Lever Brothers

Soap Company's model worker city, as 'corresponding to a Slave Compound'.[31] Upon hearing of the threatened libel action Bernard Shaw wrote Chesterton a letter of support, offering financial help to fight the case. Chesterton also wrote to Wells, apparently at the instigation of his solicitor:

Dear Wells,

I am asked to make a suggestion to you that looks like, and indeed is, infernal impudence: but which a further examination will rob of most of its terrors. Let not these terrors be redoubled when I say that the request comes from my solicitor. It is a great lark; I am writing for him when he ought to be writing for me.

In the forthcoming case of Lever v. Chesterton & Another, the Defendant Chesterton will conduct his own case; as his heart is not, like that of the lady in the song, Another's. He wants to fight it purely as a point of the liberty of letters and public speech; and to show that the phrase 'slavery' (wherein I am brought in question) is current in the educated controversy about the tendency of Capitalism today. The solicitor, rather to my surprise, approves this general sociological line of defence; and says that I may be allowed one or two witnesses of weight and sociological standing – not (of course) to say my words are defensible, still less that my view is right – but simply to say that the Servile State, and servile terms in connection with it, are known to them as parts of a currrent and quite unmalicious controversy. He has suggested your name: and when I have written this I have done my duty to him . . . Do you care to come and see the fun?[32]

In the event the suggested line of defence was so successful that Wells's testimony was not needed. The case was withdrawn and no apology was sought. In any case, it was certain that no apology would be given, since Chesterton, under the acerbic influence of his brother, had become more militant than ever. The previous year, at a meeting organised by the Church Socialist League in support of a miners' strike, he had expressed regret that England had not experienced a civil war, adding that if there were a civil war, it would be a good thing. Immediately after the meeting a procession of some six hundred people walked to Lambeth Palace, led by the Labour MP George Lansbury, who was carrying a cross. The meeting was also noteworthy for being the first occasion on which Chesterton's hymn 'O God of Earth and Altar' was sung. This hymn, normally sung to a traditional English melody arranged by Vaughan Williams,

combined a complex mixture of theological humility with the anger
of Christ in the temple:

> O God of earth and altar,
>   Bow down and hear our cry,
> Our earthly rulers falter,
>   Our people drift and die;
> The walls of gold entomb us,
>   The swords of scorn divide,
> Take not Thy thunder from us,
>   But take away our pride.
>
> From all that terror teaches,
>   From lies of tongue and pen,
> From all the easy speeches
>   That comfort cruel men,
> From sale and profanation
>   Of honour and the sword,
> From sleep and from damnation,
>   Deliver us, good Lord.
>
> Tie in a living tether
>   The prince and priest and thrall,
> Bind all our lives together,
>   Smite us and save us all;
> In ire and exultation
>   Aflame with faith and free,
> Lift up a living nation,
>   A single sword to Thee.

The theme of an English civil war, or an English revolution, was
one to which Chesterton returned in *The Victorian Age in Literature*:

It is no idle Hibernianism to say that towards the end of the eighteenth
century the most important event in English history happened in
France. It would seem still more perverse, yet it would be still more
precise, to say that the most important event in English history was
the event that never happened at all – the English Revolution on
the lines of the French Revolution. Its failure was not due to any
lack of fervour or even ferocity in those who would have brought
it about . . . The revolution failed because it was foiled by another
revolution; an aristocratic revolution, a victory of the rich over the

poor ... And the effect of this in turn was that from the middle of
the eighteenth century to the middle of the nineteenth century the
spirit of revolt in England took a wholly literary form. In France
it was what people did that was wild and elemental; in England it
was what people wrote. It is a quaint comment on the notion that
the English are practical and the French merely visionary, that we
were the rebels in arts while they were rebels in arms.[33]

It is clear that Chesterton saw himself as part of this living tradition.
He too was a rebel in arts and he believed that he and Cecil were
brothers in arms in a single struggle for justice. Yet the romantic
notion of an English civil war would soon be eclipsed by the grim
reality of a very uncivil world war.

« 13 »

Magic and Miracles

On 7 November 1913 Chesterton's first play opened at the Little Theatre in London. *Magic*, described as 'a fantastic comedy in three acts', was performed together with a one-act farce, *Germinae*, by George Calderon, and a programme of music by a string trio that included Brahms's Hungarian dances in its repertoire. A vivid account of the play's opening night was given by Ada Jones, Cecil's fiancée:

One of G. K.'s most attractive points was his complete freedom from any literary affectation. He was always quite honestly astonished at his success, and incredulous of his genius. I have never seen him more responsive than he was to the congratulations of his friends that night . . .

It was a memorable evening. Gilbert and Frances were almost mobbed in the foyer, and at every interval were eagerly surrounded. She wore a quite charming gown of a pre-Raphaelite cut in blue and gold, and I think was genuinely overcome by their reception . . .

The performance all round was exceptionally fine. Fred Lewis, that matchless actor, was supreme as the Duke, and muddled irresistibly all over the stage. Patricia was played by Grace Croft, who gave a very delicious sketch of a young girl . . .

There was an immense ovation when the curtain rang down, and Gilbert made one of his wittiest and most delightful speeches. There were demands from the management that he and his wife should go to supper at the Savoy with the members of the company, and the author, I know, would have accepted the invitation. But it was not to be, and the Chestertons returned with us to Warwick Gardens, where a huge sheaf of wires attracted G. K.'s attention.[1]

Encouraged by her husband, Frances set about opening these and read them aloud to the assembled company. One can visualise the scene being re-enacted the following morning: Frances eagerly reading the reviews in the daily newspapers while Gilbert looked on, wryly amused. By and large, Frances would have been pleased with what she saw because the critics generally approved of Chesterton's début as a playwright. The public were equally impressed; *Magic* had to be reprinted five times within four months of the opening performance. To celebrate the hundredth performance Bernard Shaw wrote a one-act play, *The Music-Cure*, which was used as the curtain-raiser at all subsequent performances. On 2 March 1914 a special souvenir edition of *Magic* was presented by Kenelm Foss, the play's director, 'to commemorate the one hundred and fiftieth performance of *Magic* by G. K. Chesterton and the fiftieth performance of *The Music Cure* by Bernard Shaw'.

Perhaps the most magnanimous praise for *Magic* came from George Moore, the Irish writer, who wrote to a friend on 24 November 1913:

> I followed the comedy of *Magic* from the first line to the last with interest and appreciation, and I am not exaggerating when I say that I think of all modern plays I like it the best. Mr Chesterton wished to express an idea and his construction and his dialogue are the best that he could have chosen for the expression of that idea: therefore, I look upon the play as practically perfect . . .
>
> I hope I can rely upon you to tell Mr Chesterton how much I appreciated his Play as I should like him to know my artistic sympathies.[2]

The enormous generosity and magnanimity of this expression of Moore's 'artistic sympathies' can be gauged by comparing it with Chesterton's earlier criticism of Moore in *Heretics*: 'Mr Moore's egoism is not merely a moral weakness, it is a very constant and influential aesthetic weakness as well. We should really be much more interested in Mr Moore if he were not quite so interested in himself.'[3] Earlier in the same essay Chesterton had complained that Moore 'has admired all the most admirable modern eccentrics until they could stand it no longer'.[4] Little did he know that eight years later he would be added to Moore's venerable list of admirable modern eccentrics.

If Chesterton's play had struck the ageing Moore as perfect, it struck the young C. S. Lewis as merely perplexing. He recorded in his diary: 'I read *Magic* through. A pleasant little play – I am not sure that I understand it.'[5]

It seems, however, that *Magic* was popular with those considerably less refined than either Moore or Lewis. When the play was read aloud to the convicts in Pentonville Prison a single line – 'I hear the vegetarians killed a policeman in Kent' – caused a spontaneous outburst of loud applause and laughter from prisoners, prison officers and the prison chaplain. When this was reported to Chesterton, he exclaimed, 'I'm so glad to have given the poor fellows a few moments of freedom.'[6] It is perhaps ironic that these words, which conveyed an almost Pythonesque absurdity and humour in Chesterton's day, should have become unwittingly prophetic in the wake of increasingly militant animal rights demonstrations today.

Inevitably, Chesterton's foray into the field of drama brought comparisons with Shaw. For instance, when the play was produced in Germany a Munich newspaper reported that 'he means more to it than the good old Shaw'.[7] However, even Chesterton's friend and biographer, Maisie Ward, questioned whether Chesterton could really be compared to Shaw, stating, 'Chesterton's superiority can hardly be entertained in the matter of technique.' Yet she maintained that Chesterton excelled in a different way: 'Chesterton once said that he suspected Shaw of being the only man who had never written any poetry. Many of us suspect that Chesterton never wrote anything else. This play is a poem and the greatest character in it is atmosphere.'[8]

Another friend, Father O'Connor, took a different view, maintaining that Chesterton's technique was indeed superior to Shaw's:

> . . . it was my good luck to listen to a week of Shavian Drama, and to be much persuaded of the perfect ear of Shaw for the spoken word. It appeared to me that he could 'get away' with almost anything by sheer beauty of diction. About one week later I came upon an amateur performance of Chesterton's *Magic* and was startled to find his dialogue even better than Shaw's. At Beaconsfield in the autumn of that year I told Chesterton my findings. 'Strange you should say it,' quoth he; 'Shaw has been telling me the same thing, urging me to go in for play-writing. He says I could do it so much better than himself.'[9]

In fact, Shaw had been urging Chesterton to write drama for years. In a letter dated 1 March 1908 he had pleaded for a play from Chesterton's pen:

> What about that play? It is no use trying to answer me in the *New Age*: the real answer to my article is the play. I have tried fair means: The *New Age* article was the inauguration of an assault below the belt. I shall deliberately destroy your credit as an essayist, as a journalist, as a critic, as a Liberal, as everything that offers your laziness a refuge, until starvation and shame drive you to serious dramatic parturition. I shall repeat my public challenge to you; vaunt my superiority; insult your corpulence; torture Belloc; if necessary, call on you and steal your wife's affections by intellectual and athletic displays, until you contribute something to the British drama. You are played out as an essayist: your ardour is soddened, your intellectual substance crumbled, by the attempt to keep up the work of your twenties in your thirties. Another five years of this and you will be the apologist of every infamy that wears a Liberal or Catholic mask ... Nothing can save you now except a rebirth as a dramatist. I have done my turn; and I now call on you to take yours and do a man's work.[10]

On 30 October 1909 Shaw was again urging his friend to write drama, this time offering practical advice:

> It can be plausibly held that you are a venal ruffian, pouring forth great quantities of immediately saleable stuff, but altogether declining to lay up for yourself treasures in heaven. It may be that you cannot afford to do otherwise. Therefore I am quite ready to make a deal with you.
>
> A full length play should contain about 18,000 words (mine frequently contain two or three times that number). I do not know what your price per thousand is. I used to be considered grossly extortionate by Massingham and others for insisting on £3. Eighteen thousand words at £3 per thousand is £54. I need make no extra allowance for the republication in book form, because even if the play aborted as far as the theatre is concerned, you could make a book of it all the same. Let us assume that your work is worth twice as much as mine: this would make £108. I have had two shockingly bad years of it pecuniarily speaking, and am therefore in that phase of extravagance which straitened means have always produced in me. Knock off 8% as a sort of agent's commission to me for starting you on the job and finding you a theme. This leaves £100. I will pay you

£100 down on your contracting to supply me within three months with a mechanically possible, i.e., stageable drama dealing with the experiences of St Augustine after re-visiting England. The literary copyright to be yours, except that you are not to prevent me making as many copies as I may require for stage use. The stage right to be mine; but you are to have the right to buy it back from me for £250 whenever you like . . . What do you say? There is a lot of spending in £100.[11]

It must be assumed that Chesterton declined the offer because the play never materialised. Two and a half years later, on 5 April 1912, Shaw was again endeavouring to get him to write drama. This time he changed tactics by writing to Frances instead of Gilbert, imploring her to persuade her husband:

Dear Mrs Chesterton,

I have promised to drive somebody to Beaconsfield on Sunday morning; and I shall be in that district more or less for the rest of the day. If you are spending Easter at Overroads, and have no visitors who couldn't stand us, we should like to call on you at any time that would be convenient.

The convenience of time depends on a design of my own which I wish to impart to you first. I want to read a play to Gilbert. It began by way of being a music-hall sketch; so it is not three-and-a-half hours long as usual: I can get through it in an hour and a half. I want to insult and taunt and stimulate Gilbert with it. It is a sort of thing he could write and ought to write: a religious harlequinade. In fact, he could do it better if a sufficient number of pins were stuck into him. My proposal is that I read the play to him on Sunday (or at the next convenient date), and that you fall into transports of admiration of it; declare that you can never love a man who cannot write things like that; and definitely announce that if Gilbert has not finished a worthy successor to it before the end of the third week next ensuing, you will go out like the lady in *A Doll's House*, and live your own life – whatever that dark threat may mean . . .

Forgive this long rigmarole: it is only to put you in possession of what *may* happen if you approve, and your invitations and domestic circumstances are propitious.[12]

Again, whether or not the proposed visit ever materialised, the proposed play didn't. Eventually, however, eighteen months later Shaw got his way and Chesterton had written a play for the London stage. Why was Shaw so doggedly persistent in his insistence that Chesterton should try his hand at drama? Was it, as Father O'Connor implied, a selfless gesture because Shaw believed Gilbert to be his literary equal or even his superior, or was there an ulterior motive? The facts appear to point to the latter conclusion because Chesterton was not the only writer being urged by Shaw to try drama. Shaw was very heavily involved with Harley Granville-Barker in the revolutionising of the London theatre and, as part of his crusade to broaden the literary base of British drama, he wrote to Conrad, Kipling and Wells, as well as Chesterton. Quite simply, Shaw was obsessed with getting as many well-known writers as possible to write plays. In the event Chesterton was the only writer to succumb to Shaw's persuasion.

Shaw did appear to rate *Magic* very highly. In a signed review of Julius West's *G. K. Chesterton: A Critical Study* in the *New Statesman* of 13 May 1916 he wrote:

I agree very heartily with Mr West as to Mr Chesterton's success in his single essay as a playwright. I shirk the theatre so lazily that I have lost the right to call myself a playgoer; but circumstances led to my seeing *Magic* performed several times, and I enjoyed it more and more every time. Mr Chesterton was born with not only brains enough to see something more in the world than sexual intrigue, but with all the essential tricks of the stage at his fingers' ends; and it was delightful to find that the characters which seem so fantastic and even ragdolly (stage characters are usually waxdolly) in his romances became credible and solid behind the footlights, just the opposite of what his critics expected. The test is a searching one: an exposure to it of many moving and popular scenes in novels would reveal the fact that they are physically impossible and morally absurd. Mr Chesterton is in the English tradition of Shakespeare and Fielding and Scott and Dickens, in which you must grip your character so masterfully that you can play with it in the most extravagant fashion . . . The Duke in *Magic* is much better than Micawber or Mrs Wilfer, neither of whom can bear the footlights because, like piping bullfinches, they have only one tune, whilst the Duke sets everything in the universe to his ridiculous music. That is the Shakespearian touch. Is it grateful to ask for more?[13]

Ironically and surprisingly, Shaw's laudatory view of *Magic* was not shared by the one man who was normally Chesterton's greatest literary advocate. Belloc had been taken to see his friend's play by Lady Juliet

Duff. He was unimpressed, believing the play got worse as it went on and that many of the speeches had nothing to do with the stage at all.[14]

The most significant criticism of *Magic* appeared in the *Dublin Review* in January 1914. Written by Chesterton himself, it illustrated the author's humour and humility – along with an ability to be ruthlessly self-critical:

> The author of *Magic* ought to be told plainly that his play . . . has been treated with far too much indulgence in the public press. I will glide mercifully over the most glaring errors, which the critics have overlooked – no Irishman could become so complete a cad merely by going to America – that no young lady would walk about in the rain so soon before it was necessary to dress for dinner . . . The Secretary disappears half way through the play . . . By the exercise of that knowledge of all human hearts which descends on any man . . . the moment he is a dramatic critic, I perceive that the author of *Magic* originally wrote it as a short story. It is a bad play, because it was a good short story.[15]

Although nobody could have known it at the time, possibly not even Gilbert himself, this critical review effectively announced the author's retirement as a playwright. Regardless of Shaw's protestations to the contrary, Chesterton was convinced that his abilities as a dramatist were severely limited. In future, apart from a few half-hearted dabblings in drama, he would stick to writing good short stories instead of bad plays.

The last word on Gilbert's brief moment of glory on the London stage belongs to the brief moment of glory itself when he took the stage on the opening night to accept the applause and to make what his brother's fiancée called 'one of his wittiest and most delightful speeches'. During the speech, in defiance of the audience's acclaim, he confessed a lack of belief in his own abilities. He did not believe he could write a good play, nor a good article, nor even a picture postcard, perhaps the hardest task of all. But he did believe in his own opinions, and so sure was he that they were right that he wanted his audience to believe them too.[16]

Whether wittingly or unwittingly, Chesterton had isolated the play's primary weakness in this speech. He had always used his art as a vehicle for his ideas. His poetry, novels, short stories and journalism had all become successfully subservient to the ideas they conveyed. Yet *Magic* had not become successfully subservient in the same way. As a vehicle for his ideas the play was heavy-handed and awkward. Either the ideas interfered with the dialogue or the dialogue dulled the ideas. In the end each cancelled out the other and neither triumphed. *Magic*, although written for the stage, was better suited for the soap-box.

Chesterton's next sortie on to the stage came in much less serious circumstances. On 7 January 1914, while *Magic* was still playing to appreciative audiences at London's Little Theatre, Chesterton starred in a mock trial at the King's Hall, Covent Garden. The trial in question was that of John Jasper, the lay precentor of Cloisterham Cathedral in the County of Kent, who was accused of the murder of Edwin Drood, an engineer. The trial was based, of course, on *The Mystery of Edwin Drood*, Dickens's last, unfinished novel. Sponsored by the Dickens Fellowship, the light-hearted project was supported by an all-star cast. Chesterton had agreed to play the judge, Cecil was the counsel for the defence, and Cecil's fiancée, Ada Jones, played Princess Puffer, the Opium Woman. J. Cuming Walters led for the prosecution and the witnesses included Arthur Waugh, father of Evelyn, who played Canon Crisparkle. The foreman of the jury was Shaw, and other members of the jury included Belloc, W. W. Jacobs, G. S. Street and William Archer. None of the amateur actors had the use of prepared scripts but they were obviously very familiar with the unfinished novel.

According to Ada Jones, the original inspiration for the trial came from Cecil, who could 'repeat parts of Edwin Drood, when the mood took him, *in extenso*. The story had always fascinated him, his contention being that the hero had not been murdered, but had just disappeared until such time as Dickens decided to reproduce him. The topic became a favourite point of controversy, and discussion raged.'[17] From these discussions arose the idea of the trial: 'Both the brothers were members of the Dickens Fellowship, which at the moment was deeply concerned with the poverty of some of the novelist's grand-children. Money was wanted to help them, and presently the bright idea occurred that funds could be raised, and entertainment provided, by staging the Trial of John Jasper for the Murder of Edwin Drood.'[18]

The proposed 'trial' caught the imagination of press and public alike so that 'applications for tickets were so heavy that the house could have been sold out six times over'. Ada Jones provided a vivid description of the whole event, stating that Cecil had immersed himself in the case 'with the same thoroughness and care that he devoted to the exposure of government scandals'. Wigs and gowns supplied by barrister friends ensured that the characters looked the part and Gilbert was 'magnificent' as the judge: 'G. K. was in his wittiest and most brilliant vein. The game was played according to rule, and every possible legal point and quibble was raised and contested. He looked very handsome in his full-bottomed wig and scarlet robe.'[19]

The drama of the evening – the cross-examinations of the witnesses by both counsels and the occasional interjections on points of law by Mr Justice Chesterton – dragged on for nearly four hours before events approached a climax:

> The Judge, assuming the essential portentousness, summed up with wit and shrewdness. His analysis of the evidence was masterly, and on the tip-toe of excitement the audience waited for the jury to retire for the consideration of their verdict.
>
> Now at last Dickensians felt that the clouds of doubt would disperse, and the actual existence or death of the missing Edwin be settled. But at that moment the verdict was snatched from the jury's mouth and the issue for ever postponed. Bernard Shaw, in his beloved role of *enfant terrible*, intervened. Posterity, he said, might accept the jury's verdict as evidence as to what Dickens had intended. We did not know – nobody knew – just what fate Edwin Drood's creator had decided for him, and it would be presumptuous and, indeed, indefensible, to decide on his behalf.
>
> Shaw's wit, charm and irresistible voice carried the day. There was indeed no possible sequel to such an anticlimax, and to the general disappointment the show ended – suspense closed down.[20]

In fact, Ada Jones, in her memory of the evening's proceedings, had omitted the fact that there was a sequel to Shaw's anticlimax. The last word, and the last laugh, belonged to the judge. In a short concluding speech, Chesterton committed everyone but himself to jail for contempt of court.

Six months later Shaw and Chesterton were again involved in a light-hearted romp, this time at Shaw's instigation. On this occasion they made their film débuts, starring as cowboys alongside William Archer and Lord Howard de Walden, in a film produced by J. M. Barrie and directed by Shaw's theatrical collaborator, Granville-Barker. Chesterton's account of this bizarre episode conjures up an atmosphere of surrealism worthy of Salvador Dali's later experiments in cinematic self-indulgence:

> We went down to the waste land in Essex and found our Wild West equipment. But considerable indignation was felt against William Archer; who, with true Scottish foresight, arrived there first and put on the best pair of trousers. They were indeed a magnificent pair of fur trousers; while the other three riders of the prairie had to be content with canvas trousers. A running commentary upon this piece of individualism continued throughout the afternoon; while we were being rolled in barrels, roped over faked precipices and eventually turned loose in a field to lasso wild ponies, which were so tame that they ran after us instead of our running after them, and nosed in our pockets for pieces of sugar. Whatever may be the strain on credulity, it is also a fact that we all got on the same motor-bicycle; the wheels of which were spun round under us to produce the illusion of hurtling like a thunderbolt down the mountain-pass. When the rest finally vanished over the cliffs, clinging to the rope, they left me behind as a necessary weight to secure it; and Granville-Barker kept on calling out to me to Register Self-Sacrifice and Register Resignation, which I did with such wild and sweeping gestures as occurred to me; not, I am proud to say, without general applause. And all this time Barrie, with his little figure behind his large pipe, was standing about in an impenetrable manner; and nothing could extract from him the faintest indication of why we were being put through these ordeals ... It was as if the smoke that rose from that pipe was a vapour not only of magic, but of black magic ... I have since heard in a remote and roundabout way certain vague suggestions, to the effect that there was some symbolical notion of our vanishing from real life and being captured or caught up in the film world of romance; being engaged through all the rest of the play in struggling to fight our way back to reality. Whether this was the idea I have never known for certain; I only know that I received immediately afterwards a friendly and apologetic note from Sir James Barrie, saying that the whole scheme was going to be dropped.[21]

On 22 January 1914, with Barrie's cinematic romp still six months away, Chesterton's latest literary romp was published. *The Flying Inn* was a return to more familiar ground following the theatrical ramblings of *Magic*. Indeed, the two works were as different stylistically as a night at the theatre compared to a night on the town.

The Flying Inn, a fictional flight of fancy in the same tradition as his earlier novels, raced riotously through an England which, under Islamic influence, had prohibited the sale of alcohol. The two heroes, a wild Irishman and the last English inn-keeper, embark on a series of adventures arising out of their spirited resistance to the imposition of this tyrannical teetotalism.

The high jinks and adventure of the plot aside, *The Flying Inn* was intended as a protest against the lobbying of the Temperance Movement for stricter licensing laws. Also, although the total ban on alcohol may seem somewhat far-fetched today, it should be remembered that at the time of the novel's publication the United States had not yet embarked on the policy of Prohibition. Consequently, *The Flying Inn* contained an element of prophecy. None the less, most people, critics and public alike, seemed to agree that the highlights of the novel were the verses, masquerading as drinking songs, which punctuated the text. These included 'Wine and Water', 'The Song Against Grocers', 'The Song of the Oak' and, most memorably, 'The Rolling English Road', which is perhaps the best-loved of all Chesterton's poetry.

On the Monday afternoon of 19 January, three days prior to the publication of *The Flying Inn*, Chesterton took part in a lively public debate on the subject of whether miracles happen. The debate took place at the Little Theatre, a singularly appropriate venue since it was being held as a response to certain controversial aspects of Chesterton's *Magic*, the play currently being performed at the theatre. The principal protagonists in the debate divided into two camps. The sceptics included Joseph McCabe, who had been branded as one of the 'heretics' in Chesterton's earlier book of that name, and the economist J. A. Hobson, who would later brand himself as an 'Economic Heretic'. The champions of the orthodox Christian belief in miracles were G. K. Chesterton, Cecil Chesterton and Hilaire Belloc. The chairman of the meeting was Kenelm Foss, the director of *Magic*, whose opening remarks illustrate Gilbert's total surprise at being asked to give the opening address: 'Ladies and Gentlemen, the first thing I have to do is to apologise, not so much to you, as to Mr Chesterton, who protests that I have been guilty of the utmost treachery. He maintains that he intended to come here and hear other people say there were no miracles, and then say there were.'[22]

In truth, Chesterton's rambling address to the meeting betrayed a woeful lack of preparation. Yet there were a number of redeeming moments, such as this confession:

I in my boyhood worked with a planchette; and, though I am perfectly willing to admit that I may have gone mad for the time being, or that there were resources in my subconsciousness I should never have imagined to exist, if anybody tells me that it was either cheating or done by my own will, I say it is nonsense. The thing ran across a table a good deal longer than this by which I am standing, with a violent pull. There was something undoubtedly behind it, and it was not either of the two people working it. I simply put that in as my own personal testimony. I also came to the conclusion afterwards that it was a bad experiment, and I would not go on with it; and that is, I fear, faintly connected with the moral of the play to which too much reference has been made.[23]

Apart from this interesting autobiographical aside, there was little in Gilbert's opening address to convince sceptics of the existence of miracles. In fact, after Joseph McCabe had skilfully and patiently dissected the loose ends in his speech, it was clear that his performance had been lacklustre. It was then that Belloc entered the fray:

Heaven knows nowadays what can be called a miracle! When those wonderful cures first took place at Lourdes it was said these cures were auto-suggestion. You could cure this and that by 'auto-suggestion', but you could not cure something else with a long scientific name; when this next cure was effected, a fresh disease was mentioned, as certainly incurable, and so on. Each miracle is called impossible *until it takes place*. When it can no longer be denied, it is given a long name and called natural.[24]

Yet Belloc was outshone on this occasion by the lesser-known of the Chesterton brothers. Cecil, in stark contrast to his brother, seemed positively inspired:

I cannot follow Mr Hobson's argument about purpose in the universe as distinct from personality ... When you say a man has 'purpose', you mean he desires a certain thing to happen and seeks to make it happen; that can only be done by a person. If there is a purpose in Nature, there is a personality; to talk about the purpose of Nature without a personality is to talk mere muddle-headed nonsense.
... but if there is a personality behind Nature, and everything that happens in the universe is the result of that personality, then, though each miracle is improbable, miracles in general are most probable ...

If you believe that there is a person or personality ruling the universe, that the things that happen are the action of that Person, and that that Person has will and freewill, as we have freewill, then it is an overwhelmingly probable thing that miracles do happen. In addition to this, you have the abundant and overwhelming testimony of history that in fact they do.[25]

It is certainly worthy of note that Cecil Chesterton, so often lurking in the shadow of his brother and Belloc, should have overshadowed both of them in this debate. Indeed, at the beginning of 1914 there was every sign that he was finally emerging as a force to be reckoned with in his own right. He had taken centre-stage the previous year during the Marconi affair, and he was widely respected in his role as a radical journalist.

It was still Gilbert, however, who took centre-stage at the Little Theatre where his play was acclaimed even if his speech on miracles had floundered. Perhaps, in this period in Chesterton's literary career when he was experimenting with drama, the final word should belong to a fellow playwright. Israel Zangwill wrote the following letter apologising for his inability to attend the miracles debate:

I am glad to hear *Magic* is producing the debate which it challenges. The stage is here doing its right work. I only regret that I am so worn out by rehearsals for my own play, *The Melting Pot*, that I am leaving town, and cannot hope to be back by Monday – unless by a miracle. And miracles do not happen. That was Matthew Arnold's formula, and I agree with it. Mr Chesterton is putting back the clock of philosophy even while he is putting forward the clock of drama. My satisfaction with the success of his play would thus be marred were it not that people enjoy it without understanding what Mr Chesterton is driving at.[26]

Although Gilbert was probably amused by Zangwill's comments, he would not have welcomed them. He always hoped that the magic of his art would show people the miracle of life. If *Magic* had failed to produce the miracle, it was a failure in itself. Thenceforth Chesterton largely spurned the theatre, dropping drama in favour of literary forms he believed better suited as a focus for his philosophy.

« 14 »

The Shadow of Death

ON 20 JANUARY 1914, the day following the debate on miracles at the Little Theatre, Gilbert and Frances paid a visit to King's Land, the home of Hilaire and Elodie Belloc. It was one of many visits made by the Chestertons to their friends in Sussex, yet this visit was more sombre than usual. Elodie Belloc had fallen suddenly ill on 23 December, being unable to swallow her food. She became progressively worse over Christmas and the doctor, arriving on Boxing Day, reported on the serious nature of her condition. Two nurses were in attendance and leeches were applied. By the 28th she had improved sufficiently to take nourishment in extract, but by the 30th she was again unable to take food. There was another slight improvement in the New Year, yet Elodie's condition remained a serious cause for concern. The nurses stayed in the house, the doctor came regularly from London and the weeks passed with very little change. One can imagine the thoughts passing through Belloc's mind as he cited the miraculous cures at Lourdes in his speech on 19 January. On the 21st he wrote to Maurice Baring:

> Elodie gets no worse and no better; certain of the symptoms have improved, but others are more distressing and I am bound here very anxiously . . . Elodie is stronger *functionally* i.e. in digestion and nutrition but weaker *nervously*. She eats almost normally but she can see no one, she can read but very little and she sleeps more and more ill. I cry and pray God to take her to the Sun. The doctor won't let her move – not even out of bed – and it will be long, long. *Priez pour elle et pour moi.*[1]

Elodie grew steadily worse during the last days of January, passing into unconsciousness on 1 February. On the 3rd Belloc sent the following telegram to Chesterton: 'Elodie entered immortality yesterday the Purification a little before midnight unconscious blessed and without pain. Pray to God for her and for me and for my children.'[2]

Belloc was overcome with grief, being sustained in the first days of his bereavement by Father Vincent McNabb, who came down to King's Land and walked with him among the flowers in the garden Elodie loved and up and down the brick path he had made for her. The memories were all around him and some were simply too hard to bear. He would never again set foot in Elodie's room. The door to it was closed and it was not used again in his lifetime. Each night, as he passed the door on his way to bed, he would pause and trace upon it the sign of the Cross. For the rest of his life he dressed in the same black broadcloth as an outward sign of his mourning, and the King's Land writing-paper was edged with black. Every year mass was offered for the repose of Elodie's soul, sometimes on the Feast of the Purification, the anniversary of her death, and sometimes on 16 June, the anniversary of their wedding.

Within three weeks of Elodie's death, Belloc set out by himself on a pilgrimage to Rome, the city his wife had loved beyond all others. During his stay he had an audience with the ageing Pope Pius X, who would himself die later the same year having written in his will: 'I was born poor, I have lived poor, and I wish to die poor.' Like Belloc, Chesterton was an admirer of Pius X, writing the following tribute to him in the *Illustrated London News* in the week after his death:

Among the many true and touching expressions of respect for the tragedy of the Vatican, most have commented on the fact that the late Pope was by birth a peasant . . . Those who admired him most, admired the simplicity and sanity of a peasant. Those who murmured against him most, complained of the obstinacy and reluctance of a peasant . . .

As has been pointed out, with subtle power and all proper delicacy, in numberless liberal and large-minded journals, the great and good priest now dead had all the prejudices of a peasant. He had a prejudice to the effect that the mystical word 'Yes' should be distinguished from the equally unfathomable expression 'No' . . . The Pope never pretended to have an extraordinary intellect; but he professed to be right – and he was. All honest atheists, all honest Calvinists, all honest men who mean anything or believe anything or deny anything, will have reason to thank their stars (a heathen habit) for the peasant in that high place. He left people to agree with his creed or disagree with it; but not free to misrepresent it. It was exactly what any peasant taken from any of our hills and plains would have said. But there was something more in him that would not be in the ordinary peasant. For all this time he had wept for our tears; and he broke his heart for our bloodshed.[3]

In fact, barely two weeks before the Pope's death, bloodshed destined to break a million hearts erupted around Europe. On 4 August the Germans refused Britain's ultimatum to withdraw from Belgium and war was declared. Chesterton had earlier experienced a premonition of the coming conflict during a trip to Germany in 1909:

> I had to visit Frankfurt, where I took on rather casually the task of lecturing on English literature to a congress of German schoolmasters. We discussed Walter Scott's *Marmion* and other metrical romances; we sang English songs over German beer, and had a very pleasant time. But there was already stirring, even among those mild and amiable Germans, something that was not so pleasant; and though they expressed it quite politely I suddenly found myself once more in the same difficulty about the national and the imperial notion . . . They formed the extraordinary idea that I was an internationalist, indifferent, or even hostile, to English interests . . . Anyhow, they began to talk more openly, but still vaguely; and there grew gradually on my consciousness the conviction that these extraordinary people really thought that I might accept or approve, on some toshy ethnological or sociological ground or other, the extension of the Teutonic Race at the expense even of the impotence or absorption of my own land. It was a somewhat difficult situation; for they said nothing definite that I had any right to resent; it was merely that I felt in the atmosphere a pressure and a threat . . . After thinking a moment, I said, 'Well, gentlemen, if it ever came to anything like that, I think I should have to refer you to the poem of Scott that we have been discussing.' And I gravely repeated the answer of Marmion, when King James says that they may meet again in war as far south as Tamworth Castle.

> Much honour'd were my humble home,
> If in its halls King James should come;
> But Nottingham has archers good,
> And Yorkshire men are stern of mood;
> Northumbrian prickers wild and rude . . .
> And many a banner will be torn,
> And many a knight to earth be borne,

And many a sheaf of arrows spent,
'Ere Scotland's king shall cross the Trent.

I looked at them and they at me, and I think they understood; and there rose up like an enormous shadow over that drinking-hall the terror of things to be.[4]

At the beginning of September 1914, barely a month after war was declared, C. F. G. Masterman, the new head of the War Propaganda Bureau, called a secret meeting of twenty-five leading writers to discuss how the *literati* could contribute to the war effort. Chesterton was one of those invited and he was in illustrious company. Others at the meeting included Arnold Bennett, James Barrie, Sir Arthur Conan Doyle, Thomas Hardy, H. G. Wells, John Galsworthy, John Masefield and John Buchan. Kipling, unable to attend, sent a message of support. The meeting bore fruit almost immediately. Bennett, Wells and Kipling were sent to France, where they were encouraged to produce books, pamphlets and articles on patriotic themes. Secret deals were struck with commercial publishers whereby suitable books were subsidised and large orders for them placed. Sir Gilbert Parker, a Canadian-born Conservative MP and successful romantic novelist, was put in charge of propaganda in America; by 1917 Masterman could claim in a report to Cabinet that Parker had a network of 13,000 influential people in the United States. As well as the literary efforts, Masterman's War Propaganda Bureau also created a successful photographic syndication service, which became highly influential in neutral countries.[5]

Chesterton's early literary contributions to the war effort included *The Barbarism of Berlin*, a short book based on articles previously published in the *Daily Mail*, and *The Martyrdom of Belgium*, a pamphlet subtitled 'An Appeal by G. K. Chesterton' for the Belgian Relief and Reconstruction Fund, which had originally been written as an article for the *Illustrated London News*. The nature of Belgium's martyrdom was summed up as follows: 'she saved France, she saved England – herself she could not save.'[6] Against this selfless heroism, Chesterton argued, the duplicity of Prussian diplomacy stood in stark contrast:

In this sense it is true that the attempts of the Prussian to be polite have something about them monstrous and amusing, like a bear on its hind-legs. He cannot keep it up – sometimes not even to the end of a sentence. It is particularly entertaining in his appeals to neutral powers. His utterances always end so very differently from the way in which they began. He says, in effect, to a country like Holland, 'We salute your delightful dykes. Our culture contemplates your pleasing canals. Your army is under the protection of our never-to-be-broken word – and lucky for it, for one Pomeranian Grenadier could kick all your waddling regiments into the Zuyder Zee.' Having put the Dutchman at his ease, the Prussian turns, let us say, to the Switzer and says, 'Schiller has written of William Tell. Hoch the William Tell! How fortunate for that hero that he did not have to face the Krupp howitzer with his little bow and arrow! As you are a neutral power, it will be unnecessary to exhibit our engines for blowing up the Rigi and removing the Lake of Geneva to the Palmen Garten at Frankfort.' Leaving the Switzer in raptures, he will turn to the philosophic Dane and say, 'My own old, humble, and grateful friend! I will protect you. I protected a bit of you just before 1870; and I'll protect a lot more unless you jolly well do as I tell you. Just look at this gun!' Without waiting for the delighted thanks of Denmark, he will turn to the United States and offer not to lay waste the whole of that country; or to Italy, and explain when and why he will not hang the Pope. Then, when he finds he is not so popular as he thought, his heart will bleed, and he will say the sword is forced into his hand, and that he 'has not a friend in the wide world'. Which is probably the case.[7]

Belgium's martyrdom was brought home to Chesterton quite literally when a family of refugees moved into a house next to Overroads. Gilbert and Frances took the newcomers, Baron Isidoor Opsomer and his wife, under their wing, becoming particularly fond of Walter, the Opsomers' nine-year-old son. In fact, Walter Opsomer's memories of his wartime childhood in Beaconsfield offer a valuable insight into the home life of the Chestertons at this time. His reminiscences begin in Ostend, where the family managed to get aboard the last ferry to Dover:

> When I think back to that time, all sorts of pictures come before my mind's eye. In the hurley-burley of that bustling port, I see English soldiers, freshly disembarked, running to and fro. Through the open window of an hotel I see Winston Churchill sitting down to a meal. I hear the great cannons rolling through the streets . . .
> In England . . . there was no greater accolade than that of 'Belgian

Refugees', as we were quickly to find ... After eight days, we were directed to Beaconsfield, a pleasant village with a thousand inhabitants ...

We arrived there on a grey day at ten o'clock in the morning. At noon, just as we were sitting down to table, we heard someone calling out: Hello! hellooo! We looked out and saw two ladies and a gentleman standing on the other side of the hedge. Father went to meet them. They were our neighbours who spoke French quite well and identified themselves as Mr and Mrs Chesterton and Mrs Chesterton's sister. They showed a great deal of interest in us, asked how the journey had gone, and wanted to know where we had come from. The fate of the Belgians touched them very much. 'As soon as you can, you must come and visit us,' they said. Father, who was well up in artistic and literary matters, soon realised who our friendly neighbour was. Later I was to hear that Chesterton had written about the plight of Belgian refugees and about the German invasion of our country.

The nine-year-old soon became fully acquainted with the 'friendly neighbour', remembering the studio 'where Chesterton came to work' with its grand piano, toy theatre and Javanese puppet show. And everywhere there were 'books, books, and yet more books'. 'I felt completely at home in Beaconsfield ... I used to go round to the Chestertons only too willingly for I was always given some sweets or asked to tea, and Mrs Chesterton was ever so nice.'[8]

At about the time the Belgian child appeared on the scene, Gilbert was putting the finishing touches to a second collection of Father Brown stories. *The Wisdom of Father Brown* was published in October 1914 and enjoyed the same success as its predecessor. The volume of twelve short stories contained not only the wisdom of the fictional priest but also the wit of his creator. Thus in 'The Paradise of Thieves', one of the characters declaims that 'to be clever enough to get all that money, one must be stupid enough to want it'.[9] In another story, 'The Head of Caesar', Father Brown shines forth as both poet and psychologist: '"What we all dread most," said the priest in a low voice, "is a maze with *no* centre. That is why atheism is only a nightmare."'[10]

There was also acerbity in some of the stories, a legacy of the libel actions of the previous year. 'The Purple Wig' commenced with a description of a newspaper editor, possibly modelled on A. G. Gardiner, and contained a thinly disguised reference to Sir William Lever who had threatened Gilbert with libel action during the preceding summer:

> Mr Edward Nutt, the industrious editor of the *Daily Reformer*, sat at his desk, opening letters and marking proofs to the merry tune of a typewriter, worked by a vigorous young lady.
>
> He was a stoutish, fair man, in his shirt-sleeves . . . It might truly be said of him, as for many journalists in authority, that his most familiar emotion was one of continuous fear; fear of libel actions, fear of lost advertisements, fear of misprints, fear of the sack.
>
> His life was a series of distracted compromises between the proprietor of the paper (and of him), who was a senile soap-boiler with three ineradicable mistakes in his mind, and the very able staff he had collected to run the paper . . .[11]

Although the reference to Sir William Lever as 'a senile soap-boiler' was hardly likely to build bridges, there was no animosity between Chesterton and Gardiner. On the contrary, both remained on friendly terms in spite of Gardiner's termination of Chesterton's employment as a *Daily News* columnist. Gilbert was aware that Gardiner was merely bowing to pressure, and Gardiner, for his part, appeared to almost envy Chesterton his freedom from George Cadbury's clutches, remarking a year later that Gilbert was 'free from the tyranny of things'.[12] If any proof was required that the two friends were reconciled, it came in April 1914, when Gardiner published a volume of character portraits entitled *Prophets, Priests, and Kings*. Those portrayed in the volume were multifarious, including Bernard Shaw, the Kaiser, Lloyd George, Winston Churchill and Rudyard Kipling. Gardiner had commenced his book with an essay on King Edward VII, yet he concluded it with a portrait of Chesterton:

> Walking down Fleet Street some day you may meet a form whose vastness blots out the heavens. Great waves of hair surge from under the soft, wide-brimmed hat. A cloak that might be a legacy from Porthos floats about his colossal frame. He pauses in the midst of the pavement to read the book in his hand, and a cascade of laughter descending from the head notes to the middle voice gushes out on the listening air. He looks up, adjusts his pince-nez, observes that he is not in a cab, remembers that he ought to be in a cab, turns

and hails a cab. The vehicle sinks down under the unusual burden
and rolls heavily away. It carries Gilbert Keith Chesterton.

Mr Chesterton is the most conspicuous figure in the landscape of
literary London. He is like a visitor out of some fairy tale, a legend
in the flesh, a survival of the childhood of the world . . . He is a
wayfarer from the ages, stopping at the inn of life, warming himself
at the fire and making the rafters ring with his jolly laughter.

Time and place are accidents: he is elemental and primitive. He
is not of our time, but of all times.[13]

If Chesterton was in illustrious company within the pages of
Gardiner's book, he was in equally grand company at the social
engagements he attended during the summer and autumn of 1914.
At a dinner at the Savoy Theatre the Chestertons brushed shoulders
with the Prime Minister and dined with Sir Edward Elgar, who
casually remarked to Frances towards the end of the meal: 'I suppose
you know you're being filmed all this time.'[14] The extent to which
Chesterton was now 'the most conspicuous figure in the landscape
of literary London' can be gauged from A. R. Orage's lament in the
New Age:

Of studies of Shaw, Chesterton, etc., we have more than enough.
Every timid little scribbler can safely write his appreciation or criticism
of these, for by this time every opinion possible of them has been well
trodden. Editors tell me that their average of manuscripts about Messrs.
Shaw and Chesterton is half a dozen a week, which, on a fair estimate,
means that fifty articles a week or over two thousand a year are being
written on these two writers. What cowards essayists must be, and
how dull! Thomas Hardy, I suppose, comes next, now that Meredith
is dead; and shortly, no doubt, Henry James and Joseph Conrad will
be suffering the tramp of a thousand feet.[15]

The number of articles being written about Chesterton was almost
matched by the number being written by him. One of his secretaries
was amazed, when she first started working for him, by his ability to
write two articles at once on totally different subjects by dictating
one to her while he scribbled away at another himself. However,
he was destined to pay a heavy price for the burden of work he
carried. Overweight and overworked, Gilbert was heading for a fall.
On 25 November he addressed a large gathering of undergraduates
at Oxford 'in defence of the English Declaration of War'. During his

speech he was suddenly overcome by a fit of dizziness and was forced to leave the platform. Later he would recall little of the meeting but he came home and attempted to write a letter to Shaw, criticising his friend's pacifism: 'You are, my dear Shaw, face to face with certain new facts but you still try to treat them as if they were old frauds . . . With the millions of British at the moment Belgium is not a pretext, but a passion . . . You are out of your depth . . . for you have jumped into this deep river to prove that it was shallow . . .'[16] Chesterton, still feeling extremely ill, left the letter unfinished and laid down his pen. He would not lift it again for months. Staggering into his bedroom, he collapsed so heavily on to the bed that it broke.

Panic-stricken at her inability to move or assist her husband physically, Frances called for the doctor. Dr Pocock discovered Chesterton lying in a grotesquely awkward position on the partially collapsed bed, his hips higher than his head. It was the beginning of a long, life-threatening illness.

Although there was scarcely any doubt about the seriousness of the illness, there remained considerable doubt as to its nature. Writing to Father O'Connor, Frances echoed the doctor's initial diagnosis: 'You must pray for him. He is seriously ill and I have two nurses. It is mostly heart-trouble, but there are complications.'[17] According to Father O'Connor, however, Chesterton 'was exhausted beyond recovery' and had 'what can only be described as gout all over. Brain, stomach, lungs were affected . . .'[18] Meanwhile, Cecil, writing to Shaw six days after his brother's collapse, offered yet another opinion:

> Gilbert has been pretty bad and we have all been anxious about him. He has been in bed with a complication of troubles, partly a sort of congestion of the larynx from which he has been suffering for some months but which has recently become worse, and partly from something wrong with his kidneys. However, I believe he is seeing a specialist today and the last reports from his wife (this morning) are that he is more comfortable and that his condition is improving.[19]

Whichever diagnosis was nearest the truth, it was clear that Gilbert had suffered a major breakdown. It was also clear that his brother's hopes of an imminent improvement were wildly optimistic. On Christmas Eve he lapsed into a long and rarely broken coma. On 29 December Frances again wrote to Father O'Connor: 'Gilbert had a bad relapse on Christmas Eve, and now is being desperately ill. He is not often conscious, and is so weak – I feel he might ask for you – if so I shall wire. Doctor is still hopeful, but I feel in despair.'[20] Evidently Father O'Connor replied immediately, asking to be able to visit his friend, because Frances wrote again on 3 January: 'If you came he would not know you, and this condition may last some time. The brain is dormant, and must be kept so. If he is sufficiently conscious at any moment to understand, I will ask him to let you come – or will send on my own responsibility. Pray for his soul and mine.'[21]

Another dilemma eating at Frances's conscience was whether her husband would desire the last rites of the Catholic Church should his condition deteriorate still further. On 7 January she expressed her worries in another letter to Father O'Connor:

> Gilbert seemed decidedly clearer yesterday, and although not quite so well today the doctor says he has reason to hope the mental trouble is working off. His heart is stronger, and he is able to take plenty of nourishment. Under the circumstances therefore I am hoping and praying he may soon be sufficiently himself to tell us what he wants done. I am dreadfully unhappy at not knowing how he would wish me to act. His parents would never forgive me if I acted only on my own authority. I do pray to God He will restore him to himself that we may know. I feel in His mercy He will, even if death is the end of it – or the beginning shall I say?[22]

Although Frances found considerable consolation in her faith, these were terribly difficult days for her. A letter to Josephine Ward, the wife of the Catholic writer Wilfrid, was a cry for help: 'Gilbert remains much the same in a semi-conscious condition – sleeping a great deal. I feel absolutely hopeless; it seems impossible it can go on like this. The impossibility of reaching him is too terrible an experience and I don't know how to go through with it. I pray for strength and you must pray for me.'[23] During one of these desperate attempts to reach her husband she sought to find out whether he was conscious by asking if he knew who was looking after him. 'God,' he replied, and lapsed into unconsciousness again. Frances confessed to Josephine Ward that Gilbert's reply had been a humbling experience.[24]

On 9 January Frances sent a hastily written postcard to Father O'Connor: 'There has been quite distinct improvement and awaking the last three days – we hope the recovery may move much more rapidly now, but we may do nothing to hasten the brain or make any suggestions. He is sleeping a great deal.'[25] The optimistic tone continued in another letter to the priest three days later: 'He is really better I believe and by the mercy of God I dare hope he is to be restored to us. Physically he is stronger, and the brain is beginning to work normally, and soon I trust we shall be able to ask him his wishes with regard to the Church. I am so thankful to think that *we* can get at his desire.'[26]

On the day Frances was writing these hopeful words to Father O'Connor, another priest was writing words of condolence to Frances. The priest in question was her husband's friend, Father Vincent McNabb, who had recently been elected prior of Hawkesyard. It was from Hawkesyard that he wrote:

> The public press has been telling us of the very serious illness of your husband.
>
> To me and to all under this roof the news comes as an overwhelming blow.
>
> Your husband's work has been to me, as to them, a unique apologetic of the great sanctities of revealed religion. When speaking of him, as I often did, I have said, 'Gilbert Chesterton makes it easier to understand what manner of man is a major prophet.'
>
> He may not have known and now alas! he may never know that we professors of theology have read out his books in class. With perfect trust we have sent our students to the pages in which his frank, unflinching wisdom was strung on a chain of brilliant epigram.
>
> As I shall be in your neighbourhood shortly, is it impertinent to ask if there is any hope of seeing you – and him – if only for a few moments – whilst he is yet with us?[27]

Father McNabb had obviously read alarmist reports in the papers stating that Gilbert was on the point of death. By mid-January, however, although the illness had very nearly claimed his life, Chesterton could have repeated the words of Mark Twain to the effect that reports of his death were greatly exaggerated. The danger was receding and he was on the long and arduous road to recovery. On 18 January an excited Frances reported further signs of progress in a letter to Father O'Connor: 'Gilbert has improved yesterday and again today . . . He *asked* for me today, which is a great advance. He is dreadfully weak, but the brain-clouds are clearing, though the doctors won't allow him to make the slightest effort to think.

Please God he will recover normally – and I can only abide in His patience. I will let you know of his welfare as often as I can.'[28] A similar report was sent simultaneously to Josephine Ward: 'Gilbert is today a little better, after being practically at a standstill for the past week. He *asked* for me today, which is a great advance, and hugged me. I feel like Elijah (wasn't it?) and shall go in the strength of that hug forty days. The recovery will be very slow, the doctors tell me, and we have to prevent his using his brain at all.'[29]

On the following day Frances met Father McNabb, complying with his request to meet her. He wrote to her upon his return to Hawkesyard:

I arrived home at about 10 p.m.

It was a great pleasure to have met you: even under the terrible circumstances of your sorrow.

Your heart and your days are in God's hands of love. You are now undergoing supreme things; experiences which bring Golgotha to our doors. The God of all consolation console you.

I want to assure you of my prayers and service . . .

The old lay-brother, Brother Joseph, told me that he says the 'five mysteries of the Rosary' every day for your husband.

God bless your husband and you.[30]

Throughout the rest of the winter Chesterton's recovery remained steady but painfully slow. On 29 January Frances was again reporting to Father O'Connor on her husband's progress: 'Gilbert moves very slowly, but so far forward, though progress is almost inappreciable, as seen day by day. We can only pray that nothing may hinder the return to complete consciousness, and the doctor says all will come right, but it will need infinite patience – I will let you know if there is any change.'[31]

One of the first visitors to be allowed to see the convalescent Chesterton was Walter Opsomer, the young Belgian refugee, now ten years old:

. . . as soon as I heard that our neighbour was so ill, I went to his house on the other side of the street where he was being nursed. On the door there was a brass knocker in the shape of a bat with its wings spread and its feet uppermost. I made no use of it, for on a placard there was written: Please do not knock as Mr Chesterton is badly ill.

A few weeks later, he was feeling better. He grew bored and
he sent the young lady to come and get me ... he was dressed
in a white nightshirt and lying, or rather more or less sitting up,
against a heap of pillows. I must have looked somewhat taken aback,
which was something that amused him. The door closed behind me,
and I was left alone with him. He looked at me, but stayed silent
for a while.

The room was whitewashed. Along the wall, there were books piled
high in stacks of a foot to over a foot-and-a-half tall. I could find no
stool. 'Sit down on the books,' was the first thing that Chesterton
said. I did what he said and took my place on one of the piles.
'Tell me,' he then asked, 'what do you really speak when you don't
speak French?' 'Flemish,' I said. 'That's the same as Dutch,' he said.
'No, it isn't,' I protested. 'Oh yes, it is, it's the same,' he said. 'No,'
I answered, 'Dutch is Dutch, but we speak Flemish.'[32]

Little did either participant in this tête-à-tête realise it would be
one of their last encounters. In March, while Chesterton was still
housebound, the Opsomer family moved to London. In May they
travelled on to Holland. It was typical of Chesterton, however, that
he kept in touch, sending the Opsomers a Christmas card with a
poem in it every year.

On 15 March Frances wrote Father O'Connor another cautiously
optimistic letter:

Things are going on satisfactorily with Gilbert though very slowly.
He has to be kept very quiet, as he is easily upset, and that affects
his heart. He is gradually clearing and is realising his surroundings.
He said to me yesterday, 'Did you think I was going to die?' I said,
'I feared it at one time, but now you are to live.' He said, 'Does
Father O'Connor know?' and I said, 'Yes.' He then wandered off
again into something else. I thought you would like to know he had
been and was evidently thinking of you.

The doctor has no doubt that before very long he will be quite
normal, though it is impossible to foretell how long it will take. So,
dear Padre, he needs your prayers still. So do I.[33]

At around the same time this letter was written, Frances met
Josephine Ward and told her that Gilbert had spoken to her about
his desire to become a Catholic. On 21 March she wrote to Mrs
Ward expressing her desire that the substance of their conversation
remain confidential:

I think I would rather you did not tell anyone just yet of what I told you regarding my husband and the Catholic Church. Not that I doubt for a moment that he meant it and knew what he was saying and was relieved at saying it, but I don't want the world at large to be able to say that he came to this decision when he was weak and unlike himself. He will ratify it no doubt when his complete manhood is restored. I know it was not weakness that made him say it, but you will understand my scruples. I know in God's good time he will make his confession of faith – and if death comes near him again I shall know how to act.

Thanks for all your sympathy. I *did* enjoy seeing you.[34]

On Easter Eve Frances was again writing to both Father O'Connor and Josephine Ward. To Father O'Connor she wrote:

All goes well here, though still very slowly – G's mind is gradually clearing, but it is still difficult to him to distinguish between the real and the unreal. I am quite sure he will soon be able to think and act for himself, but I dare not hurry matters at all. I have told him I am writing to you often and he said, 'That is right – I'll see him soon. I want to talk to him.' He wanders at times, but the clear intervals are longer. He repeated the Creed last night, this time in English.

I feel I understand something of the significance of the resurrection of the body when I see him just consciously laying hold of life again.[35]

As soon as Frances had finished the letter to Father O'Connor it seems she commenced writing to Josephine Ward:

I feel the enormous significance of the resurrection of the body when I think of my dear husband, just consciously laying hold of life again. Indeed, I will pray that your dear ones may be kept in safety. God bless you for all your sympathy. I am so glad that Gilbert's decision (for I am sure it was a decision) has made you so happy. I dare not hurry anything, the least little excitement upsets him – last night he said the Creed and asked me to read parts of Myers's *St Paul*. He still wanders a good deal when tired but is certainly a little stronger. Love and Easter blessings to you all.[36]

For the first time since her husband's collapse a genuine spirit of joyfulness permeated Frances's words. The previous months had been traumatic, but the great weight of anxiety was slowly lifting from her wearied and worried shoulders. Her ordeal, which had begun the previous November and had become worse on Christmas Eve when Gilbert slipped into a coma, ended on Easter Eve when the shadow of death had finally passed them by.

« 15 »

The Valley of Death

'Forward, the Light Brigade!'
Was there a man dismay'd?
Not tho' the soldier knew
    Some one had blunder'd:
Their's not to make reply,
Their's not to reason why,
Their's but to do and die:
Into the valley of Death
    Rode the six hundred.
ALFRED LORD TENNYSON, 'The Charge of the Light Brigade'

As SOON AS HE had fully recovered, Chesterton picked up the pen which had lain dormant for six months and, brandishing it like a sword, resumed his life's work with gusto. In fact, he restarted as he'd finished – by defending the war effort against the pacifism of Shaw:

My Dear Bernard Shaw,
    I ought to have written to you a long time ago, to thank you for your kind letter which I received when I had recovered, and still more for many other kindnesses that seem to have come from you during the time before the recovery. I am not a vegetarian; and I am only in a very comparative sense a skeleton. Indeed I am afraid you must reconcile yourself to the dismal prospect of my being more or less like what I was before; and any resumption of my ordinary habits must necessarily include the habit of disagreeing with you . . . You probably know that I do not agree with you about the War; I do not think it is going on of its own momentum; I think it is going on in accordance with that logical paradox whereby the thing that

is most difficult to do is also the thing that must be done. If it were an easy war to end it would have been a wicked war to begin . . . I have always thought that there was in Prussia an evil will; I would not have made it a ground for going to war, but I was quite sure of it long before there was any war at all. But I suppose we shall some day have an opportunity of arguing about all that. Meanwhile my thanks and good wishes are as sincere as my opinions . . .[1]

Shaw replied on 22 June:

My Dear Chesterton,

I am delighted to learn under your own hand that you have recovered all your health and powers with an unimpaired figure. You have also the gratification of knowing that you have carried out a theory of mine that every man of genius has a critical illness at 40, Nature's object being to make him go to bed for several months. Sometimes Nature overdoes it: Schiller and Mozart died. Goethe survived, though he very nearly followed Schiller into the shades. I did the thing myself quite handsomely by spending eighteen months on crutches, having two surgical operations, and breaking my arm . . .

It is perfectly useless for you to try to differ with me about the war. NOBODY can differ with me about the war: you might as well differ from the Almighty about the orbit of the sun. I have got the war right; and to that complexion you too must come at last, your nature not being a fundamentally erroneous one . . .

As to the evil will, of course there is an evil will in Prussia. Prussia isn't Paradise. I have been fighting that evil will, in myself and others, all my life. It is the will of the brave Barabbas, and of the militant Nationalists who admired him and crucified the pro-Gentile.[2]

With the wisdom of hindsight it is difficult to side with Chesterton against Shaw on the issue of the First World War. However, most of the worst excesses of the war had yet to materialise by the early summer of 1915, and Chesterton's words were written a year before the slaughter of the Somme forced many to reappraise their patriotism. None the less, Chesterton's view of the war was coloured far too much by images akin to Tennyson's glorious 'Charge of the Light Brigade'. This poem, written as a tribute to the six hundred cavalrymen who charged obliviously into an artillery ambush during the Crimean War, belonged to a previous age. The reality of similar military blunders during the First World War, when troops were sent 'over the top' into far worse 'valleys of Death', would be recorded in the poems of Owen and Sassoon with bitterness and anger.

In fact, the blunders had already begun in earnest in 1915, as H. G. Wells recorded in a reply to an earlier letter from Chesterton:

Dear Old G. K. C.,

I'm so delighted to get a letter from you again. As soon as I can I will come to Beaconsfield and see you. I'm absurdly busy in bringing together the Rulers of the country and the scientific people of whom they are totally ignorant. Lloyd George has never heard of Ramsey – and so on, and the hash and muddle and quackery on our technical side is appalling. It all means boys' lives in Flanders and horrible waste and suffering. Well, anyhow if we've got only obscure and cramped and underpaid scientific men we have a bench of fine fat bishops and no end of tremendous lawyers. One of the best ideas for the Ypres position came from Robert Mond but the execution was too difficult for our officers to attempt. So we've got a row of wounded and mangled men that would reach from Beaconsfield to Great Marlow – just to show we don't take stock in these damned scientific people.[3]

Meanwhile, life in England carried on in relatively blissful ignorance of the horror unfolding on the other side of the Channel.

During her husband's illness, Frances had corrected the proofs of Chesterton's poems and these were published under the simple title *Poems* by the Catholic publishing house Burns & Oates in April 1915. However, *Poems* had not included the drinking songs from *The Flying Inn*, a sin of omission rectified in August when they were published separately in a slim volume entitled *Wine, Water and Song*. This little book proved immensely popular and went into fifteen editions before the author's death. It even enjoyed success in certain unlikely circles. Shaw wrote to Chesterton of 'a scandalous orgy' he had witnessed at the headquarters of the Fabian Society:

As I descended the stairs I was stunned by the most infernal din I have ever heard ... coming from the Fabian Hall ... On rushing to this temple I found the young enthusiasts sprawling over tables, over radiators, over everything except chairs, in a state of scandalous abandonment, roaring at the tops of their voices and in a quite unintelligible manner a string of presumably obscene songs, accompanied on the piano with frantic gestures and astonishing musical skill by a man whom I had always regarded as a respectable Fabian Researcher . . . As they went on (for I regret to say that my presence exercised no restraint whatever) they sang their extraordinary and incomprehensible litany to every tune, however august its associations, which happened to fit it . . .

But I have not told you the worst. Before I fled the building I did at last discover what words it was they were singing. When it first flashed on me, I really could not believe it. But at the end of the next verse no doubt or error was possible. The young maenad nearest me was concluding every strophe by shrieking that she didn't care where the water went if it didn't get into the wine. Now you know.

I have since ascertained that a breviary of this Black Mass can be obtained at the Fabian Office, with notes of the numbers of the hymns Ancient and Modern, and all the airs sacred and profane, to which your poems have been set.

This letter needs no answer – indeed, admits of none. I leave you to your reflections.[4]

Although Shaw, albeit light-heartedly, was seeking to reprove his friend for creating poetry capable of such abuse, Chesterton would have been highly amused at the thought of young Fabians enjoying his verse so riotously. After all, the poem in question, collected in *Wine, Water and Song*, had been written originally as a drinking song:

The cataract of the cliff of heaven fell blinding off the brink
As if it would wash the stars away as suds go down the sink,
The seven heavens came roaring down for the throats of hell to drink,
And Noah he cocked his eye and said, 'It looks like rain, I think,
The water has drowned the Matterhorn as deep as a Mendip mine,
But I don't care where the water goes if it doesn't get into the wine.'

During the late summer of 1915 the *New Witness* began to print advertisements for classical music concerts and opera performances, a new diversion for the paper and a million miles from the drinking songs at Shaw's 'scandalous orgy'. The reason for the sudden interest shown by the *New Witness* for matters musical was the arrival on the scene of the young conductor Thomas Beecham. As a keen supporter of the paper who was also a member of the family which owned the pharmaceutical company of that name, Beecham was in a position to give much needed financial assistance. According to Ada Jones, his arrival couldn't have come at a better time because the *New Witness*, suffering from financial constraints, had been forced to relapse into twenty and sometimes sixteen pages:

> And then the tide suddenly and whirlingly turned . . . a dazzling backer came upon the scene . . . that brilliant and original personality, Sir Thomas Beecham. He had sent occasional letters to our correspondence columns, but that had been our only contact, until one day he rang up and asked Cecil to lunch . . . Sir Thomas was keen on the paper and decided to invest capital in the company, and would join the Board and instruct his man of business to act on his and our behalf.
>
> Beecham was full of ideas and suggested right away that Ernest Newman should write us a weekly article on music. This fresh access of influence and capital sent us sky high with hope.[5]

Meanwhile, Gilbert was returning to the serious business of supporting Britain's war effort. In November 1915 *The Crimes of England* was published. Written as a reply to a fictional German professor, it contained polemic of a biting and bitter character: 'By all means say that Germany is unconquerable and that we cannot really kill you. But if you say that we do not really want to kill you, you do us an injustice. You do indeed.'[6]

The central argument of the book was that England's crimes were often caused by German influence. Thus, the author argues, 'the negative Germanism of the Reformation, its drag towards the north, its quarantine against Latin culture, was in a sense the beginning of the business'.[7] Even the 'crime' of English involvement in Ireland is blamed, in part at least, on the Germans. Although admitting that 'telling the truth about Ireland is not very pleasant to a patriotic Englishman', Chesterton argued that 'we should hardly have seen such a nightmare as the Anglicising of Ireland if we had not already seen the Germanising of England'. To illustrate his point, the ascension to the throne of a Protestant German monarchy in England and the use of Protestant German mercenaries in Ireland were cited:

> A village vicar was slain with inconceivable stripes, and his corpse set on fire with frightful jests about a roasted priest. Rape became a mode of government. The violation of virgins became a standing order of police . . . In its bodily aspects it became like a war of devils

upon angels; as if England could produce nothing but torturers, and Ireland nothing but martyrs . . .

But Germany was not merely present in the spirit: Germany was present in the flesh. Without any desire to underrate the exploits of the English or the Orangemen, I can safely say that the finest touches were added by soldiers trained in a tradition inherited from the horrors of the Thirty Years' War, and of what the old ballad called 'the cruel wars of High Germanie' . . . When the Irish say, as some of them do say, that the German mercenary was worse than the Orangemen, they say as much as human mouth can utter . . .

The practice of using German soldiers, and even whole German regiments, in the make-up of the British army, came in with our German princes, and reappeared on many important occasions in our eighteenth-century history . . . When that very typical German, George III, narrow, serious, of a stunted culture and coarse in his very domesticity, quarrelled with all that was spirited, not only in the democracy of America but in the aristocracy of England, German troops were very fitted to be his ambassadors beyond the Atlantic.[8]

Neither, according to Chesterton, were the abuses of German mercenaries confined to Ireland or America. After recounting that William Cobbett had been thrown into prison for complaining about the flogging of English troops by their German officers, he concludes that

Teutonic mercenaries did not confine themselves solely to torturing Irishmen. They were equally ready to torture Englishmen: for mercenaries are mostly unprejudiced. To Cobbett's eye we were suffering from allies exactly as we should suffer from invaders. Boney was a bogey; but the German was a nightmare, a thing actually sitting on top of us. In Ireland the Alliance meant the ruin of anything and everything Irish, from the creed of St Patrick to the mere colour green. But in England also it meant the ruin of anything and everything English, from the Habeas Corpus Act to Cobbett.[9]

In the person of William Cobbett, Chesterton had discovered his ideal English hero. Cobbett 'saw the beginning of Capitalism in the Tudor pillage and deplored it; he saw the triumph of Capitalism in the industrial cities and defied it'.[10]

Cobbett would have asked nothing better than to bend his mediaeval bow to the cry of 'St George for Merry England' . . . But if we take that old war cry as his final word (and he would have accepted it) we must note how every term in it points away from what the modern plutocrats call either progress or empire. It involves the invocation of saints, the most popular and the most forbidden form of mediaevalism. The modern Imperialist no more thinks of St George in England than he thinks of St John in St John's Wood. It is nationalist in the narrowest sense; and no one knows the beauty and simplicity of the Middle Ages who has not seen St George's Cross separate, as it was at Crécy or Flodden, and noticed how much finer a flag it is than the Union Jack. And the word 'merry' bears witness to an England famous for its music and dancing before the coming of the Puritans, the last traces of which have been stamped out by a social discipline utterly un-English. Not for two years, but for ten decades Cobbett has been in prison; and his enemy, the 'efficient' foreigner has walked about in the sunlight, magnificent, and a model for men. I do not think that even the Prussians ever boasted about 'Merry Prussia'.[11]

Perhaps it was this inability to be merry which Chesterton disliked most about the Puritanism of Prussia. He believed that its seriousness was taken to such an extreme that it bordered on insanity: 'The Germans cannot really be deep because they will not consent to be superficial. They are bewitched by art, and stare at it, and cannot see round it. They will not believe that art is a light and slight thing – a feather, even if it be from an angelic wing. Only the slime is at the bottom of a pool; the sky is on the surface.'[12]

Finally, towards the end of *The Crimes of England*, the author gets to grips with the key to his own anti-Prussianism. The Germans, through their idolisation of the strong at the expense of the weak and their worship of Nietzsche's Superman, had turned morality on its head:

By this time there was in the North German brain an awful inversion of all the legends and heroic lives that the human race has loved. Prussia *hated* romance. Chivalry was not a thing she neglected; it was a thing that tormented her as any bully is tormented by an unanswered challenge. That weird process was completed . . . whereby the soul of this strange people was everywhere on the side of the dragon against the knight, or the giant against the hero. Anything unexpected – the forlorn hopes, the eleventh-hour inpirations, by which the weak can elude the strong, and which take the hearts of happier men like trumpets – filled the Prussian with a cold fury, as of a frustrated fate.[13]

The Crimes of England is indispensable as a means of understanding Chesterton's wholehearted support for the war effort. In the final analysis, however, it is not so much a work of intelligent rhetoric as a piece of anti-Prussian propaganda:

> Prussia, now at last armed to the teeth and secure of triumph, stood up before the world, and solemnly, like one taking a sacrament, consecrated her campaign with a crime. She entered by a forbidden door, one which she had herself forbidden – marching upon France through neutralised Belgium, where every step was on her broken word . . . The statistics of non-combatants killed and tortured by this time only stun the imagination. But two friends of my own have been in villages sacked by the Prussian march. One saw a tabernacle containing the Sacrament patiently picked out in a pattern by shot after shot. The other saw a rocking-horse and the wooden toys in a nursery laboriously hacked to pieces. Those two facts together will be enough to satisfy some of us of the name of the Spirit that has passed.[14]

It was inevitable that *The Crimes of England* should cause controversy, yet it was ironic that the writer who commented loudest was A. R. Orage, who had earlier complained that too much was being written about Chesterton. Orage, who had bemoaned the fact that 'every opinion possible' on Chesterton had been 'well trodden', now ventured to offer his own opinion on *The Crimes of England*:

> It is too late to expect Mr G. K. Chesterton to change his style, or, rather, to adapt it to his subject; so it must be said, *tout simplement*, that the style of *The Crimes of England* is a deplorable misfit. In the tradition of literature there is an established rule that the matter and the manner must be somehow in harmony; and, moreover, the particular harmonies are by this time pretty well fixed as well. For instance, you would not expect to find an epic in limerick-metre; nor would you expect to find puns in a funeral oration. Mr G. K. Chesterton has, however, one manner (I am speaking of his prose only), which he applies to every matter. Let the subject be naturally cheerful, fanciful, serious or tragic, the same style may confidently be looked for from him – and consequently the same result will be achieved. As an exhibition of Mr Chesterton's miraculous cleverness, Mr Chesterton's

almost fanatical earnestness, Mr Chesterton's knowledge and insight, *The Crimes of England* is, I venture to say, one of his two best works; but as an *exposé* of the crimes of England or, for the matter of that, of Germany either, it is unconvincing. The *truth* of what Mr Chesterton says is the last thing the reader thinks about. So dazzled are we by the verbal sparklings of Mr Chesterton's wit that it is as if we were trying to read by the light of fireworks; we can read nothing for the explosions and the coloured spectacles.[15]

Whether or not Orage's criticism is justified, *The Crimes of England* owed as much to the influence of Belloc as to the style of Chesterton. In championing Cobbett's view of English history, Chesterton was merely echoing Belloc's endorsement of that viewpoint in *The Servile State*, published three years earlier. Indeed, it is clear that Chesterton regarded Belloc's grasp of history very highly and that he learned much from the long historical discussions they shared together. Neither was Chesterton alone in his admiration for Belloc's historical learning. During the war, editors of magazines and newspapers were beseeching him for articles in which he drew on his extensive knowledge of European history to shed light on the progress of the current conflict. The editor of *Pearson's Magazine* wrote the following praise for 'a remarkable article' by Belloc in the May 1915 issue:

In this masterly article Mr Belloc . . . analyses the motives of the Germanic powers, and shows clearly the domination that they would exercise over the Continent in the event of victory for their armies. He inquires into the ideals animating the Allies, and shows what they hope to achieve – a reconstruction of Europe on a basis of national boundaries, of freedom for the little nations, and of restricting Prussian power. His exposition of the subject is a triumph of lucidity and sound reasoning.[16]

Almost eighty years later this praise of Belloc was ratified by Norman Stone, Professor of Modern History at Oxford. In his review of David Cannadine's biography of the historian G. M. Trevelyan Professor Stone concluded: 'Cannadine's is a good book, and he convinces me to have another try at reading Trevelyan. But I think that, in the end, I shall go to Trevelyan's enemies, Hilaire Belloc or Lord Acton, both Catholics, for an understanding of modern England.'[17]

Christmas 1915 was celebrated at Overroads in far happier

circumstances than those of the previous year, when Chesterton had slipped into a coma on Christmas Eve. There was the traditional children's party, with Ethel, Frances's sister, bringing her children over from Fernley, near Maidenhead. Also invited to the party were the five children who had recently moved into Boyne House, almost opposite Overroads and next door but one from the Studio. The eldest daughter of this family was Hilary and the second daughter was Charity. Chesterton teased them both mercilessly. Pretending to get their names mixed up, he caused much laughter by calling the one Chillary and the other Harrity.

Early in the new year the Society of SS Peter and Paul, publishers to the Church of England, brought out a small pamphlet by Chesterton entitled *Divorce versus Democracy*, which had appeared originally in *Nash's Magazine*. It was not one of his most lucid offerings and began, predictably enough, with an attack on Prussia, claiming that 'the North Germans have become the peculiar champions of that modern change which would make the State infinitely superior to the Family'.[18] Other pamphlets published by the Society of SS Peter and Paul at this time included several by Ronald Knox, the chaplain of Trinity College, Oxford. These had been enthusiastically reviewed by the *Church Times*; Knox was lauded as 'a devotional writer of real piety and distinction'.[19] A year later, when Knox became a Roman Catholic, his conversion proved as controversial as that of Newman, shocking and shaking the establishments of both Canterbury and Oxford.

If the Anglican establishment was about to lose one of its pillars in the person of Ronald Knox, the Roman Catholic establishment was also to lose one of the staunchest members of its laity in 1916 with the death of Wilfrid Ward. Ward was the son of William George Ward, a leading light in the Oxford Movement, who was deprived of his degree and forced out of Oxford for publishing *The Ideal of a Christian Church* in 1844. His son Wilfrid had become a prominent member of the Catholic laity in England, and it was Wilfrid's wife, Josephine, who had been such a help and confidante to Frances during Chesterton's illness the previous year. Following her husband's death, Gilbert wrote to Josephine, seeking to console her in her grief:

> I fear I have delayed writing to you, and partly with a vague feeling that I might so find some way of saying what I feel on your behalf and others'; and of course it has not come. Somewhat of what the

world and a wider circle of friends have lost I shall try to say in the *Dublin Review*, by the kindness of Monsignor Barnes, who has invited me to contribute to it; but of all I feel, and Frances feels, and of the happy times we have had in your house, I despair of saying anything at all.[20]

Chesterton found constant consolation for the loss of such close friends in the exuberance of the literary life of London. An insight into this literary scene in the spring of 1916 is given in the diary of Marie Belloc Lowndes, Hilaire Belloc's sister, who was herself enjoying considerable success as a novelist at the time:

> Yesterday my Elizabeth and I went to the most remarkable Poets' Reading I have ever attended. It was held at Lord Byron's beautiful house in Piccadilly, lent by Lady d'Erlanger, in aid of the Star and Garter Home at Richmond.
> Mr Augustine Birrell was in the Chair . . . I was moved by Mr de la Mare reading five poems of great beauty. Elizabeth was thrilled at seeing for the first time W. H. Davies, a strange tiny poet. He read *Love's Silent Hour* and three others. Hilary read *The Poor of London* and *The Dons*. He got a big reception.
> G. K. Chesterton proposed the vote of thanks.[21]

Unknown to Augustine Birrell, who was Irish Secretary in the coalition Government, the chairing of this light-hearted gathering would be an idyllic calm before the storm. Within weeks the Easter uprising by Sinn Féin in Dublin would lead to his resignation.

Surprisingly perhaps, considering Chesterton's sympathetic stance towards the suffering of the Irish in *The Crimes of England*, the uprising was condemned vociferously in the *New Witness*. The 'rebellion' had obviously been fomented by the Prussians and was the work of 'a rather unbalanced and fanatical minority in Ireland'. Several weeks later, Cecil wrote: 'The "rebellion" organised by a small minority in Ireland is, to all intents and purposes, over, and we may indulge in the hope that we have seen the last blood to be shed in that unfortunate island.'[22]

Without doubt, Cecil was blinded by his own propaganda and one wonders whether the editorial policy of the *New Witness* would have been different if Britain and Ireland had not been at war with Germany. But they were at war, and Cecil was making every effort to enlist. In fact, he had been given an added incentive to join the fighting because his fiancée, Ada Jones, had promised to marry him if he was sent out to the front. Eventually, in the autumn, he was passed fit to join the East Surrey Regiment.

The last issue of the *New Witness* to be edited by Cecil was that of 12 October. The following week he wrote 'An Au Revoir to *The New Witness*', in which he thanked his brother, 'who, at no little personal sacrifice, has consented to undertake the editorship in my absence, and to allow his name to appear on the front page of the paper'.

Gilbert was, of course, far too unfit to enlist, but if he couldn't join the fighting himself, he could at least assist the war effort at home. As well as writing war propaganda and taking over the editorship of the *New Witness* in his brother's absence, he began to visit wounded servicemen in hospital. On one occasion, in autumn 1916, he and Frances visited the Royal Flying Corps Hospital in Bryanston Square, London, where they met Hugh Paynter, a twenty-three-year-old pilot who was suffering from multiple fractures. Before they left, Frances invited him to Beaconsfield as soon as he was well enough. It was the beginning of a friendship destined to last the rest of their lives. Paynter visited Beaconsfield shortly before returning to the front and remembered a conversation he had with Chesterton: 'I was alone with him and mentioned some doubts which were troubling me about the after-life. He was not a Catholic then, of course, but I remember so vividly the firmness of his convictions and how I went away feeling reassured.'[23]

Despite his fears, Paynter survived the war and lived a long and happy life. Others were not so fortunate. On 3 November 1916 Auberon Herbert, another pilot in the Royal Flying Corps and a close friend of both Chesterton and Belloc, was killed. On 7 December Belloc wrote to Chesterton from Boulogne: 'Pray for Bron Herbert continually and he will help you from heaven. I do not know how these things are. (Neither does any man outside dogma, which is mathematical, therefore of God), but in human words he was the most chivalrous, the bravest and the best, and will help us all out of heaven. God has received him with the fighting men of the Pyrenees whom he loved.'[24]

The war was also claiming the lives of other friends. Raymond Asquith had been killed in September 1915, and both Edward Horner and Basil Blackwood were killed in 1917. On 9 April 1917 Chesterton lost his old schoolfriend, R. E. Vernede, who had been one of the early members of the Junior Debating Club. The following month the *New Witness* mourned Edward Thomas, who had been an occasional contributor: 'A beautiful and essentially noble figure died for England.'

Another victim was the Secretary for War, Lord Kitchener, who died when HMS *Hampshire* was mined off the coast of Orkney on 5 June 1916. The following year Chesterton's short biography of Kitchener was published. The book was essentially a panegyric – Kitchener was hailed as a latter-day Hannibal destined 'to war against the eagles of Germany' – but there was still room for the customary and mandatory attack on Prussia: 'In truth the whole of that great European movement which we call the cause of the Allies is in itself a homeward journey. It is a return to native and historic ideals, after an exile in the howling wilderness of the political pessimism and cynicism of Prussia.'[25]

Amid all the death and despondency there was an event of great joy in the Chesterton family in June 1917. At long last, after years of courtship, Ada Jones kept her promise and married Cecil the moment he was passed for active service:

> He rushed up to London, coming straight to the flat where I was living with my niece. It was past midnight when he arrived, and ringing loud and fiercely at the bell he almost fell into the hall in his excitement, and seizing me tightly shook me in his eagerness.
>
> 'I'm through,' he said. 'I'm through. I'm A1 and I'm going to the front, and I've three days' leave. You'll marry me, Kiddy – now?'
>
> His hands trembled and his eyes were full of a deep questioning, which in a moment turned to unbelievable radiance. At last, at long last he had won his wife.[26]

The next days were hectic as Cecil rushed to get a special licence to marry. Then there was the problem of a new uniform. He had been transferred from the East Surreys to the Highland Light Infantry, and although the kilt looked admirable enough, the tunic was ill-fitting. He rushed round to as many friends as possible, lunched with Shaw and went in and out of numerous newspaper offices and taverns. Tommy Pope, Cecil's best man, relieved Ada of her job at the *New Witness* office, so she could pack for the journey to Sandwith, near Whitehaven, where Cecil was camped. She was to stay at the nearest hotel.

Marie Louise, Chesterton's mother, was 'inexpressibly dear and sweet', telling Ada that she had always wished to have her as a daughter. Her future father-in-law was 'equally affectionate' and gave the couple a hundred pounds for a wedding present. According to Ada, 'Cecil joyously paid it into his account, where it did not remain for long. In the afternoon he rushed to the tailors, bought the wedding ring and an opal to go with it, depositing all the parcels at the office, where by special request I met him for dinner.'[27]

They were married the following day, first at a civil ceremony at the Register Office in Covent Garden and then at a nuptial mass at Corpus Christi, Maiden Lane. Ada's account of the ceremony is both detailed and vivid:

The Actor's Church, as it is called, was decorated for Whitsun, and red roses flamed from the high altar and on the little shrines and the church was filled to the doors, though we had only expected a handful of friends. But the papers had splashed the announcement of the wedding, and it seemed as if everyone we knew were there. Fleet Street had turned up in force – army, navy and the air; Conrad Noel made a special journey from the wilds of the country to see us married at what he always called the Church of the Italian Mission to London. He was with the parents, Gilbert and Frances, Mrs Belloc Lowndes and a tall distinguished old lady, with a lovely carriage and a lace head-dress, whom I recognised as Madame Belloc, mother of Hilaire. She was a remarkable woman with a particularly clear and bell-like voice, and she gave us her blessing and good wishes.

When I reached the altar and my brother handed me over, Cecil leaned forward and said a few impressive words.

'I warn you,' he remarked, 'they'll sprinkle you with Holy Water and you'll say my beastly religion has spoilt your hat. But don't worry, I'll buy you a new one!'

I was sprinkled all right, just after I was endowed with the ritual gold and silver. But the hat wasn't hurt, and we walked down the aisle, talking to people all the way. Indeed, in his delight at the whole proceedings Cecil swept up the spectators in a comprehensive invitation to the Cheshire Cheese. There had been no time to arrange any special festivities, and we had planned to have a small luncheon there. But this quiet suggestion went by the board, and the management, who only expected a few guests, found that the famous lark pudding had run short. But they produced alternative dishes, and there was plenty to drink.

Everyone made speeches – Hilaire Belloc, Raymond Radclyffe, Conrad Noel, Gilbert and Sir Thomas Beecham . . .

234

We left the Cheshire Cheese amid a tumultuous send-off, and went to the Waldorf for the night.[28]

In October 1917, with Cecil in France and the revolution raging in Russia, Chatto & Windus published *A Short History of England*, Gilbert's latest literary offering. He had written the book with great reluctance. In fact, when the publishers first suggested he should write a history, he had refused resolutely on the grounds that he was not an historian. Later, he signed a contract with the same publisher for a book of essays before discovering that he was already under contract to give this book to another firm. He asked Chatto & Windus to cancel their contract and offered to write something else for them instead. Frank Swinnerton, who was employed by Chatto at the time, remembered his employers' response:

The publishers, concealing jubilation, sternly recalled their original proposal for a short history of England. Shrieks and groans were distinctly heard all the way from Beaconsfield, but the promise was kept. The *Short History of England* was what Chesterton must have called a wild and awful success. It probably has been the most generally read of all his books. But while the credit for it is his, he must not be blamed for impudence in essaying history, when the inspiration arose in another's head (not mine) and when in fact no man ever went to the writing of a literary work with less confidence.[29]

Whether Chesterton deserved to be blamed for impudence, he was attacked by Professor Pollard, holder of the Chair of Constitutional History at University College, London, for daring to write a history without the necessary academic qualifications. Professor Pollard dismissed the book as being of interest 'only as an expression of Mr Chesterton's mentality and as an illustration of the whimsical visions of the past which appear to the agitated and the agitators'.[30] Not everyone was so dismissive as Professor Pollard, however. Other history professors at London University told Chesterton's friend Lawrence Solomon that although the book contained inaccuracies, 'He's got something we hadn't got.'[31]

Chesterton defended himself against the charge of whimsy in an introduction to a later edition of the *History*:

When I was invited, some years ago, to write the little volume that bears the title of *A Short History of England*, I was well aware that there would seem to be a certain impudence in accepting the challenge; though in reality the title is more impudent than the book. I had intended it to be called *A Sketch of English History*, or *An Essay on English History*, though I did not think either the title or the book a worthy subject for solemn dispute. But the task as I conceived it involved no swagger of sham scholarship. The neglected side of English history does not consist of little things which the learned obscurely conceal, but rather of large things which the learned frequently ignore. Much of it can be learned, not only without any prodigy of book learning, but practically without any books. It can be learned from large and obvious things, like the size of Gothic churches or the style of classical country houses. It needs no very abstruse learning to know that a squire is not an abbot, while his house is called an abbey. It needs no very elaborate logic to deduce that a place called a Common was common land. The difference is not about the facts but about the importance of the facts; and that must be left to a general criticism of the general view.[32]

In fact, Chesterton's 'general criticism of the general view' was something of a personal crusade against the established Whig view of history. This view, generally accepted at the time, was, according to Chesterton, a classic case of history being written by the victors to justify their own position. Specifically, it was a justification by the landed aristocracy of their theft of church and common land.

Typically and topically, the pro-German bias of established historical teaching, and especially that of the schools of thought led by William Stubbs and John R. Green, was also attacked in Chesterton's book. For example, Green's *History of the English People* begins with the claim that 'the Fatherland of the English race' is Lower Hanover, where 'our ancestors with their fierce, free energy . . . took part in the general attack of the German race on the Empire of Rome . . .'[33] Stubbs is even more adulatory: 'The English . . . are a people of German descent . . . We owe the leading principles . . . worked out in [our] constitutional history . . . to the Germanic races . . . The constructive elements of our life are barbarian or Germanic . . .'[34]

Although Chesterton accepted that Germanic tribes were the most prominent of those settling in England after the exodus of the Romans, he felt the German influence was overstated: 'German history had simply annexed English history, so that it was almost counted the duty of any patriotic Englishman to be proud of being German.'[35]

Thankfully, however, the author did not allow his obsessive aversion to all things Prussian to colour his *History* unduly, and the main thrust of his attack was on the distortions of the Whig historians:

> The tide which thus burst through the breach and overwhelmed the King as well as the Church was the revolt of the rich, and especially of the new rich. They used the King's name, and could not have prevailed without his power, but the ultimate effect was rather as if they had plundered the King after he had plundered the monasteries. Amazingly little of the wealth, considering the name and theory of the thing, actually remained in royal hands . . . By marrying into the Seymour family, and thus providing himself with a son, Henry had also provided the country with the very type of powerful family which was to rule merely by pillage . . . We talk of the dissolution of the monasteries, but what occurred was the dissolution of the whole of the old civilisation. Lawyers and lackeys and money-lenders, the meanest of lucky men, looted the art and economics of the Middle Ages like thieves robbing a church. Their names (when they did not change them) became the names of the great dukes and marquises of our own day. But if we look back and forth in our history, perhaps the most fundamental act of destruction occurred when the armed men of the Seymours and their sort passed from the sacking of the Monasteries to the sacking of the Guilds. The mediaeval Trade Unions were struck down, their buildings broken into by the soldiery, and their funds seized by the new nobility.[36]

All in all, and regardless of the response of certain academic historians, *A Short History of England* was a huge popular success. Nine editions were printed within the first seven years of publication and Bernard Shaw, writing in the *Observer*, was sufficiently impressed to dub Chesterton 'the most concise and the fullest historian this distressful country has yet found'.[37]

With another successful book under his belt Chesterton seemed to be waltzing through 1918 on the crest of a wave of popularity. All was well with the world and, as the months passed, it appeared that all was well with the war. As autumn approached it looked as though the allies finally had victory within their grasp. The war, however, had a sting in its tail. On 26 August Louis Belloc, Hilaire's son, was killed, only weeks before his twenty-first birthday, during a Royal Flying Corps bombing raid over enemy lines. His body was never found.

Worse was to follow.

The war ended on 11 November and Chesterton, in his role as temporary editor, reported in the *New Witness*, 'The Prussian devil is defeated.' It was time for rejoicing, and Ada remembered that 'Fleet Street on Armistice evening was an excited mass of khaki and friendship.'[38] Yet there was a shadow over the celebrations as she worried about Cecil's safe return from France:

> ... there was no word from him that day, nor any answer to my telegram of joy. His letters had come so regularly, always brim full of love and anticipation, that I felt terribly anxious. But day followed day without a line, in spite of my frantic appeals for news ...
>
> ... An alarming note from Cecil arrived by the late post, which, inexplicably delayed, should have reached me days earlier. He explained that he had not been feeling at all well, but had not gone sick until after the Armistice, when he felt he could be spared from the line. He wrote from a hospital at Wimereux, and there was an underlying note of pain and disappointment that gave me a queer foreboding, which deepened as the night wore on.
>
> He did not say, what I afterwards learned, that on reporting sick he had had to march from Ypres for twelve miles in the heavy rain, until at last the Officer Commanding, seeing how ill he was, told him to fall out. He was by then soaked through and through and when, after a long train journey and a bumpy passage in a lorry, he finally reached the base, he was seriously ill with nephritis ...
>
> ... On Monday morning I had more serious news. I received a telegram from the War Office which should have reached me on the previous Friday. It stated that Private Chesterton was on the danger list, but regretted that owing to transport difficulties I could not be allowed to visit him.[39]

Close to despair, Ada tried frantically to find a means of getting to France. All official channels remained firmly closed, but Maurice Baring, at Gilbert's behest, used his diplomatic contacts to arrange transport. Eventually, after a tortuously long journey, she arrived at the field hospital at Wimereux:

> I was half across the ward when Cecil's voice rang out clear and strong as on his marriage day.
>
> 'Kiddy!' he said. 'You've come.'
>
> He talked and laughed, and declared he felt much better. But he said nothing of the future and asked a little wistfully about Fleet Street and the Cottage, his mother and our friends.

After a while he grew tired and closed his eyes. One by one the lights went out, till only a glimmer of lampshine remained. Vast shadows flickered across the ceiling; the Nissen hut seemed to crouch lower on the ground and in the distance the sea broke softly on the shore.

'He's sleeping now,' said a nurse, and asked me to come to another room.

Before the dawn I was back again. There was a change – for the worse. And when the first pale gleams of lovely sunshine crept through the windows I knew it was the end.

'It's goodbye, Kiddy darling,' he said smiling, and clutched my hand . . .

Cecil looked up and smiled. Life was all round him and me: only in the brave face that still kept courage was it ebbing little by little, until it passed beyond the last faint breath.

Suddenly the consciousness came down on me that all our hopes and dreams, light-hearted plans, ambitious undertakings had gone. The future – our future – had ended. I should never hear him speak again. I should never feel his touch, or watch the light in his eyes when unexpectedly he saw me.[40]

Gilbert was utterly devastated by the news of his brother's death and completely unconsolable. Eaten by a bitterness fed with despair, he found it a cruel injustice that his brother was dead when his brother's persecutors, Rufus and Godfrey Isaacs, were still alive. In an open letter to Rufus Isaacs his pain spilled over with uncharacteristic violence, verging on hatred: 'It would be irrational to ask you for sympathy but I am sincerely moved to offer it. You are far more unhappy; for your brother is still alive.'[41]

The article was headed 'At the Sign of the World's End'. In the wake of his brother's death it was singularly appropriate.

« 16 »

Life After Death

CECIL CHESTERTON WAS BURIED in a French military cemetery on 6 December 1918. His recently wed and newly widowed bride was the only member of the family present as his body was lowered into one of the hundreds of narrow graves that lined the coastal hillside.

Back in England, on 13 December Gilbert reported his brother's death in the *New Witness* editorial:

> It is already known that the late Editor of *The New Witness* has died in France of the effects of the last days of the fighting. He lived long enough to march to victory which was for him a supreme vision of liberty and the light. The work which he put first he did before he died. The work which he put second, but very near to the other, he left for us to do. There are many of us who will abandon many other things, and recognise no greater duty than to do it.

In the same issue, Belloc penned a tribute to Cecil's courage:

> His courage was heroic, native, positive, and equal . . . He never in his life checked an action or a word from a consideration of personal caution, and that is more than can be said of any other man of his time . . . He was incapable of neglecting an act from lack of courage or even from a modification of courage, as most men are incapable of a public act which would involve them in danger, and by the measure of the one you may take the measure of the other. Courage possessed and displayed in that degree is by definition heroic.

This sentiment was echoed by Gilbert many years later when, in his *Autobiography*, he recalled the nature of his brother's sacrifice:

For my brother was destined to prove, in a dark hour of doom, that he alone of all the men of our time possessed the two kinds of courage that have nourished the nation; the courage of the forum and of the field. In the second case he suffered with thousands of men equally brave; in the first he suffered alone. For it is another example of the human irony that it seems easier to die in battle than to tell the truth in politics.[1]

On 14 December a requiem mass was held for Cecil at Corpus Christi, Maiden Lane, the church in which he had been received into the Catholic fold and in which the nuptial mass had been celebrated six months earlier. Father Vincent McNabb preached the panegyric, the central theme of which was Cecil's overriding passion for justice. Belloc always considered Father McNabb's sermon on that day the finest piece of sacred oratory he had ever heard.

Cecil's death also inspired Gilbert to write one of his finest pieces of poetry. His 'Elegy in a Country Churchyard' may lack the subtlety and finesse of the more famous poem by Thomas Gray, but its bitterness gives it potency:

> The men that worked for England
> They have their graves at home:
> And bees and birds of England
> About the cross can roam.
>
> But they that fought for England,
> Following a falling star,
> Alas, alas for England
> They have their graves afar.
>
> And they that rule in England,
> In stately conclave met,
> Alas, alas for England
> They have no graves as yet.[2]

The poem marked something of an artistic conversion for Chesterton. The harshness and indignation of his 'Elegy' had nothing in common with Tennyson's imperial optimism but, on the contrary, was strikingly similar in sentiment to Sassoon's 'Fight to a Finish':

The boys came back. Bands played and flags were flying,
And Yellow-Pressmen thronged the sunlit street
To cheer the soldiers who'd refrained from dying,
And hear the music of returning feet.
'Of all the thrills and ardours War has brought,
This moment is the finest.' (So they thought.)

Snapping their bayonets on to charge the mob,
Grim Fusiliers broke ranks with glint of steel.
At last the boys had found a cushy job.

I heard the Yellow-Pressmen grunt and squeal;
And with my trusty bombers turned and went
To clear the Junkers out of Parliament.[3]

A few months after the tragedy of his brother's death, Gilbert was able to remember him more dispassionately. In 1919 Cecil's book *A History of the United States* was published and Gilbert, at the request of the publishers, wrote a 'Biographical Note on the Author':

Cecil Edward Chesterton was born on 12th November 1879; and there is a special if a secondary sense in which we may use the phrase that he was born a fighter. It may seem in some sad fashion a flippancy to say that he argued from his very cradle. It is certainly, in the same sad fashion, a comfort to remember one truth about our relations: that we perpetually argued and that we never quarrelled. In a sense it was the psychological truth, I fancy, that we never quarrelled because we always argued. His lucidity and love of truth kept things so much on the level of logic, that the rest of our relations remained, thank God, in solid sympathy . . .[4]

It was this 'lucidity and love of truth' which, according to Gilbert, led his brother to the Catholic Church:

. . . having for some time held an Anglo-Catholic position, he joined the Roman Catholic Church. It is notable, in connection with the general argument, that . . . he was . . . characteristically amused and annoyed with the sentimentalists, sympathetic or hostile, who supposed he was attracted by ritual, music, and emotional mysticism. He told such people, somewhat to their bewilderment, that he had been converted because Rome alone could satisfy the reason. In his case, of course, as in Newman's and numberless others, well-meaning people conceived a thousand crooked or complicated explanations, rather than suppose that an obviously honest man believed a thing because he thought it was true.[5]

Gilbert ended his short biographical note with an apology for its inadequacy: 'This note, necessarily so broken and bemused, must reach its useless end . . . A portrait is impossible; as a friend he is too near me, and as a hero too far away.'[6]

But there was life after his brother's death and Gilbert, however desolate, never despaired. He continued his brother's work as editor of the *New Witness* with a dutiful determination. W. R. Titterton, a member of the *New Witness* staff, remembered that he 'never exhibited his grief' but, on the contrary, was as courteous and kind as ever 'because he liked people and liked being with them and because, for all his sorrow, he thanked God for being alive . . .'[7]

The *New Witness*, under Gilbert's editorship, played an important part in launching the young Dorothy L. Sayers in a literary career. A collection of her poems had been published in September 1918 by Basil Blackwell. Previously, however, she had offered the poems to Chesterton in the hope that he would accept them for publication in the *New Witness*. No doubt her hopes were based upon the fact that her poetry was similar in style and sentiment to Chesterton's own poetry. According to Barbara Reynolds, Sayers's friend and biographer, 'the poems are much in his style and to a large extent inspired by his own robust and hearty expressions of faith'.[8] Although Chesterton failed to publish the poems, he did publish a review of them by the Catholic poet Theodore Maynard, who was singularly unimpressed. Basing his criticism on theological grounds, Maynard complained that Sayers's poems paganised Christianity. Seizing her opportunity, and working on the principle that all publicity is good publicity, Sayers masterminded a letter-writing campaign to the *New Witness*. She asked her friend Muriel Jaeger to reply to the review under an assumed name, agreeing with Maynard, and then to follow this with another letter putting the opposite view. Dorothy herself would write in at a later stage and there would be 'a scrumptious row', which would make the book 'go like wildfire'. The plan worked admirably. Muriel Jaeger, as requested, wrote the pseudonymous letters and her efforts were rewarded when several genuine correspondents entered the debate. Wilfred Rowland Childe, a writer whose poetry had also been published by Blackwell, objected to Maynard's 'patronising clericalism', stating that he had noticed the same attitude towards 'Mr Charles Williams, whose truly noble poetry he vilified from the same standpoint'.[9]

It is likely that Chesterton remained blissfully ignorant of the way Sayers had duped him into being an unwitting launchpad for her own career. He would also have been unaware of his influence on a young soldier in a field hospital in France in the closing stages of the war. In the winter of 1918 C. S. Lewis, a nineteen-year-old second lieutenant in the Somerset Light Infantry, spent three weeks recovering from trench fever in a hospital at Le Tréport:

> It was here that I first read a volume of Chesterton's essays. I had never heard of him and had no idea of what he stood for; nor can I quite understand why he made such an immediate conquest of me. It might have been expected that my pessimism, my atheism, and my hatred of sentiment would have made him to me the least congenial of all authors. It would almost seem that Providence, or some 'second cause' of a very obscure kind, quite over-rules our previous tastes when It decides to bring two minds together. Liking an author may be as involuntary and improbable as falling in love. I was by now a sufficiently experienced reader to distinguish liking from agreement. I did not need to accept what Chesterton said in order to enjoy it. His humour was of the kind which I like best – not 'jokes' imbedded in the page like currants in a cake, still less (what I cannot endure), a general tone of flippancy and jocularity, but the humour which is not in any way separable from the argument but is rather (as Aristotle would say) the 'bloom' on dialectic itself. The sword glitters not because the swordsman set out to make it glitter but because he is fighting for his life and therefore moving it very quickly. For the critics who think Chesterton frivolous or 'paradoxical' I have to work hard to feel even pity; sympathy is out of the question . . .
>
> In reading Chesterton, as in reading MacDonald, I did not know what I was letting myself in for. A young man who wishes to remain a sound Atheist cannot be too careful of his reading. There are traps everywhere – 'Bibles laid open, millions of surprises', as Herbert says, 'fine nets and stratagems'. God is, if I may say it, very unscrupulous.[10]

Only one new Chesterton book was published during 1919, and that didn't appear until November. *Irish Impressions* contained the author's opinions on the growing turmoil in Ireland. His views on the subject had been voiced in *The Crimes of England,* and a visit to Ireland at the invitation of W. B. Yeats during the early autumn of the previous year had only served to reinforce these convictions. Sociologically, the rustic lifestyle of the south was superior to the industrialism of the north, and theologically the Catholicism of the south was superior to the Calvinism of the north. In one memorable passage Chesterton contrasted Protestant pride with Catholic humility:

> In so far as the Ulster Protestant really has a faith, he is really a fine fellow; though perhaps not quite so fine a fellow as he thinks himself. And that is the chasm; and can be most shortly stated as I have often stated in such debates: by saying that the Protestant generally says, 'I am a good Protestant,' while the Catholic always says, 'I am a bad Catholic.'[11]

From this typically Chestertonian paradox sprang a typically Chestertonian conclusion: 'There is a religious question; and it will not have an irreligious answer. It will not be met by the limitation of Christian faith, but rather by the extension of Christian charity.'[12]

At the end of the previous year's visit, Chesterton had looked back at the Wicklow hills as the ferry sailed for England. The view of the receding coastline inspired an evocative description of Ireland:

> As the long line of the mountain coast unfolded before me I had an optical illusion; it may be that many have had it before. As new lengths of coast and lines of heights were unfolded, I had the fancy that the whole land was not receding but advancing, like something spreading out its arms to the world. A chance shred of sunshine rested, like a riven banner, on the hill which I believe is called in the Irish the Mountain of the Golden Spears; and I could have imagined that the spear and the banner were coming on. And in that flash I remembered that the men of this island had once gone forth, not with the torches of conquerors or destroyers, but as missionaries in the very midnight of the Dark Ages; like a multitude of moving candles, that were the light of the world.[13]

However, Chesterton's most evocative image of Ireland was produced not in prose but in a solitary picture, sketched in charcoal. Captioned 'How I felt when I went to Ireland and met St Patrick', it depicts a minuscule self-portrait aghast and in awe as he is confronted with the overpowering presence of Ireland's patron saint. It is a timely reminder that Chesterton's creative talent was not confined to the written word.

Irish Impressions was reviewed by Bernard Shaw in the *Irish Statesman*:

> These Irish impressions are not, as the title page states, impressions by Mr Chesterton. They are impressions by Ireland on Mr Chesterton. I am tempted to recommend the book in which he has recorded them as a proof that an Englishman is a much pleasanter, jollier, kindlier human variety than an Irishman; and though I am checked by the reflection that all Englishmen are unfortunately not like Mr Chesterton, and that he describes himself as a blend of Scotch, French, and Suffolk Dumpling, still, the net result is the sort of man that England can produce when she is doing her best.[14]

The final paragraph of Shaw's review described *Irish Impressions* as 'delightful, deep, and spiritually nutritious'. Furthermore, Chesterton, although

> pretending all the time to be nothing but a carelessly jolly Englishman . . . is enormously robust and exquisitely subtle . . . as funny as a harlequinade and as serious as an epic, and doing it all with an immense good humour which prevents his prodigious cleverness from ever wearying or tiring you . . . The world is not half thankful enough for Chesterton; and I hope Ireland will not be among the ingrates; for no Irishman alive or dead has ever served her better and more faithfully with the pen than he.

Shaw's words were those of reconciliation, an attempt to illustrate to his fellow Irishmen that all Englishmen were not ogres. Many were unconvinced, and British policy in Ireland served to reinforce their anger. Chesterton entered the fray by writing articles condemning government policy. Two of these, *What are Reprisals?* and *The Danger to England*, were published as leaflets. In the former he criticised the Government for the harsh nature of its reprisals, comparing its methods with those of the Prussians during the war:

> The Prussians adopted the destructive method in Belgium; and the English have now adopted it in Ireland. They have crossed a line and the whole world has seen them do it . . .

When men in our uniform shoot a woman with a baby in her arms, or kill a little girl of eight, it is a confusion of thought to profess that it was an accident, or even to discuss whether it was an accident. The whole system is designed to produce such accidents, even if you call them accidents . . .

Of the morality of the proceedings something may be said later, if indeed anything needs to be said. But keeping to the line of logical distinction, it is necessary to note even here that the particular problem is not affected at all by any proper horror of atrocities on the other side. It is not relevant even to denounce the original crime; because by hypothesis we are not dealing with the original criminal. In discussing whether it is to the public advantage to hang Mr Jones because Mr Smith has killed his wife in the next street, it is illogical to insist that Mr Smith has not shot her but poisoned her, or not poisoned her but burned her alive. The question at issue is not how much harm Mr Smith has done, but how much good we are doing by pretending that Mr Jones is Mr Smith.[15]

This theme was reiterated in *The Danger to England*: 'The principle of reprisals is the very opposite of the principle of law and order. Law is based on the idea that the criminal can be punished; reprisals are based on the idea that he cannot be punished. They consist of striking at random at a crowd of strangers . . .'[16]

The key to Chesterton's opposition to the Government's policy in Ireland was his support for the rights of small nations against the imperial claims of their larger neighbours. In *The Danger to England* he put the matter succinctly: 'Our rulers tell us they can never recognise Ireland as a separate nation. But, in fact, they are recognising it as a separate nation. They are paying the plainest possible compliment to its independence; they are invading it.'[17]

The belief in the rights of small nations was held by Chesterton as a fundamental principle and was enshrined as sacrosanct in *The Napoleon of Notting Hill*. This championing of the underdog in international affairs won him many admirers throughout Europe. By 1918 *The Man Who was Thursday* had been translated into Hungarian and proved very popular. Soon afterwards *Orthodoxy* had been translated into Hungarian also and, later still, an anthology of extracts from *Orthodoxy*, *Heretics* and *What's Wrong with the World* was on sale in Budapest. These books were read avidly by Aurel Kolnai, a young man destined to become one of his country's most respected philosophers. He confessed a debt of gratitude to Chesterton: 'Like so many other converts of my time, I was won for Catholicism largely, if not chiefly, by the wisdom and wit of Gilbert Keith Chesterton . . . Of the many intellectual influences I have undergone, none by far has been so powerful and formative as his.'[18]

Chesterton's books were also gaining widespread popularity in Poland, and by 1919 *The Man Who was Thursday* and *The Club of Queer Trades* had been translated into Russian – though they were soon to be suppressed by the Bolsheviks.

In the summer of 1919, Chesterton wrote to Maurice Baring in the hope that his friend could use his contacts to secure the relevant documentation to allow him and Frances to visit Jerusalem. It had been scarcely seven months since Chesterton had sought Baring's help to permit his sister-in-law to visit Cecil on his death-bed in France. Now, however, it was the health of his wife which was causing concern:

> . . . could you possibly do me a great favour? It is very far from being the first great favour you have done me; and I should fear that anyone less magnanimous would fancy I only wrote to you about such things. But the situation is this. An excellent offer has been made to me to write a book about Jerusalem, not political but romantic and religious, so to speak; I conceive it as mostly about pilgrimages and crusades, in poetical prose . . . The offer includes money to go to Jerusalem but cannot include all the political or military permissions necessary to go there. I have another motive for wanting to go there, which is much stronger than the desire to write the book . . . Frances is to come with me, and all the doctors in creation tell her she can only get rid of her neuritis if she goes to some such place and misses part of an English winter. I would do anything to bring it off, for that reason alone . . . If you could possibly help in this matter, I really think you would be helping things you yourself care about; and one person, not myself, who deserves it. I will not say it would be killing two birds with one stone, which might seem a tragic metaphor; but bringing one bird at least to life; and allowing the other bird, who is a goose, to go on a wild goose-chase.[19]

Chesterton also claimed in the letter that Baring was 'a man who knows everybody'. It was certainly true that he knew the right people because General Allenby, who had liberated Jerusalem from the Turks two years earlier, replied to Baring personally, stating that he would be delighted to welcome the Chestertons in Jerusalem, and that every possible facility would be afforded for easy travel throughout Palestine. Consequently, on 29 December, immediately after the traditional Christmas celebrations in Beaconsfield, the Chestertons set off for France *en route* to Palestine.

Following a fairly good Channel crossing, they found there was 'an awful confusion at Boulogne' as they took the train to Paris. From Paris they took a sleeper to Rome. On New Year's Day they toured the city, visiting the Forum in the morning and the Colosseum in the afternoon. The same evening they departed for Brindisi, where they discovered that they would have to wait a day longer than expected for the boat to Alexandria. From the evening of 3 January until the early morning of the 7th they were at sea. Frances was seasick for the first two days. Finally arriving in Alexandria, they visited the Catholic cathedral of St Catherine, where Christmas was still being celebrated. Frances recorded in her diary that the cathedral contained one of the most beautiful cribs she had ever seen. From Alexandria they took the train to Cairo and thence to Jerusalem, their final destination.

Upon his return to England, Chesterton recorded his impressions of the visit in a book entitled *The New Jerusalem*: 'Various cultivated critics told me that I should find Jerusalem disappointing; and I fear it will disappoint them that I am not disappointed.'[20]

Predictably, *The New Jerusalem* was much more than a run-of-the-mill travelogue. Filled to the brim with his own opinions on a multitude of subjects, the book began with a spirited defence of the Crusades:

> When people talk ... as if the Crusades were nothing more than an aggressive raid against Islam, they seem to forget in the strangest way that Islam itself was only an aggressive raid against the old and ordered civilisation in these parts. I do not say it in mere hostility to the religion of Mahomet; as will be apparent later, I am fully conscious of many values and virtues in it; but certainly it was Islam that was the invasion and Christendom that was the thing invaded.[21]

Islam was also criticised for its attitude to women: 'Islam asserts admirably the equality of men; but it is the equality of males ... On the road to Cairo one may see twenty groups exactly like that of the Holy Family in the pictures of the Flight to Egypt; with only one difference. The man is riding the ass.'[22] In case the reader should gain the impression that the author had been converted to the cause of the suffragettes, he is quick to dismiss feminism as equally fallacious: '. . .

the Suffragettes no more established a philosophy of the sexes by their feminism than the Arabs did by their anti-feminism. A woman can find her home on the hustings even less than in the harem . . .'[23]

Elsewhere Chesterton criticises the outlook of the educated English tourist who, lacking either sympathy or understanding of the indigenous culture and traditions of the Middle East, sees only the ritual on the surface and not the mysticism beneath:

> . . . it is the educated Englishman who is the idolater. It is he who only reverences the place, and does not reverence the reverence for the place. It is he who is supremely concerned about whether a mere object is old or new, or whether a mere ornament is gold or gilt. In other words, it is he who values the visible things rather than the invisible; for no sane man can doubt that invisible things are very vivid to the priests and pilgrims of these shrines.[24]

As far as Chesterton is concerned, any religion is preferable to the blind and bland materialism of the modern agnostics:

> . . . my sympathies, when I go beyond the things I myself believe, are with all the poor Jews who do believe in Judaism and all the Mahometans who do believe in Mahometanism, not to mention so obscure a crowd as the Christians who do believe in Christianity. I feel I have more morally and even intellectually in common with these people, and even the religion of these people, than with the supercilious negations that make up the most part of what is called the enlightenment.[25]

This superciliousness is attacked vehemently in a spirited defence of traditional theology:

> The truth is that the things that meet today in Jerusalem are by far the greatest things that the world has yet seen. If they are not important nothing on this earth is important, and certainly not the impressions of those who happen to be bored with them . . .
>
> For instance, the critic generally begins by dismissing these conflicts with the statement that they are all about small points of theology. I do not admit that theological points are small points. Theology is only thought applied to religion; and those who prefer a thoughtless religion need not be so very disdainful of others with a more rationalistic taste. The old joke that the Greek sects only differed about a single letter is about the lamest and most illogical joke in the world. An atheist and

250

a theist only differ by a single letter; yet theologians are so subtle as
to distinguish definitely between the two.[26]

Chesterston's perception of the nature of the situation in Jerusalem
led, inevitably perhaps, to a premonition of the human tragedy about
to unfold in the Middle East:

> There was a movement in my own mind that was attuned to these
> things . . . for the sense of crisis is not only in the intensity of the ideals,
> but in the very conditions of the reality . . . And the burden of it is the
> burden of Palestine . . . A voice not of my reason, but rather sounding
> heavily in my heart, seemed to be repeating sentences like pessimistic
> proverbs. There is no place for the Temple of Solomon but on the
> ruins of the Mosque of Omar. There is no place for the nation of
> the Jews but in the country of the Arabs. And these whispers came
> to me first not as intellectual conclusions upon the conditions of the
> case . . . but rather as hints of something immediate and menacing
> and yet mysterious. I felt almost a momentary impulse to flee from
> the place, like one who has received an omen. For two voices had
> met in my ears; and within the same narrow space and in the same
> dark hour, electric and yet eclipsed with cloud, I had heard Islam
> crying from the turret and Israel wailing at the wall.[27]

In the summer of 1920, a few months after his return from Palestine,
Chesterton addressed the first Anglo-Catholic Congress, which met in
the Albert Hall. Although he was still officially an Anglican, he now
felt his position to be awkwardly and increasingly incongruous. He
wrote to Maurice Baring about his feeling of unease at being asked
to speak to such a large gathering of Anglo-Catholics:

> . . . before my present crisis, I had promised somebody to take part
> in what I took to be a small debate on labour. Too late, by my
> own carelessness, I found to my horror it had swelled into a huge
> Anglo-Catholic Congress at the Albert Hall. I tried to get out of it, but
> I was held to my promise . . . So I spoke very briefly, saying something
> of what I think about social ethics. Whether or not my decision was
> right, my experience was curious and suggestive, though tragic; for
> I felt it like a farewell. There was no doubt about the enthusiasm
> of those thousands of Anglo-Catholics. But there was also no doubt,
> unless I am much mistaken, that many of them besides myself would
> be Roman Catholics rather than accept things they are quite likely
> to be asked to accept – for instance, by the Lambeth Conference

... I am at least sure that much turns on that Conference, if not for me, for large numbers of those people at the Albert Hall. A young Anglo-Catholic curate has just told me that the crowd there cheered all references to the Pope, and laughed at every mention of the Archbishop of Canterbury. It's a queer state of things. I am concerned most, however, about somebody I value more than the Archbishop of Canterbury; Frances, to whom I owe much of my own faith, and to whom therefore (as far as I can see my way) I also owe every decent chance for the controversial defence of her faith. If her side can convince me, they have a right to do so; if not, I shall go hot and strong to convince her. I put it clumsily, but there is a point in my mind. Logically, therefore, I must await answers from Waggett and Gore as well as Knox and McNabb; and talk the whole thing over with her, and then act as I believe.

This is a dusty political sort of letter, with nothing in it but what I think, and nothing of what I feel. For that side of it, I can only express myself by asking for your prayers.[28]

These were difficult days for Chesterton as he agonised over the nature of his faith. In another letter to Baring he seemed to have reached certain conclusions which edged him still closer to Rome:

As you may possibly guess, I want to consider my position about the biggest thing of all, whether I am to be inside it or outside it. I used to think one could be an Anglo-Catholic and really inside it; but if that was (to use an excellent phrase of your own) only a Porch, I do not think I want a Porch, and certainly not a Porch standing some way from the building. A Porch looks so silly, standing all by itself in a field.[29]

In the same letter Gilbert complained about his workload, 'which really seems to bury me day after day. I never realised before that business can really block out much bigger things.' The workload in question included his continued editorship of the *New Witness* and the writing of the regular column in the *Illustrated London News*. Also in the autumn of 1920 another collection of essays, entitled *The Uses of Diversity*, was published. In one of the essays Chesterton attacked the underlying pessimism of much modern poetry: 'I will not write any more about these poets, because I do not pretend to be impartial, or even to be good-tempered on the subject. To my thinking, the oppression of the people is a terrible sin; but the depression of the people is a far worse one.'[30]

Amid all the work there was still time for play. In November Chesterton was again involved in a mock trial. As before, he was bewigged and berobed as the judge, presiding at the trial of the publisher Cecil Palmer, who was accused of the charge of 'sobriety'. Throughout the trial *The New Jerusalem* replaced the Bible for the purposes of the oath and Chesterton, in his summing up at the conclusion of the evening, pronounced that the prosecution had established the case for the defence and the defence the case for the prosecution. The accused was found guilty as charged, and Chesterton sentenced him to 'three years in a Turkish harem'. The proceedings prompted the *Daily Dispatch* to comment that law courts would be 'much more entertaining . . . if judges were as Mr Gilbert Chesterton on the bench . . . In his wig and gown G. K. C. was imposing, and only a long white beard need have been added to have in him an ideal "Father Christmas". Such is his universality.'[31]

Chesterton also made many appearances as a public speaker at this time. In one such engagement, at a meeting of the Architects Club, he said he had always wanted to organise a fancy-dress ball where all the costumes represented buildings. He had already chosen the costume he would wear: 'Of course, *I* shall go as the Albert Hall.'[32]

Towards the end of the year Gilbert was again writing to Maurice Baring:

This is the shortest, hastiest and worst written letter in the world. It only tells you three things: (1) that I thank you a thousand times for the book; (2) that I have to leave for America for a month or two, earlier than I expected; but I am glad, for I shall see something of Frances, without walls or work between us; and (3) that I have pretty well made up my mind about the thing we talked about. Fortunately, the thing we talked about can be found all over the world.[33]

On Christmas Eve, a similar letter was sent to Father O'Connor:

I feel I must scribble you a line, with incongruous haste and crudity, to send you our love at Xmas and to ask for your prayers. Frances and I are going away to America for a month or two; and I am glad of it, for I shall be at least free from the load of periodical work that has prevented me from talking properly to anybody, even to her; and I want to talk very much. When it is over I shall probably want to talk to you, about very important things – the most important things there are. Frances has not been well, and though I think she is better, I have to do things in a considerate way, if you understand me; I feel it is also only right to consult with my Anglo-Catholic friends; but I have at present a feeling that it will be something like a farewell. Things have shaken me up a good deal lately – especially the persecution of Ireland. But of course there are even bigger things than that.[34]

Apart from concerns about his faith, which constituted 'the most important things there are', Chesterton was clearly worried about his wife's health. Recent X-rays had revealed arthritis in her spine, causing almost constant pain and suffering, but she had decided to accompany Gilbert on the proposed lecture tour of America. They departed on a transatlantic liner, the *Kaiserin Augusta Victoria*, which left Liverpool on New Year's Day 1921. The vessel met 'fresh gales and rough seas' as it headed into the Atlantic and, on 8 January, two days before arriving at New York, the weather became decidedly 'squally'.

Although Gilbert was aware that his books were very popular in the United States, he was completely unprepared for the hero's welcome he received on his arrival. The American press had heralded the visit of 'the World Famous Literary Genius and his wife' with extensive and enthusiastic gusto, so much so that Frances remarked, 'I did not know I was the wife of a great man until I came to America.'[35] Chesterton's first impressions of American hospitality were revealed through the eyes of Father Brown in a story published five years later:

> When Father Brown first stepped off an Atlantic liner on to American soil, he discovered . . . that he was a much more important person than he had ever supposed . . . America has a genius for the encouragement of fame . . . and he found himself held up on the quay by a group of journalists, as by a gang of brigands, who asked him questions about all the subjects on which he was least likely to regard himself as an authority, such as the details of female dress and the criminal statistics of the country that he had only that moment clapped his eye on.[36]

The novelty of press attention soon wore off, and Gilbert began to regard the journalists, the 'gang of brigands' who pestered him and his wife outside their hotel rooms, with considerable trepidation. Frances, essentially a very private person, found the constant media pressure particularly difficult to cope with, and this fuelled the homesickness she was feeling. As we have noted, 'The real truth is,' she told one reporter, 'that I care more for my dog, donkey and garden in the little English village where we live than for all the publicity in the world.'[37]

None the less, the extensive media coverage ensured enormous interest in the lectures Gilbert was giving. These began in New York and were followed by others in Boston. He returned to New York at the end of January to give two further lectures at the Times Square Theatre. By this time the major newspapers of both cities were singing his praises:

New York Herald: 'A large crowd stormed the doors of the Times Square Theatre to hear the British essayist.'

New York Evening Post: 'His basic kindliness is infectious; his vast mirth appeals to many hearts. Few English authors could have been more certain of an affectionate welcome.'

New York World: 'What he said was wholly to the liking of the really choice audience that gathered to hear him and he received sincere tributes of appreciation.'

New York Evening World: 'Mentally he is a crackling electric spark, the only man who can give the cleverest radical debaters a Roland for their Oliver.'

Boston Post: 'Britain's famous jester ridiculed in rollicking fashion; with rapier-like thrusts he drew what seemed to be the life-blood from popular scientific conceits.'

Boston Transcript: 'The reaction of the audience to his wit and wisdom was expressed in merriment and applause.'

Boston Globe: 'He talked in a humorous vein, his facetious remarks on a wide range of topics evoking roars of laughter from the audience.'

Boston Herald: 'Whether he speaks on prohibition, ping-pong or the Pentateuch he has always something to say. His epigrams and witty sayings were repaid in bursts of laughter and applause.'[38]

Although many of the lectures were relatively mundane in their subject matter, such as the talk on 'Fads' on 30 January in the

Times Square Theatre, New York, and the address on 'Literature as Luggage' at the same venue the following week, many more captured the imagination through the incorporation of a paradox in the title; thus Chesterton lectured on 'The Ignorance of the Educated', 'The Perils of Health', and 'Shall We Abolish the Inevitable?' The *New York Sun* observed that 'a superficial observer merely sees the Chestertonian paradox; the man who looks deeper sees the underlying truth.'[39] This theme was taken up by a cartoonist in the *New York Herald*, who depicted Chesterton supplying 'Paradoxygen to the World'. The cartoon was accompanied by a less sympathetic satirical poem called 'Paradoxygen', by Edward Anthony:

> O Gilbert, I know there are many who like
> Your talks on the darkness of light,
> The shortness of length and the weakness of strength
> And the one on the lowness of height.
>
> My neighbour keeps telling me 'How I adore
> His legality of the illicit
> And I've also a liking intense for his striking
> Obscurity of the explicit.'
>
> But I am unmoved. What's the reason? Oh, well,
> The same I intend to expound
> Some evening next week, when I'm going to speak
> On the shallowness of the profound.[40]

After New York the Chestertons visited Chicago, Philadelphia, Baltimore, Nashville, Oklahoma, Omaha and Albany. Gilbert received a rapturous response everywhere he went, and the success was repeated when he crossed the border into Canada. Through it all he remained totally unaffected by events and as self-effacing as ever. For example, when an enthusiastic reporter asked him which of his works he considered the greatest, he replied instantly, 'I don't consider any of my works in the least great.'[41]

'Thank Heaven,' Frances told another reporter, 'my husband is thoroughly normal and unaffected; he doesn't care for popularity any more than I do, and we are just terribly homesick for our home in England.'[42]

Eventually, though evidently not soon enough for Frances, the Chestertons returned home on the liner *Aquitania* on 12 April 1921.

Chesterton's account of the American trip was published the following year under the appropriate, if unimaginative, title *What I Saw in America*. Meanwhile, an account of the couple's return to England was recorded by their secretary, Kathleen Chesshire:

> Not yet long back from their American lecture tour, Mrs G. K. C. could hardly accustom herself to it all. Dear familiar Beaconsfield, her garden, friends dropping in, the steady even tempo of life in England's countryside. When the Secretary had met her at Waterloo, there had been two arms flung around her, 'You don't know how refreshing you look, my dear, in your blue straw hat. I've been thinking of bluebells and England all the way from Southampton.'[43]

Back in Beaconsfield the Chesterton home reaped the benefits of the money earned in America. Gilbert had been paid up to $1,000 for each lecture he gave in the United States, and this extra income enabled him and Frances to finish the conversion of the studio into Top Meadow, their new home. They added a wing with a kitchen, a bathroom and small bedrooms at the top of a narrow, winding stair. Built in stages, at first merely a studio and den, where Chesterton found the solitude to write, it evolved into the house of their dreams where they would live out the rest of their lives.

A vision of the homeliness of Top Meadow was given by Ada Chesterton, who described the 'open brick fireplace with space for a small low chair on either side, where Frances would sit for hours, watching the logs crumble into fiery particles'.[44] Ada also recalled Frances's love for the garden: 'The gardens stretching luxuriantly at the back were always a joy. Frances I think found undiluted happiness in their superintendence. They were lavishly kept and a local man worked unremittingly. I remember one gorgeous summer day when flaming pokers, delphiniums, lupins, peonies, sunflowers – all the piled-up wealth of scent and colour – streamed across the lawn.'[45]

Somewhat in contrast to the array of colour on the summer day when Ada visited, Frances was bemused one spring to discover nothing in the borders except wallflowers. When she remonstrated with Mr Childs, the elderly gardener, at the lack of variety, he replied, 'Master, he do like a bit of wall-flower. It's the only flower he knows the name of.'[46] The gardener's judgment that Gilbert was botanically ignorant was ratified when the 'Master' wrote a poem for Frances about wild flowers:

I know you would have known the names
     Of all the flowers that fire the moor
Names that seem coloured from your soul
     So elvish and perverse and pure.

Names that you might have made yourself,
     As quaint as clouds, as kind as showers,
If Adam named the brutes and birds
     I know 'twas Eve that named the flowers.

The dog rose bends, a stricken saint,
     Its fiery aureole rent and riven
The larkspur spurns the earth and climbs
     Until it catch the tints of heaven.

The goatsbeard gilds the gloaming meads;
     The foxglove – bells and steeple bent –
O'er this still chapel of the fields
     Shakes out, instead of music, scent.

But you – in you are all the flowers
     Not only in your body rare –
Those blue and starry flowers, your eyes,
     That brown and fragrant flower, your hair.[47]

Regardless of the poem's other merits, Frances would have been highly amused at the catalogue of botanical errors it contained. The larkspur, far from being a tall moorland plant that 'spurns the earth and climbs', is a small and rare plant growing near cornfields. The goat'sbeard, said to 'gild the gloaming meads', is popularly called 'go-to-bed at noon' because no blossom is open in the afternoon. Meanwhile the foxglove, in spite of Chesterton's assertions to the contrary, is not a sweet-scented flower.

If Gilbert failed to share his wife's love for gardening, he did share her love for animals. Mary Rushton, a housemaid who was with the Chestertons for many years, remembered Gilbert with the family pets – the two dogs, Winkle and Quoodle, and Perky the cat:

He was mad on old Quoodle. He'd sit with his arm round him. Mrs Chesterton said Quoodle mustn't get on the couch. But he knew he wouldn't be turned off while his master was there. He'd look at me as if he was daring me to turn him off if Master was in the room.

If Quoodle let out the least little squeak, he'd drop everything and rush to the door . . . He loved kippers for breakfast. One day Perky got on the table, and I caught him getting at the kippers. I was going to throw them out, but he said: 'I don't mind eating after Perky.'[48]

The measure of Chesterton's affection for animals can be gauged by the fact that one of the most sympathetically portrayed characters in any of his novels was not a human being but a dog. The dog, given the name of Quoodle in honour of the Chestertons' family pet, was one of the heroes in *The Flying Inn*:

Dalroy, as he sang this, actually began to dance about like a ballet girl, an enormous and ridiculous figure in the sunlight; waving the wooden sign round his head. Quoodle opened his eyes and pricked up his ears and seemed much interested in these extraordinary evolutions. Suddenly, with one of those startling changes that will transfigure the most sedentary dogs, Quoodle decided that the dance was a game; and began to bark and bound round the performer . . .[49]

During 1921 Chesterton had been elected president of the Dickens Society, and the last Christmas at Overroads, before they finally moved into Top Meadow the following spring, was celebrated in true Dickensian style. Children were supplied in quantities by friends and relatives, and the toy theatre took pride of place alongside the Nativity crib. Amid these festivities Chesterton turned his attention to a matter which was becoming ever more pressing. On Christmas Day he wrote to Maurice Baring:

I have been troubled for some time about a particular problem in connection with the great subject (which has hardly left my thought for an hour) and I hope the decision I have come to does not sound abrupt and incoherent in this hasty note. I should very much like to see you, but I should also like to see some priest of your acquaintance, about what is involved in a certain case. What I mean is this: he may very well be a friend of yours, and even know what has passed between us so far. But I don't particularly want him to be a friend of mine; I know several Catholic priests, and though of course I know they would consider principles and not friendship, I don't want to burden their friendship till I know it is necessary . . . If you could let me know after the end of this week, or preferably after Epiphany (to preserve the twelve days of Xmas) I would arrange an appointment at your convenience and his.[50]

In another, undated, letter to Baring, Gilbert broached the same subject even more cautiously:

> I am moved somehow to send you a very hasty and, I fear, inconsequent scrawl, for I have been working hard till midnight, to tell you I have not forgotten the things we talked of last year; though they have had further complications; and that I shall soon probably have more to tell you about them. For deeper reasons than I could ever explain, my mind has to turn especially on the thought of my wife, whose life has been in many ways a very heroic tragedy; and to whom I am so much in debt of honour that I cannot bear to leave her, even psychologically, if it be possible by tact and sympathy to take her with me. We have had a very difficult time lately; but the other day she rather abruptly faced the thing herself in a new way, and spoke as if she knew where we would both end. But she asked for a little time; as a great friend of hers is also (with the approval of the priest whom she consulted) delaying for the moment till she is more certain. She and Frances want to meet and have it out, I think, and I cannot imagine any way in which Frances is more likely to be moved in that direction than by an Anglican or ex-Anglican friend of exactly that type . . . I only write this to tell you the thing may look rather stationary, and yet it moves.[51]

Early in 1922 Gilbert was again burning the midnight oil when he wrote to Father Ronald Knox:

> Please excuse the journalistic paper, but the letter-block seems undiscoverable at this time of night. I ought to have written before; but we have been in some family trouble; my father is very ill, and as he is an old man, my feelings are with him and my mother in a way more serious than anything except the matter of our correspondence. Essentially, of course, it does not so much turn the current of my thoughts as deepen it; to see a man so many million times better than I am, in every way, and one to whom I owe everything, under such a shadow makes me feel, on top of all my particular feelings, the shadow that lies on us all. I can't tell you what I feel of course; but I hope I may ask for your prayers for my people and for me. My father is the very best man I ever knew of that generation that never understood the new need of a spiritual authority; and lives almost perfectly by the sort of religion men had when rationalism was rational. I think he was always subconsciously prepared for the next generation having less theology than he has;

and is rather puzzled at its having more. But I think he understood my brother's conversion better than my mother did; she is more difficult, and of course I cannot bother her just now.[52]

By the time Gilbert wrote this letter his father was seriously ill. Yet his condition was the culmination of a long, protracted illness which began as nothing more than an obstinate cold. At first, according to Ada Chesterton, 'there was nothing sinister or alarming in his symptoms'.[53] Slowly, however, his condition worsened. He took to his bed and began to leave it less and less frequently. The doctors recommended a change of air but he refused to move, lacking either the inclination or the energy. Ada described his final days: 'Little by little his mental keenness was over-clouded, and he drifted into lassitude and inertia, so that when at last he went out the end was not wholly a surprise.'[54]

A few days after his father's death Chesterton was again writing to Father Knox:

I was just settling down three days ago to write a full reply to your last very kind letter, which I should have answered long before, when I received the wire that called me instantly to town. My father died on Monday; and since then I have been doing the little I can for my mother . . . I only send you this interim scribble as an excuse for delaying the letter I had already begun; and which nothing less than this catastrophe would have prevented me finishing. I hope to finish it in a few days. I am not sure whether I shall then be back in Beaconsfield; but if so it will be at a new address: Top Meadow, Beaconsfield.[55]

Thus ended an episode in Chesterton's life in which death followed death: the deaths of his friends in the war; the death of his brother at the war's end; and, finally, the death of his father. Yet it was also an episode epitomising the triumph of life after the tragedy of death. Indeed, 1922 was to be a year of new beginnings for Chesterton. As well as the new home at Top Meadow, he would also find the spiritual home for which he had been searching for many years.

« 17 »

Word Made Flesh

On 29 May 1922 Maurice Baring sent Chesterton his condolences:

> I only heard just lately the very sad news about your father.
>
> I have been meaning to write to you ever since and the silence and delay has been due to no want of sympathy or thought of you; on the contrary I have lately felt strangely near to you, and I have had (quite wrongly perhaps) the impression that your buffetings were over and that your ship was in calm waters, well in sight of the harbour. Forgive me if this is all wrong.
>
> I admired your father very much. He reminded me of my own father in being intensely English.
>
> Dear Gilbert, I know what these things are and what one feels and I am so sorry for you.
>
> God bless you.[1]

There is no doubt that the 'calm waters' to which Baring referred expressed his belief that Chesterton had finally found peace in a firm resolution to resolve the anomalous nature of his religious position. It is clear also that the 'harbour' in question was the Roman Catholic Church. When Baring had converted thirteen years earlier he recorded his own feelings in verse:

> One day I heard a whisper: 'Wherefore wait?
> Why linger in a separated porch?
> Why nurse the flicker of a severed torch?
> The fire is there, ablaze beyond the gate.
> Why tremble, foolish soul? Why hesitate?'[2]

The questions, answered so finally by both Baring and Cecil many years earlier, still required an answer from Gilbert, whose prolonged procrastination continued. His lingering concerns and fears, centred principally on the attitude of Frances, were voiced in a series of undated letters to Father Ronald Knox, another who had previously taken the step of conversion, in his case in highly controversial circumstances:

> I feel horribly guilty in not having written before, and I do most earnestly hope you have not allowed my delay to interfere with any of your own arrangements. I have had a serious and very moving talk with my wife; and she is only too delighted at the idea of your visit in itself; in fact she really wants to know you very much. Unfortunately, it does not seem very workable at the time to which I suppose you referred. I imagine it more or less corresponds to next week; and we have only one spare bedroom yet, which is occupied by a nurse who is giving my wife a treatment that seems to be doing her good and which I don't want to stop if I can help it . . . In our conversation my wife was all that I hope you will some day know her to be; she is incapable of wanting me to do anything but what I think right; and admits the same possibility for herself: but it is much more of a wrench for her, for she has been able to practise her religion in complete good faith; which my own doubts have prevented me from doing.
>
> I will write again very soon.[3]

Although he did write again soon afterwards it was 'only a wild and hasty line', repeating that Father Knox's visit was still difficult to arrange because of 'a nurse who is staying here giving my wife a treatment of radiant heat – one would hardly think needed in this weather; but it seems to be doing her good, I am thankful to say'.[4]

As well as with concerns over his wife's health, Gilbert was still preoccupied with his duties as an executor in the wake of his father's death. Also, as was illustrated by the shortage of spare bedrooms, the correspondence with Father Knox coincided with the move to Top Meadow, which was still in the process of construction. One can imagine the chaotic circumstances in which the Chestertons were living and the way this would make any arrangements very difficult. Indeed, Gilbert explained to Father Knox that 'my normal chaos is increased by moving into a new house, which is still like a wastepaper basket'.[5] Added to this was another lecture tour, this time to the Netherlands, which prompted yet another apology:

Just as I am emerging from the hurricane of business I mentioned to you, I find myself under a promise a year old to go and lecture for a week in Holland; and I write this almost stepping on the boat. I don't in the least want to go; but I suppose the great question is there as elsewhere. Indeed, I hear it is something of a reconquered territory; some say a third of this heroic Calvinist state is now Catholic ... I will write to you again and more fully about the business of instruction when I return, which should be in about ten days.[6]

The practicalities of instruction, and the psychology behind Gilbert's desire for it, were discussed in yet another letter to Knox:

I cannot tell you how much I was pleased and honoured even by the suggestion that you might possibly deal with the instruction yourself; it is something I should value more vividly and personally than I can possibly express. But as this was so long ago, before so many delays and interruptions, I fear your margin of Sundays in London must now be very narrowed. But I think there must be a Sunday or two left on your list; and with your permission, I propose to come up next Sunday, if I could have the pleasure of seeing you then. I have no doubt it could be arranged through Maurice Baring or somebody, supposing you have no arrangements of your own which you would prefer ...

... I am in a state now when I feel a monstrous charlatan, as if I wore a mask and were stuffed with cushions, whenever I see anything about the public G. K. C.; it hurts me; for though the views I express are real, the image is horribly unreal compared with the real person who needs help just now. I have as much vanity as anybody about any of these superficial successes while they are going on; but I never feel for a moment that they affect the reality of whether I am utterly rotten or not; so that any comments on my religious position seem like a wind on the other side of the world; as if they were about somebody else – as indeed they are. I am not troubled about a great fat man who appears on platforms and in caricatures, even when he enjoys controversies on what I believe to be the right side. I am concerned about what has become of a little boy whose father showed him a toy theatre, and a schoolboy whom nobody ever heard of, with his brooding on doubts and dirt and day-dreams of crude conscientiousness so inconsistent as to [be] near to hypocrisy; and all the morbid life of the lonely mind of a living person with whom I have lived. It is that story, that so often came near to ending badly, that I want to end well. Forgive this scrawl; I think you will understand me.[7]

It seems, however, that by July, following further discussions with Frances, Gilbert had decided that he should receive instruction from Father O'Connor rather than Father Knox. He wrote to Father Knox explaining his decision:

I ought to have written long ago to tell you what I have done about the most practical of business matters . . . I have managed to have another talk with my wife, after which I have written to our old friend Father O'Connor and asked him to come here, as he probably can, from what I hear. I doubt whether I can possibly put in words why I feel sure this is the right thing, not so much for my sake as for hers. We talk about misunderstandings; but I think it is possible to understand too well for comfort; certainly too well for my powers of psychological description. Frances is just at the point where Rome acts both as the positive and the negative magnet; a touch would turn her either way; almost (against her will) to hatred, but with the right touch to a faith far beyond my reach. I know Father O'Connor's would be the touch that does not startle, because she knows him and is fond of him; and the only thing she asked of me was to send for him. If he cannot come, of course I shall take other action and let you know.[8]

For his part, Father Knox seemed unperturbed by what may have been perceived as a rebuff. Far from taking the matter personally, he wrote to Chesterton on 17 July expressing delight at his friend's decision: 'I'm awfully glad to hear that you've sent for Father O'Connor and that you think he's likely to be available. I must say that, in the story, Father Brown's powers of neglecting his parish always seemed to me even more admirable than Dr Watson's powers of neglecting his practice; so I hope this trait was drawn from the life.'[9]

Chesterton's letter to Father O'Connor was undated, but post-marked 11 July:

I ought to have written to you long before in reply to your kind letter; but indeed I do not answer it now in order to agree with you about Ireland or disagree with you about France; if indeed we do disagree about anything. I write with a more personal motive; do you happen to have a holiday about the end of next week or thereabouts; and would it be possible for you to come south and see our new house – or old studio? This sounds a very abrupt invitation; but I write in great haste, and am troubled about many things. I want to talk to you about them; especially the most serious ones, religious and concerned with my own rather difficult position. Most of the difficulty has been my own fault, but not all; some of my difficulties would commonly be called duties; though I ought perhaps to have learned sooner to regard them as lesser duties. I mean that a Pagan or Protestant or Agnostic might even have excused me; but I have grown less and less of a Pagan or Protestant, and can no longer excuse myself . . . Anyhow, you are the person that Frances and I think of with most affection, of all who could help in such a matter. Could you let me know if any time such as I name, or after, could give us the joy of seeing you?[10]

Father O'Connor replied immediately to the effect that he would hold himself at Gilbert's disposal any day during the ensuing fortnight. However, Frances wrote a letter on 23 July which betrayed some of the underlying tension caused by the issue of her husband's conversion:

I just want to know if you can send *me* a line as to how long you can stay in Beaconsfield. I have a spare bed for Wednesday night, but after that I must get a room out or at one of the inns for you. Please don't think me inhospitable. I am only too pleased that G. wants you – and I am sure that you will now be able to give him all the advice and help he wants. But I must make arrangements, and I want you to have all the time you may need together.[11]

It seems that Father O'Connor made use of the spare bed on the Wednesday night because that was the day he arrived in Beaconsfield. It must also be assumed that Frances made arrangements for his accommodation elsewhere in the town thereafter because he stayed until the following Sunday.

On the Thursday morning Father O'Connor accompanied Frances on a trip to the village and took the opportunity of broaching the subject of Gilbert's desire for conversion. He told her that her husband's deepest concern was the effect his conversion may have on her. Frances's response, tempered no doubt by her fondness for the priest, was reassuringly positive: 'Oh! I shall be infinitely relieved. You cannot imagine how it fidgets Gilbert to have anything on his mind. The last three months have been exceptionally trying. I should be only too glad to come with him, if God in His mercy should show the way clear, but up to now He has not made it clear enough to me to justify such a step.'[12]

The fact that Frances had finally given her blessing was all the reassurance Gilbert needed to take the final plunge. He and Father O'Connor discussed at length any remaining questions and the priest told him to read through the Penny Catechism to make sure there were no further difficulties. Father O'Connor recalled that it was 'a sight for men and angels all the Friday to see him wandering in and out of the house with his fingers in the leaves of the little book, resting it on his forearm whilst he pondered with his head on one side'.[13]

Not surprisingly for a man who had been defending Catholic orthodoxy for nearly twenty years, there were no final doubts or difficulties, only a sense of apprehension at the size of the step he was about to take: 'I had no doubts or difficulties just before. I had only fears, fears of something that had the finality and simplicity of suicide.'[14]

Thus all was set for his long-awaited reception into the Church. Father Ignatius Rice, OSB, one of Chesterton's oldest and keenest admirers who had become one of his dearest friends, had hoped that Gilbert would be received at the Douai Abbey School where he was the headmaster. This was not to be. Instead Chesterton chose a far more humble venue. His choice was the Railway Hotel in Beaconsfield, the dance-room of which had been converted into a makeshift chapel in the absence of any Catholic church in the town. In truth it was little more than a shed with a corrugated-iron roof and wooden walls, fitted with chapel fixtures by Sir Philip Rose and made available by the hotel's Irish landlady, Mrs Borlase. However, if Father Rice had failed to persuade Chesterton to be received in more luxurious surroundings, he was compensated amply when Gilbert requested that he be present with Father O'Connor at his reception on Sunday, 30 July. The two priests breakfasted together at the inn at which Father O'Connor was staying before walking together to Top Meadow. According to Father Rice, they found Gilbert in an armchair reading the catechism, 'pulling faces and making noises as he used to do when reading'.[15] Greeting his two friends, he got up and stuffed the catechism in his pocket. At lunch he drank water and poured wine for everyone else, and at about three o'clock they set out for the church. While Gilbert was making his confession to Father O'Connor, Frances, who was weeping continually, was comforted by Father Rice.

After the baptism the two priests left the chapel while Gilbert and Frances remained inside. When Father Rice returned to collect something he had forgotten he saw them coming down the aisle together. Frances was still weeping and Gilbert, his arm round her, sought to offer comfort. Recalling the day's events, Father O'Connor remembered Frances's emotional response: 'dear Frances – my eyes fill to think of it, was present, in tears which I am sure were not all grieving'.[16] Whether the tears were all grieving, there can be little doubt that grief was one of the emotions she was feeling. In the practice of their faith, the most important thing in their lives, she and her husband were now separated.

For Gilbert, however, the day was a liberation and, as with Maurice Baring before him, the occasion of his conversion inspired one of his best sonnets:

> . . . The sages have a hundred maps to give
> That trace their crawling cosmos like a tree,
> They rattle reason out through many a sieve
> That stores the sand and lets the gold go free:
> And all these things are less than dust to me
> Because my name is Lazarus and I live.[17]

Father Thomas Walker, the parish priest at Beaconsfield, remembered the occasion of Chesterton's First Communion: 'It was one of the most happy duties I had ever to perform . . . That he was perfectly well aware of the immensity of the Real Presence on the morning of his First Communion, can be gathered from the fact that he was covered with perspiration when he actually received Our Lord. When I was congratulating him he said, 'I have spent the happiest hour of my life.'[18]

In a letter to Father Walker, both undated and never actually sent, Chesterton conveyed his humility in the face of the mystery of the Real Presence:

I do hope you will forgive me if I bother you by asking whether I might see you some time soon, about a thing that has got between me and my best happiness for some little time; which I want to see straight before I go to the Blessed Sacrament, as of course I shall do within the Easter period somehow. Even if I could be back in Beaconsfield in time, which is uncertain, I would not delay confessions at such a busy time: for it is not exactly a sin, save in so far that I repent abjectly having postponed this explanation of it. Nor is it a doubt of the Faith: on the contrary, the trouble with me is that I am too much frightened of that tremendous Reality on the altar. I have not grown up with it and it is too much for me. I think I am morbid: but I want to be told so by authority.[19]

These sentiments were reiterated ten years later in *Christendom in Dublin*: 'The word Eucharist is but a verbal symbol, we might say a vague verbal mask, for something so tremendous that the assertion and denial of it have alike seemed a blasphemy; a blasphemy that has shaken the world with the earthquake of two thousand years.'[20]

Moving from the mysterious to the mundane, Gilbert dutifully informed his mother of his conversion. It was a difficult letter to write, coming so soon after the death of her husband, because Gilbert was aware that his actions would not be met with approval:

I write this (with the worst pen in South Bucks) to tell you something before I write about it to anyone else; something about which we shall probably be in the position of the two bosom friends at Oxford, who 'never differed except in opinion'. You have always been so wise in not judging people by their opinions, but rather the opinions by the people. It is in one sense a long story by this time; but I have come to the same conclusion that Cecil did . . . and I am now a Catholic in the same sense as he, having long claimed the name in its Anglo-Catholic sense. I am not going to make a foolish fuss of reassuring you about things I am sure you never doubted; these things do not hurt any relations between people as fond of each other as we are; any more than they ever made any difference to the love between Cecil and ourselves. But there are two things I should like to tell you, in case you do not realise them through some other impression. I have thought about you, and all that I owe to you and my father, not only in the way of affection, but of the ideals of honour and freedom and charity and all other good things you always taught me: and I am not conscious of the smallest break or difference in those ideals; but only of a new and necessary way of fighting for them. I think, as Cecil did, that the fight for the family and the free citizen and everything decent must now be waged by [the] one fighting form of Christianity. The other is that I have thought this thing out for myself and not in a hurry of feeling. It is months since I saw my Catholic friends and years since I talked to them about it. I believe it is the truth. I must end now, you know with how much love; for the post is going.[21]

In view of the continuous correspondence with Father Knox and Maurice Baring during the previous months, Chesterton's claim that he hadn't discussed the issue with his Catholic friends was, at best, Jesuitical equivocation, inasmuch as he hadn't literally *seen* or *talked* to them but had only *written* to them. At worst, it was plainly and simply a lie, albeit a white lie to spare his mother's feelings.

Having fulfilled the unenviable task of delivering more unwelcome news to his grieving mother, Chesterton wrote to Maurice Baring, to whom the news of his conversion would be most welcome indeed. Referring to his reception as 'this wonderful business, in which you have helped me so much more than anyone else', he also cited Father Knox as the other person whose help had been invaluable.[22]

Knox wrote of Chesterton's conversion that

> he had found his home. Just as the hero of his own book *Manalive* walked round the world to find, and to have the thrill of finding, the house which belonged to him, so Chesterton probed all the avenues of thought and tasted all the philosophies, to return at last to that institution which had been his spiritual home from the first, the Church of his friend, Father Brown. He would, I think, have done so before, if he had not been anxious to spare the feelings of his wife, the heroine of all his novels . . .[23]

Baring, joyful that his friend's 'ship had arrived at its port', wrote to Chesterton with a candour which would have been inconceivable before his reception:

> Nothing for years has given me so much joy. I have hardly ever entered a church without putting up a candle to Our Lady or to St Joseph or St Anthony for you. And both this year and last year in Lent I made a Novena for you. I know of many other people, better people far than I, who did the same. Many Masses were said for you and prayers all over England and Scotland in centres of Holiness. I will show you some day a letter from some Nuns on the subject. A great friend of mine, one of the greatest saints I have known, Sister Mary Annunciation of the Convent Orphanage, Upper Norwood, used always to pray for you. She, alas, died last year.
>
> Did I ever quote you a sentence of Bernard Holland on the subject of Kenelm Henry Digby when the latter was received?
>
> 'Father Scott . . . at last, guided him through the narrow door where one must bend one's head, into the internal space and freedom of the eternal and universal Catholic Church.' *Space* and *freedom*: that was what I experienced on being received; that is what I have been most conscious of ever since . . .

Well, all I have to say, Gilbert, is what I think I have already said to you, and what I have said not long ago in a printed book. That I was received into the Church on the Eve of Candlemas 1909, and it is perhaps the *only act* in my life which I am quite certain I have never regretted. Every day I live, the Church seems to me more and more wonderful; the Sacraments more and more solemn and sustaining; the voice of the Church, her liturgy, her rules, her discipline, her ritual, her decisions in matters of Faith and Morals more and more excellent and profoundly wise and true and right, and her children stamped with something that those outside Her are without. There I have found Truth and reality and everything outside Her is to me compared with Her as dust and shadow. Once more God bless you, and Frances. Please give her my love. In my prayers for you I have always added her name.[24]

Another Catholic friend who spoke with uncharacteristic candour following Chesterton's conversion was Hilaire Belloc. Writing on 1 August, only two days after Gilbert's reception, his letter discussed the more personal aspects of faith far less reticently than was usual:

The thing I have to say is this (I could not have said it before your step: I can say so now. Before it would have been like a selected pleading). The Catholic Church is the exponent of *Reality*. It is true. Its doctrines in matters large and small are statements of what is. This it is which the ultimate act of the intelligence accepts. This it is which the will deliberately confirms. And that is why Faith through an act of the Will is Moral. If the Ordnance Map tells us that it is 11 miles to Wookey Hole then, my mood of lassitude as I walk through the rain at night making it *feel* like 30, I use the Will and say 'No. My intelligence has been convinced and I compel myself to use it against my mood. It is *11* and though I feel in the depths of my being to have gone 20 miles and more, I *know* it is not yet 11 I have gone.'
I am by all my nature of mind sceptical, by all my nature of body exceedingly sensual. So sensual that the virtues restrictive of sense are but phrases to me. But I accept these phrases as true and act upon them as well as a struggling man can. And as to the doubt of the soul I discover it to be false: a mood: not a conclusion. My conclusion – and that of all men who have ever once *seen* it – is the faith. Corporate, organised, a personality, teaching. A thing, not a theory. It.
To you, who have the blessing of profound religious emotion, this statement may seem too desiccate. It is indeed not enthusiastic. It lacks meat. It is my misfortune. In youth I had it: even till lately. Grief has drawn the juices from it. I am alone and unfed. The more

do I affirm the Sanctity, the Unity, the Infallibility of the Catholic Church. By my very isolation do I the more affirm it as a man in a desert knows that water is right for a man: or a wounded dog not able to walk yet knows the way home . . .

But beyond this there will come in time, if I save my soul, the flesh of these bones – which bones alone I can describe and teach. I know – without feeling (an odd thing in such a connection) the reality of Beatitude: which is the goal of Catholic Living.

> In hac urbe lux solennis
> Ver aeternum pax perennis
> Et aeterna gaudia.[25]

Ironically, Belloc had always believed that Chesterton would never actually become a Catholic. In a letter to Baring he expressed his belief that, although their mutual friend possessed the Catholic *mood*, he would never possess the *will* to convert:

People said that he might come in at any time because he showed such a Catholic point of view and so much affection for the Catholic Church. That always seemed to me quite the wrong end of the stick. Acceptation of the Faith is an act, not a mood. Faith is an act of will and as it seemed to me the whole of his mind was occupied in expressing his liking for and attraction towards a certain mood, not at all towards the acceptation of a certain Institution as defined and representing full reality in this world. There is all the difference between enjoying military ideas . . . and becoming a private soldier in a common regiment.[26]

In fact, Belloc was so convinced of his own viewpoint that he endeavoured, in the week prior to Gilbert's conversion, to persuade Father O'Connor of the futility of any efforts to sway him. Once proved wrong, he was almost dumbstruck. On 12 August he wrote to Father O'Connor, 'it is very great news indeed . . . I am overwhelmed by it.' On 23 August he again wrote to Father O'Connor:

I still remain under the *coup* of Gilbert's conversion. I had never thought it possible!

The Catholic Church is central, and therefore approached at every conceivable angle! I have written to him and shall write again – but I am a poor hand at such things.[27]

Chesterton as a child.

Gilbert, aged six or seven, poses for a studio photograph.

Gilbert, aged seven, with Cecil.

This drawing, made when he was only seven years old, reveals both a developing artistic talent and an uncanny awareness of the religious issues which would dominate his later life.

The Junior Debating Club, 1891. From left to right: Lucian Oldershaw,
E. W. Fordham, Lawrence Solomon, G. K. Chesterton, Digby D'Avigdor,
B. N. Langdon-Davies and Waldo D'Avigdor.

Two motions, handwritten by Chesterton and debated by the
Junior Debating Club in 1892.

Sir David Wilkie a painter of distinguished merit, born at Cupar in Fifeshire 1785; died 1841. He attracted notice by the excellence of his earliest efforts, and in 1804 brought out his "Blind Fiddler", "Rent Day"; Chelcy Penchoners

By By By By By By By
Fiddler Fiddler Fiddler Fiddler
Chelsea Chelsea Chelsea Chelsea
Pensioners Pensioners Pensioners

A page from Gilbert's schoolbook. Note the eight-year-old Chesterton's singular spelling of 'Chelsea Pensioners'.

At the seaside with his mother and brother, *c.* 1885.

Frances Chesterton at around the time of her marriage.

Frances with Winkle, the family pet, *c.* 1910.

Frances and Gilbert in the garden of Overroads, *c.* 1910, with the wife
and daughters of the novelist Archibald Marshall.

A family photograph taken in the gardens of Overroads on 6 May 1911.
Chesterton's parents are in the centre, and Cecil,
Frances and Gilbert are on the right.

Chesterton receiving an honorary doctorate from
Notre Dame University, Indiana.

Shaw, Belloc and Chesterton before the
highly publicised debate at Kingsway Hall in 1927.

Gilbert and Frances with a young friend, Spain, 1935.

Ending with a bang? Gilbert and Frances at a children's party at the
Decca Studios in Chelsea, January 1936.

Two days later, still scarcely able to believe the evidence of his own eyes, Belloc wrote to Father O'Connor yet again: 'The more I think on Gilbert the more astonished I become!' On 9 September he reported to Father O'Connor that he had seen Gilbert at Top Meadow and had stopped the night: 'He is very happy. In the matter of explanation you are right. But I have no vision.'[28]

Years later Belloc wrote that 'he advanced towards the Faith over many years and was ultimately in full communion with it' . . . 'He approached the Catholic Church gradually but by a direct road. He first saw the city from afar off, then approached it with interest and at last entered. Few of the great conversions in our history have been so deliberate or so mature. It will be for posterity to judge the magnitude of the event. We are too near it to see it in scale.'[29]

Another of Gilbert's friends who wrote to Father O'Connor following the conversion was Father Vincent McNabb:

> How good of you to make me so soon a partner in the good news of Gilbert's home-coming. He has sat on the door-step too long for the patience of his friends who love him; if not for God who loves him more than his friends. As Mrs Chesterton has not, for the moment, found herself able to go where he has gone his will must have been fast set on the Will of God! There was a time when his wife seemed so undeniably sent of God that he had no will to go elsewhere than where she went. If now he has loved God more than 'father and mother and wife' I feel sure that this love of God must be a sword piercing him to the very division of the soul and spirit.
>
> We must pray that the pain he is suffering on her account will be to her profit. Ever since I spoke with her and heard from others some of the sad stories of a convert kinsman of hers I have felt that her difficulties were psychological rather than logical; and that nothing would be so strong to help her as prayer to God.[30]

There is an element of imbalance and injustice in Father McNabb's assertion that Gilbert was suffering on account of Frances's failure to follow him into the Catholic fold. In fact, however much Gilbert may have been suffering, it would be true to say that Frances was suffering more. He at least had the comfort and consolation of his new-found faith, whereas she had been left behind and alone by his conversion. None the less, it is interesting to note Father McNabb's observation that Frances was still haunted by the death of her brother Knollys sixteen years earlier. Knollys, the 'convert kinsman' referred to in

273

the letter, had suffered from deep and prolonged depression and had committed suicide shortly after being received into the Catholic faith in 1906.

Father McNabb's letter to Father O'Connor was dated 2 August. On the same day he wrote to Chesterton:

> I have just been to Our Blessed Lord in the chapel to say the Te Deum and to *sing* the Veni Sancte Spiritus for you, so often my brother-in-arms and now my brother.
>
> Fr. O'Connor's postcard telling me the news came this morning. I open my arms and heart to welcome you.
>
> I want to give you the welcome of Truth. Again and again as I have studied the works of St Thomas – that Pontiff of Truth – I have thought of you as his brother; and I have prayed to him that one day you who have served truth so long and well out on the ramparts might be summoned into Truth's council-chamber or by its hearth. Thank God, you are standing, a little dazed no doubt, at the hearth-stone and we, the household are weeping tears of welcome to our brother!
>
> I want to give you the welcome of charity. We who have heard your war-cries and the noise of your untiring sword-work in defence of the sacred little-things of God, have loved you more than we dared say even to ourselves. We loved you to the foolish point of impatience at what we thought your slowness to wake up to the morning light. And now our love has put on the quality of gratitude – it is not merely a holocaust of all we have but a thank-offering for all we owe to you.[31]

The news of Chesterton's conversion soon became known to the Catholic press, and the *Tablet*, after checking the authenticity of the story by telegram, published the news in a spirit of jubilation. Letters of congratulation flooded in from every corner of the English-speaking world, and it says something for Chesterton's selflessness that he spent a lot of time replying to as many as possible. Thus, for instance, he replied, and even apologised for the delay in replying, to an Irishman who sent him a missal:

> I do not know how to thank you for your most beautiful and generous present; or how to apologise for having delayed this inadequate attempt so long. I can honestly say however that it was largely through a faint and futile hope of finding time to make it a little more adequate. I had to acknowledge a great pile of congratulations, only less great

than the reason of the congratulations, and if I dealt with others first, it was partly because they were easier to deal with.[32]

To a non-Catholic, who responded to his reception into the Church by writing to him on the purpose of ritual, the use of reason and the ideas of Wells, Chesterton replied with typical lucidity:

> Please forgive the extreme haste of this line on the large matters you mention. I ought to say first that, saving the grace of God, my own conversion to Catholicism was entirely rational; and certainly not at all ritualistic. I was received in a tin shed at the back of a railway hotel. I accepted it because it *did* afford conviction to my analytical mind. But people can see the ritual and are seldom allowed to hear of the philosophy.
>
> About ritual itself I think the truest thing was said by Yeats the poet, certainly not a Catholic or even a Christian; that ceremony goes with innocence. Children are not ashamed of dressing-up, nor great poets at great periods, as when Petrarch wore the laurel. Our world does feel something of what Wells says, because our world is as nervous and irritable as Wells himself. But I think the children and the poets are more permanent.[33]

The recipient of this reply was obviously convinced by Chesterton's arguments because, three years later, he followed him into the Church. Others, however, were considerably less enthusiastic about the decisive step Chesterton had taken. Wells, for instance, was not amused: 'I love G. K. C. and hate the Catholicism of Belloc and Rome . . . If Catholicism is still to run about the world giving tongue, it can have no better spokesman than G. K. C. But I begrudge Catholicism G. K. C.!'[34] Another friend who begrudged Catholicism G. K. C. was Bernard Shaw. In fact, Shaw was so dismayed at Chesterton's step that the bitterness it provoked in him threatened to sully their friendship. On first hearing the news he was stung sufficiently to ask sardonically whether Chesterton had been drunk. 'My dear G. K. C.,' he wrote, 'This is going too far.'[35]

Whether Chesterton's conversion was going too far, few except Shaw were surprised by it. On the contrary, the surprising aspect of the whole affair in the eyes of most people was the seemingly endless delay in its coming to pass. Father O'Connor, in spite of the patience he exhibited when dealing with Gilbert directly, had felt frustrated that his friend had loitered outside the Church for years without entering. He began to despair of his ever taking the final step and confided to Josephine Ward that 'he will need Frances to take him to church, to find his place in the prayer-book, to examine his conscience for him when he goes to Confession. He will never take all those hurdles unaided.'[36]

If Father O'Connor had been correct in his assumption, it is probable that Chesterton would never have entered the Church at all. Certainly Frances was a long way from the desire to convert, confessing to Kathleen Chesshire, her husband's secretary, that 'there are three things I shall never do: cut off my hair, engage an efficient secretary, or become a Roman Catholic'.[37]

Regardless of whether Father McNabb was correct in stating that Frances's difficulties were psychological rather than logical, it was undeniably true that Gilbert's difficulties were not metaphysical but physical. He had been convinced of the metaphysical truth of Catholicism for years, but becoming a Catholic required a physical act as well as a metaphysical conviction. He relied so heavily on others, and particularly Frances, for all the practical demands of life that he found all physical activity a real effort. Hence his obesity; hence his reverence and respect for men of action like his brother and Belloc; and hence his complete and utter dependence on Frances to make his practical decisions for him. So his conversion, the only major practical step he took without his wife's assistance, has something of the quality of heroism. Indeed, he admitted as much when he wrote, 'there is in the last second of time or hairbreadth of space, before the iron leaps to the magnet, an abyss full of all the unfathomable forces of the universe. The space between doing and not doing such a thing is so tiny and so vast.'[38]

Indeed it was. From the Catholic standpoint he now professed, it was the difference between the word, of which he was a master, and the word made flesh, of which he was a servant. It was the difference between a man who preached and a man who practised what he preached. It was a spiritual and practical incarnation, the act upon which his whole life hinged. His life prior to conversion, seen in this light, was an old testament leading inexorably to its fulfilment within the Church. One hears insistently the refrain of an old love letter Gilbert wrote to Frances during their courtship: 'Here ends my previous existence. Take it: it led me to you.'[39]

« 18 »

Gratitude and Grief

Conversion is like stepping across the chimney piece out of a Looking-Glass world, where everything is an absurd caricature, into the real world God made; and then begins the delicious process of exploring it limitlessly.

EVELYN WAUGH[1]

'I KNOW THAT CATHOLICISM is too large for me,' wrote Chesterton of his conversion, 'and I have not yet explored its beautiful and terrible truths.'[2] The rest of his life would be devoted to the exploration of the truth he'd discovered and the enjoyment of the inner peace it bestowed. Indeed, he was so at home with his adopted faith that he would soon write, 'I cannot explain why I am a Catholic; because now that I am a Catholic I cannot imagine myself as anything else.'[3] However, whether it be called a contradiction or a Chestertonian paradox, he spent most of the rest of his life explaining what he couldn't explain.

In his *Autobiography* he wrote the following confession of faith or, more specifically, a confession of faith in the act of confession:

When people ask me ... 'Why did you join the Church of Rome?' the first essential answer, if it is partly an elliptical answer, is 'To get rid of my sins.' For there is no other religious system that does *really* profess to get rid of people's sins. It is confirmed by the logic, which to many seems startling, by which the Church deduces that sin confessed and adequately repented is actually abolished; and that the sinner does really begin again as if he had never sinned ... Thus the Sacrament of Penance gives a new life, and reconciles a man to all living, but it does not do it as the optimists and the hedonists and the heathen preachers of happiness do it. The gift is given at a price, and is conditioned by a confession. In other words, the name of the price is Truth, which may also be called Reality; but it is facing the reality about oneself. When the process is only applied to other people, it is called Realism.[4]

These words were written fourteen years after his conversion, but the extent to which his views had remained substantially unchanged can be gauged by a comment he made in the *Daily News* fourteen years before his conversion: 'According to [a contemporary critic], it is morbid to confess your sins. I should say the morbid thing is not to confess them. The morbid thing is to conceal your sins and let them eat your heart out, which is the happy state of most people in highly civilised communities.'[5]

This view was bolstered by an unlikely source when the eminent psychiatrist, Carl Gustav Jung, commented on the way that Catholics were conspicuous by their absence from the psychiatrist's couch: 'During the past thirty years, people from all the civilised countries of the earth have consulted me. I have treated many hundreds of patients, the larger number being Protestants, a smaller number Jews, and not more than five or six believing Catholics.'[6]

In the months and years following his conversion Chesterton was asked to explain his decision on many occasions. Needless to say, he seldom, if ever, found that he was bereft of an explanation. To the French paper *La Vie Catholique* he recounted the rationale behind the move to Rome:

Before arriving at Catholicism I passed through different stages and was a long time struggling. The various stages are hard to explain in detail. After much study and reflection, I came to the conclusion that the ills from which England is suffering: Capitalism, crude Imperialism, Industrialism, Wrongful Rich, Wreckage of the Family, are the result of England not being Catholic. The Anglo-Catholic position takes for granted that England remained Catholic in spite of the Reformation or even because of it. After my conclusions, it seemed unreasonable to affirm that England is Catholic. So I had to turn to the sole Catholicism, the Roman. Before my conversion I had a lot of Catholic ideas, and my point of view in fact had but little altered.

Catholicism gives us a doctrine, puts logic into our life. It is not merely a Church Authority, it is a base which steadies the judgment ... To be a Catholic is to be all at rest! To own an irrefragable metaphysic on which to base all one's judgments, to be the touchstone of our ideas and our life, to which one can bring everything home.[7]

To the *Toronto Daily Star*, his exposition was even more forthright:

The change I have made is from being an Anglo-Catholic to being a Roman Catholic. I have always believed, at least for twenty years, in the Catholic view of Christianity. Unless the Church of England was a branch of the Catholic Church I had no use for it. If it were a Protestant Church I did not believe in it in any case. The question always was whether the Church of England can claim to be in direct descent from the mediaeval Catholic Church. That is the question with every Anglo-Catholic or Higher Churchman . . .

It appears to me quite clear that any church claiming to be authoritative, must be able to answer quite definitely when great questions of public morals are put. Can I go in for cannibalism, or murder babies to reduce the population, or any similar scientific and progressive reform? Any Church with authority to teach must be able to say whether it can be done.

But the point is that the Church of England does not speak strongly. It has no united action. I have no use for a Church which is not a Church militant, which cannot order battle and fall in line and march in the same direction.[8]

This theme was reiterated in an article Chesterton wrote for the *New Witness* in reply to a newspaper suggestion that the Church ought to 'move with the times':

The Church cannot move with the times; simply because the times are not moving. The Church can only stick in the mud with the times, and rot and stink with the times. In the economic and social world, as such, there is no activity except that sort of automatic activity that is called decay; the withering of the high flowers of freedom and their decomposition into the aboriginal soil of slavery. In that way the world stands much at the same stage as it did at the beginning of the Dark Ages . . .

We do not want, as the newspapers say, a Church that will move with the world. We want a Church that will move the world. We want one that will move it away from many of the things towards which it is now moving; for instance, the Servile State. It is by that test that history will really judge, of any Church, whether it is the real Church or no.[9]

There is no doubt that Chesterton considered the Church of England as having failed the test categorically. Indeed, in the article in the *Toronto Daily Star* he had expressed a debt of gratitude to the liberals within the Anglican hierarchy, such as the Dean of St Paul's, W. R. Inge, and the Bishop of Durham, H. Hensley Henson, for making it clear to him by their theological vagueness that Anglicanism was not a part of the Catholic Church. Another prominent Anglican who had incurred his ire was E. W. Barnes, who was to become Bishop of Birmingham in 1924. Barnes was typical of the Anglican Modernists who were satirised by Father Ronald Knox for the manner in which they

> . . . tempering pious zeal
> Corrected 'I believe' to 'One does feel'.[10]

Barnes had attacked the Catholic doctrine of the Eucharistic Presence as a recrudescence of fetish worship little better than the devotion of a 'cultured Hindu idolater'.[11] Chesterton responded by comparing Barnes, in his repugnance of the Blessed Sacrament, to the Manichaeans. Neither was Chesterton alone in his disapproval, since Barnes's insistence on the absolute profanity of the Eucharistic elements of Christianity went far further than the accepted Anglican concepts of receptionism (a presence in the receiving of the sacrament) and virtualism (a presence of the power, *virtus*, of Christ). There was talk of Barnes's enforced resignation and Hensley Henson was speaking only partly in jest when at a crowded Lambeth gathering, with no chair free for the newly arrived Barnes, he hailed him with the words: 'Ah, my Lord of Birmingham, come in: sit on the fire; and anticipate the judgment of the Universal Church.'[12] (Henson's own consecration as Bishop of Durham, it should be noted, had been delayed by a controversy over his apparent rejection of the Virgin Birth and of the Gospel miracles.)

This, then, was the backdrop to Chesterton's conversion. It is scarcely surprising, therefore, that Father Woodlock, the Jesuit who preached at a Mass of Reparation for Barnes's attack on the Real Presence, claimed that Chesterton's reception into the Catholic Church was a direct result of his disgust at the 'unchecked Modernism and heretical teaching' of Henson and Inge. Father Woodlock repeated the same claim in his book *Modernism and the Christian Church*: 'His logical mind drew its conclusions about the alleged Catholicity of Anglicanism from its complacent toleration of heresy in its dignitaries and official teachers.'[13]

Meanwhile in September 1922, eight weeks after his reception into the Church, Chesterton received the Sacrament of Confirmation. An invaluable handwritten account of the events leading up to the Confirmation ceremony is recorded in the Beaconsfield parish records:

September 23. His Lordship . . . arrived on the 5.24 pm train to make his Visitation of the Mission & administer the Sacrament of Confirmation. He heard Confessions in the evening.

September 24. His Lordship said the 8 o/c Mass assisted by the Rev Father Walker, the P.P. of the Mission. About 70 parishioners received Holy Communion . . .

At 6.30 His Lordship held the Confirmation Service. He preached a delightful & helpful sermon. Thirty-nine persons were presented for Confirmation, amongst whom was G. K. Chesterton, the famous journalist, who was received into the Church by Father John O'Connor at the Railway Hotel, Beaconsfield, on the 30th of July this year. He also made his First Communion on this day at Beaconsfield. His Lordship concluded the day's services with Pontifical Benediction of the Most Blessed Sacrament. A reception was afterwards held in the Sacristy. His Lordship made the personal acquaintance of G. K. Chesterton Esq. on this occasion in the Presbytery.[14]

A portentous postscript to the ceremony was provided by Chesterton's choice of Francis as his confirmation name. Although the most obvious motive for the choice was a desire to show love and respect for his wife, there was also another significant reason. St Francis of Assisi had always been a favourite of Chesterton, and at the time of his confirmation he was planning a biography of the saint.

In the interim, however, other books were published. During the previous February, while the author was in the throes of dilemma over his religious future, Cassell had published *Eugenics and Other Evils*. This was a controversial volume in which Chesterton had bemoaned the fact that 'Materialism is really our established Church.' In particular, he singled out 'the great but disputed system of thought which began with Evolution and has ended in Eugenics'.[15]

The science of eugenics had been formulated originally by Francis

Galton, Darwin's cousin, who had propagated the theory that human society would be improved and human progress promoted by a policy of selective breeding – that is, by encouraging persons of superior abilities to have more children while encouraging the less able to have fewer. By the time of his death in 1911 Galton had acquired a great deal of personal prestige and could claim many influential disciples. One such disciple was H. G. Wells, who had written in 1903: 'The conclusion that if we could prevent or discourage the inferior sort of people from having children, and if we could stimulate and encourage the superior sorts to increase and multiply, we should raise the general standard of the race, is so simple, so obvious, that in every age I suppose there have been voices asking in amazement why the thing is not done.'[16]

Meanwhile, Major Leonard Darwin, Charles Darwin's son and president of the Eugenics Society, had stated in *The Need for Eugenic Reform* that there were three possible means of eliminating the less fit. These were the gas chamber, sterilisation or life-long compulsory segregation. Although he rejected the first method on moral grounds, he welcomed the two other methods as desirable. There would, however, be practical difficulties caused by the huge numbers designated as unfit by Major Darwin: 'The number of those who could be eliminated with advantage is so large that it affords no basis on which any practical scheme could be built.'[17] His own suggestion was that financial help should be given to those living on public assistance on the strict condition that the recipients produce no more children. Those failing to comply would be segregated in public institutions and released only at the price of sterilisation.

Chesterton became embroiled in the eugenics debate when he denounced the Mental Deficiency Act of 1913, which had been hailed by the *Eugenics Review* as 'the only piece of English social law extant, in which the influence of heredity has been treated as a practical factor in determining its provisions'.[18] Under the provisions of this Act various categories of 'degenerates' could be placed in institutions on the strength of two medical certificates and a magistrate's order. Grounds for certification were extremely vague, so that adults could be certified if they required 'care, supervision and control for their own protection or the protection of others' and children if they appeared 'incapable of receiving proper benefit from the instruction in ordinary schools' or if they were 'morally defective', that is to say, having 'strong vicious or criminal propensities'.[19]

It is noteworthy, in the light of Chesterton's opposition to the Modernist theologians in the Church of England, that several of them were leading advocates of the Mental Deficiency Act. Indeed, the committee to further the Mental Deficiency Bill of 1913 was headed by the archbishops of Canterbury and York and included a substantial proportion of the bench of bishops. There were Anglican clerics in abundance ready to endorse eugenics in the name of Christianity, including two of Chesterton's most vocal enemies, namely Dean Inge and Bishop Barnes of Birmingham. The latter's Galton Lecture to the Eugenics Society was particularly outspoken:

> Christianity seeks to create the Kingdom of God, the community of the elect. It tries to make what we may call a spiritually eugenic society . . .
> When religious people realise that, in . . . preventing the survival of the socially unfit, they are working in accordance with the plan by which God has brought humanity so far on its road, their objections to repressive action will vanish.[20]

Such views were condemned unequivocally by the Catholic Church, and it is perhaps appropriate that Chesterton's last book before he left the communion to which Barnes belonged for the communion of Rome should be a scathing attack on Eugenics:

> What is novel and what is vital is this: that the *defence* of this crazy Coercion Act is a Eugenic defence. It is not only openly said, it is eagerly urged, that the aim of the measure is to prevent any person whom these propagandists do not happen to think intelligent from having any wife or children. Every tramp who is sulky, every labourer who is shy, every rustic who is eccentric, can quite easily be brought under such conditions as were designed for homicidal maniacs. That is the situation; and that is the point.[21]

The publication of *Eugenics and Other Evils* resulted in one of the rare occasions when Chesterton and Shaw actually agreed publicly. Shaw, reviewing the book in the *Nation*, found much that was praiseworthy:

> It is a graver, harder book than its forerunners . . . but there is plenty of compensating gain; for this book is practically all to the good . . . The use of the word Eugenics implies that the breeding

of the human race is an art founded on an ascertained science. Now when men claim scientific authority for their ignorance, and police support for their aggressive presumption, it is time for Mr Chesterton and all other men of sense to withstand them sturdily. Mr Chesterton takes the word as a convenient symbol for current attempts at legislative bodysnatching – live bodysnatching – to provide subjects for professors and faddists to experiment on when pursuing all sorts of questionable, ridiculous, and even vicious theories of how to produce perfect babies and rear them into perfect adults.[22]

Although six months elapsed after the appearance of *Eugenics and Other Evils* before there was any new offering from Chesterton's pen, three new books were published in quick succession between September and November 1922. The first of these was *What I Saw in America*, a collection of essays recording the author's impressions of the United States during his lecture tour of the previous year. The second, published in October by Cecil Palmer, was a new collection of poetry entitled *The Ballad of St Barbara and Other Verses*. Although the title poem was not so successful as previous ballads such as 'Lepanto', it did embody the two central threads or themes which characterised the whole collection. These were the contrasting, though not contradictory, emotions of gratitude and grief. Chesterton had felt both in large measure throughout the preceding years, the period during which the poems were being written, and the whole collection abounds with the alternating presence of pain and joy. Hence 'The Ballad of St Barbara' is a bitter-sweet poem of life in the trenches interwoven with the story of St Barbara, the patron saint of those in danger of sudden death. Hence also the bitterness of his 'Elegy in a Country Churchyard', written so soon after Cecil's death in a military hospital, with its complaint that 'they that rule in England . . . have no graves as yet', is followed by the gratitude of 'The Sword of Surprise':

> Give me miraculous eyes to see my eyes,
> Those rolling mirrors made alive in me,
> Terrible crystal more incredible
> Than all the things they see.

The same sentiments are expressed in 'The Mystery':

> Witness, O sun that blinds our eyes,
> Unthinkable and unthankable King,

> That though all other wonder dies
> I wonder at not wondering.

These were poems on an old theme; the synthesis of innocence and wisdom which Chesterton made the foundation of his whole philosophy. Indeed, the mood of humility in the presence of wonder was captured in a poem, appropriately titled 'A Second Childhood':

> Behold, the crowning mercies melt,
> The first surprises stay;
> And in my dross is dropped a gift
> For which I dare not pray:
> That a man grow used to grief and joy
> But not to night and day.

Many years earlier, Chesterton had written that 'the secret of life lies in laughter and humility'[23] and the new selection of poetry contained a great deal of both. In 'The Convert', another poem collected in the book, he had written, 'my name is Lazarus and I live', yet Lazarus, raised to life, still sought to raise a laugh. Thus, for instance, a report in the press that a chief constable had 'issued a statement declaring that carol singing in the streets by children is illegal, and morally and physically injurious' brought from Chesterton a humorous response:

> God rest you merry gentlemen,
> Let nothing you dismay:
> The Herald Angels cannot sing,
> The cops arrest them on the wing,
> And warn them of the docketing
> Of anything they say.

> God rest you merry gentlemen,
> May nothing you dismay:
> On your reposeful cities lie
> Deep silence, broken only by
> The motor horn's melodious cry,
> The hooter's happy bray.

> So, when the song of children ceased
> And Herod was obeyed,

In his high hall Corinthian
With purple and with peacock fan,
Rested that merry gentleman;
And nothing him dismayed.

The spirit of fun continued in several 'Songs of Education', all of which showed the author at his wittiest and best. The first of these was a poetical postscript to his *Short History of England*, a sort of Shorter History of England in Verse':

The people lived on the land, the land,
They pottered about and prayed;
They built a Cathedral here and there
Or went on a small crusade:
Till the bones of Becket were bundled out
For the fun of a fat White Czar,
And we all became, in spoil and flame,
The intelligent lot we are.

Chorus
The intelligent lot, the intuitive lot,
The infallible lot we are.

O Warwick woods are green, are green,
But Warwick trees can fall:
And Birmingham grew so big, so big,
And Stratford stayed so small.
Till the hooter howled to the morning lark
That sang to the morning star;
And we all became, in freedom's name,
The fortunate chaps we are.

A month after the publication of *The Ballad of St Barbara and Other Verses* a collection of short stories was published as *The Man Who Knew Too Much*. The stories, which had appeared originally in *Cassell's Magazine* and the *Storyteller*, were linked through the character of Horne Fisher, a tall, aristocratic detective with contacts in the highest echelons of society, modelled allegedly on Maurice Baring.

Evidence that the character in the stories was based on Baring is circumstantial. Three years earlier, when Chesterton had sought

Baring's help to facilitate entry into Palestine, he had written: 'You are a man who knows everybody; do you know anybody on Allenby's staff; or know anybody who would know anybody who would know anything about it?'[24] On that occasion Baring had obtained the permission necessary from General Allenby himself. (On a previous occasion, as we have seen, he had pulled strings to enable Ada Chesterton to visit Cecil in France.) Further allusions by Chesterton to Baring's contacts were made in a letter dated 14 February 1923, three months after *The Man Who Knew Too Much* was published: '. . . we are men who have talked to a good many men about a good many things, and seen something of the world and the philosophies of the world and that we have not the shadow of a doubt about what was the wisest act of our lives'.[25] However, the best evidence that Baring was the model for *The Man Who Knew Too Much* comes from the opening pages of the book itself when the character of Horne Fisher is introduced. The physical similarities between the fictional Fisher and the factual Baring are striking: 'He was a tall, fair man, cadaverous and a little lackadaisical, with heavy eyelids and a high-bridge nose. When his face was shaded with his wide white hat, his light moustache and lithe figure gave him a look of youth. But the panama lay on the moss beside him, and the spectator could see that his brow was prematurely bald . . .'[26]

Regardless of whether Chesterton had described his friend accurately in a literal sense, however, in a literary sense he had failed to do him justice. *The Man Who Knew Too Much* was one of the least memorable of Chesterton's books, and perhaps the author knew as much because he killed off the hero at the end of it.

With three new books published in as many months, for Gilbert 1922 had ended with a flourish. Yet 1923, in stark contrast, didn't so much start as stall. The first months of the year were dominated by continuing worries about the future of the *New Witness*. On 12 January Chesterton had alerted his readers to the possibility of 'a new *New Witness*'. Admitting that the fortunes of the paper had gone into decline, he lamented that it had been 'crippled by the death of the only man who could really do it'. Following his brother's death the *New Witness* had 'lost the one great controversialist against corruption who was materially, mentally and morally on the spot'. Compared to Cecil, Gilbert confessed to being 'an amateur'. But all was not lost, and Chesterton appealed for money to resurrect the paper as a 'sixpenny weekly':

I do think it possible that men with a little money to spare might club together in support of such potential success, when they would not do it for our present avowed failure. I mean that they might subscribe enough to put the paper on the ordinary basis of paying people reasonably to write and direct it, with some hope that they would not lose and might well gain. The very atmosphere of the new adventure would be quite different from the inevitable and trailing tragedy of the old one.[27]

It soon became apparent that most people believed that a new guise for the *New Witness* also required a new name. Chesterton discovered to his dismay that the desired name for the new venture was *G. K. C.'s Weekly*. He was horrified at the prospect: 'If I may be allowed to relieve my feelings by saying that I execrate, abominate and anathematise the new name, that I renounce and abjure it, that I blast it with lightning and curse it with bell, book and candle . . .'[28] None the less he was persuaded, albeit reluctantly, that his international literary reputation made his own name the paper's biggest asset and selling point. He was forced to admit that 'it is certainly the best name we can take', but he made it abundantly clear that he disliked the new name intensely:

> In this day and hour I haul down my flag, I surrender my sword, I give up a fight I have maintained against odds for very long. No; I do not mean the fight to maintain the *New Witness*, though that was a fight against impossible odds and has gone on for years. I mean a more horrid but hidden conflict, of which the world knew nothing; the savage but secret war I have waged against a proposal to call a paper by the name of *G. K. C.'s Weekly* [later, *G. K.'s Weekly*]. When the title was first suggested my feeling was one of wild terror, which gradually softened into disgust.[29]

In spite of the editor's protestations, the advice of his friends proved correct. The readership of the *New Witness*, and admirers of Chesterton from around the world, rallied to the newly unfurled banner of *G. K.'s Weekly*. Subscriptions poured in, and the financial future of the new venture seemed secure. However, the ringing in of the new required the ringing out of the old, and the last issue of the *New Witness* appeared on 4 May. Wells, who wrote that the *New Witness* had been 'a decent wrong-headed old paper, full of good writing', was among those whose valedictory letters were published. Another was written by Belloc: 'It is twelve years since Mr Cecil Chesterton and I founded the paper as *The Eye-Witness* (a title which

Mr Gilbert Chesterton suggested), and during that astonishing long life – attack has never, I think, been so long sustained.'

It is scarcely surprising that the demise of the *New Witness* should elicit nostalgia from Belloc and those who had been closely involved with it. It was in this same spirit that Arthur Ransome remembered fondly the early days of the paper:

> This little paper was a pleasure to all of us and replaced the old *Week's Survey* in our affections. Tuesday was the meeting-day for its contributors, and on that day the pageboy of the Adelphi Hotel in John Street used to stand on the steps of the hotel scanning the hansom-cabs that turned into John Street from the Strand. He knew us all by sight and was nimble in darting down the steps and holding up the hansom with the cry, 'The Editor's in the cellar!' And there in a basement room we would hear them and find them, Belloc talking like his books (I used to listen for a reference to 'a bullet-headed French gunner'), G. K. Chesterton shaken by internal laughter, quivering like a gigantic jelly, and Cecil Chesterton, who could out-argue either of them, though he could not write so well, laughing until his eyes disappeared at things slid into the conversation by the much quieter Maurice Baring.[30]

As part of the discussions on the new name for the *New Witness*, Shaw had written to Chesterton voicing his own view that the resurrected journal should be called simply *Chesterton's*. Although the suggestion was ultimately rejected, Gilbert was at least interested enough in his friend's suggestion to request permission to publish it as part of the ongoing debate. Shaw replied on 16 February, 'of course you may publish any letter of mine that you care to, at your discretion'. However, amid the friendly phraseology of this particular letter, Shaw had inserted several scathing references to his friend's recent conversion:

> . . . the Roman Catholic Church, embarrassed by recruits of your type . . . will quietly put you on the unofficial index . . . Your ideal Church does not exist and never can exist within the official organisation . . . and I know that an officially Catholic Chesterton is an impossibility . . . I believe that you would not have become a professed official Catholic if you did not believe that you believe in transubstantiation; but I find it quite impossible to believe that you believe in transubstantiation . . .

You will have to go to Confession next Easter; and I find the spectacle
– the box, your portly kneeling figure, the poor devil inside wishing
you had become a Fireworshipper instead of coming there to shake
his soul with a sense of his ridiculousness and yours – all incredible,
monstrous, comic . . . Now, however, I am becoming personal (how
else can I be sincere?).[31]

However much this vitriolic venting of his spleen, so uncharacteristic of the usual tone of his correspondence, betrayed Shaw's violent
disapproval of Chesterton's recent conversion, it did nothing to dull
Gilbert's affection for him. On the contrary, in spite of the depth
of their differences the phrase Chesterton employed to sum up his
relationship with his brother was equally applicable to his relationship
with Shaw: they argued but they never quarrelled. The fact was that
Gilbert's sense of laughter and humility applied as much to the cut
and thrust of controversy as to any other area of life. His fencing
was always fooling and his jousting was always jesting. Neither did
he mind if playing the fool made him look foolish, or if his jesting
made him look like the court jester. If others saw, as Shaw had done,
'a sense of his ridiculousness . . . all incredible, monstrous, comic', he
was more likely to laugh it off as a compliment than treat it as an insult.
He was, in fact, consciously playing the part of God's juggler, playing
the fool for Christ. It was in this spirit that he was inspired to write
his biography of St Francis of Assisi, the archetypal *jongleur de Dieu*.

« 19 »

Jongleur de Dieu

To most people . . . there is a fascinating inconsistency in the position of St Francis. He expressed in loftier and bolder language than any earthly thinker the conception that laughter is as divine as tears. He called his monks the mountebanks of God. He never forgot to take pleasure in a bird as it flashed past him, or a drop of water as it fell from his finger: he was, perhaps, the happiest of the sons of men. Yet this man undoubtedly founded his whole polity on the negation of what we think the most imperious necessities; in his three vows of poverty, chastity, and obedience, he denied to himself and those he loved most, property, love, and liberty. Why was it that the most large-hearted and poetic spirits in that age found their most congenial atmosphere in these awful renunciations? Why did he who loved where all men were blind, seek to blind himself where all men loved? Why was he a monk and not a troubadour? These questions are far too large to be answered fully here, but in any life of Francis they ought at least to have been asked; we have a suspicion that if they were answered we should suddenly find that much of the enigma of this sullen time of ours was answered also.[1]

THESE WORDS, WRITTEN IN 1900 at the very outset of Chesterton's literary career, could have served as the introduction to his biography of St Francis published twenty-three years later. Indeed, the sentiments expressed in the former essay are indistinguishable from those expressed two decades afterwards, a striking indication of St Francis's lasting influence on Chesterton's spiritual formation.

The roots of this influence stretch back to the dawn of Gilbert's consciousness, to the days in the nursery when his parents first read him the story of St Francis. The memories of childhood endured so that he could write many years later that the figure of St Francis 'stands on a sort of bridge connecting my boyhood with my conversion to many other things'.[2]

Instances of the Franciscan influence can be found throughout his adolescence. One of his earliest poems, 'St Francis of Assisi', published in the *Debater* in November 1892 when he was only eighteen years old, revealed the romance of the saint acting as an antidote to the gloom and despondency of his teenage years. Two years later, when he was a student at the Slade School, he penned a short story entitled 'Jongleur de Dieu' in his private notebook.[3] In the same year, writing from a hotel in Milan to his old schoolfriend E. C. Bentley, he listed St Francis among those he most admired.[4] A few years later still, probably some time between 1895 and 1899, he wrote another poem in honour of St Francis. Also entitled 'Le Jongleur de Dieu', this poem was seemingly lost to posterity until it was discovered under articles of clothing in an old trunk at Top Meadow. It has never been published. The following stanza is fairly representative of the poem as a whole:

> O'er giant hills and valleys,
>   With shifting skies above,
> I carry for Earth and all men,
>   My heart's fantastic love,
> Over the road and pinewood,
>   Over the field and hill,
> Over the world and round it,
>   Crazily laughing still.[5]

Many years later Gilbert was deeply affected by the role of modern-day Franciscans in the Holy Land. After he and Frances had visited the Mount of Olives, during their trip to Jerusalem in 1919, he wrote:

At the foot of the hill is the garden kept by the Franciscans on the alleged site of Gethsemane . . .

Around this terrible spot the Franciscans have done something which will strike many good and thoughtful people as quite fantastically inadequate; and which strikes me as fantastically but precisely right. They have laid out the garden simply as a garden . . . They have made flower-beds in the shape of stars and moons, and coloured them with flowers like those in the backyard of a cottage. The combination of these bright patterns in the sunshine with the awful shadow in the centre is certainly an incongruity in the sense of a contrast. But it is a poetical contrast, like that of birds building in a temple or flowers growing on a tomb. The best way of suggesting what I for one feel about it would be something like this; suppose we imagine a company of children, such as those whom Christ blessed in Jerusalem, afterwards put permanently in charge of a field full of his sorrow; it is probable that, if they could do anything with it, they would do something like this. They might cut it up into quaint shapes and dot it with red daisies or yellow marigolds. I really do not know that there is anything better that grown up people could do, since anything that the greatest of them could do must be, must look, quite as small. 'Shall I, the gnat that dances in Thy ray, dare to be reverent?' The Franciscans have not dared to be reverent; they have only dared to be cheerful. It may be too awful an adventure of the imagination to imagine Christ in that garden. But there is not the smallest difficulty about imagining St Francis there; and that is something to say of an institution which is eight hundred years old.[6]

This admiration of St Francis, which Chesterton had carried with him throughout his life, was inextricably bound up with his belief in the superiority of childlike innocence over all forms of cynicism. It was a reiteration of his belief in the synthesis of laughter and humility, a belief that playing and praying go hand in hand.

In 'The Song of the Children', one of his earliest poems, he expressed the fact that Christ is accepted easily through the innocent eyes of children but that He is rejected and condemned through the cynical eyes of adults:

> The grown folk mighty and cunning,
>   They write his name in gold;
> But we can tell a little
>   Of the million tales he told.
>
> He taught them laws and watchwords,
>   To preach and struggle and pray;
> But he taught us deep in the hayfield
>   The games that the angels play.
>
> Had he stayed here for ever,
>   Their world would be wise as ours –

And the king be cutting capers,
And the priest be picking flowers.

But the dark day came: they gathered:
On their faces we could see
They had taken and slain our brother,
And hanged him on a tree.

It was with these ideas and images in mind that he began, in 1923, to write his biography of St Francis of Assisi.

A vivid and evocative description of the writing of the book was given by Kathleen Chesshire, Chesterton's secretary at the time. It was a sunny midsummer morning and, having been told that Gilbert would not require her services until about ten o'clock, Miss Chesshire had bicycled into the village to pay her bills. Returning to Top Meadow, she found Frances among her flowers. In the midst of the garden a statue of St Francis appeared to preach to the birds as they hopped around it. Meanwhile Gilbert, seemingly oblivious to all around him, paced the garden path, lost in thought. Noticing the return of his secretary, Gilbert settled down to the day's work:

> 'Now, I think, if you're ready,' said G. K. C. The Secretary followed him into what had once been a tomato shed, and they started work. The Life of St Francis was to appear that autumn, and this month they were pledged to finish it. They were also pledged to present themselves for rehearsals of the Dream at Hall Barn every evening of this wonderful June, necessitating the polishing off of St Francis early in the day.[7]

Although Chesterton's main priority throughout the summer was the writing of *St Francis*, its publication was preceded in September by *Fancies versus Fads*, another collection of essays culled from his journalism. Appearing originally in the *London Mercury*, the *New Witness* and the *Illustrated London News*, the essays contained the usual concoction of Chestertonian wit and wisdom:

> When you meet a millionaire, the cornerer of many markets, out at dinner in Mayfair, and greet him (as is your custom) with the exclamation 'Scoundrel!' you are merely shortening for convenience some such expression as: 'How can you, having the divine spirit of man that might be higher than the angels, drag it down so far as to be

a scoundrel?' When you are introduced at a garden party to a Cabinet Minister who takes tips on Government contracts, and, when you say to him in the ordinary way 'Scamp!' you are merely using the last word of a long moral disquisition; which is, in effect, 'How pathetic is the spiritual spectacle of this Cabinet Minister, who being from the first made glorious by the image of God, condescends so far to lesser ambitions as to allow them to turn him into a scamp.' It is a mere taking of the tail of a sentence to stand for the rest like saying 'bus for omnibus. It is even more like the case of that seventeenth century Puritan whose name was something like 'If-Jesus-Christ-Had-Not-Died-For-Thee-Thou-Hadst-Been-Damned Higgins;' but who was, for popular convenience, referred to as 'Damned Higgins'.[8]

One can imagine Chesterton chortling to himself as he wrote articles such as this, and the picture painted by Charles Masterman of his laughing at his own work comes to mind. Masterman told Frank Swinnerton of a time when Gilbert was scribbling an article in a Fleet Street café, 'sampling and mixing a terrible conjunction of drinks', while waiters hovered about him, partly in awe and partly in case he should leave without paying. Finally, the head waiter approached Masterman: 'Your friend,' he whispered admiringly, 'he very clever man. He sit and laugh. And then he write. And then he laugh at what he write.'[9] Neither was Chesterton embarrassed to be seen laughing at his own jokes. 'If a man may not laugh at his own jokes,' he once asked, 'at whose jokes may he laugh? May not an architect pray in his own cathedral?'[10] Another who described the memory of Chesterton's laughter was the writer and literary critic, Patrick Braybrooke: 'What a wonderful laugh Chesterton has. It is like a clap of thunder that suddenly startles the echoes in the valley; it is the very soul of geniality. There is nothing that so lays bare a man's character as his laugh . . .'[11]

Yet the laughter was not all levity. *Fancies versus Fads* contained much that was both confrontational and controversial. Thus Arnold Bennett's allegation that Chesterton's dogmatism illustrated a lack of intellect was met with the following response: 'In truth there are only two kinds of people, those who accept dogmas and know it and those who accept dogmas and don't know it. My only advantage over the gifted novelist lies in my belonging to the former class.'[12]

Although there was nothing particularly new in Chesterton's defence of dogma, his defence of the traditional devices of poetry (rhyme, metre and stanzaic form) was more daring. By 1923 the ideas of Ezra Pound and T. S. Eliot had revolutionised the writing of English poetry. Their modernist ideas called for a rejection of regular rhythms in favour of a free verse that, they claimed, was capable of subtler and more sophisticated results. Pound had urged poets to 'compose in sequence of the musical phrase, not in sequence of a metronome',[13] and Eliot had called for an obscurantist approach to poetry through an 'objective correlative'.[14] In *Fancies versus Fads* Chesterton leapt to the defence of traditional poetic forms:

> The whole history of the thing called rhyme can be found between those two things: the simple pleasure of rhyming 'diddle' to 'fiddle', and the more sophisticated pleasure of rhyming 'diddle' to 'idyll'. Now the fatal mistake about poetry, and more than half of the fatal mistake about humanity, consists in forgetting that we should have the first kind of pleasure as well as the second . . . we should have the first pleasure as the basis of the second.[15]

It is the old Chestertonian premise that all wisdom, be it philosophical wisdom or poetical wisdom, is based on innocence. Poetical sophistication must be based on, and must build on, this primeval innocence. If it fails to do so, it will be devoid of meaning or, as Chesterton puts it, 'when poets put away childish things they will put away poetry'.[16] Later, lest anyone should mistake his innocence for ignorance, he makes the same point with subtlety: 'Song is not only a recurrence, it is a return. That labouring caravan is always travelling towards some camping ground that it has lost and cannot find again. No lover of poetry needs to be told that all poems are full of that noise of returning wheels . . . It is in this deeper significance of return that we must seek for the peculiar power in the recurrence we call rhyme.'[17]

For all the controversy contained within its pages, *Fancies versus Fads* was eclipsed within a month of its publication by the appearance of Chesterton's *St Francis of Assisi*. From the very outset the author confessed his debt of gratitude to the saint:

> Many thousand things that I now partly comprehend I should have thought utterly incomprehensible, many things I now hold sacred I should have scouted as utterly superstitious, many things that seem to me lucid and enlightened now they are seen from the inside I should honestly have called dark and barbarous seen from the outside, when long ago in those days of boyhood my fancy first caught fire with the glory of Francis of Assisi.[18]

In the chapter entitled 'Le Jongleur de Dieu' Chesterton attempted to explain the psychology of the saint:

> Many signs and symbols might be used to give a hint of what really happened in the mind of the young poet of Assisi. Indeed they are at once too numerous for selection and yet too slight for satisfaction. But one of them may be adumbrated in this small and apparently accidental fact: that when he and his secular companions carried their pageant of poetry through the town, they called themselves Troubadours. But when he and his spiritual companions came out to do their spiritual work in the world, they were called the Jongleurs de Dieu . . .
>
> . . . St Francis was talking the true language of a troubadour when he said that he also had a most glorious and gracious lady and that her name was Poverty.
>
> But the particular point to be noted here is not concerned so much with the word Troubadour as with the word Jongleur. It is especially concerned with the transition from one to the other . . . A jongleur was not the same thing as a troubadour, even if the same man were both a troubadour and a jongleur. More often, I believe, they were separate men as well as separate trades. In many cases apparently the two men would walk the world together like companions in arms, or rather companions in arts. The jongleur was properly a joculator or jester; sometimes he was what we should call a juggler.[19]

However, to call St Francis and his followers the jokers or jugglers of God was only half the story. For Chesterton, and for Francis, all the laughter in the world was worthless unless accompanied by humility. The secret of the saint's success was this synthesis of humility and laughter:

> It was in a wholly happy and enthusiastic sense that St Francis said, 'Blessed is he who expecteth nothing, for he shall enjoy everything.' It was by this deliberate idea of starting from zero, from the dark nothingness of his own deserts, that he did come to enjoy even earthly things as few people have enjoyed them; and they are in themselves the best working example of the idea. For there is no way in which a man can earn a star or deserve a sunset.[20]

This is Chesterton at his best. The feeling of wide-eyed wonder ascribed to the Franciscans is instantly recognisable as the Chestertonian 'wonder at not wondering' with which his recent poems were imbued. In extracts such as this the Franciscan and the Chestertonian become blurred, almost merged, into an indistinguishable whole. It is difficult to tell when Chesterton is describing the Franciscan spirit and when he is defining the Chestertonian philosophy: '. . . we talk about a man who cannot see the wood for the trees. St Francis was a man who did not want to see the wood for the trees. He wanted to see each tree as a separate and almost a sacred thing, being a child of God and therefore a brother or sister of man.'[21]

Following its publication in October 1923, a reviewer in the *New York Times* observed that the book showed 'a more restrained and less paradoxical Chesterton'.[22] Although it was certainly true that the biography conveyed the author spiritually at rest, it was not true that Chesterton had forsaken paradox as a method of illuminating truth. For example, his readers were informed of the eccentric nature of St Francis's eccentricity: 'Even among the saints he has the air of a sort of eccentric, if one may use the word of one whose eccentricity consisted in always turning towards the centre.'[23]

Characteristically, Chesterton had been self-effacing when he had commenced writing the book, stating that 'though I am certain of failure I am not altogether overcome by fear; for he suffered fools gladly'.[24] However, if Chesterton was the fool, his readers suffered him very gladly indeed. The book was an instant success, receiving laudatory acclaim from critics and public alike. Patrick Braybrooke enthused about 'Mr Chesterton's astoundingly brilliant book about Saint Francis of Assisi . . . The Catholic Church has found in Mr Chesterton the greatest interpreter of her greatest saint.'[25] Elsewhere he wrote:

> In writing of Saint Francis, Mr Chesterton has written a beautiful book: it is a beautiful book about a beautiful Saint. There are many points of beauty in the Catholic Church, but one outstanding part of this beauty is the lives of the Saints. Saint Francis was one of the most picturesque, he is better known to non-Catholics than any other Saint. Mr Chesterton's book proves that the story of the life of a Saint can be a far greater romance than the most brilliant of novels.[26]

One suspects that Chesterton would have been mildly embarrassed at the over-zealous nature of such commendation, but Braybrooke touched upon the truth when he observed that the book 'succeeds admirably in doing what Mr Chesterton means it to do. That is, it is the type of book which will make the ordinary man and the ordinary woman interested in a Saint.'[27] Considering that *St Francis of Assisi* became one of Chesterton's best-loved and best-selling books, it is clear that he did succeed in this regard. Neither was Braybrooke alone in his praise. A Franciscan professor described the book as worth all others on the subject,[28] and the young C. S. Lewis recorded in his diary the impression the biography made on him, especially 'the chapter about naturalism and what it led to among the pagans, wh. I thought pretty true . . .'[29]

Perhaps the most unlikely accolade came from Alan Watts, guru of the San Francisco counter-culture of the 1960s and doyen of what became known as the New Age. At first glance Chesterton and Watts appear diametrical opposites. Watts, the populariser of Oriental mysticism, would appear to have little in common with Chesterton's crusading love for Christendom, yet, writing soon after Gilbert's death, Watts confessed a love for Chesterton based upon the latter's spiritual *joie de vivre*. In an article titled 'G. K. Chesterton: the Jongleur de Dieu', he wrote: 'Although I am anything but a Roman Catholic, the recent death of G. K. Chesterton felt almost like a personal loss. For with no writer of today did I find myself in deeper sympathy. It was not that I agreed with all his ideas, but rather that I felt myself in complete accord with his basic attitude to life.'[30] After stating that Chesterton's conversion to Catholicism 'was, perhaps, unfortunate', Watts went on to write that he would be

> the last to quarrel with anyone for his love of romance, because it indicates a certain childlike attitude to life which is the passport to the kingdom of heaven. It is, in fact, the sense of wonder, the sense which transforms every littlest thing in the universe into a divine mystery . . . The sense of wonder expresses itself in gratitude, and I know of no finer exposition of the mysticism of gratitude than the concluding pages of Chesterton's *Autobiography*.
>
> 'The aim of life,' he says, 'is appreciation; there is no sense in not appreciating things; and there is no sense in having more of them if you have less appreciation of them.'[31]

There is something beguiling about this unlikely bonding of Watts's Buddhism and Chesterton's Christianity, yet, according to Watts himself, it was the spirit of St Francis, battling against the sophistries of the world, which bound them together: 'Chesterton came as one of St Francis' "Jongleurs de Dieu" (God's Merry Men) and blew aside this pettiness with "a great, rollicking wind of elemental and essential laughter", with *joie de vivre* perhaps a little like the feeling which God had when He looked at His universe and "saw that it was good".'[32]

Although St Francis, in the persons of Chesterton and Watts, had reconciled the irreconcilable, Chesterton, in the writing of his biography of the saint, had failed to explain the inexplicable. In spite of his efforts, the Franciscan spirit remained as mysterious as ever. Gilbert's biography did not answer the questions it had set out to answer. He had written of his suspicion 'that if they were answered we should suddenly find that much of the enigma of this sullen time of ours was answered also'. The enigma remained because the enigma of St Francis remained. Chesterton chased the saint recklessly through the pages of his book, complaining that all explanations were 'too slight for satisfaction'. It was a heaven-sent game of hide-and-seek, similar to the plot of *The Man Who was Thursday*, with the Man who was Francis remaining as difficult to pin down as the Man who was Sunday. Yet, as with the plot of the novel, there was something thrilling in the chase.

Gilbert's friend and biographer, Maisie Ward, recounted the medieval story of a tumbler who converted and became a monk. Finding himself inept at the offices of choir and scriptorium, he went before a statue of the Blessed Virgin and there played all his tricks. Finally, quite exhausted, he looked up at the statue and said, 'Lady, this is a choice performance.' 'There is,' wrote Mrs Ward, 'more than a touch of Our Lady's tumbler in Gilbert.'[33]

There was certainly more than a touch of the tumbler in Gilbert's writing of *St Francis of Assisi*. Whatever the book's shortcomings as an explanation of the saint, it was most emphatically successful as a romance and a romp in the true Franciscan spirit. A choice performance. From start to finish Chesterton played cat and mouse with the Jongleur de Dieu. And, in keeping with the poetry of the saint, it didn't much matter if sister cat failed to catch brother mouse. What mattered was that Gilbert had paid his tribute to his childhood hero. Our Lady's Tumbler had performed for God's Juggler.

« 20 »

Wells and the Shallows

On 29 May 1924 Chesterton celebrated his fiftieth birthday. As was their custom, Gilbert and Frances commemorated the occasion in low-key fashion and the milestone failed to merit so much as a mention in his *Autobiography*. By contrast, the fiftieth birthday of his friend Maurice Baring, celebrated at the Royal Albion Hotel in Brighton only five weeks earlier on 27 April, was recounted with gusto in Chesterton's *Autobiography*, with Gilbert paying homage to the 'godlike joy of life that induced a gentleman to celebrate his fiftieth birthday in a Brighton hotel at midnight by dancing a Russian dance with inconceivable contortions and then plunging into the sea in evening dress'.[1] Although the evening ended in the riotous fashion described so graphically by Gilbert, it had started serenely enough as a dinner for fifty-two guests, including Chesterton, Belloc and E. V. Lucas. Baring made a rhyming speech, and more prosaic addresses were delivered by Chesterton, Lady Juliet Duff and Harry Preston, the owner of the hotel.[2]

It was around this time that Gilbert appeared with Wyndham Lewis in an anarchic play. Lewis remembered how he and the rest of the cast had been upstaged by Chesterton:

> It was a unique dramatic experiment on the pattern of the Commedia dell' Arte, devised and arranged by Mrs Cecil. It took place one winter night in 1923 or 1924, in a hall in or off Drury Lane. The play was called 'The Witch of Fleet Street', its basic idea being a satiric survey of the cheaper Press; and as in the Italian Comedy, the actors were given a rough outline of the probable plot and left to make up their own dialogue on the stage, as they went along.
>
> We got along rather lamely – the Witch being played, and how inadequately, by myself – until G. K. C. came on and lifted the whole thing at once into brilliant fantasy, as you might expect. It

301

fell to my unfortunate lot to engage him in dialogue for the first
five minutes, after which he took charge, thank God, and the rest
was a long and enchanting monologue. For some reason I forget, his
enormous figure was swathed in black muslin rags and tinsel, and he
was supposed to represent Famine, flying from Fortnum and Mason.
All I remember of his performance is an attack on the *Daily Mail* for
reducing him to a skeleton. The audience loved it all.[3]

One could be forgiven for believing that Chesterton's life, at the
ripe age of fifty, was nothing but an endless round of riotous parties and
impromptu play-acting. Certainly, apart from his regular journalistic
commitments, there was nothing to show in the way of published
work during the entire year. The following year was very different.
On 21 March 1925, after many delays and false starts, the first issue
of *G. K.'s Weekly* was finally published. A large part of the first issue,
which sold for sixpence, was written by Chesterton himself, but other
notable contributors were Belloc and Walter de la Mare.

The second issue contained a memorable short poem by Chesterton,
'On Professor Freud':

> The ignorant pronounce it Frood,
> To cavil or applaud.
> The well-informed pronounce it Froyd,
> But I pronounce it Fraud.

At the time, Sigmund Freud was being hailed as a prophet, almost
universally, and his psychoanalytical theories were treated with the
greatest respect. In calling the eminent founder of psychoanalysis a
false prophet Chesterton was kicking against the intellectual spirit
of the age. Today, with many of Freud's theories being revised or
rejected, Chesterton's poem has itself taken on something of the
nature of prophecy.

Although the circulation of *G. K.'s Weekly* was somewhat disappointing at around 5,000 copies per issue, the few who did invest their
sixpences were treated to some of Chesterton's finest journalism. In
the fourth issue, published on 11 April, he was moved to respond
to an attack on the Catholic Church by the Home Secretary:

The Home Secretary is reported as saying 'We want no priestly
interference, we ask for no purgatory, and we will submit to
no compulsory confessional.' The last clause of this declaration

is especially a great relief to our minds. No longer shall we see a policeman seizing a man in the street by the scruff of the neck and dragging him to the nearest confessional-box. No longer will our love of liberty be outraged by the sinister bulk of the Black Maria taking its daily gang of compulsory penitents to Westminster Cathedral . . . But the passage that interests me . . . is the singular phrase that comes before it . . . the very remarkable phrase 'We ask for no purgatory' . . . It seems to imply that when Sir William reaches the gates of another world, St Peter or some well-trained angel will say to him in a slightly lowered voice, in the manner of a well-trained butler, 'Would you be requiring a purgatory?'

. . . it never occurs to Sir William Joynson-Hicks that . . . Purgatory may exist whether he likes it or not. If it be true, however incredible it may seem, that the powers ruling the universe think that a politician or a lawyer can reach the point of death, without being in that perfect ecstasy of purity that can see God and live – why then there may be cosmic conditions corresponding to that paradox, and there is an end of it. It may be obvious to us that the politician is already utterly sinless, at one with the saints. It may be evident to us that the lawyer is already utterly selfless, filled only with God and forgetful of the very meaning of gain. But if the cosmic power holds that there are still some strange finishing touches, beyond our fancy, to put to his perfection, then certainly there will be some cosmic provision for that mysterious completion of the seemingly complete. The stars are not clean in His sight and His angels He chargeth with folly; and if He should decide that even in a Home Secretary there is room for improvement, we can but admit that omniscience can heal the defect that we cannot even see.

In June 1925 the first new Chesterton book for more than eighteen months was published. *Tales of the Long Bow* was a collection of magazine stories, each of which revolved around well-known English phrases such as 'I'll eat my hat', 'set the Thames on fire', and 'when pigs have wings'. During the course of the tales, set against the backdrop of an agrarian revolution, Chesterton contrived to make water burn and pigs fly. It was flippant and fantastic, yet even as this volume was published the author was working on a far more serious project.

The Everlasting Man, published on 30 September, grew out of the controversy that had raged between Belloc and H. G. Wells ever since the latter had published his *Outline of History*. It was no mere coincidence that Chesterton's *Everlasting Man* should be published in the same year that Wells's *Outline of History* was published for the first time in a single, complete volume. Previously, Wells's book had been published in separate sections, each of which had been attacked vehemently and vociferously by Belloc. In the first instance Belloc objected to the book's tacitly anti-Christian stance, according to which Christ warranted far less space than the Persians' campaign against the Greeks. Yet Belloc's principal objection was to the materialistic determinism which formed the foundation of Wells's *History*. As far as Wells was concerned human 'progress' was both blind and beneficial, unshakeable and unstoppable. He perceived history as the product of invisible and immutable evolutionary forces which were coming to fruition in the twentieth century. The history of man had begun in the caves and was reaching a climax in the modern age with the triumph of science over religion. This, in turn, heralded a new dawn, a brave new world where happiness would be ushered in by technology.

To Belloc the first editions of *The Outline of History*, published in 1920, had been like a red rag to a bull. Predictably, he charged. His first attacks were published in the *London Mercury* and the *Dublin Review*, where he lambasted Wells for being inaccurate and for writing 'howlers'. Thereafter he clinically dissected Wells's *History* in a long series of articles in the *Universe*. He began with 'Mr Wells and the Creation of the World (Man)' and continued with 'Mr Wells and the Fall of Man', 'Mr Wells and God', 'Mr Wells and the Incarnation', 'Mr Wells on Priesthood' and so on. In fact, the analogous reference to Belloc as a charging bull is not wholly accurate. He was not so much a bull as a bulldog who bit hard and refused to let go.

In Belloc's view, Wells's book was the product of a prejudiced provincialism. After complaining that 'his book is Provincial' and that 'a schoolboy ought to know better than to write this', he wrote that Wells had 'not kept abreast of the modern scientific and historical work . . . not followed the general thought of Europe and America in matters of physical science', and 'in history proper, he was never taught to appreciate the part played by Latin and Greek culture, and never even introduced to the history of the early Church'. After raining blow upon blow upon his opponent, Belloc finished his attack in merciless mood: 'With all this Mr Wells suffers from the very grievous fault of being ignorant that he is ignorant. He has the strange cocksureness of the man who only knows the old conventional textbook of his schooldays and mistakes it for universal knowledge.'[4]

The controversy reached a conclusion and a climax in 1926 when Belloc's articles for the *Universe* were collected into a single volume and published as *A Companion to Mr Wells's 'Outline of History'*. Wells responded with *Mr Belloc Objects* and Belloc, determined to have the last word, replied with *Mr Belloc Still Objects*. At the end of the six-year struggle, Belloc claimed to have written over 100,000 words in refutation of the central arguments of Wells's book.

Not surprisingly, the conflict between Belloc and Wells soured their relationship irreparably. The two erstwhile friends became bitter enemies, but Chesterton, typically, remained on friendly terms with both combatants. An insight into the relationship of Belloc and Chesterton to Wells, two years after the controversy commenced, was afforded when Wells stood for Parliament in 1922. The *Daily News* invited both Chesterton and Belloc to give their comments on Wells's candidature. The difference is striking; Chesterton's affability stands in stark contrast to Belloc's sardonic sarcasm:

> *G. K. Chesterton:* I wish Wells all possible luck, but I can't say that is exactly the same as wishing he will get into Parliament. The question is not whether Wells is fit for Parliament, but whether Parliament is fit for Wells. I don't think it is. If he has a good idea, the last place in the world where he would be allowed to talk is the House of Commons. He would do better to go on writing.

> *Hilaire Belloc:* Of the effect of election upon Mr Wells's style I am not competent to pronounce. But in morals, temperament, instruction, and type of oratory, I know him to be admirably suited for the House of Commons.[5]

It was amid this acrimony and controversy that Chesterton wrote *The Everlasting Man*. Intended as an answer to Wells but wholly different in tone from Belloc's bellicosity, it was Gilbert's own attempt at an 'outline of history': 'I have . . . divided this book into two parts: the former being a sketch of the main adventure of the human race in so far as it remained heathen; and the second a summary of the real difference that was made by it becoming Christian.'[6]

The opening chapter of the book began with a discussion of evolution:

> Most modern histories of mankind begin with the word evolution, and with a rather wordy exposition of evolution . . . There is something

slow and soothing and gradual about the word and even about the idea. As a matter of fact, it is not, touching these primary things, a very practical word or a very profitable idea. Nobody can imagine how nothing could turn into something ... It is really far more logical to start by saying 'In the beginning God created heaven and earth' even if you only mean 'In the beginning some unthinkable power began some unthinkable process.'

... But this notion of something smooth and slow, like the ascent of a slope, is a great part of the illusion. It is an illogicality as well as an illusion; for slowness has really nothing to do with the question. An event is not any more intrinsically intelligible or unintelligible because of the pace at which it moves ... Yet there runs through all the rationalistic treatment of history this curious and confused idea that difficulty is avoided, or even mystery eliminated, by dwelling on mere delay or on something dilatory in the process of things.[7]

Following the laying of these foundations as a necessary prerequisite for any realistic study of mankind through the ages, Chesterton requested that his readers 'make with me a sort of experiment in simplicity. And by simplicity I do not mean stupidity, but rather the sort of clarity that sees things like life rather than words like evolution.'[8] He proceeded to parallel Wells's *History* by beginning with prehistoric man:

Today all our novels and newspapers will be found swarming with numberless allusions to a popular character called a Cave-Man. He seems to be quite familiar to us, not only as a public character but as a private character. His psychology is seriously taken into account in psychological fiction and psychological medicine. So far as I can understand, his chief occupation in life was knocking his wife about, or treating women in general with what is, I believe, known in the world of the film as 'rough stuff'. I have never happened to come upon the evidence for this idea; and I do not know on what primitive diaries or prehistoric divorce-reports it is founded.[9]

After mocking the prejudiced presumptions of those who had psychoanalysed a mythical prehistoric patient, Chesterton requested an unprejudiced, objective look at the physical evidence available:

In fact, people have been interested in everything about the cave-man except what he did in the cave. Now there does happen to be some real evidence of what he did in the cave. It is little enough, like all the prehistoric evidence, but it is concerned with the real cave-man and his cave and not the literary cave-man and his club. And it will be valuable to our sense of reality to consider quite simply what that real evidence is, and not to go beyond it. What was found in the cave was not the club, the horrible gory club notched with the number of women it had knocked on the head. The cave was not a Bluebeard's Chamber filled with the skeletons of slaughtered wives; it was not filled with female skulls all arranged in rows and all cracked like eggs . . . This secret chamber of rock, when illuminated after its long night of unnumbered ages, revealed on its large walls large and sprawling outlines diversified with coloured earths . . . They were drawings or paintings of animals; and they were drawn or painted not only by a man but by an artist. Under whatever archaic limitations, they showed that love of the long sweeping or the long wavering line which any man who has ever drawn or tried to draw will recognise; and about which no artist will allow himself to be contradicted by any scientist. They showed the experimental and adventurous spirit of the artist . . . as where the draughtsman had represented the action of the stag when he swings his head clean round and noses towards his tail, an action familiar enough in the horse. But there are many modern animal-painters who would set themselves something of a task in rendering it truly. In this and twenty other details it is clear that the artist had watched animals with a certain interest and presumably a certain pleasure.[10]

Thus, with the keen knife of clarity, Chesterton had cut clean through the mythology of the pseudo-scientists who had moulded the cave-man into the image of their own preconceptions. Instead, looking at nothing but the physical evidence available, he deduced that man's ancient ancestors were civilised enough to be artists, that they observed and loved nature and, the most shocking revelation of all, that they may even have loved their wives. Yet even the physical evidence was open to abuse if facts were turned into fiction:

Another distinguished writer, again, in commenting on the cave-drawing attributed to the neolithic men of the reindeer period, said that none of their pictures appeared to have any religious purpose; and he seemed almost to infer that they had no religion. I can hardly imagine a thinner thread of argument than this which reconstructs the very inmost moods of the prehistoric mind from the fact that somebody who has scrawled a few sketches on a rock, from what motive we do not know, for what purpose we do not know, acting under what customs or conventions we do not know, may possibly have found it easier to draw reindeers than to draw religion. He may have drawn it because it was his religious symbol. He may have drawn it because it was not his religious symbol. He may have drawn anything except his religious symbol. He may have drawn his real religious symbol somewhere else; or it may have been deliberately destroyed when it was drawn. He may have done or not done half-a-million things; but in any case it is an amazing leap of logic to infer that he had no religious symbol, or even to infer from his having no religious symbol that he had no religion. Now this particular case happens to illustrate the insecurity of these guesses very clearly. For a little while afterwards, people discovered not only paintings but sculptures of animals in the caves. Some of these were said to be damaged with dints or holes supposed to be the marks of arrows; and the damaged images were conjectured to be the remains of some magic rite of killing the beasts in effigy; while the undamaged images were explained in connection with another magic rite invoking fertility upon the herds. Here again there is something faintly humorous about the scientific habit of having it both ways. If the image is damaged it proves one superstition and if it is undamaged it proves another. Here again there is a rather reckless jumping to conclusions; it has hardly occurred to the speculators that a crowd of hunters imprisoned in winter in a cave might conceivably have aimed at a mark for fun, as a sort of primitive parlour game. But in any case, if it was done out of superstition, what has become of the thesis that it had nothing to do with religion? The truth is that all this guesswork has nothing to do with anything. It is not half such a good parlour game as shooting arrows at a carved reindeer for it is shooting them into the air.[11]

Chesterton was tearing away the fabric of falsehood which shrouded much modern scientific speculation. Yet it was not science he objected to but the patronising arrogance of many scientists. Continuing the theme of cave-drawings, he wondered what future scientists would make of twentieth-century hieroglyphics, commonly known as graffiti:

> ... the time will come when these inscriptions will really be of remote date. And if the professors of the future are anything like the professors of the present, they will be able to deduce a vast number of very vivid and interesting things from these cave-writings of the twentieth century. If I know anything about the breed, and if they have not

fallen away from the full-blooded confidence of their fathers, they will be able to discover the most fascinating facts about us from the initials left in the Magic Grotto by 'Arry and 'Arriet, possibly in the form of two intertwined A's. From this alone they will know 1. That as the letters are rudely chipped with a blunt pocket-knife, the twentieth century possessed no delicate graving-tools and was unacquainted with the art of sculpture. 2. That as the letters are capital letters, our civilisation never evolved any small letters or anything like a running hand. 3. That because initial consonants stand together in an unpronounceable fashion, our language was possibly akin to Welsh or more probably of the early Semitic type that ignored vowels. 4. That as the initials of 'Arry and 'Arriet do not in any special fashion profess to be religious symbols, our civilisation possessed no religion.[12]

The Everlasting Man fulfilled its purpose. It was an answer to Wells's *Outline of History* and an attack on the shallowness of modern thought. Yet it was not as popular with the public as Chesterton's biography of St Francis had been. It was more esoteric, harder to grasp and, in dealing with the shallows, it plumbed the depths. In short, it was never really destined for a mass audience. The underlying reason for its relative lack of popularity was summed up by the critic Patrick Braybrooke:

> Perhaps it is really unfair to compare *The Everlasting Man* and *St Francis of Assisi*. Yet in a sense, both are apologies for the Catholic Church. Suppose a sceptic were to read these two books. Suppose after perusal he was led to give his allegiance to the Church. I think that the book which had performed this miracle of conversion would be the story of the miraculous Saint Francis. *St Francis of Assisi* is a simple beautiful book, *The Everlasting Man* is never beautiful, it is never simple, it is profound. Wherefore, it may be asked, which is the most worthy of praise, a beautiful and simple book, or a profound and difficult book? The answer may be, that the book which achieves most will be worthy of the more merit. As I have said, both these books are in the nature of Catholic propaganda. I have no hesitation whatever in saying that I think *Saint Francis* will help the Catholic Church more than *The Everlasting Man*, because we can weep with *Saint Francis*, but we can only be amazed at *The Everlasting Man*, and perhaps weeping leads to conversion more quickly than mere amazement. *Saint Francis* appeals to the heart more than the head, *The Everlasting Man* appeals more to the head than the heart.[13]

None the less, *The Everlasting Man*'s lack of popular success did not necessarily indicate a lack of literary success. Two recent biographers of Chesterton, Michael Ffinch and Michael Coren, express the opinion that *The Everlasting Man* was Gilbert's 'masterpiece', and their view was shared by many of the author's contemporaries. Father O'Connor sang its praises enthusiastically:

> It is in the middle, close and difficult reading because of the *density* of the matter. He took the whole jungle of Comparative Religion (the 'Science' of) upon his hayfork, and made hay. But anthologies not yet dreamed will produce pages as discoveries of what English prose can be. He had at last a thesis worthy of his declamatory powers, and he was not teaching himself philosophy, he had mastered all that. Peace! His triumph shall be sung by some yet unmoulded tongue, far on in summers that we shall not see.[14]

Father Ronald Knox was 'firmly of the opinion that posterity will regard *The Everlasting Man* as the best of his books'[15] and his view was echoed by Evelyn Waugh:

> Chesterton is primarily the author of *The Everlasting Man*. In that book all his random thoughts are concentrated and refined; all his aberrations made straight. It is a great, popular book, one of the few really great popular books of the century; the triumphant assertion that a book can be both great and popular. And it needs no elucidation. It is brilliantly clear. It met a temporary need and survives as a permanent monument.[16]

Perhaps the literary figure who was affected most profoundly by *The Everlasting Man*, however, was C. S. Lewis. Lewis had been a long-standing admirer of Chesterton but could not accept his Christianity. In his own words, 'Chesterton had more sense than all the other moderns put together; bating, of course, his Christianity.'[17] At this time Lewis described himself as a theist whose 'God' was very different from 'the God of popular religion':

> There was, I explained, no possibility of being in a personal relation with Him. For I thought He projected us as a dramatist projects his characters, and I could no more 'meet' Him than Hamlet could meet Shakespeare. I didn't call Him 'God' either; I called Him 'Spirit'. One fights for one's remaining comforts.

Then I read Chesterton's *Everlasting Man* and for the first time saw the whole Christian outline of history set out in a form that seemed to me to make sense.[18]

Many years later, during the Second World War, Charles Gilmore, the Commandant of the Chaplains' School of the RAF, remembered that Lewis 'would bid me study again Chesterton's *Everlasting Man*; would anxiously ask if the chaplains had really got it into their heads that the ancients had got every whit as good brains as we had . . . He certainly made his mark on the Chaplains save on those who themselves made no mark on anyone.'[19]

If Lewis had made his mark as a lecturer with the RAF, it was due in no small part to the mark Chesterton, and particularly *The Everlasting Man*, had made on him. One recalls Braybrooke's belief that Chesterton's *St Francis* would win more converts to Christianity than *The Everlasting Man* and his assertion that 'the book which achieves most will be worthy of the more merit'. Considering the importance of *The Everlasting Man* to both C. S. Lewis and Evelyn Waugh, it must be arguable that this book and not the more popular biography of Saint Francis was the more important. One can but wonder to what extent the course of twentieth-century literature would have altered had *The Everlasting Man* not been written. If this one link in the chain had not materialised, would the world have been blessed with the *Chronicles of Narnia* or *Brideshead Revisited*? It is, of course, impossible to say and idle perhaps to conjecture, but one can at least be a witness to the fact that from Wells and the shallows of his *Outline of History* emerged Chesterton and the depths of *The Everlasting Man*.

The Outline of Sanity

WHETHER OR NOT CHESTERTON'S *Everlasting Man* had any direct influence on the later literary output of Lewis and Waugh, there seems little doubt that his invention of Father Brown was having a definite influence on the genesis of one of the twentieth century's most popular writers of detective fiction. In October 1925 Dorothy L. Sayers had been sent a copy of a Chesterton article on the writing of detective stories. It was to prove pivotal in Sayers's development of her craft. She found the article 'one of the soundest and most useful pieces of constructive criticism' she had met for a long time, adding that 'G. K. C. has put his finger at once on the central difficulty', that of making the solution neither too obscure nor too obvious. Although, on the whole, she did not care for the presence of a love-interest in a detective story, she admitted the truth of Chesterton's claim that it is useful as camouflage. The stories in which it is most successful, she considered, are those in which it forms an integral part of the plot, as in Wilkie Collins's *The Moonstone* and E. C. Bentley's *Trent's Last Case*. She applauded Chesterton for upholding the strictly classic form of detective story and quoted his recommendation: 'The thing that we realise must be the thing that we recognise; that is, it must be something previously known, and it ought to be prominently displayed.' Commenting on this Chestertonian axiom, she wrote: 'That excellent sentence should be illuminated in letters of gold and hung above the desk of every mystery-story writer.' She concluded by citing an example of one of Chesterton's own Father Brown stories, 'The Invisible Man': 'But there! once started on the fascinating subject of technique, one could go on for hours.'[1] Sayers, whose own sleuth, Lord Peter Wimsey, had made his first public appearance two years previously, embroidered and embellished these Chestertonian themes in her essay on the history of detective fiction, published as an introduction to her anthology *Great Short Stories of Detection, Mystery and Horror*.

In the same month that Dorothy L. Sayers was captivated by Chesterton's views on detective fiction, Chesterton was attempting to captivate the students at Glasgow University. At the behest of many of the students themselves he had been persuaded to stand as one of the three candidates in the university's rectorial election. E. C. Bentley, whose book had been praised so highly by Sayers, was among those enlisted to speak on Chesterton's behalf at one of the many public meetings organised during the election campaign. Chesterton himself told the students at one such meeting, 'England has taken refuge in Utopia after Utopia of ever-mounting insanity, believing a world in which all labour and sorrow had vanished, with reforms by which every man could live to be three hundred years old . . . And now, after a century of such nonsense, we stand where we did . . .'[2]

The meetings were often riotous affairs as Ada Chesterton, who had been invited to speak in support of her brother-in-law, remembered:

> I was warned that the students might hotly resent being addressed by a woman, and that they would be tempted to launch a bombardment of peasemeal, if not haddocks' heads and bags of Reckitt's blue, as tokens of disapprobation . . . I was warned not to expect attention, let alone respect, from the audience . . .
>
> How should I hold them? I resolved all kinds of expedients, and at last, just as we were crossing the threshold to take the Professor's car to the University, I had an inspiration. With a muttered apology I darted back into the dining-room, took an apple from the sideboard, and dropped it into my bag.
>
> I have never heard anything more rampant than the noise which greeted us when we entered the great building . . .
>
> Bentley captured attention and was heard in comparative quiet . . . And then it was my turn, and I clambered up to the wildest reception that can be imagined. Howls of derision greeted me, every and any noise was added – whistles, mouth organs. But I remembered my directions, and stood smiling and silent.
>
> But they were quite merciless. They did not want a woman to talk to them: they would not have a woman. So I opened my bag, produced the big red apple and took a bite. It was the funniest sensation to watch the sudden surprised faces, the gradual slackening of noise as I methodically munched.

And then a clear, boyish voice called from high up, near the ceiling:

'Carry on, Eve – we've fallen!'

And they had. I never met a more appreciative audience, and when I finished they broke into cheers . . .[3]

Ada Chesterton had gained an unlikely victory over the boisterous anarchy which prevailed during the election, but Gilbert had one ally who was singularly at home in such riotous surroundings. Hilaire Belloc, taking time off from his battles with Wells, made the greatest contribution in time and effort to Chesterton's campaign, speaking twice in the Men's and once in the Women's Union, as well as contributing regularly to *G. K. C.*, the daily news-sheet produced by Chesterton's student supporters. No transcript exists of any of Belloc's speeches but newspaper reports testify to the energy and wit with which he conducted himself. At 1.15 p.m. on 15 October he entered the Debating Hall to the traditional welcome of ear-splitting cheers, cat-calls and tin whistles – though he was spared the bags of flour that were hurled at Father Ronald Knox when he appeared for Chesterton on the following Monday and the oatmeal with which the students greeted David Kirkwood, a Member of Parliament, when he appeared for the Labour candidate. The chairman shouted an unheard and unheeded introduction and Belloc stood motionless, waiting for the noise to subside. The mayhem was heightened when those at the back, their view impaired, began to chant, 'Get on the table.' His response, in a moment of relative calm, was to caution his audience that they were dealing with age and timidity: 'I never go to sea in a boat or mount a horse without being frightened and I could no more mount that table than fly.' Another heckler he parried with a rebuke: 'Never make fun of old men, or bears will come out of the woods and devour you.'[4] From that moment, the noise subsided and the audience seemed prepared to give him a hearing. They were further intrigued by Belloc's expressed intention of explaining that they should *not* vote for the candidate on whose behalf he was officially speaking:

All the causes that I have taken up during my life have failed. It is with this in mind that I am here to give you reasons why you should not vote for Chesterton . . . Chesterton is a poet and a great poet. He has written the best poem within living memory, and such a man is, of course, to be avoided at all costs. To read and understand a great poet always demands thought, and thought inevitably brings discomfort. It is good for individuals to keep away from poets, and the same can be said about Corporations and Universities. There is something nefarious and disreputable about good poetry, and it is up to you to mark your displeasure of it. Another reason for not voting for Chesterton is that he is not a party politician. In this he is distinct from the other two – both of whom are party politicians with labels attached. Let us not break the tradition: let us vote, not for the man but for the label – possibly the two labels at once.[5]

According to the following morning's edition of the *Glasgow Herald*, Belloc's speech 'was all accomplished with such skill that the students, as quick in the appreciation of a good thing as mercilessly censorious of an indifferent, made of him quite a popular hero at the finish'.[6]

Belloc was back in the arena the following day with more students than ever crowding the Debating Hall: 'At 1.15 p.m., standing room was a myth. The corridors were packed. The sliding doors at the back of the hall had to be opened. The very Union walls seemed to bulge and creak.'[7] A report in the *Daily Record* captured the atmosphere of the evening:

> ... through the gloom of the Union's thick atmosphere – a combination of fog and tobacco smoke, in which one viewed things as in a glass, darkly – Mr Belloc's wit shone brilliantly ... Through the din that was caused by the unruly spirit present, Mr Belloc was heard saying that one great advantage of raising a rumpus was that the speaker could not be heard, and as he had nothing to say – well, it didn't really matter. After a frank confession of that sort, of course, what could his youthful audience do but listen to what their speaker had to say? He had spiked their guns.[8]

Belloc concluded his address by saying that he believed he had created a record in speaking on two successive days in the Union – and coming out alive. An hour later, he was telling the women students in the Queen Margaret Union that it was as sensible to vote for a man according to his party as to vote for him according to his initial in the alphabet:

> It would be ridiculous to vote for a poet laureate in this way. It is ridiculous to choose a Lord Rector in this way. Chesterton was the representative of literature. Mr Shaw was right when he said the other day that G. K. C. was worthy of standing alongside Dr Johnson. He was truly a great man with an enormous output, much

of which was superlative. Not only was his production apparently inexhaustible, but it had a consistent philosophy behind it all. With his excellency of workmanship and firmly held philosophy, Gilbert Chesterton's work was bound to last. Read *Lepanto* before you go to the poll, and you cannot fail to vote for G. K. Chesterton . . . If G. K. is rejected, the Rectorial of 1925 will be remembered for the defeat of G. K. Chesterton, not for who had defeated him.[9]

This last sentiment was reitereated on the eve of the poll in 'A Final Letter to the Students of Glasgow University from Hilaire Belloc': 'If Mr Chesterton is not elected, it certainly will have an odd effect on posterity and the future generations will find it difficult to understand the mind of a time in which chance men, then forgotten, were preferred (by a University, of all electorates!) to a permanent name in the first rank of English letters.'[10]

Belloc's pleading was to no avail. Chesterton lost the election to Sir Austen Chamberlain, the Conservative candidate, by 274 votes. The result was scarcely surprising. As Foreign Secretary at the time of the election, Chamberlain was riding a wave of popularity for his negotiating of the Locarno Pact. This pact, signed by Britain, France, Germany, Belgium and Italy, amounted to a common agreement by all parties to the maintenance of the boundaries of the Treaty of Versailles. It also allowed Germany into the League of Nations in return for her promise never to repossess the Rhineland or the Saar. The pact was seen as a major cornerstone in the building of a lasting peace, and Chamberlain took the credit for both negotiating it with the other powers and for signing the agreement on Britain's behalf. He was rewarded with both a knighthood and the Nobel peace prize.

Chesterton, however, failed to share the optimism and euphoria that surrounded the signing of the pact. Instead he saw a nightmare vision of a resurgent and unrepentant Prussia. Within weeks of the Locarno Pact being signed he was writing a Christmas play about St George and the Dragon which contained a prophetic vision of the Second World War. Written nearly fifteen years before the nightmare became reality, the prediction of blitz and blackout is uncannily accurate in the light of later events:

> SAINT GEORGE: I know that this is sure
> Whatever man can do, man can endure,
> Though you shall loose all laws of fight, and fashion

A torture chamber from a tilting yard,
Though iron hard as doom grow hot as passion,
Man shall be hotter, man shall be more hard,
And when an army in your hell fire faints,
You shall find martyrs who were never saints.

(They wound each other and the doctor comes to the help of the Turkish knight.)

PRINCESS: Why should we patch this pirate up again?
  Why should you always win and win in vain?
  Bid him not cut the leg but cut the loss.
SAINT GEORGE: I will not fire upon my own red cross.
PRINCESS: If you lay there, would he let *you* escape?
SAINT GEORGE: I am his conqueror and not his ape.
DOCTOR: Be not so sure of conquering. He shall rise
  On lighter feet, on feet that vault the skies.
  Science shall make a mighty foot and new,
  Light as the feather feet of Perseus flew,
  Long as the seven-leagued boots in tales gone by,
  This shall bestride the sea and ride the sky.
  Thus shall he fly, and beat above your nation
  The clashing pinions of Apocalypse,
  Ye shall be deep-sea fish in pale prostration
  Under the sky foam of his flying ships.

When terror above your cities, dropping doom,
Shall shut all England in a lampless tomb,
Your widows and your orphans now forlorn
Shall be no safer than the dead they mourn.
When all your lights grow dark, their lives grow gray,
What will those widows and those orphans say?

SAINT GEORGE: Saint George for Merrie England.[11]

In Chesterton's eyes, Merrie England was an idealised view of what England had been and what she could be. It was an England free from post-Reformation Puritanism and post-industrial proletarianism. It was an England where the majority of people would own the land on which they lived and worked. It was Blake's green and pleasant land liberated from the dominion of dark, satanic mills. Neither was St George the only champion of this Merrie England. Others throughout history had shared Chesterton's view and one of these, William Cobbett, was the subject of a biography by Chesterton, published in November 1925. According to Christopher Hollis, Chesterton's *William Cobbett* was 'in many ways the most satisfactory of his biographies'.[12] A reviewer in the *Observer*, R. Ellis Roberts, noted that no book

> ... will give the student of history so clear a view of what Cobbett wanted, what he meant, and why he said the things he did. In Mr Chesterton's view – and he will find a good many people to agree with him – Cobbett stood for England: England unindustrialised, self-sufficient, relying on a basis of agriculture and sound commerce for her prosperity, with no desire for inflation.[13]

In fact, Chesterton's fascination with Cobbett was such that it is a little surprising that the biography was so late in coming. Many years earlier, in 1912, he had afforded Cobbett a place of honour at the dawning of the Victorian age:

> Three years before the young queen was crowned, William Cobbett was buried at Farnham. It may seem strange to begin with this great neglected name, rather than the old age of Wordsworth or the young death of Shelley. But to any one who feels literature as human, the empty chair of Cobbett is more solemn and significant than the throne. With him died the sort of democracy that was a return to nature, and which only poets and mobs can understand. After him Radicalism is urban – and Toryism suburban. Going through green Warwickshire, Cobbett might have thought of the crops and Shelley of the clouds. But Shelley would have called Birmingham what Cobbett called it – a hell-hole.[14]

This theme was taken up with gusto in the biography:

> What he saw was not an Eden that cannot exist, but rather an Inferno that can exist, and even that does exist. What he saw was the perishing of the whole English power of self-support, the growth of cities that drain and dry up the countryside, the growth of dense dependent populations incapable of finding their own food, the toppling triumphs of machines over men, the sprawling omnipotence of financiers over patriots, the herding of humanity in nomadic masses whose very homes are homeless, the terrible necessity of peace and the terrible probability of war, all the loading up of our little island like a

sinking ship; the wealth that may mean famine and the culture that may mean despair; the bread of Midas and the sword of Damocles.[15]

For Cobbett, as for Chesterton, the problems of the present were caused by the crimes of the past; and for Cobbett, as for Chesterton, the principal crime was the Reformation, which had unleashed a plague of land-grabbing and money-grubbing in England:

> He was simply a man who had discovered a crime: ancient like many crimes; concealed like all crimes. He was as one who had found in a dark wood the bones of his mother, and suddenly knew she had been murdered. He knew now that England had been secretly slain. Some, he would say, might think it a matter of mild regret to be expressed in murmurs. But when he found a corpse he gave a shout; and if fools laughed at anyone shouting, he would shout the more, till the world should be shaken with that terrible cry in the night.
>
> It is that ringing and arresting cry of 'Murder!', wrung from him as he stumbled over the bones of the dead England, that distinguishes him from all his contemporaries.[16]

The murder of Merrie England was not, however, a cause for despair because, like the phoenix, England could rise from the ashes. Indeed, only three months earlier, in *The Everlasting Man*, Chesterton had written, 'Christianity has died many times and risen again; for it had a god who knew the way out of the grave.'[17] What was true of Christianity in general was true of Christianity in England. Merrie England was, first and foremost, a Christian land and, as such, it was capable of resurrection.

This spirit of hope was the inspiration for Chesterton's next novel, *The Return of Don Quixote*, which began appearing in serialised form in *G. K.'s Weekly* from December 1925 onwards. The novel's theme was typically fantastic, a flight of fancy like all his other works of fiction. The elaborate plot begins with the rehearsing of a medieval play and is complicated when one of the actors, an eccentric librarian, throws himself, heart and soul, into the project and studies the period thoroughly, the better to interpret his part. When the play is over, he refuses to change his costume, resolving to live his real life in the medieval spirit, because, as he confesses at the end of the story, 'I found the play you acted much more real than the life you led.'[18] The rest of the book revolves around the battle between the Medievalists and the Moderns to control society. However fanciful the flight, the novel remains a parable containing a kernel of truth. Chesterton's art as a writer of fiction lies in the way he wields the sledgehammer to crack the nut.

The Return of Don Quixote continued appearing in *G. K.'s Weekly* until November 1926 but was not actually published as a book until 1927. Meanwhile, *G. K.'s Weekly* was itself becoming an outspoken mouthpiece for the ideals of Merrie England. As editor, Chesterton was self-consciously aware of his duty to maintain the crusading spirit of his late brother, whose editorship of the *New Witness* a decade earlier had been militant in its criticism of many aspects of modern society. No doubt, in the wake of his biography of Cobbett, he was also aware of a parallel between his own paper and Cobbett's *Register*, which had fulfilled a similar function, that of criticising the establishment a century earlier. In short, Chesterton perceived *G. K.'s Weekly* as being part of a long tradition of radical opposition to plutocracy. This fact was highlighted in the lead article on the front page of the very first issue of *G. K.'s Weekly*, appropriately titled 'The First Principle':

> This single adventure in weekly journalism cannot compete with our wealthy and world-wide press in resources and reports. [But] it exists to demand that we fight Bolshevism with something better than plutocracy . . . The thing behind Bolshevism . . . is a new doubt . . . not merely a doubt about God, it is rather specially a doubt about man. The old morality, the Christian religion . . . really believed in the rights of man . . . These [new] sages cannot trust the normal man to rule in the home; and most certainly do not want him to rule in the State . . . We alone have the right to call ourselves democratic. That is what we think; and Bolshevism and Capitalism are absolutely at one in thinking the opposite . . . We at least have seen sanity, if only in a vision, while they go forward chained eternally to enlargement without liberty and progress without hope.[19]

In another article Chesterton wrote that choosing between socialism and capitalism 'is like saying we must choose between all men going into monasteries and a few men having harems'.[20] The logic of the argument struck a chord with many of Chesterton's readers who rallied to the political position adopted by *G. K.'s Weekly*. Soon, however, it was argued that the creed would gain credence if it found expression in a political organisation. Thus on 17 September 1926, at the Essex Hall in the Strand, the Distributist League was born. Quoting Francis Bacon's assertion that 'property is like muck, it is good only if it be spread', Chesterton told the inaugural meeting that the League's 'simple idea was to restore possession'.[21] The following week the first committee meeting took place, and Chesterton was duly elected president. Alternative names were discussed, such as the Cobbett Club, the Luddite League or the League of Small Property, and the discussion continued in articles in *G. K.'s Weekly*:

> The Cow and Acres, however suitable as the name of a public house at which we could assemble, is too limited as an economic statement . . .
> The League of the Little People (President, Mr G. K. Chesterton) may seem at first too suggestive of the fairies; but it has been strongly supported among us.
> And again: Suppose we call our movement 'The Lost Property League' . . . the idea of the restoration of lost property is far more essential to our whole conception than even the idea of liberty, as now commonly understood. The Liberty and Property Defence League implies that property is there to be defended. 'The Lost Property League' describes the exact state of the case.[22]

In spite of such Chestertonian word-play it was decided that the name of the new organisation should be the Distributist League, which, although more prosaic than other suggestions, was more precise as a description of its aim to distribute property.

In October another meeting of the central branch was held in Essex Hall, and branches had been established in Croydon, Birmingham, Manchester and Glasgow. The first meeting of the Bath branch was chaired by the city's mayor, and the meeting had to overflow into a very large hall. The leading article in *G. K.'s Weekly* on 6 November announced that the price of the paper was being slashed from sixpence to twopence to facilitate a greater propagation of the League's principles: 'Every reader who has been buying one copy at sixpence, must take three copies at twopence until his two surplus copies have secured two new readers . . . The League would have to make itself responsible for the success of this experiment and save the paper which gave it birth, or die of inanition, for it is certainly not yet strong enough to leave its mother.'[23]

Although this was a bold and risky move, the gamble paid off and the circulation of *G. K.'s Weekly* rose, almost overnight, from 5,000 to 8,000 copies. Fired by this initial success, Gilbert's report of a League meeting in the following week's edition bubbled over with enthusiasm:

> We find it difficult to express the effect the meeting had upon us. We were astonished, we were overwhelmed. Had we anything to do with the making of this ardent, eager, indefatigable creature? The answer is, of course, that though we had something to do with the shaping of the body, we had nothing to do with the birth of the soul. That was a miracle, a miracle we had hoped for, and which yet, when it happened, overwhelmed us. We have the happy feeling that we have helped to shape something which will go far above and beyond us.[24]

In the following weeks further branches of the League were established in Liverpool, Chatham, Worthing, Chorley, Cambridge and Oxford. It looked as though the movement, formed only weeks earlier, could achieve anything it wished. The central branch of the League, calling for a boycott of large chainstores, sensed a new dawn: 'And that is only a beginning. We hope to enlist the support of the small farmer and the small master craftsman. We hope, little by little, to put the small producer in touch with the small retailer. We hope in the end to establish within the state a community, almost self-supporting, of men and women pledged to Distributism, and to a large extent practising it.'[25]

It was in this spirit of hopeful optimism that Chesterton wrote *The Outline of Sanity*. Published on 2 December, the book was a collection of essays on distributism culled from his regular articles in *G. K.'s Weekly*. The tone and the purpose of the book were laid down on the very first page:

> I have been asked to republish these notes – which appeared in a weekly paper – as a rough sketch of certain aspects of the institution of Private Property, now so completely forgotten amid the journalistic jubilations over Private Enterprise. The very fact that the publicists say so much of the latter and so little of the former is a measure of the moral tone of the times. A pickpocket is obviously a champion of private enterprise. But it would perhaps be an exaggeration to say that a pickpocket is a champion of private property.[26]

Having distinguished between private property and private enterprise, Chesterton develops the argument by giving capitalism a definite definition:

Capitalism is really a very unpleasant word. It is also a very unpleasant thing. Yet the thing I have in mind, when I say so, is quite definite and definable; only the name is a very unworkable word for it. But obviously we must have some word for it. When I say 'Capitalism', I commonly mean something that may be stated thus: 'That economic condition in which there is a class of capitalists, roughly recognisable and relatively small, in whose possession so much of the capital is concentrated as to necessitate a very large majority of the citizens serving those capitalists for a wage'. This particular state of things can and does exist, and we must have some word for it, and some way of discussing it. But this is undoubtedly a very bad word, because it is used by other people to mean quite other things. Some people seem to mean merely private property. Others suppose that capitalism must mean anything involving the use of capital. But if that use is too literal, it is also too loose and even too large. If the use of capital is capitalism, then everything is capitalism. Bolshevism is capitalism and anarchist communism is capitalism; and every revolutionary scheme, however wild, is still capitalism. Lenin and Trotsky believe as much as Lloyd George and Thomas that the economic operations of today must leave something over for the economic operations of tomorrow. And that is all that capital means in its economic sense. In that case, the word is useless. My use of it may be arbitrary, but it is not useless.[27]

In introducing his case by getting at the literal root of the terms under discussion Chesterton was being radical in the strict sense of the word. However, it necessitated a drier approach, somewhat alien to his natural style, and the Chestertonian paradox and parable, hidden among the economic discussions, emerges as comic relief:

All of us, or at least all those of my generation, heard in our youth an anecdote about George Stephenson, the discoverer of the Locomotive Steam-Engine. It was said that some miserable rustic raised the objection that it would be very awkward if a cow strayed on the railway line, whereupon the inventor replied, 'It would be very awkward for the cow.' It is supremely characteristic of his age and school that it never seemed to occur to anybody that it might be rather awkward for the rustic who owned the cow.

Long before we heard that anecdote, however, we had probably heard another more exciting anecdote called 'Jack and the Beanstalk'. That story begins with the strange and startling words, 'There once was a poor woman who had a cow.' It would be a wild paradox in modern England to imagine that a *poor* woman could have a cow; but things seem to have been different in ruder and more superstitious ages. Anyhow, she evidently would not have had a cow long in the sympathetic atmosphere of Stephenson and his steam-engine. The train went forward, the cow was killed in due course; and the state of mind of the old woman was described as the Depression of Agriculture.[28]

However, if 'Jack and the Beanstalk' was a memory of a Merrie England that had passed away, Chesterton believed that many desired a return to a Merrie England in the future:

I should maintain that there is a very large element still in England that would like a return to this simpler sort of England. Some of them understand it better than others, some of them understand themselves better than others; some would be prepared for it as a revolution; some only cling to it very blindly as a tradition; some have never thought of it as anything but a hobby; some have never heard of it and feel it only as a want. But the number of people who would like to get out of the tangle of mere ramifications and communications in the town, and get back nearer to the roots of things, where things are made directly out of nature, I believe to be very large.[29]

Although Chesterton had accepted the presidency of the Distributist League, he would have been the first to concede that he was not, by any means, the founder of distributism. In fact, *The Outline of Sanity* appeared more than a decade after Belloc's *The Servile State*. It was singularly apt, therefore, that Chesterton expressed distributism's debt of gratitude to Belloc in an 'Open Letter': 'Now at the fountain of that river, at the root of that genealogical tree, your figure will stand in the history of England. You were the founder and father of this mission; we were the converts but you were the missionary . . . you first revealed the truth both to its greater and its lesser servants . . . Great will be your glory if England breathes again.'[30]

Yet Belloc did not deserve all the glory either. He was, after all, merely expounding, and expanding upon, the social doctrine laid down by Pope Leo XIII in his encyclical letter *Rerum Novarum*. Published in 1891, this document, with its explicit call for the restoration of property, can claim to be the originator of distributism:

The law, therefore, should favour ownership and its policy should be to induce as many people as possible to become owners. Many excellent results will follow from this; and first of all, property will certainly become more equitably divided . . . If workpeople can be encouraged to look forward to obtaining a share in the land, the result will be that the gulf between vast wealth and deep poverty will be bridged over, and the two orders will be brought nearer together.[31]

There is no doubt that Belloc's own distributism had its roots in the Pope's teaching. As early as 1909 he had written *The Church and Socialism* and this was followed by *The Catholic Church and the Principle of Private Property* (1920) and *Catholic Social Reform versus Socialism* (1922). It is hardly surprising, therefore, that many members of the Distributist League were practising Catholics. 'For us Catholics,' wrote Father Vincent McNabb, 'the Distributist State is not something we discuss, but something we have to propagate and institute. No advance in social thought or social action is possible if we are seeking to prove ourselves as a theory what we should be trying to realise in fact.'[32]

These views would have found wholehearted support from Eric Gill, himself both a convert to Catholicism and a dedicated distributist. Gill treated the modern industrial system with disdain, claiming that it 'makes good mechanics, good machine-minders, but men and women who in every other respect are morons, cretins, for whom crossword puzzles, football games, watered beer, sham half-timbered bungalows and shimmering film stars are the highest form of amusement'.[33] In contempt of, and in contrast to, the world at large, Gill had founded a distributist community at Ditchling in Sussex, quite literally putting his beliefs into practice. In August 1924, however, he moved to Wales, despatching Chesterton a brusque notification of his change of address: 'I do think you make a bit of a bloomer in 1. supporting Orpenism as against Byzantinism and 2. in thinking that the art of painting *began* with Giotto – whereas Giotto was really much more the end. We are leaving Ditchling Common and after this week my address will be Capel-y-ffin, nr. Abergavenny, S. Wales.'[34]

In spite of these evident differences of opinion, Chesterton appointed Gill as art editor of *G. K.'s Weekly* the following year. Yet Gill remained singularly self-opinionated, only agreeing to Chesterton's request that he write about Epstein if both the editor and Belloc promised not to disagree with him. Instead they must 'accept my doctrine as the doctrine of *G. K.'s Weekly* in matters of art – just as I accept yours in other matters'.[35]

On 12 August 1925 Gill purchased forty-nine shares in G. K.'s

Weekly Limited at a cost of £24.10s.0d.[36] Almost immediately he used his status as a shareholder to his advantage: 'I don't intend to write for you as an outsider (have I not put almost my last quid into your blooming company?).'[37] Surprisingly, perhaps, by brushing the brusqueness aside with characteristic good humour Chesterton remained on friendly terms with his art editor.

Perhaps the Distributist League's finest hour came in late October 1927 when Belloc chaired a public debate between Chesterton and Shaw at the Kingsway Hall in London. Organised by the League, the debate was broadcast live by the BBC. Shaw and Chesterton discussed the theme, 'Do We Agree?', and, needless to say, they didn't. Shaw still argued for socialism, Chesterton for distributism and never the twain did meet. There was something almost stale about the stalemate until Belloc stole the show with his summing up:

> I was told when I accepted this onerous office that I was to sum up. I shall do nothing of the sort. In a very few years from now this debate will be antiquted. I will now recite you a poem:
>
> > Our civilisation
> > Is built upon coal.
> > Let us chaunt in rotation
> > Our civilisation
> > That lump of damnation
> > Without any soul,
> > Our civilisation
> > Is built upon coal.
> >
> > In a very few years
> > It will float upon oil.
> > Then give three hearty cheers,
> > In a very few years
> > We shall mop up our tears
> > And have done with our toil.
> > In a very few years
> > It will float upon oil.
>
> In I do not know how many years – five, ten, twenty – this debate will be as antiquated as crinolines are. I am surprised that neither of the two speakers pointed out that one of three things is going to happen ... The industrial civilisation, which, thank God, oppresses only the small part of the world in which we are most inextricably bound up,

will break down and therefore end from its monstrous wickedness, folly, ineptitude, leading to a restoration of sane, ordinary human affairs, complicated but based as a whole upon the freedom of the citizens. Or it will break down and lead to nothing but a desert. Or it will lead the mass of men to become contented slaves, with a few rich men controlling them. Take your choice. You will all be dead before any of the three things is going to happen, or a mixture of two, or possibly a mixture of the three combined.[38]

Little could anyone that night at the Kingsway Hall know it, but Belloc, in ringing down the curtain on the debate, was also ringing down the curtain on the Distributist League. Certainly, the League's existence dragged on for several more years, but it had lost its momentum and its way. Soon there would be internal dissent over the role of machinery; there would be tension between Catholics and non-Catholics over the importance or otherwise of religion; and there would be widespread frustration at the League's general lack of progress. In short, there would soon be many who would leave the organisation disillusioned with distributism. Some sought other alternatives to capitalism or socialism; some chose the blind alley of fascism. One thing, however, was certain. The Distributist League was finished as a force for change.

One wonders whether Chesterton recalled his own words to the students at Glasgow University as he witnessed the League disintegrating: 'England has taken refuge in Utopia after Utopia of ever-mounting insanity . . .'

As the Utopian dreamers within the Distributist League talked themselves into oblivion, their president watched the outline of sanity fade away.

« 22 »

Daughter of Desire

THERE WAS LITTLE TO celebrate at Top Meadow at the start of 1926. Frances's health had deteriorated and the arthritis of the spine from which she'd suffered for years was causing concern. While in Bath at the beginning of the year she had consulted a specialist, who had warned her to live 'very quietly and rest as much as possible'. This was merely repeating the advice of Dr Bakewell, her doctor in Beaconsfield, who had finally persuaded her at the end of the previous year to go into a rest home for a spell of recuperation. Another specialist praised Dr Bakewell for prevailing on Frances to go into the home: 'How you ever got her into a Home for a decent spell . . . I cannot imagine, and therefore can only congratulate you. Mrs Chesterton ought to go away for several months . . .'[1]

A welcome respite from the worries over Frances's health was provided in early January by another Mrs Chesterton. Cecil's widow, Ada Chesterton, had, in collaboration with Ralph Neale, written a play of Gilbert's novel *The Man Who was Thursday*. The play, which opened at the Everyman Theatre on 19 January, created quite a stir and prompted the *Observer* to interview the novel's author. Asked about his motivation for writing the novel, Chesterton replied at length:

> It was, of course, a protest against the pessimism of the 'nineties. And though I didn't know much about God, I was ready to stick up for Him against the jury of Cockney poets who had brought Him in guilty. It was a bad period when it was unfashionable to believe in innocence, and we were all supposed to worship Wilde and Whistler, and everything twisty and strange. I suppose it was a natural revolt . . .
>
> The peculiar interest of this play for me, apart from the fact that my sister-in-law has had a hand in writing it, is that we are

under a wave of pessimism just now. And if you agree to take my extravaganza seriously, you will find an interest, too, in comparing the pessimism of my Anarchist with that of the young men of today. To my mind, our pessimism is much more noble. The sad souls of the 'nineties lost hope because they had taken too much absinthe; our young men have lost hope because a friend died with a bullet in his head.[2]

During the course of the interview it emerged that Gilbert had himself written another play: 'Yes, it is true that I have written a play called *Doctor Johnson*, which, my agent tells me, after having found a temporary lodging in Mr Basil Dean's Play Box, has been accepted by Sir Barry Jackson.'[3] The play's full title would actually be *The Judgment of Dr Johnson* and it would not appear in print until the following year. It had been thirteen years since Chesterton's only other play, *Magic*, had premièred in London and this prompted an obvious question from the interviewer, to which Chesterton responded:

You ask why I haven't written more plays? Frankly, I don't know. I do naturally find myself writing in dialogue form. But I have been always busy with journalism, apart from which I was put to writing novels at an early age ... I suppose I followed the line of least resistance. Knowing almost nothing of the way you get a play on the stage, it yet has appeared to me that the line in that direction is foggier than on the good old route to the good old publisher.[4]

The first new Chesterton book of 1926 was *The Incredulity of Father Brown*, a further collection of detective stories, published in June by Cassell. The book was well received, with the *Yorkshire Post* enthusing on 23 June that it showed 'the old ingenuity of construction, the same credible impossibilities, the same thrill and the same magic' as the earlier Father Brown books. Furthermore, the reviewer suggested, Chesterton's detective had become a real threat to the supremacy of Sherlock Holmes: 'Holmes might have the attractive eccentricities, but he never talked mystical philosophy to the attentive Watson. But Father Brown can expound the cosmos at the same moment that he explains a murder.'[5]

Four days prior to the *Yorkshire Post*'s enthusiastic tribute, Father Brown's creator was expounding the cosmos in an attack on the 'New Heresy'. This latest heresy, Chesterton claimed, would 'simply be an attack on morality; and especially on sexual morality'. It would come '*not* from a few Socialists surviving from the Fabian Society; but from the living exultant energy of the rich resolved to enjoy themselves at last, with neither Popery nor Puritanism nor Socialism to hold them back'. Unlike the thin theory of collectivism which was doomed to failure because it lacked any real roots in human nature, this new heresy was more dangerous because it was rooted in the lower depths of humanity. It was a heresy 'whose flower is lust of the flesh and the lust of the eye and the pride of life'. A man who was unable to see this was unable to see the signs of the times or, as Chesterton put it, 'the sky-signs in the street', that were the new sort of signs in heaven: 'The madness of tomorrow is not in Moscow, but much more in Manhattan – most of what was in Broadway is already in Piccadilly.'[6]

He asserted that the earlier heresy that had underpinned this new outbreak of promiscuity was the materialism of the eighteenth and nineteenth centuries. The champions of this materialism in 1926 included Bishop Barnes, in England, who had sought to scientifically analyse the Consecrated Host, and Thomas Edison, in the United States, who had claimed that he could discover whether there was a soul by some scientific test. In two articles on 'The Yankee and the Chinaman' Chesterton contrasted the philosophic spirit of truth with the scientific claim to omniscience: 'Any philosophic Chinaman would know what to think of a man who said, "I have got a new gun that will shoot a hole through your memory of last Monday," or "I have got a saw sharp enough to cut up the cube root of 666," or "I will boil your affection for Aunt Susan until it is quite liquid." '[7]

Chesterton's outspoken attacks on the modernism of Bishop Barnes had not gone unnoticed by the bishop himself. When asked by the Empire Poetry League to attend a garden fête in Birmingham in late June at which Chesterton, who was the League's president for the year, was going to speak, Bishop Barnes wrote the following discourteous refusal: 'I know nothing of Mr G. K. Chesterton's poetry; but I do know the nature of his religious propaganda, and I firmly decline to be associated with any Society of which he is President.'[8] the *Universe* was quick to criticise the intolerant nature of the bishop's snub to the Society:

Considering that the Empire Poetry League is an entirely secular and non-political affair (Sir Arthur Quiller-Couch was the President last year), and that Mr Chesterton was invited to be its President simply because he is a great Englishman of letters, and author of more than one justly famous patriotic poem; also that the Bishop of Birmingham was asked to take the chair on Saturday, not as an Anglican controversialist, but as a leading personage of the City of Birmingham, His Lordship's attitude seems odd, almost to the point of ludicrous ... To a representative of *The Universe* who sought his views upon the incident, Mr Chesterton had nothing to say but that it had given him the enjoyment of a hearty laugh.[9]

A week later, on 28 June, Gilbert and Frances celebrated their silver wedding anniversary. They were still deeply devoted to each other and Gilbert expressed the eternal freshness of their love affair in a verse he wrote to commemorate the occasion:

> I need not say I love you yet
> You know how doth my heart oppress
> The intolerable tenderness
> That broke my body when we met.
> I need not say I love you yet.
>
> But let me say I fear you yet
> You the long years not vulgarise,
> You open your immortal eyes
> And we for the first time have met.
> Cover your face; I fear you yet.[10]

The anniversary was the answering of Gilbert's 'strangest prayer', conveyed in verse to Frances in the early days of their relationship:

> A wan new garment of young green,
>   Touched, as you turned your soft brown hair;
>   And in me surged the strangest prayer
> Ever in lover's heart hath been.
>
> That I who saw your youth's bright page,
>   A rainbow change from robe to robe,
>   Might see you on this earthly globe,
> Crowned with the silver crown of age.[11]

At this time it seemed that another of Gilbert's prayers was about to be answered. On 20 June Frances wrote to Father O'Connor expressing her readiness to follow her husband into the Church:

I want now, as soon as I can see a few days clear before me, to place myself under instruction to enter the Church. The whole position is full of difficulties and I pray you Padre to tell me the first step to take. I *don't* want my instruction to be here. I don't want to be the talk of Beaconsfield and for people to say I've only followed Gilbert. It isn't true and I've had a hard fight not to let my love for him lead me to the truth. I knew you would not accept me for such motives. But I am very tired and very worried. Many things are difficult for me. My health included, which makes strenuous attention a bit of a strain. I know you understand – Tell me what I shall do.[12]

Three weeks later, on 12 July, Frances wrote again to Father O'Connor, on this occasion, ostensibly, to thank him for his anniversary gift:

We have had such a week of alarums and excitements that I had not even time to thank you for the spoons. They are just what I like and incidentally just what I wanted. I feel so hopeless at getting out of this net of responsibilities in which I am at present enmeshed and to find time for instruction. I feel I have a lot to learn and I think after all I had better go quietly to Father Walker and talk to him. Gilbert is writing to you himself. I know he thinks I have made myself rather unhappy about things – and he is so involved with the paper (I pray he gives it up) we have not been able to talk over things sensibly. Please be very patient with me, because it is so difficult to get clear. My nephew Peter is very ill and I have to spend a lot of time with my poor sister.[13]

In her following letter to Father O'Connor, Frances informed him that she had written to Father Walker, the local parish priest, and 'after having seen him and had a talk I shall know what I ought to do'.[14] Indeed, after meeting Father Walker, she decided to ask for instruction and on 1 November, All Saints Day, she was finally received into the Catholic Church at Beaconsfield.

There are no extant eye-witness accounts of the emotional reaction of either Frances or Gilbert on the day of their union in the Church, but Gilbert recorded his own feelings about his wife's conversion in verse:

But not as distance, not as danger,
   Not chance, and hardly even change,
You found, not wholly as a stranger,
   The place too wondrous to be strange.

Great with a memory more than yearning,
 You travelled but you did not roam,
And went not wandering but returning
  As to some first forgotten home.

The mystic city, many-gated,
 Monstrously pillared, was your own;
Herodian stories gave words and waited
 Two thousand years to be your throne.

Strange blossoms burned as rich before you
 As that divine and beautiful blood;
The wild flowers were no wilder for you
 Than bluebells in an English wood.[15]

These words were echoed by Maisie Ward, who wrote of Frances that she had 'never known a happier Catholic . . . once the shivering on the bank was over and the plunge had been taken. One would say she had been in the Church all her life.'[16] Neither were the benefits Frances derived solely of the spiritual kind. Her specialist wrote to Dr Bakewell that there had been a remarkable difference in her condition: 'How immensely she has improved from a general point of view.'[17]

Of course, in a strictly practical sense, Frances's conversion meant that she and Gilbert could practise their faith together and, as with all practicalities, Frances seemed more at ease than her husband. For example, Gilbert allowed Frances to take the lead, especially in the case of going to confession. He would come downstairs on a Saturday morning and Frances wouldn't say a word, but the look in her eye said: we are both going to confession. She never forced it, but the look was enough. Once at church and seated outside the confessional, Gilbert would watch Frances using her book with the utmost diligence. Her examination of conscience would be thoroughly scrupulous, while his own would fly off wildly at a tangent. He would become fascinated by the very nature of sin itself, its history through the ages and the way it was viewed by different cultures. He would dwell on the theological definition of pride and recall the teaching of the fathers and the doctors of the Church. He would then return to the matter at hand: 'I know Frances is just finding her own sins while I'm lost in all these speculations, and that worries me because I'm far behind.'[18]

During mass, also, Gilbert felt in awe at the way Frances's participation was 'a perfect gesture' compared with what he perceived as his own woeful inadequacy. Quite simply, Frances's conversion was seen by Gilbert as the final seal and consummation of their sacramental union as husband and wife. He had never been happier. Now, as Father O'Connor had put it, he could let Frances take him to church, find his place in the prayer-book and examine his conscience for him. After four years in exile, Frances had returned to him, and he could once again rest in total and blissful dependence.

Perhaps, in the wake of his wife's reception, it was singularly appropriate that Chesterton's short book, *The Catholic Church and Conversion*, should be published in December. The penultimate chapter of the book began with the assertion that 'the Catholic Church is the only thing which saves a man from the degrading slavery of being a child of his age' and continued with an attack on those 'progressive' religions which *were* the slaves of their age:

> Anyhow, the New Religions are suited to the new world; and this is their most damning defect . . . Thus they all profess to be progressive because the peculiar boast of their particular period was progress; they claim to be democratic because our political system still rather pathetically claims to be democratic. They rushed to a reconciliation with science, which was often only a premature surrender to science. They hastily divested themselves of anything considered dowdy or old-fashioned in the way of vesture or symbol. They claimed to have bright services and cheery sermons; the churches competed with the cinemas; the churches even became cinemas.[19]

Chesterton's attack on those who had chained themselves to the spirit of the age was a reiteration of points raised earlier in the year in an essay entitled 'The Reason Why':

> Nine out of ten of what we call new ideas are simply old mistakes. The Catholic Church has for one of her chief duties that of preventing people from making those old mistakes; from making them over and over again for ever, as people do if they are left to themselves . . . The Catholic Church carries a sort of map of the mind which looks like the map of a maze, but which is in fact a guide to the maze. It has been compiled from knowledge which, even considered as human knowledge, is quite without any human parallel. There is no other

334

case of one continuous intelligent institution that has been thinking about thinking for two thousand years. Its experience naturally covers nearly all experiences, and especially nearly all errors. The result is a map in which all the blind alleys and bad roads are clearly marked, all the ways that have been shown to be worthless by the best of all evidence; the evidence of those who have gone down them.

. . . By this means, it does prevent men from wasting their time or losing their lives upon paths that have been found futile or disastrous again and again in the past, but which might otherwise entrap travellers again and again in the future. The Church does make herself responsible for warning her people against these . . . She does dogmatically defend humanity from its worst foes, those hoary and horrible and devouring monsters of the old mistakes.[20]

In another essay published in 1926, 'Upon This Rock', Gilbert had argued that the Church had prevented Christian devotion to the Mother of God from becoming excessive:

If Catholics had been left to their private judgment . . . they would long ago have exalted Our Lady to a height of superhuman supremacy and splendour that might really have imperilled the pure monotheism in the core of the creed. Over whole tracts of popular opinion she might have been a goddess more universal than Isis. It is the authority of Rome that has prevented such Catholics from indulging in such Mariolatry; the strict definition that distinguished between a perfect woman and a divine Man.[21]

The essay concluded abruptly with Gilbert stating that anything he wrote 'of the doctrine touching the Virgin . . . might be defaced with enthusiasm'.

In fact, just before Christmas, he allowed his enthusiasm to bubble over into verse with a short book of twenty-four poems dedicated to the Blessed Virgin, *The Queen of Seven Swords*. The title poem alluded to the seven swords of sorrow which pierced Mary's heart as she witnessed the sufferings of her Son. They were the symbols of a mother's passion. However, the best of the poems in this collection was 'The Return of Eve', in which Chesterton paid homage to the Immaculate Conception. In the view of the Jesuit C. C. Martindale, this particular poem had 'out-passed' Francis Thompson.

The Queen of Seven Swords marked the end of an important year

335

in the life of the Chestertons. They had celebrated twenty-five years of marriage and Gilbert had rejoiced at the return of his Eve when she had joined him in the Church. Frances, however, was about to receive a further blessing beyond her wildest hopes. Against all expectations, she was finally to find the daughter she had long desired.

At this time, according to Maisie Ward, 'what Frances needed was a daughter who – completely trustworthy – yet stood unhesitatingly on her own feet, who understood her as well as being understood by her in an equal exchange of affection; one who could penetrate her intense reserve: one who could support her as well as lean upon her love. In short she needed Dorothy Collins.'[22]

In 1926 Dorothy Collins came to Top Meadow to become Gilbert's new secretary. She was thirty-two years old and, unlike all the previous secretaries, she was trained and fully proficient. She had nine years' experience and had been secretary and accountant at the Educational Training College at Lincoln since 1922. Not only was she able to take down shorthand and type at considerable speed, but she could also drive, which, in spite of Chesterton's aversion to motor cars, revolutionised his life. From now on, he would be driven to London for engagements and through England, Europe and America on holidays and lecture tours.

Gilbert would never need another secretary because Dorothy Collins would stay with him for the rest of his life. Yet she was to become much more than a secretary. 'Not only did she bring order out of chaos,' wrote Maisie Ward, 'but she became first the very dear friend of both Frances and Gilbert and finally all that their own daughter could have been.'[23] In his *Autobiography* Gilbert wrote of Dorothy Collins that she acted 'as secretary, courier, chauffeuse, guide, philosopher and above all friend . . .'[24]

Frances, in particular, developed a deep love for Dorothy. Soon she would write a heartfelt poem entitled 'To D. E. C. – A Daughter':

> My soul went groping all the past years through
> Searching the barren deserts, for a dream
> A mirage, some foreknowledge or a gleam
> Of that long-waited day that should bring you.
>
> Where were you hiding, daughter of desire?
> In some far convent hidden from the sun?

Was I an abbess, you perchance a nun
Wedded to charity, as flame to fire?

And you have brought a long dead hope to birth
That I should hold a daughter by the hand
Like to myself – and I should see her stand
With serious eyes – and answering smiles of mirth.[25]

This poem, written in 1929 when Frances had known Dorothy for three years, was quoted in Maisie Ward's *Return to Chesterton* with the mistaken title 'To Dorothy in Gratitude'. In fact, this was the title of another poem Frances had written during the previous year:

Did you dream there was a room in which
Your heart might live?
That I was poor and you were rich
With gifts to give?

Gifts from a countless store to load
An empty shrine;
Flowers of sacrifice that glowed
Like altar wine.

* * *

I took the gifts; I so hard driven
The road I ride
And saw the little door in heaven
Stand open wide.

For these dear things you are confessed
As one apart,
Whose purpose holds, whose soul is blessed
Who has my heart.[26]

Dorothy, for her part, was a wholehearted recipient of Frances's maternal love, reciprocating her own feelings in verse:

I am your spirit daughter,
Conceived of thought and mind;
And through the years my path has led
To this most precious find.
Full many a moon did wane
Before this bond was grown,

337

But in that fallow season
A living seed was sown.
And did you feel the growing;
And did you give the thought,
To make the substance of a dream
This gift which time has wrought?
Slowness of growth gives depth of root,
Too strong to wither now;
And so my spirit mother,
A daughter's love I vow.[27]

On 28 June 1931 Dorothy again expressed her love for her 'spirit
mother' in a 'Doggerel for F. C. on her birthday':

Each bead a prayer for you, my love
On this your day of birth;
For joy of spirit – God's rare gift –
For peace of soul and mirth;
For grace and health and length of days
And your *own* wish come true
My prayers in number as the beads
I offer God for you.[28]

It was significant that Dorothy's poetical prayer should be centred
on the rosary because, although she wasn't a Catholic when she came
to work for the Chestertons in 1926, she had, by 1931, reached the
brink of conversion herself. In a letter to Frances, written from
Avignon on 18 September 1932, while on holiday in France, she
discussed her imminent reception into the Church:

Thank you so much for all the dear things you say. As you know, I
shall be dreadfully harassed by my family – or rather by my parents
and Kath etc about joining the Catholic Church – but after all, what
does all that matter? I am much too sensitive about disapproval and
ought not to mind, as I feel I am right. Mother remarked in her last
letter that nothing could be further from Christ's teaching, apropos
of the pilgrims at Chartres which I thought would interest her, but
evidently stirred up her latent Protestantism. And then she is hurt
and surprised when I do not tell her things . . .
I went to Mass this a.m. in the Cathedral which is attached to
the Papal Palace. Nobody knelt from beginning to end and many
were talking and whispering all the time. This evening I had quite a

different experience. I found a tiny little church served by Franciscans which was packed to bursting point for the Rosary, a sermon and Benediction. It was quite perfect. All the people looked poor, dear old peasant women in their white caps, little children and young people. They sang hymns and the *Tantum Ergo* and knelt on the cold stones. You would have *loved* it. I think so often of you.[29]

As well as being a candid confession of faith, the letter offers a unique insight into the relationship between Frances and Dorothy. She expressed concern over Gilbert's health and affirmed, in the light of his ailing condition, that she and Frances had been right in being 'really firm about autumn and winter engagements'. Meanwhile she had 'been dreadfully bitten by mosquitoes and flies' and pestered by strangers: 'I find that it is best to keep in fairly populated parts. I have been accosted and followed by strange men several times. They are awful – just like flies. I walk away and leave them to it.'[30]

Four months later, in January 1934, the mother–daughter relationship inspired Frances's best and most ingenious poem. Entitled 'Maria Immaculata: A Sonnet to D. E. C.', it is an acrostic, the initial letters reading downwards forming the name Dorothy Collins. Frances wrote that 'this was written in memory of the statue of Our Lady in the Piazza di Spagna in Rome which was decorated for the feast of the Immaculate Conception, 1929, when we were in Rome':[31]

> *Do* you remember how we walked the streets
> *Of* Rome and saw the Queen of Heaven high,
> *Ra*ised and superb upon her throne, and threw
> *Ou*r roses to her as we passed her by?
> *The* swinging bells rang out the Angelus,
> *Her* head a glory with its starry crown;
> *You* knew She stood for us and all the world
> *Chr*ist's kingdom regnant in the sacred town.
> *Of* all my visions let this never fade
> *La*dy of Stars, the new moon at your feet.
> *Le*t us beloved find Her once again
> *In* Her bright setting in the dusty street,
> *Ne*arer and holier to us whose souls have met
> *So* that you too remember, and I may not forget.[32]

Clearly Maisie Ward had been right when she said that Frances needed a daughter. Although she had coped admirably and stoically in the absence of any children of her own, bestowing her maternal affections on the offspring of friends and relatives, they were an inadequate substitute for the daughter she desired. Dorothy Collins filled the void and fulfilled the desire.

« 23 »

Poland and Prophecy

CHESTERTON BEGAN 1927 IN controversial mood, writing two articles for *Lansbury's Labour Weekly* on the subject of birth control. These were later published together as a pamphlet entitled *Social Reform versus Birth Control*:

> Everybody believes in birth control, and nearly everybody has exercised some control over the conditions of birth. People do not get married as somnambulists or have children in their sleep. But throughout numberless ages and nations, the normal and real birth control is called self control ... In so far as there is a local evil of excess, it comes with all other evils from the squalor and despair of our decaying industrialism. But the thing the capitalist newspapers call birth control is not control at all. It is the idea that people should be, in one respect, completely and utterly uncontrolled, so long as they can evade everything in the function that is positive and creative, and intelligent and worthy of a free man.[1]

To illustrate the point more potently Chesterton drew an unusual parallel with practices in ancient Rome:

> The nearest and most respectable parallel would be that of the Roman epicure, who took emetics at intervals all day so that he might eat five or six luxurious dinners daily. Now any man's common sense, unclouded by newspaper science and long words, will tell him at once that an operation like that of the epicures is likely in the long run even to be bad for his digestion and pretty certain to be bad for his character. Men left to themselves have sense enough to know when a habit obviously savours of perversion and peril. And if it were the fashion in fashionable circles to call the Roman expedient by

the name of 'Diet Control', and to talk about it in a lofty fashion as merely 'the improvement of life and the service of life' (as if it meant no more than the mastery of man over his meals), we should take the liberty of calling it cant and saying that it had no relation to the reality in debate.[2]

Although many advocates of birth control would doubtless argue that Chesterton's comparison with ancient epicureans was not only obscure but irrelevant, he remained defiant:

The fact is, I think, that I am in revolt against the conditions of industrial capitalism and the advocates of Birth Control are in revolt against the conditions of human life. What their spokesmen can possibly mean by saying that I wage a 'class war against mothers' must remain a matter of speculation. If they mean that I do the unpardonable wrong to mothers of thinking they will wish to continue to be mothers, even in a society of greater economic justice and civic equality, then I think they are perfectly right. I doubt whether mothers could escape from motherhood into Socialism. But the advocates of Birth Control seem to want some of them to escape from it into capitalism. They seem to express a sympathy with those who prefer 'the right to earn outside the home' or (in other words) the right to be a wage-slave and work under the orders of a total stranger because he happens to be a richer man. By what conceivable contortions of twisted thought this ever came to be considered a freer condition than that of companionship with the man she has herself freely accepted, I never could for the life of me make out.[3]

If the provocative and controversial rhetoric of his journalism had alienated the 'progressives' in materialistic countries like England and America, he was hailed as a hero and literary giant when he visited Poland in the spring. Travelling by train via Berlin, Gilbert, Frances and Dorothy Collins arrived at the Central Railway Station in Warsaw on 28 April. The warmth of the welcome they received made a lasting impression on Dorothy in particular:

On arrival at Warsaw we were met at the station by an escort of Cavalry Officers and representatives of the PEN Club which had been made responsible by the Government for arranging the visit. This was during the time of Marshall Pilsudski, so everything in Warsaw was very dashing and military. A romantic speech in French was made by one of those gorgeously clad cavalry men, and we were driven with cavalry escort to the Europyski Hotel. The welcoming speech on the station extolled the callings of poet and cavalry officer as being the finest in the world for a layman, which amused G.K. and appealed to the romantic side of his nature. This officer said, 'I will not say you are the chief friend of Poland, for God is our chief friend,' in those words summing up the spirit of the country.[4]

Clearly the panache of the cavalry officer appealed to the romantic side of Dorothy's nature also. However, a less flattering account of the same event was given by Adam Harasowski, an engineering student who acted as an interpreter for Chesterton during the visit:

At the time of G. K. C.'s visit to Poland, all Polish newspapers were full of accounts and stories about this most distinguished of Poland's friends in England; they listed the many personalities and organisations that invited and entertained him, quoted speeches made in his honour and G. K. C.'s replies. Honesty compels me to admit that many Poles were annoyed and frankly disgusted with the very first speech of welcome made on 28 April, 1927 at the Warsaw Central Railway Station by the notorious *bon vivant*, drunkard and womaniser, Colonel Wieniawa-Dlugoszewski, who was then the 'blue-eyed boy' of Marshall Pilsudski, the strong man of Poland at that time. There was a reception committee of the Polish PEN Club, with many illustrious and distinguished men and women, all waiting at the station, but they did not get the chance to speak. The curious thing is that the colonel was not invited to greet Chesterton at the station; he just pushed himself forward, together with a group of Polish cavalry officers – and because he enjoyed the protection of Marshall Pilsudski, nobody dared to stop him. To give him his due, Colonel Wieniawa-Dlugoszewski made quite a witty speech, in passable French, welcoming Chesterton, not as a famous writer, not even as a friend of Poland, but as a born cavalry officer who just missed his profession. Chesterton was very amused and laughed his head off, but the representatives of the PEN Club were understandably not amused.[5]

Thwarted from greeting Chesterton upon his arrival, the feelings of Poland's *literati* found expression in the *Literary News*:

. . . But this admiration would never have reached such an intensity had it not been for a truly exceptional affinity which exists between our distinguished guest and the Polish nation. No other Western writer understands Poland's aspirations and movements as Chesterton does.

He understands her today and understood her in the past, during the years of bondage. Only an intuition that sprang from so great a heart and mind as his could span the abyss that exists at the time between fortunate free England and the tragically struggling Polish nation . . . When we fought for and won our independence, Chesterton always stood for us, a staunch friend, wielding his pen for our cause and branding our bondage as an historical crime . . .

This has brought it about that, alongside of Conrad, Chesterton today is our most popular English writer. Just as he found a deep spiritual relationship in us, so have we found it in the heart of the author of *The Ballad of the White Horse*. This explains why each of his books has been received by us with especial enthusiasm. For our love for the great English writer is based not upon esteem and admiration alone, but upon a deep spiritual and mental kinship.

And this enables us to extend an exceptionally hearty welcome to a great poet and friend . . .[6]

Thus began a five-week courtship between Chesterton and the Polish people, during which he was welcomed in Warsaw, Poznań, Kraków, Lwów and, finally, Vilnius, which was just over the border in Lithuania. From Kraków he made an excursion to the salt mines of Wieliczka and he also found time to visit the mountain resort of Zakopane in the Tatra range. Dorothy wrote in her diary how she was moved by people kneeling and praying in the street at the shrine of Ostra Brama in Vilnius and she also mentioned an excursion to Troki, an old town situated on the shores of the lake bearing the same name. In Troki they visited the temple of the Karaites, a Jewish sect which settled in the region in the fourteenth century and which rejects rabbinical tradition and interprets Scripture literally. Although Chesterton failed to comment on this particular episode of his Polish tour, one can't help but wonder what his wit and theological perception would have made of this Jewish equivalent of Protestantism. They were also taken off the beaten track, their hosts driving them into the countryside to show them the small-scale farms and rural villages where home-based industries produced brightly woven garments and pottery for use locally. Chesterton's heart must have rejoiced to see a nation of peasant proprietors putting distributism into practice. Meanwhile Dorothy, displaying her talent for depicting vividly the sights and sounds of foreign climes, remembered the stay in Lwów and the arduous journey from Warsaw to Vilna (Vilnius):

At Lwów we stayed at the Hotel George, where we were served by peasant women in their national costume and with bare feet – national costume as was worn daily and not put on for tourists. There were no air services in those days and we travelled all over the country in Wagon-Lits by night. From Warsaw to Vilna on the Russian border, I had to share with a Russian woman and in advising me as to whether to take the upper or lower berth, Gilbert remarked, 'What you have to consider is whether you prefer to be stabbed through the front or the back.' I decided for the back and took the upper berth. My companion turned out to be charming! At Vilna where there were still many signs of the oppressive Russian domination, we saw a procession in the Catholic Cathedral and I have never seen such a collection of down and outs, led by an old priest with St Vitus's dance. It was a truly tragic sight.[7]

Dorothy also recounted how Chesterton's charity caused problems in Warsaw:

While we were in Warsaw the entrance of the hotel suddenly became full of beggars of every nationality, with a result that the manager came to see Chesterton to ask him not to give money in the street, as he was acting as a magnet and they found it quite impossible to get rid of the army of beggars who were finding the foreigner such a splendid source of income. This sort of thing happened everywhere he went and, I need not say, in England as well, with this most generous of men, who could never keep ten shillings in his pocket.[8]

According to Adam Harasowski, Dorothy Collins was 'the ideal, super-efficient secretary', and it was certainly true that she was a great help to Frances as well as Gilbert during the Polish trip. In a letter to her mother-in-law, Frances explained that Dorothy could take down dictation so easily that she was able to compose much longer letters home: 'I find Dorothy the greatest possible help, and she is excellent with foreigners and manages to do a great deal for both of us.'[9] In one respect in particular Dorothy was a great help; she was able to accompany Gilbert on some of the taxing evening engagements which Frances found so gruelling:

In the evening Gilbert and the energetic Dorothy Collins went off to have supper in the very famous wine-cellar of the Fukier family which dates from 1610. There apparently they drank Tokay and

Mute (I think that is Mead) and there was a great deal of singing and national songs, both the peasant ones and the military ones and at the end, I am told, a sort of 'He's a jolly good fellow' which is called 'Live for a hundred years' in honour of Gilbert.[10]

It was a great relief to Frances, both physically and emotionally, to be able to offload some of these late-night duties on to Dorothy's shoulders. Physically it was a relief because her health was such that she preferred to remain in the hotel and rest rather than burn midnight oil, but emotionally it was also a relief because she had never been enamoured with the more raucous evening events which were part and parcel of her husband's literary life. The extent to which Frances sometimes found it awkward, and even unpleasant, at these occasions can be gauged from a report of such an evening in a letter to her mother:

The PEN Club Dinner was, I fancy, considered by the Poles a huge success. If numbers indicate anything, it certainly was. I found it a little embarrassing to have to eat hot kidneys and mushrooms standing about with hundreds of guests, and this was only the preliminary to a long dinner that followed and refreshments that apparently continued until two o'clock in the morning. The speeches were really perfectly marvellous and delivered in English quite colloquial and very witty, and showing a detailed knowledge of Gilbert's works which no Englishman of my acquaintance possesses. Gilbert made an excellent, in fact, a very eloquent speech in reply, which drew forth thunders of applause.[11]

Frances's unease at such engagements was recalled by Adam Harasowski:

I remember being very nervous before meeting such a famous man as Chesterton and making my maiden speech of welcome. I need not have been, as from the word 'go' he was very cordial, charming and extremely witty, with a strong sense of humour. I remember that he asked me (after my speech) what Polish word would be most useful for him to remember. I told him he must learn to say: *psia krew*, which means 'dog's blood' and is really a mild swearword, but it is used often to express anger, as well as surprise or admiration. All students roared with laughter and Chesterton laughed with us. Mrs Chesterton did not laugh and was far less at ease during the rest of her stay in Lwów.[12]

The highlight of the Chestertons' two-and-a-half-day sojourn in Lwów was the evening of 19 May, although on this occasion their busy itinerary meant that they were separated from each other. Gilbert was guest of honour at a reception given by the Kasyno i Kolo Literacko-Artystyczne, a club of local writers and artists, while Frances was a special guest of Princess Maria Lubomirska.

On the following day a great crowd of students accompanied their honoured guests to the main railway station to wish them a fond farewell as they caught a train going north to Vilnius. Thus in Lwów, as in the rest of Poland, they had been treated with a reverence and respect beyond their wildest epectations. At Kraków, for instance, where a special performance of *Acropolis* was given in their honour, the manager of the theatre had come in front of the curtain to thank Chesterton in the name of the citizens of Kraków for his defence of Poland 'now and in the past'.[13]

He might have thanked him for his defence of Poland in the future also because as soon as Gilbert arrived back in England in the middle of June, after a week in Belgium recuperating, he agreed to give a lecture on his Polish visit at the Essex Hall. It became something of a prestigious occasion, with the Archbishop of Westminster and many members of the Polish Embassy, including the Minister, in the audience. The title of the lecture had been advertised as 'What Poland is' but this, Chesterton said, was unfortunate. He did not for a moment profess to know what Poland is: 'I should be very sorry if any brilliant Pole asked me what England is. I think it was Aristotle who said you cannot define a living thing, least of all such a living thing as Poland, one of the most living things in the world, because nothing can be so living as a thing which has risen from the dead.'[14]

After Chesterton had delivered his speech, the Professor of English from the University of Kraków, Roman Dyloski, stood up to speak about Gilbert's visit to his country. Dyloski, who according to Chesterton knew all about Polish literature and more about English literature than he did, said that the visit had not only made the Poles admire England – they had always done that – he had made them sincerely love her. He was also glad that Chesterton had realised that they had a sense of humour. The Poles, he said, 'had always had to stand before Europe in a lachrymose attitude, telling the world of their woes. Even during the terrible times when Poland was divided they had produced several humorous writers.'[15] He went on to say that the Polish inheritance of Catholicism, and the fact that they

347

had remained united to Rome, had bound them to the centre of the ideas of civilised Europe.

Gilbert would have agreed heartily with his friend's analysis. Indeed, while he was in Poland he had written the following inscription in the Polish PEN Club album: 'If Poland had not been born again, all the Christian nations would have died.' Although this statement suffers from over-enthusiasm it does contain an essential element of prophecy. If it was true in 1927, it was even more so during the early months of the Second World War, when Belloc wrote, 'the Test is Poland. The determination to save Poland, which is a determination not only to defeat Prussia but to oust the vile and murderous Communism of Moscow, is the moral condition of victory. If we waver we are lost.'[16]

In fact, when Chesterton told those at the Essex Hall that 'nothing can be so living as a thing which has risen from the dead', he was stating something more profound than his audience realised. In the half-century that followed, Poland would die twice more under both German and Soviet occupation, only to rise again. However, although Chesterton would have been less surprised than most to see the rise of the Solidarity trade union in Poland, he would not in a million years have dared to prophesy a Polish pope.

Perhaps the last words on the Polish trip should be left to Gilbert himself, whose most poignant memory was expressed in his *Autobiography*:

I made the acquaintance of a young Count whose huge and costly palace of a country house . . . had been burned and wrecked and left in ruins by the retreat of the Red Army after the Battle of Warsaw. Looking at such a mountain of shattered marbles and black and blasted tapestries one of our party said: 'It must be a terrible thing for you to see your old family home destroyed like this.' But the young man, who was very young in all his gestures, shrugged his shoulders and laughed, at the same time looking a little sad. 'Oh, I do not blame them for that,' he said. 'I have been a soldier myself, and in the same campaign; and I know the temptations. I know what a fellow feels, dropping with fatigue and freezing with cold, when he asks himself what some other fellow's arm-chairs and curtains can matter, if he can only have fuel for the night. On the one side or the other, we were all soldiers; and it is a hard and horrible life. I don't resent at all what they did here. There is only one thing that I really resent. I will show it to you.'

And he led us out into a long avenue lined with poplars; and at the end of it was a statue of the Blessed Virgin, with the head and the hands shot off. But the hands had been lifted; and it is a strange thing that the very mutilation seemed to give more meaning to the attitude of intercession; asking mercy for the merciless race of men.[17]

Amid the general joy and triumphalism that surrounded Chesterton after his return from Poland there was one small but powerful plaintive voice crying in the wilderness. Karel Capek, the Czech author, wrote mournfully from Prague: 'You wrote me that it would be difficult for you to come to Prague this spring. But it was in the newspapers that you were last month in Warsaw; why in Heaven's sake did you not come to Prague on this occasion? What a pity for us! Now we are waiting for a compensation.'[18]

In fact, Capek was a great admirer of Chesterton and wrote on several other occasions beseeching him to come to Prague:

It is just Christmas Eve; my friends presented me with some of your books, and I cannot omit to thank you for the consolation and trust I found there as already so many times. Be blessed, Mr Chesterton.

I wrote you twice without getting any answer; but it is Christian to insist, and so I write you again. Please, would you be so kind to tell me, if it shall be possible for you to come next year to Prague? Our PEN club is anxious to invite you as our guest of honour. If you would like to come next spring, I beg you to be my guest. You are fond of old things: Prague is one. You shall find here so many people who cherish you. I like you myself as no other writer; it's for yours sake that being in London I went to habit in Notting Hill and it is for yours sake that I liked it. I cannot believe that I should not meet you again. Please, come to Prague.

I wish you a happy New Year, Mr Chesterton. You must be happy, making your readers happier. You are so good.[19]

It is difficult to imagine Chesterton failing to be charmed by such a letter, not so much by the praise and flattery as by the gallant and earnest endeavours of a great writer to express himself in a foreign language. Sadly, however, Gilbert never got to Prague. Neither did he ever get to Australia where similar letters besought him to come and lecture, nor Austria where the Vienna PEN Club sought him.

The fact was that he had become a literary figure of truly international standing. His books had been translated into French, German, Dutch, Czech, Polish, Spanish, Italian and Hebrew, and a letter from Russia asked for his photograph for the *Magazine of International Literature* as his works were well known in the Soviet Union. The writer and historian Philip Guedalla wrote the following letter illustrating Chesterton's position in Argentina: 'The Argentine Intelligencia is acutely aware of your writings. Local professors terrified me by asking me on various occasions to explain the precise position which you occupied in our Catholic youth . . . A visit from you would mean a very great deal to British intellectual prestige in these parts.'[20] It is interesting to note that this particular legacy lingers on, since the recent call for Chesterton's canonisation emerged, somewhat surprisingly, from the Argentinian intelligentsia.

Two weeks after his return from Poland, on Tuesday, 28 June, Gilbert gave the seventh in a series of centenary addresses in the Great Hall of University College, London. Bearing in mind his international standing it was perhaps no surprise that Sir Gregory Foster, the Provost of the College and chairman of the meeting, should introduce his guest speaker in glowing terms:

> Ladies and Gentlemen, there is probably no country in the world in which it is necessary to introduce Mr Gilbert Chesterton. There is certainly no place in this country in which he is not known. We have the proud satisfaction of knowing that he is specially well known here. He was a member of the Slade School. I believe that during his period of studentship he frequented lectures in other Faculties almost as much as he frequented the Slade School. At all events, whether that was strictly according to rule or not, we know that it was a very wise proceeding.
>
> Without more ado I welcome Mr Gilbert Chesterton, in your name, back to the College, and I invite him to give his address, 'Culture and the Coming Peril'.[21]

There then followed a speech by Chesterton which was arguably the best he ever gave. Certainly it exhibited his charm, his wit, his humour and his wisdom to great effect. Above all, it exhibited an uncanny perception of the future – the hallmark of a prophet. If he had been hailed as a prophet in Poland, he was now clearly cast in the role of a prophet at home.

After an introduction imbued with humility and humour it was

not long before the speaker got round to the serious business of his
argument:

> ... you will hear a vast amount about the danger of Bolshevism.
> When I talk about the coming peril a very large number of people
> will probably imagine that I do mean Bolshevism. I quite agree that
> Bolshevism would be a peril, but I do not think it is coming. I do
> not think that, especially in England, we have either the virtues or
> the vices of a revolution. The kind of thing that I want to suggest
> to you is something that is coming of itself, or at least it is capable
> of coming of itself ... I suppose that the very simplest name for it
> is 'vulgarity' ... I do not know whether it would be safe in such a
> connection to whisper the word 'America', now by far the wealthiest
> of States and, in the degraded conditions of our day, therefore the
> most influential.[22]

Having defined what exactly he meant by 'vulgarity and its war
against Culture', he returned to the crux of the matter:

> To put it shortly, the evil I am trying to warn you of is not excessive
> democracy, it is not excessive ugliness, it is not excessive anarchy. It
> might be stated thus: It is standardisation by a low standard.
> Consider, as I say, that example of advertisement ... The first thing
> that strikes one about it is the space occupied, the insensibility to the
> idea of size. The spaces that are now occupied by an advertisement
> of some highly dubious wine or some practically poisonous quack
> medicine are large enough to have been the shrines of gods or great
> saints, to have been a place for the emblazonment of great national
> coats-of-arms, to have held the proclamations of Napoleon or of the
> French Revolution, to have been used for a hundred striking and
> dominant purposes by our fathers in the past. They are now entirely
> surrendered to trivialities.[23]

Towards the end of his address Chesterton hinted that his analysis of
the problem had only scratched the surface of any solution. However,
without being drawn into a discourse on either religion or politics, it
was clear that he knew where the solution was to be found:

> That danger of standardisation by a low standard seems to me to
> be the chief danger confronting us on the artistic and cultural side
> and generally on the intellectual side at this moment.
> I am not going to attempt, as I have already talked far too long,

to argue at any great length about the remedy. If I were to mention my own social remedies, I should be talking politics; and if I were to mention my own deeper remedies, I should be talking theology . . .

My only purpose this afternoon is to bear my testimony to the fact that there never was a time in the whole history of the human race when it was more necessary to defend the intellectual independence of man than this hour in which we live.[24]

If these were the words of one speaking as a prophet, he found, in the tradition of many of his predecessors, that a prophet at home is seldom given a hearing. Like the Czech writer Čapek, Chesterton had a powerful and plaintive voice that went unheeded. However, whether this was true in the wider context of England as a whole, it would be unfair to suggest that it was true of his audience at the Great Hall of University College. On the contrary, his address was greeted with 'loud and continued applause'. Indeed, the most fitting tribute to his performance that evening was given by Sir Gregory Foster in his concluding remarks. Any other comment would be superfluous:

I will only just put into words what you have already expressed by your applause, namely, our thanks to Mr Chesterton for his address. Like most things that Mr Chesterton does, it was unexpected. I do not suppose that any one of us reading the title of his address was able to forecast at all accurately what he has so brilliantly said, and for that very reason we have all enjoyed it immensely. We thank you very much.[25]

« 24 »

Home and Homelessness

IN THE SUMMER OF 1927 Chesterton's *Collected Poems* were published by Cecil Palmer. Yet the volume, the most extensive collection of his verse to have appeared in print thus far, was by no means complete. On the contrary, there were many curious omissions, and none of the poems from *The Queen of Seven Swords* was included. Gilbert, home again at Top Meadow after the tour of Poland, inscribed a copy of the *Collected Poems* to Dorothy Collins:

> Here you watch the Bard's Career,
> Month by month and year by year,
> Writing, writing, writing verse,
> Worse and worse and worse and worse.[1]

One suspects that Chesterton was far happier being the Bard of Beaconsfield than he was being the Prophet of Poland or any other role involving too much travel or trauma. Certainly Frances was happier in her English country garden during the long summer months than she was touring the world as the wife of an internationally famous husband. Back in Beaconsfield, therefore, they began once again to settle into a secluded domestic routine. Yet the seclusion was only partial, since they still received guests regularly at Top Meadow and were invited often by friends elsewhere. For example, soon after their return from Poland they were guests at the wedding of Peter Belloc, Hilaire's son. Among the other guests was Father Vincent McNabb, who wrote to Gilbert on 18 August: 'At Peter Belloc's wedding I remember we talked a little on Blessed Thomas More. I spoke of his *Dyalogue of Comforte* written in the Tower. I picked up a copy for a few pence. If you have no copy I should be honoured if you would keep the copy I now send.'[2]

One imagines that Gilbert would have been delighted to receive this addition to his library, since he was a great admirer of St Thomas More, described by Father Vincent in his letter as 'the genius, hero, saint who began his *Dyalogue of Comforte* in an English Prison in winter and finished it (the writing gear having been taken from him) with a burnt stick'. In fact, Father Vincent would later compare Chesterton to More, commenting that they 'were both Cockneys', and the Franciscan, Father Cuthbert, remarking on the mental resemblance between More and Chesterton, said that he could quite well imagine them sitting together making jokes, some of them very good and some of them very bad.[3] Certainly in one key respect they shared a bond, for Chesterton and More were both laymen who had a great love for the world and its legitimate pleasures – even if ultimately they preferred the things of heaven.

In October Gilbert was again offering public support to his sister-in-law, though on this occasion he was supporting her in a project far removed from the play she had written the previous year. Ada was working as a journalist for the *Sunday Express*, and one evening she had become involved in a heated discussion about the plight of London's homeless women. Incensed by the suggestion that any woman could get work as a domestic servant if she wanted it, she decided to prove the matter for herself:

> I would be a homeless woman – with all that it implied – and discover for myself what really happened ... The Editor agreed, and it was arranged that for a fortnight I should leave my home, without a penny in my pocket, chance my luck on what I could earn or beg, and not until the time was up go back to the Cottage ...
>
> I have had many adventures ... But of all my experiences I think the first night as a down-and-out remains the most vital and discovering. It is a queer feeling to shed your habits, identity, clothes, customs, and without protective social covering emerge in the raw.
>
> During that fortnight I went right to the depths of penury and hunger, sampled filthy beds, met thieves and prostitutes, hard-working and respectable women whose only crime was poverty. I found mere girls completely down and out, the bloom still on their cheeks, though hope was dead in their hearts.
>
> I had to walk the streets when I could not get a bed, for I found there were too few beds for the destitute, and I tramped and tramped, until I was drugged with tramping and my sodden clothes clung to my tired body. I was walking

drunk, and hungry drunk, and could not look a well-fed human in the face.[4]

She recorded her experiences in a series of articles for the *Sunday Express* and subsequently in a book entitled *In Darkest London*. The response from a shocked public was overwhelming, and Ada decided that she would establish a fund to raise money to help alleviate the plight of London's destitute women. Her cause was helped when the Bishop of London preached a sermon on her book, and she was given added assistance when Queen Mary sent a sizeable cheque for the project. Eventually the laudable ideals became translated into bricks and mortar as the first public lodging house for homeless women was opened. The rules were simple; any woman could get a clean bed with plenty of hot water for baths, tea and biscuits, for one shilling a night – and even this small fee was waived if the applicant did not possess a shilling. The one other rule was that no questions were ever asked of any applicant, the need of a bed being the only qualification required. Five such homes were eventually opened and they became known as Cecil Houses, the name Ada had chosen as 'a memorial to my husband who had always fought on the side of the poor'.[5] The homes were a fitting memorial indeed, since they are still performing a valuable service nearly seventy years later in Lambeth, Holborn and Ealing. Many celebrities from the worlds of literature, drama and music queued up to assist in the financing of these Cecil Houses, including Bernard Shaw, Hugh Walpole, Clemence Dane, Edith Evans, Louis Golding, Sir Cedric Hardwicke, Aldous Huxley, Sir Thomas Beecham, Ian Hay, Alec Waugh, Sheila Kaye Smith and Harold Nicolson.

According to Ada, Frances showed 'sympathy' and 'enthusiasm' for the project and she reviewed *In Darkest London* 'very beautifully' in *G. K.'s Weekly*.[6] Frances also accompanied her husband to a meeting in support of the Cecil Houses at Wyndham's Theatre, chaired by John Galsworthy. Speakers at the meeting, at which it was announced that nearly £1,600 had been secured in donations towards new houses, included John Drinkwater, Sir Gerald du Maurier, Lady Lovat and Margaret Bondfield, the Labour MP. Sybil Thorndike also spoke, making 'an earnest appeal on behalf of . . . her less fortunate sisters'.[7] However, it was Chesterton who stole the show, and the headlines in the following morning's papers, with a humorous speech in which he descibed the comfort and hospitality of the Cecil Houses: 'I have often

355

wanted to stay at one myself, because of its friendly atmsophere, and have wondered if I could secure admission as a pinched and starving seamstress, or perhaps a jolly Irish apple woman.'[8] The vision of Chesterton's vast frame in the guise of an Irish apple woman was too much of a temptation for at least one Fleet Street cartoonist, and the caricature of Gilbert in that unlikely disguise appeared in the next day's papers.

During the same month, October, yet another collection of Father Brown stories was published. *The Secret of Father Brown* was dedicated to Father O'Connor, 'whose truth is stranger than fiction with a gratitude greater than the world'.[9] In Father O'Connor's personal copy of the book, presented to him by the author, Chesterton had inscribed the following:

> Some sneer; some snigger; some simper;
> In the youth where we laughed, and sang.
> And *they* may end with a whimper
> But *we* will end with a bang.[10]

In fact, this verse has often been dated erroneously as late as 1936 when Chesterton recited it during a radio broadcast, but its origination in 1927 has singular significance. It was intended as a riposte 'to young pessimists', and there was no doubt that Chesterton had one particular 'pessimist' in mind. T. S. Eliot had proclaimed in his poem *The Hollow Men*, published two years earlier, that the world would end 'not with a bang but a whimper'. This, to Chesterton, was cynical defeatism and an example of post-war decadence.

Meanwhile, Eliot, for his part, was not particularly impressed with Chesterton. In fact, when Gilbert's biography of Robert Louis Stevenson was published in November, Eliot, reviewing it for the *Nation and Athenaeum*, admitted to finding Chesterton's style 'exasperating to the last point of endurance'. However, he was full of praise for Chesterton's appreciation of Stevenson's style, and the way he had sought 'to expound a Roman Catholic point of view towards *Dr Jekyll and Mr Hyde*'.[11]

Eliot had ended his review with the wry observation that Stevenson was an author well enough established to survive Chesterton's approval. The same might equally be said of Chesterton with regard to Eliot. Yet Eliot's main complaint had little to do with Stevenson but sprang from his feeling that Chesterton had been unfair to the new generation of young poets: 'We are not all so completely immersed in ignorance, prejudice and heresy as Mr Chesterton assumes. He seems always to assume that what his reader has previously believed is exactly the opposite of what Mr Chesterton knows to be true.'[12]

He had a valid point. His own poetry was not as it seemed, and beneath the sardonic surface of his verse sprang a hopefulness which was the very reverse of the decadence and despair of which he stood accused. Eighteen months later he wrote to Chesterton in a spirit of reconciliation: 'I should like extremely to come to see you one day. I do not expect to have the leisure, or the brain power, before July ... May I mention that I have much sympathy with your political and social views, as well as (with obvious reservations) your religious views? And that your study of Dickens was always a delight to me.'[13]

Regardless of whether his original review was coloured by an artificial antagonism, it is clear that Eliot had not been impressed with Chesterton's *Robert Louis Stevenson*. Not everyone was so dismissive. Sir Edmund Gosse wrote to Gilbert, thanking him for writing it:

> I have just finished reading the book in which you smite the detractors of R. L. S. hip and thigh. I cannot express without a sort of hyperbole the sentiments which you have awakened of joy, of satisfaction, of relief, of malicious and vindictive pleasure . . .
>
> It is and always since his death has been impossible for me to write anything which went below the surface of R. L. S. I loved him, and still love him, too tenderly to analyse him. But you, who have the privilege of not being dazzled by having known him, have taken the task into your strong competent hands. You could not have done it better.
>
> The latest survivor, the only survivor, of his early circle of intimate friends thanks you from the bottom of his heart.[14]

It was announced in the Stevenson book that two further 'Intimate Biographies' by Chesterton, of Savonarola and Napoleon, would be published in the near future. Sadly, neither ever materialised. Instead Chesterton would be preoccupied throughout the following year with financial worries over the future of *G. K.'s Weekly*. On 24 February 1928 he wrote an appeal to all shareholders of the paper:

> I am venturing to send you this statement at what is admittedly a crisis in the history of the paper; but is also even more certainly a crisis in

357

the controversy for which this paper exists . . . For us the crisis may be the end; in the sense of the end of this journalistic experiment. But in the larger field also it is the beginning of the end; not perhaps the end of journalism; but certainly the end of independent journalism. That movement towards a millionaire monopoly of the press, which was lately called impossible, is now called inevitable. There are few organs of which any wise man will now say that they may not pass sooner or later into a plutocratic combine. One of the few exceptions is our own . . . This organ of opinion may be smashed, but it will not be sold; it may be annihilated, but it will not be amalgamated . . .

I should never have agreed to start this paper if it had merely been a matter of profit. I should not be making such an appeal now if I were attempting to pretend that it is in the ordinary sense profitable. We are near the end of our resources; and we do not promise that such resources as we may gain can do anything but sustain the effort for its own sake. But there is a reasonable and practical chance of doing more; and if we save ourselves we may even perhaps save our country.[15]

Times were certainly difficult for the paper, and matters reached a crisis point after it became apparent that a deficit of £1,000 had been concealed from Chesterton in the hope that increased advertising might reduce it. For a time there were real fears that Gilbert might finally call it a day and close the paper down. Such a decision would have met with wholehearted approval from Frances, who had confided to Father O'Connor that she prayed that he would give it up. She was concerned that *G. K.'s Weekly* was 'dissipating his energies' and that it was thrusting his other work into the background or, in the case of the proposed biographies of Savonarola and Napoleon, into oblivion. Gilbert, however, listened to the advice of a group of young members of the central branch of the Distributist League who had far-reaching plans for putting the paper on to a sound financial footing. W. R. Titterton resigned as assistant editor, was replaced by Edward Macdonald and the paper emerged to fight another day. One League member, Desmond Gleeson, remembered ruefully how Chesterton's position had appeared a little incongruous: 'The young men from the Central Branch with their awareness that finance mattered must have seemed a little alien to the Bohemian spirit of Chesterton.'[16]

An invaluable account of Gilbert's editorship of the paper was given by Brocard Sewell who was a wide-eyed sixteen-year-old fresh from public school when, in September 1928, he took his first job as 'office-boy and general factotum to *G. K.'s Weekly*'.[17] Many years later, writing as an eighty-year-old Trappist monk, Sewell still retained a vivid and childlike memory of his days at the paper:

> Our editor, Mr Chesterton, we saw once a month only, apart from his occasional appearance at Distributist meetings in London . . . With his great size and girth, the ascent of our steep and shaky old staircase was trying for him, and we could hear him wheezing and groaning on his way up, until he came through the office door and sank into the editorial swivel-chair, which was just, but only just, big enough and strong enough to support him. His 'absentee' editorship worked very well, for there was an assistant editor in charge on the spot who put the paper together each week and saw it through the press. Mr Chesterton's 'copy' . . . always arrived in good time by post, or, if he had been delayed in writing it, by train, from which I collected it at Marylebone Station . . .
>
> When he appeared in the office our editor was always in genial mood, for he enjoyed being in London, and his conversation was always of a rare brilliance, and highly entertaining. I think Chesterton's conversation must have been even better than Oscar Wilde's; but it had been less well received. Wilde was not really a conversationalist; more of a solo performer. Chesterton's jests and quips were spontaneous; Wilde's were often carefully prepared beforehand and held in reserve until opportunity for their use arose.[18]

Further anecdotal memories of Chesterton at this time were provided by his assistant editor, Edward Macdonald: 'He loved all the jokes about his size. He was the first to see the point and to roar with laughter when Douglas Woodruff introduced him to a meeting as "Mr Chesterton who has just been looking round in America . . ."'[19] On another occasion, seeing the disordered pile of papers on his assistant editor's desk and complimenting him on having a filing system that demanded a keen memory, he remarked ruefully that he wished they'd let him have a desk like it at home. Macdonald also recalled that Chesterton didn't want a cartoon of himself printed unless it was 'highly satirical, insulting and otherwise unflattering'. After assurances that the cartoon was far from flattering (it depicted an obese Chesterton perched precariously on a stool, attempting to milk a cow), he permitted it to be published – on the front page!

Although Brocard Sewell had remembered that Chesterton enjoyed being in London, the fact was that he enjoyed his trips to the city only because they were comparatively rare. As with all his travels, they were either enjoyed as a novelty or endured as a necessity. They were never undertaken for their own sake or as an escape from home. On the contrary, as Chesterton got older he grew increasingly dependent on the company and security of his wife in Beaconsfield. It wasn't only in the field of politics that he was a firm advocate of Home Rule. For this reason he seldom attended the regular meetings of the central branch of the Distributist League, which took place at the Devereux Inn, just outside the Temple, a minute's walk from the offices of *G. K.'s Weekly*. Again, Brocard Sewell recalled Chesterton's rare visits to London:

> Chesterton himself did not come often to The Devereux. The meetings did not finish until 9.30, when the Distributists and their guests descended to the bar on the ground floor for a final social half-hour. By 9.30 it would have been too late and too tiring for him to have to make the journey back to Beaconsfield, and he did not care to be away from his home for a night unless it was unavoidable. When he did have to spend a night, or a few days, in town he usually stayed at Artillery Mansions, in Victoria Street, where I sometimes had to take him proofs that needed immediate attention, or collect from him an article for the *Weekly*.[20]

The best description of Gilbert's life in Beaconsfield at this time is provided by Dorothy Collins:

> He was completely unselfconscious about his work and could work anywhere I could balance a typewriter. In the most unlikely places he would suddenly say, 'I think we will do a little work, if you're sure you don't mind.' When he was at home, he never missed a day's work. He went very late to bed and was equally late in the morning, having his breakfast at about 10 and coming into the study by 10.30 where he worked all day. On the occasions when the Catholic Church demanded attendance at Mass on a weekday, as it was a small parish there would be only an early morning Mass and he would drag himself from his bed. As he got fasting into the car, I have heard him say, 'What but religion would bring us to such a pass?' But never did I know him miss a Day of Obligation either at home or abroad . . .
>
> When he was at home, he worked from about 10.30 until dinner-time, with small pauses for lunch and tea. After dinner, he would sit at a table with his books and his cigars, either reading a

detective story or making a few notes for the next day's work in a shorthand of his own invention which no one else could read. He talked about his work quite often before he started, but never when he was actually dictating, which he did straight to the machine, reading each page as it came off the typewriter. As he knew exactly what he wanted to say there was only an occasional alteration. He had a prodigious memory and could quote from readings of his youth without further reference, especially from Dickens. He would map out a book with the headings, and would dictate chapter by chapter, though not always in the final order.

There were many calls on his purse, as he was educating various children in whom he and Frances were interested. To this pressure and to large printer's bills for *G. K.'s Weekly*, we owe some of the Father Brown stories. I would say, 'We have only got £100 in the bank.' 'Oh, well. We must write another Father Brown story,' and this would be done at lightning speed a day or two later from a few notes on the back of an envelope.[21]

The fact that the ever-popular Father Brown books were churned out in such a carefree fashion probably indicated Chesterton's carefree, or even careless, approach to the writing of detective fiction. Certainly he did not share the opinion of the critic who believed Father Brown a worthy rival to Sherlock Holmes. In *Generally Speaking*, a further collection of his journalism from the *Illustrated London News* and the only new Chesterton title to appear in 1928, he declared the undisputed superiority of Holmes:

> When all is said and done, there have never been better detective stories than the old series of Sherlock Holmes; and though the name of that magnificent magician has been spread over the whole world, and is perhaps the one great popular legend made in the modern world, I do not think that Sir Arthur Conan Doyle has ever been thanked enough for them. As one of many millions, I offer my own mite of homage.[22]

Another 'magnificent magician' analysed in *Generally Speaking* was Peter Pan. Yet Chesterton had considerably less respect for J. M. Barrie's creation than he had for Conan Doyle's:

> A very fine problem of poetic philosophy might be presented as the problem of Peter Pan. He is represented as a sort of everlasting elf, a child who never changes age after age, but who in this story falls in

love with a little girl who is a normal person. He is given his choice between becoming normal with her or remaining immortal without her; and either choice might have been made a fine and effective thing. He might have said that he was a god, that he loved all but could not live for any; that he belonged not to them but to multitudes of unborn children. Or he might have chosen love, with the inevitable result of love, which is incarnation; and the inevitable result of incarnation, which is crucifixion; yes, if it were only crucifixion by becoming a clerk in a bank and growing old. But it was the fork of the road; and even in fairyland you cannot walk down two roads at once. The one real fault of sentimentalism in this fairy play is the compromise that is ultimately made; whereby he shall go free for ever but meet his human friend once a year. Like most practical compromises, it is the most unpractical of all possible courses of action. Even the baby in that nursery could have seen that Wendy would be ninety in no time, after what would appear to her immortal lover a mere idle half-hour.[23]

There were many other examples of Chesterton's finest journalism in this collection, most notably a devastating attack on the materialism of Thomas Edison and a discussion of the causes behind the pessimism of Thomas Hardy. *Generally Speaking* was published on 18 October 1928. Two days later an article in *G. K.'s Weekly* returned to the theme of pessimism:

There is a sense in which men may be made normally happy; but there is another sense in which we may truly say, without undue paradox, that what they want is to get back to their normal unhappiness. At present they are suffering from an utterly abnormal unhappiness. They have got all the tragic elements essential to the human lot to contend with; time and death and bereavement and unrequited affection and dissatisfaction with themselves. But they have not got the elements of consolation and encouragement that ought normally to renew their hopes or restore their self-respect. They have not got vision or conviction, or the mastery of their work, or the loyalty of their household, or any form of human dignity. Even the latest Utopians, the last lingering representatives of that fated and unfortunate race, do not really promise the modern man that he shall do anything, or own anything, or in any effectual fashion be anything. They only promise that, if he keeps his eyes open, he will see something; he will see the Universal Trust or the World State or Lord Melchett coming in the clouds in glory. But the modern man cannot even keep his eyes open. He is too weary with toil and a long succession of unsuccessful Utopias. He has fallen asleep.[24]

With this article Chesterton could have been writing a prophetic introduction to the future pessimistic visions of George Orwell. In fact, however, he was unwittingly raising the curtain on Orwell's literary career. On 29 December 1928 Orwell's first published work in English appeared in *G. K.'s Weekly*. Entitled 'A Farthing Newspaper', it was a bitterly ironic attack on the launch, and rapid rise in popularity, of a heavily subsidised newspaper in Paris. The *Ami du Peuple* was sold at a remarkably low price and purported to be published in the interest of 'the people' but was, in fact, the property of a millionaire industrialist who was using it to 'sell' the concept of paternalistic capitalism:

> And supposing that this sort of thing is found to pay in France, why should it not be tried elsewhere? Why should we not have our farthing, or at least halfpenny newspaper in London? While the journalist exists merely as the publicity agent of big business, a large circulation, got by fair means or foul, is a newspaper's one and only aim ... Here, then, is a worthy example for our English Press magnates. Let them imitate the *Ami du Peuple* and sell their newspapers at a farthing. Even if it does no other good whatever, at any rate the poor devils of the public will at last feel that they are getting the correct value for their money.[25]

The parallels between Orwell's article in *G. K.'s Weekly* and Chesterton's appeal to the paper's shareholders earlier in the year to fight 'the millionaire monopoly of the press' are striking. It is scarcely surprising, therefore, that Orwell should have received a sympathetic hearing in Chesterton's paper. However, although *G. K.'s Weekly* had given Orwell his first break into English journalism, he had already made minor inroads in France. On the day that his article was published in England, the radical journal *Le Progrès Civique* published an article he had written on unemployment. In January the same journal published two more of his articles – one on tramps, one on beggars. He was certainly qualified to write such an article because he was living in abject poverty on the streets of Paris at the time, experiencing the same squalor and despair that Ada Chesterton had depicted in *In Darkest London*. Later, of course, Orwell was to enjoy literary success with *Down and Out in Paris and London*, his own account of personal deprivation. Yet Orwell's homelessness was never merely physical; it was metaphysical also. He never found an intellectual or ideological home and even when he began to mix with the Trotskyists who influenced him temporarily during the Thirties, he maintained an enigmatic independence. Indeed, as late as 1935 he told a friend that 'what England needed was to follow the kind of policies in Chesterton's *G. K.'s Weekly*'.[26]

« 25 »

Rome and Romance

On 23 March 1929 Chesterton wrote an article for *G. K.'s Weekly* on modern advertising. The article had been prompted by an essay which proclaimed that good salesmanship made 'everything in the garden beautiful'. Using the example of Eden as an ideal testing-ground for such a theory, Gilbert explained why he failed to be sold on the idea:

> There was only one actor in that ancient drama who seems to have had any real talent for salesmanship. He seems to have undertaken to deliver the goods with exactly the right preliminaries of promise and praise. He knew all about advertisement: we may say he knew all about publicity, though not at the moment addressing a very large public. He not only took up the slogan of Eat More Fruit, but he distinctly declared that any customers purchasing his particular brand of fruit would instantly become as gods. And as this is exactly what is promised to the purchasers of every patent medicine, popular tonic, saline draught or medicinal wine at the present day, there can be no question that he was in advance of his age. It is extraordinary that humanity, which began with the apple and ended with the patent medicine, has not even yet become exactly like gods. It is still more extraordinary (and probably the result of a malicious interpolation by priests at a later date) that the record ends with some extraordinary remarks to the effect that one thus pursuing the bright career of Salesmanship is condemned to crawl on his stomach and eat a great deal of dirt.[1]

This article was typical of Chesterton's writing at the time, since it seemed that he ascribed a religious significance to every subject he came across. It was not surprising, therefore, that six weeks later he wrote to Maurice Baring offering his praise for the latter's latest religious novel, *The Coat Without Seam*. Earlier Virginia Woolf had attacked Baring's 'superficiality', and he had been attacked by others who believed his novels were merely a front for Catholic propaganda. Such an accusation was scarcely likely to elicit an attack from Chesterton, who announced that he had been 'much uplifted' by his friend's latest book:

> It is, as you say, extraordinary how the outer world can see everything about it except the point. It is curiously so with much of the very good Catholic work now being done in literature, especially in France. The Protestant English, who prided themselves on their common sense, seem now to be dodging about and snatching at anything except the obvious ... I am only a vulgar controversial journalist, and never pretended to be a novelist; my writing cannot in any case be so subtle or delicate as yours. But even I find that if I make the point of a story stick out like a spike, they carefully go and impale themselves on something else. But there are plenty of people who will appreciate anything as good as *The Coat Without Seam*.[2]

In fact, Chesterton had long been an admirer of Baring's fiction. Five years earlier, when Baring's *C* had been published, he had written of his friend's realism and his ability to appreciate that 'medieval men were men and medieval minds were minds': 'God moves in a mysterious way; and considering that most people would expect Catholic literature to be rather romantic, it will be very amusing if the new Catholic literature turns out to be strictly realistic; and beats the realists at their own game.'[3]

In the following decades, the novels of Evelyn Waugh and Graham Greene would epitomise the realism of twentieth-century Catholic literature. In the meantime, Chesterton was content to let Baring and a handful of others practise the art of the Catholic novel while he concentrated on controversy. He did, however, publish a volume of short stories in July 1929 entitled *The Poet and the Lunatics*. The stories were both romantic and fantastic, the apparent antithesis of the realism he had praised in Baring's novels. Yet realism shone through the romance and fact through the fantasy, as the poet Gabriel Gale, the central character of all the stories, proved his sanity in the face of the lunacy of his adversaries. In one of the stories a character named Saunders is cured of his belief that he is God when Gale drags him to a tree and pins him there with a pitchfork. Helplessly humiliated in this position, and in considerable discomfort, Saunders becomes aware of his own limitations and ultimate mortality. It is then that Chesterton, through the character of Gale, delivers the profundity of his message. His violence was the only remedy for Saunders who needed the 'acute, practical, painful discovery that he could not control matter or the elements'.[4] Appeasement would have served only to reinforce his delusions: 'There is no cure for that nightmare of omnipotence except pain; because that is the thing a man *knows* he would not tolerate if he could really control it.'[5] The extent of this statement can be gauged by the fact that Chesterton was here suggesting a solution to the problem of pain, on which C. S. Lewis wrote a whole book, in a single sentence. It illustrates his remarkable perception and, as important, an uncanny ability to communicate it succinctly.

Another example of realism in *The Poet and the Lunatics* was provided in the complaint of a hermit who accosts the agents of the law in the market place: 'Do you imagine because you kill men now by modern machinery and modern law, that we do not know that you are as likely to kill unjustly as Herod or Heliogabulus? Do you think we do not know that the powers of the world are what they always were, that your lawyers who oppress the poor for hire will shed innocent blood for gold?'[6]

It was in his capacity as a short-story writer that Gilbert was asked to join the Detection Club when this was founded by Anthony Berkeley, the mystery writer, in 1929. Berkeley had written to Chesterton that the Club 'would be quite incomplete without the creator of Father Brown'.[7] Other members of the original group were Dorothy L. Sayers, Freeman Wills Crofts, Austen Freeman, Father Ronald Knox, E. C. Bentley and Agatha Christie. Eventually others were invited to join, including Margery Allingham, Gladys Mitchell, Ngaio Marsh and John Dickson Carr.

Chesterton was elected as its first president, or Ruler, so that he had the fun of officiating at the club's whimsically bizarre initiation ceremony for new members. To qualify, prospective members had to have written two mysteries and to have been sponsored by two existing members. At this annual rite, first held at the Northumberland Hotel in a large basement party room, Gilbert sat waiting in total darkness, enthroned and robed ceremoniously in the style of Fu Manchu in a scarlet and black Mandarin coat and tiny pillbox hat. The doors were flung open and the members entered in a procession, the first carrying Eric the skull on a black cushion, flanked by torch bearers, and followed by other wardens with the implements of their trade – daggers, guns, vials of poison and blunt instruments. Chesterton, as Ruler, then cried out in a loud voice: 'What mean these lights, these ceremonies, and this reminder of our mortality?' At this point the initiation ceremony commenced in earnest.[8] Carried out by candlelight, with proper and preposterous decorum, the whole affair was a self-conscious parody of the pomp of Masonic ritual. Indeed, when Gilbert publicised the initiation ceremony in an article he wrote about the club, he made a particular point of reprinting the ritual in full, 'thereby setting a good example to the Mafia, the Ku Klux Klan, the Illuminati . . . and all the other secret societies which now conduct the greater part of public life, in the age of Publicity and Public Opinion'.[9]

The authorship of the initiation ceremony has been a matter of some dispute. James Brabazon, Sayers's biographer, maintained that Sayers had written it in the style of the Book of Common Prayer, while Evelyn Waugh, in his biography of Father Ronald Knox, claimed that it was simply an adaptation of a code of rules set out by Knox in 1928 in his introduction to *The Best Detective Stories of the Year*. Barbara Reynolds, in her more recent biography of Sayers, was content to compromise, claiming that Sayers 'was at least part author of their amusing initiation ceremony'.[10] Perhaps it is appropriate that the authorship of the Detection Club's ceremony should remain a mystery, yet it is certainly beyond doubt that its substance is no longer a secret because of Chesterton's decision to publish it. It is worth reprinting in full for both humorous and historic reasons:

The Ruler shall say to the Candidate:

M.N. Is it your firm desire to become a Member of the Detection Club?

Then the Candidate shall answer in a loud voice:

That is my desire.

Ruler:

Do you promise that your detectives shall well and truly detect the crimes presented to them using those wits which it may please you to bestow upon them and not placing reliance on nor making use of Divine Revelation, Feminine Intuition, Mumbo Jumbo, Jiggery-Pokery, Coincidence or Act of God?

Candidate:

I do.

Ruler:

Do you solemnly swear never to conceal a vital clue from the reader?

Candidate:

I do.

Ruler:

Do you promise to observe a seemly moderation in the use of Gangs, Conspiracies, Death-Rays, Ghosts, Hypnotism, Trap-Doors, Chinamen, Super-Criminals and Lunatics; and utterly and for ever to forswear Mysterious Poisons unknown to Science?

Candidate:

I do.

Ruler:

Will you honour the King's English?

Candidate:

I will.

Then the Ruler shall ask:

M.N. Is there anything you hold sacred?

Then the Candidate having named a Thing which he holds of peculiar sanctity, the Ruler shall ask:

M.N. Do you swear by *(here the Ruler shall name the Thing which the Candidate has declared to be his Peculiar Sanctity)* to observe faithfully all these promises which you have made, so long as you are a member of the Club?

But if the Candidate is not able to name a Thing which he holds sacred, then the Ruler shall propose the Oath in this manner following:

M.N. Do you, as you hope to increase your Sales, swear to observe faithfully all these promises which you have made, so long as you are a member of the Club?[11]

Perhaps the Detection Club's initiation ceremony gave Chesterton the inspiration for the title of his next book. Entitled *The Thing*, it consisted of thirty-five essays which had been published previously either in magazines or in the Catholic newspaper the *Universe*. The Thing which Chesterton 'declared to be his Peculiar Sanctity' was, of course, the Catholic Faith, and his defence of the faith was the common thread and theme which bound the essays together. From the very outset Chesterton had stated the reasoning behind the book, almost beginning with an apology for his apologetics:

I am very sorry if this little book of mine seems to be controversial on subjects about which everybody is allowed to be controversial except ourselves. But I am afraid there is no help for it; and if I assure the reader that I have tried to start putting it together in an unimpaired spirit of charity, it is always possible that the charity may be as one-sided as the controversy. Anyhow, it represents my attitude towards this controversy; and it is quite possible that everything is wrong about it, except that it is right.[12]

The alternative to writing such a book was to ignore, in an arrogant or patronising fashion, the varying criticisms of the Church. This, according to Chesterton, was not a justifiable option:

The great temptation of the Catholic in the modern world is the temptation to intellectual pride. It is so obvious that most of his critics are talking without in the least knowing what they are talking about that he is sometimes a little provoked towards the very un-Christian logic of answering a fool according to his folly . . . So when somebody says that a fast is the opposite to a feast, and yet both seem to be sacred to us, some of us will always be moved merely to say, 'Yes,'

370

and relapse into an objectionable grin. When the anxious ethical enquirer says, 'Christmas is devoted to merry-making, to eating meat and drinking wine, and yet you encourage this pagan and materialistic enjoyment,' you or I will be tempted to say, 'Quite right, my boy,' and leave it at that. When he then says, looking even more worried, 'Yet you admire men for fasting in caves and deserts and denying themselves ordinary pleasures; you are clearly committed, like the Buddhists, to the opposite or ascetic principle,' we shall be similarly inspired to say, 'Quite correct, old bean,' or 'Got it first time, old top,' and merely propose an adjournment for convivial refreshment.

Nevertheless, it is a temptation to be resisted. Not only is it obviously our duty to explain to the other people that what seems to them contradictory is really complementary, but we are not altogether justified in any such tone of superiority.[13]

Instead it was the duty of the Catholic to unravel, as far as possible, the mysteries of the faith so the unenlightened could understand: 'All science, even the divine science, is a sublime detective story. Only it is not set to detect why a man is dead; but the darker secret of why he is alive. The Catholic Church remains in the best sense a mystery even to believers. It would be foolish of them to complain if it is a riddle to unbelievers.'[14]

The imagery of the detective story is continued in another essay, 'The Mask of the Agnostic', and it is appropriate that the choice of title is resonant of one of the author's Father Brown stories:

There is always a certain irony, even in the simple pages of my favourite detective stories, in the fact that everybody rushes for a doctor as soon as they are quite certain that a man is dead. But in the detective story there may at least be something to be learnt by the doctor from the dead body. In the doctrinal speculation there is nothing whatever; and it does but confuse the eternal detective story for the doctor of medicine to pretend to be a doctor of divinity. The truth is that all this business about 'a medical man' is mere bluff and mystagogy. The medical man 'sees' that the mind has ceased with the body. What the medical man sees is that the body can no longer kick, talk, sneeze, whistle or dance a jig. And a man does not need to be very medical in order to see that. But whether the principle of energy, that once made it kick, talk, sneeze, whistle and dance, does or does not still exist on some other plane of existence – a medical man knows no more about than any other man.[15]

Elsewhere, Chesterton returned to the defence of Catholic novelists which had animated his correspondence with Maurice Baring:

> I see that Mr Patrick Braybrooke and others, writing to the *Catholic Times*, have raised the question of Catholic propaganda in novels written by Catholics. The very phrase, which we are all compelled to use, is awkward and even false. A Catholic putting Catholicism into a novel, or a song, or a sonnet, or anything else, is not being a propagandist; he is simply being a Catholic. Everybody understands this about every other enthusiasm in the world. When we say that a poet's landscape and atmosphere are full of the spirit of England, we do not mean that he is necessarily conducting an Anti-German propaganda during the Great War. We mean that if he is really an English poet, his poetry cannot be anything but English.[16]

Alongside the more obvious attacks on the Church addressed by Chesterton in *The Thing*, an ominous new threat began to receive his attention:

> A book was sent me the other day by a gentleman who pins his faith to what he calls the Nordic race; and who, indeed, appears to offer that race as a substitute for all religions. Crusaders believed Jerusalem was not only the Holy City, but the centre of the whole world. Moslems bow their heads towards Mecca and Roman Catholics are notorious for being in secret communication with Rome. I presume that the Holy Place of the Nordic religion must be the North Pole . . . The only thing that puzzles me is that the Englishmen who now call themselves Nordic used to call themselves Teutonic; and very often even Germanic. I cannot think why they altered this so abruptly in the autumn of 1914. Some day, I suppose, when we have diplomatic difficulties with Norway, they will equally abruptly drop the word Nordic. They will hastily substitute some other – I would suggest Borealic. They might be called the Bores, for short.[17]

Throughout the rest of this essay, arguably the best in the book, Chesterton really excels. Whereas the worshippers of the Nordic race 'would substitute one race for all religions', Catholics 'are ready to offer one religion to all races'. Then, after stating that 'it is not very clear what is to be done with the people who do not happen to belong to the race,' Chesterton concludes, in the words of the essay's title, that the Nordic idea is nothing but 'the call to the Barbarians': '. . . the religion of race that he proposes is exactly what he himself calls the Dark Ages . . . It is very doubtful if there ever was any Nordic race. It is quite certain that there never was any Nordic common sense. The very words "common sense" are a translation from the Latin.'[18]

In the article 'Obstinate Orthodoxy' Chesterton contrasted the sin of cynicism with the realism of romance:

> It does sometimes happen that a man of real talent has a weakness for flattery, even the flattery of fools. He would rather say something that silly people think clever than something which only clever people could perceive to be true. Oscar Wilde was a man of this type. When he said somewhere that an immoral woman is the sort of woman a man never gets tired of, he used a phrase so baseless as to be perfectly pointless. Everybody knows that a man may get tired of a whole procession of immoral women, especially if he is an immoral man. That was 'a Thought'; otherwise something to be uttered, with uplifted hand, to people who could not think at all. In their poor muddled minds there was some vague connection between wit and cynicism; so they never applauded him so warmly as a wit as when he was cynical without being witty. But when he said, 'A cynic is a man who knows the price of everything and the value of nothing,' he made a statement (in excellent epigrammatic form) which really meant something. But it would have meant his own immediate dethronement if it could have been understood by those who only enthroned him for being cynical.[19]

Against this shallowness stood the eternal reality of romance – or, if one preferred, the romance of reality:

> In short, what the critics would call romanticism is in fact the only form of realism. It is also the only form of rationalism. The more a man uses his reason upon realities, the more he will see that the realities remain much the same . . . If the real girl is experiencing a real romance, she is experiencing something old, but not something stale. If she has plucked something from a real rose-tree, she is holding a very ancient symbol, but a very recent rose. And it is exactly in so far as a man *can* clear his head, so as to see actual things as they are, that he will see these things as permanently important as they are. Exactly in so far as his head is confused with current fashion and aesthetic modes of the moment, he will see nothing about it except that it is like a picture on a chocolate-box . . . Exactly in

so far as he is thinking about real people, he will see that they are really romantic. Exactly in so far as he is thinking about pictures and poems and decorative styles, he will think that romance is a false or old-fashioned style. He can only see people as imitating pictures; whereas the real people are not imitating anything. They are only being themselves – as they will always be. Roses remain radiant and mysterious, however many pink rosebuds are sprinkled like pips over cheap wallpapers. Falling in love remains radiant and mysterious, however threadbare be the thousandth repetition of a rhyme as a valentine or a cracker-motto. To see this fact is to live in a world of facts. To be always thinking of the banality of bad wallpapers and valentines is to live in a world of fictions.[20]

The publication of *The Thing* in October 1929 was not likely to enamour those who criticised Chesterton for dragging 'Catholic propaganda' into his books. In many ways the whole volume could be described as a work of propaganda, and it was, at the very least, a plaintive plea for the use of reason in religion. Not surprisingly, therefore, Hilaire Belloc became the book's most vociferous champion. In his short study *On the Place of Gilbert Keith Chesterton in English Letters* Belloc described *The Thing* as 'his best piece of work. Of all his books it is by far the most profound and the most clear.' None the less, Belloc didn't believe that its intrinsic merits would necessarily lead to either critical or popular success: 'I am curious and even meditative upon its probable fate. If it is read by the generation now rising, that will mean that England is beginning to think. If it is forgotten, that will mean that thought is failing; for nowhere has there been more thorough thinking or clearer exposition in our time.'[21]

Another anthology of Chesterton's prose appeared in the same October. *G. K. C. as M. C.* was a collection of his prefaces to other people's books, dating back as far as 1903, and included essays on such diverse characters as Job, Cecil Chesterton and George MacDonald.

In the month that both *The Thing* and *G. K. C. as M. C.* were published in London, Gilbert, Frances and Dorothy were in Rome. It was not the Chestertons' first visit, as they had both passed through on their way to the Holy Land a decade earlier. Yet now they would have three months in the city instead of only a few days; and now they were both seeing it as Roman Catholics, which neither had been during the previous visit. On both the temporal and the spiritual level, therefore, they were able to appreciate the Eternal City from a new and a fresh perspective.

They stayed in the Hotel Hassler overlooking the Spanish Steps, where, according to Dorothy Collins, 'in a first floor room Chesterton wrote *The Resurrection of Rome* while below the windows a stream of every nationality passed to and fro on those lovely steps, at the foot of which stands the house where Keats lived and died'.[22] In this setting, for perhaps the first and only time, the artist looked upon a canvas too large to paint:

> ... I suddenly saw lie open before me a book that I cannot write. This book is the printed proof that I cannot write it. I could, I suppose, if I liked, go back and write another book, full of the details of Rome and the hundred accidents of travel ... Or I might begin again and write a better book about all the human contacts of the place, and the curious and interesting persons to be found there ... A greater obligation, and an even greater pleasure, would lie in acknowledging all the forms of hospitality and courtesy which I received, if they were not too numerous to be acknowledged ... Perhaps the most impressive incident, which would require a book to itself, was the experience of visiting the College of Propaganda, with its friendly crowd of every race and colour under heaven; a real League of Nations – which did not quarrel. On some, and possibly many, of these incidents or aspects I shall touch in their turn; but I am conscious that I could have written a much more amusing book if I had confined myself entirely to these many-coloured experiences.[23]

In this one paragraph Chesterton gave a tantalising taste of the books he could have written. Perhaps they might have been entitled 'What I Saw in Rome', 'Who I Met in Rome' or, continuing the theme of *The Thing*, 'The Romance of Rome'. None of these ever materialised, prompting Maisie Ward to ask whether 'perhaps Rome was too big even for Chesterton'.[24] Certainly *The Resurrection of Rome*, the book he did write in the Hotel Hassler during the closing months of 1929, was a disappointment. The prose wanders off in all directions, following endless theological or historical tangents, and, in the words of Maisie Ward, 'gives an impression of being thrown together hastily before the ideas had been thought through to their ultimate conclusions'.[25]

In fact, Chesterton was well aware of the book's inadequacies. He had hoped to cover 'the general historical or philosophical notion I had in mind, as I looked on that luminous evening from the obelisk of the Trinità across to the dome of St Peter's. Only the complete thing I had seen broke as I saw it; and all that follows here is but a litter of the fragments.'[26] But *The Resurrection of Rome* does have one or two saving graces, not least Chesterton's entertaining account of his meeting with Benito Mussolini, the Italian dictator:

> I went into the black cavernous entry of one of those great castles or palaces, some of them very ancient, which are still used for many of the public offices, and showed a sentinel an order I had received from headquarters, granting me an interview ... with the present head of the Italian State. I passed from official to official, a little more rapidly than is my experience in such attendances; and was eventually shown into a large room which seemed to me like a vast wilderness of tessellated pavement.[27]

At the far end of the room, seated at a small table, was Mussolini, 'an alert, square-shouldered man in black', who 'got up very rapidly and walked equally rapidly right across the room, till we met not far from the door. He shook hands and asked me in French if I minded talking in that language. I said I did it badly but would do my best.'

> ... the very first thing he did was to dump me down in a chair and ask me about the Disestablishment of the Church of England.
>
> In short, to put it one way, I did not interview him because he interviewed me. He put a rapid succession of questions covering a wide field, but mostly concerned with my country and not his ... Something I said about Imperialism and Internationalism seemed to arrest his attention sharply ... I told him, in increasingly halting French, that I knew it was difficult, or perhaps nearly impossible; but I did desire England to be more self-supporting and less dependent on the ends of the earth, for I thought such dependence had become very perilous. Before I knew where I was, I found myself talking at large about my own fad of Distributism; and now, between my embarrassment and my excitement, my French went all to pieces. God alone knows in what language the last part of the conversation found expression on my side ... Thinking it not improbable that Signor Mussolini might think I was mad, I rose as if to bow myself out. He rose also and said, with what was probably irony but was none the less most polished courtesy, 'Well, I will go and reflect on what you have told me' ...

As we parted, I said, '*Vous me pardonnez, Excellence, que je parle français si mal*'; at which he laughed again and said, '*Ah, vous parlez français comme je parle anglais.*'

. . . I hated the idea of having talked too much, instead of listening to a more interesting person; but I could not quite get it out of my mind that the interesting person had possibly intended that I should talk a great deal about my politics, rather than he talk about his.[28]

Following such an enjoyable and entertaining description of the meeting with Mussolini, Gilbert became lost in an incoherent and haphazard discussion of the rights and wrongs of fascism. It was a perfect example of the litter of fragments for which he apologised at the book's outset. Expressing the concern that his discussion 'may be mistaken for a defence of Fascism', he countered that his natural sympathies were with the pre-fascist Popular Party, 'which was specially the party of the Catholic Democrats' and which was 'chiefly criticised for having been too democratic'.[29] Yet he went on to depict fascist Syndicalism as a preferable alternative to multinational capitalism:

I do not mean that the Italian government is my ideal of justice, or that it does not ever support the employers, or that it might not support them where I should oppose them. I mean that it may support them, but it *can* oppose them. The ordinary modern government cannot. The ordinary regular respectable representative government, by Wall Street via Washington, cannot. The ordinary British government, by the Party Fund via the Parliamentary group, cannot. The new Italian government can; and it has again and again adopted a policy quite unparalleled in the whole political world of today; which is worthy of a sharp and close attention which it has hardly received. It is not Socialism; it is not Distributism; but it is distinguished and divided in a most startling manner from anything to which we are accustomed as Capitalism.[30]

It seems that Chesterton was painting the Blackshirts whiter than they deserved merely because anything, or almost anything, was preferable to multinational plutocracy. Yet he was not completely blinded to the error of Mussolini's ways:

. . . I think there is a case for saying that this revolution is too much of a reaction. I mean it in the psychological sense of a recoil; that he does sometimes recoil so much from anarchy as to talk only of authority;

that he does recoil from mere pacifism as to seem to endorse mere militarism; that he does recoil so much from the babel of tongues talking different heresies and contrary forms of nonsense as to make his own moral thesis a little too much on one note.[31]

Fascism, therefore, was first and foremost the politics of frustration. Ultimately, however, although Chesterton could sympathise fully with the frustration, he could not sympathise fully with the politics:

> I am well aware that two black shirts do not make a white. But I assure the reader that I am not, in this case, in the least trying to prove that black is white. I wish there were in the world a real white flag of freedom, that I could follow, independently of the red flag of Communist or the black flag of Fascist regimentation. By every instinct of my being, by every tradition of my blood, I should prefer English liberty to Latin discipline.[32]

Finally, after muddling his way through fifty pages of arguments both for and against the position of Mussolini in Italy, Chesterton eventually arrived at the 'logical case against Fascism': 'The intellectual criticism of Fascism is really this; that it appeals to an appetite for authority, without very clearly giving the authority for the appetite.'[33] Having reached a conclusion, and being aware of the inadequacies of his initial arguments, Chesterton felt the need for an appendix to make his position perfectly clear. Stating that he 'may have the appearance of labouring and yet missing the point', he wanted 'the English reader to understand my meaning, and above all my motive':

> I can assure him that I am very far from being what is usually understood as a British Fascist . . . My motive in this matter is very simple to the point of violence; it is to point out, as emphatically as I can, that the whole political and financial world in which we live has been goading Fascism into revolt for the last fifty years. In this sense my remarks might rather be called a warning against Fascism, as a wise man in the early eighteenth century might have uttered a warning against the French Revolution.[34]

From Roman reaction Chesterton returned to Roman romance. He believed passionately that the central reality of Rome did not reside with Il Duce but with Il Papa. Fascism would fade away but the Pope would remain. Hence thousands of goose-stepping Blackshirts on the secular streets of Rome were not so powerful as a handful of Swiss Guards on the steps of St Peter's. The paradox pleased Chesterton immensely, so much so that his first sight of a Swiss Guard at the Vatican inspired a delightful flight of fancy:

> . . . as I watched him, and the pale light from one of Rome's stormy days striking his streaks of colour as he turned and shifted the hand upon the halberd, something else stirred within me, to which I could not as yet put a name. As these idle thoughts had been drifting aimlessly through my mind, there was an undercurrent in them that was somehow less international and nearer home; something nameless connected with my own nation and even my own experience. I could not imagine why this romantic Roman halberdier should in any way remind me of England . . . And then suddenly I remembered that long ago, in my older days of scribbling, I had written a ridiculous story about Notting Hill; of which the joke was that a man might die for a little suburb as if for a holy city; and that I had equipped the men fighting for it with the same sort of halberds and heraldic colours. The man standing on the great stairway was, among a myriad other more important things, one of my own little dreams come true. And I realised with something rather like alarm at the coincidence, that the comparision might really have been pressed further. For the Guard of the Vatican City really was defending a place almost parochial in size though the reverse of parochial in importance. That here in the heart of Christendom, on the high place of the whole world, on a plane above all earthly empires and under the white and awful light that strikes on an eternal town, was really a model state no larger than Notting Hill.[35]

Without doubt, the highlight of the whole visit for Chesterton was his audience with the Pope. Yet, surprisingly, Maisie Ward, in her biography of Gilbert, stated that he had 'left no record of his Papal audience'.[36] This is a curious remark because Chesterton saw Pope Pius XI on three separate occasions during his stay in Italy and all three are documented in *The Resurrection of Rome*. Indeed, he began by attempting to describe 'the personal experience of approaching the very centre of such pomps or ceremonies, and meeting the personal ruler who oversees them all'.[37] Yet, before doing so, he was at pains to stress that even the Pope was only a servant of the servants of God and that all the pomp and rituals of the Church were only an outward expression of the central mystery of Faith:

... I am particularly anxious to affirm, at the start, that though of course these shows and pageants meant immeasurably much to me, and profoundly affected my emotions, yet I do not base my belief on such emotions, still less on such pageants or shows. I was myself received into the Catholic Church in a small tin shed, painted brick-red, which stood among the sculleries and outhouses of a railway Hotel ... And the Pope would be the first to say that the step I took in entering that shed was inconceivably more important than the step of entering St Peter's, or the Vatican, or his own presence. [38]

Having put the pomp of the papal audiences into perspective, it is clear that his meetings with the Pope affected him profoundly, so much so that Dorothy Collins remembered that he could do no work for two days before and two days after the first, private audience:

I saw His Holiness Pius XI three times; the first time in private audience; the second in a semi-private assembly of various notables; and the third time among the crowds that thronged St Peter's on the day of the Beatification of the English Martyrs. On the first occasion a dignitary who was the head of one of the National Colleges kindly helped to introduce me; and I have seldom been more grateful for human companionship. It is altogether inadequate to say I was nervous ... He came suddenly out of his study, a sturdy figure in a cape, with a square face and spectacles, and began speaking to me about what I had written, saying some very generous things about a sketch I wrote of St Francis of Assisi ... Then he made a motion and we all knelt; and in the words that followed I understood for the first time something that was once meant by the ceremonial use of the plural, and in a flash I saw the sense of something that had always seemed to me a senseless custom of kings. With a new strong voice, that was hardly even like his. own, he began, *'Nous vous bénissons,'* and I knew that something stood there infinitely greater than an individual; I knew that it was indeed 'We'; We, Peter and Gregory and Hildebrand and all the dynasty that does not die. Then, as he passed on, we rose and found our way out of the Palace, through knots of Swiss and Papal Guards, till we were again under the open sky. I said to the clerical dignitary, 'That frightened me more than anything I have known in my life.' The clerical dignitary laughed heartily. [39]

There is something disarming in the simple sincerity of such sentiments, conveying a wisdom beyond worldliness through that innocence which is the very kernel of truth. They were the words of Chesterton the Child.

Two other encounters with the Pope were to follow during the stay in Rome. First, Gilbert was present with various other dignitaries when Pope Pius heard the documents of the Beatification of the Forty Martyrs of England and Wales read for his approval:

> I heard the very long list of those English heroes, who resisted the despotic destruction of the national religion, read in due order; and listened to a number of names that sounded like Smith or Higgins pronounced with a perfect Italian accent. Then the Pope himself spoke, in a manner rather conversational than rhetorical, but with not a little Italian gesture and vivacity, by the standard of English conversation. What moved me very much, as an Englishman and an exile, was that he spoke with peculiar warmth and vividness in praise of England, and like one who had seen it rather than heard of it. He dwelt even more strongly on the words 'so beautiful a country' than on the words 'so great a nation'. He also emphasised the fact that the last witnesses in England were men of every class and condition, poor as well as rich, and agricultural labourers as well as the first noble of the land. He spoke in Italian; but so clearly and with such exact gesture that I could understand nearly every word.[40]

Finally, Gilbert was present with thousands of others at the Beatification ceremony at St Peter's when the Pope 'in the fullest blaze of publicity . . . came to consummate the Beatification before a colossal congregation, and to conclude it by celebrating Benediction at the High Altar'.[41]

Thus the tripartite highlight of the Italian visit was concluded with a climax close to Chesterton's heart; the honouring by Rome of those Englishmen who had sacrificed their lives for the Church. However, the Pope was to have another telling influence on Chesterton, an influence that transcended national loyalties and national prejudices. Gilbert had been impressed by the Pope's call for worldwide evangelisation, and this led him to question his own attitudes towards non-Europeans. He realised that Pius XI's 'enthusiasm for missions' was, in fact, 'a very strong antagonism to the contempt for the aboriginal races and a gigantic faith in the fraternity of all tribes in the light of the Faith'.[42] This realisation led, in turn, to something of a watershed; a shedding of certain patronising and prejudiced assumptions:

A distinguished Scandinavian, whom I met later, was so warm an upholder of this humanitarianism that he said, with shining eyes as one who beholds a vision, 'We may yet have a black Pope.' In a spirit of disgraceful compromise, I suggested meekly that (if not quite ready for that) I should be delighted to see a black Cardinal ... Then I remembered the great King who came to Bethlehem, heavy with purple and crimson and with a face like night; and I was ashamed.[43]

Towards the end of the visit, on 6 December 1929, Chesterton was guest of honour at the North American College. After dinner he gave a speech which met with a very mixed response. According to Robert MacNamara, in his history of the college, Gilbert's performance was less than inspiring: '... perhaps because of his casual English platform-manner and his chuckling paradoxical style, the great British champion of the Catholic Church rather disappointed the American seminarians. "Nothing special as a speaker," one of them afterward commented.'[44] A different view was given by Charles Boldrick, another seminarian, who made the following entry in his diary on the night of Chesterton's speech:

> We were all anticipating Chesterton's visit tonight. When we came down to supper, he was at the post of honour, and among several Bishops. He is a towering man of colossal proportions, with a gray mane of hair and a black string on his eye-glasses. He eats with his left hand. At the lecture following, the library was nicely decorated, and crowded with ourselves and alumni ... He referred amusingly to the Pilgrim Fathers, to Glorious Maryland, and Virginia, and Sir Walter Raleigh who was the only approximately respectable person who ever had anything to do with Queen Elizabeth ... Everyone enjoyed him immensely. I was so glad to see and hear him who, I think, is the outstanding Catholic writer of today, one of the world's greatest minds, perhaps the greatest convert since Newman. The Church is fortunate in calling him her son.[45]

Two days later, Gilbert, Frances and Dorothy were enjoying the celebrations throughout the city for the feast of the Immaculate Conception. It will be remembered that this festival had a marked and lasting effect on Frances, who would write a sonnet to Dorothy inspired by their shared memory of it:

Do you remember how we walked the streets
Of Rome and saw the Queen of Heaven high,
Raised and superb upon her throne, and threw
Our roses to her as we passed her by? . . .[46]

Gilbert shared the same memories, commenting that the city 'was illuminated everywhere for the festival' and that there was 'every kind of decoration and display': 'There were fireworks; and I have always been as fond of fireworks as a child or a Chinaman. Nor could I, at any time of my life, have found it easy to maintain that the love of Mary was a less worthy motive than the hatred of Guy Fawkes.'[47]

Gilbert's most vivid memory of the festival, however, was similar to that of his wife and revolved around the statue of the Blessed Virgin bedecked with flowers. In a florid flight of the imagination, he described a 'paradise where, far above the roofs of Rome in winter, She walked upon the flowers of spring'.[48]

Their stay in Rome was almost at an end, but before returning to England the Chestertons and Dorothy paid a visit to Max Beerbohm and his wife, who lived in a villa overlooking the Bay of Rapallo. Beerbohm had been an old friend of Gilbert, making his acquaintance in the early years of the century when both were earning a living on Fleet Street, but he had married in 1910, had gone to Italy on his honeymoon and had stayed there ever since. During the visit, according to Dorothy Collins, Beerbohm took great pleasure in demonstrating his favourite toy. It was a small white bear, purchased from a Parisian sweet shop, which was sitting up with a little drum round its neck. When wound up sufficiently it banged away on its drum to everybody's intense satisfaction. He also showed his guests an amusing fresco he had painted on the wall over the dining-room door, depicting many of his friends going in to a meal. In pride of place, at the front of the column, was Chesterton.[49]

During their sojourn in Rapallo they took the opportunity of visiting Ezra Pound and his wife who were also living there. Pound had become an outspoken fascist but he was also interested in the Social Credit ideas of Major C. H. Douglas, which were very influential in Canada at the time, and he discussed these at length with Chesterton.[50]

Having made the acquaintance of Pound, and having revived Gilbert's old friendship with Max Beerbohm, it was time for the long-awaited return to England. It was inconceivable that Gilbert and Frances should ever follow in the footsteps of either of these happily exiled couples by moving to Italy. The Chestertons were already filled with home thoughts from abroad and finally returned home on 20 December, in good time for the traditional Christmas celebrations at Top Meadow. Regardless of whether the feast of the Immaculate Conception was best celebrated in Rome, a true Dickensian Christmas could only be celebrated in England's bleak midwinter.

« 26 »

At Home in America

In December 1929, on the day the Chestertons left Rome, one of the young seminarians from the North American College went to Gilbert's hotel to make 'one more attempt to show my appreciation of him'. The young man, who would become a priest of the Archdiocese of Louisville, Kentucky, had received a hickory-nut cake as a Christmas gift from home, a large slice of which he had cut and wrapped with the intention of presenting it to Gilbert before his departure. After attaching 'an appropriate note' to his small gift, he delivered it to the Hotel Hassler himself 'as a sort of votive offering'. However, he was informed upon his arrival that the Chestertons had left already: 'Alas! The concierge told me that Signor Chesterton had just departed. I was disappointed. I know he would have enjoyed it.'[1]

This small token of American hospitality may have gone unnoticed and untasted, but it was none the less a foretaste of the hospitality Gilbert would receive from his American hosts when he visited the United States nine months later. In the meantime he was back in England and writing for *G. K.'s Weekly* about a new threat in Germany:

> When we are told that the ancient Marshall Hindenburg is now Dictator of Germany we suspect a note of exaggeration ... Hindenburg never was the dictator of anything and never will be. He is, however, the man who keeps the seat warm for a Dictator to come. Hindenburg has led us back to Frederick the Great ...
>
> Hindenburg has now given rein to the extreme Nationalists, with the delivered provinces to support him in the flush of patriotism. And the extreme Nationalists have only one policy: to reconstitute the unjust frontiers of Germany, which Europe fought to amend.[2]

Written in July 1930, three years before Hitler finally rose to power, these words were truly prophetic, offering an ominous and gloomy picture of the dark days ahead. However, any cause for concern in Germany was forgotten on 27 July by a cause to celebrate closer to home. Gilbert's old ally, Hilaire Belloc, had reached his sixtieth birthday, and his friends were determined to ensure it would be a day to remember. Chesterton described the dinner which was organised in Belloc's honour at the Adelphi Hotel as 'one of the most amusing events of my life', and he recounted the evening at considerable length in his *Autobiography*:

> There were about forty people assembled, nearly all of them were what is called important in the public sense, and the rest were even more important in the private sense; as being his nearest intimates and connections. To me it was that curious experience, something between the Day of Judgment and a dream, in which men of many groups known to me at many times all appeared together as a sort of resurrection . . . There was my old friend Bentley, who dated from my first days at school; and Eccles, who reminded me of the earliest political rows of the Pro-Boers; and Jack Squire (now Sir John) who first floated into my circle in the days of the *Eye-Witness* and my brother's campaign against corruption; and Duff Cooper, a rising young politician I had met but a month or so before, and A. P. Herbert of somewhat similar age; and the brilliant journalist I had long known as 'Beachcomber', and only recently known as Morton. It was to be, and was, a very jolly evening; there were to be no speeches. It was specially impressed upon me that there were to be no speeches. Only I, as presiding, was to be permitted to say a few words in presenting Belloc with a golden goblet modelled on certain phrases in his heroic poem in praise of wine, which ends by asking that such a golden cup should be the stirrup-cup of his farewell to friends:

> And sacramental raise me the divine
> Strong brother in God and last companion, wine.[3]

The actual words from Belloc's poem which were engraved on the goblet couldn't have been more appropriate:

> Open, golden wide
> With benediction graven on its side.[4]

In presenting this birthday gift to his friend, Gilbert had said that the bestowing of such a loving-cup 'might have been as fitting thousands of years ago, at the festival of a great Greek poet'. Furthermore, Chesterton was 'confident that Belloc's sonnets and strong verse would remain like the cups and the carved epics of the Greeks'.[5]

Belloc, in accepting the gift, stated that he had found, by the age of sixty, that he had ceased to care very much whether his verse remained or not: 'But I am told that you begin to care again frightfully when you are seventy. In which case, I hope I shall die at sixty-nine.'[6]

After the presentation the cup was passed from guest to guest, with each, in turn, drinking from it as a mark of their affection for its owner. It was a lasting tribute to Belloc that, although he made so many enemies, he also enjoyed the love and loyalty of so many friends.

The feast then commenced in earnest until someone whispered in Chesterton's ear that, as chairman, he should say a few words to thank A. D. Peters, Belloc's literary agent, for organising the dinner. At first he was reluctant, remembering the resolution that there should be no speeches. Eventually he relented and said a few words. Peters than rose briefly to acknowledge Gilbert's gratitude but added that the event was in fact organised by J. B. Morton, alias 'Beachcomber', who sat immediately on his right. Morton then rose with a mixture of surprise and mock-solemnity to acknowledge the abruptly transferred applause. There then commenced an impromptu party game in which each of the guests rose to greet the applause of the other guests for allegedly organising the dinner before making a short speech explaining that the person to their right had in fact organised the event. Eventually all forty diners had made a speech with varying degrees of imagination and improvisation. A. P. Herbert impersonated a trade-union orator, and Duff Cooper, the Conservative MP, pretended to be a Liberal politician. D. B. Wyndham Lewis, who had attempted to avoid his turn in this round-table of spoof speeches by hiding under the table, was dragged out schoolboy fashion and forced to play the game. Perhaps Maurice Baring stole the show by reciting an Horatian ode, composed by Ronald Knox, while balancing a glass of Burgundy on his bald head. During the recital he had to brave a barrage of pellets of bread which other guests threw at him in unsuccessful efforts to dislodge the precariously positioned wine glass.[7]

The last word of tribute to Belloc should be left to Chesterton, who concluded his account of the 'most amusing' evening with a quatrain of Victorian verse which expressed his sincere gratitude for their lasting friendship:

> It is the only dinner I have ever attended, at which it was literally true that every diner made an after-dinner speech. And that was the very happy ending of that very happy dinner, at which there were to be no speeches.
>
> I did not myself make another speech; though I was far from thinking there had been too much speechifying. Only certain fragmentary words, a memory of a late Victorian poet whom I knew, Sir William Watson, floated on the surface of the mind; and it was those words that I should have said, if I had said anything. For what the poet said to his friend is all that I could have added, in a merely personal spirit, to the many things that were said that night about Hilaire Belloc; and I should not have been ashamed if the words had sounded like a vaunt:

> > Not without honour my days ran,
> > Nor yet without a boast shall end;
> > For I was Shakespeare's countryman,
> > And were not you my friend.[8]

In August a loosely connected collection of four Chesterton novelettes was published. Entitled *Four Faultless Felons*, the book contradicted its own title by being far from faultless. It was, in fact, completely forgettable and not worthy of the author. A more endurable and far more enjoyable volume was published on 2 October under the title *Come to Think of It*. This was yet another collection of Chesterton's journalism, gleaned for the most part from his regular column in the *Illustrated London News*. The essays were arranged and selected to commemorate Gilbert's twenty-five years as a columnist with the paper, and he dedicated the book 'To Captain Bruce S. Ingram, MC, OBE, Editor of the *Illustrated London News*, for suffering me week after week for twenty-five years on that paper'. It seemed an appropriate time for reminiscence, and Chesterton concluded his introductory essay by making a connection with his youth: 'It was enough for our youth to show that our ideas were suggestive; it is the task of our senility and second childhood to show that they are conclusive.'[9]

Although Chesterton may indeed have been in his second childhood – if indeed he had ever left his first – the quality and poignancy of the writing in *Come to Think of It* belied any suggestion of senility on the author's part. As usual, his writing encompassed a multitude of subjects but always from a singular and single-minded viewpoint. In the essay 'On What We Would Do with Two Million (If We Had It)' he defined the difference between a philanthropist and a Christian: 'Philanthropists would give it to the deserving poor; Christians would give it to the undeserving poor. For the first thought of the Christians, if they were really Christians, would be that they themselves were examples of the undeserving rich.'[10]

Throughout the rest of the book Chesterton chased the errors of the age relentlessly. Whether he was writing on psychoanalysis, the new poetry, the classics or the mythology of scientists, the same spirit of provocative paradox prevailed. In short, the essays were a fitting tribute to the continuing popularity of his *Note-Book* column.

Two weeks prior to the publication of *Come to Think of It*, Gilbert, Frances and Dorothy were again setting out for foreign climes. This time their destination was the United States, via Canada, and they embarked from Liverpool aboard the White Star Line's SS *Doric* on 19 September. Dorothy, in particular, had fond memories of the voyage:

There was a very jolly party on board of all ages and Chesterton thoroughly enjoyed the fun. On one occasion a treasure hunt was suggested and he was provided with reams of brown paper and coloured chalks and was asked to make the clues. He spent a whole day writing verses and drawing pictures to be hidden around the decks. The whole thing was an uproarious success and when I went round afterwards to collect up the clues there was not one left. Others had been before me, and they are now most probably collectors' pieces.[11]

Frances, who had been a notably poor traveller on previous occasions, also appeared to enjoy the transatlantic voyage, informing her mother-in-law, Marie Louise, that she and Gilbert were being kept luxuriously: 'We have a delightful suite on board (paid for by Gilbert's University People) – a bedroom with two beds, a sitting room and a bath room, and Dorothy's room is quite near. We are fed like fighting cocks – as is always the way on these great liners.'[12]

As well as dictating his regular newspaper articles to Dorothy, Chesterton passed the time at the horse-racing games played on board. His 'horse' was 'Anecdote', whose pedigree was 'by Memory out of Repertoire', while Frances's horse was called 'Safety Match'. 'The excitement was quite thrilling,' she told Marie Louise. 'This morning I was photographed with my horse. The horses you understand are wooden ones on stands with numbers and jockeys complete and they are made to move by the numbers thrown by the dice like the children's game of Race Horses we used to play.'[13]

The purser, 'a rather remarkable man, very full of good animal spirits and very amusing', asked Chesterton to act as chairman at the ship's Grand Concert, to which Gilbert readily agreed. The concert took place on the evening of 27 September, after which Chesterton made an appeal on behalf of sailors' charities. According to Frances, his speech was 'a little serious, and humorous too'. The night ended with national songs of America, Canada, Scotland, Ireland and England, and the Chestertons did not finally retire to their cabin until after one o'clock in the morning, which Frances remarked was hardly 'a Christian hour'.[14]

Other highlights of the voyage were the sighting of an iceberg off the coast of Newfoundland, the Aurora Borealis and what Frances described as a school of 'spouting whales' but which the captain assured her were only porpoises.

Arriving in Canada, the *Doric* sailed up the St Lawrence to Quebec, from whence Gilbert, Frances and Dorothy would proceed to Toronto and Montreal. Although the stop in Quebec was very short, the Chestertons were given a lightning tour of the city in a motor car, visiting the Wolfe and Montcalm monuments. The visit to these two landmarks made a lasting impression on Gilbert, who recounted his memory of them during a speech he gave a few years later at a luncheon given for Rudyard Kipling by the Canadian Literary Society:

> . . . anybody sailing up the St Lawrence will see where the legend of
> Canada begins . . . and I cannot tell you, least of all in this brief and
> inadequate speech, what my feelings were when I mounted to those
> Heights of Abraham where the great battle was fought and where I

was . . . uplifted in the worthy sense in which great poetry, or great music, or even great mathematics or philosophy can lift a man, by finding that from that crest they had set up a monument in noble Latin, in the original international language of Christian men, which commemorated together the names of James Wolfe and Montcalm; and I remembered that great French gentleman who died in arms and that bourgeois boy of genius, the most generous and full of the most genial fighting spirit of all the heroes of England alone to be named with Nelson . . . that those two great heroes are celebrated together in the universal language of Europe upon the height that is called the Height of Abraham, upon the battlefield, that is what I call a legend . . .[15]

At Toronto and Montreal Chesterton commenced the dozens of lectures he would give during his visit. At both cities he spoke to audiences of between 4,000 and 5,000 people, a measure of his tremendous popularity.

On 11 October the Montreal periodical *World Wide* published an article by Chesterton called 'Should Science Take a Holiday?' Again, he was cast in the role of prophet, with the grim reality of scientific warfare in the twentieth century standing in stark contrast to his romantic vision of the eighteenth-century battle at Quebec:

Blasts of poison gas . . . were suddenly let loose on living men in the middle of the war from laboratories where they had been manufactured and kept absolutely secret and controlled by a privileged few. The men on whom they were loosed had never a word to say about whether this new weapon was or was not to be tolerated among the weapons of honourable war. The men who are likely to suffer from it, that is the men who are poor, ignorant and courageous, have never had a word to say about it since.

The specialist perfection of aviation, the specialist perfection of explosives, have decided that the men and women of undefended civilian towns are to be wiped out with flame and poison . . . The women and children have not expressed an ardent desire for it; the civilian towns have but rarely passed a democratic vote desiring or inviting these visits. Mankind as such has had absolutely nothing to say about the change; it has never consented to it in the smallest degree. It is simply the law of scientific progress. The machines are better and therefore the massacres must be worse.[16]

Chesterton's sojourn in Canada was extremely brief because he was due to give a series of lectures over a period of six weeks at the University of Notre Dame in Indiana. His hosts at Notre Dame, 'Gilbert's University People', as Frances had referred to them in the letter to her mother-in-law, had engaged him to talk to a group of 500 students on the subject of Victorian history and literature.

For the duration of their stay at Notre Dame Gilbert, Frances and Dorothy lodged with an estate agent and his family, who lived at South Bend. They were made to feel at home almost instantly and Frances wrote to tell Marie Louise of her first impressions:

> There is a grandfather, a husband and wife and two small children – kindness itself, but so utterly unlike people of the same position at home. Here we have the true democracy at work and we shall all lead the family life I can see. Miss Collins is already nursing the baby and Gilbert is conversing with the grandfather about the Civil War and Lincoln, while I must help Mrs Bixler to clear the table.[17]

Predictably, Frances fell in love with both the children and made particular friends with Delphine, who was four years old. Many years later Dorothy remembered the relationship between Delphine and 'Auntie Frances':

> Delphine seldom went to bed till midnight and got up in the morning when she felt inclined and danced about all the morning in her pyjamas and dressing-gown. Mrs Chesterton sometimes took her for a walk but she was worn out before they had walked half-a-mile.
>
> Knowing Mrs Chesterton's love of children, you can imagine how happy she was during our six weeks stay at South Bend.[18]

The Bixlers quite literally made the Chestertons feel 'at home' in America, enabling Gilbert to gain a greater insight into the American way of life than would have been possible if he had simply stayed in hotels. Meanwhile an insight into the life of the Chestertons in this home from home was offered by Mrs Bixler, who had many fond memories of their stay with her. She recalled that Gilbert would stand in the living-room 'with his hands clasped behind his back, looking perfectly relaxed and gazing at baby Frances – sometimes for quarter of an hour at a time'. He would do this 'again and again', and when he wasn't gazing at the baby he would sit Delphine, her sister, on his lap. His working day was similar to the routine adhered to in Beaconsfield: dictating from breakfast to lunch and lunch to tea. Each weekday evening he left for the university at about seven o'clock to deliver his lecture, accompanied by both Frances and Dorothy, returning at about nine thirty. Initially they were scheduled to have their meals at the university, but Frances besought Mrs Bixler to let them eat at home. Subsequently they ate breakfast and lunch with the family in the kitchen but dined alone in the evening.[19]

Mrs Bixler also remembered that her husband made home-brew and that Gilbert 'kept Daddy busy making home-brew for him'. She remembered a time when they had gone to a banquet and Frances had written saying how artificial it was and how she wished she was back home, by which she meant back home with the Bixlers, not back home in England. The fact that both Gilbert and Frances soon began to refer to the Bixler household as home pleased their hostess very much. She recalled with pleasure that they had gone to dinner with 'some very rich people' but that Gilbert had arrived back at the house sighing, 'Oh, I'm glad to be home.' Frances then remarked that he was 'wanting to go home' all evening. 'After that they didn't go out at night. They both loved simplicity.'[20]

Mrs Bixler spoke at length of the Chestertons' affection for her four-year-old daughter:

> They were always buying Delphine something. My, how fond they were of her . . .
>
> He bought for Delphine one of those Russian toys – one doll inside another, perhaps six in all. He had one himself and would take it apart and put it together by the hour while he was thinking up something. His was tiny, hers quite big. Sometimes they would sit together taking their dolls apart and putting them together again. He never went past Delphine without noticing her, chuckling or something. They played *a lot* together. He carried his little doll with him all the time.
>
> When they left, Gilbert kissed the babies good-bye and tears came to his eyes. Frances cried.
>
> I think he loved everybody. He'd never say an unkind word or think an unkind thing about anybody. You can't but pick up something of a character living under the same roof for six weeks. He was most tender-hearted.[21]

None the less, Mrs Bixler confessed that Gilbert 'was way over my head' and that she was amazed at his intellectual abilities: 'He'd write three or four articles and they were as clean as A.B.C. I've often wondered if that man's mind stopped working any time, if he ever relaxed completely. Looking at the baby, bouncing Delphine on his knee, he had an extremely different – a relaxed expression. But I wondered if his mind wasn't still working in another sphere.'[22]

However much the Chestertons enjoyed their home from home, they still managed to make many friends at the university where Gilbert lectured five nights a week. At the time America was in the throes of Prohibition and Professor Engels recalled that Chesterton 'would sit around consuming home-made ale by the quart' and that he remarked that 'the head of the philosophy faculty made the best brew in the college'.[23] On another occasion he was persuaded to go to an informal gathering after his hosts mentioned that they had some illicit Canadian ales. Gilbert didn't take much persuading: 'The ales have it,' he quipped. There can be little doubt that episodes such as these were in Chesterton's mind when he wrote: 'If I ever meet anybody who suggests there's something Calvinistic or Puritanical in Catholicism I shall ask, "Have you ever heard of the University of Notre Dame?"'[24]

Gilbert's chauffeur for the duration of the six weeks remembered how he liked to be driven out to the countryside:

> He'd just talk about the country, he'd admire the streams and things like that. I took him to the Virgin Forest and I could hardly get him back. He even got out to notice the trees. He spent almost an hour. The women raved at me and said I must get him back at a certain time. He'd ask me the names of the trees. He loved rivers and would ask me about the fish. At one time Father O'Donnell thought he should drive to Chicago or some big town but he didn't care for towns, said they all looked alike to him, so after that we always went to the country.[25]

The chauffeur also recalled that Chesterton's vast bulk made it very difficult for him to get in and out of the car. Once, when he was struggling even more than usual, he remarked that he couldn't get out sideways because he had no sideways.

He also seemed to enjoy life on the campus, being impressed particularly by the golden-domed church of the Blessed Virgin which overlooked the arena where he enjoyed watching the students playing American football, urged on by cheer-leaders. The contrast between the spiritual and sporting activities of the students inspired his poem 'The Arena', which he dedicated to the University of Notre Dame and which was probably written while he was there:

> She too looks on the Arena,
> Sees the gladiators in grapple,
> She whose names are Seven Sorrows and the Cause
> of All Our Joy,
> Sees the pit that stank with slaughter
> Scoured to make the courts of morning
> For the cheers of jesting kindred and the scampering
> of a boy.[26]

The 'scampering' of the footballers impressed Chesterton in a way that sport seldom had in the past. In the poem he described the physical aspect of the game as 'hateless war and harmless mirth'.

Although Chesterton lectured every weekday evening at Notre Dame, he was free at weekends to accept lecturing engagements elsewhere. It was during these weekends that he visited Milwaukee, Detroit and Chicago. In Chicago the bishop introduced him by quoting the lines of Oliver Herford's verse:

> When plain folks such as you and I
> See the sun sinking in the sky,
> We think it is the setting sun:
> But Mr Gilbert Chesterton
> Is not so easily misled;
> He calmly stands upon his head,
> And upside down obtains a new
> And Chestertonian point of view.
> Observing thus how from his nose
> The sun creeps closer to his toes
> He cries in wonder and delight
> How fine the sunrise is tonight![27]

It was at Chicago also that Gilbert won the affection of the audience with his quick-witted *ad libs*. For instance, when someone yelled from the audience that he couldn't hear, Chesterton glanced up and said, 'Good brother, don't worry, you're not missing a thing.'[28]

On 5 November, as his series of lectures was drawing to an end, Chesterton was made an honorary Doctor of Laws in the first special convocation of the faculty of Notre Dame. The citation called him a 'man of letters . . . defender of the Christian tradition, whose keen mind, right heart, and versatile literary genius have been valiantly devoted to eternal truth, goodness, and beauty, in literature and in life . . .'[29] It was the first of many honorary doctorates he would collect during the remainder of his stay in America and Canada.

A few days later, and about three or four days before his final lecture, Chesterton announced to the students that they could bring books to the Bixler house to be autographed. Mrs Bixler remembered that the students took advantage of this offer for themselves and their friends on an immense scale: 'They kept us busy answering the door. Students would come with three and four books. Others sent them in large boxes.' According to Mrs Bixler, there were between six and seven hundred books in total and Chesterton signed them all.[30]

On 15 November, his six weeks at Notre Dame completed, Gilbert's extensive lecture tour commenced in earnest. They were sad to leave, and Frances wrote in a letter home that 'every thing and everyone has been so nice and the lectures so successful and Gilbert is beloved by the students'.[31]

Their first engagement was at Cincinnati, where they were given the royal suite where Queen Marie of Romania had stayed. Indeed, as Dorothy recalled, they were treated like royalty with Gilbert's welcome being fit for a king:

> The Union Jack was flying, and the entrance hall was decorated with Union Jacks and a large illuminated sign saying 'Welcome G. K. Chesterton'.
>
> As soon as we had unpacked, the manager appeared with one of the staff with a huge cake made as an exact reproduction of Mr Chesterton's latest book, *The Resurrection of Rome*. We could never have eaten it had not the Chesterton Club turned up in force that evening and they made short work of it.[32]

The Club added to Chesterton's luggage by presenting him with a framed etching so large that two taxis were now required to transport the Chestertons, Dorothy and the luggage. The etching was carried everywhere they went until, in a taxi in New York, Gilbert finally sat on it, smashing the glass.

It was from the St Moritz Hotel in New York that Frances wrote on 25 November to a friend:

> Since we arrived in New York our life has been a nightmare. Publicity men, reporters, interviewers, photographers, even film producers, dog our uneasy footsteps.
>
> I have not had a moment to thank you before this for the lovely

embroidered Polish Eagle. (His American brother faces me on the hotel bedspread.) But you will understand and forgive the delay. The poems too we are very proud to possess.

We have nothing but happy memories of Notre Dame – in spite of football excitements it seems compared with the conditions of hotel life in New York like the classic groves of Hellas.[33]

It is clear that, as far as Frances was concerned, the six weeks at Notre Dame were the blissful calm before the dreaded storm. She was now back in the tedious and tiring routine which she had found so irritating during the previous visit to America.

The Chestertons spent Thanksgiving Day in New York and it is likely that it was here that Gilbert made the remark, which infuriated some and delighted others, that the English should institute their own special Thanksgiving Day to celebrate the fact that the Pilgrim Fathers had left.

Throughout December Chesterton lectured in various cities in the north-east. In Pittsburgh he won the audience over with joking references to his obesity: 'I want to assure you I am not this size, really, dear no, I'm being amplified by the [microphone].'[34] Other lectures were given at Philadelphia, Cleveland, Ohio and Buffalo, where he received another honorary degree. At Albany he told the Americans that their worship of economic activity was unsound:

The people are too eager to build up: they spend their energy in building up something that will be taken down in a few years. It has grown to be almost a religion with the people here.

It is a very subtle thing. I don't know where it came from. It is the outgrowth of history, of the exhilarating climate and the pioneer spirit, I suppose. The Puritans came here full of ideals of religion as if a new light shone.

That passionate energy for religion with which they came to this country passed away and the people have thrown their tremendous energy into business. It is the worship of activity for its own sake. They worship it without an objective. In England the rich classes that worship laziness are as bad. Neither is sound. It is a false religion.[35]

Perhaps one of the warmest welcomes Chesterton received was from Holy Cross College at Worcester, Massachusetts. Upon his arrival on 12 December, he was greeted outside the library by seven students dressed up to represent giants of literature, namely Newman, Shakespeare, Cervantes, Chaucer, Dante, Virgil and Homer. He was also presented with 'a dim print of a Greek painting on vellum, now in Athens, of the Battle of Lepanto', the college having 'secured the services of an artist to bring into clearer relief the obscure details on the print'.[36]

Chesterton was to give the inaugural lecture of the winter course, and, to commemorate the occasion, a special souvenir brochure entitled *Chestertoniana* was published. The foreword, written by Michael Earls, SJ, stated that the college was 'especially elated that the inaugural lecture for the ensuing course is by the distinguished man of letters, admired and beloved, Mr G. K. Chesterton'.[37] The students themselves expressed their hospitality in a 'Salutation to the Crusader G. K. C. from Crusaders at Holy Cross in Accents of Their Forefathers'. The salutation was then given in a truly cosmopolitan cross-section of languages by students whose ancestors came from all four corners of the world. Gilbert was saluted in Arabic, Armenian, Chinese, French, Gaelic, German, Greek, Hungarian, Italian, Lithuanian, Polish, Portuguese, Spanish and Syriac. However, the most prestigious tribute came from Paul Claudel, the poet, dramatist and essayist, who was the French ambassador to Washington at the time of Chesterton's visit:

> I am delighted to bring my salutations to the great poet and the great Christian, G. K. Chesterton, during his tour of the United States. His books, for the past twenty years, have never failed to bring me joy and refreshment: and this feeling of regard is so tender and unusual that approbation is linked with admiration.
>
> During the past century, Catholicism almost everywhere has had to sustain an attitude of defense: it preferred to take shelter in the past and in forms of refuge, or, as one might say, in chapels severely cloistered and ornamented with rigid refinery. Chesterton thoroughly understands that in our religion Mystery is wed with Evidence, and our eternal responses with the most pressing and present exigencies. He is the man that threw the doors wide open: and upon a world pallid and sick he sent floods of poetry, of joyousness, of noble sympathies, of radiant and thundering humor, – all drawn from unfailing sources of orthodoxy. His onward march is the verification of that divine saying: 'The Truth will make you free.'
>
> If I were to state his essential quality, I would say that it is a sort of triumphant common sense – that *gaudium de veritate*, of which

philosophers discourse; – a joyous acclaim towards the splendor and the powers of the soul, those faculties that were overburdened and numbed by a century of false science, of pedantic pessimism, and of *counterfeit* and *contra-fact*. In the sparkling and irresistible dialectics of a great poet, he keeps always bringing us back to that infallible promise of Christ: – And I will refresh you: *Et Ego reficiam vos*.[38]

Most of the remainder of the souvenir-brochure was devoted to reprints of two Chesterton poems and one of his essays. The two poems were 'The House of Christmas' and 'Lepanto', while the essay, 'Some Heresies of Our Mass Production', returned to the theme of over-production discussed in Albany. Taking the example of mass-produced walking sticks, Chesterton waxed lyrical on the absurdities of modern economic practices:

> Then the same demoniac logic begins to extend itself in every direction. As there is a machine for making the stick, there must also be a machine for making the machine. As the machine as well as the stick must be sold as often as possible, it must be broken as often as possible. And the inverted and insane progress, which began with a perfect wheel turning out an imperfect stick, may even end in the turning out of a more and more imperfect wheel. To this there is added salesmanship, which means inducing people to buy imperfect wheels as if they were perfect wheels; and mergers, which means making sure there shall be only one imperfect sort of wheel; and publicity, which means proclaiming this preposterous state of things through ten thousand trumpets of brass, as if it were the age of gold.[39]

The extent to which Chesterton enjoyed his visit to Holy Cross College can be gauged from a letter Charles Murphy wrote from the Canadian Senate to the English novelist Wilfrid Meynell on 16 January 1931:

> Through the courtesy of Reverend Michael Earls, S.J., of Holy Cross College, Worcester, Mass., I am enabled to send you, under separate cover, a copy of *Chestertoniana*, the brochure which was issued by Holy Cross College in commemoration of the visit of Mr G. K. Chesterton last month. I am sure you will be interested in this unique publication.
>
> When Mr Chesterton was in Ottawa at Christmas time I had a conversation with him about everything in general, and nothing in particular. However, he spoke of his visit to Holy Cross College

with enthusiasm, and referred specifically to the pageant which was organised in his honor, and in which a group of the Great Ones in the literature of the world were impersonated by a number of the students at the College.

Since the copy of the brochure was sent to me Father Earls and I have exchanged correspondence . . . I understand that Mr Chesterton is likely to pay a return visit to Holy Cross College, and I am hopeful that we may have the pleasure of hearing him in a lecture here in Ottawa sometime in the Spring.[40]

Returning to New York City, Chesterton took part in a much publicised debate at the Mecca with the religiously sceptical Chicago lawyer Clarence Darrow. The subject to be debated was the story of creation in the Book of Genesis and many believed that the sharp mind of the acclaimed lawyer would be too much for Chesterton. One of those who attended the debate, Frances Taylor Patterson, believed that Chesterton's arguments 'might seem somewhat literary in comparison with the trained scientific mind and rapier tongue of the famous trial lawyer'.[41] Gilbert, however, had always been more at home in open debate than he was in delivering a monologue, and he had learned the art of holding his own in conflicts of this sort with Bernard Shaw among others. He was more than a match for Darrow, as Patterson was to witness:

> I have never heard Mr Darrow alone, but taken relatively, when that relativity is to Chesterton, he appears positively muddle-headed.
> As Chesterton summed it up, he felt as if Darrow had been arguing all afternoon with his fundamentalist aunt, and simply kept sparring with a dummy of his own mental making. When something went wrong with the microphone, Darrow sat back until it could be fixed. Whereupon G. K. C. jumped up and carried on in his natural voice, 'Science, you see, is not infallible!' . . . Chesterton had the audience with him from the start, and when it was over, everyone just sat there, not wishing to leave. They were loath to let the light die![42]

As Christmas approached it would have been expected that the Chestertons would finish their tour and return to Beaconsfield. No doubt this was their desire and certainly one suspects that Frances, in particular, was itching for a return to domesticity. However, the leading American lecture agent, Lee Keedick, had persuaded Chesterton to embark on a longer tour than Gilbert had originally either envisaged or desired. Consequently, with a string of engagements still beckoning during the early months of 1931, the Chestertons were confined to New York City for the Christmas and New Year celebrations.

On 6 January they headed for the South *en route* for the West Coast. While they were at Chattanooga in Tennessee Frances suddenly began to feel ill. At first her condition wasn't felt to be too serious, and Gilbert left her in the charge of Dorothy while he continued to travel. However, Frances ran a very high temperature and the care and attention of both Dorothy and the hotel doctor brought no discernible improvement. She was admitted to hospital, where she had a private room and two nurses. Two specialists were called in and for four days, as Dorothy recorded, 'it was doubtful whether she would get better'.[43] Chesterton hastened back to Chattanooga to be at Frances's side and many lectures in the South had to be cancelled at short notice. According to the terms of his contract, Chesterton was required to pay Keedick £100 for each cancellation. In consequence, Frances, who was now recovering well, insisted that Dorothy should accompany Gilbert to the West Coast to try to salvage what was left of the tour. She would follow as soon as she could. Chesterton was due to commence lecturing on 12 February, so it was necessary to leave immediately. After travelling for three days and nights, Gilbert and Dorothy arrived in Los Angeles on the 10th. For the next week, wrote Dorothy, 'we rushed up and down the Californian coast and Mr Chesterton gave a lecture at a different place every night'.[44]

Frances finally arrived on 17 February, accompanied by one of her nurses, and Dorothy managed to locate, in the Californian hills only a few miles outside the city, a small Spanish hotel which she believed would be ideal for a happy convalescence. It was from this hotel that Gilbert found time to write to Clare Nicholl, one of the family of young sisters he had met originally at Lyme Regis five years earlier. Clare had been a child when he had first met her but she was now a rapidly maturing teenager, a fact borne out by the tone of Chesterton's letter:

If you only knew how we long to be home in England you would not accuse us of wandering wilfully . . . The trouble is that [Frances] got ill rather quickly and gets well rather slowly: two good doctors have told me there is nothing wrong and it is a matter of time: but as an exile I learn to hate time, as you do. I see a new and savage sense in the figure of Killing Time. I handle the large knife in my pocket.

I will dramatise for you a real scene, farce, comedy or miracle play: which occurred in Chattanooga in the State of Tennessee (which is Puritan and very Dry) . . . Frances in bed. To her enters a perfectly gigantic Popish Priest, swarthy as a Spaniard . . .

Priest (after a boisterous greeting) I was told ye were ill: but I didn't know how ill. I've brought the Holy Oils.

Frances (somewhat tartly) Then you can take 'em away again. I don't want *them* just yet. But I wish you'd give me your blessing, Father.

Priest I'll give ye some whiskey first.

(Produces an enormous bottle of Bootleg Whiskey and flourishes it like a club). Don't ye believe all that yer told about the stuff we get – you've only got to know your Bootlegger. This is perfectly sound mellow Canadian stuff and the nurse says ye need a little stimulant.

(Administers a little stimulant with a convivial air.)

You drink that down and ye'll be all the better.

Frances (rather faintly) . . . and the Blessing?

Priest (straightens himself and gabbles in a strong guttural voice) *Benedicat te Omnipotens Deus*, etc. etc., or whatever is the form for sickbeds.

. . . Frances is much better this morning and we shall probably resume normally the homeward march. For we are now really turning homeward, though so far away: we shall never, please God, go farther away. The idea is to lecture at San Francisco . . . and then work up the coast by Oregon . . . then pause by Vancouver where we have a friend or two: and then bang back to New York and Old England. Amen.[45]

It is clear from the general tone of this letter that Gilbert and Frances were now thoroughly homesick for England. The warmth of the welcome and the memories of the homeliness and hospitality they had received at the outset of the tour had now receded into the realms of dim and distant memory. Gilbert was also rather too optimistic about the state of his wife's health, as she was far from fit enough to travel with him on the next round of lecturing engagements. Reluctantly, he and Dorothy were forced to leave Frances to recuperate in the Spanish hotel while they travelled to

San Francisco, Seattle and Portland, Oregon; and thence across the Canadian border to Vancouver and Victoria, British Columbia. (Dorothy remembered a particularly dramatic episode during the visit to Portland, where she and Gilbert nearly witnessed a gangland killing: 'The thuggery which resulted from Prohibition was at its height. At Portland there was a hold-up and a killing outside our hotel which, much to the distress of the taxi-driver, we just missed by minutes.')[46]

Upon their arrival in Vancouver it was evident immediately that Chesterton was as popular on the west coast of Canada as he had been on the east of the country six months earlier. The two Vancouver newspapers publicised his visit extensively and when, on 11 March, Gilbert travelled across the water to Victoria the reception at the hands of the press was even more enthusiastic. Indeed, on 8 March, three days before his arrival, the *Daily Colonist* had reported the growing interest in Chesterton's lecture in terms bordering on hero-worship:

> Gilbert K. Chesterton, the brilliant English essayist, dramatist, novelist, and philosopher . . . will speak at the Royal Victoria Theatre, Wednesday, March 11, his subject being 'The Ignorance of the Educated'.
> Mr Chesterton's views on this topic are certain to hold the interest of the large audience he will undoubtedly attract. His ideas have always been original and oftentimes startling, for he is admittedly the greatest prophet of our generation. What will particularly impress his audience will be his pronounced optimism, the sparkling epigrams with which he brightens his discourse, and his broad vein of humor. He will also furnish every evidence that he is a man of supreme genius, a clear thinker, whose ideas impress and fascinate every hearer while the message he brings will be virile and uplifting.[47]

On the afternoon of 11 March a journalist with the *Victoria Daily Times* obtained a pre-lecture interview with Chesterton at the Empress Hotel. Although not as fawning in his approach as the *Daily Colonist*'s reporter, the journalist was none the less impressed by Chesterton's presence. He was a 'ponderous form in a voluminous black cloak' who

> had a ruddy, somewhat rounded face with a high, broad forehead; thin slightly grey hair that embraced the upper part of his ears; a moustache of a sandier color that hooked down below his mouth. His large eyes twinkled. They branded Chesterton as unavoidably

genial, in spite of his heavy eyebrows, his aggressive nose. Layers of chin tapered down into the folds of an ample winged collar. His skin was fair, delicate ... His replys [*sic*] to the interviewers were often followed by a cavernous chortle, and his whole body shook and shifted around on the settee ...

Chesterton stood up to shake hands and was over six feet. His massive shoulders curved under his long cloak, and he walked with a slow amble. Not a man to be passed in a crowd – rather a Dr Samuel Johnson come to life in this twentieth century, able to talk on most things, dictatorially perhaps, but readily and optimistically.[48]

Meanwhile, hundreds of miles to the south, Frances was writing to Marie Louise from the Spanish hotel, situated not far from Hollywood, that some film producers were 'very anxious to get hold of some Father Brown stories for filming. It would be splendid financially ... and a great help, as naturally my illness has been a bit expensive. Everything out here is about 4 times as much as in England.'[49]

Gilbert, however, was typically oblivious to any financial considerations. Upon his return to Los Angeles, he devoted a great deal of his precious little spare time to writing and illustrating a children's book as a personal gift to Sheila Matier, the young daughter of a friend in the city. The book, entitled 'The Three Conquistadors', recounted in verse the stories of 'Red Bison of the Hokum Tribe', 'Juan the Dago' and 'The Chinese Pirate'. It was dedicated to 'Sheila Matier, who is too old for such picture books, and her father, who is too young for them, and her mother, to whom I offer these childish thanks for hospitality'.[50] Some time later the handwritten volume was shown to a writer from the *Los Angeles Times*: 'It seemed to us such a revelation of Chesterton, such a priceless expression of his kindliness and courtesy and humor – for how many men whose writings are worth a round price per word would give so much time and effort to making a book for a child?'[51]

Chesterton would probably have been embarrassed by such public praise for a volume he had intended to remain strictly private, but as he had left Los Angeles long before the praise was printed, in July 1931, it is likely that he remained blissfully ignorant of its publication. In fact, the Chestertons had finally left California on 23 March, dropping Frances's nurse off at Kansas City before continuing to New York. Arriving in New York on 29 March, they had to endure a final series of lectures before making the long-awaited journey home.

« 27 »

On Air in England

ALTHOUGH CHESTERTON HAD ARRIVED home from America in a state of physical and mental exhaustion, his long absence meant that he was in greater demand than ever in England. By the second week of May 1931 he was speaking to the City Literary Institute on Mary Queen of Scots, and the following evening he attended the Detection Club dinner at L'Escargot Bienvenu, in Greek Street. On 21 May he was at the Oxford Union proposing the motion 'That the Law is an Ass'.

Frances and Dorothy were understandably concerned that Gilbert's workload was having a detrimental effect on his health and they were determined to cut down his lecture schedule to a more manageable size. They met with some success because Ronald Knox wrote plaintively to Chesterton on 1 July that Dorothy had turned down an invitation of his:

> Now it seems your secretary refuses to let you lecture for the next few months, because you've got so bored with it in America.
>
> It is so maddening, after five years of being told you wouldn't come because you were lecturing too much, to be told now that you won't come because you're lecturing too little. I shall begin to believe you have a down on me, or Newman, or something.[1]

One suspects that the tone of Father Knox's letter would have been radically different had he realised that his friend was close to collapse. By the end of the summer Chesterton was effectively confined to Top Meadow. Maurice Baring, having learned of Gilbert's illness, wrote a letter of condolence to Frances: 'I am so sorry Gilbert has been so unwell. Every man of his age and mine seems to be unwell at the moment. Tell him that although he does not write to me he sometimes does better: he sends me a wave and a smile in his articles in the *Illustrated London News* by sometimes mentioning things we have talked about or something I have written about him . . . It is like getting a message on the wireless.'[2]

In fact, Chesterton's articles for the *Illustrated London News* were the source for his only book during the whole of 1931. Published on 22 October by Methuen, its title, *All is Grist*, was particularly apt considering the way his health had suffered under the millstone of his commitments. It was also appropriate, and unwittingly prophetic, that Baring had compared Gilbert's articles to 'a message on the wireless' because on Christmas Day 1931 Chesterton made his first ever radio broadcast. The fledgling BBC was obviously aware of Gilbert's popular success during his lecture tour of America twelve months earlier and had asked him to make a fifteen-minute broadcast to the United States on the subject of Christmas and Charles Dickens. This was a singular honour, inviting comparison with the King's Christmas broadcast to the Empire. Yet, although it is scarcely remarkable that Chesterton should be at home with the subject of Christmas and Dickens, it is somewhat surprising that he proved such an instant success as a broadcaster. His transatlantic audience was charmed instantly by the jovial personality and the clarity of his voice:

> I have been asked to speak to you . . . on Dickens and Christmas; or as I should prefer to say, on Christmas and Dickens. Why . . . Christmas and Dickens? Perhaps the official organisers do not know me very well. Perhaps they have a grudge against you. Why, on this day of holiday, am I made to work? Why, on this day of rejoicing, are you made to suffer? . . . Dickens was separated by centuries of misunderstanding from that mysterious revelation that brought joy upon earth; but . . . he was resolved to enjoy it . . . And now in the name of all such things, let us all go and do the same.[3]

Towards the end of 1931 and during the early weeks of 1932 Chesterton, Belloc and Baring were brought together for sittings at the studio of the artist James Gunn. The result was Gunn's well-known *Conversation Piece*, which was a great success at the Academy Summer Exhibition in April and which today can be seen in the National Portrait Gallery. On 11 May *Punch* captioned a cartoon of the portrait 'Mr Chesterton takes a note of another Sussex tavern, discovered by Mr Belloc, where they sell very good ale.'[4]

It was also in May that Gilbert's next book, entitled *Sidelights*, was published by Sheed & Ward. The volume's full title was *Sidelights on New London and Newer York and Other Essays*, and it consisted, as the title suggested, of three loosely connected sections. The first of these, 'New London', comprised eight essays concerned principally with the follies of the 'Bright Young Things' who adorned the social scene of contemporary London. In truth, however, he rarely succeeded in his professed goal of illustrating the fundamental errors of their ways, and his efforts paled into insignificance beside the novels of Evelyn Waugh, which were exposing the follies of contemporary high society with more wit and greater effectiveness. Yet there were one or two highpoints among the 'Sidelights on New London', most notably in the essay on 'The Unpsychological Age':

> Many human beings ... have in the past managed to enjoy themselves a great deal without bothering about Psychology. Still, if a whole human generation is going to bother and bewilder itself with Psychology, it might as well know something about it. The present generation knows nothing about it.
>
> What the present generation knows is a number of catch phrases taken from one particular theory, which happens to be the last theory, and which will therefore be blown to bits by the next theory. But even before it is blown to bits, the culture of our time has never had anything except bits of it. It has learnt for instance, to use the phrase 'Inferiority Complex' to describe what Christians used to call Modesty and gentlemen good manners. But if you stop somebody who has just used the phrase 'Inferiority Complex', and ask him whether there is such a thing as 'Superiority Complex', he will gape and gobble and gurgle unmeaning sounds and his legs will give way beneath him. His inferiority complex, anyhow, will be instantly and appallingly apparent. For he has never thought about the phrase he uses; he has only seen it in the newspapers. The new phrase is not in the newspapers; and he has never heard of it. But the much older and much more profound Psychology of the Christian Religion was founded on the very ancient discovery that a superiority complex was the beginning of all evil.[5]

Chesterton returned to the subject of psychology, affirming that realism trod a path between the extremes of optimism and pessimism, during the first of the 'Other Essays' which formed the third and final section of the book:

> ... there was a truth behind the impatient discovery of the Millennium, as well as behind the belated rediscovery of the Fall. Nor will man be

permanently satisfied with the pessimism of Huxley, any more than with the optimism of Whitman. For man knows there is that within him that can never be valued too highly, as well as that within him which can never be hated too much; and only a philosophy which emphasises both, violently and simultaneously, can restore the balance to the brain.[6]

The best section of *Sidelights* was neither the first nor the third but the middle section, 'on Newer York'. Inspired by his experiences in America, many of the essays in the middle of the book are highly entertaining. For example, in 'A Plea for Prohibition' Chesterton observed that the prohibition of alcohol by the American state had led to a welcome increase in the number of people brewing their own beer:

> ... the private brews differ very widely; multitudes are quite harmless and some are quite excellent. I know an American university where practically every one of the professors brews his own beer; some of them experimenting in two or three different kinds. But what is especially delightful is this: that with this widespread revival of the old human habit of home-brewing, much of that old human atmosphere that went with it has really reappeared ... Prohibition has to that extent actually worked the good, in spite of so malignantly and murderously willing the evil. And the good is this: the restoration of legitimate praise and pride for the creative crafts of the home.
>
> This being the case, it seems that some of our more ardent supporters might well favour a strong, simple and sweeping policy. Let Congress or Parliament pass a law not only prohibiting fermented liquor, but practically prohibiting everything else. Let the Government forbid bread, beef, boots, hats and coats; let there be a law against anybody indulging in chalk, cheese, leather, linen, tools, toys, tales, pictures or newspapers. Then, it would seem by serious sociological analogy, all human families will begin vigorously to produce all these things for themselves; and the youth of the world will really return.[7]

The whimsically sardonic humour continued in a contrasting vein in the following essay:

> When we say that this is the age of the machine, that our present peace, progress and universal happiness are due to our all being servants of the machine, we sometimes tend to overlook the quiet and even bashful presence of the machine gun ...

In one sense, of course, the machine gun is, like many modern things, so familiar as to be almost old-fashioned. Governments have long used it, of course, against barbarians so brutal and ignorant as not instantly to surrender their own mines or oil fields to the foreign millionaires who govern most of the governments. So an early poem of Mr Belloc summed up for ever the moral qualities that make for world mastery and the really essential virtues of a conquering race:

> Whatever happens we have got
> The Maxim gun and they have not.[8]

In the essay 'Skyscrapers' it is clear that Chesterton was still haunted by the memory of the large and depersonalised hotels in which he had stayed during the American trip. He imagined that some of these hotels were so large that they could almost, in a flight of fancy at least, have their own civil war:

A fine American epic might be written about the battle in the big hotel, with its multitudinous cells for its swarming bees. It might describe the exciting battle for the elevators; the war of the nameless and numberless guests, known only by their numbers. It might describe the gallant sally of 55783, who succeeded in seizing and working the thirty-second lift; the heroic conduct of 62017, in bringing up an armful of yams and sweet potatoes by the fire-escape; of the deathless deeds of 65991, whose name, or rather number, will resound for ever in history.[9]

Amid the flippancy there was, of course, a serious underlying message. England was being Americanised and London was 'being made to look like a bad imitation of New York'. This was Chesterton's primary concern, even though he was well aware of 'the simpler and saner elements of American life, which are almost as far from New York as from London'.[10] This concern was of paramount importance to Gilbert and he returned to it on several occasions elsewhere in the book:

Strange as it may seem, some are puzzled because I hate Americanisation and do not hate America. I should have thought that I had earned some right to apply this obvious distinction to any foreign country, since I have consistently applied it to my own country ... I am myself an Englishman ... and I have done my best to praise and glorify a number of English things: English inns, English roads,

English jokes and jokers; even to the point of praising the roads for being crooked or the humour for being Cockney; but I have invariably written, ever since I have written at all, against the cult of British Imperialism.

And when that perilous power and opportunity, which is given by wealth and worldly success, largely passed from the British Empire to the United States, I have applied exactly the same principle to the United States. I think that Imperialism is none the less Imperialism because it is spread by economic pressure or snobbish fashion rather than by conquest; indeed I have much more respect for the Empire that is spread by fighting than for the Empire that is spread by finance.

Anyhow, in both cases there is one constant factor: that it is invariably the worst things that are spread . . . A man can watch in every detail, day after day and year after year, the Americanisation of London, and there will never come to him, even as a faint and far-off breath of any wind of the prairies, a whisper of the real virtues of America.[11]

Sheed & Ward had published *Sidelights* a month after Faber & Faber had published Chesterton's biography of Chaucer. This book was the most lucrative Gilbert would write in his career, with Faber paying him an advance of £1,000. The idea for Chesterton's *Chaucer* had been that of Richard de la Mare, the son of the poet, who was enthusiastically promoting a series for Faber & Faber under the general heading of 'The Poets on the Poets'. Inevitably, many critics condemned the biography because it failed to meet certain scholarly criteria. Chesterton, however, was merely being true to form and following the familiar style that had characterised all his previous biographies. His intention, as he confessed candidly on the very first page of the book, was to point to the general truth without being bogged down by too many specific facts:

. . . I feel tempted to write, 'Beware!' or some such melodramatic phrase, in large letters across the frontispiece. For I do really desire to warn the reader, or the critic, of some possible mistakes in or about this book: touching its real purpose and its inevitable pitfalls.

It were perhaps too sanguine a simplicity to say that this book is intended to be popular; but at least it is intended to be simple. It describes only the effect of a particular poet on a particular person . . . It makes no claim to specialism of any sort in the field of Chaucerian scholarship. It is written for people who know even less about Chaucer than I do. It does not, in any of the disputed details, dictate to those who know much more about Chaucer than I do. It is primarily concerned with the fact that Chaucer was a poet. Or, in other words, that it is possible to know him, without knowing anything about him. A distinguished French critic said of my sketch of an English novelist that it might well bear the simple title, 'The Praise of Dickens'; and I should be quite content if this tribute only bore the title of 'The Praise of Chaucer'. The whole point, so far as I am concerned, is that it is as easy for an ordinary Englishman to enjoy Chaucer as to enjoy Dickens.[12]

Whether or not the last assertion was true for ordinary Englishmen, it was certainly true for Chesterton. He did find it as easy to enjoy Chaucer as to enjoy Dickens and, considering his love for Dickens, this was praise indeed. In fact, at the very outset of the book he awarded Chaucer a place of honour among the greatest writers of English literature:

Chaucer was a poet who came at the end of the medieval age and order; which certainly contained fanaticism, ferocity, wild asceticism and the rest. There are some who really suggest that it contained only fanaticism, ferocity and the rest. Anyhow, I was faced with the fact that Chaucer was the final fruit and inheritor of that order. And I was also confronted with the fact, which seems to me quite as certain a fact, that he was much *more* sane and cheerful and normal than most of the later writers. He was less delirious than Shakespeare, less harsh than Milton, less fanatical than Bunyan, less embittered than Swift. I had in any case to construct some sort of theory in connexion with this practical problem and this practical fact. Therefore in this book I advance the general thesis; that, in spite of everything, there was a balanced philosophy in medieval times; and some very unbalanced philosophies in later times.[13]

Gilbert concluded the first chapter, 'The Greatness of Chaucer', with an inspired and inspiring revelation of his own philosophy of gratitude. The potency of the prose, carried along on a wave of youthful exuberance and enthusiasm, belied any suggestion that his later writing had become tired or turgid:

There is at the back of all our lives an abyss of light, more blinding and unfathomable than any abyss of darkness; and it is the abyss of actuality, of existence, of the fact that things truly are, and that we ourselves are incredibly and sometimes almost incredulously real.

It is the fundamental fact of being, as against not being; it is the unthinkable, yet we cannot unthink it, though we may sometimes be unthinking about it; unthinking and especially unthanking. For he who has realised this reality knows that it does outweigh, literally to infinity, all lesser regrets or arguments for negation, and that under all our grumblings there is a subconscious substance of gratitude . . . This is something much more mystical and absolute than any modern thing that is called optimism; for it is only rarely that we realise, like a vision of the heavens filled with a chorus of giants, the primeval duty of Praise.[14]

The charm of Chesterton's *Chaucer* resided in this irrepressible enthusiasm. The author was clearly in love with the poet who was the subject of his book; as well as being in love with the medieval age to which the poet belonged and the medieval philosophy which the poet inherited.

Writing in the *Sunday Times* on 18 April, Desmond MacCarthy had nothing but praise for the newly published biography: 'When this book on Chaucer came into my hands I realised that there was no author in English literature, after Dickens, who was a better subject for Mr Chesterton; no other with whom he would find himself more instantly at home, and in criticising whom this sense of proportion would be more illuminating.' Lord David Cecil was even more impressed, proclaiming that Chesterton had brought out more forcibly than anyone the scale of Chaucer's genius.[15]

In the same month that *Chaucer* was published a short Chesterton article entitled 'If Christ Should Come' appeared in *Good Housekeeping*. Although it is little known and did not appear in John Sullivan's *Bibliography*, it is important because of its concise exposition of the relationship between the author's religion and his politics:

> If I am to answer the question, 'How would Christ solve modern problems if He were on earth today?', I must answer it plainly; and for those of my faith there is only one answer. Christ is on earth today; alive on a thousand altars; and He does solve people's problems exactly as He did when He was on earth in the more ordinary sense. That is, He solves the problems of the limited number of people who choose of their own free will to listen to Him . . .

Having introduced his article in orthodox fashion, Chesterton went on to discuss the Church's social teaching. 'The Catholic Church,' he explained, 'continues to advise men as Jesus advised men,' and problems arose because people ignored the teaching of the Church as they ignored the teaching of Christ. Specifically, the Church's condemnation of the excesses of capitalism were being ignored:

> ... the head of the Catholic Church, whom we call the Vicar of Christ, sent forth a proclamation commonly called *Rerum Novarum*, in which he subsequently stated three things: 1. That the existing concentration of wealth in the Capitalist 'laid upon the labouring millions a yoke little better than slavery'. 2. That we must not escape from this by the further concentration of Communism, as it denies even the natural forms of property, freedom and the home. 3. That, while wage-earners are entitled to combine and even to strike, on certain conditions of justice, it would be better if 'the poor so far as possible should become owners'; that is, small capitalists or possessors of the means of production. That is not an old Greek text from the Synoptics; neither is it a purely theological counsel addressed to the isolated soul. It is a perfectly clear outline of a general course of action; and there was nothing wrong with it, except that nobody acted on it ...
>
> Now I will maintain without hesitation that *if* the modern world had taken the Pope's advice even forty years ago, had really made a violent effort to decentralise Capitalism without accepting Communism; to make full ownership more of an ordinary thing for ordinary people, we should not be in the ghastly mess we are in at present. We should have a decent and dignified condition of property, which Christians could really defend against Communists. Having gone our own horrible heathen way, we have now to defend something nearly indefensible; only because the remedy is even worse than the disease.[16]

Chesterton, it seemed, was never more at home than when he was called upon to defend the faith, and he would have been gratified to know that to some people, at least, his defence was being particularly well received. One such person was C. S. Lewis, who was composing autobiographical verse during the spring of 1932 describing his conversion to Christianity. Only thirty-four lines have survived, in a letter written to his friend Owen Barfield on 6 May 1932, but his biographers, Roger Lancelyn Green and Walter Hooper, have labelled what remains of the verse a 'Chestertonian "voyage"': 'As Lewis had read most of Chesterton's theological books by this time it does not seem fanciful to suppose that Lewis's idea of a spiritual

413

"voyage" was based on an idea suggested by Chesterton in his book on *Orthodoxy*.'[17]

Another person who had been greatly influenced by Chesterton was the historian Christopher Dawson. On 1 June 1932 Dawson sent Chesterton a copy of his new book, *The Making of Europe*, 'in the hope that it may be of interest to you'. Dawson had converted to Catholicism many years earlier, partly due to Chesterton's literary influence, and he wrote in his letter that *The Making of Europe* 'gives a proper place to spiritual factors'. However, he confided to Gilbert his concern that the book was 'in danger of falling between two stools – being too popular for the academic public and too abstruse for the general reader'.[18] He needn't have worried because *The Making of Europe* was soon on the reading list in the history faculties of many universities and was translated into several European languages. The Belloc–Chesterton school of history now had a new academic champion.

On 18 June Gilbert and Frances sailed from Holyhead to attend the Eucharistic Congress in Dublin. As they drove from the quay through the streets of the city towards the Viceregal Lodge, where they would be staying as official guests, Chesterton was recognised by some of the crowd, who shouted out: 'God bless him. Three cheers for G. K.' Frances found the experience both 'exciting and embarrassing'.[19]

Upon arrival at the Lodge, Frances was pleased to find they had been given spacious rooms and she and Gilbert were delighted to learn that the tenor, John MacCormack, whom they had met the previous year in California, would also be a house guest. On 21 June the Irish hierarchy gave a garden party at Blackrock for some 30,000 people. Frances wrote to her mother, who was in ailing health and residing in a nursing home in Beaconsfield, that she and Gilbert had been spotted by Cardinal Bourne, who had been 'very gracious' to them both. Chesterton was also accosted by a priest from Eastern Europe who was full of praise for his writing. When the priest requested that they be photographed together, Chesterton remarked with characteristic wit that perhaps it was considered lucky in Eastern Europe to be seen with an idiot. The fact that this aside was more than a mere flippancy can be gauged by Chesterton's view that the Congress had made him realise that there was 'something disproportionate in finding one's own trivial trade, or tricks of the trade, amid the far-reaching revelations of such a trysting-place of all the tribes of men'.[20]

The apex of the Congress was the Pontifical High Mass in Phoenix Park. John MacCormack sang at the service, and Chesterton wore the scarlet robe, green hood and black velvet cap of a Doctor of Letters of the National University of Ireland, 'an honorary degree given some time ago'. At the Consecration there was an awesome stillness as the faint sound of St Patrick's bell, which had been silent for centuries, broke the silence. Typically, however, although he felt due reverence at such occasions, Gilbert's fondest memories of Dublin were of the spontaneous outbursts of little altars and amateur decorations in the poorest parts of the city. A story he loved to tell was that of an old woman who said, when the clouds looked threatening on the last day: 'Well, if it rains now He will have brought it upon Himself.'[21]

Back in England Gilbert's health began to deteriorate again, and by early September he had suffered a further collapse. Dorothy, who was on holiday in the south of France, expressed her concern in a letter to Frances from Carcassonne on 15 September: 'It seems almost inevitable that he should have these attacks at stated intervals. I suppose it is Nature's warning to him that he is not made of cast-iron and that he must be careful.'[22] Three days later she was writing again, this time from Avignon:

> It was lovely to find your dear letter waiting for me and to hear that he is going on well. Is the doctor going to be very severe about a future regime for him? He is generally so good after he has been ill for a little while. I do hope he will be careful. It would be so awful if he got properly ill again. I always wonder that he does not. What a good thing we were really firm about autumn and winter engagements.[23]

The letter concluded with a desire that Frances should 'give him my love and best wishes for a speedy recovery'. Her wishes were granted sooner than she dared hope because the letter crossed with one from Frances to say that Gilbert was better. Dorothy wrote back immediately: 'I am glad he is really better, but sorry to hear that your feelings do not entirely coincide with the doctor's opinions. What is worrying you now? I can't help feeling that possibly his nervousness is bound to react on you and you may worry in sympathy with him when there is not any cause. It will do you both a lot of good to get away.'[24]

Dorothy's previous letter had contained a vivid description of

Avignon, the streets and alleys of which reminded her of Naples: 'It is all very, very old and picturesque and there are fine views from the Public Gardens over the Rhône and the valley to the mountains beyond. The colouring at sunset tonight was magnificent.'[25]

Within a couple of months she was able to share these views with Frances and Gilbert even more vividly because Avignon was on their itinerary when she drove the Chestertons through France in the autumn. She obviously hoped that a non-working holiday in a milder climate would be beneficial to both of them. They also stayed at Nîmes and Perignon before returning to England.

Dorothy's principal worry during Gilbert's illness was that she may have contributed to his collapse by overworking him. She expressed this concern to Frances:

> I am glad he feels that I am moderately reasonable, because so often I feel he would be much happier with someone who was more haphazard about the work and did not bother him about dates, and getting letters answered, and so on. It could be done on those lines I realise quite well, and I often wonder if I try to drive it too much along a road instead of letting it wander in the woods. He is more than patient with me, whatever he thinks. Please give him my love.[26]

In fact, Gilbert was intensely grateful for the discipline and efficiency Dorothy instilled into his working practices. This gratitude was expressed most poignantly in the personal inscriptions he wrote in the books he had recently dictated to her, such as this personal dedication written in a copy of *Chaucer*: 'To Dorothy Collins without whom this book would have been published upside down'.[27] However, the inscription Dorothy treasured most was the one he wrote in his next book, *Christendom in Dublin*, published in November 1932. This time it took the form of a poem, ostensibly written for her birthday but concerned primarily with congratulating her on her recent reception into the Catholic Church:

> As you were better than a friend
> In more than friendship we agree –
> Friendship at best may be a bond:
> And Truth has made us free.

Who enters by that Door alone,
However dubious or afraid
For that one hour is that one Mind
For which the world was made . . .[28]

Christendom in Dublin was a short collection of essays giving the author's impressions of the Eucharistic Congress earlier in the year. The essays had been written originally for the *Universe* and these, together with an essay on 'The Mission of Ireland', which had appeared in a magazine called *Studies*, were published together by Sheed & Ward. The book contained some moments of true inspiration and it is likely that he was thinking of Dorothy's conversion as well as his own when he wrote of the role of reason in the convert's ultimate decision to embrace the faith of the Catholic Church:

A man who finds his way to Catholicism, out of the tangle of modern culture and complexity, must think harder than he has ever thought in his life. He must often deal as grimly with dry abstractions as if he were reading mathematics . . . He must often face the dull and repulsive aspects of duty, as if he were facing the dreariest drudgery in the world . . . He must feel all the counter-attractions of Paganism at least enough to know how attractive are those attractions. But, above all, he must think; above all, he must preserve his intellectual independence; above all, he must use his reason . . .

I say that *when* you are convinced, when you are rationally convinced, when you have come to the end of the long road of reason, when you have seen through the tangled arguments of the time, when you have found the answer to them – *then* you will find yourself suddenly in the morning of the world. Then you will find yourself among facts and not arguments . . .[29]

Christendom in Dublin concluded with a description of an Irish statue of the Madonna and Child which Chesterton had purchased in London and presented to his local parish church in Beaconsfield:

She was a peasant and she was a queen, and in that sense she was a lady; but not the sort of sham lady who pretends to be a peasant, nor the sort of sham peasant who pretends to be a lady. She was barefoot like any colleen on the hills; yet there was nothing merely local about her simplicity. I have never known who was the artist and I doubt if anybody knows; I only know that it is Irish, and I almost think that I should have known without being told . . . She looks across the church with an intense earnestness in which there is something of endless youth; and I have sometimes started, as if I had actually heard the words spoken across that emptiness: *I am the Mother of God, and this is Himself, and He is the boy you will all be wanting at the last.*[30]

On 31 October 1932 a new milestone was reached in Chesterton's career when he gave the first of a series of broadcasts for the BBC. His talk was entitled 'Some Famous Historical Characters' and was inspired by recently published biographies of Philip of Spain, William of Orange, Bonnie Prince Charlie, Talleyrand, Napoleon and the King of Rome. He was an instant success, his convivial and conversational approach capturing the affection of his listeners. A letter from Broadcasting House on 2 November expressed the Corporation's delight:

> The building rings with your praises! I knew I was not alone in my delight over your first talk. I think even you in your modesty will find some pleasure in hearing what widespread interest there is in what you are doing. You bring us something very rare to the microphone. I am most anxious that you should be with us till after Christmas. You will have a vast public by Christmas and it is good that they should hear you. Would you undertake six further fortnightly talks from January 16th onwards?[31]

The extraordinary success continued throughout the rest of the series of broadcasts, prompting further letters from the BBC remarking that he was 'quite superb at the microphone' and that his work on the radio was 'unique'.[32] 'You are a born broadcaster,' wrote the Director, 'and we must have much more of it.'[33] Although he was asked to submit a manuscript before each broadcast he was told that he was not expected to keep to the letter of it: 'We should like you to make variations as these occur to you as you speak at the microphone. Only so can the talk have a real show of spontaneity about it.'[34]

As these talks were meant to be book reviews, and as each talk dealt with between four and ten books, a lot of reading and a principle of selection were required. In fact, a great deal of this was undertaken by Dorothy: 'Much of the non-fiction sent to the BBC came to him for review . . . As the books came in, I would sort them and mark the passages which I knew would interest him, and quickly before each talk he would take a pile and make a talk which introduced and briefly reviewed a few, and mentioned some of the others. These were published as full-page articles in the *Listener*.'[35]

Needless to say, the fact that he was supposed to be reviewing other people's books seldom stopped him from introducing views of his own. For instance, a selection of various Victorian memoirs elicited the following view of the Victorian age:

> It is said young people were humbugged in Victorian times. I can only say that young people are being very thoroughly humbugged now on the subject of the Victorian times. Nothing can be more absurd than to say that the Victorians were merely prim, prosaic and respectable; on the contrary, they were the only people, before or since, who lived in a happy topsy-turveydom. It may be a hundred years before we again produce the mood that produced Lewis Carroll and Lear's Nonsense Rhymes.[36]

Similarly when Gilbert commenced his second series for the BBC in January 1933 a review of architectural books was an excuse for an elucidation of his own views on modern architecture:

> Those rows of new villas in the suburbs are built for anybody, that is nobody . . . the speculative builders do not know what people would really like so they build all the houses exactly the same in a style that nobody could like very much . . . There is nothing to show that suburban people really like suburban villas, indeed I strongly suspect that most of the satire against suburban villas is written in suburban villas . . . Now all this is to say what most of these books largely agree in saying, that there is not any modern style that is popular in the sense that most people like to look at it, let alone that most people would actually try to build it . . . Today, that is, we have things that a few people admire and we have things that a lot of people put up with, but we have not anything that can be called the taste of the age . . .[37]

The regular radio broadcasts helped to make Chesterton even more of a household name than he had been previously. Many who had never read a Chesterton book came to know his voice on the radio, whereas others who knew his books wanted to hear his voice. Dorothy Collins recalled how some people had bought their first radios solely so they would be able to hear Gilbert's talks: 'There was still a certain amount of resistance in those days among diehards who would not have a wireless set in the house, but news was reaching us in Beaconsfield of those who had bought sets just to listen to Chesterton.'[38] Dorothy also recalled the simple secret behind his phenomenal success:

> In spite of his success he was always very nervous beforehand and he would not undertake the series each year without a promise that his wife or I or both of us should sit in the studio with him. He liked it best that way and talked direct to us, which gave his talks the intimate character which the public so much enjoyed. He had Stuart Hibberd as his introducer who was always arrayed in a dinner-jacket, a custom of the BBC of those days for the evening talks, even though the announcer could not be seen. He would watch the green light turn to red and with an agonised glance at us, he would begin, and immediately be oblivious of his surroundings as he read and improvised his script as he went along.[39]

The effect which Chesterton had on his radio audience was exemplified by the reaction of a barber who rushed out of his shop to offer his condolences to one of Gilbert's friends on the morning after his death: 'I just wanted to say I was sorry to hear the news. He was a grand man.' Upon being asked whether he knew Chesterton well, the barber replied that he had 'never read a word he wrote, but I always listened to him on the wireless. He seemed to be sitting beside me in the room.'[40]

The irony was that Chesterton, in spite of all his warnings against the possible abuses of science, had found himself at the vanguard of a new age of technology. For the remainder of his life his popularity in England would have as much to do with his words on air as his words in print. Yet, regardless of whether the pen was mightier than the sword, Gilbert was now concerned that the microphone had become more powerful than both. As early as 1928 he had warned that the radio could very easily be used as an instrument of tyranny:

> Suppose you had told some of the old Whigs, let alone Liberals, that there was an entirely new type of printing press, eclipsing all others; and that as this was to be given to the King, all printing would henceforth be government printing. They would be roaring like rebels, or even regicides, yet that is exactly what we have done with the whole new invention of wireless. Suppose it were proposed that the king's officers should search all private houses to make sure there were no printing presses, they would be ready for a new revolution. Yet that is exactly

what is proposed for the protection of the government monopoly of broadcasting . . . There is really no protection against propaganda . . . being entirely in the hands of the government . . . It is wicked to nationalise mines or railroads; but we lose no time in nationalising tongues and talk.[41]

In principle, Gilbert's warnings may have been fair enough. In practice, however, the BBC was fair-minded and free enough to allow his dissident voice to fill the airwaves throughout the length and breadth of the country.

« 28 »

Dumb Ox and Donkey

On 21 March 1933 *G. K.'s Weekly* celebrated its tenth anniversary. To commemorate the event Chesterton composed an article in which he proposed 'to write about birthdays in a futile and irresponsible manner, as befits a festive occasion'. Two days later, *All I Survey*, another collection of his journalism for the *Illustrated London News*, was published. In one of the essays, 'On Saint George Revivified', he argued that 'the disadvantage of men not knowing the past is that they do not know the present. History is a hill or a high point of vantage, from which alone men see the . . . age in which they are living.'[1] He also remarked that the chief fact he could adduce from history was the living Christian tradition in which Augustine and Aquinas were one 'communion' and in which the mind of Aristotle still laboured on like a 'mighty mill'.[2]

On 29 March Dorothy L. Sayers wrote to Chesterton from Witham in Essex to say, 'We are so delighted that you can come and preside at the D. C. Guestnight Dinner on May 10th.'[3] However, although Gilbert continued to find time throughout the following months for the Detection Club and other social events, his mind was on other things or, rather, his mind was on another mind. In fact, his words in the essay in *All I Survey* about Augustine and Aquinas were an allusion to the book on St Thomas which would keep him occupied for the greater part of the year, during which he would labour like a 'mighty mill' to get to grips with what he had described in his biography of Chaucer as 'the colossal common sense of St Thomas Aquinas'.[4]

The biography of St Thomas was written at the request of Hodder & Stoughton, who wanted to publish it as a companion volume to Chesterton's highly successful biography of St Francis of Assisi, which had been published a decade earlier. Consequently in the spring of

1933 he commenced the writing of *St Thomas Aquinas*. It was destined to be the last full-length book he would write, with the exception of the posthumously published *Autobiography*.

Bernard Shaw was delighted when he heard that his friend had been asked to write the book. 'Great news this,' he wrote in a letter to Frances, 'about the Divine Doctor. I have been preaching for years that intellect is a passion that will finally become the most ecstatic of all the passions; and I have cherished Thomas as a most praiseworthy creature for being my forerunner on this point.'[5] Others viewed the prospect of a Chesterton biography of Aquinas with a great deal less enthusiasm. Even those normally considered his greatest friends and admirers had their doubts. Maisie Ward reported that she and her husband were filled with fear and trepidation when informed of the forthcoming book: 'When we were told that Gilbert was writing a book on St Thomas and that we might have the American rights my husband felt a faint quiver of apprehension. Was Chesterton for once undertaking a task beyond his knowledge? Such masses of research had recently been done on St Thomas by experts of such high standing, and he could not possibly have read it all.'[6]

Chesterton, of course, had been much maligned for the lack of scholarship in his previous biographies, not least in the study of Chaucer published the previous year. Furthermore, whereas his other biographies had concentrated on those who had plied the same trade as the author – writers such as Dickens, Browning and Robert Louis Stevenson – the new study, dealing as it did with one of history's greatest philosophers, was straying on to ground that many felt Chesterton had not charted and on which he was not qualified to wander. This being so, it was not surprising that even Catholic publishers such as Sheed & Ward were seriously concerned about the book's prospects.

These fears would scarcely have been allayed had the publishers known Chesterton's carefree approach to the writing of the book. Dorothy Collins recalled that 'after clearing the weekly articles he would suddenly say, "Shall we do a bit of Tommy?"'[7] In this fashion he dictated half the biography without consulting any books whatsoever. He finally asked Dorothy 'to go to London and get me some books'. When asked which he required he replied that he didn't know. Dorothy wrote hastily to Father O'Connor and received by return a list of classic and more recent books on St Thomas. According to Dorothy, when Gilbert was given these he 'flipped them rapidly through' and then proceeded to dictate to her the rest of his own book without consulting any of them again.[8]

None the less, echoing Shaw's conviction that 'intellect is a passion that will finally become the most ecstatic of all the passions', Chesterton hoped that the biography would gain in passion whatever it lacked in precision. He *loved* St Thomas with both his heart and mind, and he *understood* St Thomas's teaching with both his heart and mind. This, he hoped, would be sufficient. Indeed, an interesting insight into his love for St Thomas was given by a friend who saw Gilbert coming out of early mass on Corpus Christi, 1933, when he was in the midst of writing the book: 'As I've been trying to write about St Thomas,' he explained, 'I thought the least I could do was to go to Communion on the day he wrote his Mass.'[9] In similar vein, friends remembered him at a Corpus Christi procession in Beaconsfield, singing St Thomas's hymn, the *Pange Lingua*, with all his heart and quite out of tune. He was blissfully unaware that he had become an object of ridicule to the dwellers in the council houses opposite the church who were watching the proceedings with puzzled amusement.[10]

In view of Dorothy Collins's description of Chesterton dictating *St Thomas Aquinas*, one can almost picture the scene in his study as he paced up and down composing the opening lines of the first chapter:

Let me at once anticipate comment by answering to the name of that notorious character, who rushes in where even the Angels of the Angelic Doctor might fear to tread. Some time ago I wrote a book of this type and shape on St Francis of Assisi; and some time after (I know not when or how, as the song says, and certainly not why) I promised to write a book of the same size, or the same smallness, on St Thomas Aquinas. The promise was Franciscan only in its rashness; and the parallel was very far from being Thomistic in its logic. You can make a sketch of St Francis: you could only make a plan of St Thomas, like the plan of a labyrinthine city. And yet in a sense he would fit into a much larger or a much smaller book. What we really know of his life might be pretty fairly dealt with in a few pages; for he did not, like St Francis, disappear in a shower of personal anecdotes and popular legends. What we know, or could know, or may eventually have the luck to learn, of his work, will probably fill even more libraries in the future than it has filled in the past. It was allowable to sketch St Francis in an outline; but with St Thomas everything depends on the filling up of the outline.[11]

Considering that Chesterton's biography of St Thomas was intended as a companion volume to his earlier book on St Francis, it was natural enough that he should commence his study with a chapter devoted to a comparison of the two saints:

St Francis was a lean and lively little man; thin as a thread and vibrant as a bowstring; and in his motions like an arrow from the bow. All his life was a series of plunges and scampers; darting after the beggar, dashing naked into the woods, tossing himself into a strange ship, hurling himself into the Sultan's tent and offering to hurl himself into the fire. In appearance he must have been like a thin brown skeleton autumn leaf dancing eternally before the wind; but in truth it was he that was the wind.

St Thomas was a huge heavy bull of a man, fat and slow and quiet; very mild and magnanimous but not very sociable; shy, even apart from the humility of holiness; and abstracted, even apart from his occasional and carefully concealed experiences of trance or ecstasy. St Francis was so fiery and even fidgety that the ecclesiastics, before whom he appeared quite suddenly, thought he was a madman. St Thomas was so stolid that the scholars, in the schools which he attended regularly, thought he was a dunce. Indeed, he was the sort of schoolboy, not unknown, who would much rather be thought a dunce than have his own dreams invaded by more active or animated dunces.[12]

This sort of schoolboy was certainly not unknown to Chesterton because, as a child, he had fitted the description perfectly himself. In his *Autobiography* he recalled his dogged determination not to stand out in the classroom.

Thomas, like Chesterton, would sit quietly for hours, listening intently but taking no part in the general discussion. It was then that his fellow students in Cologne, unable to get a single word out of him and marvelling at his huge head and ponderous frame, gave him the nickname of the Dumb Ox. Chesterton recounted this episode in St Thomas's life and clearly relished the autobiographical parallels:

Among the students thronging into the lecture-rooms there was one student, conspicuous by his tall and bulky figure, and completely failing or refusing to be conspicuous for anything else. He was so dumb in the debates that his fellows began to assume an American significance in the word dumbness; for in that land it is a synonym for dullness. It is clear that, before long, even his imposing stature began to have only the ignominious immensity of the big boy left behind in the lowest form. He was called the Dumb Ox. He was the object, not merely of mockery, but of pity. One good-natured student pitied him so much as to try to help him with his lessons; going over the elements of logic like an alphabet in a horn-book. The dunce thanked him with pathetic politeness; and the philanthropist went on swimmingly, till he came to a passage about which he was himself a little doubtful; about which, in point of fact, he was wrong. Whereupon the dunce, with every appearance of embarrassment and disturbance, pointed out a possible solution which happened to be right. The benevolent student was left staring, as at a monster, at this mysterious lump of ignorance and intelligence; and strange whispers began to run round the schools.[13]

There is a story of how one of Thomas's fellow students looked out of the window during a recess between lectures and cried, 'Look, look, there is a bull flying overhead!', whereupon Thomas stuck his head out of the window, only to be greeted by howls of derisive laughter. This innocent credulity was paralleled by incidents in Chesterton's childhood but he didn't appear to suffer adversely from these episodes. On the contrary, he seemed to rejoice in being seen as an object of fun, once depicting himself in a cartoon as being tethered beside Trotsky, the pet donkey he and Francis kept in Beaconsfield, with the caption 'Mrs Chesterton's Donkeys in waiting'. It is scarcely surprising, therefore, that he should be attracted by the paradox of a philosophical genius being known as the Dumb Ox (indeed, all the American editions of *St Thomas Aquinas* were even subtitled *The Dumb Ox*):

> ... before we come to those aspects of St Thomas that were very severely intellectual, we may note that in him as in St Francis there is a preliminary practical element which is rather moral; a sort of good and straightforward humility; and a readiness in the man to regard even himself in some ways as an animal; as St Francis compared his body to a donkey. It may be said that the contrast holds everywhere, even in zoological metaphor, and that if St Francis was like that common or garden donkey who carried Christ into Jerusalem, St Thomas, who was actually compared to an ox, rather resembled that Apocalyptic monster of almost Assyrian mystery, the winged bull. But again, we must not let all that can be contrasted eclipse

what was common; or forget that neither of them would have been too proud to wait as patiently as the ox and ass, in the stable of Bethlehem.[14]

One can't help but see Chesterton reflected again in his subject when he deals with St Thomas's girth or his absent-mindedness:

His bulk made it easy to regard him humorously as the sort of walking wine-barrel common in the comedies of many nations; he joked about it himself. It may be that he, and not some irritated partisan of the Augustinian or Arabian parties, was responsible for the sublime exaggeration that a crescent was cut out of the dinner-table to allow him to sit down . . . It is universally attested that Aquinas was what is commonly called an absent-minded man. That type has often been rendered in painting, humorous or serious; but almost always in one of two or three conventional ways. Sometimes the expression of the eyes is merely vacant, as if absent-mindedness did really mean a permanent absence of mind. Sometimes it is rendered more respectfully as a wistful expression, as of one yearning for something afar off, that he cannot see and can only faintly desire. Look at the eyes in Ghirlandajo's portrait of St Thomas, and you will see a sharp difference. While the eyes are indeed completely torn away from the immediate surrounding, so that the pot of flowers above the philosopher's head might fall on it without attracting his attention, they are not in the least wistful, let alone vacant. There is kindled in them a fire of instant inner excitement; they are vivid and very Italian eyes. The man is thinking about something; and something that has reached a crisis; not about nothing or about anything, or, what is almost worse, about everything. There must have been that smouldering vigilance in his eyes, the moment before he smote the table and startled the banquet-hall of the King.[15]

For all Chesterton's attraction to the saint's eccentric personality, and regardless of any psychological affinity he felt, his principal concern was with the saint's philosophy. Above all, St Thomas Aquinas was the Philosopher of Life:

He did, with a most solid and colossal conviction, believe in Life; and in something like what Stevenson called the great theorem of the livableness of life. It breathes somehow in his very first phrases about the reality of Being. If the morbid Renaissance intellectual is supposed to say, 'To be or not to be – that is the question,' then the massive medieval doctor does most certainly reply in a voice of thunder, 'To be – that is the answer.'[16]

One of the great attractions of Chesterton's biography is his treatment of philosophy not merely as a prosaic science but as a romantic adventure in search of truth. If Chesterton's *Chaucer* had been a poet's view of a great poet, his *St Thomas Aquinas* was a poet's view of a great philosopher. For example, the Incarnation, the Word made Flesh, had many romantic ramifications:

> There really was a new reason for regarding the senses, and the sensations of the body, and the experiences of the common man, with a reverence at which great Aristotle would have stared, and no man in the ancient world could have begun to understand. The Body was no longer what it was when Plato and Porphyry and the old mystics had left it for dead. It had hung upon a gibbet. It had risen from a tomb. It was no longer possible for the soul to despise the senses, which had been the organs of something that was more than man. Plato might despise the flesh; but God had not despised it. The senses had truly become sanctified; as they are blessed one by one at a Catholic baptism. 'Seeing is believing' was no longer the platitude of a mere idiot, or common individual, as in Plato's world; it was mixed up with real conditions of real belief. Those revolving mirrors that send messages to the brain of man, that light that breaks upon the brain, these had truly revealed to God himself the path to Bethany or the light on the high rock of Jerusalem. These ears that resound with common noises had reported also to the secret knowledge of God the noise of the crowd that strewed palms and the crowd that cried for Crucifixion. After the Incarnation had become the idea that is central in our civilisation, it was inevitable that there should be a return to materialism; in the sense of the serious value of matter and the making of the body. When once Christ had risen, it was inevitable that Aristotle should rise again.[17]

Yet the poetic approach lacks precision, and throughout the book there is a want of detail in his discussion of philosophical theories. We are told that it was unlikely that St Thomas understood Effective Causality at the age of six: '. . . or even that he had worked out, as he did in later life, the whole theory by which a man's love of himself is Sincere and Constant and Indulgent; and that this should be transferred intact (if possible) to his love of his neighbour. At this early age he did not understand all this.'[18] Chesterton assumed, however, that the reader did 'understand all this' because there was no effort to discuss these Thomist principles. He did discuss briefly that the understanding of the concept of being is hampered by the inadequacy of translation from the Latin word *ens*. He also endeavoured to explain the important difference between form and matter, but always in terms of vague poetic imagery. The same poetic treatment was brought to bear in the discussion of the objective and subjective:

> The *strangeness* of things, which is the light in all poetry, and indeed in all art, is really connected with their otherness, or what is called their objectivity. What is subjective must be stale; it is exactly what is objective that is in this imaginative manner strange. In this the great contemplative is the complete contrary of that false contemplative, the mystic who looks only into his own soul, the selfish artist who shrinks from the world and lives only in his own mind. According to St Thomas, the mind acts freely of itself, but its freedom exactly consists in finding a way out to liberty and the light of day; to reality and the land of the living. In the subjectivist, the pressure of the world forces the imagination inwards. In the Thomist, the energy of the mind forces the imagination outwards, but because the images it seeks are real things. All their romance and glamour, so to speak, lies in the fact that they are real things; things *not* to be found by staring inwards at the mind. The flower is a vision because it is not only a vision. Or, if you will, it is a vision because it is not a dream. This is for the poet the strangeness of stones and trees and solid things; they are strange because they are solid. I am putting it first in the poetical manner, and indeed it needs much more technical subtlety to put it in the philosophical manner.[19]

However, for all Chesterton's lack of technical subtlety, the subtlety of his literary analogies made complex philosophical issues more accessible to the general reader:

> The mind is not merely receptive, in the sense that it absorbs sensations like so much blotting-paper; on that sort of softness has been based all that cowardly materialism, which conceives man as wholly servile to his environment. On the other hand, the mind is not purely creative, in the sense that it paints pictures on the windows and then mistakes them for a landscape outside. But the mind is active, and its activity consists in following, so far as the will chooses to follow, the light outside that does really shine upon real landscapes. That is what gives the indefinably virile and even adventurous quality to this view of life; as compared

with that which holds that material influences pour in upon an utterly helpless mind, or that which holds that psychological influences pour out and create an entirely baseless phantasmagoria. In other words, the essence of the Thomist common sense is that two agencies are at work; reality and the recognition of reality; and their meeting is a sort of marriage. Indeed it is very truly a marriage, because it is fruitful; the only philosophy now in the world that really is fruitful. It produces practical results, precisely because it is the combination of an adventurous mind and a strange fact. M. Maritain has used an admirable metaphor, in his book *Théonas*, when he says that the external fact *fertilises* the internal intelligence, as the bee fertilises the flower. Anyhow, upon that marriage, or whatever it may be called, the whole system of St Thomas is founded; God made Man so that he was capable of coming in contact with reality; and those whom God hath joined, let no man put asunder.[20]

In contrast, Chesterton argued, those modern philosophies which denied this relationship of the mind with objective reality were so barren that they could not really be called philosophies at all: 'Most modern philosophies are not philosophy but philosophic doubt; that is, doubt about whether there can be any philosophy.'[21] Furthermore these modern philosophers were utterly unable to practise what they preached because what they preached was utterly impractical:

No sceptics work sceptically; no fatalists work fatalistically; all without exception work on the principle that it is possible to assume what it is not possible to believe. No materialist who thinks his mind was made up for him, by mud and blood and heredity, has any hesitation in making up his mind. No sceptic who believes that truth is subjective has any hesitation about treating it as objective.[22]

Against this illogical and unworkable doubt, St Thomas is the champion of fact:

Long before he knows that grass is grass, or self is self, he knows that something is something. Perhaps it would be best to say very emphatically (with a blow on the table), 'There *is* an Is.' That is as much monkish credulity as St Thomas asks of us at the start. Very few unbelievers start by asking us to believe so little. And yet, upon this sharp pinpoint of reality, he rears by long logical processes that have never really been successfully overthrown, the whole cosmic system of Christendom.[23]

This passage begs an obvious question. If there is an Is, *what* is the Is? Surprisingly, Chesterton fails to elaborate on St Thomas's arguments for the existence of God: 'This is, in a very rude outline, his philosophy; it is impossible in such an outline to describe his theology. Anyone writing so small a book about so big a man must leave out something. Those who know him best will best understand why, after some considerable consideration, I have left out the only important thing.'[24]

Regardless of whether this conscious omission was justifiable, it does render Chesterton's study of St Thomas frustratingly incomplete. The reader is left clasping the fundamental principles but groping helplessly in the direction of the 'long logical processes' upon which St Thomas constructed 'the whole cosmic system of Christendom'. Instead he or she is left a few scraps in the form of passing allusions to the necessity of God's existence. The reader is told, for instance, 'that if there has been from the beginning anything that can possibly be called a Purpose, it must reside in something that has the essential elements of a Person'.[25]

Notwithstanding its obvious shortcomings, *St Thomas Aquinas*, published on 21 September 1933, was acclaimed by authoritative Thomist scholars as a major work on the subject. Maisie Ward, so sceptical beforehand of Chesterton's ability to do justice to Aquinas, described the biography as perhaps the 'most important book of his life'.[26] Others who recognised instantly the integration of Chesterton's thought with that of Aquinas were his friends Father John O'Connor and Father Vincent McNabb. Father O'Connor wrote of Chesterton: 'He is quite soberly estimated by those who know best to be a portent of the Philosophia Perennis, since he discovered it himself and adorned it all his life, so that a Dominican professor said his works would do for footnotes to the "Philosophy of St Thomas". Thomas was so pleasant to even tiresome persons that he was called the Angelic Doctor. Call Chesterton the Angelic Jester.'[27] Without doubt Gilbert would have considered it a great compliment to have his life's work labelled merely as footnotes to St Thomas and, to continue Father O'Connor's analogy, the Angelic Jester would have happily played the fool at the feet of the Angelic Doctor. Father Vincent McNabb also found a remarkable comparison between Chesterton and Aquinas: 'A quality at once felt but not at once analysable in the thought of St Thomas Aquinas is to be found in the words of Gilbert Chesterton. With both men thought becomes consecration: their intellectual activities have a dominantly moral character.'[28]

Although Father O'Connor had not named the Dominican professor who believed that Chesterton's work would serve as footnotes to the works of Aquinas, it is known that the Master-General of the Dominican Order, Père Gillet, OP, was so impressed with the book that he lectured on and from it to large meetings of Dominicans.[29] Considering that St Thomas Aquinas was himself a Dominican – is indeed the jewel in the Dominican crown – such affirmation of the merits of Chesterton's book by the international head of the Dominican order was praise that could scarcely be surpassed.

Yet perhaps an even more prestigious tribute was given by Etienne Gilson, arguably the world's most highly esteemed Thomist scholar. Gilson had long been an admirer of Chesterton's writing, considering *Orthodoxy* 'the best piece of apologetic the century had produced', yet he was still utterly astonished by the publication of *St Thomas Aquinas*: 'Chesterton makes one despair. I have been studying St Thomas all my life and I could never have written such a book.'[30] A few years later he reiterated these sentiments at greater length:

> I consider it as being without possible comparison the best book ever written on St Thomas. Nothing short of genius can account for such an achievement. Everybody will no doubt admit that it is a 'clever' book, but the few readers who have spent twenty or thirty years in studying St Thomas Aquinas, and who, perhaps, have themselves published two or three volumes on the subject, cannot fail to perceive that the so-called 'wit' of Chesterton has put their scholarship to shame. He has guessed all that which they had tried to demonstrate, and he has said all that which they were more or less clumsily attempting to express in academic formulas. Chesterton was one of the deepest thinkers who ever existed; he was deep because he was right; and he could not help being right; but he could not either help being modest and charitable, so he left it to those who could understand him to know that he was right, and deep; to the others, he apologised for being right, and he made up for being deep by being witty. That is all they can see of him.[31]

Neither did Gilson ever modify or moderate his praise for Chesterton's biography. In 1965 he replied to a letter sent by Father Kevin Scannell, a priest of the diocese of Leeds:

First, you cannot speak too highly of G. K. for my taste. My reason for admiring his Thomas Aquinas as I do, precisely is that I find him *always right* in his conclusions about the man and the doctrine even though, in fact, *he knew so little about him.* The case is identically the same you so perfectly describe in your letter under the name of common sense. I must refrain from commenting because the subject would overpower me. But I do believe that our mind has a natural feeling for truth quite apart from dialectical reasoning – in fact dialectical reasoning often clouds us to truth: G. K. always argues *from* his intellectual perception of truth, never towards it. In the case of Thomas Aquinas – a mere incident in his colossal production – I always feel him nearer the real Thomas than I am after reading and teaching the Angelic Doctor for sixty years. The worst for me is, that *I shall never be* with Thomas in the same kind of intimate communion G. K. was after just looking at him the way he did.[32]

Gilson, writing from the Pontifical Institute of Mediaeval Studies in Toronto, concluded by paying Chesterton a singular compliment: 'with Chesterton more than literature is at stake – We love him here for his importance as a *theologian* at least as much as a writer.'[33]

Ten years later still, in 1975, James A. Weisheipl, OP, another Thomist scholar at the Pontifical Institute in Toronto, revealed that Chesterton's *St Thomas Aquinas* was as much loved and as influential as ever. Weisheipl, who was himself the author of a biography of St Thomas, wrote a review of Chesterton's biography in the *Archives Internationales d'Histoire des Sciences*:

The year 1974 marks the seven-hundredth anniversary of the death of St Thomas Aquinas. This occasion is being celebrated throughout the Christian world by congresses, conferences, discussions, books, sermons, and articles of all kinds. To mark this occasion, Doubleday has published not only my large biography of Friar Thomas d'Aquino, but it has reissued this classic gem first published in 1933 with the new subtitle 'The Dumb Ox'. The master of English prose, paradox, wit, and penetrating insight has rightfully attracted appreciation from such professional Thomists as Etienne Gilson, Jacques Maritain, and Anton C. Pegis. Unanimously they have proclaimed this book the best ever written on Aquinas. While others have laboured a life-time to portray the genius of St Thomas, Chesterton in the space of a very little book has brilliantly revealed the optimism, realism, and common sense of the Angelic Doctor in such a way that the reader cannot help but want more. As for myself, I cannot praise it enough, for this was the first book I had ever read on Aquinas thirty-five years ago; it led me to become a Dominican and a Thomist.[34]

The reprint of *St Thomas Aquinas* reviewed by Weisheipl was destined to have a profound effect on a young student at the University of California:

I first encountered the writings of Chesterton in 1983, while I was enrolled in a class in the History of Christianity at the University of California.

Though the teaching of a particular faith in a confessional context is forbidden in a public university such as the University of California, my professor had seen fit to include Chesterton's book about St Thomas Aquinas entitled in its American edition *The Dumb Ox* on his supplemental reading list. I had seen Chesterton's name mentioned with great respect in C. S. Lewis's *Surprised by Joy*, a book which was instrumental in bringing me to Christianity. Consequently, I decided to read Chesterton's book.

My reaction to the book was mixed, but intense. Chesterton's description of the mind of Luther as a 'dot' on the map of the mind of St Thomas was disturbing to my thoroughly German-Protestant upbringing. I also found the use of his alliteration distracting. My primary sensation, however, was that of having encountered one of the most insightful minds I had ever encountered. Chesterton's study of St Thomas made the concept of 'Saint' meaningful to a Protestant who knew nothing about Saints.[35]

Almost a decade later, in 1991, the same student 'rediscovered Chesterton by picking up a second-hand copy of *The Everlasting Man*'. He then read, in rapid succession, *Orthodoxy*, *Heretics*, *St Francis of Assisi* and Chesterton's *Autobiography*. Feeling 'as though my entire life had been a preparation for exposure to this thought', he became a Catholic at the Easter Vigil Mass at the University of San Diego's Immaculata Chapel.

This last example of the enduring influence of his biography of St Thomas would have given Chesterton more pleasure, one suspects, than all the praise of the experts. Indeed, he hadn't written *St Thomas Aquinas* to receive the adulation or approval of scholars but to introduce the saint to those who had possibly never heard of him and to elucidate Thomist teaching to the public at large. Upon its initial publication it would have been impossible to foresee the extent to which he would succeed in this aim, but an unsigned review in *The Times Literary Supplement* on 5 October 1933 was indicative of its general reception by the readership at which it was aimed:

> Mr Chesterton's little volume makes one of the pleasantest introductions to St Thomas that could be desired, though it will be read more because it is by the wit of Beaconsfield than because it is about the Dumb Ox of Sicily; and, indeed, it tells us as much about the one as about the other.
>
> ... Mr Chesterton not only awakens the mind in this little volume but keeps it awake ... St Thomas, of course, has become the official philosopher of the Communion of which Mr Chesterton is a member. And Mr Chesterton takes a malicious pleasure in pointing out the huge bulk of the Dumb Ox. But that is not – in the scholastic sense – a substantial likeness. More important is the fact that Mr Chesterton has already written in this series a book on St Francis of Assisi, and he has been led on to write about the great complementary friar, and, indeed, begins with an acute comparison of the two. There is a world of wisdom in one of his observations: 'As the nineteenth century clutched at the Franciscan romance, precisely because it had neglected romance, so the twentieth century is already clutching at the Thomist rational theology, because it has neglected reason.'[36]

Echoing this Chestertonian perception, Christopher Hollis believed that Chesterton had forged a unique synthesis between the 'sentimentalism' of the Franciscans and the 'rationalism' of the Thomists: 'With Saint Francis, in his belief, the Catholic religion, having purged itself and come of age, dared to annex to itself the delights of Nature. With Saint Thomas the Catholic religion, having purged itself, dared to annex to itself the delights of reason.'[37]

In other words, in Chesterton's view the Catholic Church, through its consistent and resolute championing of the causes of romance and reason, had come to embody these two spirits in the one flesh. Yet Chesterton also appeared, in microcosm, to embody these same two spirits. He had become an incarnation of the ideas he espoused: a synthesis of the Franciscan and the Thomist. No less than the Church of which he was a member, Chesterton was the fruit of the mystical marriage between St Francis the Romantic and St Thomas the Rationalist.

435

« 29 »

Germany and Justice

DURING THE CLOSING WEEKS of 1933 a friendly exchange of letters between Chesterton and H. G. Wells illustrated the depth of their mutual affection. Indeed, considering Chesterton's consistent and resolute opposition to Wells's ideas, and considering Wells's inclination to quarrel publicly and personally with his opponents, it was a tribute to Chesterton's tact and amicability that his friendship with Wells was both lasting and intact. The correspondence arose out of an article by Chesterton praising Wells in the *Illustrated London News*:

Dear Old G. K. C.

An *Illustrated London News* Xmas cutting comes like the season's greetings. If after all my Atheology turns out wrong and your Theology right I feel I shall always be able to pass into Heaven (if I want to) as a friend of G. K. C.'s. Bless you.

My Dear H. G.,

I do hope my secretary let you know that at the moment when I got your most welcome note I was temporarily laid out in bed and able to appreciate it, but not to acknowledge it. As to the fine point of theology you raise – I am content to answer (with the subtle and exquisite irony of the Yanks) I should worry. If I turn out to be right, you will triumph, not by being a friend of mine, but by being a friend of Man, by having done a thousand things for men like me in every way from imagination to criticism. The thought of the vast variety of that work, and how it ranges from towering visions to tiny pricks of humour, overwhelmed me suddenly in retrospect: and I felt we had none of us ever said enough. Also your words, apart from their generosity, please me as the first words I have heard for a long time of the old Agnosticism of my boyhood when my brother Cecil and my friend Bentley almost worshipped old Huxley like a god. I think I have nothing to complain of except the fact that the other side often forgot that we began as free-thinkers as much as they did: and there was no earthly power but thinking to drive us on the way we went. Thanking you again a thousand times for your letter . . . and everything else.[1]

My Dear Chesterton:

You write wonderful praise and it leaves me all aquiver. My warmest thanks for it. But indeed that wonderful fairness of mind is very largely a kind of funk in me – I know the creature from the inside – funk and something worse, a kind of deep, complex cunning. Well anyhow you take the superficial merit with infinite charity – and it has inflated me and just for a time I am an air balloon over the heads of my fellow creatures.[2]

Gilbert's reference to his being 'temporarily laid out in bed' was more ominous than the dismissive tone of his letter suggested. During the previous year he had been plagued by one illness after another and the following year was destined to see a continuance in his physical decline. None the less at the beginning of 1934, during a respite in the periods of ill health, his talks on the radio continued to extol the joys of everyday life:

Unless we can bring men back to enjoying the daily life which moderns call a dull life, our whole civilisation will be in ruins in about fifteen years. Whenever anybody proposes anything really practical, to solve the economic evil today, the answer always is that the solution would not work, because the modern town populations would think life dull. That is because they are entirely unacquainted with life. They know nothing but distractions from life; dreams which may be found in the cinema; that is, brief oblivions of life . . . Unless we can make daybreak and daily bread and the creative secrets of labour interesting in themselves, there will fall on all our civilisation a fatigue which is the one disease from which civilisations do not recover. So died the great Pagan Civilisation; of bread and circuses and forgetfulness of the household gods.[3]

Soon, however, the joys were once again mingled with suffering. Gilbert fell ill during the early months of the year, this time afflicted with jaundice, and in the spring both Gilbert's and Frances's mothers

437

had become seriously ill. Mrs Blogg was residing at the Yews, a nursing home within easy reach of Top Meadow, enabling Frances to visit her every day, while Marie Louise Chesterton was still living at Warwick Gardens in Kensington. Frances's daily vigil at her mother's bedside precluded her from being able to accompany Gilbert on his visits to his own ailing mother in London. Blanche Blogg, who at the end was almost totally blind, died at Beaconsfield, and Marie Louise Chesterton died at around the same time at home in London. According to her daughter-in-law, Ada Chesterton, her final passing was both peaceful and painless: 'Gilbert and Frances arrived early in the morning, and later, a smile on her face, a last tender look in her eyes, Marie Louise fell asleep – and did not waken.'[4]

Chesterton had been left sufficient money in his mother's will to leave legacies of his own to all his nieces and nephews, and he also had enough left over to make a substantial donation towards the building of a new Catholic church in Beaconsfield which would not be completed until after his own death.[5]

On 22 May 1934 Chesterton received an honour which he cherished considerably more than all the honorary degrees he had been awarded throughout the years. The honour in question was the Knighthood of the Order of St Gregory, bestowed on both him and Belloc at the same time by Pope Pius XI, 'in recognition of the services' which they had rendered to the Church by their writings. The two knights were dubbed by Cardinal Bourne, who then handed them a certificate signed by the Vatican's Secretary of State, Cardinal Eugenio Pacelli, who would later become Pope Pius XII. The handbook which accompanied the certificate was inscribed by Frances Cardinal Bourne of Westminster with his 'heartfelt congratulations', and it contained intriguing and tantalising coloured illustrations of the ornate uniform, regalia and ceremonial sword which both Belloc and Chesterton thereupon became entitled to wear.[6]

Three days later, on 25 May, Father Vincent McNabb wrote to congratulate Chesterton:

> I feel I want to hug the Pope – and you – for what he has done for you. We all feel, so to say, that he has taken the word out of our mouth. He has done exactly and even punctually what we had wanted him to do.
>
> I think there never was a time when your heart was not a catholic

heart. You were an 'anima naturaliter catholica'. If, for a time, you remained like St John 'outside the Latin Gate', your hesitation like that of the Apostle Thomas (to quote your new overlord St Gregory) was more profitable to us than the quick belief of others.[7]

The only new Chesterton book to be published during 1934 was *Avowals and Denials*, yet another selection of his weekly journalism for the *Illustrated London News*. Many of the essays merely shed light on familiar territory with Chesterton sounding forth 'On the Fallacy of Eugenics', 'On the Science of Sociology' and 'On the Return to the Land'. There were the seemingly mandatory criticisms of Shaw and Wells and the predictable defence of tradition over modernism: 'man should be a prince looking from the pinnacle of a tower built by his fathers, and not a contemptuous cad, perpetually kicking down the ladders by which he climbed'.[8] This last view was encapsulated brilliantly in the essay 'On Facing Facts':

We talk of people living in the past; and it is commonly applied to old people or old-fashioned people. But, in fact, we all live in the past, because there is nothing else to live in. To live in the present is like proposing to sit on a pin. It is too minute, it is too slight a support, it is too uncomfortable a posture, and it is of necessity followed immediately by totally different experiences, analogous to those of jumping up with a yell. To live in the future is a contradiction in terms. The future is dead; in the perfectly definite sense that it is not alive. It has no nature, no form, no feature, no vaguest character of any kind except what we choose to project upon it from the past. People talk about the dead past; but the past is not in the least dead, in the sense in which the future is dead. The past can move and excite us, the past can be loved and hated, the past consists largely of lives that can be considered in their completion; that is, literally in the fullness of life. But nobody knows anything about any living thing in the future, except what he chooses to make up, by his own imagination, out of what he regrets in the past or what he desires in the present.[9]

There was, however, one relatively new and less familiar theme throughout the book which arose from Chesterton's increasing concern about the rise to power of the National Socialists in Germany. Hitler had become Chancellor in January of the previous year and the following month he had engineered the burning of the

Reichstag. By the time that *Avowals and Denials* was published Hitler had assumed dictatorial powers and was busy silencing all dissident voices. In Chesterton's view, Hitler and the Nazis represented 'the Return of the Barbarian':

> The common or garden German may be described as the beer-garden German. As such, I love and embrace him. Just lately, and at historic intervals, he becomes the bear-garden German. As such I regard him with a love more mystical and distant, and would prefer to avoid his embrace. For the embraces of bears, even in the most festive and gorgeously illuminated bear-gardens, are apt to show that over-emphasis, or excess of pressure, which is the fault of the German temperament.
>
> Now, ever since Herr Hitler began to turn the beer-garden into a bear-garden, there has been an increasing impression on sensitive and intelligent minds that something very dangerous has occurred. A particular sort of civilisation has turned back towards barbarism.[10]

In the essay 'On the Fossil of a Fanatic' he alleged that the roots of National Socialism could be traced to the void which followed the decay of religion in the Protestant parts of Germany. Although the view is idealised and simplistic, omitting the stark reality that Hitler was as popular in Catholic Bavaria as in the Protestant parts of the *Reich,* his argument that National Socialism developed from post-Reformation scepticism is persuasive:

> The old fanatics who followed Gustavus Adolphus and William of Orange were not ethnologists or evolutionists. They did not imagine that they belonged to a Nordic race; they most certainly did not imagine that they or theirs had ever been bothered with a swastika . . . They were thinking about their own strictly religious scruples and schisms. They were really fighting fiercely and savagely for points of doctrine; and I should be the last to blame them for it. But these doctrines did not last; they were the very doctrines that have now long been dissolving in the acids of German scepticism; in the laboratories of the Prussian professors. And the more they evaporated and left a void, the more the void was filled up with new and boiling elements; with tribalism, with militarism, with imperialism and (in short) with that very narrow type of patriotism that we call Prussianism.
>
> Most of us would agree that this kind of patriotism is a considerable peril to every other kind of patriotism. That is the whole evil of the

ethnological type of loyalty. Settled States can respect themselves, and also respect each other; because they can claim the right to defend their own frontiers and yet not deny their duty to recognise other people's frontiers. But the racial spirit is a restless spirit; it does not go by frontiers but by the wandering of the blood . . . You can have a League of Nations; but you could hardly have a League of Tribes. When the Tribe is on the march, it is apt to forget leagues – not to mention frontiers. But my immediate interest in this flood of tribalism is that it has since poured into the empty hollows left by the slow drying up of the great Deluge of the Thirty Years' War, and that all this new and naked nationalism has come to many modern men as a substitute for their dead religion.[11]

This analysis of the phenomenon of National Socialism, viewed with the wisdom of hindsight, is phenomenal in itself. Whether one accepts Chesterton's historical perspective, his vision of 'the wandering of the blood' conjures images of the wanderlust that all too soon became the blood-lust sweeping through Europe. It also represented a prophecy of Hitler's demands for *Lebensraum* which precipitated the marching of the Tribe across frontiers.

Neither did Chesterton leave the subject of Hitler and his policies there. On the contrary, his writing of *Avowals and Denials* was as preoccupied with the Nazis in Germany as his writing of *The Resurrection of Rome* four years earlier had been preoccupied with the Fascists in Italy. However, where he had found sympathy with some aspects of Mussolini's Fascism, even if these were not palatable in the last analysis, he found absolutely nothing agreeable about Hitler's Nazism. Instead he condemned Hitler's return to 'the stale theories of Eugenics; the talk of compulsory action to keep the breed in a certain state of bestial excellence; of nosing out every secret of sex and origin, so that nobody may survive who is not Nordic; of setting a hundred quack doctors to preserve an imaginary race in its imaginary purity'.[12] From this imaginary purity the Nazis had resurrected an imaginary deity: 'Mythology has returned; the clouds are rolling over the landscape, shutting out the broad daylight of fact; and Germans are wandering about saying they will dethrone Christ and set up Odin and Thor.'[13]

Towards the end of *Avowals and Denials*, in an essay entitled 'On the Great Relapse', Chesterton predicted with uncanny accuracy the principal aggressors in a war that would not start for another five years:

These are not views that have of late been common; perhaps they are not views that can even now be popular. But they are views in which I myself have never wavered, and in which I have of late been very strongly confirmed. Long ago, before the Balkan Wars or the Russo-Japanese War, I remember writing in this general sense: that there were two forces in the world threatening its peace, because of their history, their philosophy and their externality to the ethics of Christendom; and they were Prussia and Japan. I remember horrifying all my Liberal friends, when I wrote for the *Daily News* in the days of my youth, by saying this about Japan. I did not, however, modify my view then. I am certainly not likely to modify it now.[14]

The essays in *Avowals and Denials* were simply the culmination of a year of attacks by Chesterton on the Third Reich. His line had been consistent throughout, and as early as 20 April of the previous year, the date of Hitler's birthday, he had written in *G. K.'s Weekly* about 'The Heresy of Race':

> ... in the lands of the new religions, rapidly turning into new irreligions, there had already sprung up a number of new tests and theories; of which the most menacing was the new theory of Race ... that a modern science of ethnology revealed a superior Teutonic type, spread everywhere from prehistoric times, and wherever that type could be recognised (by square heads, saucer blue eyes, hair like tow or other signs of godhood) there the new German Kaiser would stamp his foot crying, 'This is German land' ...
>
> I think this wild worship of Race far worse than even the excessive concentration on the nation, which many Catholics rightly condemn. Nationalism may in rational proportion help stability, and the recognition of traditional frontiers. But Anthropology gone mad, which is the right name for Race, means everlastingly looking for your own countrymen in other people's countries.[15]

In the following edition of *G. K.'s Weekly* Chesterton resumed his attack. Hitler had built a successful career 'by raving against Catholicism and hounding the Jews like rats' and by 'making his great speeches about Race':

> Oh those speeches about Race! Oh the stewed staleness and stupidity of the brains of a thousand boiled owls, diluted and filtered through the brains of a thousand forgotten Prussian professors! The German is not only a German. He is an Aryan. His heart leaps up when he

beholds a Swastika in the sky; because Professor Esel found it carved on quite a number of prehistoric stones in Northern Europe. The Jew, on the other hand, is not an Aryan. Most of us imagined that it was enough, for general common sense, that he was a Jew; but, alas, he is a Semite. Show him a Swastika and he remains cold . . . Need even a new Religion fall back on anything quite so faded and threadbare as the notion that nobody is any good but a Teuton? Are even the learned so ignorant as still to believe that Odin and Thor were great cosmic deities more ancient than Christianity? Must these golden-haired giants (like Mr Hitler) go on calling on the German God exactly and unalterably as of old?[16]

Although the whole tone of the article was softened with satire, this was Chesterton in uncharacteristically savage mood. He concluded by branding the Nazism of Hitler as 'one huge and howling Heresy: a Heresy run quite wild and raving: Race and the pride of Prussia'.

Four months later, on 17 August 1933, Chesterton had written another article for *G. K.'s Weekly* on 'The British Fascist'. This was an altogether more delicate affair. Fascism was growing in popularity in Britain, and a number of members of Chesterton's Distributist League, disillusioned with its lack of progress, had started to look to the Fascists in their search for a realistic alternative to communism and capitalism. Hence Chesterton's weighted attack on British Fascism was courageous and, in some circles, very unpopular. Although he reserved judgment on Sir Oswald Mosley, stating that it was 'difficult to discover what he and his party do actually propose to do', he had no reservations about condemning the more rabid elements in the British Fascist movement:

I suppose Sir Oswald Mosley is a British Fascist . . . I am sure he means well, just like Mr MacDonald; and there my knowledge of the Mosley mind, as of the MacDonald mind, abruptly becomes a blank. But perhaps it is not quite fair for me to judge, because I have really seen very little in the way of exposition or propaganda coming from this central or relatively moderate branch of British Fascism. On the other hand, the lesser branches grow much more wild. I have seen several pamphlets produced by the other British Fascists who know not Mosley. And these are very extraordinary documents indeed. The writers seem to be rather British Hitlerites than British Fascists; and even then more Hitlerite than British. For instance, they even write in a sort of semi-German . . . Splashed on the very cover of the leaflet are the words in large letters 'Hail Hitler! Hail Henry Ford! Hail Japan!' . . . But this is not talking like a very British Fascist. We English people do not suddenly say 'Hail!' to anybody we happen to admire. I do not go about abruptly shouting 'Hail Belloc!' – 'Hail Eric Gill!' – 'Hail Father Vincent McNabb!' It is not a very English thing to do at all; but if you do do it, the English idiom is 'Hurrah for Belloc!' All this raises doubts in me about the British Fascists; and the doubts increase when I read what they conceive to be a defence of typical British institutions. For instance, they were furiously Anti-Semite. Well, I have been called an Anti-Semite myself and even mistaken for a furious one; and I know all about it, and all that there really is to be said for it.[17]

Although Chesterton failed to name the group that had produced this literature, it was probably Arnold Leese's Imperial Fascist League. This organisation was always far more rabid in its attacks on the Jews than Mosley's relatively more moderate British Union of Fascists. Yet it is significant that Chesterton should find the anti-Semitism as abhorrent as the pro-Prussianism. Chesterton remained suspicious of Jewish financial power, and the rest of the article traced his view of the Jews in terms which trod dangerously close to going beyond candour to callousness. Yet in concluding the article he made it abundantly clear that his criticisms of the Jews bore no similarity to the anti-Semitism of the Fascists:

> . . . in Holland re-arose the great modern power of the Jews. Cromwell brought the Jews back into England; as early as that they were bound up with the building of the Whig aristocratic state. I can understand a man believing now that this aristocratic state has brought us to ruin, or that this aristocratic state is still our only hope of avoiding ruin. But if anybody thinks that the defence of it can follow the antics of foreign fanatics who murder Jews in the street – then I tell him plainly, in crude, coarse, outspoken words, that he is a British Fascist.[18]

In fact, the accusation that Chesterton was an anti-Semite springs principally from the bitterness he felt in the wake of what became known as the Marconi Scandal. The climax of this affair in 1913 had led to his brother Cecil being tried on criminal libel charges at the behest of Godfrey Isaacs. Chesterton, believing that Cecil had been persecuted unjustly, allowed a lingering resentment to ferment which, reinforced by his brother's death in 1918, spilled over into several venomous attacks on Isaacs and his Jewishness. However, these bitter outbursts were rare aberrations, alien to Chesterton's natural good humour. Indeed, even his attacks on the Jews were normally intended light-heartedly rather than heavy-handedly:

> I am fond of Jews
> Jews are fond of money
> Never mind of whose.
> I am fond of Jews
> Oh, but when they lose
> Damn it all, it's funny.

There can be little doubt that such sentiments have more in common with the cracking of jokes than the cracking of skulls. In similar vein is his poem from *The Flying Inn*:

> Oh I knew a Dr Gluck
> And his nose it had a hook
> And his attitudes were anything but Aryan.
> So I gave him all the pork
> That I had upon a fork
> Because I am myself a vegetarian.

It is clear that such verses may cause offence, but it is equally clear that they were not intended to do so. Indeed, in the latter poem one shouldn't forget that Chesterton always despised 'Aryan attitudes', and the poem was intended primarily as a jocular attack on vegetarianism. In short, the poem was written while the poet's tongue was emphatically embedded in his cheek. If it appears tasteless to the sensitivities of those who recall the worst excesses of the Second World War, it must be remembered that it was written long before the war.

For Chesterton it was all a question of justice. He had attacked the Jews when he felt that they were the perpetrators of injustice, but as soon as he saw that they had become the victims of injustice he was swift in their defence. As early as 1923 he had written an editorial in *G. K.'s Weekly* entitled 'Sanity and Semitism'. He said that those responsible for the *New Witness*, principally Belloc and his brother Cecil, had been the first to attack the Jews at the time of the Marconi Scandal, but now that the Jews were being attacked on

445

all sides *G. K.'s Weekly* might yet be the first to defend them: 'With Beaverbrook himself denouncing Jews, with Rothermere himself denouncing financiers, it would seem at first as if there were little more for us to say.' Newspapers that had been talking nothing but nonsense about Bolshevism, he said, were not likely to begin talking sense about Jews.[19]

This was a pertinent point because even the most respectable newspapers were publishing anti-Semitic articles at the time. An article on the murder of the Tsar in *The Times* on 1 September 1920 was typical of the anti-Jewish stance of many Fleet Street newspapers. According to *The Times*'s 'Special Correspondent', 'Jewish murderers and their accomplices' had carried out 'the hellish design of the Jew fiend, Yankel Sverdlov – to exterminate all the Romanovs'. On 4 September *The Times* continued its vitriol by blaming the Tsar's murder on a conspiracy between the German government and the Jews: 'But, morally, as well as practically, the German hand which had brought the Jew murderers into Russia controlled and directed the assassins' work. Only when Berlin realised that the Romanovs were irrevocably on the side of the Entente did they release the hands of the murderers.' This pseudo-respectable backdrop of crude anti-Semitism must be taken into account in any assessment of Chesterton's attitudes, which were relatively moderate compared with the views of many of his peers.

Another important factor in assessing Gilbert's attitudes must be the extent to which he had personal and personable relationships with Jewish friends. Perhaps the best known of these was his friendship with Israel Zangwill, that most quintessential of Jewish writers. They had remained good friends from the early years of the century until Zangwill's death in 1926. He had also met, and had formed a friendship, with André Maurois, the French Jewish novelist. Maurois had considered Gilbert's study of Dickens one of the best biographies ever written, which was praise indeed, considering that Maurois himself was a biographer of rare distinction. (Maurois's family – his real name was Emile Herzog – had already suffered at the hands of Prussian expansionism, moving to Normandy from Alsace at the time of the Franco-Prussian war in 1870.)

However, the most important of these relationships with Chesterton were not the high-profile public friendships of his literary peers but the little-known private friendships that had enriched his life. These stretched back to his schooldays when Waldo and Digby d'Avigdor and Lawrence and Maurice Solomon were among the handful of Gilbert's schoolfriends with whom he had formed the Junior Debating Club. Chesterton remained close to the Solomon brothers throughout his life, and the Solomons eventually moved to Beaconsfield to be closer to their friend.

In the early years of his literary career, as we have seen, Chesterton, through Frances, had become friendly with Mr and Mrs Steinthal. A Jewish businessman in Yorkshire, Mr Steinthal owned a large house in Ilkley. Frances had known Mrs Steinthal from her days at the Parents' National Education Union, where she had worked before she was married, and she had stayed with the Steinthals in Ilkley before her marriage. Following their wedding, she and Gilbert often spent short holidays with them. Gilbert loved the moors and would take long walks before returning home in time for delightful evenings with the Steinthals discussing topics of artistic or philosophic interest. Often the Steinthals would employ the services of a pianist or singer to entertain their guests, and it is recorded that a lady virtuoso from Frankfurt gave them the Bach Great Organ Fugue on the piano. On another, less formal, occasion Frances sang 'O Swallow, Swallow Flying South' from *The Princess*, while Chesterton worked at a crayon blazon for the local poetry league. He used crayons liberally at the Steinthals', and the attic walls were in time covered with his murals.[20] He also wrote a short playlet for the amusement of his hosts, a copy of which is now at the G. K. Chesterton Study Centre in Bedford. Over the years the Steinthals showed their love for him by amassing a large collection of his books and memorabilia, and this (now known as the Steinthal–Petrie Family Collection) formed a significant part of the 1974 Chesterton Exhibition at the National Theatre in London. Most important of all, however, was the fact that the Steinthals were destined to play a crucial role in the future development of Chesterton's life and career when they introduced Gilbert to Father John O'Connor.

There are other examples of the lasting friendships he formed with Jewish acquaintances. When Margaret Halford first met him she was worried whether he would want to know her. She wrote: 'I'm a stiff-necked viper on the Jewish question. I wasn't really "afraid" about my own welcome – but though I had for years been an enthralled admirer of G. K.'s, I'd have forgone the pleasure of personal friendship, if his true attitude had not become manifest.'[21] His true attitude was, of course, to display the same warmth he tended

447

to show to everybody he met, and Halford became a good friend and regular guest of the Chestertons. Similarly, on his travels to the United States and Canada, Gilbert was entertained by many Jewish people, all of whom were anxious to play host to him again.

Yet it is true that the adage 'some of my best friends are Jewish' is not, in itself, an adequate defence against the charge of anti-Semitism. Therefore it is interesting that an archivist at the Wiener Library in London, Britain's foremost Jewish library which houses a unique collection of material on anti-Semitism, regarded Chesterton as a friend, not an enemy:

> The difference between social and philosophical anti-semitism is something which is not fully understood. John Buchan, for example, was charming towards Jewish people he met, but undoubtedly possessed a world view of anti-semitism. With Chesterton we've never thought of a man who was seriously anti-semitic on either count. He was a man who played along, and for that he must pay a price; he has, and has the public reputation of anti-semitism. He was not an enemy, and when the real testing time came along he showed what side he was on.[22]

Following Chesterton's death, Rabbi Wise, a leading and respected figure inside the American Jewish community, wrote the following tribute:

> Indeed I was a warm admirer of Gilbert Chesterton. Apart from his delightful art and his genius in many directions, he was, as you know, a great religionist. He as Catholic, I as Jew, could not have seen eye to eye with each other, and he might have added 'particularly seeing that you are cross-eyed'; but I deeply respected him. When Hitlerism came, he was one of the first to speak out with all the directness and frankness of a great and unabashed spirit. Blessing to his memory![23]

Further praise came from the Jewish poet Humbert Wolfe, who had initially attacked Chesterton as an anti-Semite but later bitterly regretted it. As a young man Wolfe had published a small volume of verse named after its longest poem, 'Shylock Reasons with Mr Chesterton':

> Jew-baiting still! Two thousand years are run
> And still it seems, good Master Chesterton,

Nothing's abated of the old offence,
Changing its shape, it never changes tense.

However, once Wolfe had actually met Chesterton a cordial relationship developed, the nature of which can be gauged from a note dated 2 November 1928:

Dear Mr Chesterton,
I send you this for your private amusement; at least I hope it may amuse you.
And it would be more than charming if I could sometime have another glimpse of you.

Yours sincerely,
Humbert Wolfe.[24]

Appropriately enough, Wolfe's most memorable tribute to Chesterton was in verse:

Like a great wind after a night of thunder
He rocked the sodden marches of the soul
And ripped the mists of cowardice asunder
With laughter vivid as an aureole.

He does not need to knock against the Gate
Who every action like a prayer ascended
And beat upon the panels. Trumpets, wait
For a hushed instant. We loved him. It is ended.[25]

The main reason for the eventual reconciliation between Chesterton and the Jews was, ironically and paradoxically, the anti-Semitism of Hitler. The Jews forgave Chesterton his earlier indiscretions because 'he was one of the first to speak out when the real testing time came', and Chesterton softened his attitude to the Jews because he was horrified to see the hardening of attitudes in Germany and its results. In 1989 two British Jews, Anthony Read and David Fisher, wrote *Kristallnacht: The Nazi Night of Terror*, in which they documented the opening of the Nazi campaign of anti-Semitic persecution. In it they wrote:

Belloc, like his friend Chesterton, like so many of the English middle class, was prejudiced against Jews. He did not like them

... Nevertheless, he was not anti-semitic – certainly not in the Nazi sense and the idea of employing physical brutality against a single Jew would have appalled him. He was an honourable man, uneasily aware that there was something going on in Germany of which, in conscience, he could not approve.[26]

Towards the end of his life Chesterton echoed these sentiments when he spoke candidly of his mellower approach:

In our early days Hilaire Belloc and myself were accused of being uncompromising anti-Semites. Today, although I still think there is a Jewish problem, I am appalled by the Hitlerite atrocities. They have absolutely no reason or logic behind them. It is quite obviously the expedient of a man who has been driven to seeking a scapegoat, and has found with relief the most famous scapegoat in European history, the Jewish people. I am quite ready to believe now that Belloc and I will die defending the last Jew in Europe.[27]

There was one final reconciliation to arise out of this particular episode in Chesterton's life. It was the most surprising reconciliation of all and one which would have pleased him immensely. He continued to attack the Nazi regime in the few years remaining to him, but he could never have believed that one day he would be reconciled to one of the most notorious Nazi leaders. Albert Speer had been Hitler's chief architect, and in 1942, at the height of the war, he had been made Minister of Armaments. After the war he was sentenced to twenty years' imprisonment in Spandau. It was during his prison sentence that Speer was introduced to the works of Chesterton. The effect this had upon him was recorded in his diary:

April 7th, 1957. Have read a great deal recently. As early as 1904 Chesterton, in *The Napoleon of Notting Hill*, dealt with the frightening consequences of a mass psychosis. In this story a pseudoking arbitrarily picked out of the London city directory succeeds in playing on the emotions of a whole people – as Hitler was to do – bringing about the most absurd actions and reactions. Such books are only read after the fact.

This evening I have been thinking of Chesterton again. Strange how such Caesarean demagogues, who really need a splintered society in which to work, were nevertheless foreshadowed in the orderly, strictly hierarchical, stable-seeming world of the *fin de siècle* ...

I wonder how Chesterton was read in his time, as a kind of prophecy or as an entertaining fantasy? After half a century, at any rate, it is clear that, with the nervous attunement of a great artist, he sensed what the future would be. This much seems certain: Art has no need of reality to bring to light the truth about an era.[28]

« 30 »

Liberty and Exile

In SUMMER 1934 GILBERT, Frances and Dorothy Collins set out for Rome, principally so that Gilbert could visit the Vatican in thanksgiving for the honour the Pope had bestowed upon him earlier in the year. After Rome, the intention had been to travel south to Sicily and thence to the Holy Land. This latter stage of their pilgrimage had to be cancelled, however, when Chesterton collapsed at Syracuse suffering from 'inflammation of the nerves of the neck and shoulders'.[1] He was forced to rest for five weeks before the three eventually returned home via Malta, where Chesterton was too ill to honour a dinner engagement at Admiralty House.

On 11 October the five-hundredth edition of *G. K.'s Weekly* was published. Two days later, Gilbert gave an interview at Top Meadow to a reporter from the *Observer* who had called to congratulate him on the achievement. The interview was published in the following morning's edition:

> Heaven knows why, but I am an editor. I am a very bad editor, I was never meant to be an editor; but I am the editor of the only paper in England which is devoted to what is a perfectly normal idea – private property.
>
> Most modern property isn't private, and ordinary capitalism makes it even less private if possible than ordinary communism. The system under which we live today is one of huge commercial combinations in which property isn't private . . . What we mean by private property is that as many people as possible should own the means of production; the ground in which to dig, the spade with which to dig, the roof under which to sleep at night, the tools and machinery of production should belong to as many separate individuals as possible.
>
> There is a case for communism; there is even a case for capitalism;

but they are both cases against private property. They both mean that it is not a good thing that separate men should own separate tools, separate farms, and separate shops, but that all should be linked together in one great machine, whether it be a communist State or a capitalist business.[2]

Asked by the reporter whether private property was really essential, Chesterton responded that 'it was one of the ordinary human hungers': 'And there is no other paper representing that ordinary point of view. You cannot take away from the ordinary man the sense that he is more dignified when he is free, when he has no master but God. And what we complain of is that in England – it is different in other countries – no one is given even a glimpse of that idea.'[3]

Concerning the practicalities of bringing about the distributist state he desired, Chesterton insisted that it could be done constitutionally without the need for violent revolution: 'Every contract by which small property would pass into the possession of large property should be prohibitively taxed, and similarly the setting up of every small business or every small ownership of land should be advantaged in the same fashion.'[4]

There was, however, a hint of frustration and regret as he alluded to the lack of progress being made by *G. K.'s Weekly* and its creed of distributism:

We have had ten years of struggle to keep the paper going, with a fine staff and no capital. We have a good circulation for our sort of paper, but we can't get out of the habit of appealing to the intelligence of the human race. That is perhaps where I am old-fashioned . . . and I have grown old in the delusion that my fellow creatures are rational as well as myself. I am afraid I can't start regarding them as a race of morons or nitwits; I shall go to my grave believing that if I meet an ordinary sane man he will agree that two and two make four.[5]

He reluctantly agreed with his interviewer that modern life was becoming more complicated and that 'the conquest was now almost complete':

The motor car has progressed because nobody is happy where he is. The idea of leisure has become the idea of getting away somewhere else in the hope that by some extraordinary chance it may be better. That principle means death and destruction, and God knows, motors

453

on the roads are death and destruction. Modern civilised life is so miserable for both rich and poor, because of its vulgar and stifling atmosphere, that people are always full of that divine human illusion that if only they rush round the corner they will find something that is a little better, and they make round the corner exactly like what they have left.[6]

This was the nearest Chesterton ever came to despairing at the ability of his fellow countrymen to change the fate that awaited them. Indeed, his frustration at their apparent indifference seemed to find expression in an almost Orwellian pessimism about the future. Although such sentiments seem somewhat alien to Chesterton, they may explain why Orwell himself felt attracted to certain aspects of distributism at around this time. It was during this period of his life that he had exclaimed, to the amazement of his Trotskyist friends, that 'what England needed was to follow the kind of policies in Chesterton's *G. K.'s Weekly*'.[7]

However, whereas Orwell may have seen the failure of *G. K.'s Weekly* as a sunset heralding a twilight followed by darkness, Chesterton saw the same sunset as a promise of a new dawn, a resurrection. It was the difference between hope and despair, and Chesterton, for all his frustration and regret, was always motivated by hope. On 6 December 1934 he wrote in *G. K.'s Weekly*:

Before the Boer War had introduced me to politics, or worse still to politicians, I had some vague and groping ideas of my own about a general view or vision of existence. It was a long time before I had anything worth calling a religion; what I had was not even sufficiently coherent to be called a philosophy. But it was, in a sense, a view of life; I had it in the beginning; and I am more and more coming back to it in the end . . . my original and almost mystical conviction of the miracle of all existence and the essential excitement of all experience.[8]

The same spirit pervaded an article in the following week's edition:

It was then no more than a notion about the point at which extremes meet, and the most common thing becomes a cosmic and mystical thing. I did not want so much to alter the place and use of things as to weigh them with a new dimension; to deepen them by going down to the potential nothing; to lift them to infinity by measuring from zero.

The most logical form of this is in thanks to a Creator; but at every stage I felt that such praises could never rise too high; because they could not even reach the height of our own thanks for unthinkable existence, or horror of more unthinkable non-existence. And the commonest things, as much as the most complex, could thus leap up like fountains of praise . . .

We shall need a sort of Distributist psychology, as well as a Distributist philosophy. That is partly why I am not content with plausible solutions about credit or corporative rule. We need a new (or old) theory and practice of pleasure. The vulgar school of *panem et circenses* only gives people circuses; it does not even tell them how to enjoy circuses. But we have not merely to tell them how to enjoy circuses. We have to tell them how to enjoy enjoyment.[9]

Although Chesterton continued to write regularly for *G. K.'s Weekly* and other periodicals, he had effectively given up any attempt to write full-length books. Consequently, those who admired his writing must have waited eagerly for the publication of *The Scandal of Father Brown* in March 1935. This, the first new collection of Father Brown stories for eight years, was reviewed by the poet, critic and novelist, Winifred Holtby, in the *London Mercury*:

Most writers of detective stories isolate their robberies and murders into a specialised world where the drama might as well consist of snakes and ladders as of human beings with nerves, souls and hearts. The crime and its discovery are everything. Mr G. K. Chesterton is too good a Catholic and humanitarian for that. To him the souls and hearts and consciences of men are so important that he prefers, if possible, to leave the crime out altogether, or to prove that, whatever its appearance, it was in truth no crime. Thus in these eight short stories of the moon-faced priest with the bulky umbrella, who has become one of our institutional literary detectives, four are concerned not with the existence of the criminal but with the non-existence of the crime.

This is good fun, and as legitimate a pursuit as any other. There are few wittier and more inventive sleuths than Mr Chesterton, and he is never happier than when he can prove that a corpse which was apparently poisoned, stabbed and hanged, really died happily and peacefully in bed from natural causes. But all tricks become a little tedious in time – those of the soft as well as those of the hard heart. Erudition, dexterity and ingenuity prevent Mr Chesterton's tales from the sin of monotony, and it is only sometimes that one wishes he would take a page out of his great contemporary's *Ruthless Rhymes for Heartless Homes.* Perhaps, however, it would not do. The creator of Father Brown must be true to his particular type of temperament, and it is only fair to say that the most impressive story in the volume (to mention its title would be to give the show away) is based upon nothing more substantial than a practical joke.[10]

In the same month that *The Scandal of Father Brown* was published in England Gilbert, Frances and Dorothy set off once again for foreign climes. This time Dorothy drove the Chestertons through France to Spain. Arriving in the busy centre of Barcelona at midday on a Saturday, Dorothy encountered traffic lights for the first time:

> There were coloured lights which at that time were unknown in England and the workings of which I did not understand, added to which, characteristically and in accord with Gilbert's idea of a holiday, we did not know where we wanted to go. With traffic to the right and to left of us, police whistles blowing, lights flashing, G. K. sat in the back of the car, quite oblivious, reading a detective story.[11]

Eventually, after Dorothy had managed to extricate her vehicle from the traffic chaos she had unwittingly caused, she remonstrated with Gilbert that he hadn't been of much assistance. His reply was typical: 'Ah, my dear Dorothy, you don't realise how much more helpful I was than I should have been if I had been shouting directions from the back seat.' By then they had all seen enough of city traffic to decide to leave Barcelona immediately and drive to Sitges, a small town on the coast where, according to Dorothy, they 'spent several happy weeks and did a great deal of work'.

Leaving Spain, they drove through the south of France to Italy, where Gilbert gave a lecture on English literature and the Latin tradition as part of the International Festival in Florence. The route home took them through Switzerland and Belgium. Dorothy recalled that the trip was a great success and that her companions were 'wonderful passengers', though Gilbert did complain to his wife on one occasion: 'Frances, I wish you wouldn't keep telling Dorothy to admire the view when we are hanging over precipices.'[12]

It was typical of Chesterton's child-like personality that the souvenir of this trip which he treasured most was a cardboard toy theatre he had brought back from Spain. Both the child-like personality and the Spanish toy theatre were remembered fondly by Emile Cammaerts, a Belgian writer and friend of Gilbert:

My little girl had lost her heart to Chesterton. The origin of this passionate feeling is somewhat obscure . . . It fed on memories of his large hat which she had handled, or his heavy stick which she had been allowed to wave about, of his knees on to which she had crept and of a particular tone in his voice which he only used when talking to small children and which, no doubt, they alone could understand. There were also deep pockets from which presents were extracted and placed slyly on the table when the child's head was turned away, and a contagious laughter which they had shared like a piece of festive cake . . . On our last visit, he showed her his toy theatre. It was a wonderful affair which he had brought back from Spain during a recent journey, with bright scenery, electric lights, and brand new stories. But the stage itself was far more exciting than the plays. It had to be inspected from every angle. We twisted our necks and bent our backs to get a better view, but the two children of the party, although one was fifty years older than the other, went down on their knees at once, assuming the humble attitude which comes naturally to children before their toys, as it comes to men before their God. It is in this attitude that we shall always remember him, crouching eagerly in front of the diminutive stage, while the small electric bulbs which brightened it rose like so many suns over the barren yellow mountains and the vivid green valleys. He had seen these landscapes and crossed these streams, but this was better than Spain . . . As I was watching him, some words of his came back into my mind, something about immortality and the next world, and I felt a pang of pain. I found these words, the same evening, in *Tremendous Trifles*: 'If I am ever in any other and better world, I hope that I shall have enough time to play with nothing but toy theatres . . .'[13]

After Gilbert's death, Frances lent the Spanish toy theatre to the Bastable family, who had long been friends. The postcard she sent with it stated that there was 'no hurry about returning it but I don't want to lose it as G was so fond of it'.[14]

Shortly after his return to England, Chesterton became embroiled once more in religious and political controversy. In fact, he was so intrigued by an article by Father C. C. Martindale, SJ, in the *Catholic Herald* on 11 May that he was inspired to write a poem. Father Martindale's article had reported on the failure of Stalin's attempts to establish anti-religious societies throughout Russia:

In January of last year Breboznik complained that anti-religious societies had been disbanded in seventy districts, while it had

457

been thought that in the region of Kovrov there was a whole system of atheist cells, the President of that region wrote . . . that neither in the town nor in the region were there any cells left – in fact, 'in the entire district there is now only one organised atheist – myself'.

Chesterton's response to this news was the satirical verse 'Comfort for Communists':

> Look west, look west, to the Land of Profits,
> To the old gold marts, and confess it then
> How greatly your great propaganda prospers
> When left to the methods of Business Men.
>
> Ah, Mammon is mightier than Marx in making
> A goose-step order for godless geese,
> And snobs know better than mobs to measure
> Where God shall flourish and God shall cease.
>
> Lift up your heart in the wastes Slavonian,
> Let no Red Sun on your wrath go down;
> There are millions of very much organised atheists
> In the Outer Circle of London town.[15]

It was in London town the following month that Chesterton crossed swords with Bertrand Russell, one of the century's most gifted atheists. The occasion was a debate, broadcast by the BBC, on 'Who Should Bring Up Our Children?'. Russell was, during this phase of his life, a keen and controversial educationist. In 1927 he had established a progressive school near Petersfield with his second wife, Dora Winifred Black, having published his educationist theories in his book *On Education* during the previous year. In 1932 he published *Education and the Social Order*, and it was the principles set out in this book which Russell sought to defend, and which Chesterton challenged, in the BBC debate. Russell contended that poor parents could not give their children the food, clothing and space they needed, while rich parents spoilt their children by giving them too much and expecting too much in return. All children should therefore be put in the care of officials, such as doctors, nurses and teachers, in especially adapted institutions. Chesterton countered that the family was a natural institution and that parents were fitted by nature to bring up their children. Instead of spending money on the special institutions desired by Russell, it could be more properly and profitably spent by providing the poor with better living conditions.[16] Maurice Baring, admittedly a biased judge, considered Chesterton 'especially brilliant' during the debate.

It was also during June 1935 that the BBC asked Gilbert to contribute to a series of radio broadcasts on the subject of liberty. It was the only time the BBC had actually requested that Chesterton speak specifically 'as a Catholic'. In his talk, which the *Listener* had entitled 'The Liberty that Matters', he defined the Free Man as 'he who is in charge of himself. He may, and does, damage himself. He may smoke too much, drink too much, work too hard, walk too little; he (or she) may starve fanatically, either for fasting or for slimming. But he (or she) decides.'[17] This libertarian approach contrasted starkly with Bertrand Russell's proposals for educational regimentation and also clashed with the ideas of Bernard Shaw, who had disagreed publicly with Gilbert on the issue: 'I am not so much concerned about their freedom as Mr Chesterton; for it is plain to me that our civilisation is being destroyed by the monstrously excessive freedom we allow to individuals.'[18]

To Chesterton, however, the idea of Liberty was always paramount. In his radio talk he had said that the absence of liberty was far worse than the presence of lice in the slums. On this issue, he said, he would have gladly spoken merely as an Englishman, but as he had been asked to speak as a Catholic, 'I am going to point out that Catholicism created English liberty; that the freedom has remained exactly in so far as the Faith has remained; and that where it is true that all our faith has gone, all our freedom is going. If I do this, I cannot ask most of you to agree with me; if I did anything else, I could not ask any of you to respect me.'[19]

Other speakers in the series had dwelt on the liberty secured to Englishmen by the parliamentary and judicial systems, both, Chesterton noted, of Catholic origin. Yet he argued that even these freedoms were being eroded and that the most important freedom of all, the freedom to have real control over one's own life, had effectively disappeared for the great mass of the people. Meanwhile, the liberty lauded so widely that followed the Reformation

has been a limited liberty because it was only a literary liberty . . .
You always talked about verbal liberty; you hardly ever talked about

459

vital liberty . . . the faddist was free to preach his fads; but the free man was no longer free to protect his freedom . . . Monarchy, aristocracy, democracy, responsible forms of rule, have collapsed under plutocracy, which is irresponsible rule. And this has come upon us because we departed from the old morality in three essential points. First, we supported notions against normal customs. Second, we made the State top-heavy with a new and secretive tyranny of wealth. And third, we forgot that there is no faith in freedom without faith in free will. A servile fatalism dogs the creed of materialism; because nothing, as Dante said, less than the generosity of God could give to Man, after all ordinary gifts, the noblest of all things, which is Liberty.[20]

This was Chesterton at his most provocative and controversial. It was scarcely surprising, therefore, that his talk elicited a lively response from many of his listeners. On 11 June, the evening of the broadcast, Mary N. Windsor, a listener from St Anne's-on-Sea, felt compelled to write the following letter:

Four of us – two Catholics and two Protestants – listened to your contribution to the 'Freedom' series tonight and enjoyed it immensely. Thank you ever so much. We chuckled with you and were serious with you, and rejoiced quite inordinately over your 'offensiveness'. But being of very ordinary intellect we found ourselves somewhat out of our depth over the fact that 'nowadays men cannot possess their houses or their shops'. If the fact that I'm merely adding another letter to your, no doubt, already weighty correspondence does not annoy you too much, I wonder if you could put me straight as to what exactly you meant by this. I tried to explain it to my Protestant co-listeners as being the difference between the Pre-Reformation peasant's 'three acres and a cow' and the present-day factory worker's home, usually rented, but my version of it didn't sound very satisfactory, somehow.[21]

Gilbert replied two weeks later, on 25 June, apologising for the delay by stating, 'I have had to deal with a huge stack of letters about the BBC talk.' Many of these letters were far from sympathetic. George H. Bull, who described himself as 'only a working man' and a die-hard Nonconformist, had attacked him bitterly. Gilbert's reply, on 17 June, exhibited a mixture of restraint and irritation:

The odd and interesting thing about your letter is that, among about ten or twelve assertions, one is actually true. The rest are all untrue, of course; things you have been told and doubtless believe in all simplicity and sincerity. When you say that penitents pay for absolution, or that money can annul any marriage, it is merely as if you had said that Margate is in Scotland, or that elephants lay eggs. It does not happen to be the fact, as you would discover if you investigated the facts. But when you suggest that there hangs on to the fringe of the Catholic Church a vast horde of outcasts, criminals, prostitutes, etc. . . . you refer to a real fact; and a very remarkable and interesting fact it is. They cannot get the Church's Sacraments or solid assurances, except by changing their whole way of life; but they do actually love the Faith that they cannot live by . . . If you explain it by supposing that the Church, though bound to refuse them Absolution where there is no amendment, keeps in touch with them and treats their human dignity rather more sympathetically than does the world, Puritan or Pagan . . . that also probably refers to a real fact. It is one of the facts that convince me most strongly that Catholicism is what it claims to be. After two thousand years of compromises and concordats, with every sort of social system, the Catholic Church has never yet become quite respectable. He still eats and drinks with publicans and sinners.[22]

On the same day he replied to another letter which contained a range of questions about the Catholic faith. In response to the suggestion that Catholics are 'bound to go to confession and buy the pardon of God for their sins', Gilbert replied: 'I do not understand what you mean by "buy the pardon". Surely you are not, like my less literate correspondents, under the ignorant delusion that we pay money to the priest for absolution. If you mean to say do we try to earn the pardon of God, by sincerity and facing the truth about ourselves, we do.'[23] Predictably, however, he saved his most emphatic response for replying to the suggestion that Catholics were not allowed to use their intelligence on questions of doctrine but must swallow them whole:

If you mean swallow them without thinking about them, Catholics think about them much more than anybody else does in the muddled modern world . . . It is precisely because most non-Catholics do *not* think, that they can hold a chaos of contrary notions at once, as that Jesus was good and humble, but falsely boasted of being God; or that God became Man to guide men till the end of time, and then died without giving them a hint of how they were to discover His decision in the first quarrel that might arise; or, alternatively, that he was not God, but only a Galilean peasant, but we are bound to submit to His

461

most startling paradoxes about peace, but not to His plainest words about marriage. Thinking means thinking connectedly. If I thought the Catholic creed untrue, I should cease to be a Catholic. But as the more I think about it, the truer I think it, the dilemma does not arise; there is no connection in my mind between thinking about it and doubting it.[24]

Perhaps the most surprising attack on Chesterton, in the wake of his talk for the BBC on liberty, was published in the *Catholic Herald*. Gilbert's response was published in the paper on 6 July:

It is with mingled respect and regret that I differ from a paper I admire so much as I do the *Catholic Herald* . . .

The BBC, much to the credit of its own relatively sound sense of liberty, having asked me specially for what I thought about Catholicism, I did certainly divulge the secret that I thought it was true, and that, therefore, even great cultures falling away from it, in any direction, had fallen into falsehood. I fully appreciate the desire to be fair or friendly that may lead anyone to deplore this disclosure, but I do not myself believe that it will do an atom of good to anyone, least of all to the English, to whitewash or conceal the bad results of heresy in history. I was therefore a little puzzled when a contributor called it 'a sectarian note'. Somehow, I had not expected anybody on the *Catholic Herald* to call the Catholic Church a sect.[25]

In the midst of the controversy Chesterton found time to attend a dinner engagement in Cambridge. It was here that the Canadian writer Marshall McLuhan, who was then a twenty-five-year-old student studying English literature, first met him:

Well, Chesterton *was* at the dinner! I had seen his pictures, heard his voice, and thought his thoughts, and knew what to expect. But I was not prepared for his quick, light-blue eye, or the refinement and definition of his features. He has much that reminds me of R. B. Bennett, but a large head, and as I say, finer features. His hair is not very long but it curls up at the back of his head – like his light moustache, it is quite white. His bulk is unexaggerated by accounts. He is six feet two or three and much thicker (at the equator) than he is wide at the shoulders, or elsewhere. His voice is not tiny or high-pitched but it is not powerful. He holds himself quite erect when he stands – necessarily he moves slowly, and because he is

GK, he imparts a sense of largesse, ample humour, tolerance, and significant dignity to the necessity which nature has laid upon him. His eye and head and face might easily, in a more portable figure, have been consonant with the speedy active agitator and leader.[26]

Three months later, when McLuhan was on the verge of joining the Catholic Church, he explained in a letter to his mother how important Chesterton had been to his conversion: 'Had I not encountered Chesterton, I would have remained agnostic for many years at least. Chesterton did not convince me of religious truth, but he prevented my despair from becoming a habit or hardening into misanthropy. He opened my eyes to European culture and encouraged me to know it more closely.'[27]

In 1948, when McLuhan had become a professor at St Michael's College in Toronto, he wrote the introduction to Hugh Kenner's critical study *Paradox in Chesterton*:

> ... in presenting him as a master of analogical perception and argument, Mr Kenner at once divorces the Toby-jug Chesterton of a particular literary epoch from the central and important Chesterton who had an unwavering and metaphysical intuition of being. The specific contemporary relevance of Chesterton is this, that his metaphysical intuition of being was always in the service of the search for moral and political order in the current chaos.[28]

Another writer who defended Chesterton vociferously at this time was André Maurois, whose book *Prophètes et Poètes* was published in Paris in 1935. Later translated into English, Maurois's book gave Chesterton a place of honour:

> Chesterton, with wonderful vigour and brilliance, has striven to reconcile intelligence with tradition. Against Shaw and Wells he is an indispensable counterpoise ...
>
> He can be accused of sometimes falling a victim to his own virtuosity. The physicist works out symmetrical formulas and finds in these the laws of the universe because God is a geometrist; similarly Chesterton, by setting paradox alongside paradox, builds up a picture of reality because reality is a totalling of paradoxes. But sometimes this juggling with formulas exhausts the reader, who is left with an uneasy feeling in his mind. He sees so clearly that Chesterton is brilliant that he no

longer sees how profound Chesterton is. In the ballet of his words
we do not always recognise the ordinary life which he would have
us love . . .

. . . Without his paradoxes, without his jokes, without his rhetorical
switchbacks, Chesterton might perhaps be a clearer philosopher. But
he would not be Chesterton. It has often been supposed that he is
not serious, because he is funny; actually he is funny because he is
serious. Confident in his truth, he can afford to joke . . . Certainty
breeds serenity.[29]

Something of the serenity Maurois detected was present in *The
Well and the Shallows*, a collection of essays published by Sheed &
Ward in September. The book was more solemn in many respects
than previous collections, and Chesterton was so intent on being
taken seriously that he was tempted to call the book 'Joking Apart':
'I was monstrously attracted by a suggestion that these essays should
bear the general title of "Joking Apart". It seemed to me a simple
and sensible way of saying that the reader of these pages must not
look for many jokes, certainly not merely for jokes, because these are
controversial essays, covering all subjects on which a controversialist
is challenged . . .'[30]

Although *The Well and the Shallows* did touch upon many controversies, both ancient and modern, it was the continuing controversy
surrounding his faith which formed the central theme of much of
the book. Indeed, the first sentence in a series of six essays, entitled
collectively 'My Six Conversions', was representative of the book as
a whole: 'At least six times during the last few years, I have found
myself in a situation in which I should certainly have become a
Catholic, if I had not been restrained from that rash step by the
fortunate accident that I was one already.'[31] There then followed
fifty pages in which Chesterton expounded his belief in the strength
of the Catholic position compared with the relative weakness of all
other positions. In the end, however, his conclusion was merely a
reiteration of the very first sentence:

I could not abandon the faith, without falling back on something
more shallow than the faith. I could not cease to be a Catholic,
except by becoming something more narrow than a Catholic. A
man must narrow his mind in order to lose the universal philosophy;
everything that has happened up to this very day has confirmed this
conviction; and whatever happens tomorrow will confirm it anew.

We have come out of the shallows and the dry places to the one deep well; and the Truth is at the bottom of it.[32]

Meanwhile, the sceptics who failed to fathom the depths were accused of causing enormous harm: '... the work of the sceptic for the past hundred years has indeed been very like the fruitless fury of some primeval monster; eyeless, mindless, merely destructive and devouring; a giant worm wasting away a world that he could not even see; a benighted and bestial life, unconscious of its own cause and of its own consequences'.[33]

Chesterton developed this argument in another essay in which he contrasted the philosophy of the Church with that of the sceptics:

There is, for instance, one influence that grows stronger every day, never mentioned in the newspapers, not even intelligible to people in the newspaper frame of mind. It is the return of the Thomist Philosophy; which is the philosophy of common sense, as compared with the paradoxes of Kant and Hegel and the Pragmatists. The Roman religion will be, in the exact sense, the only Rationalist religion. The other religions will not be Rationalist but Relativist; declaring that the reason is itself relative and unreliable; declaring that Being is only Becoming or that all time is only a time of transition; saying in mathematics that two and two make five in the fixed stars, saying in metaphysics and in morals that there is a good beyond good and evil. Instead of the materialist who said that the soul did not exist, we shall have the new mystic who says that the body does not exist. Amid all these things the return of the Scholastic will simply be the return of the sane man ... But to say that there is no pain, or no matter, or no evil, or no difference between man and beast, or indeed between anything and anything else – this is a desperate effort to destroy all experience and sense of reality; and men will weary of it more and more, when it has ceased to be the latest fashion; and will look once more for something that will give form to such a chaos and keep the proportions of the mind of man.[34]

He believed that the shallowness of modern philosophy had spilled over into the field of economics. In 'Reflections on a Rotten Apple', one of the few essays in the book which did not deal primarily with a religious theme, he began his attack on the modern obsession with trade by reiterating his attack on the modern mind's inability to grasp essentials:

Our age is obviously the Nonsense Age; the wiser sort of nonsense being provided for the children and the sillier sort of nonsense for the grown-up people. The eighteenth century has been called the Age of Reason; I suppose there is no doubt that the twentieth century is the Age of Unreason . . .

For it seems that we live today in a world of unreason, in which the orchards wither because they prosper, and the multitude of apples on the apple-tree of itself turns them into forbidden fruit, and makes the effort to consume them in every sense fruitless. This is the modern economic paradox, which is called Over-Production, or a glut in the market . . .[35]

After citing Oscar Wilde's maxim that 'a cynic is a man who knows the price of everything and the value of nothing', Chesterton concluded his article by stating that the chief error of the modern economic theory of trade was 'that things are to be judged by the price and not by the value':

And since Price is a crazy and incalculable thing, while Value is an intrinsic and indestructible thing, they have swept us into a society which is no longer solid but fluid, as unfathomable as a sea and as treacherous as a quicksand. Whether anything more solid can be built again upon a social philosophy of values, there is now no space to discuss at length here; but I am certain that nothing solid can be built on any other philosophy; certainly not upon the utterly unphilosophical philosophy of blind buying and selling; of bullying people into purchasing what they do not want; of making it badly so that they may break it and imagine they want it again; of keeping rubbish in rapid circulation like a dust-storm in a desert; and pretending that you are teaching men to hope, because you do not leave them one intelligent instant in which to despair.[36]

These are the words of a man thoroughly disillusioned with the prevailing philosophy and economics of his day. He was an exile, out of place in the sceptical intellectual atmosphere which was as 'treacherous as a quicksand'. As an outsider, he observed the 'dust-storm in a desert' from the still waters running deep within his own faith and philosophy. 'We Catholics must realise,' he wrote in one of the essays in *The Well and the Shallows*, 'that by this time we are living in pagan lands; and that the barbarians around us know not what they do.'[37]

On 1 November Hugh Paynter, the serviceman who was befriended by Gilbert and Frances when he was recovering from a wound in a London hospital during the war, was received into the Catholic Church along with his wife. It was an event which must have brought great joy to both the Chestertons. Ever since they had first met Paynter in the Royal Flying Corps Hospital in 1916, Gilbert and Frances had kept in touch and they had formed a lasting friendship. Yet at the time of their first meeting none of them had been Catholics. Now, nineteen years on, he was following them into the Church:

It was on All Saints day 1935 that they came over for the great occasion of our lives. That was the day my wife and I both had the great happiness of being received into the Church. It was a wonderful day for us. G. K. and Frances were there as our Godparents at the little church at Stonor Park associated with the Blessed Edmund Campion which is now recognised as a place of pilgrimage. When we got back to the farm a festive lunch had been prepared and there were several people invited to it. Unfortunately the wind was blowing from the wrong direction or the chimney wanted sweeping. Smoke belched out into the room all through the meal. But that sort of thing never worried G. K. Even while his eyes were streaming he was still laughing and entertaining us. That laugh of his, once heard you never forgot it. He seemed to put all the jollity of his nature into it. In a theatre people would turn from the play to listen to it. It was spontaneous, sincere, appreciative – no words can do credit to it. It was more than the laugh of a poet, an artist, or a genius, though he was all these. It was just part of himself and when he went he left the echo of it as a memory behind.[38]

On 9 November Father Vincent McNabb wrote to Gilbert, thanking him for an introduction he had written to one of his books:

When this morning, I read for the first time your words of Introduction I felt inclined to say: 'God forgive you – for you know not what you do.' But I stifled it into a 'God bless you!' because I knew your exaggerations and mistakes were only the exaggerations and mistakes of love.

Perhaps you had read or had divined without reading what I had written in *The Call of St Patrick*. You knew that if I loved Ireland as a man loves his mother, I loved England as a man loves his wife. And ever since God gave me to know you, I could not help thinking that you were England – the Merry, chivalrous, simple-hearted, fearless

England that I loved. In the love that I bear you I can forgive the exaggerations of the love that you bear me.

May God have you and your dear wife ever in His keeping.

Pray for me.[39]

As 1935 drew to a close, it was time for Chesterton's customary Christmas articles. This year, however, the festivities were overshadowed by the festering spectre of Fascism:

> We live in a terrible time, of war and rumour of war . . . International idealism in its effort to hold the world together . . . is admittedly weakened and often disappointed. I should say simply that it does not go deep enough . . . If we really wish to make vivid the horrors of destruction and mere disciplined murder we must see them more simply as attacks on the hearth and the human family; and feel about Hitler as men felt about Herod.[40]

Christmas 1935 was Chesterton's last. It was also one of the happiest he ever spent. Much of it was passed at the appropriately named Christmas Cottage in Beaconsfield, home of the Nicholl family. Clare Nicholl, who had been the recipient that year of a hand-drawn Christmas card from Chesterton which depicted the Nicholl sisters 'bringing in the bore's head' (i.e. Chesterton's) on a salver, remembered Twelfth Night:

> We always made a great feature of our table decorations and used to compete with each other to think up new things every year. This particular Christmas the table was a concerted family effort. We made them wait in the hall while we arranged the final dramatic effect. When the door to the dining-room was opened, the room was in darkness except for the firelight. In the middle of the table was a seascape (the big looking glass from the hall) and a ship in full sail towards a high rocky harbour (representing the Cobb at Lyme). On the edge of the harbour wall was a toy lighthouse. The windows revolved and a night-light inside made miniature beams shoot through the darkness and lit up the sea and the ship, its sails full set for home.
>
> We of course expected pleasure and surprise and plenty of appreciation of our labours. What we were not prepared for was G. K.'s reaction. He came in last, being 'taken into dinner' by one of us. He said no word at all, but paused in the doorway and stared and stared. And the sister whose arm was in his was stirred out of all

proportion and heard herself muttering her thoughts aloud to G. K. (one of his rarest qualities was that one could literally think aloud to him without fear or self-consciousness). 'It reminds me,' she said, 'of the *Salve Regina*.' And G. K. said below his breath, 'Yes – *nobis, post exilium ostende* . . .'[41]

« 31 »

End of the Beginning

NOBIS, POST EXILIUM OSTENDE . . . As Chesterton's life drew nearer its end he came to believe, more potently than ever, that man's life on earth was a time of exile and that the fullness of his existence was to be found elsewhere. According to the Nicholl sisters,

> the writing of his book on St Thomas marked a great change in G. K. . . . While he was writing it, he had apparently got the Corpus Christi sequence by heart, and time and again he recited to us the last two stanzas:

> > Bone pastor, panis vere,
> > Jesu nostri miserere;
> > Tu nos pasce, nos tuere:
> > Tu nos bona fac videre
> > In terra viventium.

> > Tu, qui cuncta scis et vales,
> > Qui nos pascis hic mortales:
> > Tuos ibi commensales,
> > Coheredes et sodales
> > Fac sanctorum civium

> which he would repeat and repeat, thumping his fist on the arm of the chair . . . Then he would say, 'What a summary of Heaven: the exact reversal of the slang expression "down among the dead men". There you have it – literally "the land of the living". Yes, my friends, we shall see all good things in the land of the living.'
> Another definition of Heaven he often quoted was the two words *in patria*: 'It tells you everything: "our native land".'[1]

Naturally enough, Chesterton began 1936 embroiled in yet another controversy. This time his opponent was the Cambridge medieval scholar at St John's College, Dr G. G. Coulton, a staunch anti-Catholic who had crossed swords with both Knox and Belloc on other occasions. This time Coulton had chosen Chesterton as his quarry, but Gilbert, uncharacteristically, was not fit for the chase. Normally, of course, he would have relished such a contest, but now he scarcely had the inclination to put pen to paper. It was left to Dorothy Collins to fob his adversary off. On 28 January Coulton replied to her letter, commenting that he was 'very sorry to hear of Mr Chesterton's indisposition'.[2]

However, if Cambridge University had produced a medieval scholar who was hostile to Chesterton, Oxford could boast a scholar who was far more favourably disposed towards him. During the early part of the year Oxford University Press had published *The Allegory of Love: A Study in Medieval Tradition* by C. S. Lewis. This book, for which Lewis was awarded the Hawthornden Prize, contained a great tribute to Chesterton's prowess as a literary critic:

> The *Furioso*, in its own peculiar way, is as great a masterpiece of construction as the *Oedipus Rex*. But nothing will finally explain, as no criticism of mine can adequately represent, the overwhelming achievement of Ariosto. There is only one English critic who could do justice to this gallant, satiric, chivalrous, farcical, flamboyant poem: Mr Chesterton should write a book on the Italian epic.[3]

Chesterton was no more able to fulfil Lewis's desire for a book on medieval romance than he was able to meet Coulton's demands for a battle over medieval Rome. He was finding it more of a struggle to meet his weekly journalistic commitments, and most of the energy he had remaining was expended in the completion of his *Autobiography*. No doubt this was made easier in February when another room, a large study, was added as an extension to Top Meadow. Dorothy Collins had complained that it was absurd for Gilbert to work in a tiny room at the far end of what had originally been the studio. Frances wrote to Father O'Connor, informing him of the latest extension to the house: 'Did you know we had built a new study? That is a great success. Gilbert says at first he had not room to swing a cat, now he has room to swing a tiger! That room is warm anyhow, and Dorothy rejoices.'[4]

In the relative comfort of the new study, Gilbert finally finished his *Autobiography*. Its completion prompted one friend to remark, *'Nunc dimittis,'* and certainly there was much in the book which sounded suspiciously as though it was intended as a swan song:

> I am here engaged in the morbid and degrading task of telling the story of my life; and have only to state what actually were the effects of such doctrines on my own feelings and actions. And I am, by the nature of the task, especially concerned with the fact that these doctrines seem to me to link up my whole life from the beginning, as no other doctrines could do . . . And they specially affected one idea; which I hope it is not pompous to call the chief idea of my life; I will not say the doctrine I have always taught, but the doctrine I should always have liked to teach. That is the idea of taking things with gratitude, and not taking things for granted . . .
>
> I began by being what the pessimists called an optimist; I have ended by being what the optimists would very probably call a pessimist. And I have never in fact been either, and I have never really changed at all. I began by defending vermilion pillar-boxes and Victorian omnibuses although they were ugly. I have ended by denouncing modern advertisements or American films even when they are beautiful. The thing that I was trying to say then is the same thing that I am trying to say now; and even the deepest revolution of religion has only confirmed me in the desire to say it. For indeed, I never saw the two sides of this single truth stated together anywhere, until I happened to open the Penny Catechism and read the words, 'The two sins against Hope are presumption and despair.'[5]

Chesterton proceeded to compare the presumption of the optimists with the despair of the pessimists, concluding that Realism trod a Hopeful path between the two. The final pages of the *Autobiography* were a reiteration of his lifelong philosophy of gratitude:

> I am finishing a story; rounding off what has been to me at least a romance, and very much of a mystery-story. It is a purely personal narrative that began in the first pages of this book; and I am answering at the end only the questions I asked at the beginning. I have said that I had in childhood, and have partly preserved out of childhood, a certain romance of receptiveness, which has not been killed by sin or even by sorrow; for though I have not had great troubles, I have had many. A man does not grow old without being bothered; but I have grown old without being bored. Existence is still a strange thing to me; and

as a stranger I give it welcome . . . This story, therefore, can only end as any detective story should end, with its own particular questions answered and its own primary problem solved . . . But for me my end is my beginning, as Maurice Baring quoted of Mary Stuart, and this overwhelming conviction that there is one key which can unlock all doors brings back to me my first glimpse of the glorious gift of the senses; and the sensational experience of sensation.[6]

However, many of the sensations Chesterton experienced at this time were not particularly pleasant because he was becoming seriously ill. His breathing was more and more laboured, he suffered perpetually from bronchial catarrh and he fell into intermittent bouts of fever. By February he appeared to have improved somewhat and Frances wrote a cautiously optimistic letter to Father O'Connor. She reported that Gilbert seemed a bit better but that she had been unwell. Her main concern at the time, however, was neither her own nor her husband's health. She confided to O'Connor that she was in the midst of a family crisis. One of her nieces had broken her engagement to marry and had run off to Australia. This had so upset the girl's mother that she had fallen gravely ill and Frances had taken it upon herself to nurse her. All this had not dampened her spirits, however, because she informed Father O'Connor that 'if the weather improves I hope to go to town tomorrow to the Lourdes Service at Westminster Cathedral, and incidentally if I can fit it in to Cruft's dog show. I want a new dog.'[7]

On 15 March Chesterton made his last radio broadcast, apart from a talk to schools on the Middle Ages a week later. Appropriately enough his final adult broadcast was entitled 'We will End with a Bang', part of a series of talks collectively titled 'The Spice of Life'. During the talk he bemoaned the fact that 'a great many people are at this moment paying rather too much attention to the spice of life, and rather too little attention to life'. None the less, he confessed to enjoying the common distractions of life as much as the next person:

I myself have even been blamed for defending the spices of life against what was called the simple life. I have been blamed for making myself a champion of beer and skittles. Fortunately, if I was a champion of skittles there was never any danger of my being a champion *at* skittles; somehow I never could aim at skittles with that precision with which I could aim at beer, but I have played ordinary games like skittles,

always badly . . . I have even played golf in Scotland before Arthur
Balfour brought it to England and it became a fashion and then a
religion. My difficulty since is that I cannot manage to regard a game
as a religion. The horrid secret of my failure is that I never could
quite see the difference between the cricket and golf, as I played
them when I was a boy, and the puss-in-the-corner and honeypots
as I played them when I was a child. Perhaps those nursery games are
now forgotten. Anyhow, I will not reveal what good games they were
lest they should become fashionable. If once they are taken seriously
in that most serious world, the world of sport, enormous results will
follow. [Shops] will sell a special shaped slipper for hunt-the-slipper,
or a caddy will follow the player with a bag full of fifteen different
slippers; moneypots will be made out of honeypots, and there will be
a corner in puss-in-the-corner. Anyhow, I have enjoyed, like anyone
else, these sports and spices of life. But I am convinced that neither
in your special spices or mine . . . nor in any other distraction from
life is the secret we are all seeking, the secret of enjoying life. All
our world will end in despair unless there is some way of making the
mind itself, the ordinary thoughts we have at ordinary times, more
happy than they seem to be just now, to judge by most modern novels
and poems. You have got to be happy in those quiet moments when
you remember that you are alive.[8]

The title of the talk was a light-hearted response to T. S. Eliot's
poem 'The Hollow Men' with its pessimistic refrain:

> This is the way the world ends
> This is the way the world ends
> This is the way the world ends
> Not with a bang but a whimper.

Such a suggestion was anathema to Chesterton:

Forgive me if I say, in my old-world fashion, that I'm damned if
I ever felt like that . . . I knew that the world was perishable and
would end, but I did not think it would end with a whimper,
but, if anything, with a trump of doom . . . I will even be so
indecently frivolous as to burst into song, and say to the young
pessimists:

> Some sneer; some snigger; some simper;
> In the youth where we laughed, and sang.

And *they* may end with a whimper
But *we* will end with a bang.[9]

Such was the emphatic climax to Chesterton's broadcasting career.
A week later his last poem was published. Printed in *G. K.'s Weekly*
on 26 March, it was entitled 'To The Jesuits (Spain, 1936)':

You bade the Red Man rise like the Red Clay
Of God's great Adam in his human right,
Till trailed the snake of trade, our own time's blight,
And Man lost Paradise in Paraguay.

You, when wild sects tortured and mocked each other
Saw truth in the wild tribes that tortured you
Slurred for not slurring all who slurred or slew,
Blamed that your murderer was too much your brother.[10]

The 'lost Paradise in Paraguay' was an allusion to the Jesuit
Reductions in South America during the seventeenth and eighteenth
centuries, which Chesterton perceived as being distributist in nature.
These Reductions were, in fact, Indian villages, largely self-governing,
where the native peoples, under the direction of Jesuit missionaries,
lived in a sort of Christian cooperative. Each family had its own house
and garden but worked together with other families on the larger
farming units, which were cultivated cooperatively. Between 1600
and 1750 there were said to be about sixty of these villages, containing
100,000 people. They eventually fell in the face of mercantile greed,
'the snake of trade, our own time's blight'.

In writing his last poem Chesterton had been animated by the same
spirit that had inspired one of his first. As early as 1892, during his last
year at St Paul's School, he had entered a competition for a prize poem
and won it. The subject on that occasion had been St Francis Xavier,
the Jesuit missionary and 'Apostle of the Indies', whose life, like that of
the Jesuit missionaries in Paraguay, had been a glorious failure among
pagan peoples. It seemed that Chesterton could claim for his poetry, as
well as for his philosophy, that 'for me my end is my beginning'.

In May it was decided that a pilgrimage to Lisieux and Lourdes
would be beneficial to Chesterton's failing health. On the evening
before he, Frances and Dorothy departed, Gilbert visited the Nicholl
sisters at Christmas Cottage for supper. He didn't stay as late as usual

and the sisters detected something portentous in the nature of his departure:

> Two of us only were at home. It was a particularly beautiful night, flower-scented, sunlit and enchanted, as only a May night in England can be. G. K. arrived looking for the first time in our memory dreadfully tired. We made the excuse of drinking him *bon voyage* to produce brandy, which brought some colour, but not much, back into his face.
>
> For some reason on this one occasion we stood together in the porch to see him off, and neither walked to the gate. The dusk was still gold in a lingering and splendid sunset. G. K. went through the wooden gate and turned, his hand still on the latch. He looked back at us; then he stretched out his hand in the strangest prolonged gesture – it was like a mixture of benediction and farewell. He stood still, for quite five minutes; then the latch clicked and we heard his footsteps crunching down the road. We stood together in the silence and my sister said, whispering, 'Do you feel horribly strange? Did you see how he stood and looked and looked, as though he were looking for the last time? I don't like it – I don't like it at all.'[11]

In that moment, immediately after he had left, one wonders whether either sister recalled the lines of the Thomas Moore poem which Chesterton was so fond of reciting during happy evenings at Christmas Cottage:

> More times than one can count, when he was sitting among us, during a pause in the long comfortable conversations, he would look round at each face in turn and quote a verse from Thomas Moore's *Farewell – But Whenever You Welcome the Hour*:
>
> > And still on that evening, when pleasure fills up
> > To the highest top sparkle each heart and each cup,
> > Where'er my path lies, be it gloomy or bright,
> > My soul, happy friends, shall be with you that night;
> > Shall join in your revels, your sports and your wiles,
> > And return to me beaming all o'er with your smiles –
> > Too blest, if it tell me that, 'mid the gay cheer,
> > Some kind voice had murmur'd, 'I wish he were here!'
>
> So often did he repeat these lines that those of us who had not known them already remembered them by heart from hearing him say them.[12]

Dorothy drove the Chestertons to Lisieux and thence to Lourdes, and it was from there that Gilbert began to write a letter which remained unfinished:

> ... I was afraid to come here, not with a holy fear (which I retain) but an unholy fear that the unholy modern world had made it vile with publicity and commercialism, as anti-Catholics say and some Catholics admit.
>
> It is not true. Lourdes is a nice little Pyrenean town, full of poor people drinking very cheap wine: much *less* transformed by touts and trippers than older shrines ...
>
> Lourdes is *not* spoilt: Our Lady came here to the very humblest, to a ragged child almost barefoot: and perhaps that is why there is a sense that she left this rocky place in a naked purity like stone: as if there were health and not wealth to be got out of it. By comparison, I hope I shall not lose the intercession of a Saint I have come to honour and understand better – and who presides in my own English town – if I say there was something a little *bourgeois* about St Thérèse of Lisieux – or rather her social setting. At Lourdes the framework is hard rock and Holy Poverty – all that Assisi ought to be. Of course there are shops that sell souvenirs: that is inevitable: for we must all sympathise with those who buy if not with those who sell ... The Grotto is not a 'blaze of gold and tinsel' as it is its duty to be for the sake of Baptist tourists from Tennessee. The Grotto is a grey forest of crutches and wooden legs hung up by ex-cripples who could only afford such things in honest wood.[13]

If the crutches left by ex-cripples provided evidence of the miraculous cures ascribed to Lourdes, no such cure was forthcoming for Chesterton. Indeed, Frances later wrote to Father O'Connor that 'Our Lady's answer to my prayers for him there was not what I expected – but right, I know, however hard.'[14] As it transpired, Dorothy Collins recalled that 'the first signs of his last illness showed at a Mass on Ascension Day at Clermont Ferrand when he had to come out before the Mass was finished and did not feel well enough to enjoy his breakfast'.[15]

Although he seemed to improve during the long drive home, serenading the ladies tunelessly with songs from Gilbert and Sullivan, his condition again deteriorated when he arrived back in Beaconsfield. He began to lose concentration and would fall asleep at his desk. The doctor was called and expressed serious concern over the condition of his heart. He was confined to bed and soon began to drift into a state of intermittent semi-consciousness, punctuated by sleep. On one occasion, emerging from a sort of reverie, he said: 'The issue is now quite clear. It is between light and darkness and every one must choose his side.'[16]

According to Dorothy, 'Frances was devastated and unable to attend to anything.'[17] In consequence, it was Dorothy who took charge. On 10 June she replied to a letter from G. G. Coulton:

> I am sure you will be sorry to hear that Mr Chesterton is very ill. He is being nursed at home by two nurses and so far we have been able to keep his illness out of the papers, but I do not expect to be able to do so much longer, as all his work has stopped. The specialist who saw him on Monday said he will not be able to work for some months, and then only on one or two of his weekly articles if he is feeling strong enough. He is suffering from cardiac weakness and complications. He was about three quarters of the way through the essay he was writing for you, but had not finished it as he was waiting to go to the British Museum for some research work. He has not been well enough for any extra exertion for some months, although he has tried to keep going. We had hoped to see a great improvement as a result of his visit to France, so this relapse is very disappointing.[18]

On 12 June Chesterton's old school friend E. C. Bentley, author of *Trent's Last Case*, came to visit. Unable to see Gilbert, he sat in the study with Dorothy. Thus far, the press had had no idea that Chesterton was seriously ill, but while Dorothy and Bentley were talking in the study, a journalist from the *Daily Mail* rang up to say he had heard the news. Dorothy confirmed that Gilbert was very ill but requested that the news remain secret because 'Mr Chesterton has to be kept very quiet and we must not have telephones and doorbells.' She extracted a promise that the *Daily Mail* would not publicise his illness: 'E. C. Bentley looked at me as if I were a newborn baby and said, "You don't expect them to keep that promise, do you?" "I do," I said, "but you know the press better than I do. I still hope they will." And they did. I wrote to the Editor after G. K.'s death to thank him for his great courtesy.'[19]

On the same day Monsignor Smith, the parish priest, called at Top Meadow to anoint Chesterton with chrism, and Chesterton was conscious enough to receive what turned out to be his last

Communion. Father Vincent McNabb arrived in the afternoon, having travelled down from St Dominic's Priory in London. Standing beside the bed where Chesterton lay unconscious, he intoned the *Salve Regina*, as was the custom in the Dominican order for a dying priest. Then, seeing Gilbert's pen on the table beside the bed, he picked it up and kissed it.

It was also on this day that Frances took a brief break from her bedside vigil to write to Father O'Connor:

> In case you hear the news from elsewhere I write myself to tell you that G. is very seriously ill. The main trouble is heart and kidney and an amount of fluid in the body that sets up a dropsical condition. I have had a specialist to see him, who says that though he is desperately ill there is a fighting chance. I think possibly he is a little better today. He has had Extreme Unction this morning and received Holy Communion.
>
> Will you, as I know you will, pray for him and get others to do so and say some Masses for him.[20]

All through the following day Frances kept a constant vigil at her husband's bedside. Consequently she was present when he eventually regained consciousness. Recognising Frances, he said, 'Hello, my darling.' Then, noticing that Dorothy was also in the room, he said: 'Hello, my dear.' These were his last words; he soon sank back into a laborious and fitful sleep and never again regained consciousness. There is real bathos in these last words of Chesterton; it is disappointing that one of the greatest wits of the century should make his exit so anticlimactically. Yet the words were sublimely apt, first, because they were addressed solely to the two most important people in his life: his wife and his surrogate daughter, and, second, because they were words of greeting and not of farewell, signifying a beginning and not an end of their relationship. Certainly, all three people in the room believed this to be the case, however hard the reality may have appeared *in extremis*. Indeed, one hears echoes of a more worldly wartime speech by Winston Churchill, which would not even be uttered for a further six years, in which he said, concerning the Battle of Egypt, that it wasn't the end, nor even the beginning of the end, but it was, perhaps, the end of the beginning.

In a mortal sense at least, the end came quickly. His condition worsened during the night, and he died soon after ten o'clock on the morning of Sunday, 14 June. Later the same day Frances wrote to Father O'Connor: 'Our beloved Gilbert passed away this morning at 10.15. He was unconscious for some time before but had received the Last Sacraments and Extreme Unction whilst he was still in possession of his understanding . . .'[21]

Many people observed wryly that there were several coincidences connected with the timing of Chesterton's death. His passing had occurred on the Sunday within the Octave of Corpus Christi, the feast upon which he had been received into the Church fourteen years earlier. Father Ignatius Rice also noted with a smile that the Introit for that day's mass, which was printed on his memorial card, contained a joke about his size: 'The Lord became my protector and He brought me forth into a large place. He saved me because he was well pleased with me. I will love thee O Lord my strength. The Lord is my firmament and my refuge and my deliverer.'[22] To these words on Gilbert's memorial card, Frances had added Walter de la Mare's tribute to her husband:

> Knight of the Holy Ghost, he goes his way
> Wisdom his motley, Truth his loving jest;
> The mills of Satan keep his lance in play,
> Pity and innocence his heart at rest.[23]

These lines found a distant echo in a stanza from *The Ballad of the White Horse*:

> People, if you have any prayers
> Say prayers for me:
> And lay me under a Christian stone
> In that lost land I thought my own,
> To wait till the holy horn is blown,
> And all poor men are free.

On the day of his funeral it was clear that many people had come to comply with this request because the tiny Church of St Teresa was filled to overflowing with friends and admirers. They had arrived from London, from all over England, and even from France, Germany and America. Hilaire Belloc, Max Beerbohm, Eric Gill, D. B. Wyndham Lewis, Ronald Knox and A. G. Gardiner were among the mourners, who numbered four hundred in total. However, as St Teresa's was not yet completed, only half the congregation could be seated. The rest, including dozens of villagers, stood throughout the requiem mass in a temporary wooden annexe, and others, for whom there was no space even in the annexe, stood outside the church in the sunshine.

The coffin, of light oak, rested among wreaths. A cross of dark red roses lay on top of it, attached to which was an inscription by Frances: '"Red roses full of rain". for you – as you would wish.'

The mass was celebrated by Monsignor Smith, rector of Beaconsfield, in the presence of the Archbishop of Westminster, Dr Hinsley, who gave the Absolution. Other clergy in attendance included Monsignor Fulton J. Sheen, of the Catholic University of America, Father Vincent McNabb, Father C. C. Martindale, Father Ignatius Rice and Father Josef Stocker from Cologne.

The Nicholl sisters were among the congregation and they remembered an earlier discussion they'd had with Chesterton about death and funerals:

> Discussing funerals, one of us said, 'To logical Christians, any funeral should really be an occasion of rejoicing. There should be no black, no dirges; the coffin should be draped in white and silver and preceded by a fanfare of trumpets. And the friends of the dead person should light every candle in the church and sing the *Te Deum*.' In 1936 we remembered this conversation . . . and there was not one candle socket empty in the Beaconsfield church during G. K.'s requiem Mass. One of us said afterwards with truth that at the moment of the Consecration of the Mass she had a sudden and most strong sense of festival and an inrush of joy – there was nothing of mourning in that requiem – it was part of a huge birthday party in Heaven.[24]

After mass, a long line of cars followed the slow procession of clergy to the cemetery, over a mile away. Many mourners followed on foot, a forty-minute walk through old and new Beaconsfield. William Titterton, a great friend of Gilbert who would later become his biographer, noted:

> Now I am at his peaceful funeral at Beaconsfield in the great company of his friends. (I have gone down by train with some of them, arguing furiously and joyously all the way about his views on machinery.) I see the coffin that holds all that is mortal of my captain. I pass with it along the little town's winding ways. It is a roundabout way we go. For the police of the place will have it that Gilbert Chesterton shall make

his last earthly journey past the homes of the people who knew him and loved him best. And there they were, crowding the pavements, and all, like us, bereaved. Yet it was almost a gala day. There was no moping, no gush of tears. Nay, there was laughter as one of us recalled him and his heroic jollity to another's ready remembrance. A policeman at the gate of the cemetery said to Edward Macdonald, 'Most of the lads are on duty, else they would all have been here.' As Edward Macdonald says, 'He was the Lord of the Manor. And he never knew it.' So we left him.[25]

They left him laughing. In fact, they left him laughing in both senses of the ambiguous phrase because Gilbert, throughout his literary life, had literally laughed at death:

> Know you what earth shall lose tonight, what rich
>   uncounted loans,
> What heavy gold of tales untold you bury with my bones?
> My loves in deep dim meadows, my ships that rode at ease,
> Ruffling the purple plumage of strange and secret seas.
> To see this fair earth as it is to me alone was given,
> The blow that breaks my brow tonight shall break
>   the dome of heaven.
> The skies I saw, the trees I saw after no eyes
>   shall see.
> Tonight I die the death of God: the stars shall die
>   with me:
> One sound shall sunder all the spears and break
>   the trumpet's breath:
> You never laughed in all your life as I shall laugh
>   in death.[26]

One of Chesterton's most famous poems, 'The Rolling English Road', had extolled the virtues of 'the decent inn of death', and an early poem, written before the world had even heard of G. K. Chesterton, had finished with the lines:

> Surely, friends, I might have guessed
> Death was but the good King's jest,
>   It was hid so carefully.

However, when the moment of his death came, not everyone was able to treat it so whimsically or philosophically. To those closest to him, care-filled, the jest, if jest it was, was hidden very carefully indeed. Hilaire Belloc was found after the funeral weeping tears of disconsolate isolation into a pint of beer outside the Railway Hotel, and Frances, unable to cope with the responsibility of playing the hostess for those mourners who returned to Top Meadow after the ceremony, hid herself in her room.

One person who was absent from the funeral was Maurice Baring, who was suffering progressively from Parkinson's disease. He was clearly upset at his inability to attend his friend's burial, and scrawled several letters to Frances which were almost illegible: 'Too paralysed with neuritis and "agitance" to hold pen or pencil. Saw incredible news in *Times*. Then your letter came. All my prayers and thoughts are with you. I'm not allowed to travel except once a week to see doctor, but I'll have a Mass said here.'[27] The following day he wrote again: 'There is nothing to be said, is there, except that our loss, and especially yours, is his gain? I wish I could come down tomorrow [to the funeral], but I cannot go even to mass here on Sundays because directly I get into a church where there are people I have a sort of attack of palpitations and have to come out at once . . . O, Frances, I feel as if a tower of strength had vanished and our crutch in life had broken.'[28]

Bernard Shaw also wrote to Frances offering his condolences: 'It seems the most ridiculous thing in the world that I, 18 years older than Gilbert, should be heartlessly surviving him . . . The trumpets are sounding for him.'[29]

Meanwhile Belloc, who had been unable to articulate his feelings at the funeral, was better able to express them when he came to conclude his study of Chesterton's place in English letters four years later:

In the appreciation of a man rather than of a writer virtue is immeasurably more important than literary talent and appeal. For these last make up nothing for the salvation of the soul and for an ultimate association with those who should be our unfailing companions in Beatitude: the Great Company. Of that Company he now is; so that it is a lesser and even indifferent thing to determine how much he shall also be of the company, the earthly and temporal company, of the local and temporarily famous.

What place he may take according to that lesser standard I cannot tell, because many years must pass before a man's position in the literature of his country can be called securely established.

We are too near to decide this. But because we are so near and because those (such as I who write this) who were his companions, knew him through his very self and not through his external activity, we are in communion with him. So be it. He is in Heaven.[30]

A host of others wrote to Frances as the news of Gilbert's death reached his many friends and admirers. Dorothy L. Sayers wrote to her on 15 June, the day after his death, 'I think, in some ways, G. K.'s books have become more a part of my mental make-up than those of any writer you could name.'[31] This was a sentiment echoed by several of his contemporaries. Ronald Knox wrote: 'To me, Chesterton's philosophy, in the broadest sense of the word, has been part of the air I breathed, ever since the age when a man's ideas begin to disentangle themselves from his education. His paradoxes have become, as it were, the platitudes of my thought.'[32] Charles Williams exclaimed, on hearing the news, that 'the last of my Lords is dead,' and, in similar vein, Sir Iain Moncreiffe recalled the praise Chesterton had been afforded by his English tutor: 'When I was at Stowe our English tutor was that remarkable falconer-pacifist-huntsman, T. H. White, who wrote *The Sword in the Stone* and *The Ill-Made Knight*. One morning Tim White came into our beautiful Georgian classroom and announced, "G. K. Chesterton died yesterday. P. G. Wodehouse is now the greatest living master of the English language."'[33] Writing to Cyril Clemens, an early Chesterton biographer, Hugh Kingsmill stated: 'My friend Hesketh Pearson was staying with me when I read of Chesterton's death. I told him of it through the bathroom door, and he sent up a hollow groan which must have echoed that morning all over England.'[34]

On Saturday, 27 June, a memorial requiem mass was celebrated at Westminster Cathedral with a congregation of about 2,000 people. Cardinal (then Archbishop) Hinsley had requested that Monsignor John O'Connor sing the mass, assisted by Father Ignatius Rice, who had been O'Connor's assistant at Chesterton's reception into the Church. Father Vincent McNabb also assisted as sub-deacon. This was a fitting tribute, not only to Chesterton but also to Monsignor O'Connor, whose friendship with Gilbert had spanned more than three decades. It was Father Brown's crowning glory.

O'Connor described the requiem at Westminster as 'the solemn commemoration of him by and for those who could not be present at Beaconsfield at his burial, myself for instance having been confined to bed all that week'. He also heard on the day at Westminster that

Wells had said that if he ever got to Heaven, 'presuming there *is* a Heaven, it will be by the intervention of Gilbert Chesterton'.[35]

The panegyric at Westminster was preached by Monsignor Ronald Knox, but the highest honour came in the form of a message from the Pope. Both Frances and Cardinal Hinsley received telegrams from Cardinal Pacelli for and on behalf of Pope Pius XI. (Pacelli was later destined, as Pius XII, to be the Pope's successor.) The telegram to Cardinal Hinsley was read to the vast crowd in the cathedral and found an echo in the hearts of all those present: 'Holy Father deeply grieved death Mr Gilbert Keith Chesterton devoted son Holy Church gifted Defender of the Catholic Faith. His Holiness offers paternal sympathy people of England assures prayers dear departed, bestows Apostolic Benediction.'[36]

There was an ironic twist to the Pope's telegram because the secular press refused to publish it on the grounds that 'the Pope had bestowed on a British subject a title held by the King'.[37] That the title of *Fidei Defensor* was originally bestowed upon the King by the Pope was, of course, overlooked, Henry VIII being awarded the title by Pope Leo X shortly before the King rebelled against the Church. No doubt Chesterton would have been highly amused at the muddle-headed response of his beloved Fleet Street to the honour the Pope had posthumously bestowed upon him. Needless to say, he had little in common with the monarch who had previously received the same honour from the Pope – except perhaps the size of their girths.

Casting controversy aside, few would dispute that Chesterton had been a defender of the Catholic faith, and one wonders what he would have thought of the assertion by one of his recent biographers, 'Certainly Chesterton would burst out of the ark in which his co-religionists have locked him.'[38] Considering that he had often described the Catholic faith as the key to intellectual freedom, it is hard to imagine his consenting to a revisionist approach which suggested that his faith had actually confined him. In fact, one can't help but wish that Chesterton was around to answer the accusation himself, to point out in his own inimitable style that anyone 'bursting out of the ark' would probably drown. Meanwhile, and contrary to such claims about the actions of his co-religionists, one of the most notable histories of the Catholic Church in England, written and published around the time of his death, barely mentioned Chesterton's name at all. David Mathew's *Catholicism in England 1535-1935* affords Gilbert's conversion in 1922 only a single sentence, while the only other reference to him in the book says more about his Englishness than his Catholicism:

> In Chesterton there arose a Catholic thinker who was really of the English people, a 'character', utterly independent, a writer with something of the touch of Dickens; a genuine upsurge of English feeling and idealism with that passion for broad justice which always receives a sympathetic and uproariously orderly hearing in this country. The torrential felicity of phrase and the bounding paradox intimately reflected the Englishman in his humours; and he was aided in his search for justice by a deep understanding of the ordinary man.[39]

One senses that Chesterton would have been pleased with such a judgment because his Englishness was always very dear to him. Yet his love for England was only a reflection of his love for something greater. Father Ignatius Rice's interpretation of 'The Rolling English Road', perhaps the most quintessentially English of all Chesterton's poems, illustrated this:

> 'The Rolling English Road' is taken to be just a drinking song. In reality it is an allegory of life. The young man is carefree and boisterously merry in the first stanza; as he grows older in the second stanza he becomes aware of social justice and patriotic duty; then he grows conscious of sin, which would blast even the material beauty of the world but for the mercy of God; and finally the approach of death expels the folly of youth and clears his vision for the good news of God.[40]

If Chesterton's life can be depicted allegorically as a rolling road, one should not forget that he never travelled alone for the greater part of the journey. In fact, no study of his life would be complete if it failed to recognise the crucial role of his lifelong travelling companion.

Frances had told friends during Gilbert's final illness that they had both considered his recovery from the near fatal collapse twenty years earlier to be a miracle. 'I did not dare,' she said, 'to pray for another miracle.'[41] In fact, she had been bracing herself for her husband's death on the earlier occasion, writing to Father O'Connor, 'I do pray to God He will restore him to himself . . . I feel in His mercy He will, even if death is the end of it – or the beginning shall I say?'[42]

No doubt, as she sought to cope with bereavement, Frances hoped to gain fortitude from her faith, and certainly her friends did the best they could to offer support. Father Ronald Knox wrote to offer his condolences with what his biographer, Evelyn Waugh, described as 'a touch of hyperbole appropriate to the occasion':

> He has been my idol since I read *The Napoleon of Notting Hill* as a schoolboy; I'll only hope that you, who know as no one else does what we have lost, will find it easy to imagine as well as believe that he is alive and unchanged. Thank God for that faith; that I have it when so many of my friends lost it was due, I think, under God to him. May he be pardoned all that remains to pardon; I don't think he can be long for Purgatory.[43]

On the day Chesterton died Father Vincent McNabb wrote to Frances the moment he heard the news:

> I feel I must write to you. But what to write I do not know . . . If gratitude could dry tears – you would shed none. But even pride in the soul you were called to wed as a wife and tend as a mother has no power against a wife and a mother's sense of loss.
>
> May the God of all consolation give what He alone can give to your aching heart![44]

Six days later Father Vincent visited Laura, Lady Lovat, who had become acquainted with the Chestertons through her close friendship with Maurice Baring. Afterwards he wrote again to Frances, seemingly at Lady Lovat's request:

> This little note is not written in my name or by my own prompting. It is written by the prompting of that purest well-spring of sympathy – a fellow sufferer's heart, one who like you still mourns the loss of the one whom God gave to them in wedlock.
>
> I have just come from the Hospital of SS. John and Elizabeth where I saw Lady Lovat who is still seriously ill after a second operation.
>
> It was with great difficulty she spoke a few words even to me her confessor for whom she had sent. In those few words with their long silences, yours was the only name mentioned.
>
> She asked feebly yet determinedly as if your sorrow had been her sorrow – 'How is Mrs Chesterton?'
>
> Then after a pause – 'I was going to write to her.'
>
> I noticed that her writing hand had not, for the moment, power to make the sign of the cross. But her widow's, mother's, sufferer's heart had the 'will' to console yours.

I thought you ought to have this jewel and scent of sisterly consolation from the bed of suffering.[45]

For all the letters and prayers of her friends, Frances found her loss practically beyond endurance. On 21 July she sent a heart-rending letter to Father O'Connor which was almost a scream of despair:

> I find it increasingly difficult to keep going. The feeling that he needs me no longer is almost unbearable. How do lovers love without each other? We were always lovers.
>
> I have a Mass said here for him every Tuesday – but I feel it is more for the repose of my soul than for his.[46]

Perhaps at such moments Frances remembered the lines that Gilbert had written for her during the early years of their marriage:

> Oh when the bitter wind of longing blows
> And all between us seems an aching space
> Think that we hold each other close, so close;
> We cannot even see each other's face.[47]

To an exceptional degree, she and Gilbert had come to embody the principle of the married couple being one flesh. The result of her husband's death, therefore, was psychologically schismatic. She survived only two years longer, prompting Bernard Shaw to ask after her death: 'What did Frances die of? Was it of widowhood?'[48] In fact, physiologically at least, the cause of death was, in Maisie Ward's words, 'a most painful cancer heroically endured'.[49]

She was cared for by Dorothy and finally, in the last stages of the illness, by the nuns of the Bon Secours. On 7 December 1938, five days before Frances's death, Father Vincent wrote to Dorothy from St Dominic's Priory:

> Your note about Frances gave me the consolation of praying for her. I also asked the prayers of the Community. As we are all in retreat I imagine she will have an unusually large wreath of prayers.
>
> I was glad to be able to see her – and see her at her best. Sickness tries even the most perfect souls. The little corners of 'self' are often laid bare. But in my last talk with Frances I could find nothing of self except her wonted self-effacement. She spoke to me as a soul speaks to a priest. But the priest to whom she spoke hidden things

. . . will remember how all her thoughts – even on her bed of death
– were for others.

If she is still alive when this reaches you give her my blessing.[50]

One of the last people to see her alive was Mrs Nicholl, mother
of the Nicholl sisters: 'Just before she died I saw her in the hospital.
She didn't see me, but the nuns had left her door open. Her arms
were spread out and there was a lovely expression of happiness on
her face. I felt that Gilbert had come to tell her everything was all
right and to welcome her.'[51]

The last words belong to Gilbert. Writing to Frances during the days
of their courtship, nearly forty years earlier, he expressed a love which
never diminished:

. . . there are four lamps of thanksgiving always before him. The first
is for his creation out of the same earth with such a woman as you.
The second is that he has not, with all his faults, 'gone after strange
women'. You cannot think how a man's self-restraint is rewarded in
this. The third is that he has tried to love everything alive: a dim
preparation for loving you. And the fourth is – but no words can
express that. Here ends my previous existence. Take it: it led me
to you.[52]

NOTES

Preface

1 W. R. Titterton, *G. K. Chesterton: A Portrait*, London, 1936, pp. 88–9.
2 Maisie Ward, *Gilbert Keith Chesterton*, London, 1944, p. 501.
3 Christopher Hollis, *The Mind of Chesterton*, London, 1940, p. 86.
4 Michael Ffinch, *G. K. Chesterton: A Biography*, London, 1988, p. 258.
5 Fr Claude Williamson (ed.), *Great Catholics*, London, 1938, p. 548.
6 John O'Connor, *Father Brown on Chesterton*, London, 1937, p. 157.
7 Ffinch, *G. K. Chesterton*, p. 5.
8 Ward, *Gilbert Keith Chesterton*, p. 362.
9 D. J. Conlon (ed.), *G. K. Chesterton: A Half Century of Views*, Oxford University Press, 1987, pp. 226–7.
10 Ward, *Gilbert Keith Chesterton*, p. 500.
11 *Chesterton Review*, vol. XVIII, no. 3., p. 439.
12 G. K. Chesterton, *Autobiography*, London, 1936, p. 238.
13 Hilaire Belloc, *On the Place of Gilbert Keith Chesterton in English Letters*, London, 1940, p. 56.
14 *Chesterton Review*, vol. XII, no. 4, p. 539.
15 D. J. Conlon (ed.), *G. K. Chesterton: The Critical Judgments*, Antwerp, 1976, p. 510.
16 G. K. Chesterton, *Heretics*, London, 1909, p. 131.
17 Christopher Hollis, *The Mind of Chesterton*, p. 8.
18 Dorothy L. Sayers, Preface to *The Surprise*, London, 1952, p. 5.
19 G. K. Chesterton, *The Innocence of Father Brown*, London, 1937, p. 81.
20 John A. O'Brien (ed.), *The Road to Damascus*, Vol. I, London, 1949, p. 271.
21 Maisie Ward, *Return to Chesterton*, London, 1952, p. 137.

1 Father of the Man

1 G. K. Chesterton, *Autobiography*, London, 1936, p. 54.
2 ibid.
3 ibid., pp. 53–4.
4 ibid., p. 54.
5 ibid., pp. 31–2.
6 ibid., p. 33.
7 ibid., p. 59.
8 *Chesterton Review*, vol. VI, no. 1, p. 30.

9 Chesterton, *Autobiography*, p. 40.
10 ibid., p. 41.
11 Michael Coren, *Gilbert: The Man Who was Chesterton*, London, 1989, p. 12.
12 Maisie Ward, *Return to Chesterton*, London, 1952, p. 17.
13 Chesterton, *Autobiography*, p. 15.
14 ibid., pp. 40–41.
15 ibid., p. 18.
16 ibid.
17 Coren, *Gilbert*, p. 8.
18 *Chesterton Review*, vol. VI, no. 1, p. 30.
19 Chesterton, *Autobiography*, p. 9.
20 Baptism Register, St George's church, Campden Hill, 1874.
21 Alzina Stone Dale, *The Outline of Sanity: A Life of G. K. Chesterton*, Grand Rapids, MI, 1982, p. 7.
22 Chesterton, *Autobiography*, pp. 35–6.
23 ibid., p. 35.
24 ibid., p. 29.
25 ibid., p. 196.
26 ibid.
27 ibid.
28 ibid.
29 Ada Chesterton, *The Chestertons*, London, 1941, pp. 19–21.
30 Chesterton, *Autobiography*, pp. 143–4.
31 ibid., p. 145.
32 ibid., p. 146.
33 ibid., p. 55.
34 Dale, *The Outline of Sanity*, p. 15.
35 John Sullivan (ed.), *G. K. Chesterton: A Centenary Appraisal*, London, 1974, p. 76.
36 Unpublished drawing, 1882, G. K. Chesterton Study Centre, Bedford.
37 Maisie Ward, *Gilbert Keith Chesterton*, London, 1944, p. 22.
38 Unpublished poem, *c.* 1886, G. K. Chesterton Study Centre, Bedford.

2 Soul in a Ferment

1 School exercise book, *c.* 1882, G. K. Chesterton Study Centre, Bedford.
2 G. K. Chesterton, *Autobiography*, London, 1936, p. 58.
3 ibid., p. 72.
4 ibid.
5 Maisie Ward, *Gilbert Keith Chesterton*, London, 1944, p. 28.
6 ibid., p. 25.
7 ibid., p. 26.
8 Michael Ffinch, *G. K. Chesterton: A Biography*, London, 1988, p. 19.
9 Chesterton, *Autobiography*, p. 70.
10 ibid., p. 61.
11 E. C. Bentley, *Trent's Last Case*, London, 1912, dedication page.
12 G. K. Chesterton, *The Man Who was Thursday*, London, 1908, dedication page.
13 Maisie Ward, *Return to Chesterton*, London, 1952, pp. 16–17.
14 Maisie Ward, *Gilbert Keith Chesterton*, London, 1944, p. 46.
15 ibid.
16 Chesterton, *Autobiography*, pp. 63–4.
17 Michael Coren, *Gilbert: The Man Who was Chesterton*, London 1989, p. 30.
18 Ward, *Gilbert Keith Chesterton*, pp. 31–2.
19 Agenda of JDC meeting, 1892, G. K. Chesterton Study Centre, Bedford.

20 Coren, *Gilbert*, p. 36.
21 Ward, *Gilbert Keith Chesterton*, p. 41.
22 Coren, *Gilbert*, p. 33.
23 ibid., pp. 34–5.
24 Ward, *Gilbert Keith Chesterton*, pp. 27–8.
25 ibid., p. 558.
26 ibid., p. 42.
27 Coren, *Gilbert*, p. 39.
28 *Debater*, vol. 3, 1893, G. K. Chesterton Study Centre, Bedford.
29 Dudley Barker, *G. K. Chesterton: A Biography*, London, 1973, p. 49.
30 *Debater*, vol. 2, 1892, G. K. Chesterton Study Centre, Bedford.
31 Coren, *Gilbert*, p. 39.
32 ibid., p. 40.
33 'Love', early 1890s, G. K. Chesterton Study Centre, Bedford.
34 Chesterton, *Autobiography*, p. 80.
35 G. K. Chesterton, *Orthodoxy*, London, 1908, p. 151.
36 Chesterton, *Autobiography*, p. 81.
37 ibid., pp. 81–4.
38 ibid.
39 Fr John O'Connor, *Father Brown on Chesterton*, London, 1937, p. 74.
40 Chesterton, *Autobiography*, pp. 84–5.
41 G. K. Chesterton, *Culture and the Coming Peril*, London, 1927, p. 6.
42 Coren, *Gilbert*, p. 44.
43 ibid., p. 45.
44 Chesterton, *Autobiography*, pp. 92–3.
45 Ward, *Gilbert Keith Chesterton*, pp. 45–6.
46 Chesterton, *Autobiography*, pp. 93–4.
47 'Thank You', mid 1890s, G. K. Chesterton Study Centre, Bedford.
48 'Parables', mid 1890s, G. K. Chesterton Study Centre, Bedford.
49 G. K. Chesterton, *The New Jerusalem*, London, 1920, p. 159.
50 Chesterton, *Autobiography*, p. 94.

3 The Chesterblogg

1 Maisie Ward, *Return to Chesterton*, London, 1952, p. 82.
2 Maisie Ward, *Gilbert Keith Chesterton*, London, 1944, p. 51.
3 ibid., p. 52.
4 Michael Ffinch, *G. K. Chesterton: A Biography*, London, 1988, p. 44.
5 Ward, *Gilbert Keith Chesterton*, pp. 54–5.
6 ibid., p. 55.
7 Ward, *Return to Chesterton*, pp. 19–20.
8 ibid., pp. 10–11.
9 'Easter Sunday', 1895, G. K. Chesterton Study Centre, Bedford.
10 'The Song of the Children', late 1890s, G. K. Chesterton Study Centre, Bedford.
11 'An Old Riddle', *c.* 1895, G. K. Chesterton Study Centre, Bedford.
12 'A Christmas Carol', *c.* 1896, G. K. Chesterton Study Centre, Bedford
13 Ffinch, *G. K. Chesterton*, p. 47.
14 Ward, *Gilbert Keith Chesterton*, p. 67.
15 ibid.
16 ibid., p. 77.
17 Ffinch, *G. K. Chesterton*, p. 49.
18 ibid.

19 G. K. Chesterton, *Autobiography*, London, 1936, p. 153.
20 Ward, *Gilbert Keith Chesterton*, p. 78.
21 Ward, *Return to Chesterton*, pp. 23–4.
22 Ward, *Gilbert Keith Chesterton*, pp. 79–80.
23 Association copies owned by David Roth in 1956, G. K. Chesterton Study Centre, Bedford.
24 Ward, *Return to Chesterton*, pp. 34–5.
25 ibid., p. 35.
26 Ward, *Gilbert Keith Chesterton*, pp. 85–6.
27 ibid., p. 104.
28 Ffinch, *G. K. Chesterton*, p. 65.
29 Ward, *Return to Chesterton*, p. 67.
30 Chesterton, *Autobiography*, pp. 152–3.
31 G. K. Chesterton, *The Ballad of the White Horse*, London, 1911, p. xvi.
32 Ffinch, *G. K. Chesterton*, p. 271.
33 John Sullivan (ed.), *G. K. Chesterton: A Centenary Appraisal*, London, 1974, p. 160.
34 *Speaker*, October 1901.
35 Ward, *Return to Chesterton*, p. 79.
36 Chesterton, *Autobiography*, p. 137.
37 *Daily News*, 13 December 1907.
38 Ward, *Gilbert Keith Chesterton*, p. 535.
39 ibid., pp. 93–4.
40 G. K. Chesterton, *Collected Poems*, London, 1927, pp. 348–9.
41 Ward, *Gilbert Keith Chesterton*, p. 451.

4 The Chesterbelloc

1 *New Age*, 15 February 1908.
2 Emma Letley, *Maurice Baring: A Citizen of Europe*, London, 1991, p. 140.
3 E. C. Bentley, *Those Days*, London, 1940, pp. 85–6.
4 Maisie Ward, *Gilbert Keith Chesterton*, London, 1944, pp. 211–12.
5 ibid., p. 113.
6 Maisie Ward, *Return to Chesterton*, London, 1952, p. 52.
7 G. K. Chesterton, *Autobiography*, London, 1936, p. 116.
8 ibid., pp. 116–18.
9 Ward, *Gilbert Keith Chesterton*, p. 113.
10 ibid., pp. 126–7.
11 Robert Speaight, *The Life of Hilaire Belloc*, New York, 1970, pp. 196–7.
12 ibid., p. 192.
13 Ward, *Gilbert Keith Chesterton*, pp. 124–5.
14 ibid., p. 134.
15 Sketch map drawn by Chesterton, *c.* 1902, G. K. Chesterton Study Centre, Bedford.
16 Alfred Noyes, *Two Worlds for Memory*, London, 1953, p. 260.
17 Ward, *Return to Chesterton*, p. 74.
18 Eleanor and Reginald Jebb, *Belloc the Man*, Maryland, 1957, p. 114.
19 Ward, *Gilbert Keith Chesterton*, pp. 134–5.
20 Chesterton, *Autobiography*, pp. 216–17.
21 ibid., p. 217.
22 ibid., pp. 219–21.
23 F. J. Sheed, *The Church and I*, London, 1976, p. 33.
24 ibid.
25 Frank Swinnerton, *The Georgian Literary Scene*, London, 1950, p. 88.

26 Christopher Hollis, *The Mind of Chesterton*, London, 1940, pp. 8–9.
27 *New Age*, 11 January 1908.
28 Hilaire Belloc, *Complete Verse*, London, 1991, p. 95.
29 Hilaire Belloc, *On the Place of Gilbert Keith Chesterton in English Letters*, London, 1940, pp. 80–82.
30 J. B. Morton, *Hilaire Belloc: A Memoir*, London, 1955, pp. 76–7.
31 ibid., p. 77.
32 ibid., p. 122.
33 Belloc, *On the Place of Gilbert Keith Chesterton in English Letters*, p. 72.
34 Fr John O'Connor, *Father Brown on Chesterton*, London, 1937, p. 143.
35 Speaight, *The Life of Hilaire Belloc*, p. 481.
36 Belloc, *On the Place of Gilbert Keith Chesterton in English Letters*, p. 36.
37 Speaight, *The Life of Hilaire Belloc*, p. 338.
38 Ward, *Return to Chesterton*, p. 113.
39 *New Age*, 15 February 1908.
40 D. J. Conlon (ed.), *G. K. Chesterton: A Half Century of Views*, Oxford, 1987, p. 71.
41 *New Witness*, 27 April 1923.
42 Karl G. Schmude, *Hilaire Belloc: His Life and Legacy*, Melbourne, 1978, p. 8.
43 *Catholic Herald*, 24 July 1970.

5 Enter G. K. C.

1 Maisie Ward, *Gilbert Keith Chesterton*, London, 1944, p. 127.
2 Maisie Ward, *Return to Chesterton*, London, 1952, pp. 54–5.
3 Frank Swinnerton, *Background with Chorus*, London, 1956, p. 87.
4 Ward, *Gilbert Keith Chesterton*, p. 124.
5 ibid., p. 125.
6 *Whitehall Review*, 27 February 1902.
7 Michael Ffinch, *G. K. Chesterton: A Biography*, London, 1988, p. 101.
8 G. K. Chesterton, *The Defendant*, London, 1901, p. 78.
9 ibid., pp. 45–6.
10 ibid., p. 49.
11 G. K. Chesterton, *Autobiography*, London, 1936, p. 159.
12 ibid., p. 157.
13 Ward, *Gilbert Keith Chesterton*, p. 121.
14 Chesterton, *Autobiography*, p. 170.
15 ibid., p. 164.
16 Ffinch, *G. K. Chesterton*, p. 107.
17 G. K. Chesterton, *Twelve Types*, London, 1902, p. 39.
18 ibid., p. 43.
19 ibid., p. 44.
20 ibid., p. 168.
21 *New Age*, 6 November 1902.
22 Ward, *Gilbert Keith Chesterton*, p. 249.
23 ibid., p. 250.
24 Ward, *Return to Chesterton*, p. 53.
25 Rupert Hart-Davis (ed.), *Letters of Max Beerbohm 1892–1956*, London, 1988, pp. 25–6.
26 Chesterton, *Autobiography*, p. 122.
27 ibid., pp. 122–3.
28 Ward, *Return to Chesterton*, p. 68.
29 ibid., p. 69.
30 Robert Speaight, *The Life of Hilaire Belloc*, New York, 1970, p. 161.

31 Michael Ffinch, *G. K. Chesterton: A Biography*, London, 1988, p. 106.
32 Ward, *Gilbert Keith Chesterton*, pp. 172–4.
33 ibid., pp. 174–5.
34 ibid., pp. 175–6.
35 Dudley Barker, *G. K. Chesterton: A Biography*, London, 1973, p. 169.
36 Ward, *Gilbert Keith Chesterton*, p. 176.
37 Copy of letter published in the *Clarion*, 1903, G. K. Chesterton Study Centre, Bedford.
38 Ward, *Gilbert Keith Chesterton*, p. 177.
39 ibid.
40 Unpublished letter, G. K. Chesterton Study Centre, Bedford.
41 *Daily News*, 12 January 1904.
42 *Daily News*, 12 December 1903.

6 Robert Browning and Father Brown

1 G. K. Chesterton, *Autobiography*, London, 1936, p. 99.
2 ibid.
3 Cyril Clemens, *Chesterton as Seen by His Contemporaries*, Webster Groves, MO, International Mark Twain Society, 1939, p. 14.
4 Walter Hooper (ed.), *All My Roads Before Me: The Diary of C. S. Lewis 1922–1927*, London, 1992, p. 297.
5 Chesterton, *Autobiography*, p. 99.
6 ibid., pp. 307–8.
7 Unpublished notebook, *c.* 1910, G. K. Chesterton Study Centre, Bedford.
8 G. K. Chesterton, *Robert Browning*, London, 1903, p. 65.
9 ibid., p. 69.
10 ibid., p. 78.
11 ibid., pp. 103–4.
12 ibid., p. 99.
13 ibid., p. 185.
14 ibid., pp. 185–6.
15 ibid., p. 185.
16. G. K. Chesterton, *G. F. Watts*, London, 1904, pp. 121–2.
17 ibid., p. 40.
18 Unpublished extract from Frances Chesterton's diary, 5 April 1904, G. K. Chesterton Study Centre, Bedford.
19 Maisie Ward, *Gilbert Keith Chesterton*, London, 1944, p. 147.
20 Hugh Brogan, *The Life of Arthur Ransome*, London, 1992, p. 31.
21 Arthur Ransome, *Autobiography*, London, 1976, p. 100.
22 Frank Swinnerton, *Background with Chorus*, London, 1956, p. 89.
23 Frances Chesterton's diary, 22 March 1904, G. K. Chesterton Study Centre, Bedford.
24 Ward, *Gilbert Keith Chesterton*, p. 152.
25 G. K. Chesterton, *The Napoleon of Notting Hill*, London, 1904, p. 42.
26 ibid., p. 34.
27 ibid., pp. 36–7.
28 ibid., p. 61.
29 ibid., p. 63.
30 Michael Coren, *Gilbert: The Man Who was Chesterton*, London, 1989, p. 147.
31 Fr Claude Williamson, OSC (ed.), *Great Catholics*, London, 1938, p. 551.
32 Chesterton, *The Napoleon of Notting Hill*, pp. 90–91.
33 Christopher Hollis, *The Mind of Chesterton*, London, 1940, p. 108.

34 *Chesterton Review*, vol. XVIII, no. 3, p. 457.
35 Terry Pratchett and Neil Gaiman, *Good Omens*, London, 1992, dedication page.
36 ibid., p. 270.
37 Frances Chesterton's diary, 31 March 1904, G. K. Chesterton Study Centre, Bedford.
38 Ward, *Gilbert Keith Chesterton*, p. 217.
39 Coren, *Gilbert*, p. 141.
40 Fr John O'Connor, *Father Brown on Chesterton*, London, 1937, pp. 1–2.
41 Chesterton, *Autobiography*, pp. 324–6.
42 Frances Chesterton's diary, 5 April 1904, G. K. Chesterton Study Centre, Bedford.
43 G. K. Chesterton, *The Secret of Father Brown*, London, 1927, dedication page.
44 Chesterton, *Autobiography*, p. 327.
45 ibid., pp. 327–8.
46 ibid., p. 328.
47 G. K. Chesterton, *The Innocence of Father Brown*, London, 10th edn 1937, p. 4.

7 Heretics and Orthodoxy

1 *Chicago Evening Post*, 9 April 1904.
2 Fr John O'Connor, *Father Brown on Chesterton*, London, 1937, p. 61.
3 ibid.
4 Maisie Ward, *Gilbert Keith Chesterton*, London, 1944, p. 165.
5 John Sullivan (ed.), *G. K. Chesterton: A Centenary Appraisal*, London, 1974, p. 161.
6 Ward, *Gilbert Keith Chesterton*, p. 148.
7 *Daily News*, 24 September 1904.
8 Letter from Aleister Crowley, 1904, G. K. Chesterton Study Centre, Bedford.
9 Aleister Crowley, *A Child of Ephraim*, privately printed, 1904.
10 Ward, *Gilbert Keith Chesterton*, pp. 45–6.
11 ibid.
12 G. K. Chesterton, *The Club of Queer Trades*, London, 1905, p. 7.
13 ibid., p. 18.
14 G. K. Chesterton, *Heretics*, London, 1905, pp. 22–3.
15 ibid., pp. 29–30.
16 ibid., pp. 88–9.
17 ibid., pp. 85–7.
18 ibid., p. 66.
19 ibid., pp. 285–6.
20 ibid., p. 286.
21 ibid., pp. 295–6.
22 ibid., p. 53.
23 ibid., pp. 51–2.
24 ibid., pp. 214–15.
25 Michael Ffinch, *G. K. Chesterton: A Biography*, London, 1988, p. 145.
26 G. K. Chesterton, *Charles Dickens*, London, 1906, pp. 22–3.
27 *Throne*, 8 September 1906.
28 Chesterton, *Charles Dickens*, pp. 62–3.
29 ibid., p. 77.
30 ibid., p. 78.
31 Ffinch, *G. K. Chesterton*, p. 144.
32 'The Crystal', unpublished, G. K. Chesterton Study Centre, Bedford.
33 Frank Swinnerton, *Background with Chorus*, London, 1956, p. 85.
34 Ffinch, *G. K. Chesterton*, p. 153.

35 *Nation*, 7 December 1907.
36 *Nation*, 14 December 1907.
37 *Daily News*, 18 January 1908.
38 G. K. Chesterton, *The Man Who was Thursday*, London, 1908, p. 24.
39 Ward, *Gilbert Keith Chesterton*, p. 169.
40 G. K. Chesterton, *Autobiography*, London, 1936, pp. 103–4.
41 D. J. Conlon (ed.), *G. K. Chesterton: A Half Century of Views*, Oxford, 1987, pp. 71–2.
42 *Chesterton Review*, vol. III, no. 1, p. 161.
43 G. K. Chesterton, *All Things Considered*, London, 1908, p. 7.
44 ibid., p. 31.
45 Chesterton, *Autobiography*, p. 177.
46 Ward, *Gilbert Keith Chesterton*, p. 181.
47 Maisie Ward, *Resurrection versus Insurrection*, London, 1937, p. 206.
48 G. K. Chesterton, *Orthodoxy*, London, 1908, p. 82.
49 ibid., p. 122.
50 ibid., p. 128.
51 ibid., pp. 134–5.
52 ibid., p. 169.
53 Barbara Reynolds, *Dorothy L. Sayers: Her Life and Soul*, London, 1993, p. 74.
54 Dorothy L. Sayers, Preface to Chesterton's play *The Surprise*, London, 1952, p. 5.
55 John A. O'Brien (ed.), *The Road to Damascus*, Vol. 1, London, 1949, p. 114.
56 Chesterton, *Autobiography*, p. 178.

8 Uncle Chestnut

1 G. K. Chesterton, *Autobiography*, London, 1936, p. 215.
2 Fr John O'Connor, *Father Brown on Chesterton*, London, 1937, pp. 123–4.
3 Maisie Ward, *Gilbert Keith Chesterton*, London, 1944, pp. 210–11.
4 Maisie Ward, *Return to Chesterton*, London, 1952, pp. 87–8.
5 Eleanor and Reginald Jebb, *Testimony to Hilaire Belloc*, London, 1956, p. 110.
6 ibid.
7 D. J. Conlon (ed.), *G. K. Chesterton: A Half Century of Views*, Oxford, 1987, p. 48.
8 Ward, *Gilbert Keith Chesterton*, p. 222.
9 John Sullivan (ed.), *G. K. Chesterton: A Centenary Appraisal*, London, 1974, p. 160.
10 *Daily News*, 17 December 1910.
11 Ward, *Return to Chesterton*, p. 88.
12 ibid., p. 97.
13 ibid., p. 91.
14 ibid., p. 97.
15 ibid., p. 98.
16 ibid.
17 ibid., p. 100.
18 ibid., p. 98.
19 ibid., p. 194.
20 ibid., pp. 161–2.
21 ibid., p. 163.
22 ibid., p. 164.
23 ibid., p. 176.
24 ibid., p. 178.
25 ibid., pp. 198–9.
26 ibid., p. 190.

27 ibid., p. 191.
28 ibid.
29 ibid., p. 200.
30 ibid., pp. 161–2.
31 ibid., p. 201.
32 ibid., pp. 201–2.
33 ibid., p. 240.
34 ibid., pp. 206–7.
35 ibid., p. 176.

9 The Chestershaw

1 G. K. Chesterton, *Autobiography*, London, 1936, p. 224.
2 *Everyman*, 20 December 1912 (*Collected Works*, vol. XI, p. 497).
3 Maisie Ward, *Return to Chesterton*, London, 1952, p. 224.
4 ibid., p. 5.
5 *G. K.'s Weekly*, 18 April 1931 (*Collected Works*, vol. XI, p. 571).
6 Maisie Ward, *Gilbert Keith Chesterton*, London, 1944, pp. 135–6.
7 ibid., p. 136.
8 Michael Holroyd, *Bernard Shaw*, Vol. II: *The Pursuit of Power*, London, 1989, p. 182.
9 Chesterton, *Autobiography*, p. 224.
10 Alzina Stone Dale, *The Outline of Sanity: A Life of G. K. Chesterton*, Grand Rapids, MI, 1982, pp. 44–5.
11 W. R. Titterton, *G. K. Chesterton: A Portrait*, London, 1936, pp. 44–5.
12 *Daily News*, 15 April 1905 (*Collected Works*, vol. XI, p. 347).
13 *New Age*, 15 February 1908.
14 *New Age*, 29 February 1908.
15 ibid.
16 G. K. Chesterton, *Orthodoxy*, London, 1908, p. 38.
17 Radio Four broadcast, 24 February 1993.
18 G. K. Chesterton, *George Bernard Shaw*, London, 1909, p. 23.
19 ibid., pp. 34–6.
20 ibid., pp. 57–8.
21 Michael Holroyd, *Bernard Shaw*, Vol. I: *The Search for Love*, London, 1988, p. 5.
22 Chesterton, *George Bernard Shaw*, pp. 37–8.
23 ibid., pp. 55–6.
24 Holroyd, *Bernard Shaw*, Vol. I, p. 7.
25 ibid.
26 ibid., p. 15.
27 ibid., p. 8.
28 ibid., p. 16.
29 ibid., p. 18.
30 ibid., p. 8.
31 Chesterton, *George Bernard Shaw*, pp. 64–5.
32 ibid., pp. 71–2.
33 ibid., pp. 94–5.
34 ibid., pp. 106–7.
35 ibid., pp. 186–7.
36 ibid., p. 130.
37 ibid., pp. 213–14.
38 ibid., pp. 197–8.
39 ibid., pp. 243–7.

40 D. J. Conlon (ed.), *G. K. Chesterton: The Critical Judgments*, Antwerp, 1976, p. 197.
41 ibid., p. 208.
42 ibid., p. 210.
43 ibid., p. 211.
44 Holroyd, *Bernard Shaw*, Vol. II, p. 213.
45 Conlon (ed.), *G. K. Chesterton*, pp. 201–4.
46 Holroyd, *Bernard Shaw*, Vol. II, p. 215.
47 ibid.
48 *Chesterton Review*, vol. XVIII, no. 3, p. 387.
49 Christopher Hollis, *The Mind of Chesterton*, London, 1940, p. 86.
50 Ward, *Gilbert Keith Chesterton*, p. 420.
51 Malcolm Muggeridge, *Conversion: A Spiritual Journey*, London, 1988, p. 132.
52 Ward, *Gilbert Keith Chesterton*, p. 500.
53 Maisie Ward, *Return to Chesterton*, London, 1952, p. 61.
54 Ward, *Gilbert Keith Chesterton*, pp. 500–501.
55 *G. K.'s Weekly*, 21 March 1933.

10 Innocence and Wisdom

1 *Westminster Gazette*, 18 December 1909.
2 *T. P.'s Weekly*, 12 November 1909.
3 G. K. Chesterton, *Tremendous Trifles*, New York, 1909, p. 134.
4 ibid., pp. 298–303.
5 ibid., pp. 138–9.
6 ibid., p. 226.
7 *Church Socialist Quarterly*, January 1909.
8 ibid., April 1909.
9 ibid., July 1909.
10 ibid.
11 Maurice Baring, *The Puppet Show of Memory*, London, 1930, p. 396.
12 *Hibbert Journal*, July 1909.
13 Dudley Barker, *G. K. Chesterton: A Biography*, London, 1973, p. 162.
14 ibid.
15 Fr John O'Connor, *Father Brown on Chesterton*, London, 1937, pp. 110–11.
16 Michael Ffinch, *G. K. Chesterton: A Biography*, London, 1988, pp. 182–3.
17 Albino Luciani, *Illustrissimi*, London, 1978, pp. 27–9.
18 Maisie Ward, *Gilbert Keith Chesterton*, London, 1944, p. 242.
19 Ffinch, *G. K. Chesterton*, p. 183.
20 *Daily News*, 7 May 1910.
21 ibid.
22 G. K. Chesterton, *What's Wrong with the World*, London, 1910, p. v.
23 Ffinch, *G. K. Chesterton*, p. 186.
24 David Cecil, *Max: A Biography*, London, pbk edn 1983, p. 307.
25 Chesterton, *What's Wrong with the World*, p. 33.
26 ibid., pp. 47–8.
27 ibid., p. 292.
28 ibid., p. 179.
29 ibid., p. 180.
30 Barbara Reynolds, *Dorothy L. Sayers: Her Life and Soul*, London, 1993, p. 58.
31 James Brabazon, *Dorothy L. Sayers: A Biography*, London,1981, p. 51.
32 Aidan Mackey, *The Wisdom of G. K. Chesterton*, Bedford, 1994, pp. 3–4.
33 *Nation*, 17 December 1910.
34 G. K. Chesterton, *Alarms and Discursions*, London, 7th edn 1939, pp. 182–5.

35 *Country Life*, 23 September 1911.
36 Alec Guinness, *Blessings in Disguise*, London, 1986, pp. 63–4.
37 Donald Spoto, *The Dark Side of Genius*, London, 1994, pp. 39–41.
38 G. K. Chesterton, *The Innocence of Father Brown*, London, 10th edn 1937, pp. 4–5.

11 A Man Alive

1 G. K. Chesterton, *Alarms and Discursions*, London, 7th edn 1939, p. 193.
2 ibid., p. 220.
3 ibid., pp. 197–8.
4 ibid., p. 197.
5 Fr John O'Connor, *Father Brown on Chesterton*, London, 1937, p. 68.
6 Dudley Barker, *G. K. Chesterton: A Biography*, London, 1973, p. 204.
7 Michael Ffinch, *G. K. Chesterton: A Biography*, London, 1988, pp. 208–9.
8 Douglas Hyde, *I Believed*, London, 1951, p. 257.
9 *Chesterton Review*, vol. IX, no. 2, p. 136.
10 George Sayer, *Jack: C. S. Lewis and His Times*, London, 1988, p. xvi.
11 *Observer*, 12 March 1978.
12 Humphrey Carpenter (ed.), *Letters of J. R. R. Tolkien*, Boston, 1981, p. 92.
13 Maisie Ward, *Gilbert Keith Chesterton*, London, 1944, p. 245.
14 *Academy*, 3 June 1911, G. K. Chesterton Study Centre, Bedford.
15 *Fortnightly Review*, July 1911, G. K. Chesterton Study Centre, Bedford.
16 *Chesterton Review*, vol. XII, no. 3, p. 286.
17 'The Future of Religion', G. K. Chesterton Study Centre, Bedford.
18 ibid.
19 ibid.
20 ibid.
21 *Cambridge Review*, 23 November 1911, G. K. Chesterton Study Centre, Bedford.
22 *Gownsman*, 25 November 1911, G. K. Chesterton Study Centre, Bedford.
23 Dan H. Laurence (ed.), *Bernard Shaw: Collected Letters, 1911–1925*, London, 1985, pp. 54–5.
24 Maisie Ward, *Return to Chesterton*, London, 1952, p. 128.
25 Frank Swinnerton, *The Georgian Literary Scene*, London, 1950, p. 46.
26 Ward, *Return to Chesterton*, pp. 130–31.
27 *Chesterton Review*, vol. XIV, no. 4, p. 542.
28 ibid., pp. 542–9.
29 G. K. Chesterton, *Manalive*, London, 1912, pp. 124–7.
30 ibid., pp. 160–61.
31 ibid., p. 365.
32 ibid., p. 372.

12 Brothers in Arms

1 *Daily News*, 5 November 1910.
2 ibid.
3 ibid.
4 *Daily News*, 13 May 1911.
5 *Daily News*, 21 August 1909.
6 *Daily News*, 4 December 1909.
7 Michael Ffinch, *G. K. Chesterton: A Biography*, London, 1988, p. 193.

8 *Daily News*, 16 July 1910.
9 ibid.
10 Maisie Ward, *Return to Chesterton*, London, 1952, p. 206.
11 Ferdinand Valentine, OP, *Father Vincent McNabb*, London, 1955, p. 184.
12 ibid., p. 264.
13 ibid., p. 200.
14 ibid., p. 129.
15 Fr John O'Connor, *Father Brown on Chesterton*, London, 1937, pp. 83–6.
16 Hilaire Belloc, *On the Place of Gilbert Keith Chesterton in English Letters*, London, 1940, p. 78.
17 Alfred Noyes, *Two Worlds for Memory*, London, 1953, p. 224.
18 Maisie Ward, *Gilbert Keith Chesterton*, London, 1944, p. 317.
19 O'Connor, *Father Brown on Chesterton*, pp. 78–9.
20 G. K. Chesterton Study Centre, Bedford.
21 G. K. Chesterton, *The Victorian Age in Literature*, London, 1913, p. 81.
22 ibid., pp. 12–13.
23 ibid., pp. 93–5.
24 ibid., pp. 110–11.
25 ibid., p. 113.
26 Ffinch, *G. K. Chesterton*, p. 212.
27 ibid., p. 215.
28 ibid., p. 216.
29 ibid.
30 G. K. Chesterton, *Autobiography*, London, 1936, p. 208.
31 Ward, *Gilbert Keith Chesterton*, p. 319.
32 ibid., pp. 320–21.
33 Chesterton, *The Victorian Age in Literature*, pp. 17–19.

13 Magic and Miracles

1 Ada Chesterton, *The Chestertons*, London, 1941, pp. 134–5.
2 Maisie Ward, *Gilbert Keith Chesterton*, London, 1944, p. 315.
3 G. K. Chesterton, *Heretics*, London, 6th edn 1905, p. 131.
4 ibid., p. 128.
5 Walter Hooper (ed.), *All My Roads Before Me: The Diary of C. S. Lewis 1922–1927*, London, 1992, p. 34.
6 Maisie Ward, *Return to Chesterton*, London, 1952, p. 114.
7 Ward, *Gilbert Keith Chesterton*, p. 315.
8 ibid., pp. 315–16.
9 Fr John O'Connor, *Father Brown on Chesterton*, London, 1937, pp. 70–71.
10 Ward, *Gilbert Keith Chesterton*, p. 196.
11 ibid., pp. 203–4.
12 ibid., pp. 207–8.
13 *New Statesman*, 13 May 1916.
14 Robert Speaight, *The Life of Hilaire Belloc*, New York, 1970, p. 338.
15 John O'Sullivan (ed.), *Chesterton Continued: A Bibliographical Supplement*, London, 1968, pp. 90–91.
16 Michael Ffinch, *G. K. Chesterton: A Biography*, London, 1988, p. 222.
17 Ada Chesterton, *The Chestertons*, p. 144.
18 ibid.
19 ibid., pp. 144–6.
20 ibid., pp. 147–8.
21 G. K. Chesterton, *Autobiography*, London, 1936, pp. 232–4.

22 The Christian Commonwealth Co. Ltd, *Do Miracles Happen?*, London, 1914, p. 1.
23 ibid., p. 5.
24 ibid., p. 10.
25 ibid., pp. 19–21.
26 ibid., p. 23.

14 The Shadow of Death

1 Robert Speaight, *The Life of Hilaire Belloc*, New York, 1970, p. 341.
2 ibid., p. 342.
3 *Illustrated London News*, 29 August 1914.
4 G. K. Chesterton, *Autobiography*, London, 1936, pp. 131–2.
5 Anne Chisholm and Michael Davie, *Beaverbrook: A Life*, London, 1992, p. 154.
6 G. K. Chesterton, *The Martyrdom of Belgium*, London, 1914, p. 4.
7 ibid., pp. 5–6.
8 *Chesterton Review*, vol. XIV, no. 4, pp. 631–3.
9 G. K. Chesterton, *The Wisdom of Father Brown*, London, 1914, p. 26.
10 ibid., p. 95.
11 ibid., p. 108.
12 A. G. Gardiner, *Prophets, Priests, and Kings*, London, 1914, p. 340.
13 ibid., pp. 331–2.
14 Chesterton, *Autobiography*, pp. 233–4.
15 Wallace Martin (ed.), *Orage as Critic*, London, 1974, p. 118.
16 Dudley Barker, *G. K. Chesterton*, London, 1973, pp. 223–4.
17 Fr John O'Connor, *Father Brown on Chesterton*, London, 1937, p. 98.
18 ibid., p. 94.
19 Barker, *G. K. Chesterton*, p. 227.
20 O'Connor, *Father Brown on Chesterton*, p. 98.
21 ibid.
22 ibid., pp. 98–9.
23 Maisie Ward, *Gilbert Keith Chesterton*, London, 1944, pp. 329–30.
24 ibid., p. 330.
25 O'Connor, *Father Brown on Chesterton*, p. 99.
26 ibid., pp. 99–100.
27 Ferdinand Valentine, OP, *Father Vincent McNabb*, London, 1955, pp. 264–5.
28 O'Connor, *Father Brown on Chesterton*, p. 99.
29 Ward, *Gilbert Keith Chesterton*, p. 330.
30 Valentine, *Father Vincent McNabb*, p. 265.
31 O'Connor, *Father Brown on Chesterton*, p. 100.
32 *Chesterton Review*, vol. XIV, no. 4, pp. 633–4.
33 O'Connor, *Father Brown on Chesterton*, pp. 100–101.
34 Ward, *Gilbert Keith Chesterton*, p. 330.
35 O'Connor, *Father Brown on Chesterton*, pp. 101–2.
36 Ward, *Gilbert Keith Chesterton*, p. 331.

15 The Valley of Death

1 Maisie Ward, *Gilbert Keith Chesterton*, London, 1944, p. 332.
2 ibid., p. 333.
3 ibid., pp. 334–5.
4 ibid., pp. 348–9.

5 Ada Chesterton, *The Chestertons*, London, 1941, p. 183.
6 G. K. Chesterton, *The Crimes of England*, London, 1915, pp. 17–18.
7 ibid., p. 48.
8 ibid., pp. 52–4.
9 ibid., pp. 62–3.
10 ibid., p. 64.
11 ibid., p. 68.
12 ibid., p. 71.
13 ibid., pp. 111–12.
14 ibid., pp. 116–17.
15 Wallace Martin (ed.), *Orage as Critic*, London, 1974, p. 188.
16 *Pearson's Magazine*, May 1915.
17 *Sunday Times*, 4 October 1992.
18 G. K. Chesterton, *Divorce versus Democracy*, London, 1916.
19 ibid., back cover.
20 Ward, *Gilbert Keith Chesterton*, p. 331.
21 Susan Lowndes (ed.), *Diary and Letters of Marie Belloc Lowndes 1911–1947*, London, 1971, p. 71.
22 *New Witness*, 11 May 1916.
23 *Catholic Truth*, Autumn 1916.
24 Robert Speaight, *The Life of Hilaire Belloc*, New York, 1970, pp. 369–70.
25 G. K. Chesterton, *Lord Kitchener*, London, 1917, p. 19.
26 Ada Chesterton, *The Chestertons*, pp. 199–200.
27 ibid., pp. 201–2.
28 ibid., pp. 203–4.
29 Frank Swinnerton, *The Georgian Literary Scene*, London, 1950, p. 93.
30 *The Times Literary Supplement*, 22 November 1917.
31 Ward, *Gilbert Keith Chesterton*, p. 355.
32 G. K. Chesterton, *A Short History of England*, London, 1929, p. v.
33 John R. Green, *A Short History of the English People*, Vol. I, New York, 1960, p. 30.
34 William Stubbs, *The Constitutional History of England*, Vol. I, London, 1874, pp. 2–3.
35 Chesterton, *A Short History of England*, p. 233.
36 ibid., pp. 149–50.
37 *Observer*, 4 November 1917.
38 Ada Chesterton, *The Chestertons*, p. 232.
39 ibid., pp. 233–4.
40 ibid., pp. 237–8.
41 Michael Ffinch, *G. K. Chesterton: A Biography*, London, 1988, p. 251.

16 Life After Death

1 G. K. Chesterton, *Autobiography*, London, 1936, p. 257.
2 G. K. Chesterton, *Collected Poems*, London, 1927, p. 65.
3 Siegfried Sassoon, *Selected Poems*, London, 1968, p. 27.
4 Cecil Chesterton, *A History of the United States*, London, 1940.
5 ibid.
6 ibid.
7 W. R. Titterton, *G. K. Chesterton: A Portrait*, London, 1936, p. 119.
8 Barbara Reynolds, *Dorothy L. Sayers: Her Life and Soul*, London, 1993, p. 81.
9 ibid.
10 C. S. Lewis, *Surprised by Joy*, London, 1991, pp. 153–4.

11 G. K. Chesterton, *Irish Impressions*, London, 1919, pp. 209–43.
12 ibid.
13 ibid.
14 *Irish Statesman*, 22 November 1919.
15 G. K. Chesterton, *What are Reprisals?*, London, 1920.
16 G. K. Chesterton, *The Danger to England*, London, 1920.
17 ibid.
18 *Chesterton Review*, vol. VIII, no. 2, p. 143.
19 Maisie Ward, *Gilbert Keith Chesterton*, London, 1944, p. 377.
20 G. K. Chesterton, *The New Jerusalem*, London, 1920, p. 58.
21 ibid., pp. 26–7.
22 ibid., p. 32.
23 ibid., p. 36.
24 ibid., p. 60.
25 ibid., p. 117.
26 ibid., pp. 96–7.
27 ibid., p. 110.
28 Ward, *Gilbert Keith Chesterton*, pp. 388–9.
29 ibid., pp. 384–5.
30 G. K. Chesterton, *The Uses of Diversity*, London, 1925, pp. 32–3.
31 *Daily Dispatch*, 22 November 1920.
32 *Architects Journal*, August 1974.
33 Ward, *Gilbert Keith Chesterton*, p. 385.
34 Fr John O'Connor, *Father Brown on Chesterton*, London, 1937, p. 268.
35 Michael Ffinch, *G. K. Chesterton: A Biography*, London, 1988, p. 271.
36 G. K. Chesterton, *The Incredulity of Father Brown*, New York, 1975, pp. 25–6.
37 Ffinch, *G. K. Chesterton*, p. 271.
38 G. K. Chesterton Study Centre, Bedford.
39 ibid.
40 Ward, *Gilbert Keith Chesterton*, p. 483.
41 ibid., p. 480.
42 Ffinch, *G. K. Chesterton*, p. 271.
43 Maisie Ward, *Return to Chesterton*, London, 1952, p. 153.
44 Ada Chesterton, *The Chestertons*, London, 1941, p. 255.
45 ibid., pp. 256–7.
46 Ward, *Return to Chesterton*, pp. 110–11.
47 ibid., p. 111.
48 ibid., p. 112.
49 G. K. Chesterton, *The Flying Inn*, London, 7th edn 1926, p. 123.
50 *Tablet*, 26 December 1953.
51 ibid.
52 Ward, *Gilbert Keith Chesterton*, p. 392.
53 Ada Chesterton, *The Chestertons*, p. 263.
54 ibid., p. 264.
55 Ward, *Gilbert Keith Chesterton*, p. 393.

17 Word Made Flesh

1 *Tablet*, 26 December 1953.
2 Maurice Baring, *Collected Poems*, London, 1925, p. 66.
3 Maisie Ward, *Gilbert Keith Chesterton*, London, 1944, pp. 393–4.
4 ibid., p. 394.
5 Undated letter, G. K. Chesterton Study Centre, Bedford.

6 Ward, *Gilbert Keith Chesterton*, p. 394.
7 Undated letter, G. K. Chesterton Study Centre, Bedford.
8 Ward, *Gilbert Keith Chesterton*, p. 395.
9 ibid.
10 Fr John O'Connor, *Father Brown on Chesterton*, London, 1937, pp. 126–7.
11 ibid., pp. 127–8.
12 ibid., p. 129.
13 ibid.
14 F. J. Sheed, *The Church and I*, London, 1976, p. 103.
15 Ward, *Gilbert Keith Chesterton*, p. 396.
16 O'Connor, *Father Brown on Chesterton*, p. 131.
17 G. K. Chesterton, *Collected Poems*, London, 1927, p. 387.
18 Ward, *Gilbert Keith Chesterton*, p. 530.
19 G. K. Chesterton Study Centre, Bedford.
20 Ward, *Gilbert Keith Chesterton*, p. 530.
21 ibid., pp. 396–7.
22 ibid., p. 397.
23 D. J. Conlon (ed.), *G. K. Chesterton: A Half Century of Views*, Oxford, 1987, p. 49.
24 Ward, *Gilbert Keith Chesterton*, pp. 404–6.
25 ibid., pp. 403–4, and Robert Speaight, *The Life of Hilaire Belloc*, New York, 1970, pp. 374–5.
26 Robert Speaight, *Letters from Hilaire Belloc*, London, 1958, p. 124.
27 O'Connor, *Father Brown on Chesterton*, p. 141.
28 ibid., p. 142.
29 Hilaire Belloc, *On the Place of Gilbert Keith Chesterton in English Letters*, London, 1940, p. 13.
30 Ferdinand Valentine, OP, *Father Vincent McNabb*, London, 1955, p. 268.
31 ibid., p. 269.
32 Ward, *Gilbert Keith Chesterton*, p. 239.
33 ibid., p. 238.
34 John O'Sullivan (ed.), *G. K. Chesterton: A Centenary Appraisal*, London, 1974, p. 136.
35 William B. Furlong, *Shaw and Chesterton: The Metaphysical Jesters*, Pennsylvania State University Press, 1970, p. 129.
36 Ward, *Gilbert Keith Chesterton*, pp. 379–80.
37 Maisie Ward, *Return to Chesterton*, London, 1952, p. 153.
38 Ward, *Gilbert Keith Chesterton*, p. 387.
39 ibid., p. 94.

18 Gratitude and Grief

1 *Literary Review*, November 1988, p. 12.
2 F. J. Sheed, *The Church and I*, London, 1976, p. 113.
3 Michael Ffinch, *G. K. Chesterton: A Biography*, London, 1988, p. 288.
4 G. K. Chesterton, *Autobiography*, London, 1936, pp. 329–30.
5 *Daily News*, 18 January 1908.
6 John A. O'Brien (ed.), *The Road to Damascus*, Vol. 3, London, 1954, p. 257.
7 Fr John O'Connor, *Father Brown on Chesterton*, London, 1937, pp. 138–9.
8 ibid., pp. 139–41.
9 Maisie Ward, *Gilbert Keith Chesterton*, London, 1944, p. 398.
10 G. K. Chesterton, *The Well and the Shallows*, London, 1935.
11 Aidan Nicholls, OP (ed.), *Chesterton and the Modernist Crisis* (Saskatoon, 1990), p. 168.

12 J. Barnes, *Ahead of His Age: Bishop Barnes of Birmingham*, London, 1979, p. 196.
13 F. Woodlock, SJ, *Modernism and the Christian Church*, London, 1925, p. 28.
14 Beaconsfield Parish Records, 1922, G. K. Chesterton Study Centre, Bedford.
15 G. K. Chesterton, *Eugenics and Other Evils*, London, 1922, pp. 76–7.
16 H. G. Wells, *Mankind in the Making*, London, 1903, p. 36.
17 Leonard Darwin, *The Need for Eugenic Reform*, London, 1926, p. 380.
18 *Eugenics Review*, vol. VI, 1914–15, p. 52.
19 Kathleen Jones, *Mental Health and Social Policy*, London, 1960, pp. 67–8.
20 *Eugenics Review*, vol. XVIII, 1926–7, pp. 11–14.
21 Chesterton, *Eugenics and Other Evils*, p. 20.
22 *Nation*, 11 March 1922.
23 G. K. Chesterton, *Heretics*, London, 1905, p. 131.
24 Ward, *Gilbert Keith Chesterton*, p. 377.
25 ibid., p. 391.
26 G. K Chesterton, *The Man Who Knew Too Much*, London, 1922, p. 2.
27 *New Witness*, 12 January 1923.
28 ibid., 9 February 1923.
29 ibid.
30 Arthur Ransome, *Autobiography*, London, 1976, p. 145.
31 Ward, *Gilbert Keith Chesterton*, pp. 416–17.

19 Jongleur de Dieu

1 *Speaker*, 1 December 1900.
2 G. K. Chesterton, *St Francis of Assisi*, London, 1923, p. 17.
3 Taken from Top Meadow in January 1990, now in the possession of the British Library.
4 Maisie Ward, *Gilbert Keith Chesterton*, London, 1944, pp. 52–3.
5 Unpublished poem, G. K. Chesterton Study Centre, Bedford.
6 G. K. Chesterton, *The New Jerusalem*, London, 1920, pp. 178–9.
7 Maisie Ward, *Return to Chesterton*, London, 1952, p. 154.
8 G. K Chesterton, *Fancies versus Fads*, London, 1923, pp. 88–9.
9 Frank Swinnerton, *The Georgian Literary Scene*, London, 1950, p. 71.
10 Michael Ffinch, *G. K. Chesterton: A Biography*, London, 1988, p. 3.
11 Patrick Braybrooke, *Gilbert Keith Chesterton*, London, 1926, p. 101.
12 Ward, *Gilbert Keith Chesterton*, p. 189.
13 Ezra Pound, *Poetry*, Chicago, 1913.
14 T. S. Eliot, *Hamlet and His Problems*, London, 1919.
15 Chesterton, *Fancies versus Fads*, p. 2.
16 ibid., p. 5.
17 ibid., p. 16.
18 Chesterton, *St Francis of Assisi*, p. 16.
19 ibid., pp. 74–7.
20 ibid., pp. 84–5.
21 ibid., p. 99.
22 *New York Times*, 2 March 1924.
23 Chesterton, *St Francis of Assisi*, p. 96.
24 ibid., p. 17.
25 Braybrooke, *Gilbert Keith Chesterton*, frontispiece.
26 ibid., p. 127.
27 ibid., p. 126.
28 Fr John O'Connor, *Father Brown on Chesterton*, London, 1937, p. 132.

29 Walter Hooper (ed.), *All My Roads Before Me: The Diary of C. S. Lewis 1922–1927*, London, 1992, p. 297.
30 Alan Watts, *The Modern Mystic*, Shaftesbury, 1990, p. 95.
31 ibid., pp. 95–6.
32 ibid., pp. 99–100.
33 Ward, *Gilbert Keith Chesterton*, p. 522.

20 Wells and the Shallows

1 G. K. Chesterton, *Autobiography*, London, 1936, p. 228.
2 Emma Letley, *Maurice Baring: A Citizen of Europe*, London, 1991, p. 200.
3 Maisie Ward, *Return to Chesterton*, London, 1952, p. 125.
4 Michael Coren, *The Invisible Man: The Life and Liberties of H. G. Wells*, London, 1993, pp. 162–3.
5 Robert Speaight, *The Life of Hilaire Belloc*, New York, 1970, pp. 397–8.
6 G. K. Chesterton, *The Everlasting Man*, London, 1947, pp. 14–15.
7 ibid., pp. 25–6.
8 ibid., p. 27.
9 ibid., pp. 28–9.
10 ibid., pp. 29–32.
11 ibid., pp. 50–51.
12 ibid., p. 52.
13 Patrick Braybrooke, *Gilbert Keith Chesterton*, London, 1926, p. 135.
14 Fr John O'Connor, *Father Brown on Chesterton*, London, 1937, p. 149.
15 D. J. Conlon (ed.), *G. K. Chesterton: A Half Century of Views*, Oxford, 1987, p. 49.
16 *Chesterton Review*, vol. XVIII, no. 3, p. 436.
17 C. S. Lewis, *Surprised by Joy*, London, 1991, p. 171.
18 ibid., p. 178.
19 Roger Lancelyn Green and Walter Hooper, *C. S. Lewis: A Biography*, London, 1987, p. 208.

21 The Outline of Sanity

1 Barbara Reynolds, *Dorothy L. Sayers: Her Life and Soul*, London, 1993, pp. 163–4.
2 Alzina Stone Dale, *The Outline of Sanity: A Life of G. K. Chesterton*, Grand Rapids, MI, 1982, p. 243.
3 Ada Chesterton, *The Chestertons*, London, 1941, p. 279.
4 *Glasgow Herald*, 16 October 1925.
5 *G. K. C.*, student paper, 16 October 1925, quoted in *Chesterton Review*, vol. XII, no. 2.
6 *Glasgow Herald*, 16 October 1925.
7 *G. K. C.*, 19 October 1925.
8 *Daily Record*, 17 October 1925.
9 *G. K. C.*, 19 October 1925.
10 *G. K. C.*, 23 October 1925.
11 Maisie Ward, *Gilbert Keith Chesterton*, London, 1944, pp. 426–7.
12 Christopher Hollis, *G. K. Chesterton*, London, 1964, p. 11.
13 *Observer*, 13 December 1925.
14 G. K. Chesterton, *The Victorian Age in Literature*, London, 1913, pp. 16–17.
15 G. K. Chesterton, *William Cobbett*, London, 1925, pp. 14–15.
16 ibid., pp. 176–7.
17 G. K. Chesterton, *The Everlasting Man*, London, 1947, p. 290.

18 G. K. Chesterton, *The Return of Don Quixote*, London, 1927, p. 284.
19 *G. K.'s Weekly*, 21 March 1925.
20 Ward, *Gilbert Keith Chesterton*, p. 433.
21 ibid.
22 ibid.
23 *G. K.'s Weekly*, 6 November 1926.
24 ibid., 13 November 1926.
25 Ward, *Gilbert Keith Chesterton*, p. 435.
26 G. K. Chesterton, *The Outline of Sanity*, London, 1928, p. 3.
27 ibid., pp. 5–6.
28 ibid., p. 107.
29 ibid., p. 123.
30 *New Witness*, 27 April 1923.
31 Ward, *Gilbert Keith Chesterton*, p. 437.
32 Michael Ffinch, *G. K. Chesterton: A Biography*, London, 1988, p. 305.
33 A. N. Wilson, *Hilaire Belloc*, London, 1986, p. 293.
34 Fiona MacCarthy, *Eric Gill*, London, 1990, p. 179.
35 Ward, *Gilbert Keith Chesterton*, pp. 422–3.
36 Copy of share certificate, G. K. Chesterton Study Centre, Bedford.
37 Ward, *Gilbert Keith Chesterton*, p. 423.
38 'Do We Agree?', London, October 1928, pp. 45–7.

22 Daughter of Desire

1 Michael Ffinch, *G. K. Chesterton: A Biography*, London, 1988, p. 303.
2 *Observer*, 10 January 1926.
3 ibid.
4 ibid.
5 *Yorkshire Post*, 23 June 1926.
6 *G. K.'s Weekly*, 19 June 1926.
7 Maisie Ward, *Gilbert Keith Chesterton*, London, 1944, p. 488.
8 *Universe*, 25 June 1926.
9 ibid.
10 G. K. Chesterton, *Collected Poetry*, Vol. I, San Francisco, 1994, p. 349.
11 G. K. Chesterton, *Collected Poems*, London, 1927, pp. 348–9.
12 Ward, *Gilbert Keith Chesterton*, p. 457.
13 ibid., p. 458.
14 ibid.
15 Unpublished poem, G. K. Chesterton Study Centre, Bedford.
16 Ward, *Gilbert Keith Chesterton*, p. 458.
17 Ffinch, *G. K. Chesterton*, p. 308.
18 Maisie Ward, *Return to Chesterton*, London, 1952, p. 244.
19 G. K. Chesterton, *The Catholic Church and Conversion*, London, 1960, pp. 78–80.
20 ibid., pp. 106–7.
21 ibid., p. 126.
22 Ward, *Return to Chesterton*, p. 192.
23 Ward, *Gilbert Keith Chesterton*, p. 459.
24 G. K. Chesterton, *Autobiography*, London, 1936, p. 315.
25 Unpublished poem, G. K. Chesterton Study Centre, Bedford.
26 Unpublished poem, G. K. Chesterton Study Centre, Bedford.
27 Unpublished poem, G. K. Chesterton Study Centre, Bedford.
28 Unpublished poem, G. K. Chesterton Study Centre, Bedford.
29 Unpublished letter, G. K. Chesterton Study Centre, Bedford.

30 ibid.
31 Ward, *Return to Chesterton*, p. 193.
32 ibid.

23 Poland and Prophecy

1 G. K Chesterton, *Social Reform versus Birth Control*, London, 1927, p. 10.
2 ibid., p. 11.
3 ibid., pp. 11–12.
4 John Sullivan (ed.), *G. K. Chesterton: A Centenary Appraisal*, London, 1974, p. 162.
5 *Chesterton Review*, vol. III, no. 2, p. 301.
6 Michael Coren, *Gilbert: The Man Who was Chesterton*, London, 1989, pp. 240–41.
7 Sullivan, *G. K. Chesterton*, p. 163.
8 ibid., pp. 162–3.
9 Michael Ffinch, *G. K. Chesterton: A Biography*, London, 1988, p. 311.
10 ibid.
11 Maisie Ward, *Gilbert Keith Chesterton*, London, 1944, pp. 488–9.
12 *Chesterton Review*, vol. III, no. 2, p. 303.
13 Ffinch, *G. K. Chesterton*, p. 311.
14 ibid., p. 313.
15 ibid.
16 *Weekly Review*, 4 January 1940.
17 G. K. Chesterton, *Autobiography*, London, 1936, pp. 317–19.
18 Ward, *Gilbert Keith Chesterton*, p. 489.
19 ibid., pp. 489–90.
20 ibid., p. 490.
21 G. K. Chesterton, *Culture and the Coming Peril*, London, 1927, p. 5.
22 ibid., pp. 8–9.
23 ibid. pp. 16–17.
24 ibid., pp. 18–19.
25 ibid., p. 19.

24 Home and Homelessness

1 Inscription, G. K. Chesterton Study Centre, Bedford.
2 Ferdinand Valentine, OP, *Father Vincent McNabb*, London, 1955, p. 269.
3 Maisie Ward, *Gilbert Keith Chesterton*, London, 1944, p. 491.
4 Ada Chesterton, *The Chestertons*, London, 1941, pp. 271–2.
5 ibid., p. 274.
6 ibid., pp. 274–5.
7 *Telegraph*, 29 October 1928.
8 ibid.
9 G. K. Chesterton, *The Secret of Father Brown*, London, 1927.
10 G. K. Chesterton Study Centre, Bedford.
11 *Nation and Athenaeum*, 31 December 1927.
12 ibid.
13 Michael Ffinch, *G. K. Chesterton: A Biography*, London, 1988, p. 318.
14 Michael Coren, *Gilbert: The Man Who was Chesterton*, London, 1989, p. 247.
15 G. K. Chesterton Study Centre, Bedford.
16 Maisie Ward, *Return to Chesterton*, London, 1952, p. 220.
17 John Sullivan (ed.), *G. K. Chesterton: A Centenary Appraisal*, London, 1974, p. 141.
18 Brocard Sewell, *The Habit of a Lifetime*, Tabb House, Cornwall, 1992, p. 38.

19 Ward, *Gilbert Keith Chesterton*, pp. 505–6.
20 Sullivan, *G. K. Chesterton*, pp. 150–51.
21 ibid., pp. 157–8.
22 G. K. Chesterton, *Generally Speaking*, London, 1930, p. 6.
23 ibid., p. 86.
24 *G. K.'s Weekly*, 20 October 1928.
25 Bernard Crick, *George Orwell: A Life*, London, 1992, p. 192.
26 ibid., p. 270.

25 Rome and Romance

1 *G. K.'s Weekly*, 23 March 1929.
2 Emma Letley, *Maurice Baring: A Citizen of Europe*, London, 1991, p. 217.
3 ibid., p. 219.
4 G. K. Chesterton, *The Poet and the Lunatics*, London, 1931, p. 129.
5 ibid., p. 130.
6 ibid., pp. 161–2.
7 Maisie Ward, *Gilbert Keith Chesterton*, London, 1944, p. 466.
8 Alzina Stone Dale, *The Outline of Sanity: A Life of G. K. Chesterton*, Grand Rapids, MI, 1982, p. 272.
9 Ward, *Gilbert Keith Chesterton*, p. 466.
10 Barbara Reynolds, *Dorothy L. Sayers: Her Life and Soul*, London, 1993, p. 275. See also Evelyn Waugh, *Ronald Knox*, Glasgow, 1962, p. 161, and James Brabazon, *Dorothy L. Sayers: A Biography*, New York, 1981, p. 144.
11 Ward, *Gilbert Keith Chesterton*, p. 467.
12 G. K. Chesterton, *The Thing*, London, 1929, p. 4.
13 ibid., pp. 128–9.
14 ibid., p. 78.
15 ibid., p. 86.
16 ibid., p. 119.
17 ibid., pp. 113–14.
18 ibid., p. 116.
19 ibid., p. 55.
20 ibid., p. 53.
21 Hilaire Belloc, *On the Place of Gilbert Keith Chesterton in English Letters*, London, 1940, pp. 66–7.
22 Dorothy E. Collins, 'Recollections', in John Sullivan (ed.), *G. K. Chesterton: A Centenary Appraisal*, London, 1974, p. 163.
23 G. K. Chesterton, *The Resurrection of Rome*, London, 1930, pp. 33–6.
24 Ward, *Gilbert Keith Chesterton*, p. 490.
25 ibid.
26 Chesterton, *The Resurrection of Rome*, p. 36.
27 ibid., p. 230.
28 ibid., pp. 232–5.
29 ibid., p. 242.
30 ibid., pp. 251–2.
31 ibid., p. 273.
32 ibid., p. 283.
33 ibid., p. 286.
34 ibid., p. 345.
35 ibid., pp. 299–301.
36 Ward, *Gilbert Keith Chesterton*, p. 493.
37 Chesterton, *The Resurrection of Rome*, pp. 317–18.

38 ibid, pp. 292–30.
39 ibid., p. 322.
40 ibid., p. 321.
41 ibid., pp. 321–2.
42 ibid., p. 320.
43 ibid.
44 Robert MacNamara, *The American College in Rome*, Rochester, NY, 1956, p. 552.
45 *Chesterton Review*, vol. X, no. 3, pp. 352–3.
46 Maisie Ward, *Return to Chesterton*, London, 1952, p. 193.
47 Chesterton, *The Resurrection of Rome*, pp. 335–7.
48 ibid., pp. 337–8.
49 Sullivan, *G. K. Chesterton*, pp. 163–4.
50 ibid., p. 164.

26 At Home in America

1 *Chesterton Review*, vol. X, no. 3, p. 353.
2 Maisie Ward, *Gilbert Keith Chesterton*, London, 1944, p. 537.
3 G. K. Chesterton, *Autobiography*, London, 1936, pp. 303–4.
4 Robert Speaight, *The Life of Hilaire Belloc*, New York, 1970, p. 480.
5 Chesterton, *Autobiography*, p. 304.
6 ibid.
7 Speaight, *The Life of Hilaire of Belloc*, pp. 480–81, and A. N. Wilson, *Hilaire Belloc*, London, pbk edn 1986, p. 324.
8 Chesterton, *Autobiography*, p. 306.
9 G. K. Chesterton, *Come to Think of It*, London, 2nd edn 1932, p. xiii.
10 ibid., p. 6.
11 Dorothy E. Collins, 'Recollections', in John Sullivan (ed.), *G. K. Chesterton: A Centenary Appraisal*, London, 1974, p. 164.
12 Michael Ffinch, *G. K. Chesterton: A Biography*, London, 1988, p. 321.
13 ibid., p. 322.
14 ibid.
15 Radio broadcast, *c.* 1934.
16 *Chesterton Review*, vol. VIII, no. 2, p. 183.
17 Ffinch, *G. K. Chesterton*, p. 323.
18 ibid.
19 Maisie Ward, *Return to Chesterton*, London, 1952, pp. 252–3.
20 ibid., p. 253.
21 ibid., p. 254.
22 ibid., p. 255.
23 Ward, *Gilbert Keith Chesterton*, p. 494.
24 ibid.
25 ibid., p. 495.
26 G. K. Chesterton, *Collected Works*, Vol. X, San Francisco, 1994, pp. 108–9.
27 Ward, *Gilbert Keith Chesterton*, p. 497.
28 Cyril Clemens, *Chesterton as Seen by His Contemporaries*, International Mark Twain Society, Webster Groves, MO, 1939, p. 71.
29 ibid., p. 106.
30 Ward, *Return to Chesterton*, p. 253.
31 Ffinch, *G. K. Chesterton*, p. 323.
32 ibid., pp. 323–4.
33 Unpublished letter, G. K. Chesterton Study Centre, Bedford.
34 Clemens, *Chesterton as Seen by His Contemporaries*, p. 71.

35 Ffinch, *G. K. Chesterton*, p. 324.
36 *Chestertoniana*, Worcester, MA, 1930, p. 4.
37 ibid., p. 3.
38 ibid., p. 15.
39 ibid., p. 27.
40 Unpublished letter, G. K. Chesterton Study Centre, Bedford.
41 Ward, *Gilbert Keith Chesterton*, p. 496.
42 Clemens, *Chesterton as Seen by His Contemporaries*, pp. 67–8.
43 Ffinch, *G. K. Chesterton*, p. 325.
44 ibid.
45 Ward, *Return to Chesterton*, pp. 247–8.
46 Collins, 'Recollections', in Sullivan, *G. K. Chesterton*, p. 165.
47 *British Columbia Chesterton Bulletin*, vol. 2, no. 2, Spring 1992.
48 ibid.
49 Ffinch, *G. K. Chesterton*, p. 325.
50 Ward, *Return to Chesterton*, p. 255.
51 ibid.

27 On Air in England

1 Michael Ffinch, *G. K. Chesterton: A Biography*, London, 1988, p. 326.
2 ibid.
3 John Sullivan (ed.), *Chesterton Continued: A Bibliographical Supplement*, London, 1968, pp. 98–104.
4 *Punch*, 11 May 1932.
5 G. K. Chesterton, *Sidelights*, London, 1932, pp. 60–61.
6 ibid., pp. 200–201.
7 ibid., p. 94.
8 ibid., p. 95.
9 ibid., p. 147.
10 ibid., p. 160.
11 ibid., pp. 164–5.
12 G. K. Chesterton, *Chaucer*, London, 1932, pp. 9–10.
13 ibid., p. 12.
14 ibid., pp. 36–7.
15 Ffinch, *G. K. Chesterton*, p. 327.
16 *Good Housekeeping*, April 1932 (*Chesterton Review*, vol. X, no. 1, pp. 9–11).
17 Roger Lancelyn Green and Walter Hooper, *C. S. Lewis: A Biography*, London, 1974, p. 127.
18 *Chesterton Review*, vol. IX, no. 2, p. 136.
19 Ffinch, *G. K. Chesterton*, p. 329.
20 G. K. Chesterton, *Christendom in Dublin*, London, 1932, p. 35.
21 Maisie Ward, *Gilbert Keith Chesterton*, London, 1944, p. 523.
22 Ffinch, *G. K. Chesterton*, p. 330.
23 Letter from Dorothy Collins, 18 September 1932, G. K. Chesterton Study Centre, Bedford.
24 Ffinch, *G. K. Chesterton*, p. 330.
25 Letter from Dorothy Collins, 18 September 1932, G. K. Chesterton Study Centre, Bedford.
26 Ffinch, *G. K. Chesterton*, pp. 330–31.
27 Maisie Ward, *Return to Chesterton*, London, 1952, p. 158.
28 ibid., p. 159.
29 Chesterton, *Christendom in Dublin*, pp. 56–8.

30 ibid., pp. 71–2.
31 Ward, *Gilbert Keith Chesterton*, p. 541.
32 ibid., p. 534.
33 Dorothy E. Collins, 'Recollections', in John Sullivan (ed.), *G. K. Chesterton: A Centenary Appraisal*, London, 1974, pp. 158–9.
34 Ward, *Gilbert Keith Chesterton*, p. 541.
35 Collins, 'Recollections', pp. 158–9.
36 Dudley Barker, *G. K. Chesterton: A Biography*, London, 1973, p. 279.
37 BBC radio broadcast, January 1933.
38 Collins, 'Recollections', p. 159.
39 ibid.
40 Ward, *Gilbert Keith Chesterton*, p. 543.
41 ibid., p. 534.

28 Dumb Ox and Donkey

1 G. K. Chesterton, *All I Survey*, London, 1933, p. 105.
2 ibid., p. 50.
3 Unpublished letter, G. K. Chesterton Study Centre, Bedford.
4 G. K. Chesterton, *Chaucer*, London, 1932, p. 242.
5 Maisie Ward, *Gilbert Keith Chesterton*, London, 1944, p. 525.
6 ibid.
7 Dorothy E. Collins, 'Recollections', in John Sullivan (ed.), *G. K. Chesterton: A Centenary Appraisal*, London, 1974, p. 158.
8 Ward, *Gilbert Keith Chesterton*, p. 525.
9 Maisie Ward, *Return to Chesterton*, London, 1952, p. 241.
10 ibid., pp. 240–41.
11 G. K. Chesterton, *St Thomas Aquinas*, London, 1933, pp. 13–14.
12 ibid., pp. 14–15.
13 ibid., pp. 76–7.
14 ibid., pp. 28–9.
15 ibid., pp. 142–5.
16 ibid., pp. 131–2.
17 ibid., pp. 138–9.
18 ibid., p. 154.
19 ibid., p. 219.
20 ibid., pp. 220–21.
21 ibid., p. 222.
22 ibid.
23 ibid., pp. 198–9.
24 ibid., p. 216.
25 ibid., p. 211.
26 Ward, *Gilbert Keith Chesterton*, p. 525.
27 Fr John O'Connor, *Father Brown on Chesterton*, London, 1937, p. 157.
28 *Chesterton Review*, vol. XI, no. 3, p. 397.
29 Ward, *Gilbert Keith Chesterton*, p. 146.
30 ibid., p. 525.
31 ibid., p. 526.
32 *Chesterton Review*, vol. XVIII, no. 2, pp. 281–2.
33 ibid., p. 282.
34 *Chesterton Review*, vol. IX, no. 1, p. 82.
35 *Chesterton Review*, vol. XVIII, no. 3, pp. 461–2.
36 *The Times Literary Supplement*, 5 October 1933.

37 Christopher Hollis, *The Mind of Chesterton*, London, 1940, p. 260.

29 Germany and Justice

1 Maisie Ward, *Gilbert Keith Chesterton*, London, 1944, pp. 513–14.
2 ibid.
3 *Listener*, 31 January 1934.
4 Ada Chesterton, *The Chestertons*, London, 1941, p. 291.
5 Michael Ffinch, *G. K. Chesterton: A Biography*, London, 1988, p. 333.
6 Certificate and handbook, G. K. Chesterton Study Centre, Bedford.
7 Ferdinand Valentine, OP, *Father Vincent McNabb*, London, 1955, p. 271.
8 G. K. Chesterton, *Avowals and Denials*, London, 1934, p. 78.
9 ibid., p. 182.
10 ibid., p. 37.
11 ibid., pp. 126–7.
12 ibid., p. 135.
13 ibid., p. 187.
14 ibid., p. 208.
15 *G. K.'s Weekly*, 20 April 1933.
16 ibid., 27 April 1933.
17 ibid., 17 August 1933.
18 ibid.
19 ibid., 13 April 1923.
20 Dudley Barker, *G. K. Chesterton: A Biography*, London, 1973, p. 153.
21 Michael Coren, *Gilbert: The Man Who was Chesterton*, London, 1989, p. 209.
22 ibid., pp. 209–10.
23 Ward, *Gilbert Keith Chesterton*, p. 228.
24 G. K. Chesterton Study Centre, Bedford.
25 Coren, *Gilbert*, pp. 211–12.
26 Anthony Read and David Fisher, *Kristallnacht: The Nazi Night of Terror*, London, 1989, p. 183.
27 *Sunday Times*, 18 August 1957.
28 Albert Speer, *Spandau: The Secret Diaries*, London, 1976, pp. 308–9.

30 Liberty and Exile

1 Michael Ffinch, *G. K. Chesterton: A Biography*, London, 1988, p. 340.
2 *Observer*, 14 October 1934.
3 ibid.
4 ibid.
5 ibid.
6 ibid.
7 Bernard Crick, *George Orwell: A Life*, London, 1992, p. 270.
8 *G. K.'s Weekly*, 6 December 1934.
9 ibid., 13 December 1934.
10 *London Mercury*, vol. XXXI, no. 186, April 1935, pp. 605–6.
11 Dorothy E. Collins, 'Recollections', in John Sullivan (ed.), *G. K. Chesterton: A Centenary Appraisal*, London, 1974, p. 166.
12 ibid.
13 Emile Cammaerts, *The Laughing Prophet*, London, 1937, pp. 141–2.
14 Postcard from Frances Chesterton to Mrs Bastable, dated 30 August 1936, G. K. Chesterton Study Centre, Bedford.

15 G. K. Chesterton, *Collected Works*, Vol. X, San Francisco, 1994, pp. 387–8.
16 *Listener*, 19 June 1935.
17 ibid.
18 George Bernard Shaw, *Pen Portraits and Reviews*, London, 1932, p. 102.
19 *Listener*, 19 June 1935.
20 ibid.
21 Letter, dated 11 June 1935, G. K. Chesterton Study Centre, Bedford.
22 Letter, dated 17 June 1935, G. K. Chesterton Study Centre, Bedford.
23 Letter, dated 17 June 1935, G. K. Chesterton Study Centre, Bedford.
24 ibid.
25 *Catholic Herald*, 6 July 1935.
26 Matie Molinaro, Corinne McLuhan and William Taye (eds.), *Letters of Marshall McLuhan*, Toronto, 1988, quoted in *Chesterton Review*, vol. XIV, no. 4, p. 607.
27 ibid.
28 Hugh Kenner, *Paradox in Chesterton*, London, 1948, pp. xi–xii.
29 D. J. Conlon (ed.), *Chesterton: The Critical Judgments*, Antwerp, 1976, pp. 511–12.
30 G. K. Chesterton, *The Well and the Shallows*, London, 1935, p. v.
31 ibid., p. 23.
32 ibid., pp. 71–2.
33 ibid., p. 83.
34 ibid., pp. 193–4.
35 ibid., pp. 220–22.
36 ibid., pp. 230–31.
37 ibid., p. 256.
38 *Catholic Truth*, Autumn 1961.
39 Ferdinand Valentine, OP, *Father Vincent McNabb*, London, 1955, p. 271.
40 Maisie Ward, *Gilbert Keith Chesterton*, London, 1944, p. 540.
41 Maisie Ward, *Return to Chesterton*, London, 1952, p. 258.

31 End of the Beginning

1 Maisie Ward, *Return to Chesterton*, London, 1952, pp. 266–7.
2 Michael Ffinch, *G. K. Chesterton: A Biography*, London, 1988, p. 342.
3 C. S. Lewis, *The Allegory of Love: A Study in Medieval Tradition*, Oxford, 1936, pp. 302–3.
4 Dudley Barker, *G. K. Chesterton: A Biography*, London, 1973, p. 283.
5 G. K. Chesterton, *Autobiography*, London, 1936, p. 330.
6 ibid., pp. 340–43.
7 Barker, *G. K. Chesterton*, p. 284.
8 BBC broadcast, 'We will End with a Bang', from the 'Spice of Life' series, 15 March 1936.
9 ibid.
10 G. K. Chesterton, *Collected Works*, Vol. X(A), San Francisco, 1994, p. 176.
11 Ward, *Return to Chesterton*, p. 268.
12 ibid., p. 283.
13 ibid., pp. 268–9.
14 ibid., p. 269.
15 Dorothy E. Collins, 'Recollections', in John Sullivan (ed.), *G. K. Chesterton: A Centenary Appraisal*, London, 1974, pp. 157–8.
16 Maisie Ward, *Gilbert Keith Chesterton*, London, 1944, p 551.
17 Collins, 'Recollections', p. 166.
18 Ffinch, *G. K. Chesterton*, pp. 342–3.
19 Collins, 'Recollections', pp. 166–7.

20 Ward, *Return to Chesterton*, p. 270.
21 ibid.
22 Ward, *Gilbert Keith Chesterton*, p. 552.
23 ibid.
24 Ward, *Return to Chesterton*, p. 267.
25 Michael Coren, *Gilbert: The Man Who was Chesterton*, London, 1989, pp. 4–5.
26 Chesterton, *Collected Works*, Vol. X(A), p. 548.
27 Barker, *G. K. Chesterton*, p. 286.
28 ibid.
29 Michael Holroyd, *Bernard Shaw*, Vol. III: *The Lure of Fantasy*, London, 1991, p. 327.
30 Hilaire Belloc, *On the Place of Gilbert Keith Chesterton in English Letters*, London, 1940, pp. 83–4.
31 Barbara Reynolds, *Dorothy L. Sayers: Her Life and Soul*, London, 1993, p. 375.
32 Ronald Knox on Chesterton in Fr Claude Williamson (ed.), *Great Catholics*, London, 1938, p. 548.
33 Barry Phelps, *P. G. Wodehouse: Man and Myth*, London, 1992, p. 200.
34 Ward, *Gilbert Keith Chesterton*, p. 553.
35 Fr John O'Connor, *Father Brown on Chesterton*, London, 1937, p. 152.
36 Ward, *Gilbert Keith Chesterton*, p. 553.
37 Ferdinand Valentine, OP, *Father Vincent McNabb*, London, 1955, p. 276.
38 Alzina Stone Dale, *The Outline of Sanity: A Life of G. K. Chesterton*, Grand Rapids, MI, 1982, p. 300.
39 David Mathew, *Catholicism in England 1535–1935*, London, 1938, pp. 238–9.
40 *Converts' Aid Society Report*, 1947, p. 28.
41 Ward, *Gilbert Keith Chesterton*, p. 551.
42 O'Connor, *Father Brown on Chesterton*, p. 99.
43 Evelyn Waugh, *Ronald Knox*, London pbk 1959, pp. 197–8.
44 Valentine, *Father Vincent McNabb*, pp. 271–2.
45 ibid., p. 272.
46 Ward, *Return to Chesterton*, p. 270.
47 ibid., p. 79.
48 Ward, *Gilbert Keith Chesterton*, p. 554.
49 ibid.
50 Valentine, *Father Vincent McNabb*, p. 274.
51 Ward, *Return to Chesterton*, p. 270.
52 Ward, *Gilbert Keith Chesterton*, p. 94.

INDEX

Index